Rhode Island Latino Political Empowerment

1996 – 2006

By Tomás Alberto Ávila

Rhode Island Latino Political Empowerment

Tomás Alberto Ávila

Milenio Publishing, LLC

Library of Congress Catalog Card Number: Pending

ISBN 978-1-928810-06-3

PRINTING HISTORY
First Edition

Milenio Associates, LLC
61 Tappan Street
Providence, RI 02908
Phone: 877-454-4049
Fax: 401-633-6535
milenioassociates@yahoo.com

Index

Introduction

Anniversaries, like birthdays, are a way of celebrating the arrival and departure of a point in time. They remind us of how long we've been somewhere, and start the clock from that moment to the next marker. My involvement in the empowerment of the Rhode Island Latino community is no different. Ten years ago, I responded to a calling and decided to put all my personal interests aside and instead involved myself in a political movement that was just developing in the state, and integrated myself among many women and men that were guiding such movement. Interestingly enough many of those individuals involved in the movement were young Latinos that had just completed their college career and were eager to put their new learned theories in practice and were challenging the status quo, mixed with members of the old guard some of whom understood what was going on and joined them while some who didn't and instead antagonized these new breed of movers and shakers.

Back in 1996 I made the personal decision to get involved in the growing Latino community of Rhode Island and joined the young revelers and put my corporate experience to their avail in drafting strategies while documenting such movement. While mulling this decision, I came across a report in the Providence Journal Entitle "Coming into Their Own: In politics, business, music and the arts, R.I. Latinos are making their presence felt". The weeklong series chronicle the fast growth of the Latino community during the 1980's and how such community was becoming a political force. In such series, I read about a 25 year old young man named Victor Capellan who had just suffered a narrow political defeat to incumbent George A. Castro by just 11 votes 297 to 286.

While reading the week long spread about the growing Latino community, I also found out about the Community Leadership Development Initiative being offered by the Center for Hispanic Policy & Advocacy (CHisPA) that trained newly arrived immigrants and individuals new to the state, directed by Betty Bernal and Francis Parra. I made the decision to sign up for such program and get to know the community in general such as the needs, political system, and society as well as members of the community.

That was the beginning of my decision to inject myself in the empowerment of the Latino community, and my successful accomplishments along great individuals that I met across the state of Rhode Island and together we change the political scene of Rhode Island. Interestingly enough during the retreat of the leadership program at the University of Rhode Island, I met the young man featured in the week long report by the Providence Journal Victor

Capellan who happened to be the facilitator of the all day retreat program that day. During the retreat's lunch, I had the opportunity to establish a conversation with Capellan, in which he further explained his candidacy experience and we spoke about the political wave sweeping the country and the state at the time.

I remembe speaking with Capellan about Loretta Sanchez victory over the Congressman Dan Dordham as an example of what the Latino community could accomplish in the political arena to gain the respect of elected officials across the country and we committed to join forces and work together in the empowerment of the Latino community into the 21st century. From that conversation we quickly learned that we shared similar vision and goals to help the young Hispanic community advance it's socio-political power. That conversation, was the beginning of very fruitful and powerful relationship we started that continued with my participation in Victor's 1998 campaign and the start of my involvement in the political empowerment of the fastest growing segment of the population in Rhode Island and the nation, the Latino community.According to the 1990 census the Rhode Island Latino population in the state of Rhode Island numbered 45,000, growing substantially from the estimated 18,000 reflected in the 1980 Census,

According to the Journal article, weeks after the primary defeat, Capellan was still excited, marveling at the powerful forces he tapped in the neighborhoods of lower South Providence and Washington Park. Capellan had no political experience, and his campaign workers were all members of the Dominican youth group called Quisqueya en Accion, of which Capellan was president. They marched down the streets, these groups of Latino youths, distributing flyers and taping posters in storefront windows, and they almost pulled off a huge upset.

Capellan's sudden emergence in South Providence was an encouraging development in a year that featured an unusual level of activism by Rhode Island's Hispanics. Their growing participation sprang in reaction to proposals in Congress to deny benefits to immigrants. They also rallied against the Rhode Island congressional candidacy of former Providence Mayor Joseph Paolino Jr., whose campaign featured a call for English as an official national language. Capellan's performance was the strongest among seven Latinos who ran in General Assembly primary races that year according to the Providence Journal.

Two other Hispanics ran in the general elections: Rep. Anastasia Williams, D-Providence, the state's first Hispanic legislator, retained her seat; Republican Daniel Garza lost to Rep. Maria J. Lopes, D-East Providence. The wave of candidates and media attention they received encouraged Latino leaders who have dreamed for years of gaining a share of political power.

The City Councils in Providence, Pawtucket and Central Falls were devoid of Latinos. Central Falls, with a public-school student population that is 51 percent Hispanic, did not have a single Hispanic teacher. So community leaders are trumpeting anything that resembles progress.

Mildred Vega, a community activist in Central Falls who ran unsuccessfully for the House District 72 seat against incumbent Rep. Joseph Faria and Vicente Caban, another Hispanic, another Latino candidate, and Leonel Bonilla, appeared on the ballot in House District 73 in Central Falls. Delia Smidt, who ran for Senate in Coventry and also lost, said at the time "We might have lost the battle but not the war. Going into the 21st century, we're going to become a very powerful political movement in Rhode Island."

Marta Martinez, chairwoman of the Governor's Commission on Hispanic Affairs added, "The fact that we lost (the primary races) was not that bad". "What's important is the fact that we came forward with seven candidates for the first time and made a mark on the political scene."

Needless to say time has proven both Delia and Marta correct in their comments and predictions at the time, since the Latino community has evolved into a powerful political movement and the experience of the losses at the time brought many of the candidates together in strategizing about the community political empowerment.

Latino Leaders credited Congregational Candidate Joseph Paolino's controversial position on English and immigration for focusing media attention on Rhode Island's own Latin Americans. All of a sudden, the rest of the state wanted to know what Latinos were thinking. His comments really empowered the community.

Latinos made politicians and the press listen when they said "no mas" (no more) to Washington's attacks on immigrants and plans to cut their benefits. They did so by rallying against Joseph R. Paolino Jr., a 2nd Congressional District candidate whose campaign featured slights against more recent immigrants and plans to make English the official language of the United States. For the first time in Rhode Island history, seven Latinos ran for seats in the House and Senate. The candidates were Puerto Rican, Dominican, Guatemalan, Panamanian, Argentinean and Mexican-American. Five lost in the primaries, and one lost and one won in the general elections. The majority of the candidates who lost said they would run again. The emergence of the Latino community in Rhode Island echoed a national trend in growth and assertion of power.

Patricia Martinez predicted, "It was the beginning". "We have been here 25 to 30 years. I see the growth in our community. As we head toward our 40th year, like any other immigrant group, you will see people taking more active roles in the political arena. I see more kids graduating from college. I see more of our people in good positions in the Health Department and in Human Services. As we saw with the Irish and the Italians, it took time before they took over."

But the biggest question was who were these Latino people who make up the largest minority group in Rhode Island? They are often lumped together into one category - "Hispanic" - but they come from 21 countries from North America to the Caribbean and South America, where political situations range from democracy in Costa Rica to Communism in Cuba. Latinos are a mixture, in varying degrees of Indian, black and Spanish blood. They are the blue-eyed blonde riding her bike down the street, the brown-skinned girl sketching in her notebook, the black boy walking to school.

After completing the Community Leadership Development Initiative in the spring of 1997, I interviewed was selected to be a participant of the Providence Plan Civic Entrepreneurs Leadership program, a year long program that taught its participants about community networking, city politics and activism. It was during this program that I met a great dynamic young lady named Alina Ocasio who was a member of the program, along with Ernesto Figueroa whom I met during our participation in CHisPA's CLDI program just 2 weeks after his arrival to the United States and Rhode Island. During this same period, I reconnected with Victor Capellan after our meeting in Kingston and through I met Juan Pichardo who together were developing an organization called Latinos for Community Advancement (LCA), which they envisioned to become a 501-C4 organization that would serve as the political advocacy organization for the existing 501-C3 Latino organizations.

Through that involvement I became involve in the political empowerment of the Rhode Island Latino community by joining forces with Victor and Juan in the development process of LCA which at the time counted as it's members: Betty Bernal, Delia Smidt (now Rodriguez-Masjoan), Executive Director of the Joslin Community Center, Patricia Martinez, Executive Director of Progreso Latino, Elvys Ruiz, President of Quisqueya In Action, Olga Noguera, President of Guatelmatecos Unidos Association (GUA) and member of the Providence Public School Department. My involvement with Capellan and Pichardo in the development of LCA provided me a great opportunity to put into action my strengths in strategic planning, management, and my engineering practices of researching, drafting, testing, retesting, planning and implementation in the development of what will eventually become the Rhode Island Latino Political Action Committee.

After several meetings started back in 1996, I worked very closely with Victor and Juan while directing the efforts of LCA and drafting of it's bylaws, and organizational structure, while at the same time investing many hours getting to know the members of the Latino community and the power brokers of the political arena. In January 1998 the planning that I had started as LCA joined forces with other Latino leaders in the political arena such as Dr. Pablo Rodriguez, Angel Taveras, Nellie Gorbea, Jose Gonzales, Ricardo Patino, Francisco Cruz, Alido Baldera, Gladys Corvera-Baker, Michelle Torres, Jenny Rosario and proceeded to join our efforts through the early part of the year and become a co-founders of the Rhode Island Latino Political Action Committee officially launched August 20 1998 and I immediately identified as the opportunity to make a huge impact in the Rhode Island political scene as it's first Treasurer and unofficial Operations Manager.

On August 20, 1998 the Hispanic community's emergence as a full, powerful partner in Rhode Island elections, folks note an event at the Roger William Park Casino. The Rhode Island Latino Political Action Committee made its debut with a fundraiser that brought in some $10,000, not a bad start on building a war chest and establishing clout. The bipartisan PAC was created to support candidates Hispanic and otherwise it considers friends. We wanted to play the game the way everybody else plays it and we were coming of age and were ready to influence and change the political scene in the state of Rhode Island.

We wanted to send a message to all politicians: You've got to pay attention to our interests and us. In other words, we became aware that money talksand many pols that flocked to the event contributed money by attending the event and becoming sponsors to the tune of $200.

It also was an eclectic evening in this sense. The founders of RILPAC were proud that we had broad representation from various Hispanic groups including Puerto Ricans, Dominicans, Argentineans, Honduran, Bolivian, Colombian and Peruvians who often have been rivals in the political arena. Alina Ocasio, a state economic development aide who was the founding PAC executive vice president, said outside challenges, such as immigration issues "are forcing us to become more united." RILPAC activities were schedule to include turning out the vote and lobbying.

In his inaugural speech Dr. Pablo Rodriguez emphasized that Hispanics are not looking for handouts but for investments in their community. "We are not here to ask for a bigger slice of the pie," he declared. "We are here to help bake a bigger one, so all of us can have a bigger slice." And he warned pols not to think that dealing with the PAC relieves them of their duty to campaign in the community they still must get out and shake hands and advertise in the Hispanic media.

During RILPAC's first endorsement in the 1998 primaries, the committee endorsed Victor Capellán, District 20 candidate for State Representative, Miguel Luna, City Council candidate in Ward 9's primary, Sheldon Whitehouse for Attorney General, and Senator Paul Tavares candidate for General Treasurer. During the General Election we endorsed Myrth York for Governor, Sheldon Whitehouse for Attorney General, Paul Tavares for General Treasurer, James Langevin for Secretary of State, David Igliozzi for State Senate and Pat Nolan for City Council in District 9.

I remember vividly the discussion about the tight finish in the City Council District 9 between incumbent Pat Nolan and challenger Miguel Luna. This race became the most controversial of all the endorsement decisions since it was a race pitting a first time Latino candidate against an incumbent who had strong support among her constituency and among the members of RILPAC's first official endorsement committee and the start of what has become a very controversial process that pits friends against each other in a democratic process of endorsing candidates for state and local office who are committed to improving the quality of life for members of the Latino community.

I also remember the controversy created when State Representative James Langevin was endorsed over Ed Lopez, a Republican Latino running for Secretary of State, Santa Espinosa not being given an opportunity to participate in the endorsement process, because she was an unknown Republican. Just as it has been questioned during this year's endorsement, the community questioned RILPAC's commitment to support and elect Latinos, regardless of their party affiliation and gave way to accusations of being a Democratic PAC rather than a nonpartisan institution which needless to say such doubt continues despite the endorsement the first Republican during 2002 and the first Green Candidate in the same year.

In 1999 after several months of agonizing in search of candidate to seek Central Falls Ward 3 City Council seat in the primary, first-time candidate Ricardo Patino made a last minute decision to run for such seat, against first-time candidate Rose Marie Canavan, a retired teacher and the wife of outgoing Council President Robert Canavan. RILPAC members gathered at Patino's home after our September meeting and scramble to put together a campaign team that went to work immediately with limited resources to assure his candidacy.

Even with the limited time span to put together this campaign we manage to mobilize Latino voters to Get out and vote within a month and were able to attained a respectable second place finish with 142 votes for Patino`, or 35 percent, in his first bid for office, against topped vote-getters Canavan with 213 votes or 52 percent. Third-time candidate Douglas Pendergrass was a distant third with 42 votes and George DeLomba, who had already effectively quit the race, received 11 votes. During her victory speech Canavan acknowledge that she "was happy to have survived the political machine" that worked behind Patino. Although we were unsuccessful in electing Patino in his first campaign, RILPAC helped set the path for his second candidacy in 2001 and through financial contributions and the participation the PAC members, succeeded in becoming the first elected Latino in Central Falls Municipal Government.

No sooner had the 1999 endorsement season ended, RILPAC was back at it again in 2000 during the PAC's third endorsement cycle in which RILPAC endorsed Juan M. Pichardo Senate District 10, Gonzalo Cuervo, State Representative District 20, Joseph Almeida State Representative District 20 and Marsha Carpenter State Representative District 18's primary elections. Once again RILPAC endorsement was questioned and criticized for not endorsing Luis Leon Tejada in District 18 against Marcia Carpenter, who was defeated by Tejada. In particular the endorsement of both State Representative District 20 candidates Gonzalo Cuervo and Joseph Almeida, rather than reaching a conclusive and determining decision for either candidate. RILPAC also faced heavy criticism for it's endorsement of Marsha Carpenter in Representative District 20 an African American female being challenged by first time Latino candidate Leon Tejada.

During the 2000 endorsement cycle RILPAC also became very controversial in regards to the candidacy of Angel Taveras as the first Latino seeking a Congregational seat running against then Secretary of State James Langevin, Activist Kaye Coyne-McCoye and Attorney Kevin McAllister. The sentiment in the community and some members of the PAC was very strong that RILPAC should have endorsed Attorney Taveras even though the organization initial board had decided to be a state PAC for the first 5 years. Just like any other races, the membership was divided as to whether the PAC should endorsed Angel or not, and as usual the issue was put for a vote with the outcome not modify the organization's operations and the decision was made not to endorsed the first Latino congregational candidate.

In 2002 the committee endorsed Myrth York, for Governor, Paul Tavares for General Treasurer, Matt Brown for Secretary of State, Patrick Lynch for Attorney General, Juan Pichardo for State Senator, District 2, Jeff Toste for

Senate District 5, David Cicilline for Mayor City of Providence, Miguel Luna City Council and Stephen Laffey for Mayor City of Cranston.

During this election season, the heated endorsement was the Democratic gubernatorial race between Myrth York and Attorney General Sheldon Whitehouse, which was narrowly decided in favor of Myrth York, creating voting controversy once again among the voting members and even caused the loosing side to form their own RILPAC supporters for Sheldon Whitehouse and going as far as organizing a press conference to announce their support for Sheldon, and their disappointment that the general membership did not endorsed Mr. Whitehouse.

Needless to say despite individual members claims that Myrth's endorsement was obtained by their individual efforts, RILPAC's endorsement of Myrth during the 1998 gubernatorial elections and Sheldon Whitehouse for Attorney General shows that both candidates had a track record of supporters in the organization prior to the 2002 endorsement process. This also shows the evolution of the endorsement process, since the majority of the PAC considered Sheldon Whitehouse a favorite.

As can be seen so far, the experience faced during RILPAC's 2004-endorsement process is nothing new or nothing different than in the past, but what has been consistent in this process is the evolution of the participants in the election process, quite interestingly producing the same results and the same controversies. Looking at the participating members in 2004 year endorsement committee, the only members that remain participating in the process from the inception of the PAC are yours truly and Betty Bernal other than that the participant have changed throughout the years which is a positive, but at the same time it has not allowed the process to evolve and mature with the agenda needs of the community rather than personal agendas. It's my opinion that if many of the senior members of the organization will remain active in the process while new membership keeps the organization growing and evolving the results may be different. During this endorsement process, RILPAC endorsed Thomas Slater, State Representative District 10, Andy Galli Senate District 7, Pedro Espinal Senate District 6 and Cranston Mayor Stephen Laffey for the primary elections.

Through my participation in the Civic Entrepreneurs Leadership program in 1998 I participated in a town meeting that gathered residents, community leaders, merchants and politicians to consider ways to meet the needs of their neighborhoods. The dilemma was how to get more resources flowing through the neighborhoods in between, and the small businesses that pepper their main thoroughfares: Broad Street and Elmwood Avenue.

The town meeting was sponsored by the University of Rhode Island and the Providence Journal's May 8 edition published the following: "Tomas Avila, a local businessman, told the audience about ``Boston Link,'' a program designed to ensure that no Boston neighborhoods would be left behind as plans to redevelop the city's downtown progressed. " "Avila suggested that such a plan be developed for Providence, under the leadership of local politicians." Interestingly enough the community of South Providence and Elmwood still struggling with the same dilemma. It was through this program that I became involved in the economic empowerment of the Latino community through my thesis for such program.

On April 17, 2 years after promising that he was going to run again, Victor Capellan announced his candidacy for State Representative in District 20 stating the following: "It was about this time two years ago this month that in the midst of writing my Action Research towards the completion of my Master Degree at URI that I got up and said "I'm going to do it, I'm running for office this fall." And it was a combination of many things that at that point culminated and came all-together. It was the people in the community who asked me to run, such as the bodegueros on Broad Street, or the members of Quisqueya in Action, and it was my friends and family who asked me to run. And to re-tell a story that I've had to re-tell over and over for the last two years- I did run and I did not get elected as Representative by a margin of only 13 votes. Immediately after the count was in, I told the campaign team - well don't worry because we are coming back in 1998. So here we are today only a few months shy of the September 15th primary continuing to work towards that goal with a vision of improvement a vision for a united community.

Many times over the last year and a half people asked me "are you running again, are you going to give it another try" and others said "you should run again", "if you run I'll definitely help you this time" – and tonight air. I will respond to all those people that have asked me to run, this time, it is the members of many other organizations, it is young people, it is whites, blacks, Latinos and Portuguese, it is family members it is old friends and new friends it is you ... so my answer tonight is YES! YES, I am running for State Representative.

I joined Victor's campaign and embarked on rematch with George Castro by then a 20-year incumbent in District 20, after Capellan's 1996 narrow loss. Once Capellan made his announcement, rumors started surfacing that Castro was considering not seeking reelection and instead recruiting ex policeman Joseph Almeida to take his place, which by the time candidates submitted their nomination turned out to be true.

On June 15, 1998 Ed Lopez announced his campaign for Secretary of State challenging incumbent James Langevin. According to Lopez, his campaign was about restoring community and citizenship. This involves much more than politicians securing open government for one another; it was about restoring the sense of citizenship necessary to ensure that the check on government was in the hands of the people. It is one thing to have open government; it is quite another to have a people who care about participating in that government. Voter participation has hit an all time low across the country. Can there be any doubt that the time to strengthen and revitalize citizenship has come? As Secretary of State Ed promised would be truly committed to increasing voter registration, voter education, and the overall activity from the average citizen in the political process.

In 1970, there were slightly fewer than 8,000 Hispanics in Rhode Island. But a few years ago the population had grown to 59,000 and is projected by the Census Bureau to reach 70,000 by 2000. Social-service agencies that work with Hispanics assert that the current population is at least 25 percent higher than officially calculated.

Hispanic leaders say obvious obstacles such as the language barrier and citizenship have delayed Hispanic political progress. Many of the Hispanics are poor, too, and the poor don't tend to vote. Groups such as the Latino Political Action Committee are doing everything they can to promote Hispanic politicians and causes while at the same time working to increase voter participation.

There were three Hispanic candidates in the city Democratic primary, but Aponte was the only winner:

Miguel C. Luna, 40, a native of the Dominican Republic who emigrated to Rhode Island as a young man and whose political ideals were inspired by the resistance to the late Dominican dictator Rafael Trujillo, ran a credible campaign for a council seat, losing 536 to 413. He is director of transitional housing and special projects for AIDS Care/Ocean State.

Victor F. Capellan, 27, a Dominican native who 15 years ago was studying English as a newcomer at Roger Williams Middle School, suffered his second straight numbingly narrow loss for state representative in District 20. Capellan, student development coordinator at the University of Rhode Island, lost by 20 votes to Castro in 1996 and by 19 votes this time to Joseph S. Almeida. He has asked for a recount.

Santa ``Chary'' Espinosa, Republican candidate for City Council in Ward 9 lost her bid the Ward 9 City Council seat held by Nolan and Ed Lopez was defeated by James Langevin for Secretary of State post.

However, as the election season came to an end, it was predicted that at the rate the Hispanic population is growing, the time might come when Hispanics can put candidates over on the strength of their vote alone. Maybe someday the Latino vote will be such that the community can elect a mayor.

After the elections were over, Victor Capellan became Executive Director of the Center for Hispanic Policy and Advocacy (ChisPA), and asked me to join the staff and help him reorganized the entity which I accepted. I became the organization's Policy Analyst, and Deputy Executive Director in charge of operations programs and the tThe Bridge School, which is an alternative school for youth that have been expelled from the Providence School system. Our work with the Bridge School was attracting attention from the media as well as from the world of academia. Some students at the Bridge School arrive via the RI Training School and we work to re-engage them into the Public Education system.

The other project that I was heavily involved what Victor envisioned to be a freestanding, policy institute that was destined to attain a reputation as the Rhode Island's "premier Latino think tank." Through its strong capacity to conduct primary and secondary data analysis, The Institute was to be uniquely position to fill the void in information that exists among policymakers and political leaders regarding the complexities that characterize the Latino population heterogeneous composition, its bilingualism, and its diverse nativity.

The Institute would analyze issues of concern to Latinos, acts as a liaison to the Rhose Island Legislature, the U. S. Congress and federal agencies, conducts seminars and studies on topical issues, presents testimony to local governments and develops working relationships with other advocacy groups.

It was during this period that I became aware of the upcoming 2000 Census and agreed with Victor that we were going to rally the Latino leadership together to prepare for the upcoming 2000 Census. The goal was the most accurate census possible, completed using the most up to date scientific methods as recommended by the National Academy of Sciences and the vast majority of the professional scientific community.

I considered the Census important because it has real impact on the lives of real people. Information gathered in the decennial census is used by states and local governments to plan schools and highways, by the federal government to distribute funds for health care and other programs, and by businesses in making their economic plans. Because the census is so important, we must do everything we can to ensure that everyone is included in the count. We know that previous censuses overlooked millions of Americans, especially children and minorities. The Census Bureau would use modern scientific methods techniques that would provide an essential quality check for Census 2000 to ensure a complete and accurate count. As part of the decision to get involved in the Census activity, I agreed to partner with the Puerto Rican Educational and Legal Defense Fund in the Regional Latino Census Campaign and became acquainted with Lucia Gomez who was the Administrator of such project and would forged a strong alliance that continue to this day.

Matt Brown, an idealistic 30-year-old Yale University Law School student who doesn't want to hear about voters turned off by negative political campaigns or young slackers too cynical to bother voting. Brown decided it was time to try to do something about the sharp decline in voter turnout among every group in the United States except for the World War II generation.

Using Rhode Island as a model, Brown organized a movement that he and his allies hope would coax to the polls 75,000 more state voters in November's general election than voted in the last presidential election, in 1996, when about 390,000 Rhode Islanders went to the polls.

Brown and the group, the Democracy Compact, were trying to reverse a decades-long slide in voting. Nationally, the 1996 presidential election attracted 49 percent of eligible voters, which except for 1924 was the 20th century's lowest. Voter participation had dropped steadily since 1960, when 63 percent of voters went to the polls in the close election between Democrat John F. Kennedy and Republican Richard M. Nixon.

The compact was started with a diverse group of 39 Rhode Island leaders from business, the media, and a wide spectrum of community organizations. Seed money and support has been provided by Taco Inc., of Cranston, The Providence Journal, the Rhode Island Foundation, and Rhode Island chapters of the League of Women Voters. The leaders were Bill Allen, executive vice president, United Way of Southeastern New England, Tomas Avila, Policy Analyst Center for Hispanic Advocacy and Policy, Rick Battistoni, executive director, Feinstein Institute for Public Service, Kip Bergstrom , executive director, Rhode island Economic Policy Council, Nicole Boothman Shepard, director, Rhode Island Service Alliance, Bernie Beaudrea, executive director, Rhode Island Community Food Bank, Elizabeth Burke Bryant, director, KidsCount, Lisa Churchville, general manager, WJAR, Barbara Cottam, senior vice president, Citizens Bank, Peter Damon, president emeritus, Bank of Newport, Jim Dodge, president, Providence Energy Corporation, Nancy Gewirtz, executive director, Poverty Institute, Jim Hagan, executive director, Greater Providence Chamber of Commerce, Peter Hocking, executive director, Swearer Center for Public Service, Liz Hollander, executive director, Campus Compact, Dean Holt, president, Fleet Bank, Diana Lam, superintendent, Providence School, Department, Dennis Langley, executive director, Urban League, Joseph Le, executive director, Socio-Economic Development Corporation, Fred Lohrum, president emeritus, BankBoston, Patricia Martinez, executive director, Progreso Latino, Jim Miller, executive director. State Council of Churches, Cliff Monteiro, executive director, NAACP, Jyothi Nagraj, executive director, City Year, George Nee, secretary-treasurer, AFL-CIO, Pablo Rodriguez, M.D., Women and Infants Hospital, Hillary Salmons, president, Providence League of Women Voters, Sovann Sam, president, Cambodian Society, Bill Shuey, executive director, International Institute, Delia Smidt, partnership specialist, Census 2000, Chery and Roland Snead, Banneker Industries, Keith Stokes, executive director, Newport County Chamber of Commerce, Howard Sutton, publisher, The Providence Journal, Sammy Vaughan , pastor, Saint James Baptist Church, Darrell Waldron, executive director, Rhode Island Indian Council, Darrell West , professor of political science, Brown University, Phil West, executive director, Common Cause, John Hazen White, president, Taco, Jack Yena, president, Johnson & Wales University. The cochairs for the compact are Dr. Pablo Rodriguez of Women & Infants Hospital and a leader in the state's Hispanic community, and Lisa Churchville, general manager of Channel 10 (WJAR).

Although present in the state since the 1960s, Rhode Island Latinos erupted into the consciousness of the region in the late 1990s with two critical facts. The first is that the growth of the Latino population in the state had been explosive. Since 1990, Latinos quadrupled their share of the population, and today, with 90,820 persons, they account for 8.7 percent of the total population and for 48 percent of the racial/ethnic minority population of the state. Without the influx of Latinos, Rhode Island would have experienced negative population growth in the 1990s[1].In Providence and Central Falls, Latinos account for a significant percent of the populations of those cities, 30 percent and 47.8 percent, respectively. In those cities, the presence of Latinos can no longer he ignored.

---

[1] In fact, in 1999, the U.S. Bureau of the Census estimated that Rhode Island would have a population loss of 1.3 percent. See http://www.dlt.state.ri.us/lmi/

Even as the numbers climbed, there appeared to have been little ac-knowledgement of the meaning of the demographic change to the institutions and politics of the state. Through the 1990s there had been some appointments to the boards of nonprofit organizations and the presence of Latinos grew in key areas, such as health care delivery. But in general, there was scant attention to the supports that this large influx of newcomers would require. At the end of that decade, Latinos faced serious barriers of access to services of all types and were caught between mainstream public and private systems of service delivery unable to serve them well and policies that strongly restricted Latinos' capacity for building service organizations of their own. The avenues used by Latinos in New York, Hartford, and Boston to meeting the communities' needs for services to support their adjustment and incorporation (such as for example, community-based service organizations) have been largely out of reach to Latinos in Rhode Island, as the growth of the Latino population largely coincided with the cuts in federal funding for the urban programs that had made those services possible in other areas of the region. In Rhode Island, meeting the community's needs has meant obtaining access to decision making at the state and city levels.

Anastasia Williams, a Panamanian woman, had represented Providence's District 9 in the State Legislature since 1992 and up to 1998 was the only elected Latina in the state. In 1998 a group of seasoned leaders founded the Rhode Island Latino Political Action Committee (RILPAC) with the purpose of raising funds to support candidates that advance Latino issues and to build a consensus around the Latino political community. Luis Aponte, a Puerto Rican, was elected city councilor for Providence's Ward 10 in 1998 on his second try. Victor Capellán ran campaigns for state representative in 1996 and 1998, which resulted in very narrow losses; Miguel Luna ran in 1998 and would be successful in 2002 in his run for the Providence City Council. Leon Tejada became state representative in Providence's District 11 in 2000, and Juan Pichardo, in his second try, was elected state senator in Providence's District 2 in 2002. In Central Falls, Ricardo Patiño, a Colombian, was elected to the city council in 2001. In Rhode Island, Latinos are running for office and getting elected. From the perspective of Latinos in other areas of New England, this was a rise to electoral success the swiftness of which was unparalleled in the region.

This introduction has discussed some of the central themes cover in this volume, but obviously not all. In the interest of brevity, I have left several topics that are cover in greater depth in the articles included in this book. For an appreciation of the historical events that have played a roll in the political empowerment process of the Latino community and the nation, I invite you to proceed on to the next pages.

Report On The Hispanic, Portuguese And Cape Verdean Populations In Rhode Island

Implications for Rhode Island Grant makers listing of Organizations

By Rita C. Michaelson
The Rhode Island Foundation
September 1986

Introduction

The Rhode Island Foundation was founded in 1916 by a group of community leaders who wrote, "... a fund could be established the income of which would be used each year to advance progressive movements in the interest of the whole...." Over the years the Foundation's interests and activities have grown as it has sought new ways to deal with problems and needs that change as the character and population of the state changes.

Several ethnic groups are growing in numbers; among these are the Hispanic, Portuguese, and Cape Verdeans. Two of these, Portuguese and Cape Verdean, make up significant segments of the population in eastern sections of Rhode Island and in neighboring Massachusetts's communities such as Fall River, New Bedford, and Cape Cod. Although Portuguese and Cape Verdeans have been in this region for several hundred years, members of the Portuguese and Cape Verdean Heritage Commissions estimate that almost a thousand Cape Verdean and several thousand Portuguese arrive each year.

The majority of the Hispanic population has been in Rhode Island for only twenty years. It is the fastest growing minority group in the United States and in Rhode Island. Coming from twenty-three Central and South American nations and from islands in the Caribbean, most Hispanics emigrated because of economic and political instability at home. Estimates are that almost forty thousand Hispanics live in Rhode Island (official 1980 census of 18,000 is a gross undercount), many with limited English language ability and minimum transferable education. Like immigrant Cape Verdean and Portuguese populations, the newer arrivals, those with a lack of language and technical skills, have a hard time adjusting to the complexities of twentieth century life in an urban technological society.

In a study of the Southeast Asian community commissioned by the Foundation in 1985, findings were that Rhode Island and its institutions were not focusing on serving the needs of refugees. Educational institutions, health care delivery systems, political, legal, economic, and social services were doing little more than making bare bones accommodations to these Rhode Islanders who come from such different cultural and ethnic backgrounds. A conference focusing on the needs of the Southeast Asian community sponsored by the Foundation in April 1986 brought together more than five hundred lay and professional policy makers to identify and solve problems. Some significant gains in awareness and action have resulted, including an Executive Order, signed by Governor DiPrete in April 1986, mandating needs assessment and services by state agencies to refugees, and educational policies designed to increase education opportunities.

The present study, commissioned by the Foundation in spring 1986, has found essentially the same situation with regard to institutional response to Hispanics and the Portuguese and Cape Verdean immigrant populations. The study hopes to focus attention on Rhode Island residents who need special services and will identify areas where such services are lacking.

In examining the Hispanic, Portuguese, defining, specifically, relationship of the overall Rhode Island community to and Cape Verdean populations, some terminology needs the words "minority" and "color."

Hispanics are an official '9minority" as defined by Federal and State law. Cape Verdeans and Portuguese, like Greeks, Armenians, Germans, and the hundreds of other nationalities who immigrate to the United States, are not considered as "minority." Asians and "Native Americans" are minorities, as are American Blacks. Under Rhode Island and federal law, it is unlawful to discriminate in employment, housing, and public accommodations, where the discrimination is based on race, religion, or country of ancestral origin.

Since "protected" the 1964 Civil Rights Act, Spanish surnamed Americans have been a class," a legal "minority. Cape Verdeans and Portuguese are not a class."

Spanish surnamed Americans, Latinos, or Hispanics are terms applied to peoples coming from Central and South American countries. Portuguese is the name used to identify people who come from the Portuguese owned Azore Islands and from Portugal. Cape Verdean describes persons from the Cape Verde Islands, located off the coast of Africa, formerly owned by Portugal. All these people represent a number of ethnic stocks and vary from light to dark skinned. Many Cape Verdeans have some African as well as Portuguese and other European backgrounds. Hispanics are often mixtures of Spanish, Indian and European stock. Skin color is not as important in their own countries and marriages are not considered interracial if the partners have differences in color. The discrimination practiced against those of color in the United States presents an unaccustomed burden to the immigrant who also faces a distrust of all newcomers. In Rhode Island, Hispanics, Portuguese, and Cape Verdeans of color are subject to the effects of discrimination in many aspects of their lives.

For most Rhode Islanders, the general term "minority" refers to people of color. American Blacks, Hispanics, and Cape Verdeans of color are lumped together in the average mind as having common characteristics and needs. Recruitment of "minorities" usually means recruitment of people of color. Rhode Island State Police, for example, have recruited "Blacks" and a woman, according to newspaper reports.

Many organizations in the community, such as the Urban League, the OIC, the NAACP, and the Urban Education Center, are focused on so-called "minority" needs. While many of this outreach, especially to the Hispanic community, they are primarily perceived as organizations dealing with the status and needs of American Blacks in the fields of employment, education, and equal opportunity.

Another term emerging in organizational and educational circles is "linguistic minority." This refers to people who lack fluency in English, thereby presenting problems of communication to the institutions ~ society which attempt to deal with them. According to studies done by the Council of Community Services in 1983 on Linguistic Minorities, Rhode Island ranks sixth out of fifty states in the percentage of its population which is foreign born and speak other languages (this figure does not include Puerto Ricans, who are not foreign born, and uses the 18,000 Hispanic figure which is inaccurate. Almost one fifth of Providence and almost one quarter of Central Falls are foreign born, for example. Over 200,000 Rhode Islanders live in homes where a language other than English is spoken daily. Children, especially in the Providence, Pawtucket, and Central Falls school systems who come from non- English speaking homes, present a special educational challenge.
A1985 study by the State Department of Education lists almost 5,000 students as Limited English Proficient. These children speak 16 languages, but almost 1,800 of that total speak Spanish, 1,200 Portuguese and 200 Creole. Spanish and Portuguese account for two thirds of the languages spoken.

Another factor to be considered in an overview of the Portuguese, and Cape Verdean immigrant is the prevailing attitude Islanders toward immigrants.

Hispanics of Rhode Island

A general commentary of many Rhode Island citizens about immigrant newcomers is that they should "sink or swim, as our folks did." While it is true that immigrants in the past were left on their own, more sank than swam. Only one out of ten completed high school, many spent their lives in menial occupations due to their lack of appropriate education, and English. English language classes are presently available, but nowhere near the numbers that are needed. International Institute turned away 250 students last year for lack of space and teachers.

As American governmental and private agencies expand, even native-born citizens need help in accessing them. Most Americans are uncertain about how much accommodation should be made to serve varied linguistic minority populations. There are heated opinions about bilingual education, notices, examinations, and personnel. Several states have already passed legislation making English the "official" language, and the State of California is now embroiled in a referendum on this point. Resentment that voting materials are printed in languages other than English seems to head the list of practices which some segments find distasteful. Yet the fact remains that 15,000,000 Americans read Spanish and little or no English.

Most Rhode Islanders are not aware of the numbers of Rhode Island residents who are immigrants with limited English. Since their presence and well being, their successful adjustment and ability to work within the framework of Rhode Island life have implications for all, it is important that they not be invisible minorities. It is important that Rhode Island planners and agencies count these populations in needs assessments and plans for future development. Economic recession in Latin America and continuing political warfare will bring more Hispanics to the United States and to Rhode Island.

A1984 Ford Foundation study found, "Most organizations which can serve the Hispanic community as advocates are very fragile and Hispanics do not totally fit into the community advocacy organizations which attempt to serve all minorities. Affirmative Action has been mainly aimed at people of color, and where Hispanics have been included, it is usually under these categories. No solid community-wide organizational structure has developed within the Hispanic community, nor may any ever develop. The effectiveness of groups dealing with the establishment, however, depends on articulate spokespersons representing bona fide community consensus on issue based matters."

The Rhode Island Foundation concurs with the Ford Foundation that policy-relevant knowledge about the Hispanic population is largely undeveloped. The same can be said for the Cape Verdean and Portuguese populations.

Such knowledge is especially important for immigrants in all three groups who face serious acculturation problems. Detailed needs assessments and policy decisions based on those needs must be implemented.

In each of these three groups are second or third generation citizens, who live in the mainstream of Rhode Island life and who, except for possible identification through ethnic features or surname, are not distinguishable from other Rhode Islanders. Some clearly identify with their backgrounds, others do not. This study focuses on the underserved segments of the Hispanic, Portuguese, and Cape Verdean populations, the recent arrivals who are not in the consciousness of policy and decision makers. Interviews and data collection extended from February through July 1986. People were contacted who had overall understanding of the communities involved and who identify with them. Also interviewed were professionals in the fields of education, business, planning and development, health, religion, and state and city government in the communities where most Hispanics, Cape Verdeans, and Portuguese live.

Education is the single most important area identified in any discussion with or about Hispanics, Portuguese, or Cape Verdeans. Achievement levels of many students are low; dropout rates high. The future prosperity of the Rhode Island community is at risk if the young immigrant of today grows into adult- hood uneducated and unable to assume a meaningful role in the life of the community. Many of these youth enter the workforce too early, sacrificing the completion of their studies. Frustration born of lack of advancement and inability to cope with English language instruction leads to social ills. Hispanic, Portuguese, and Cape Verdean youth deserve an education that prepares them for future growth. Their parents need to learn how to work with the schools to advance education. Across the nation, schools that work with parents of minority children succeed in raising levels. All community members and groups stress that education is their prime concern, yet few know how to work within the current system to solve the problem.

Summary

The Hispanic Population

Almost forty thousand residents of Rhode Island have arrived since 1950 from twenty-three South and Central American countries and Caribbean Islands. In 1990 the census is likely to record 50,000 Hispanics in Rhode Island. They and their American-born children represent Rhode Island's fastest growing minority groups. Called Hispanics because Spanish is their common language, many are not citizens, but most are productive members of the community.

Although Hispanics settled in the United States before the establishment of either the Plymouth, Massachusetts or Jamestown colonies, there were only a few hundred in Rhode Island before 1960.   At that time1 Blackstone Valley mill   owners went to Colombia to recruit manual   labor   at cheap wages.   Colombians settled in the towns of Central Falls and Pawtucket. Over the past twenty-five years, about 30,000 more Hispanics have arrived, most often from other eastern cities, moving to Rhode Island because life here is perceived to be "mas tranquilo," housing is cheaper, there is less crime, jobs requiring few skills and little education are available, relatives and friends are already here.

The Rhode Island Hispanic population comes from twenty-three different countries.   Puerto Ricans, Colombians, and Dominicans make up the largest groups.   Others come from the eight major countries of South America, the nine countries of Central America, and the Caribbean Islands.   México, Cuba,   El Salvador,   Ecuador, Perú, and Nicaragua all are represented. "Hispanic" itself is a new term.   "Spanish surnamed Americans" is the U.S. government's designation of this protected minority.   l'Latino" is also a term used.   In most states, one group dominates: Cubans in Florida, Mexicans in California, and Puerto Ricans in New York City. Rhode Island has a mix.

Hispanics live in three main communities, half in Providence in the three neighborhoods known as South Providence, the West End, and Elmwood. Most of the remainder lives in Central Falls and Pawtucket. Colombians account for more than three quarters of Central Falls' Hispanic population. Guatemalans are mostly in the West End of Providence.   Dominicans, considered by some to be the largest group, are centered in Providence.

Hispanics are a young population, with twice as many persons aged 17 or younger as the population at large.   Medical care for children, adolescents, and especially for women of childbearing age is crucial.   High fertility rates are usually attributed both to Catholic upbringing and general cultural back-grounds, which promote teen-age marriage.   Recent statistics show 20 percent teen-age mothers among Hispanics compared to 12 percent in the rest of the population. Teen-age, out of wedlock pregnancy is a concern to this community, as it is in the general community.

Lack of English language skills is the single most important deterrent to the recent delivery of services to Hispanics, and keeps many in the low paying, unskilled job classifications. ESL classes are available, but too few and too inconvenient.

Education is seen by members of the Hispanic community as the most important matter to address. The dropout rate for Hispanics is almost fifty percent. Many Hispanic students are not achieving. School systems are not able to fully address needs. Roadblocks exist for the hiring of bilingual staff. Legislation on bilingual education has not been implemented, although the community successfully advocated for passage of a Bilingual Education bill in 1981.

Many Hispanic organizations exist -- social, political, religious, and cultural. They tend to consist of members of one national group. Puerto Ricans, Colombians, Dominicans, Guatemalans, and others form groups for their own countrymen. All have small memberships, except for Casa Puerto Rico. Although a few Hispanic leaders have begun to work with community groups around issues of common concern, no coalition of Hispanic leaders exists. In the late 1970's, the United Way funded an organization, which was a coalition of Hispanics. Lack of technical assistance to this group, lack of organizational support and the unfamiliarity of the Hispanic community board members with structure, budgeting, planning, and program development led to the coalition's breakdown, the withdrawal of support by the United Way, and the demise of the coalition.

Most Hispanics are first generation and have strong ties to their native lands. The neighborhoods where they live contain the churches, stores, restaurants, and other institutions of daily life. Two local Spanish newspapers exist in Rhode Island, as does radio programming and cable television in Spanish.

The Hispanic community sought legislation in 1985 to create a Hispanic study commission. The bill passed, the commission was created under the chairmanship of Representative George Castro. No funding and no staff were included in the legislation. Two public meetings were held. Some questionnaires collected data. A short report, released in the spring of 1986 gave several recommendations, but was received with little publicity and enthusiasm in the general community.

In general, Hispanic organizations designed to meet social, cultural, educational, and religious needs are still forming.

An effective and growing organization is the Hispanic Social Services Committee. A Directory, printed in 1985 by this group of mostly Hispanic social service agency professionals, states they are "dedicated to improving the delivery of human services to the Spanish speaking people of this state." The bilingual directories list churches, community action programs, education, health, employment, legal, and other services for Hispanics and the bilingual capacities of each. Portuguese and Creole language capabilities are included as well. The Directory's Introduction states that it is attempting to organize services that have bilingual resource people and to strengthen the network of those bilinguals who are working with Hispanics.

Monthly meetings of the Hispanic Social Services Committee and two highly successful conferences by this dedicated group have attested to its competence. Without staffing or much funding, the Committee has maintained an ongoing organization providing networking, services, conferences and directories that help connect all agencies, public and private, which deal with the state's Hispanics.

Another organization dealing almost exclusively with Hispanics is Progresso Latino in Pawtucket. It was formed in 1977 by a group of Hispanic leaders as an organization, which would offer a range of social services to Hispanics, especially new immigrants. Case management, Day Care, English as a Second language, and a senior citizens program are Progresso Latino's main programs. Originally funded by the Campaign for Human Development, Progresso Latino now receives the majority of its funds from the United Way with supplements from The Rhode Island Foundation, the state legislature, and the cities of Pawtucket and Central Falls. However, many Board of Directors and staff changes over the few years of Progresso Latino's operation have affected its organizational stability.

A Hispanic appointment to the Board of Regents, a Hispanic Advisory Committee to Lt. Governor Richard Licht, one to Congresswoman Claudine Schneider and the appointment of several Hispanics to Minority Affairs Commissions show some organizational movement. A Hispanic is on the Providence School Committee, and on the Board of Regents. "Ethnic issues" committees at some hospitals, utilities, and community groups show beginning awareness. Bilingual personnel at some service providers are being recruited and state and city agencies have begun adding bilingual personnel. The Department of Health and Human Services added a community liaison position in 1985 and has bilingual staff, as do the Department of Employment Security and other state agencies.

Puerto Ricans, one of the larger subgroups, are United States citizens. They have a highly visible organization, Casa Puerto Rico, with its own building and staff. Dominicans and Colombians form the other two largest groups, but do not have comparable organizations. Many Hispanics are not citizens. Many believe citizenship requires total English proficiency. Others expect eventually to return to their homelands; some own land which they will have to forfeit if they become U.S. citizens.

Ninety-five percent of Rhode Island Hispanics, though born Catholics, no longer practice. Many of those who attend church belong to Pentecostal and small Protestant churches serving Spanish speaking congregations with traditional Spanish services. Several large Catholic churches have Hispanic congregations. The Rhode Island Diocese studied their service to Hispanics and recently set up a fund for parishes that want to outreach and serve the Hispanic community. Funds were diminished, however, for advocacy programs at several Catholic churches presently serving the community in South Providence.

Most of the Hispanic population holds jobs in factories producing jewelry, textiles, or toys. Others work in low paying service jobs. Many plants employ numbers of Hispanics and a few of these conduct employment interviews in Spanish and even some ESL classes. Many Hispanics work 50 to 70 hours per week. National surveys reports Hispanics are the poorest group in the United States. The Rhode Island Hispanic population is younger than the general population. It has the largest percent of population less than 25 years of age.

The sale and use of drugs by Hispanics is of general concern to all. Law enforcement officials speak guardedly of the Latin American "cocaine connection." The dissemination of drugs by dealers is perceived to be more prevalent in the Hispanic community than in the rest of the population. This is probably not true. Substance abuse is considered to affect 117%, of the population at large and the percent is probably the same among Hispanics. The Hispanic alcohol and other drug abuser are not being served by the agencies which work in this field. Dealers are repeatedly arrested in Hispanic neighborhoods and have varied ethnic backgrounds, not Hispanic exclusively.

Nevertheless, use of drugs by Hispanics is a growing concern within the community. The trauma of readjustment to a new land, the regular stresses related to poverty, unemployment, and all social ills are given as the reasons for drug abuse. It is conceded that drugs are sold openly on Broad Street in Providence and in Central Falls and Pawtucket as well. Central Falls has instituted a program called "Drop a Dime," asking people to report wrongdoing by making a telephone call.

Casa Puerto Rico is one of the organizations, which is trying to run programs for teenagers to teach them about drug use. The Lt. Governor's Advisory Committee has chosen this as one of their priorities and worked to advocate for a bill passed by the Legislature, which allocated more funds for the control of substance abuse. This group sponsored a conference in the fall of 1986 on the subject and seeks to work with state agencies.

It is generally conceded that a more aggressive and coordinated effort among all law enforcement officials should be made.

Illegal immigration and the sanctuary movement are important subjects in the Hispanic community, but because of their complexity will not be addressed in this paper.

The Portuguese and Cape Verdean Populations

There is strong evidence that Portuguese explorers such as Miguel Corte-Real sailed into Narragansett Bay and around Cape Cod one hundred years before the landing of the Pilgrims. Portugal was then one of the leaders of navigation and exploration, and had colonized the Azores, the Madeira Islands and the Cape Verde Islands, as well as parts of Africa and areas of India, China, and Indonesia.

The Portuguese and Cape Verdean communities have had a presence in Rhode Island since the eighteenth century, when sailing ships stopped at the islands of the Azores and in the Cape Verde Islands to replenish crews. The older Portuguese communities in Rhode Island are Azoreans. There has been a steady stream of immigrants from the Portuguese mainland, Azore Islands, and the Cape Verde Islands, due to economic hardships.

Approximately one hundred thousand Rhode Island residents trace their ancestry as Portuguese, of the population. Of that number, it is estimated that 20,000 still hold Portuguese passports. In Rhode Island, Portuguese represent the largest population of non-English speakers. Seventy percent of Bristol, Rhode Island, and fifty to seventy percent of the Fall River and New Bedford, Massachusetts populations are Portuguese. Rhode Island Portuguese identify with those communities as well as their own.

Approximately 300,000 Cape Verdeans are in the United States, about 40,000 in Rhode Island, another 100,000 in the New Bedford, Fall River, *and Cape* Cod area. Thus, almost half the Cape Verdean population in the U.S. is in the Rhode Island area. Fox Point in Providence is the cultural center of the Cape Verdean population. Pawtucket has 10,000 Cape Verdeans and the largest Cape Verdean church, the Church of the Immaculate Heart of Mary. Many Cape Verdeans speak Creole, the primary language of the Cape Verde Islands. Many Rhode Islanders think Cape Verdeans speak Portuguese exclusively.

Portuguese live in Fox Point in Providence, in East Providence, the Black-stone Valley, Bristol County, and Aquidneck Island. Cape Verdeans live in Providence, Pawtucket, Central Falls, and most of the East Bay communities.

Teachers, educational administrators, lawyers, doctors, and other professionals abound in the Portuguese community. Others often seek those on the top rungs of their professions for counsel as part of the networking, which is characteristic of this community. Many Portuguese will only do business with others of their nationality. It is reported, for example, that a bank in Massachusetts holds much of the savings of the Rhode Island community because it is Portuguese managed.

Many immigrants work in the lowest unskilled jobs because of their lack of knowledge of English. To make up for the low hourly wages, many heads of households work two jobs. Teenagers are encouraged to work at very young ages to help the family and to earn funds to supply their own needs. This sometimes leads to decline in schoolwork or dropping out of school altogether.

Portuguese newspapers, television, and radio serve the community. More than three hundred New England based organizations, more than forty Rhode Island organizations, and almost a dozen churches provide a range of services to the Portuguese community. Cape Verdeans also have many organizations, and also have radio programming. A New Bedford newspaper serves the Rhode Island Cape Verdean community.

Bilingual Creole or Portuguese speakers can be found in many state and city offices and are called upon to act as translators when the need arises. Some cities and towns in Rhode Island most notably Central Falls and Pawtucket have worked to outreach to these communities, and have bilingual help available in city halls and in some city agencies. Many state employment offices have Portuguese language capability, usually because some staff speaks the language.

Neither the Portuguese nor the Cape Verdean communities are satisfied with the quality of education their children are receiving, especially the quality of bilingual, vocational, and special education. Recently some leaders have joined with other community groups to make their concerns known. However, many parents do not understand the traditions of working with schools and feel hesitant to approach administrators.

Cape Verdeans and Portuguese are well represented in the governing and political structures of the communities where they reside, in the Blackstone Valley, East Providence, Bristol, and Warren, for example. Cape Verdeans and Portuguese are members of the state legislature. Hispanics have not yet reached this step, although several are running for ward committee posts. All three groups, however, are underrepresented in the numerous community boards and commissions, which do significant work. Family and church rather than government or not-for profit agencies are expected to meet social service needs and little attention is paid to outside organizations.

Many organizations exist within the Portuguese and Cape Verdean communities, the most important of which are church related. Much of the life of the community revolves around the church and the celebration of holidays, feasts, and festivals. Portuguese language and cultural training, supported by the Portuguese government, is held in many churches.

Most Portuguese are Catholics, and eight parishes exist in Rhode Island with Portuguese speaking priests. These are bastions of Portuguese culture and learning. The first, Our Lady of The Rosary, was established in 11966 and the newest, Our Lady of Fatima in Cumberland, established in 1953. Preserving ethnic and religious traditions is of prime importance to the churches. The Portuguese government sponsors well attended classes in language and culture. Recreation and social needs are often centered on church pasts and holidays, which also serve to unite the communities and tie them to their common heritage. A Portuguese Cultural Foundation insures ties to Portugal.

A strong patriarchal family is considered a characteristic of both communities. All relatives, uncles, aunts, cousins, and grandparents are united in mutual dependency. Getting jobs for the newcomers, helping them with everything from babysitting to translation at hospitals or physician's offices, at Social Security and governmental offices, is delegated to family. Incoming families often live with relatives who provide the necessities for starting life in America. The elderly and infirm are usually cared for within the family unit.

The sense of self-sufficiency and family, which are characteristic of the Portuguese, also means that social service needs are often taken care of within the community in times of need, have been used as Benefits and raffles are held to help individuals or a family Churches, social groups, and even the beloved soccer clubs vehicles to meet unmet needs.

Ethnic and social clubs are also important in the life of the Portuguese community. Organizations were founded in the 1800's when individuals from the same area of Portugal formed a club for mutual assistance. Informal meetings evolved into structured organizations, which bought or built their own buildings instituted health and welfare plans, and sponsored activities. Today, more than forty organizations function in Rhode Island and more than three hundred in New England.

Some Cape Verdeans identify only with the Rhode Island Cape Verdean community. Others consider themselves Portuguese. Most Rhode Islanders consider those from the Cape Verde Islands, the Azores and mainland Portugal as Portuguese, even though Cape Verdeans speak Creole, a different language than Portuguese. Notices in Portuguese sent home with Cape Verdean schoolchildren might not be understood. Many agencies expect all Cape Verdean immigrants to speak Portuguese.

Language and culture set Cape Verdeans apart from mainland and Azorean Portuguese communities. The Cape Verdean culture is basically African. Cape Verde is now a member of the African community of nations. Many Rhode Island Cape Verdeans also identify with the discrimination suffered by American Blacks and have worked in the Civil Rights movements from the 1960's onward. A Cape Verdean was President of the National Association for the Advancement of Colored People (NAACP), Rhode Island Chapter. At the present time there is some involvement by Cape Verdeans with organizations of the minority community, but a feeling of ambivalence about the role by some. Cape Verdeans have maintained a strong sense of their own identity. Churches, social organizations, radio programs, and newspapers have helped to unify the community.

A Cape Verdean American Federation, Cape Verdean Progressive Association, and a Cape Verdean subcommittee of the Rhode Island Heritage Commission function actively.

Many Cape Verdeans still work in occupations connected to the sea, such as longshoremen, fishermen, or sailors. Others are employed throughout Rhode Island in factories and service sector jobs. Newcomers are integrated into the workforce through networking and helped to find employment by those members of the community already here.

Throughout Rhode Island, the Portuguese have been noteworthy as especially hard working and diligent employees and because of this; members of the community have usually been able to find jobs for newcomers. Portuguese work in textile and other mills, in sea-related occupations and in agriculture.

Recommendations

This report will make recommendations, similar to recommendations made by other studies, including the Rhode Island Legislative Commission to Study Issues Confronting the Hispanic Community. In order for the recommendations to be implemented, a strong effort on the part of the Hispanic, Cape Verdean, and Portuguese communities, with cooperation from powerful advocacy groups, will be required. Programs must be developed to accomplish goals. The Rhode Island citizenry as a whole must be educated to understand that suitable education and job training will insure a future that will enhance the quality of life for all of Rhode Island.

Recommendation I

Involvement in Government

Hispanics, Portuguese, and Cape Verdeans must be elected, appointed, and employed positions in state, represented in all city, and town governments.

As population trends change, the state and municipal governments must provide adequate representation for Hispanics, Portuguese, and Cape Verdeans in policy-making positions and as part of the governmental workforce.

Involvement is a two-way street, and members of the Hispanic, Portuguese, and Cape Verdean communities must work with the leadership of cities and towns and the State to supply qualified candidates for all positions, and to assure that all institutions deliver services to their populations in an appropriate manner.

Recommendation II

Bilingual Staff

Bilingual staff should be hired by all public agencies.
A genuine effort is required to secure Hispanic bilinguals in all agencies, which deal with the public, especially the schools. Portuguese and Creole speakers are presently more likely to be available in public agencies, but efforts should be made to make sure that they are in fact available whenever they are needed. Hispanic bilinguals must be recruited and trained. Government employees should receive monetary incentives for learning needed languages. Ability to speak languages other than English should be one of the skills desired if not required for employment in public and private agencies. All agencies; private and public, to determine the service requirements of these populations, should do assessments and realistic appraisals of the requirements to meet the needs must be undertaken.

Recommendation III

Leadership Training

Leadership training should be made available to limited English populations.

Public and private organizations and agencies in Rhode Island need the input on boards and committees of the three communities covered by this study.

To prepare for leadership roles, members of the Hispanic, Cape Verdean, and Portuguese communities should seek leadership training. Training is especially important so that board members can be effective spokespersons to represent the views of their community. As a national community foundation study points out, "People need skills to conduct productive and democratic community meetings and to learn to acquire the knowledge to examine and act on public issues."

Organizations such as the United Way should be prepared to give leadership training and technical assistance to individuals who hold or want to hold office or serve on boards of their own or other organizations.

The Portuguese and Cape Verdean communities have been in Rhode Island for many years and have many organizations; The Hispanic community is of more recent vintage and has not reached maturity in terms of organizations. It needs technical assistance in staffing its community organizations so that they can be successful.

All organizations need to know and understand how state and city governments, the private sector, and the not-for-profit sectors operate. In dealing with the agencies and organization~ which make our state function, a knowledge of who, where, how and why things are done is essential. Leadership training could make organizational activity effective and thus encourage more participation in organization projects.

Recommendation IV

Education

The education needs of the Hispanic, Cape Verdean, and Portuguese populations should be established as a priority.

School committees, teachers, administrators, and parents must address education for ethnically diverse, limited English speaking students in all communities. Programs must be developed to reach students by working through parents and the community. Schools must take the initiative to build links with the Hispanic, Portuguese, and Cape Verdean communities, especially with those students and parents who are recent arrivals. All national studies affirm the importance of working with parents, if any success is to be achieved. Hispanic youth are caught between Hispanic culture at home and U.S. culture at school.

The dropout rate for minority and linguistically limited students especially for Hispanics must be made a top priority in educational planning. Bilingual counselors can be an important factor in keeping present students in school. At the present time, they do not exist. Roadblocks, such as certification regulations, must be cast aside and creative methods used to put appropriate personnel in schools.

Curriculum, which stresses English capability, coupled with retention of native languages, and which stresses ethnic diversity and bicultural sensitivity1 must be developed.

Work should be linked to school as early as junior high school. Part time and summer strategies to link work and school have been developed elsewhere. Part time employment has been found by many national studies to keep students in schools, improve grades, and introduce students to the world of work. Educators must work with the business community to motivate youngsters and convince them that staying in school will provide better employment opportunities.

English must be taught more effectively to adult Hispanics, Cape Verdeans, and Portuguese who are new immigrants and to those who are limited English speakers. Tutorial and ESL programs at work sites should be considered.

All students should be encouraged to reach high academic achievement and to seek higher education. Programs at community colleges and institutions of higher education should offer support; services for these populations where appropriate. Seeking to enroll students from these groups without offering counseling, remedial work and the chance for tutorials will not allow them to have a successful experience.

Community-wide groups, which promote education, should seek representation from Hispanic, Portuguese, and Cape Verdean communities. Sensitivity to the needs of these groups is most important. An atmosphere of mutual respect and dignity must be established. Members of these communities, on the other hand, must be willing to work with already established groups around common issues and must learn lobbying techniques.

Studies indicate that success at school affects post--high school and those non-graduates require more public assistance. Our no longer absorb the non-graduate. Even the armed forces are not catchall for minority school dropouts since they require skilled experiences, economy can longer the technologists.

Volunteers, especially those from within the ethnic communities, used by the schools to foster English language literacy for student's adult members of the neighborhood community. Leaders of each ethnic should be involved with neighborhood schools and work to help their realize school's importance to their children's future success should be and for community Inter group relations -- the ability of students of all races and nationalities to live harmoniously and to understand and- respect each other -- should be an important goal in each school. At present there is great divisiveness in schools. No concentrated effort to deal with this problem is in place.

Involvement of the business community and strategies for work opportunities integrated into the curriculum of inner-city schools has to be part of overall education policy.

Hispanic, Cape Verdean, and Portuguese immigrant youth with limited language facility from low-income homes face little prospect for employment either after school, or during summer vacations. Yet numerous studies have shown that where work was integrated into education and where social skills, language proficiency and technical training were offered, success was achieved.

In most areas where programs are considered model, industry has helped to provide access, work experience, and world of work skills training which could increase the employment and income prospects of the youth. In Hartford, for example, insurance and banking companies, which have developed financial support to supplement government funding, have provided training sites and internships and have offered employment to those who completed programs. San Antonio gives pre-employment and work readiness training to juniors in high school.

The San Antonio Alliance for Business provided summer work sites for students who spend half their summer time in workshops while working and being paid by the companies. Boston has just announced a community-wide plan, supported by major funds from the corporate sector, to assure educational opportunities for minority students, including funds for college and jobs afterwards.

In Pawtucket, the Pawtucket Housing Authority instituted a work program for youngsters who live in the housing projects, most of them Hispanic youth. It was called "The Big Green Clean Machine." Anyone who wanted to sign up for the program was given a T-shirt and hat, and paid to work twenty hours a week in grounds keeping and maintenance. At the end of the summer, participants had earned money and were treated to a party or ball game.

Recommendation V

Health

The health delivery system must deliver services to different population groups, especially limited English speakers.

The Hispanic, Portuguese, and Cape Verdean communities in Rhode Island generally do not have their health needs addressed by the health delivery system if they are not fluent English speakers. The ability to speak several languages should be part of the desired qualifications of front line medical personnel. Medical personnel should be trained to be bilingual or trilingual. Cultural sensitivity also needs to be taught.

Hispanics, because that population is growing so rapidly, need special attention. Hispanic birth rates are high and prenatal care is rarely adequate. The population is younger than other population groups.   Drug and substance abuse programs, teenage pregnancy programs, and other concerns of the general community should also relate to the concerns of the ethnic populations.

Area hospitals and mental health facilities need to make accommodation for limited English patients, especially in emergency room personnel, where around the clock translators are required. Mental health professionals should be trained to understand and be sensitive to cultural differences.

Recommendation VI

Employment

Coordination of employment services to linguistic minorities is vital to future economic planning.

There are no meetings for employment-related groups or individuals working with Hispanics, Portuguese, or Cape Verdean immigrants such as there are in the field of social services.   Professionals working in the field of employment with special concerns for these communities have no mechanism with which to pass on materials.

The workforce in Rhode Island includes, among others, tens of thousands of immigrants who have arrived over the past ten years from Central and South America, Portugal, the Azores, and the Cape Verde Islands. Many have a limited knowledge of English and possess few marketable skills upon arrival. While jobs are available in unskilled categories in factories and in the service sector -- indeed this is the reason many move to Rhode Island -- there is little chance for advancement unless English language training and bilingual technical training is available and accessible.

Economic predictions point to a diminution of manufacturing jobs and a rise in the numbers of skilled technical positions. If this workforce is to be employed in the future and if employers coming in to Rhode Island are to find qualified help, plans must be made to upgrade capabilities. Underemployed and unemployed minorities do not add to the stability of the workforce, although it is the very fact of available unskilled; low paying jobs, which brings immigrants to Rhode Island.

Organizations involved with employment -- including Chambers of Commerce, business and labor organizations, the Department of Employment Security, the Rhode Island Department of Labor and all vocational training groups -- should direct their attention to these populations. Data needs to be gathered, programs planned and coordinated.

The populations themselves need to lobby effectively to ensure their needs are being met and that training programs adequately prepare participants for employment. Affirmative action plans should include all minorities. Accommodations should be made in pre-employment testing for limited English speakers if tests do not reflect the person's intelligence, education, or ability to do the job.

Employment of youth, with incentives to remain in school, with programs that work in concert with education and which involve the private sector, must be made a top priority for the community and the State. A generation of uneducated, unskilled, unfulfilled youth is emerging, and unless the problem is addressed, the price paid by the entire community will be very high. Since CETA programs were eliminated, no federal program has emerged for disadvantaged youth. JPTA, which succeeded CETA, has not really filled this gap. Public policy has not addressed job training for youth. Only a few short-term programs exist in Rhode Island. Boston has just announced a community-wide plan with money raised in the corporate sector to address the same problem.

Recommendation VII

Technical Assistance

Technical assistance should be provided to viable organizations. Most organization which have as their goal provision of services to recent Hispanic, Portuguese, and Cape Verdean immigrants are un-staffed, volunteer, citizen-directed efforts. If these groups had funding for part time, paid, professional staff or consultants, they could be helped to achieve some of their goals. Technical assistance could aid in fostering liaisons with other community agencies and afford the community groups some opportunity to accomplish their objectives.

The Hispanic Social Services Committee, for example, has run two highly successful conferences involving a number of public and private service providers to Hispanics. Without paid staff, the leadership of that group will find it difficult this year to mount a third. A newly formed Hispanic Chamber of Commerce might also use some assistance. Paid technical staff would be particularly useful for the grant application process to secure public or private funding.

Recommendation VIII

Drug and Alcohol/Substance Abuse

Illicit drug, alcohol, and other substance abuse services must be made available.

If there is heavy involvement within the Hispanic community with drugs and alcohol it should be identified, documented, and addressed by the public and private agencies that deal with this issue. Whether some programs can be set up that are exclusively aimed at the Hispanic population or whether some modifications can be made to existing programs will have to be determined. Since a substance abuse problem in any segment of the population is a problem for the entire population, it must be addressed.

Implications For Rhode Island Grantmakers

Of the three ethnic communities discussed emerge, as the group most in need of support from are the fastest growing population in the United in the State of Rhode Island. In this study, the Hispanics local grant makers. Hispanics States, in the Northeast, and a Latino Institute study indicates that nationally, foundation awards have been in eight major areas: education, civil rights, research, community organization, health, social services, arts, and religion. Most grants were small. Community foundations were over represented and corporate foundations were underrepresented. This report goes on to state that Hispanics have been obliged to present a united front in order to attract support, in spite of the differing needs of the groups. It is suggested that grant makers often find it frustrating to try to sort out different groups with different agendas. Most foundations limit their funds to programs, but not to coalition building. If this were not the case, Hispanic organizations might be encouraged to coalesce. They could set their own agendas, defray the costs of meeting, and be provided with some technical assistance. Specifically, the foundations could encourage coalitions around important issues, such as education and provision of social services.

In Rhode Island, two groups -- the Hispanic Education Committee, headed by attorney Juan Saez Burgos, and the Hispanic Social Services Committee, chaired by Dr. Cynthia Garcia Coll -- have already proved their effectiveness, but have not begun to scratch the surface in terms of work to be done. Another group has just been formed to act in an advocacy role to further the work of groups whose funds have been curtailed. The work of these three groups covers areas of concern to the Rhode Island community and to the Hispanic community the challenge to grant makers is to make their funds accessible to groups such as have been mentioned, to help Hispanics to form organizations to deal with their issues, to help Hispanic leaders develop the skills to form community organizations and to work within other community groups in areas of mutual concern. Grant makers should support and sustain any credible advocacy groups.

The acquisition of 501(c) (3) status and the development of organizations with sound budgeting, effective leadership and structured organization is a formidable task for new groups in our community. Foundations need to help in nurturing groups and in moving them forward.

The Rhode Island Foundation and other Rhode Island grant makers should also be willing to fund research on the needs of Hispanics, research conducted by Hispanics to identify issues and collect data on their communities. The grant- makers need also to develop working relationships with the community. The Hispanic community needs to understand and educate the foundations to deal with it as a growing but diverse segment of the population. Grant makers need to reach out and to understand that most Hispanic groups are not equipped to write proposals or to initiate comprehensive plans to solve problems. They both need to translate their wishes into mutually acceptable mechanisms.

Organizations need to hire staff knowledgeable about the Hispanic community and to encourage more boards, organizations, commissions, and philanthropic groups to have Hispanics as members. Hispanics must be integrated into the community network, which can assist them in their quest for a better life.

To accomplish a representative usually defined as life, and with sound relationships this task, grant makers perhaps should convene a meeting with group from the Hispanic community, not necessarily those leaders, but persons representing the segments of Hispanic this group seek to define ways in which they could establish

And grant makers could also make it clear to the many groups they fund that they expect these groups to be aware of the need of services to this segment of the community. For example, in collecting data from grant applicants, data on service to Hispanics in Rhode Island -- where appropriate -- could be requested. The request would certainly alert the organizations that the prestigious foundations were interested, and might make them realign their goals to include Hispanics.

Finally grant makers should encourage the corporate sector of the community to establish linkages, programs, and participation with Hispanic groups and organizations as a part of their civic responsibilities. Corporate Rhode Island should be encouraged to provide opportunities for the advancement of the aims of the Hispanic community with programs such as work-study for Hispanic youth to reverse the almost fifty percent dropout rate, with employee programs and incentives and through cooperation with community groups working to assist the Hispanic community.

The civil rights movement of the 1960s placed Blacks into the business of community life; the women's movement of the 1970s did the women. The present task is to place Hispanics into the mindset of Island community, not as a shadowy unwanted group, but as an underserved population.

Resource List

1. William Allen, United Way
2. Marian Avarista, United Way
3. Hispanic Monitoring Committee, United Way
4. Virginia DaMota, R.I. Department of Education
5. Commissioner Troy Earhart, RI Department of Education
6. Olga Escobar, R.I. Department of Health and Human Services
7. Mathies Santos, R.I. Department of Administration
8. Juan Francisco, R.I. Human Rights Commission, R.I. Board of Regents
9. Hispanic Advisory Committee, Office of the Lt. Governor
10. Lorraine Biggs, Affirmative Action Office, City of Providence
11. Pershing Rodriguez, Providence School Department
12. Phyllis Pacheco, Fox Point Branch, Providence Public Library
13. Bruce Keiser, City of Pawtucket
14. Paul Mowrey3 City of Pawtucket
15. Gloria Duggan, Pawtucket Neighborhood Health Center
16. William Siemens, City of Central Falls
17. R.I. Advisory Committee to U.S. Civil Rights Commission
18. Eva Nelson, Rhode Island Heritage Commission
19. Rep. George Castro, Hispanic Affairs Commission

20. Victor Mendoza, Hispanic Cultural Arts Committee
21. B.J. Clanton, Urban League
22. Dr. Cynthia Garcia-Cole, Hispanic Social Services Committee, Woman & Infants Hospital, Brown University
23. Virginia Neves Gonzalez, New England Bilingual Education Center
24. Juan Saez, R.I. Legal Services
25. Paul Jones, International Institute
26. William Shuey, International Institute
27. Sandra Smith, Project Persona
28. Sarah Murphy, Girl Scouts of Rhode Island
29. SER -- Jobs for Progress
30. Dania Keisling, SER
31. Patricia Martinez, SER
32. Carlos Pedro, SER
33. Al Braz, Cape Verdean Progressive Association
34. Oling Jackson, Cape Verdean Heritage Commission
35. Antonio Lopes, Cape Verdean Heritage Commission
36. Robert Candon, La Palabras
37. Progreso Latino
38. Gabriel Quirles, Casa Puerto Rico
39. Juanita Sanchez, Project Rainbow, Hope High School
40. Prof. Oneismo Almeida, Portuguese Studies, Brown University
41. Father Raymond Tetreault, St. Michael's
42. Ferdinand Cunha, Esq.
43. Rachel Cunha
44. Rev. Moises Mercedes
45. Katy Castagna, Brown University
46. Roberto Gonzalez, Urban Education Center
47. Jose Gonzalez, University of Rhode Island
48. Marguerita Baez Lt Governor's Office

Activist Undaunted By Odds In His Quest To Become Governor

Gregg Krupa
Journal-Bulletin Staff Writer.
Providence Journal Providence,
CAMPAIGN '86
Oct 30, 1986

PROVIDENCE Anthony D. Affigne sits in his campaign headquarters, a storefront in South Providence, surrounded by the remnants of all of his campaign advertising, $1,000 in wooden signs and $800 in bumper stickers and buttons.

Affigne, the Citizens Party of Rhode Island candidate for governor, leads a campaign with far less resources than the two major contenders and has few illusions about electoral realities.

But the 31-year-old teacher and social activist says his candidacy represents the unrepresented constituents like labor, the poor, women and the disabled that the major parties have forgotten, and that gives him more support than people think.

"If there were ever an election in which Rhode Island voters were being asked to choose between Tweedledum and Tweedledee, it's the 1986 gubernatorial election," Affigne said.

"There's no doubt in my mind that win or lose, the political experts will be very surprised by how well I do on Election Day."

Activism began early

Affigne's social activism dates from early confrontations with prejudice and his teenage years in rural Pennsylvania, when federal public works projects chased residents from the county in which he grew up.

"I was the only Puerto Rican for hundreds of miles around and, along with a lot of Italo-Americans, who were moving into rural sections from the metropolitan areas, I was frequently the target of prejudice and discrimination," he said.

He said residents eventually discovered that the real reason for a water project was not to provide drinking water but a dry-season source of cooling for a nuclear power plant.

"I think it certainly helped stimulate a sense of activism on my part to have my hometown destroyed by fiat of the federal government, and to see the people in the region become virtually powerless in their own lives and in their own community," Affigne said. "That all happened the year I came to Brown."

Family life

Affigne has lived in Providence since his freshman year at Brown University in 1972.

Since then, his activism led him to roles with Rhode Island Workers' Association, the Coalition for Consumer Justice, People Acting through Community Effort (PACE) and the Fox Point Community Organization.

He was chairman of the Fox Point Steering Committee, vice chairman of the Mount Hope Neighborhood Association and chairman of the Providence Citizens Review Board.

Affigne and his wife, Suzanne, live in the Mount Hope section with their two children. Another child is due just after Election Day. When he talks about the things he enjoys most in life, his hobbies and his future, Affigne mentions his family.

His daughter, Carmen Celeste, who is 3 1/2 years old, was born with multiple birth defects. She has had 11 operations and been hospitalized 13 times.

"She's a very feisty, outgoing little girl," Affigne says. "She lives with herself and is very happy with herself, and that's a real encouragement to us, that if she can find the strength and desire to live everyday, then so can I.

"I think I can do as good a job, a better job, than any of the people in the race right now, not because I was the mayor of a medium-size city in Rhode Island or because I was the chairman of the board of a major corporation, but because I have genuine compassion for the people, and genuine compassion for people with disabilities, people who are poor, people who are elderly."
Housing is big issue

Affigne resigned an adult education teaching position at Rhode Island College to campaign for governor. He teaches mathematics, and has a great deal to do with computers.

"That's what I enjoy, computers. Find ways to get computers to take some of the drudgery out of life, and to help people learn, to ease some of the drudgery in their lives."

He says his spare time often finds him with a computer book in hand and riding bicycles or playing with his children.

New housing and economic policies are issues that Affigne stresses.

If his candidacy is not successful this time, he says, he will not consider it a loss but will work toward the future.

"I intend to run for governor until I win the governor's office," he said. "Now millionaires or people who have a million dollars to spend apparently can do that the first time around. Maybe Tony Affigne's going to have to do it more than once.

"But I am 20 years younger than either of the major party candidates.

I am going to be around for a long, long time."

ANTHONY D. AFFIGNE

Age: 31

Office sought: Governor

Education: Brown University

Family: Married, daughter, 3 1/2, son, 11.

Occupation: Teacher

Latinos and the Remaking of American Politics

> At every hour of the day and night my countrymen ran to me
> for protection against the assaults or exaction of those adven-
> turers. Sometimes, by persuasion, I prevailed on them to desist;
> sometimes, also, force had to be resorted to. How could I have
> done otherwise? Could I leave them defenseless, exposed to the
> assaults of foreigners who, on the pretext that they were Mexi-
> cans, treated them worse than brutes?
>
> *-Juan Seguin[1]*

Every American recognizes the name Davy Crockett, the frontier legend who died defending the Alamo, but Juan *Seguin,* who fought with Crockett and survived, is virtually unknown.

Seguin's ancestors settled present-day San Antonio fifty years before the American Revolution. A rich landowner and federalist opposed to Mexican president Santa Anna, *Seguin* was part of the small group of Mexicans who joined the Texas rebels at the Alamo, but he was dispatched from the fort with a message to Sam Houston before the shooting began and thus escaped the massacre. Seguin went on to fight with Houston's army at the Battle of San Jacinto, was later elected a senator of the Texas Republic and served several terms as mayor of San Antonio. Then, in 1842, Anglo newcomers chased him from office at gunpoint, seized his land, and forced him to flee to Mexico, making him the last Hispanic mayor of San Antonio until Henry Cisneros took office 140 years later.[2]

Seguin is the forgotten father of Latino politics in the United States. The story of his life and career has left Mexican Americans with a somewhat different political legacy than that which Washington, Jefferson, and the Founding Fathers bequeathed to white Americans, or which Nat Turner, Sojourner Truth, and W. E. B. Du Bois symbolize for black Americans. How our nation comes to terms with that legacy will determine much of American politics during the twenty-first century.

The reason is simple. The political influence of Hispanic Americans is growing at breakneck speed. Between 1976 and 1996, Hispanic voter registration in the United States increased 164 percent compared to only 31 percent among non-Hispanics; voter turnout among Hispanics grew by 135 percent compared to only 21 percent among non-Hispanics. The number of votes cast by non-Hispanic whites decreased by 9,887,000 from 1992 to 1996, while it increased by 690,000 among Hispanics and only by 15,000 among blacks.[3]

In a mushrooming democratic revolution that is echoing what African Americans accomplished in the 1970s and 1980s; Latino candidates have been gaining majority control of school boards and rural governments throughout the Southwest, while Florida, the Northeast, and Midwest are experiencing similar upheavals. By the end of the decade, several Hispanics will be sitting in the US. Senate; four of the country's ten biggest cities-New York, Los Angeles, Dallas, and San Diego-will witness formidable campaigns for City Hall by Latino candidates; and the mayors of state capitals as scattered as Hartford, Sacramento, and Trenton could be Hispanic.

This political revolution will not be halted by the rise of anti-Hispanic sentiment among some white and black Americans nor by the spate of restrictive immigration laws Congress passed in the mid-1990s. It will not be turned back by Supreme Court decisions that negated as "racial gerrymandering" a handful of congressional districts redrawn after the 1990 census, If anything, the anti-Hispanic backlash at the end of the century-most symbolized by the English-only and anti-immigration, movements-has only heightened the clamor of Latinos for full equality.

Several new factors have fueled the spread of this peaceful revolution:
1. *A rush to citizenship.* Legal Hispanic immigrants, fearing the from initiatives like California's Proposition 187, moved in record numbers to acquire full citizenship during the 1990s rather than remain to laws that targeted non citizens.

2. *Demographics.* With a median age far younger than the rest of
U.S. Population, Hispanics are rapidly increasing their portion of the electorate, a trend that will continue throughout the first half of this century regardless of changes in future immigration levels.

3. *The consolidation of a cohesive national Latino lobby* disparate Hispanic ethnic groups have begun to master the art of intra-Latino coalitions to affect the policies of Washington lawmakers.
4. *The emergence of a socially oriented Hispanic middle class.* During : 1980s, a significant Latino professional and business class arose that perhaps with the unique exception of the Cuban American wing till identifies both its roots and its future with the masses of blue-collar Latinos, Those Latino professionals, marginalized for years by white critics who kept labeling them the inferior products of affirmative action, have now spent decades

accumulating wealth and technical skills, and :you have matured into a burgeoning middle class that is insisting on accountability to the Latino population by both government and other institutions within society.

5. The rise of the Latino Third Force. The growing ability of Latino leaders and voters to function as an unpredictable "swing factor" in the political landscape-refusing to be taken for granted by either the Democratic or Republican parties, or by those who see all politics in the country through the flawed prism of a white-black racial divide.

Fifty years ago, Latino registered voters in the United States could be counted in the thousands; today, they number more than 6.5 million. 1950, there were a few hundred Latino elected officials, almost none in major cities. Today, there are more than six thousand; and Latinos comprise the biggest ethnic voting blocs in Los Angeles, New York; San Antonio, and Miami. Fifty years ago, no presidential candidate bothered to worry about issues affecting Hispanics, while in the presidential campaign of 2000, both George W. Bush and Al Gore, the early favorites for the Republican and Democratic nominations, boast of their bilingualism and heavily court Latino voters.

This revolution did not happen overnight. It has been building since the end of World War II and has passed through several stages during that time. Unfortunately, the way those stages unfolded have until now escaped most political observers, for there have been few systematic studies of Latino politics in the US.

In this chapter, I identify and analyze each stage of the modem· Latino political movement: the people, organizations, ideas, and methods that dominated each stage, and the important lessons each generation carried from one stage to another, Hopefully, my effort will prod others more comprehensive studies. While the periods of development exactly coincide for each Latino group, the parallels among them far more striking than the differences. I have divided the past into five major periods:

- The Integration Period: 1950-1964
- The Radical Nationalist Period: 1965-1974
- The Voting Rights Period: 1975-1984
- The Rainbow Period: 1985-1994
- The Third Force Period: 1995-present

The Integration Period: 1950-1964

The most decisive influence on Latino politics this century was World War II. Thousands of Mexican Americans and Puerto Ricans who served their country in that war-and in the Korean War a few years returned from the battlefield with a new confidence regarding rights as Americans. These veterans refused to accept the blatant Hispanic segregation that had been the rule for generations, especially the Southwest. In 1949, for instance, when a funeral home in Rivers, Texas, refused to bury war veteran Felix Longoria, civic such as Dr. Hector Garcia, attorney Gus Garcia, and other founded the American GI. Forum, a civil rights and veterans group that won a wide following among Mexican Americans.[4] The Longoria incident, much like the controversy over Sergeant Jose Mendoza, Congressional Medal of Honor winner from Brownsville, Mexican American anger throughout the nation.

The veterans not only threw themselves into organizations like rum and the older League of United Latin American Citizens, but also turned to politics and began to challenge the historic Mexicans from the voting booth.

The infamous Texas poll tax and other measures to restrict ballot access (such as the· all white primary and annual voter registration months before an election before an election) had been ram through the Texas legislature at the beginni1lg of the century Democratic Party's white elite to counter· the growth of the movement among blacks, Mexicans, and poor whites. At the People's Party in 1896, for instance, its candidate for governor of Texas carried 44 percent of the vote, with an amazing 88 percent of adults going to the polls. But after the poll tax became law, Texas elections plummeted by as much as two-thirds and it failed reached higher than 40 percent for the first half of the twentieth century. Poor whites, blacks, and Mexicans simply could not afford to pay a tax that in some cases equaled almost 30 percent of the average weekly factory wage in the South.[5] The tax remained in effect until 1966, federal judge ruled it unconstitutional. Its elimination made it possible for blacks and Mexican Americans to finally return to the voting rolls in large numbers.

Before World War II, only New Mexico could claim any tradition of Mexican Americans holding federal elected office. Dennis Chavez, for instance, served in the U.S. House of Representatives from 1935 to 1962. But few Hispanics held public office anywhere else in the country. Puerto Rican Oscar Rivera Garcia, the only example in New York, was elected to the state assembly in 1937. After the war, the giant *barrios* of Los Angeles and San Antonio emerged as the centers of Hispanic ferment. In San Antonio, Henry B. Gonzalez, a war veteran and former juvenile probation officer, began organizing the *tejanos* of the West Side through his Pan American Progressive Association, while in Los Angeles, social worker Edward Roybal, another war veteran, rallied *mexicanos* to register and vote. They were the first Latino councilmen in their respective cities since the mid-nineteenth century-Roybal in 1949 and Gonzalez in 1953.

John F. Kennedy's nomination as the Democratic Party's presidential candidate in 1960 was the watershed moment of the Integration Period. Until then, Mexican Americans had backed liberal candidates in state elections but had made no visible impact on a national election. In Texas, for instance, Mexicans were loyal backers of populist Democratic senators Ralph Yarborough and Lyndon B. Johnson. But the campaign of Kennedy, a charismatic, liberal Catholic, gave Roybal, Gonzalez, and the World War II veterans the opportunity to show the growing clout they formed Viva Kennedy clubs throughout the Southwest the young Massachusetts senator against Vice President Richard Nixon.

In a close election, Kennedy swept 91 percent of the 200,000 Mexican in Texas, which helped him carry the state. And while he managed a minority of the white vote in neighboring New Mexico, he gar70 percent of the Mexican vote, enough for a razor-thin margin Nationwide, he amassed 85 percent of the Mexican vote. Kennedy, threw his support to Gonzalez in his victorious turn for Congress special election the following year; and he provided similar support in 1962, enabling him to win a congressional· seat from a district was only 9 percent *mexicano.* Then, in the Democratic landslide Lyndon Johnson to victory over Barry Goldwater in 1964, "Kika" de la Garza won a second Texas congressional seat and Montoya, the congressman from New Mexico, captured a U.S. seat.

That handful of victories during the early 1960s opened the gates for the modern Hispanic political movement. At the time De la Garza was elected, *tejanos* held only 31 of 3,300 elected positions in the state and only 5 of 11,800 appointed posts. By 1994, just three decades later, the number of Texas Hispanic officeholders had skyrocketed to 2,215.[6] To this day, you will find Mexican homes in the Southwest where a faded photo of John Kennedy hangs prominently near one of the Virgin of Guadalupe a testament to Kennedy's role as the first US. President to address the concerns of Latinos within the American family.

Those early political gains, however, were largely confined to Mexican Americans. Although nearly a million Puerto Ricans lived in the United States by the late 1950s, they were concentrated in New York City and more concerned with political events on the island than with those in their new home. In August 1936, for instance, more than ten thousand people joined a march for Puerto Rican independence organized by radical East Harlem congressman Vito Marcantonio, and throughout the 1950s, the debate over the status of Puerto Rico dominated the *barrios* of New York:

After Marcantonio's ouster, the few Puerto Ricans who won elective office in that city were all handpicked by the old-line Tammany Hall machine. None had the pioneering zeal exhibited by Mexican Americans Gonzalez and Roybal at the other end of the country. Among those machine candidates were Felipe Torres, who captured a Bronx state assembly seat in 1954, and J. Lopez Ramos, who went to the assembly from East Harlem in 1958.[8] The first citywide Puerto Rican civic associations, the Puerto Rican Forum, the Puerto Rican Family Institute, and the Puerto Rican Association for Community Affairs, were founded around that time. The machine's grip on Puerto Rican voters was not challenged until 1965, when Herman Badillo won the borough presidency of the Bronx as a candidate of the reform wing of the Democratic Party, thus becoming the first Puerto Rican to hold a major city post. Badillo's victory, however, depended largely on liberal Jewish and voters instead of Puerto Ricans, who remained a tiny electoral force.

During the 1960s, the Johnson administration, under pressure from rising civil rights movement and from the rioting of disaffected blacks, pushed a series of landmark bills through Congress. Those laws, the Civil Rights Act of 1964, the Voting Rights Act of 1965, and the Fair Housing; Act of 1968, toppled the legal underpinnings of discrimination against both blacks and Hispanics. Some conservatives challenged the inclusion of Hispanics under those laws, especially under the Voting Rights and they continue to do so to this day. Linda Chavez, for instance, in book *Out of the Barrio,* claims that "Hispanics had never been subject to the same denial of their basic right to vote that blacks had suffered."[9] That assertion somehow ignores the genuine obstacles to political representation faced from the caste system in place since the days of Juan Seguin.

Chavez even ignores major federal court decisions that finally struck down that cask system in 1954, two weeks before its *Brown .Board of Education* decision, the Supreme Court decided a seminal case affecting in *Peter Hernandez* v. *Texas,* and the Court ruled that Mexicans were "a distinct class" who could claim protection from discrimination. The Court found that of six thousand jurors called in the years in Jackson County, Texas, none had been a Mexicans comprised 14 percent of the county's To attribute that to "mere chance:' wrote Chief Justice Earl Warren for the court's majority, "taxes our credibility," instead, the Court found that the political system of the county discriminated as a distinct class from either whites or blacks.

A restaurant in town, Warren noted, had signs saying: NO MEXICANS SERVED, toilets in the local courthouse were segregated, with one men's toilet marked COLORED MEN and HOMBRES AQUI (MEN HERE) and "until children of Mexican descent were required to attend a school for the first four grades" .

The court thus reversed the murder conviction of plaintiff Peter Hernandez due to the systematic exclusion of Mexicans from juries in the country. In doing so, the Court's majority noted that "the Fourteenth is not directed solely against discrimination due to a 'two that is, based upon differences between 'white' and Three years later, in *Hernandez dill.* v. *Driscol Consolidated School! System,* a federal district court outlawed segregated schools for Mexicans, which the court said had been a fact of life in Texas since the Anglo settlers' first arrived.[11]

While new laws and federal court decisions during the Kennedy- era Latino political involvement by eliminating legal they did little to alter the economic and social inequities accumulated from both the Mexican caste system and Jim Crow the pervasive new influence of television stories of dilapidated Harlem tenements, Bull Watts suddenly made social inequity more m fact, signaled the end of the incremental with everyone else in America, entered a new psychological and political era one of rebellion and social polarization.

The Radical Nationalist Period: 1965-1974

Watts sparked the greatest period of civil unrest in the United States during the twentieth century. For several years, riots became an annual reality for the inner cities, and, as they did, many white Americans began to regard protests by blacks and Hispanics as a threat to the nation's stability. At the same time, African American and Latino youth conduced that their parents' attempt at integration within the political system had failed. Only through massive protests, disruptive boycotts, and strikes or even riots, the new generation decided, could qualitative (some called it revolutionary) change be accomplished.

Within a few years, a whole gamut of new organizations arose to compete with the more established groups such as LULAC, the GI Forum; and the Puerto Rican Forum. 'The brash new groups-the Brown Berets, La Raza Unida, the Alianza, the United Farm Workers, the Young Lords, Los Siete de La Raza, Crusade for Justice, Movimiento Pro Independencia, MECHA, August Twenty-ninth Movement-were invariably radical, their membership younger and usually from lower class than the established civic organizations, they saw the older organizations as too tied to the status quo, too concerned with appearing to be respectable and reasonable to Anglo society.

The radical groups sprang up almost overnight in every urban and southwest farm community, rarely with much organizational connection. Inspired by the black power and anti-Vietnam War at home and by the anti-colonial revolutions in the Third World, especially the Cuban revolution, most offered a utopian, vaguely socialist vision of changing America, and all of them called for a reinterpretation the Latino's place in US History. They insisted that both Puerto and Mexicans were descendants of conquered peoples who had forcibly subjugated when America annexed their territories during expansion. Because of those annexations, the rebels insisted, Puerto cans and Mexicans were more comparable to the Native Americans the African Americans than to Scotch, German, Irish, or Italian immigrants.

This was also the period when the Latino community itself more ethnically diverse. Dominican and Cuban refugees arrived in massive numbers to New York and Florida in the late 1960s, Colombians, Salvadorans, Guatemalans, and Nicaraguans in decades. Meanwhile, Mexican immigrants-both legal and well as Puerto Ricans, spread beyond their original enclaves in Southwest and Northeast.

The Mexican Americans and Puerto Ricans tended to form nationalist left-wing orientations, while the Cubans formed groups with right-wing outlooks. For Cubans, the failed Bay of in 1961 was a seminal moment. Many blamed lack of support the Kennedy administration for its failure. That resentment resulted in Cuban leaders allying themselves with the Republican Party.

For the next two decades, the overriding goal of Cuban immigrants was returning to a homeland free from Castro and Communism. That obsession gave them more the character of an exile group than a traditional immigrant community.[12] The organizations they formed reflected that preoccupation. They had names like Omega 7,Alpha 66, Comando Acción Cubana, and at one time they even formed a grand coalition under the name Bloque Revolucionario. Their threats, bombings, assassinations against those within the exile community whom they considered traitors, or against those in the broader society whom they perceived as agents of Communism, had enormous impact in forcing near unanimity in the public posture of the exile community.[13]

It did not take long for Cubans to make their presence felt in local politics· to Public Law 89-732,which Congress· passed in 1966.The law made it easier for Cubans to secure U.S. visas and it shortened the normal five-year waiting period for citizenship. An instant surge of naturalizations followed and with it an explosion of Cuban voting power. [14] By the early 1970s-only a decade after their immigration started-Cuban Americans had captured their first seats on the Miami Board of Education, the city governments of Miami and Hialeah, and Dade County judicial system. By contrast, Dominicans waited more than twenty five years to elect their first city councilman, and by 1998, Colombians still did not have a single elected official.

The Hispanic population was growing rapidly, but only Mexican Americans in the Southwest, Puerto Ricans in New York, and the Cubans .of South Florida boasted a sufficient number of voters by the mid-1970s to draw the attention of Anglo politicians. Leaders of the three groups thus took on the role, for better or worse, of socializing agents and political advocates for the newer Latino immigrants. Because the three groups were concentrated in separate regions of the country, a tense competition arose between their leaders when it came to influencing national policy, with each group's spokesmen fearing that their specific interests or power would be sacrificed under the broader banners of "Hispanic" or "Latino."

As the civil rights movement and anti-Vietnam War movement deepened however, divisions took root among the Latino radicals. The Young Lords, Los Siete de La Raza, August Twenty-ninth, and the Berets refused to participate in the traditional electoral process sought alliances instead with revolutionary groups outside the community, such as the Black Panther Party, the Students for a Democratic Society, and other New Left organizations,

Eventually, those coalitions splintered and evolved into scores fringe Marxist factions, and in the case of Puerto Ricans, those splinters included several clandestine urban groups that resorted to terrorist bombings, such as the FALN (Fuerzas Armadas de Liberación Nacional de Los Macheteros, In the Cuban community, the most extreme counter revolutionaries began taking actions jointly with other non-Cuban anti-Communist movements in the United States and Latin America., often with CIA sponsorship.[15] These radical factions, whether from the left or from the right, became increasingly divorced not only from each other but from the everyday reality that Latinos were facing; All failed to understand that despite the inequality and stubborn racism Latinos in the United States, conditions here, even for the most destitute, were substantially better than in the· Latin American nations from which they'd emigrated, a reality that to this day has doomed Marxist movements in our country to tiny followings.

A second trend was represented by Rodolfo "Corky" Crusade for Justice in Colorado, by Reies Tijerina's Alianza de los Pueblos and by La Raza Unida Party in Colorado and Texas. While their rhetoric mirrored the militant nationalism of the Marxists, these groups working within the system of U.S. elections. But they rejected Democratic and Republican parties as bankrupt and sought instead to build independent Chicano organizations that would try to win office in what the movement called Aztlán, the original Aztec homeland that encompassed the old territory ceded by the Treaty of Guadalupe Hidalgo. As we have seen, the party they formed, La Raza Unida made some impressive showings in small towns in South Texas, but it unable to spark widespread *mexicano* desertions from the Democrat Party.

A third trend was represented by Cesar Chavez's United Farm Workers Organizing Committee, by the National Council of La Raza and by Puerto Rican civic leaders like Gilberta Gerena Valentin. Members of that trend concentrated on winning the basic rights Puerto Ricans had as American citizens the right to Vote, the right to basic government services like schools, public housing, sewers, and drinking water. Chavez, the foremost representative of that trend, eventually became the most admired Hispanic leader in the country.

Out of NCLR's work emerged two pivotal organizations, the Mexican American Legal Defense and Education Fund (MALDEF), formed in .967 by Pete Tijerina and Gregory Luna, and the Southwest Voter Registration and Education Project (SVREP), whose founder was San Anonio's Willie

Velazquez. While NCLR became the main lobbying group or Hispanic issues in Washington, MALDEF and SVREP concentrated n the Southwest, where they provided Mexican Americans at the grassroots level the legal and organizational tools to enter the third period of Hispanic political development.

Meanwhile, Puerto Ricans in several Northeast cities were founding similar new civil rights groups. Gilberto Gerena Valentin, a longtime labor leader, united the various island hometown social clubs into a loose federation that pressured city government for better services; educator Antonia Pantoja founded Aspira, a youth organization to train a new generation of leaders; John Olivero, Cesar Perales, and Luis Alvarez founded the Puerto Rican Legal Defense and Education Fund. Where P*uertorriqueños* lagged behind *mexicanos* was in failing to involve themselves significantly in electoral politics, the major exception being Herman Badillo, who in 1969 became the first Puerto Rican elected to Congress.

The Voting Rights Period: 1975-1984

After 1975, Latino involvement with revolutionary organizations and nationalistic independent politics declined. Most leaders returned to integrationist and reformist goals, a stage I have labeled the Voting Rights period. Once again, the movement reverted to political equality as a primary goal, only now it was infused with the cultural and ethnic pride awakened by 1960s radicalism. Admittedly, the militancy was more muted, for America had changed. The reforms the federal government conceded to the civil rights, feminist and peace movements during the Vietnam War era had in turn spawned a New Right backlash. That backlash began in 1964 with Barry Goldwater, gathered force with George Wallace's presidential campaign in 1968, and spread with the aid of Protestant fundamentalist sects into a nationwide conservative populist movement.

Meanwhile, on the economic front, US. companies in search of cheap labor began relocating industrial jobs to the Third World. Faced with rising unemployment and a declining standard of living, white searched for someone to blame, so African Americans and Hispanics became the convenient scapegoats. The issues minority community leaders were raising-equal housing opportunity, school busing for de· segregation, affirmative action, equal political representation, bilingual education-were all blamed for subverting established "old values'? and principles of fairness in American society. The nation entered a conservative period wherein millions of whites called for restoring that traditional America, yet few stopped to consider how a good portion of that tradition had been based on the subjugation of others.

In this new climate, the second generation of postwar Latino leaders discarded its illusion of overthrowing political power and sought instead a proportional share of it. But theirs was not simply a replay of the earlier Integration Period, for each generation absorbs lessons from its predecessors. Several new factors distinguished the Voting Rights Period first, Latino leaders filed an unprecedented number of federal civil rights lawsuits; second, they formed the first lasting national coalitions across ethnic and racial lines; third, they expanded their movement beyond just middle-class professionals into poor Latino communities by combining 1960s-style mass protests with voter registration and election campaign

On the legal front, the Southwest Voter Registration and Education Project, the Mexican American Legal Defense and Education Fund, some years later,. The Mid-West Voter Registration and Education Project filed and won numerous voting rights suits against at-large systems that prevailed in many municipalities. Those systems had effectively shut out Mexican Americans from office for decades. Since Latinos were historically segregated into barrios, they could best representation by electing candidates from compact geographic not at-large ones.

Those court victories, together with massive voter registration launched by SVREP in Mexican American towns and counties Texas, produced a virtual revolution in that state's politics, one best symbolized by the 1982 election of Henry Cisneros in San Antonio.[16]

At the other end of the country, Puerto Ricans renewed their own efforts at building civil rights or advocacy groups. By then, their had spread to many Rust Belt cities and farming counties. The new groups devoted considerably more attention to voter lobbying than had previously occurred in the Puerto Rican communities. Among that new generation of organizations were the Rican Coalition (formed by Luis Alvarez, Luis Nunez, and Amalia Bettanzos in 1973 with seed money from the Ford Foundation), the Coalition in Defense of Puerto Rican and Hispanic Rights (founded in New York City in the late 1970s by lawyer Ramon Jimenez, Manuel Ortiz, and others); the National Congress for Puerto Rican Rights (founded in 1981 by scores of former Young Lords and other 1960s radicals, including myself), and the Institute for Puerto Rican Policy (a research and public policy think tank founded by political scientist Angelo Falcon).

The new groups worked closely with the Puerto Rican Legal Defense and Education Fund on several voting rights suits. As a result, in both New York and Chicago, federal judges ruled in the early 1980s that apportionment of municipal districts had discriminated against Hispanics and African Americans. In Chicago, that led to the creation of seven new aldermanic districts-three with majority black populations and four majority Hispanic. A special election in 1984 resulted in the number of Hispanic aldermen increasing from one to four: Miguel Santiago (the only incumbent), Jesus Garcia, Juan Soliz, and Luis Gutierrez. The Gutierrez victory rocked the city because it gave a one-vote majority in the city council to the new black mayor, Harold Washington, and thus symbolized the potential of a developing alliance between black and Hispanic politicians.[17]

In New York, the Puerto Rican Legal Defense and Education Fund was able to halt the 1981 municipal elections and get the federal courts to eliminate at-large council seats.[18] The redrawn council districts opened the way for increases in Puerto Rican representation on the council. Since New York has always been the trendsetter for Puerto Ricans, the battle sparked a new awareness of voting rights throughout the East Coast. As a result of both the activism of the new organizations and other voting rights court victories, by the mid-1980s, New York had a new, more independent group of Puerto Rican officials, such as city councilman Jose Rivera and state assemblymen Jose Serrano and Israel Ruiz. Similar victories occurred in other eastern and mid west cities.[19] Usually, the victories resulted from alliances the Hispanic candidates struck with a strong African American electoral campaign. Such was the case with Gutierrez in Chicago, with Angel Ortiz, who won an at-large city council seat as part of Wilson Goode's victorious 1983 mayoral campaign, and with Nelson Merced, the first Hispanic to capture a seat in the Massachusetts House of Representatives, from a predominantly black Boston district.

The climax of the Voting Rights Period came in 1983, with the stunning mayoral victories of Harold Washington in Chicago and Wilson Goode in Philadelphia. Suddenly, the nation awoke to a new reality. Power in the Democratic Party's urban areas had slipped from organizations of white politicians and their ethnic constituencies to coalitions of African Americans and Hispanics. In both Chicago and Philadelphia, Hispanic voters, who until then had been ignored by political candidates, demonstrated a newfound ability to tip an election by registering and voting in startling numbers. Washington, who had received only 25 percent of the Hispanic vote in winning a hard-fought Democratic primary, went on to capture 74 percent of that vote-the margin of his victory in the general election against conservative Republican Bernard Epton.[20]

Likewise, in Philadelphia, Goode eked out a victory in a close Democratic primary against former mayor Frank Rizzo, thanks to a black Hispanic-liberal alliance, then he romped against a weak Republican opponent. In both cases, Hispanic voters, mostly Puerto Rican, opted for Goode by more than two to one.

In South Florida, meanwhile, Cuban exile leaders, who at first had limited their political goals almost exclusively to ousting Castro and returning to Cuba, began a drastic change in the mid-1970s. That change was sharply influenced by the new generation of Cubans who had been born or raised in this country. Between 1973 and 1979, according to one study, those who said they planned to return to Cuba if Castro should be over thrown plummeted from 60 to 22 percent.[21] 'l'his changing perception by Cuban émigrés was reflected in politics. By 1974, some 200,000 Cubans in South Florida had become citizens and many were voting regularly. After several unsuccessful attempts, the first two Cubans were elected to office in 1973-Manolo Reboso to the Miami City Commission and Alfredo Duran to the Dade County School Board. Not surprisingly, both were Bay of Pigs veterans. Then, in late 1975, Cuban professionals, aided by Hispanic media personalities, launched a citizenship campaign. The following year more than 26,000 exiles were naturalized. By 1980, more than 55 percent of the exiles had become citizens, double the percentage in 1970.[22]

Those new citizens quickly made their presence felt. At first, it was largely in symbolic ways. On April 15, 1973, the Metro Dade County Commission, which had no Hispanics among its nine members, bowed to Cuban pressure and declared the county "officially bilingual." But the symbols quickly turned real. In 1978, Jorge Valdes became the country's first Cuban American mayor when he captured the Sweetwater City Hall, and he was followed by Raul Martinez in Hialeah.[23]

This growth of Cuban voting power, together with the new wave of immigrants brought by the Mariel exodus, soon touched off a backlash among whites in Dade County, who struck back with a 1980 referendum to nullify their commission's earlier bilingual declaration. The new referendum, which proposed to prohibit "the expenditure of county funds for the purpose of utilizing any language other than English, or promoting any culture other than that of the United States," instantly catapulted the issue of language onto the national stage. It passed handily, with the vote polarized almost exclusively along ethnic lines-71 percent of non Hispanic whites voted for it and 85 percent of Latinos voted against.[24]

While they found increased resistance from whites on their domestic agenda, Cuban politicians had great success in pushing their anti Communist initiatives. The Miami City Commission passed twenty-eight resolutions or ordinances against Communism in Latin America during one sixteen-month period before May 1983.[25]

The anti-Cuban backlash, however, prompted some soul-searching by first- and second-generation immigrant leaders, who decided to counter the negative image of their community in the English-speaking press. In 1980, civic leaders founded both the Spanish American League Against Discrimination (SALAD) and the Cuban American National Foundation (CANF), and two years later they launched Facts About Cuban Exiles (FACE).[26]

Ronald Reagan's election as president in 1980 signaled a new era for the solidly anti-Communist Cuban Americans. With a friend like Reagan in the White House, powerful Miami groups like CANF and the Latin American Builders Association perfected a well-bankrolled behind-the scenes lobby in Washington for their special projects-Radio Marti, TV Marti, and aid to the Nicaraguan Contras. At the same time, they adopted a new pragmatism in public, focusing less on controversial issues like bilingual education.[27]

Cuban voters diverged from Puerto Ricans and Mexican Americans in another crucial way-their posture toward the black community. While *mexicanos,* and even more so Puerto Ricans, managed to build tenuous alliances with blacks in several major cities, Cuban Americans and African Americans in Dade County turned into bitter enemies, especially as the much older black community of Miami watched the newer Cuban immigrants catapult over them economically. During the early 1970s, a Puerto Rican, Mauricio Ferro, the blond, blue-eyed scion of one of the island's richest families, won the Miami mayor's seat by building an alliance of black and liberal Jewish community to stave off the burgeoning conservative Cuban political movement.

When riots erupted in Miami's black communities several times in the 970s and 1980s, allegations by blacks of mistreatment by Cubans were ally raised as underlying factors. By the mid-1980s, Cuban immigrants had turned South Florida into the center of Hispanic conservative power throughout the country. Nothing reflected that more than the election of the first Cuban American to Congress in 1989. Ileana Ros Lehtinen, a conservative Republican, narrowly won the race despite her Democratic opponent's getting 88 percent of the Anglo vote and 94 percent of the black vote. Ros-Lehtinen's margin of victory was made possible by a Latino turnout of nearly 60 percent.[28]

The Rainbow Period: 1985-1994

When Jesse Jackson began his first campaign for the Democratic nomination for president in 1984 by calling for a new "Rainbow Coalition," Washington experts dubbed his attempt a meaningless protest. He promptly shocked all the experts by winning the majority of African American votes and a substantial minority of Latino and white votes. Jackson, who had witnessed the power of a black-Latino-liberal white coalition in both Chicago and Philadelphia, was determined to replicate it at the national level. Four years later, this time with widespread support from black and Latino politicians who had not supported him in 1984, Jackson garnered 7 million votes against the eventual Democratic presidential candidate, Michael Dukakis. In places like New York and Connecticut, Jackson won the majority of votes among Latinos, while in California, Texas, and elsewhere in the Southwest; he improved his showing but remained below 50 percent.[29]

The 1984 and 1988 Jackson campaigns, in addition, brought millions of first-time voters to the polls in the South and the northern ghettos, and those same voters sent blacks and Hispanics to Congress in record numbers. In some states, blacks showed higher election turnouts than white voters for the first time, and candidates who identified themselves as part of Jackson's Rainbow Coalition started to win isolated local elections. In Hartford, Connecticut, for instance, a Rainbow alliance captured control of the city council in the late 1980s and elected that city's first black mayor.

Then in 1989 came the most electrifying of local victories for the Rainbow movement. David Dinkins won the mayoralty of New York City the first black to hold the post--and he did so by capturing 88 percent of the black vote, 64 percent of the Hispanic vote, and less than 35 percent of the white vote.[30] As blacks and Hispanics gained greater influence within the Democratic Party, however, white middle-class and suburban voters kept deserting the party.

The Rainbow's revolutionary potential came from its appeal to those of the nation's voting-age population that had remained alienated and disenfranchised throughout most of the twentieth century blacks, Hispanics, the young, and the poor. Our country has had for decades one of the lowest voter turnout rates of any industrial democracy, assuring that those elected to office, from either the Democratic or Republican party, represent only a minority of the voting-age adults. In 1972, for instance, 77 percent of middle-class property owners voted compared to 52 percent of working-class Americans. And well-educated Americans usually vote at twice the rate of less educated citizens.[31]

Jackson's Rainbow movement, by contrast, placed prime importance not only on registering new voters but on removing legal obstacles in many states to simple and universal voter registration. But in both the 1988 and 1992 elections, Democratic presidential candidates chose to continue competing with the Republicans for the same small number of already registered voters who had fled the Democrats-the so-called Ragan Democrats-in the hope of getting them to "swing" back. Little attention was paid to Jackson's strategy

70

of getting millions of new voters from the lower classes-where blacks and Hispanics are disproportionately concentrated-onto the rolls, where they could become the basis of new political majority.

After that initial breakthrough of the late 1980s, however, the Rainbow Coalition stalled. In a country so long fixated on the contradictions between white and black society, the Rainbow fell victim to similar division. Jackson and many of the veteran black officeholders around him started treating the white, Hispanic, and Asian members of the Rainbow as permanent junior partners who could be mobilized as allies but who could not be permitted autonomy or opportunity to shape organizational strategy and policy. At the same time, a few black and Hispanic leaders started promoting ethnic competition for jobs and elected posts variety of cities. "The blacks want everything for themselves," was a common phrase of some Hispanic leaders, and "Latinos just want to ride to power on our coattails" was a refrain of too many of their black counterparts.

While the leaders argued, their followers clashed over government acts and patronage jobs. The steady rise in the number of Hispanics elected to office, for instance, was not mirrored by a rise in the number who were appointed to jobs in local governments, as had happened with Irish, Italian, and African American urban political machines of the past. After the riots of the 1960s, federal and municipal government employment had turned into a prime vehicle for many blacks to rise into the middle class. But Hispanics, perhaps in part because of the language barrier some had to overcome, did not witness a parallel progress. The few who did land government jobs invariably perceived blacks who were in supervisory positions over them as reluctant to aid their progress.

Differences in attitude toward race also tore at the Coalition. Jackson portrayed the Rainbow as a "common ground" for all Americans seeking economic justice; he urged an inclusive approach toward all minorities. Many African Americans, however, believe Latinos aspire to consider white, while many Hispanics regard blacks as obsessed race; and a good number, especially among Mexican Americans, even harbor deep prejudice toward blacks. In fact, Latinos simply view relations from a historically different perspective. This country's stark white-black dichotomy is alien to Latinos. Rather, to varying based on the country of origin and even the region within the home country, ethnic identification, or nationality, remains much more the core of Latino identity. This view is even mirrored by the locations of many Latino communities in U.S. cities; often, they emerged almost as buffer areas between black and white neighborhoods. Rather than air these different views and resolve them through debate and education, the Rainbow swept them under the rug, thus undermining its own unity.

The sudden death of Chicago mayor Harold Washington in 1987 was the first signal that keeping the Rainbow Coalition together would be even harder than constructing it. Within a few years, some of the very Latino leaders who backed Washington deserted his splintered movement and joined a new alliance with the old Democratic Party machine; now headed by Richard Daley, son of the legendary mayor. Among those was Luis Gutierrez, an activist in the Puerto Rican independence movement.[32] As a result of his switch, Gutierrez would later win Daley' support for a new congressional seat created by reapportionment. A the same time, in New York City, another Puerto Rican leader, Nydia Velazquez, fought to keep the Rainbow Coalition together, winning key support from both Jackson and the Reverend Al Sharpton in a race for new congressional seat. In 1992, Gutierrez and Velazquez became second and third Puerto Rican voting members of Congress, yet used different electoral alliances to come to power.

In Philadelphia, the black-Latino alliance started to rupture in 1991. Of those Puerto Ricans who had supported Wilson Goode throughout his two terms, some backed a liberal black Democratic leader who a tempted to succeed him, John White, Jr., while others backed the more moderate white Democrat, and eventual winner, Ed Rendell.

Finally, in 1993, the coalition of African Americans and Latinos in New York City foundered during the reelection campaign of David Dinkins.

While Dinkins retained a majority of Latino votes, his percentage was reduced, as was the voter turnout in the Latino community, enabling Republican Rudy Giuliani to squeak to victory with a very slim margin. us, by 1995, the mayoralty in four of the country's largest cities-New ark, Los Angeles, Chicago, and Philadelphia-had passed from a liberal or moderate black incumbent to a more conservative white leader. In each case, Hispanic voters shifted in significant percentages from the previous black mayor to the new white candidate, and each time, the argument of those who switched sounded the same: "We weren't treated as equal by the black leaders." Meanwhile, the failure of Jesse Jackson to and his Rainbow Coalition through a third presidential campaign in 2 left the movement organizationally adrift at the national level. ıı as the number of black and Hispanic leaders in Congress reached a record number, the cohesiveness of the alliance fractured, especially as ck voters along with whites grew increasingly uneasy about the country's population of Hispanics and Asians; In November of 1994, for instance, a majority of blac1c Californians voted for Proposition 187 to cut all public benefits to illegal immigrants.

Thus, the Rainbow Coalition was dead as a vehicle for a new progressive alliance by early 1995, even though Jackson never officially declared demise but simply folded it into his old Operation PUSH organization.

The Third Force Period, 1995-Present

Following the disintegration of the Rainbow, Latinos entered a new stage that I have dubbed the Third Force Period. The hallmarks of this new stage have been a massive rush to citizenship by Latino immigrants, a huge increase in voter participation levels, and a newfound independence by Latino leaders.

From 1994 to 1997, citizenship applications to the INS nearly tripled, 543,353 to 1,411,981, the overwhelming majority from Hispanics.[33] This stampede to citizenship was caused by several factors. First and most important was the spate of restrictive immigration laws that began with Proposition 187 in California and then spread across the country. Until then, Mexicans had the lowest naturalization rates of any immigrant group. One study showed that only 3 percent of Mexicans admitted into the country in 1970 had become citizens by 1979.[34] Many Mexicans lived and worked in this country for years, but since they invariably expected to return home someday, they rarely sought citizenship. Likewise, the Central Americans who fled civil wars in the 1980s expected to return once those wars ended.

But the new immigration laws sparked a Latino backlash. Of the 3 million illegal immigrants who became legal U.S. residents under the amnesty provisions of the Immigration Reform and Control Act of 1986 (IRCA), for instance, 2.6 million were from Latin America, and as soon as they were eligible for citizenship in 1992, most opted for i1.[35] In addition, the Republican-sponsored ban in 1996 on federal benefits for legal permanent residents (it was later partially repealed) prompted hundreds of thousands who were here legally to seek citizenship. As soon as they were sworn in, those new citizens registered to vote.

The second factor in the rush to citizenship was the peace accords in Nicaragua, Salvador, and Guatemala, which ended the fighting but not the economic chaos in those countries. Once the wars ended, the Central American refugees suddenly turned into the main source of economic aid to their beleaguered countries through the billions of dollars in remittances they sent home each year. Because of that, both the immigrants and their home governments resisted their repatriation.

A third factor was the transformation of citizenship laws in Latin America, with governments there increasingly adopting dual laws that allowed their nationals to retain home country rights they became U.S. citizens. Colombia,

Mexico, and the Dominican public have already taken major steps in that direction.[36]

The combination of all those factors turned the dormant potential Latino politics into reality starting in 1996, when the Hispanic vote astounded political experts with both its explosive growth and its unpredictability.[37] More than 5 million Latinos went to the polls that year, astounding 20 percent increase over 1992.[38]

And turnout was higher in the new immigrant neighborhoods than more established Latino areas. In New York City, for instance, overall Latino turnout was 48 percent of registered voters, but it reached 63 per cent in the Dominican area of Washington Heights, and 60 percent in the Colombian section of Jackson Heights.[39]

Those who came to the polls voted overwhelmingly for Bill Clinton and the Democratic Party. Clinton garnered 72 percent of the Lat" vote compared to 61 percent in 1992.[40] Even in Florida, where Cuba had always voted solidly Republican, he grabbed 44 percent to 49. Dole's 46 percent.[41] The seismic shift was best exemplified in California where a relative unknown, Loretta Sanchez, narrowly defeated wing congressman Robert Dornan in Orange County, a conservative Republican stronghold.

The following year, local elections in many cities repeated the same pattern of high Hispanic turnout but also showed the Latino vote was becoming less predictable than in the past. In the New York and Los Angeles mayoral races, for instance, not only did the number of Latino votes exceed that of blacks for the first time, but Latinos gave substantial backing to victorious Republican incumbents-45 percent to New York's Rudy Giuliani and 48 percent to LA's Richard Riordan-while blacks voted heavily against both.[42]

Overall, the Latino nationwide vote has more than doubled since 1980 (from 2.1 million to 5 million), and it seems sure to continue that phenomenal rate of increase even if current immigration restrictions remain in force. The demographics leave no alternative. Those 5 million voters, after all, amount to less than a third of the 17.5 million voting-age Latinos in the country today, since many Hispanic adults are still not citizens, and a good portion of those who are have yet to register. Furthermore, with nearly half of all Latinos in the United States under twenty-five compared to just a third of non-Latinos, and with Hispanic fertility rates higher than non-Hispanics, the pool of potential voters will mushroom irreversibly for decades.[43]

Most experts argue that the new Latino electorate will never function in nearly the unified fashion that blacks have done historically. The terms "Hispanic" or "Latino," they note, are useless umbrella categories masking huge ethnic differences, and Latinos will gradually adopt voting patterns closer to the old European immigrants. While the first conclusion is certainly true, the second fails to grasp the emergence during the last several decades of a rich new Latino identity on U.S. soil. From what was at first largely a Mexican American population in the Southwest and a Puerto Rican enclave in New York City, the different Hispanic groups have undergone, and continue to undergo, cultural amalgamation among themselves-through intermarriage, through shared knowledge of one another's music, food, and traditions, through common language, through a common experience of combating anti-Hispanic prejudice and being shunted into the same de facto segregated neighborhoods. No longer do a handful of Mexican American or Puerto Rican or Cuban groups dominate the national political debate on Hispanics; rather, the leaders of once disparate groups are now speaking with a more unified voice through organizations like the National Association of Latino Elected and Appointed Officials, the National Hispanic Agenda, the National Hispanic Chamber of Commerce, the Labor Council for Latin American Advancement, and the National Hispanic Political Action Committee.

In 1994, nearly fifty years after Ed Roybal and Henry B. Gonzalez pioneered modern Latino politics; there were 5,459 Latino elected officials in the nation. But that still represented little more than 1 percent of all elected officials in the country at a time when Latinos were 10 percent of the population.[44]

Some studies claim the Latino electorate is conservative at heart, but I would urge caution before accepting such conclusions. True, wherever Hispanic communities achieve relative prosperity-in places like and Orlando, northern New Mexico, Contra Costa County, they inevitably become more conservative in their voting patterns. But Hispanics remain overwhelmingly concentrated among the country's working-class and lower-middle-class sectors. The economic quest of the majority for a better standard of living necessarily brings it into conflict with corporate America's drive to achieve maximum profit from fewer and fewer workers. Latinos are constantly influenced by news of how people in their homelands are struggling to survive within the new global economy. Those economic realities, together with the anti-Hispanic bias they confront each day in the United States, continually force Hispanic of all nationalities to bind together to defend their interests.

Furthermore, Latin American immigrants are more politically sophisticated than most of us realize. They come from countries where wars and political strife have forced them to pay attention to politics. Puerto Rico, among the most peaceful of Latin American homeland more than 80 percent of the voting-age population regularly goes to polls. Everyone follows politics there with fervor more typical of foot fans here. There, Election Day is a holiday; all establishments are shuttered, even movie theaters and restaurants, until the polls close; and social and family pressures on everyone to vote are immense. The same kind of fanatical approach to voting exists in the Dominican and many other Latin American countries.

Because the continuing economic crisis in Latin America means immigrants will keep coming, and because of the maturing of interethnic Hispanic identity here, I have no doubt that the twenty century will lead to a full awakening of the voting power of Latinos. During the next few years, Hispanic Americans will continue to register vote in record numbers, energized by the historic sense that "our time has come." According to one recent study, by 2025, Latinos Americans will constitute 52 percent of the population of Texas; 50 percent in California and New Mexico, 43 percent in New York,41 in Florida, 36 percent in Arizona, 34 percent in Nevada, in Illinois; and in each of those states, Latinos will be the dominant group.

Hispanic political leaders who understand this, and who refuse to fall into the ever-recurring black-white divide on racial issues or to be taken for granted as a permanent reserve of the Democratic Party, will succeed 'n turning the Hispanic voter, along with the growing number of Asian American voters, into the basis of a new interracial coalition, or "Third fee," in American political life, Such a Third Force movement would seek to build a genuinely multiracial, multiethnic civic majority. Its aim would be not just getting more people to vote, but getting them to participate actively in social and civic institutions, creating space and voice r citizens of all races and ethnic groups. Because such a coalition would reach out to those who so far have been alienated and disenfranchised, it would necessarily change the terms of national debate, providing an alternative to the corporate-conservative minority that has financed and n both major political parties for the past thirty years,

By building such a coalition to renew American politics, the descendants of Juan Seguin will not merely reclaim their role in American his they will rewrite it.

Bibliography

1.   *A Revolution Remembered: The Memoirs and Selected Correspondence of Juan Seguin,* ed. Jesus F. de la Teja (Austin: State House Press, 1991), 90.

2.   Ibid., 1—70. De La Teja provides an excellent summary of Seguin's life. For Cisneros's election, see Thomas Weyr, *Hispanic USA.: Breaking the Melting Pot* (New York: Harper & Row, 1988), 116.

3.   United States Hispanic Leadership Institute, *Latino Electoral Potential 2000— 2025,* Report No. 312 (Chicago: 1998).

4.   Juan Gómez Quiñones, *Chicano Politics: Reality & Promise, 1940—1990* (Albuquerque: University of New Mexico Press, 1990), 60.

5.   The average factory wage in the South in the early 1900s was $10 a week, while the city and state poll taxes sometimes totaled $2.75. See Chandler Davidson, *Race and Class in Texas Politics* (Princeton: Princeton University Press, 1990), 18—23.

6.   Gómez Ouinones. *Chicano Politics,* 53—60. 73; and National Association of Latino Elected Officials, *1996 Election handbook,* 20.

7.   James Jennings and Monte Rivera, *Puerto Rican Politics in Urban America* (Westport. Conn.: Greenwood Press, 1984). 31—32.

8.   Sherrie Bayer, "Puerto Rican Politics in New York City: The Post—World War II Period," in Jennings and Rivera, *Puerto Rican Politics in Urban America,* 44.

9.   Linda Chavez. *Out of the Barrio: Toward a New Politics of Hispanic Assimilation* (New York: Basic Books. 1991). 40.

10. *Rodriguez v. Texas* May 3. 1954,347 U.S. 475.

11. Gómez Quiñones. 87. Also Manuel Del Valle, "Developing a Language-Based National Origin Discrimination Modality." in *Journal of Hispanic Policy,* John F Kennedy School of Government, Harvard University. vol. 4, p. 75, n. 22.

12. John F Stack and Christopher L. Warren, "Ethnicity and the Politics of Symbolism in Miami's Cuban Community," *Cuban Studies* 20 (Pittsburgh: University of Pittsburgh Press. 1990), 13.

13. Examples were the Miami assassinations of Luciano Nieves and Rolando Masferrer in 1975 and of Ramon Donesteves in 1976; and the murders of Car-los Muñiz Varela and Eulalio Negrin in Union City, New Jersey, in 1979; for furthering dialogue with Cuba. see Max Azicri, "The Politics of Exile: Trends and Dynamics of Political Change Among Cuban-Americans," *Cuban Studies* I 1 (Pittsburgh: University of Pittsburgh Press, 1981 and 1982), 62—66.

14. From 1961 to 196.5, an average of 2,400 Cubans became citizens each year, but after the new law; those numbers grew steadily each year. In 1970 alone, 20,888 Cubans became citizens. Sec Silvia Pedraza Bailey, "Cubans and Mexicans in the United Slates: The Functions of Political and Economic Migration," *Cuban Studies* 11 (Pittsburgh: University of Pittsburgh Press. 1981), 89.

15. Among the most well known of many actions taken by members of the Cuban underground in non-Cuban issues were: the 1973 Watergate break-in, which included three former CIA Cubans in Howard Hunt's "plumbers'" group; the fatal bombing that same year of the Chilean ambassador to Washington, Orlando Letelier. where two members of the Cuban Nationalist Movement were initially convicted, then acquitted in a retrial. See Azicri. "The Politics of Exile" &—ñ6: also Peter Dale Scott and Jonathan Marshall, *Cocaine Politics: Drugs, Politics, Armies the CIA in Central America* (Berkeley: University of California Press. 1991), 23—50.

16. Dan Balz. "Hispanics Use New Voting Rights Act to Reshape Texas Politics," *Washington Post,* April 25, 1983.

17. Gary Rivlin, *Fire on the Prairie: Chicago's Harold Washington and the Politics of Race* (New' York: Henry Holt, 1992), 348—57.

18. Jennings and Rivera. *Puerto Rican Politics,* 54.

19. Among the victories were those of Ralph Acosta and City Councilman Angel Ortiz in Philadelphia, State Representative Americo Santiago in Bridgeport, City Councilman Eugenio Caro in Hartford, State Representative Nelson Merced in Boston, Board of Education member Nancy Padilla in Rochester, Gutierrez and Santiago in Chicago.

20. But even among Hispanic voters, Puerto Ricans (79 percent) were the most pro-Washington. Followed by Mexicans (68 percent) and Cubans (52 percent). Rod Bush. *The New Black Vote: Politics and Power in Four American Cities* (San Francisco: Synthesis, 1984), 151)—Si.

21. Alejandro Portes, Juan M. Clark. and Manuel M. Lopez, "Six Years Later, the Process of Incorporation of Cuban

Exiles in the United States: 1973—1979," in Cuban Studies, July 1981—January 1982, 11.

22. Maria Cristina Garcia, *Havana USA: Cuban Exiles and Cuban Americans in South Florida, 1959—1994* (Berkeley: University of California Press, 1996), 113—15.

23. Thomas D. Bowell and James R. Curtis, *The Cuban American Experience: Culture, Images and Perspectives* (Roman & Allan held Publishers), 69.

24. Stack and Warren, "Ethnicity and the Politics," 16—17.

25. Ibid... 19.

26. Alejandro Portes, "The Rise of Ethnicity: Determinants of Ethnic Perceptions Among Cuban Exiles in Miami," *American Sociological Review* 49, no.3 (June 1984): 395.

27. Ibid.. 20—24.

28. Stack and Warren, "Ethnicity and the Politics."

29. Institute for Puerto Rican Policy, *The Puerto Rican and Latino Vote in the 1984 NYS Democratic Presidential Primary* (New York: April 5, 1984); also Institute for Puerto Rican Policy, "Puerto Ricans and the 1988 Presidential Elections" (New York: November 7, 1988); also Univision Network Poll, June 1, 1988.

30. Institute for Puerto Rican Policy, *The 1989 Mayoral Election and the Charter Revision Vote in New York City* (New York: November 1989).

31. Frances Fox Cloward and Richard A. Piven, *Why Americans Don't Vote* (New York: Pantheon, 1988), 115—16.

32. Institute for Puerto Rican Policy, *The Dinkins Administration and the Puerto Rican Community: Lessons from the Puerto Rican Experience with African-American Mayors in Chicago and Philadelphia* (New York: February 1990).

33. Author's interview with INS spokesman, March 1998; also "A Record Backlog to Get Citizenship Stymies 2 Million," *New York Times,* April 20, 1998.

34. Alejandro Portes and Ruben G. Rumbaut, *Immigrant America: A Portrait* (Berkeley: University of California Press, 1996), 117—18.

35. *Hispanic Americans Today,* U.S. Census Bureau Current Population Reports, P23—183 (Washington, D.C.: U.S. Government Printing Office, 1993), 15.

36. Louis Aguilar, "Mexican Congress Approves Dual Nationality," *Hispanic Link Weekly Report,* December 23, 1996; also Deborah Sontag and Larry Rohter "Dominicans May Allow Voting Abroad," *New York Times,* November 15, 1997.

37. *New York Times,* November 10, 1996: "The Expanding Hispanic Vote Shakes Republican Strongholds."

38. National Association of Latino Elected Officials, *1996 Latino Election Handbook,* 4.

39. Angelo Falcón, "Beyond *La Macarena:* The New York City Latino Vote," *His₄₀panic Link Weekly Report,* November 25.1996,4.

40. *New York Times,* "Expanding Hispanic Vote Shakes Republican Strongholds"; also *Wall Street Journal,* September 30, 1996, "Despite Rapid Growth, Hispanic Vote May Play Only a Limited Role in Fall Presidential Contest."

41. Falcón, "Beyond *La Macarena.*"

42. Los Angeles voter exit poll conducted by the Tomas Rivera Policy Institute, *La Opinion,* and KVEA-TV, April 8, 1997.

43. *Hispanic Americans Today,* U.S. Census Bureau, 7.

44. *1994 National Roster of Hispanic Elected Officials* (NALEO Education Fund, 1995). viii.

Coming into their own

In politics, business, music and the arts, R.I. Latinos are making their presence felt

By Tatiana Pina
Journal-Bulletin Staff Writer
11/17/96

When Raymond Lavandier came to Providence from the Dominican Republic in 1964, he went straight to the second floor of a three decker at 145 Chester Ave. There the aroma of rice and beans wafted down the hallway. Spanish voices welcomed newcomers. On that second floor, Josefina and Tony Rosario, who had moved there four years earlier, shared their apartment with newly arrived compatriots while they looked for work and got settled.

Josefina, known as "Fefa," accommodated the extra people by putting up curtains to create new spaces in her roomy apartment. She would pack her three children in her blue station wagon and go on forays to New York City to purchase the platanos, yuca, coffee and spices Dominicans could not find in Rhode Island. She provided warm clothes for her guests, accustomed only to the tropics.

When he lived with the Rosarios there was an average of five families staying there, Lavandier says. "We never needed to talk on the telephone, there were so many people around," he laughs. The couple helped their guests find jobs in restaurants, jewelry factories and textile mills, jobs that at the time were so abundant that bosses took to the streets to look for workers. Fathers or mothers who had come to the United States alone sent home word of the employment opportunities with the money tucked inside their letters.

Word spread fast.

The Rosarios saw their Latino community grow from a handful of Caribbean families to cities that now teem with Latino markets, travel agencies, newspapers, social service agencies, boutiques. Today, people from all over Latin America live in Rhode Island. The number of Hispanics has grown from nearly 8,000 in 1970 to 58,598 today. That number is projected to grow to 70,000 by the year 2000, according to the U.S.
Census Bureau. Agencies that work with Latinos, however, say the numbers are a quarter to a third higher. After more than 30 years of being called "new immigrants" and shouldering the growing pains and backlash that historically

come with that name, Latinos here are slowly starting to assert their potential.

And people are taking notice.

This year, Latinos made politicians and the press listen when they said "no mas" (no more) to Washington's attacks on immigrants and plans to cut their benefits. They did so by rallying against Joseph R. Paolino Jr., a 2nd Congressional District candidate whose campaign featured slights against more recent immigrants and plans to make English the
official language of the United States.

For the first time in Rhode Island history, seven Latinos ran for seats in the House and Senate this year. The candidates were Puerto Rican, Dominican, Guatemalan, Panamanian, Argentinian and Mexican-American. Five lost in the primaries, and one lost and one won in the general elections. The majority of the candidates who lost say they will try again. The emergence of the Latino community in Rhode Island echoes a national trend in growth and assertion of power. Patricia Martinez of Progreso Latino, a Central Falls social agency that helps Latinos, says this year's events were a window into the future.

"It was the beginning," Martinez says. "We have been here 25 to 30 years. I see the growth in our community. As we head toward our 40th year, like any other immigrant group, you will see people taking more active roles in the political arena. I see more kids graduating from college. I see more of our people in good positions in the Health Department and in Human Services. As we saw with the Irish and the Italians, it took time before they took over."

But who are these Latino people who make up the largest minority group in Rhode Island? They are often lumped together into one category - "Hispanic" - but they come from 19 countries from North America to the Caribbean and South America, where political situations range from democracy in Costa Rica to Communism in Cuba. Latinos are a mixture, in varying degrees of Indian, black and Spanish blood. They are the blue-eyed blonde riding her bike down the street, the brown-skinned girl sketching in her notebook, the black boy walking to school. The biggest groups in Rhode Island are the Puerto Ricans, Dominicans, Colombians, Guatemalans and the Mexicans, whose community church officials say is rapidly growing. The state is also home to Salvadorans, Bolivians, Peruvians, Cubans, Chileans, Ecuadoreans and others.

Like most immigrants, the majority came looking for a better life.

Little written history is available about their arrival in Rhode Island because they are a relatively young group. The Catholic Diocese, which first witnessed the growth of Latinos through its congregations, is one of the few institutions to recognize the growth of the Latino community. In 1970 Bishop Russell J. McVinney, at the Latinos' request, established the Latin American Apostelate of the Diocese of Providence to serve the community with Father Raymond Tetrault as the director.

Aida Hidalgo, director of Hispanic Ministries, says there are 13 churches in Providence, Pawtucket and Central Falls that celebrate Mass in Spanish. She estimates that in 10 years these churches will be completely Spanish because the Anglo members are older and their children are attending churches in the suburbs, she says. "Latinos are bringing faith to this country," she says. "If it were not for Latinos, the Catholic Church would not exist." One person who has watched the Latino community grow over the last 20 years is Providence Mayor Vincent Cianci Jr. He has seen them gain a presence in businesses on Broad Street, noted their steady participation in housing programs, and their pride in their culture. "Eventually Latinos will make up the backbone of the city," he says.

Latinos often mention Cianci as the one politician who attended their festivals and cultural events years ago when nobody else came. While their community presence has strengthened, their political clout has not reached its full potential, in part due to poor voter turnout, Cianci says. But that, too, is changing. Cianci points to the District 20 General Assembly race, in which Latinos came out in the September primary to vote for Victor Capellan, 25, in his bid to unseat 16-year incumbent Representative George A. Castro, D-Providence. Capellan fell just 11 votes short of victory.

"That was a race that shows some movement," Cianci says. "They are a force to be reckoned with.

Latinos Becoming Political Force

By Christopher Rowland
Journal-Bulletin State House Bureau
11/22/96

PROVIDENCE -- At his campaign headquarters in a vacant apartment above the Spanish bodegas of Broad Street, Victor Capellan is cleaning up the refuse of an unsuccessful bid for state representative.

Crumpled posters are strewn across the bare wood floors, marking a path toward a heap of old food, empty cartons and voting lists. Garbage cans are stuffed to overflowing.

You'd think Capellan, 25, a native of the Dominican Republic who learned English in Providence's public schools, would be downcast in the wake of his narrow Democratic primary defeat in September. He lost to incumbent Rep. George A. Castro, D-Providence, by just 11 votes, 297 to 286.

But weeks after the primary, Capellan is still excited, marveling at the powerful forces he tapped in the neighborhoods of lower South Providence and Washington Park.

Capellan had no political experience, and his campaign workers were all members of a Dominican youth group called Quisqueya en Accion, meaning motherland in action, of which Capellan is president. They marched down the streets, these groups of Latino youths, distributing flyers and taping posters in storefront windows.

And they almost pulled off a huge upset.

"It was everybody's first time," says Capellan. "They didn't see us as a voting power in the past."

Capellan's sudden emergence in South Providence was an encouraging development in a year that featured an unusual level of activism by Rhode Island's Hispanics.

Their growing participation sprang in reaction to proposals in Congress to deny benefits to immigrants. They also rallied against the Rhode Island congressional candidacy of former Providence Mayor Joseph Paolino Jr., whose campaign featured a call for English as an official national language.

Capellan's performance was the strongest among seven Latinos who ran in General Assembly primary races this year. The state's first Hispanic Eagle Scout, Capellan has a master's degree from the University of Rhode Island. He promises to run again.

Two other Hispanics ran in the general elections: Rep. Anastasia Williams, D-Providence, the state's first Hispanic legislator, retained her seat; Republican Daniel Garza lost to Rep. Maria J. Lopes, D-East Providence.

A Puerto Rican candidate for Providence City Council, Luis Aponte, ran strongly against the incumbent and lost by a tiny margin for the second year in a row.

The wave of candidates and media attention they received has encouraged Latino leaders who have dreamed for years of gaining a share of political power.

The City Councils in Providence, Pawtucket and Central Falls are devoid of Latinos. Central Falls, with a public-school student population that is 51 percent Hispanic, does not have a single Hispanic teacher. So anything that resembles progress is being trumpeted by community leaders.

"The clique is no more," declares Mildred Vega, a community activist in Central Falls who ran unsuccessfully for the House District 72 seat against Vicente Caban, another Hispanic, and incumbent Rep. Joseph Faria. Another Latino candidate, Leonel Bonilla, appeared on the ballot in House District 73.

"Times are changing," Vega said, "and in the near future there will be representation."

"The fact that we lost (the primary races) was not that bad," adds Marta Martinez, chairwoman of the Governor's Commission on Hispanic Affairs. "What's important is the fact that we came forward with seven candidates for the first time and made a mark on the political scene."

Says Delia Smidt, who ran for Senate in Coventry: "We might have lost the battle but not the war. Going into the 21st century, we're going to become a very powerful political movement in Rhode Island."

Leaders credited Paolino's controversial position on English and immigration for focusing media attention on Rhode Island's own Latin

Americans. All of a sudden, the rest of the state wanted to know what Latinos were thinking.

"I think it really empowered a lot of people," says Martinez. "I often got the impression that people thought all Hispanics were recent immigrants on welfare and sitting around and not doing much.

"I don't think people realized how strong and educated the Hispanic community was until this year," she says.

In Providence, voting patterns seem to indicate growing participation by Latinos.

The neighorhoods where Capellan and Aponte ran are both within the 2nd Congressional District, where Paolino lost to Lt. Gov. Robert Weygand. In the voting precincts where Capellan and Aponte did well, Paolino did poorly.

But still, these active voters number in the hundreds, not the thousands. As they seek an increased share of political power, Latinos must grapple with the same problems that have held them back for at least two decades.

For instance, while the Hispanic population is growing, the number of people becoming citizens, and thereby winning the right to vote, is not keeping pace.

In Central Falls, Vega says, only about 25 percent of Hispanic residents are citizens of the United States - making it difficult to find someone eligible to vote.

Another obstacle is that many urban Latino families rent their homes. They frequently move in and out of voting districts, making them difficult to track from election to election.

Their transient nature also contributes to a certain lack of attachment, or lack of ownership, in the communities where they live, say Hispanic leaders. Persuading them to vote is not easy, even when they become citizens.

Vega, in Central Falls, said she tracked down 70 new citizens and registered them to vote. But she said it is doubtful many of them turned out to cast a ballot.

"They say, 'What for? What does the mayor do for us? What does the council do for us?' And it's hard to break them out of that," says Vega.

Ethnic differences play a role in city politics, Vega adds, and it is difficult for Latinos to break down those barriers.

In Central Falls, French-Canadians and Portuguese have forged an alliance over the years that controls city government. In Providence, an African-American middle-class, with a longer history in the city, is better established in minority neighborhoods than the Hispanics.

Aponte, the Providence City Council candidate who lost to incumbent John H. Rollins by a mere four votes, describes some of the political problems Latinos face.

"It's difficult to build coalitions when, rightfully so, African- Americans have seen themselves disenfranchised for so many years," says Aponte. "They have some sort of political power, and there's a new group challenging for it."

Finally, Hispanics are sometimes their own worst enemies when it comes to developing a unified movement, Latino leaders say. Immigrants closely identify with their homelands - the Dominican Republic, Puerto Rico, Guatemela, Mexico, Colombia and at least 15 other Latin American countries - making it difficult to agree on a single agenda.

Among the frequent mistakes Hispanic candidates have made over the years, says Aponte, is concentrating on immigrants from their own country, instead of attempting to bridge differences.

"Candidates and campaigns tend to focus on that one community, and ignore the importance of all the other votes," said Aponte. "You can't count on just one community to get elected."

Born To Be Mild

Rhode Island's college republicans defy the stereotype of hard-core party animals

By Mark Bazer
December 18 - 25, 1997

It's always great fun to hear about young Republicans loosening their neckties, unbuttoning their collars, and getting down, dirty – and downright drunk. In an article in the January 1, 1996 issue of the Nation, Eric Alterman quotes a frequenter of Republican parties, "You haven't lived until you've seen a line of college Republicans dance the electric slide."

In the March 31, 1997 New Republic, Stephen Glass's more scathing account of the College Republicans, a national group, at the Conservative Political Action Conference (CPAC) reveals that many young conservatives are too busy partying to take their Party seriously. Many of them at the conference, Glass observed, skipped the speeches to drink and smoke marijuana in their hotel rooms, getting so soused that they spilled their drinks and their most idiotic thoughts. "Conservatives -- we're like a guy who has to pee lost in the desert, searching for a tree," one Iowa College Republican told him.

But the portrait Glass paints is ultimately more disturbing than funny. He tells of one slimy College Republican who picked up an overweight and unattractive woman at a bar, got her drunk, and brought her home. Then, the second she took off her bra, he had all of his friends jump out from behind the bed to take pictures. For the College Republicans Glass met, the chance to pull this type of shenanigan was the primary draw to the convention. He concludes that young Republicans in '97 are "like a lost generation."

The leaders of Republican college students in Rhode Island, however, are not the cruel, drunken morons described above. This is not to say that the state's young conservatives aren't slightly misguided, naive, and sometimes even selfish. It is also not to say that some of these guys don't drink or party like most college kids do from time to time. But disillusioned and directionless Rhode Island's young Republicans are not.

After all, what would be the point of being a Republican in a Democratically-controlled state such as Rhode Island (and in college of all places) if you weren't actually committed to your ideas? Being a Republican isn't exactly a normal matter of course here. In fact, most of the college Republicans I talked to didn't even grow up with conservative parents.

Instead, these Rhode Island Republicans have chosen their own beliefs based on a mix of political analysis, fears for their future, and a blind faith in the words of conservative elder party leaders. And in a state where few come to the same political conclusions as they do, a few college Republican leaders are already on their way to becoming party leaders here.

Take the plain-faced, plain-clothed, and earnest Ed Lopez. At 23, he is the chairman and founder of the Rhode Island Republican Assembly. Only a junior at the University of Rhode Island, he has already gathered a team to help him run for the state Senate position in Cranston in 1998 or in Providence in 2000.

He is also an honors political science/finance double major, and a devout Mormon who has completed a two-year mission in the Dominican Republic. Next month, Lopez also should have a real estate license. All this guy has is direction.

"I don't have many friends my own age," he admits. "I feel that in some ways I have been missing out on my youth -- mostly due to the politics -- but it's worth it." As for fun, well, he watches The X-Files at his quiet Cranston home, where he lives with his parents.

In some ways, it's hard to tell where Lopez got his political ambition. Lopez 's mother isn't very politically-minded and "probably votes Democrat," he says, while his father, a college professor and an author of Spanish literature, stays away from politics altogether. Lopez's parents are also Catholics, not Mormons -- Lopez converted to the Church of Latter Day Saints at 18 while a freshman at the University of Utah.

Already involved with the College Republicans as a freshman, Lopez says that Mormonism's strict moral code only reinforced his conservatism. He truly believes that the choices he has made in both politics and religion are helping him improve the world. Possibly the rarest breed of all, Lopez is genuine, unbelievably selfless, and a Republican.

Californian Luc Morris is another deep thinker. A slightly awkward 19-year-old sophomore at Brown, he is studying (often on weekend nights) to become a doctor. But like his studies, he takes politics very seriously and refers to himself as a "principled Republican."

"I'm a Republican mostly because the Republican Party does a better job at protecting individual rights and opposing governmental power than the Democratic Party." Usually, such an opinion would hardly get noticed at Brown, a bastion of liberalism where other points of view often get swallowed up by the majority. But as secretary of the school's chapter of the College Republicans, Morris has raised the club's profile. He constantly writes letters to the school paper (his most recent defended anti-affirmative action author Dinesh D'Souza's right to speak on campus), and he has spearheaded a joint campaign with, of all groups, the American Civil Liberties Union to put an end to the administration's speech code, which he feels censors students.

Unlike Lopez, Morris doesn't seem primarily interested in helping people. As far as he is concerned, freedom is the bottom and only line. And to hear Morris explain his college experiences, Brown has only reinforced his fear of people infringing on his rights as an individual. Although he says he believes most Brown students are not intolerant, he harps on the few who are.

"[As freshmen], we have a week-long orientation program. We discuss racism, sexism; we discuss homophobia, heterosexism, all these different 'isms' that they've decided are important," he explains. "But these discussions really aren't discussions. They're discussions led by counselors, who are upperclassmen with a certain agenda -- the university agenda. And students are molded to match that impression. Any kind of dissent is stifled."

Tim Costa is also big on individual rights. But his reasons seem to be driven first out of fear for his future. The intellectual reasoning comes later. A sophomore at Catholic University in Washington, DC, Costa, a 19-year-old Providence native, is the treasurer of the College Republicans at his school, and he works for the DC Republican Committee and serves from afar as the Rhode Island chair of the Young Republicans.

Quick-talking and brash, Costa is the Rush Limbaugh of the bunch. When you ask him why he's against the Democrats, the zingers come flying. "Take the Department of Education," he tells me over the phone from DC. "It came around in the late 1970s because Jimmy Carter wanted to pay off the teachers union." To be fair, Costa can be equally harsh about the military. "Now, I support defense, but even that -- $200 toilet seats. A waste of money is a waste of money."

His money, that is. Peel away the sarcastic layers and you've got a guy who is mainly concerned about his economic future. "None of my friends like going to work and getting their paycheck and finding 30 to 40 percent of it going to some welfare program that they don't even support," he says. "Nobody I know my age believes Social Security is going to be around [when we're due to collect]."

And indeed, Costa's concerns are legitimate. Chances are Social Security won't be around when he's older. What's more, the economy may be strong now, but finding a good job is harder than ever. Politics, as with his non-conservative father, are Costa's passion. But unlike his father, Costa is growing up in an age of less certainty. And that has him looking out for numero uno.

For all college Republicans, having their beliefs taken seriously by adult Republicans in Rhode Island only reinforces their political commitment. "The state party has really recognized us as a very useful and viable organization that they can use and respect at the same time," says Mark Ramia, a senior at Providence College and the state chairman of the College Republicans. "That's really important to me."

Part of the reason the young Republicans in the New Republic story are so disillusioned is a lack of feeling like they belong to the party. Glass quotes a College Republican from North Carolina, "Now there is no Reagan, no one to lead us. So there's a cynicism and a depression that has set in." But for Rhode Island's Republican Party -- a party without much of a past and not too impressive a future -- the last thing they can afford to be is disconnected from conservative youth.

In fact, at times they've gone too far. Two years ago the Providence Ward 8 Republican Committee sponsored a Little League team. In an issue of the Providence Republican newsletter, Dave Talan, editor and now acting chairman of the party's City Committee, wrote, "15 boys & girls age 6 to 8 . . . proudly wore T-shirts identifying them as members of the `8th Ward Republicans' team this spring."

Talan also devotes considerable room in his monthly newsletter to college Republicans. With the exception of Morris (Brown is a "world of its own," says Talan), he keeps in close contact with Providence's leading young Republicans. And he's already excited about the prospect of running Lopez and Costa for public office.

"They're energetic enough and aggressive enough," says Talan. "In a small state like Rhode Island with small electoral districts, if you're not too shy about going door to door and ringing strangers' doorbells and making a good impression, absolutely, you can win."

Winning a public election. It is something Talan has never done in a lifetime of political involvement. And now, like a father who never accomplished much in his own life and is banking on his "sons" to give his life's work purpose, he speaks of college Republicans with a mixture of pride and incredulity at their accomplishments.

Tim Costa is "brilliant," according to Talan. Ed Lopez is also "brilliant." Mark Ramia will have to settle for just being "smart." Talan recalls getting to know Costa as a member of the teenage Republicans. "He actually went to adults who he thought were potential Republican candidates
-- ones he didn't know that well -- and asked them about being candidates. Can you imagine a 15-year-old kid having the balls to do something like that?"

Costa downplays his role: "The main purpose I see for young people is to be volunteers for campaigns. If I do nothing else but recruit volunteers for [Governor Lincoln] Almond and [Lieutenant Governor Bernard] Jackvony and for whoever else is running, I'll be happy."

But as far as Talan is concerned, "whoever else is running" may soon be Costa himself. "I'd say as soon as he graduates from college and comes back here when he's 20 or 21, we'll be recruiting him to run for the state legislature or City Council right away."

The prospect of Lopez running for office brings Talan a joy similar to how he felt during black state Representative Mary Ross's campaign."Obviously, because he's Hispanic, he gets attention beyond what he would get even for being a brilliant, young man," says Talan. "And he'll make good use of it."

With Hispanics the fastest growing minority in the state, Talan should thank his lucky stars that he's got Lopez on his side. And sometime in the not-so-distant future, the Democrat Party is really going to lament the fact that Lopez isn't on theirs. When the Dems see some of the issues he's campaigning on -- cleaning up the environment, helping minorities establish businesses, providing job-training programs for welfare recipients, and perhaps even building statewide bike paths -- they'll scratch their heads with puzzlement as to why he's not.

But Lopez considers himself a staunch Republican, and he buys their rhetoric hook, line, and sinker. Morris, Costa, and Ramia all mimic the lines of their conservative elders as well. According to these guys, Republicans value families more than the Democrats do; tax cuts and
decreased funding for social programs are what's best for both rich and poor; and Ronald Reagan is a god.

Never mind the millions of poor people, minorities, homosexuals, and women for whom the Reagan era was a nightmare. How could these kids

know anything about that? In the '80s, after all, they were children watching Nickelodeon, not the evening news. Today, they can read and
repeat Reagan's words, but sadly, they don't seem to understand the consequences of his actions.

Luc Morris, for instance, would like Americans to have the legal right to discriminate against others on the basis of race or gender. "I don't know if America is ready for the repeal of the discrimination laws, but purely in principle, I think they're wrong," he argues. "If a business owner wants to exclude blacks from his store, I would say that he ought to be able to do that because it's his store. If he doesn't want to take their money, it's his right."

In other words, the government (elected by a majority of Americans) should not have the right to uphold the equality of all its citizens. But has Morris ever considered what would happen if the phone company decided not to service black people? In an ideal society, this would never happen. But in an ideal society, everyone also would be well-fed, treated equally, and have equal opportunity. Obviously, we don't live in such a society. So to improve society -- and it's not clear Morris understands this -- we have government.

What's so weird about a guy like Ed Lopez is that he's getting into government for idealistic reasons. He thinks government intervention is necessary when it comes to programs he deems worthy. "Politics is how much you care about people," he says. "It boils down to creating sound
legislation. If it's something that's really going to help people and it's not a waste of money and you're not encouraging drug use or something else, then I think you should definitely support those kinds of programs."
He goes on to explain, "If there's a lot of Hispanics in my district and I feel the need for them to learn English, then I'm going to support those programs. That's just the way it is. A congressman from South Dakota, he's probably not going to care much about bilingual education. In the end, that's democracy working."

Lopez's conservative social values (he's anti-choice, anti-pre-marital sex for himself, and thinks homosexuality is not a "correct lifestyle") fit in quite well with many Republicans. But he also sees his party as the true champion of minorities and the environment.

Tim Costa and Mark Ramia are also socially conservative. While neither claims to discriminate against homosexuals, Ramia definitely gets uneasy around the subject and Costa doesn't believe gays and lesbians should be able to marry or adopt children. But like Lopez, they're not full of hate. In fact, they're quite likable people, respectable citizens and hard workers. They bear no resemblance to their fellow college Republicans described by Glass.

Still, neither is quite as idealistic as Lopez. Costa, for instance, dismisses the question of whether his views are selfish with a quote. "Whether it's selfish or not, it's still my money," he says. "I think Ronald Reagan said, and this is a paraphrase, `Government's there to protect us from someone else, and we shouldn't want, nor can we afford, a government to protect us from ourselves."

And that's pretty much all of these guys' general attitude -- even though a "You do what you want and let me do what I want" attitude won't help Lopez accomplish all his goals. It won't create the ideal society Morris would like to see either. And if any of them are ever down and out, jobless, or homeless, it's doubtful their fellow Reaganites will be there to help them get back on their feet.

A Latino Launches House Candidacy And Maybe Career

M. CHARLES – BAKST
The Providence Journal
4.23.98

Ann Morrissey, a University of Rhode Island official who was emcee for the evening, had it exactly right. She said, ``This is not your run of the mill political event."

This was the launching the other night of Victor Capellan's 1998 campaign for the Rhode Island House. Remember that name, pronounced Kap-e-YAHN. He is a 27-year-old Dominican Republic native who lost to incumbent George Castro by only 13 votes in a 1996 Democratic primary in District 20 (lower South Providence and Washington Park) and intends to take the seat this time around.

We may see a primary rematch, although Castro, who is black, is less than definitive. ``As of right now, I'm still running," he says.

Another Democrat, Joe Almeida, a black retired Providence policeman who owns the Essence Rare Lounge, also is eying a bid. Almeida, 40, says he likes Castro but ``I'm going to decide what I think is good for the community."

Capellan, coordinator of student leadership at URI, is a key player in the state Hispanic community's incipient flexing of political muscle. At first it will be a House seat here, a city council seat there. Eventually they will be a major presence. By then, Capellan may be onto much bigger things.

Like the U.S. Senate.

He has been groomed, or groomed himself, for a political career. An Eagle Scout, he has bachelor's and master's degrees from URI. Working with students, he holds workshops on team building and teaches a class in leadership.

Dr. Pablo Rodriguez, who attended Capellan's '98 kickoff, told me, ``He represents the youth of the Hispanic community." As soon as he met Capellan, then a college student, Rodriguez began telling people to keep their eye on him, that he'd be going places.

While most of those at the kickoff were Hispanics, there were some exceptions. Morrissey, a white who works in the URI professional development office, was one. But more intriguing was Rep. Marsha Carpenter, the black woman who holds the seat in District 18 (Elmwood), which adjoins Castro's district. Democrat Carpenter is Capellan's honorary chair. She says she's for Capellan because she regularly receives phone calls from Castro's constituents asking for help. ``I guess they hear that if they call me, I return the phone call," she says.

This dovetails with Capellan's assertion that Castro is ``not around" and that ``people don't see him except at election time." Castro, 61, sells real estate and has a weekly WSNE radio program. He insists, ``I'm always around."

Capellan blends pragmatism and idealism. His plan to announce earlier in the day outdoors in Washington Park fell victim to rain. He then made the announcement part of a $40-a-person fundraiser at the Providence Marriott, fancy digs far from the district. Why do an event at the hotel? ``We wanted to bring some money into the campaign," he said evenly, and there isn't a similarly glitzy venue back home.

His announcement language was that of a man on the doorstep of destiny. ``I have been preparing myself for this," he said. ``Personally, professionally and politically -- I am prepared to lead this neighborhood into the 21st century."

He prides himself on working on gritty issues like homelessness and yet mixing with movers and shakers. His being Latino gives his campaign a special air. His speech included Spanish passages. And while he talks of being everyone's representative, his election would be a form of what he calls Hispanic ``empowerment." He told me, ``It is not just about me."

Still, it could be the start of heady things for him. His dream is to be a U.S. senator. Anybody can say that; Capellan admits it's partly fantasy. But maybe not. ``You never know," he says. ``I'm young. I have a lot of support." If things continue to break his way and people want him, he says, ``Maybe that'll make my dream a reality."

Victor Capellán Announcement Speech

April 17, 1998

Thank you Ann; Good evening Ladies and Gentlemen.

Buenas Noches a todos y gracias por su apoyo en esta noche. Es un placer para mi compartir con todos ustedes.

It is certainly a pleasure to be among family, friends and supporters as we gather here tonight with one common goal with one common purpose; that of improving our community. Because this is what is all about, continuing to develop and helping to grow a community.

It was about this time two years ago this month that in the midst of writing my Action Research towards the completion of my Master Degree at URI that I got up and said "I'm going to do it, I'm running for office this fall." And it was a combination of many things that at that point culminated and came all-together. It was the people in the community who asked me to run, such as the bodegueros on Broad Street, or the members of Quisqueya in Action, and it was my friends and family who asked me to run. And to re-tell a story that I've had to re-tell over and over for the last two years- I did run and I did not get elected as Representative by a margin of only 13 votes. Immediately after the count was in, I told the campaign team - well don't worry because we are coming back in 1998.

So here we are today only a few months shy of the September 15th primary continuing to work towards that goal with a vision of improvement a vision for a united community.

Many times over the last year and a half people asked me "are you running again, are you going to give it another try" and others said "you should run again", "if you run I'll definitely help you this time" – and tonight air. I will respond to all those people that have asked me to run, this time, it is the members of many other organizations, it is young people, it is whites, blacks, Latinos and Portuguese, it is family members it is old friends and new friends it is you ... so my answer tonight is YES! YES, I am running for State Representative. And now let me tell you why I am running for State Representative in District 20. It is because the areas of Washington Park and South Providence are areas that are usually neglected by many. We are neglected, although we have an incredible amount of resources and a great potential as a community.

We are bordered by some of the best resources in the State, that being Roger Williams Park and the Narragansett Bay. Our neighborhoods are along Broad Street which will be transformed thanks to the Broad Street/Main Street project, we are only a short ride from Downtown Providence and everything that is going on there and we are also adjacent to another great neighborhood - Edge wood in the City of Cranston. Simply our location and its borders provide the ingredients for a growing and developing neighborhood. Unfortunately that is not the case. Because we are neglected by the very same people that we elected to represent us, never mind others that are at a higher level and have other responsibilities. We are not getting the representation that we need and that we as a community deserve and that is why I am running for State Representative.

And let me tell you some other reasons why I'm running: It is because I believe that I can have an impact on our education system. By fighting to ensure that educational opportunities from its most basic level K-12 to higher education and advance degrees is available for all. As an immigrant here in this country, I have been witness to the wonders that an education can have and what a college degree can do for you. I want to be a part of the struggle that will ensure that these same opportunities are afforded to others. It is Here that I believe the key to our success as a community as a people lies. It is harnessing the benefits of an education and that is why I am running for State Representative.

Furthermore, we need to bring more resources to our small business entrepreneurs and we need to do that in a comprehensive and systematic way.

Our small business leaders up and down Broad, Eddy, Allens, Prairie must have access to resources - such as loans, technology, and expansion opportunities among others in order to be successful and to help our community continue to grow. I can remember that as a child walking along Broad Street with my Mom and Brother there were hardly any businesses on that Street even a short 12-14 years ago. Today that street is booming with businesses, it is the source of many jobs for people in our community, and it has been a catalyst for change in our community. I give them the credit for those changes and I want to help them to continue growing and expanding and that is why I am running for State Representative.

And there are more reasons, such as ensuring that when the State brings businesses into Rhode Island we in Washington Park and South Providence can have access to some of those jobs. It is by giving someone a quality good paying job that we will be able to grow. Yes, right now our State as it is with national trends has a very low unemployment rate, but you know that most of those jobs are only paying $5.15 an hour and they have no benefits. Many of them are available through Temporary Agencies that are exploiting our people. It is sad to see that a person must go and work at a booming Rhode Island business through an agency of course and be paid $5-6-7 an hour and be expected to provide for their family with only $200-300 a week. I want to help create partnerships between businesses and the community and provide other innovative job options for people. I want to continue working with groups like the United Workers Committee from Progreso Latino in order to regulate these temp agencies and the companies that are exploiting are people and that is why I am running for State Representative.

Also, we must provide a decent, safe and affordable place for people to live. I want to continue working with groups such as the Washington Park Foundation and others that are working to improve the housing situation in the neighborhoods. And I will work to continuing raising the quality of life in that area.

I know that if we unite; Blacks, Whites, Latinos, Portuguese, Asians, Old and Young we can create a neighborhood a community we can all be proud to work and live in. I want to help make those ties and foster that bond that can allow our diverse population to work together for the betterment of our community and that is why I am running for State Representative.

And you know how I'm planning to do that? It is your help! It is with the help of the people of Washington Park and South Providence. It is with every single voter that will go and cast a vote for the future, a vote for an improved neighborhood on September 15th. I have been preparing myself for this. Personally, Professionally and Politically - I am prepared to lead this neighborhood into the 21st Century. Personally, I know that there will be many hours of service and hard-work and there will be certain sacrifices to be made, but you know that I am no stranger to work and sacrifice so I am willing to do just that for my community.

Professionally, I have dedicated years to educating myself inside and outside the classroom. I have bee able to tap into many resources such as the University of Rhode Island, which has been my source of education and is now were I am developing my career.

Politically, I have the experience gained from 1996 race, and I have a Political Science degree, but that is not enough. In the past couple of years I have undergone political training both formal and informal at a local/state and national level. My campaign team has been attending political training, and I along with Juan Pichardo my campaign manager have tapped into many resources in order to improve our team and ourselves when it comes to political know-how. And I will continue to learn about politics and continue to develop and grow, but I am ready, anxious and willing to serve the people of the State of Rhode Island.

Another thing is that I have not stopped working for my community.

I stayed active in organizations and have provided long hours of service. When I lost in 1996 1 told the people that I will continue working no matter what to improve our. Neighborhood. And I did just that by working - at a local level with the Washington Avenue Resident Association, working on social issues such as homelessness with Amos House and at a national level with the National Dominican-American Roundtable and many other efforts. So I am ready to work!

And as I reach the end, I want to let you know that all this was not possible, is not and will be possible without the help of my family, friends, campaign team, supporters and without the people of Washington Park and South Providence and of course without your help. Both financially and morally it means a great deal to me to have such wonderful committed people who have worked with me. It is thanks to the groups I work with like Latinos for Community Advancement, Ocean State Action, thanks to my Sigma Class of Leadership Rhode Island (many of whom could not be here, but have definitely helped by sending their contributions), thanks to the Latino community for their support over the years and many, many other people that have seen me grow and develop over the years.

It is because of these people and their actions that I am able to stand before you today, the many teachers both inside and outside the classroom that I have had over the years, it has just been incredible the number of people that make it possible for me to be here today.

It is to them that I dedicate this campaign to my teachers, mentors that have helped me some directly others just by being by my side and others have helped me and don't even know it. I want to let them know that everything they have taught me will be put to good use to represent the people in my district and to bring to that district the appropriate representation it needs and that it deserves.

En verdad quiero agradecer a todos los que me han ensenado tanto y me han dando tanto, porque gracias a ellos estoy hoy aqui con ustedes. En especial quiero agradecer a mi Mama y mi Hermano por toda su ayuda y paciencia por todos estos anos.

And finally I will leave you with a challenge and a pledge. I will like to pose a challenge to all those here today and the many others who support me that could not join us tonight; And that .to continue fighting in your own ways for the betterment of our community. To join together and unite in order to accomplish our goals and objectives and to continue to accept your responsibility within the political process. I know that many times we are turned off by politics, unfortunately, as with many things a few rotten apples spoil the bunch. But there are many great people that are involved in politics in one way or another and it is up to us to ensure that we put into office people that will work for us and that will represent us to the best of their abilities and that will make us proud. Ladies and Gentlemen that is up to us.

My pledge to you tonight is that when the people of Washington Park and South Providence elect me I will represent them to the best of my abilities, that although, I will enter a system that has its flaws; I will not falter in the face of fear or doubt; I pledge to you that during my political career, I will remain true to the principles that guide me today! I will make you proud and that is why I am running for State Representative.

Thank you for your support!

Victor F. Capellan Biography

Victor F. Capellan, was born in the Dominican Republic on December 23, 1970. He came to the United States on August 8, 1983 with his brother Robert, to rejoin with their mother. He attended Roger Williams Middle School and Central High School in Providence.

After graduation he went to the University of Rhode Island through the Talent Development program. In 1992 Victor earned his Bachelors degree in Political Science. It was at this time that Victor became very involved in his community in Providence. He had been an active student leader and was now ready to serve his neighborhood.

After working for 2 years at URI and at Brown University he decided to return to school and attain a Masters Degree in College Student Personnel which he achieved in 1996. He focused on working with Latino Students and Leadership Development. In his present position at URI he is the Coordinator at the Center for Student Leadership Development.

Victor has served on several boards and organizations. Some of his positions include: President of Quisqueya In Action, Co-Chair and Founder of Latino for Community Advancement, he serves on the Amos House Board of Directors, and he is the current President of the Washington Park Foundation.

Victor is an active leader in the National Dominican-American Roundtable, he has coached Little League for 4 years and his Fraternity La Unidad Latina continues to sponsor a team. Victor has been actively politically since his attempt at becoming an assemblyman in 1996 and he is involved in various political committees and efforts to involve people in politics. He is committed to work for the improvement of our community and we believe that he will be elected this coming fall as the Representative for District 20 in Providence.

Chatting With District 20 Candidate Victor Capellan

By Anna M. Ferrara
The Providence American
August 1, 1998

Providence, RI-Victor F Capellan, was born in the Dominican Republic December 23, 1970, which makes him just five months shy of his 28th birthday. He's a young fella to be sure but he exudes a type of self confidence found in men twice his age.

But while his biography is almost as brief as his political career to date, it soon becomes evident to anyone talking with Victor that he's a force to be reckoned with. His record speaks for itself.

On his first time out of the political starting gate in 1996, with no political experi-ence at all and a campaign staff comprised almost entirely of a youth group from Quisqueya en Accion (Motherland in Action), he almost managed to unseat veteran lawmaker Rep. George Castro. He lost his bid to represent District 20, which includes several neighborhoods in South Providence and all of Washington Park by a mere 11 votes. Not bad for a greenhorn.

That was two years ago and Capellan is back with a vengeance, more experience and with a new agenda. This time around, however, he's not up against Rep. Castro but retired Providence Police Officer and local hero Joe Almeida. He's also been named one of "Ten to Watch in Rhode Island" by RI Monthly Magazine (January 1998).

During a sweltering heatwave last week, candidate Capellan sat down with a reporter *from The* Providence American to talk about where he came from and where he's going. Following are excerpts from that interview.

TPA: Your bio is quite brief. Tell me a little about Victor.
Capellan: "I was born in the Dominican Republic and came to Providence in 1983. I've lived in Providence ever since except for my years down at URI...We came here to look for the better life and that for us was education. I went from Roger Williams Middle School to Central High School and then to URI through the Talent Development Program. I graduated from URI in '92 with a degree in Political Science. And then I worked there for a year and a half in Alumni Affairs. I spent a little time at Brown work-ing as the coordinator of the Third World Center and then I returned to URI to get my master's degree which I finished in 1996 in Human Development and Family

Studies. . . .I returned to URI once again as Coordinator of Student Leadership Development which is my current position. I'm single, no kids."

TPA: Do you think that being single with no kids will in any way hamper your chances at winning?
Capellan: "No. I'm definitely a family man. I'm still very close to my mom and my brother. And the other part of being single just gives me a lot more time to devote to community work and politics. I don't have anybody waiting for me at home at night so I can stay out at meetings and at headquarters as long as I want."

TPA: Tell me about your platforms.
Capellan: "Education was an opportunity given to me when I came to this country and from what I've been able to see not only for minority inner-city youth but specially with that population I think that we have so many negative things and so many pressures to go in other directions that education is the way for us. But also I see what it's been able to do for myself...The reason I want to focus on mostly education is because we are neglecting it. We all talk education especially during political season because it's a nice topic but I think we have to go beyond being a nice topic and really looking at the dropout rate being so high especially among Hispanics and Blacks. Looking at the Providence School System we have a lot of potential and we have a lot of committed and hardworking people within the system but I don't think were receiving the resources necessary from the state in order to have the school system prepare our students to attend places like the University of Rhode Island."

TPA: Do you think perhaps the students aren't motivated because they fail to see role models who look like them in the school system?
Capellan: "I think that's one part of it. The school system does need to have more people of color. I think they need to make hiring more minorities a priority and the past year with the hiring of Rickie Wilson and Thomas Ramirez they've made great strides. If we could see a few more years like this one we'll be all right. But aside from that I think the kids are motivated to learn. If they are given the proper resources and environment they will learn. When we see the end product it makes sense to invest in education up front, in the elementary, in the middle schools and in the high schools. So that's why education is so important to me."

TPA: Moving on to a somewhat more difficult topic, namely the rising number of homicides in the city. Do you have an action plan in place to help combat this situation?
Capellan: "It is a difficult question. I mean what do you do? It's a crisis that we're in and I think that's how you have to deal with it. We've been too slow

to react to it. I think that supporting things like Rep. Marsha Carpenter's work with the gun control bills and things like that. Another thing to look at is a program like the one in Washington Heights, New York where they keep the schools open at night....they have a gym, they have computers, everything a kid needs during the day is also available at night. But key to this is bringing the parents in as well. The parents had to be a part of it.

TPA: Do you think such a plan is feasible for Providence?
Capellan: 'I think it's feasible. I think it's something where we can build some partnerships with local businesses to pay for it. But also if we can get some volunteers and the parents to run the programs I think it can be done. We could partner with the Americorps programs and they would be perfect to help us run a program like this."
TPA: How long has the Washington Heights program been running and how did you hear about it?
Capellan: "One of the partners is a friend of mine. We don't need to reinvent the wheel here. What we need is a multi-di-mensional approach to combat all violence, not just gun violence. We're in a crisis situation and go at it from every angle."

TPA: Tell me about your work with children.
Capellan: "My favorite is little league. I had to take this year off because of my campaign but that's one of the things I do is helping kids through sports. I was also a big brother. I'm active in Quisqueya in Action where I ran a leadership program. I'm also active with youth at Progresso Latino where I run the youth program over there. At URI one of the things I do is make sure we bring kids from different schools to the campus so they can see what it's like to be on a college campus. And every year I go back to Roger Williams and Central to speak to the kids and spend time in the ESL classes or wherever the teachers want me to go.

TPA: Do you think your age works against you?
Capellan "No. I think we have revitalized the community. Maybe it's because of the naiveness that we have but we have provided leadership to our community. We have not only excited the young people but people who have been here for 20, 30, 40 years... .they come and say things like who's that guy, Castro, he's been there forever. So they say I'm gonna go out and vote."

TPA: Speaking of voting, tell me about your door-to-door voting campaign.
Capellan: "We're running a three pronged campaign. We're definitely running an electoral campaign so I can get elected. But at the same time we know the need that we have in the community to educate them as far as the electoral process. We went door to door not just to people who were registered voters

because we wanted to bring them information. When we look at the numbers one of the lowest voter turnout districts is District 20 which is dangerous because when the state is allocating resources they'll say those people don't vote. The biggest obstacle we found to people not voting is that they didn't think their vote matters.

I want them to register to vote. I would hope they vote for me but I want them to come and vote because it's so important. Beyond my campaign it's important for the neighborhood in the long run."

TPA: Last question. What do you say to critics who claim that you're only out to represent the Hispanic population of District 20?

Capellan: "As far as my campaign and people asking am I going to be for Latinos only. I'm Latino. I'm Dominican. But I'm not a Latino candidate, I'm a candidate for state representative in District 20, period. And the fact that I'm a candidate is not going to take out the Latino part. But what I do is going to determine what kind of a representative I'm going to be and it would be a disservice to the people of this community for me to come and only work for the people who are Latinos....I want to come in and show people what I've been able to do in the many organizations I'm involved in...I want to take that same kind of energy and do the same thing for this neighborhood."

Capellan's involvement in the community is one of his biggest accomplishments. He's involved with no less than ten community and statewide organizations including: president of the Washington Park Foundation; Advisor, Quisqueya In Action; Sigma Class, Leadership Rhode Island; Steering Committee National Dominican-American Roundtable; Washington Avenue Resident Association and a Board Member of Amos House to name but a few.

Closing the interview with a pitch for volunteers Capellan says volunteers are still needed and always welcome.

Paolino Apologizes For Offense To Immigrants

Joseph Paolino Jr. says he never meant to insult or demean the immigrant community by his stands during a political campaign two years ago.

By TATIANA PINA
Journal-Bulletin Staff Writer
5.5.98

Two years after he antagonized the Hispanic community with his support for making English the nation's official language, during an unsuccessful campaign for the 2nd District House seat, Joseph Paolino Jr. has apologized.

The apology came during a speech April 25 at the International Institute of Rhode Island's annual ball at Rhodes-on-the-Pawtuxet in Cranston.Paolino and his wife, Lianne, chaired the event, a task Paolino said he undertook as a way of making amends.

The institute serves new immigrants and refugees, providing casework and citizenship counseling, as well as employment, housing and other assistance.

``I wanted through my work for this important cause to symbolically and sincerely apologize to anyone in the immigrant community whom I may have offended during my congressional campaign two years ago," Paolino said at the ball. ``I certainly never wanted my views to be seen as insulting or demeaning to the community."

Paolino, a former Providence mayor who had a reputation as a friend of the Hispanic community, surprised many during his campaign when he proposed dismantling bilingual education and making English the official language of the United States, thereby requiring all government business to be conducted in English.

He suggested that recent immigrants are more likely to go on welfare and less likely to learn English than his own immigrant forebears. Then he invited Italian-American leaders to a party at the Alpine Country Club in Cranston, saying they should vote for one of their own -- him – because they had not been represented since the 1976 retirement of Sen. John O. Pastore.

Paolino insisted at the time that he had been misunderstood. Although he had been favored in the race, he lost handily to then-Lt. Gov. Robert A. Weygand in the Democratic primary. Weygand went on to win the congressional seat in the general election.

At the International Institute ball, Paolino, now out of politics and a private real-estate developer, sought to put it all behind him.

``I just believed the English language could express all things, but in the end it failed me," Paolino said. ``I would never want anyone to abandon his or her culture, heritage, customs or language. I said English is the native language of the country we have all adopted. You know when you adopt a country, you never abandon your culture, but we all make certain adjustments, and one of those adjustments is language. Common language allows clear communication which becomes the roadmap of everyday life.

``I wish I had been able to use my own language to communicate more clearly."

Paolino said in an interview that he still feels strongly that English is the best way for a new immigrant to ``transition into America" but that it cannot be forced. The process he said he favors, however, is not English Only, but English Plus.

English Plus acknowledges that English is the main language of the United States, but promotes diversity and encourages immigrants to maintain their customs and language while adapting to this country.

``The biggest thing I failed to explain is that our Constitution protects freedom of speech in that you can't force people. It's good to give them every opportunity but not impose," Paolino said during the interview.

``Once this political firestorm took off, I knew there was no way the storm was going to be put out until the election was over," Paolino added.

Contributing to his problem, Paolino said during the interview, was the national anti-immigrant emotion sparked by Republican efforts to trim social benefits for immigrants.

``With all the stuff the Republicans were doing nationally [the English Only message] wasn't received well by the immigrant community. They felt there was a harshness to what I was saying," Paolino said. ``I felt no matter how I tried to explain it, the more I talked I would either be misunderstood or I would say it wrong and dig a deeper hole."

Paolino said his motivation for mending fences with the immigrant community was not that he wants to run for office again.

``If Yogi Berra were a politician, he would tell you that my political future is behind me," Paolino said.

The reconcilation began when Bill Shuey, director of the International Institute, asked the Paolinos to chair the annual ball. Shuey said that Paolino had called him after his defeat in 1996 to say that he wanted to do what he could to repair the damage done during the campaign.

``He asked me to facilitate a meeting with some of those who had criticized his ill-judged stance regarding English Only, simply because he felt bad about being perceived as anti-immigrant," Shuey recalled. ``He emphasized that he had no political agenda, that on a personal level he felt very bad about the negativity that had surfaced during his campaign given his impressive record of public service."

Shuey agreed to a meeting, but said that by then the campaign was over and none of Paolino's critics was particularly interested in meeting with him on this subject, so no meeting took place.

Paolino said he even discussed the possibility of teaching an English class at the institute. Shuey told him he could serve the institute better as chairman of this year's spring carnival, the institute's annual fundraiser.

``I believe it to be a sincere effort on his part to put the campaign of nearly two years ago behind him and to do something positive for the immigrant community," Shuey said.

The effort almost backfired. Some Hispanics still felt the sting of Paolino's comments two years ago, and threatened to boycott the annual ball. Shuey argued that Paolino, with his connections and desire, could help raise money for the institute.

In the end, there was no organized boycott, but a few of the people in the Hispanic community who would normally go to the ball instead stayed away. Many of those who did attend seemed willing to accept the apology at face value.

Concerned about the division in the community, Juan Pichardo, president of the Dominican American Political Committee, said he had urged Paolino to include an apology in his speech ``to clear the air once and for all."

``This has gone in a circle that has not closed yet," Pichardo said. ``There is time for Mr. Paolino to follow up on what he agreed to, to continue mending ties with the community."

Victor Mendoza, a long-time activist in the Hispanic community who criticized Paolino's stance during the campaign, said that Paolino's apology has already brought closure.

``You have to recognize his courage for coming before the public," Mendoza said. ``There are people who do bad things who never come before the people they offended to apologize. It is a very responsible thing for him as a human being and we as humans must learn to forgive."

Ed Lopez Announcement Speech

Building the Future Leadership of Rhode Island

Ed Lopez for Secretary of State Campaign
June 15, 1998

Good morning, and thank you all for joining us. I am pleased that State Republican Party Chair Joan Quick and so many other state and local Party leaders have made it a point to be here. Well, if you haven't heard, I'm Ed Lopez, and I'm running for Secretary of State. I am here with an able group of volunteers to embark on a great journey -- a ground-breaking journey that will culminate in an historic victory in November -- a victory not of an individual candidate, but rather a victory for the people of Rhode Island - as we earn your support.

This campaign is about restoring community and citizenship. This involves much more than politicians securing open government for one another; it is about restoring the sense of citizenship necessary to ensure that the check on government is in the hands of the people. It is one thing to have open government; it is quite another to have a people who care about participating in that government. Voter participation has hit an all time low across the country. Can there be any doubt that the time to strengthen and revitalize citizenship has come? As Secretary of State I will be truly committed to increasing voter registration, voter education, and the overall activity from the average citizen in the political process.

The mission I have set out to accomplish is one that is not easy, and yet it is critical to the restoration of community and citizenship, which are the key ingredients in the recipe for effective, efficient, honest, and pro-active government.

The level of voter apathy is an issue that concerns many of us-- we must make sure we lay a solid foundation for leadership in the future. We must work hard to restore an understanding, among all of our citizens, of the election process, of how our government is organized and how it works. We must revitalize citizenship by revitalizing our citizens - by bringing back the sense of community that enables a people to thrive and move boldly toward a stronger economy and a better government. We must have open doom in our government, but we must also have a people who care about leadership. We must elect those who are like us to direct the issues of the state: the average citizen -- the student, the parent, the school teacher, the nurse -- people from all walks of life who must no longer feel disenfranchised in our state. We must work hard to breathe a new sense of optimism about the Ocean State into our neighborhoods; we must do so in a way that feels close to home; we need to make sure tat the average citizen becomes a driving force in the decisions of the state and that such decisions are not limited to the folks on Smith Hill. The Secretary of State's office is a gateway for this kind of progress. Let us open tat gate this November; let us move on from small issues that are only important to the political elite, and let us begin to address the concerns of people like you and me. With your vote, in the next four years, we will reach out to the average citizen.

As your Secretary of State, I will work hard not only to restore a sense of citizenship, but I will also advance Governor Almond's efforts to break down those barriers that stand in the way of economic growth. It has been our goal as Republicans to decrease government regulation to ensure positive economic progress. With your vote we will add strength to the governor's agenda. I will be an advocate not only for businesses that employ thousands of Rhode Islanders, but of small businesses that are beginning to grow along the crowded areas of Broad Street, Cranston Street, Smith Hill, the cities of Pawtucket and Central Falls, and other areas of our state. Because I see economic stability and environmental consciousness as two sides of the same coin, I will work hard to be an advocate for environmentally friendly development. I am determined to see that the quality and condition of our natural environment is maintained as a source of both economic and spiritual renewal for generations to come.

I will work hard to earn the vote of those who have never before voted for a Republican. I will bring a new Republican message to the people of Rhode Island. It is time to wake up and realize that decades of a government controlled by one party have not adequately served those who are starting out, those who are struggling to learn English, or those living paycheck to paycheck, with little consideration from those who sit comfortably in the chambers of the State House. Governor Almond has done a great job restoring efficiency in our government and in making it accessible to the average citizen. Now we need to put more people on his team - we need to put more people on YOUR team. With your vote I will become the next Secretary of State - the youngest in the history of Rhode Island and the first Hispanic elected to statewide office -- thus reflecting the changing nice of the state of Rhode Island while bringing energy and vision to our state government. I am a progressive Republican. My vision reflects a changing Republican Party. I bring to this election a new agenda - an agenda that transcends partisan lines - one tat is less about now, and more about the future, about building the leadership necessary to ensure that we have a new generation of Rhode Islanders - a generation that cares about the old and the young, a generation that cares about the environment and business, a generation that cares about development.

I am grateful to those who are joining me in this campaign because their faith is set on ensuring that each individual has the freedom to exercise his or her conscience, the basic right to property, and the protection of life. In order to preserve these precious rights, we must raise up a new generation of Rhode Islanders, and Lord bless us to be an example to the rest of the nation as we set foot in each school to teach our children the value of citizenship and the importance of community. Let us reach out to them, not only through the internet, or the media, but through the basic relationship we should have with them as human beings. My friends, this campaign is about building leadership for the fixture of Rhode Island. Let us become a government that relates to its citizens, not as customers, but as family. Let us become interested in each other again, committed to helping each other, and committed to becoming leaders, even for the nation, in the restoration of the basic principles and ideals that have united us as Americans.

My campaign is about a new vision for Rhode Island. I am here with this dedicated and talented team of people to make history. We have charted a course for victory, and with your help, the perpetual ebb and flow of our state's political status quo will soon be swallowed up by the rising tide of renewal. My fellow Rhode Islanders, I am here to present you with a clear alternative, a true opportunity for change. I am young; I am conservative; I am progressive, and those who are with me on this campaign are not part of the political machine that has controlled our state government. They share with me a vision of a participatory, citizen-driven government -- a government of the people, that we pledge to deliver to the people. So mark your calendars; the delivery date is November 3rd. Thank you very much, and God bless.

Ed Lopez Biography

Ed Lopez was born on June 26, 1974, the son of two college professors, Xae Reyes de Lopez and Tomas Lopez. Tomas Lopez is now primarily an author of Spanish literature. His mother came from a long tradition of military and public service, his father from an immigrant family whose stories have inspired many of his writings. Lopez' maternal grandfather served in the U.S. Army more than 20 years as an infantry man with active duty in World War II, Korea and Vietnam.

During his childhood, Ed Lopez lived across the country as his parents pursued higher educational goals to help sustain the family Through their example, he learned the value of hard work and education. Lopez began working at age 16, sometimes working close to sixty hours a week after school. His responsibilities included ushering at a university auditorium, counseling at a YMCA after school program for young children, and working the butcher block at a supermarket

After graduating from high school Ed Lopez began his own pursuit for a bachelor's degree in Political Science. Ed Lopez is a member of Alpha Sigma Lambda, Epsilon Rho Chapter of the University of Rhode Island, an honor society for students who have excelled academically while maintaining full time responsibilities in the private and public sector. As a student, Lopez was a member of the Student Senate, was actively involved in journalism and was Chairman of the College Republicans, as well as National Treasurer of Students for a better America. Ed Lopez took two years off from college to serve as a full time missionary for the Church of Jesus Christ of Latter-day Saints in the Dominican Republic, an experience be feels provided him with the richest lessons of his life, including the importance of service to our fellow beings.

Lopez became actively involved with the Republican Party when he was eighteen. Having gained an appreciation for hard work through the example of his family and his own full time work after school, Lopez felt the Republican Party stood for the principles and values of the blue collar and middle class American. In addition, Lopez felt that the Republican Party stood for principles that have helped preserve those elements of our society that unite us all as Americans. Ed Lopez worked as a volunteer leader in United States Senator Robert Bennett's first campaign in Salt Lake City, Utah, and volunteered in several campaigns throughout college for Republican Candidates. Lopez was the founder of the Republican Hispanic Assembly of Rhode Island, an auxiliary of the Rhode Island Republican State Committee. It is the youngest chapter of the Republican National Hispanic

Assembly ever to qualify and bid for the Republican National Hispanic Assembly Convention. Lopez has also worked for Senator Hank Brown and Senator John H. Chafee.

Ed Lopez is a strong supporter of Eco-economic development, believing strongly that business and environmentalism must go hand in hand. He believes that the greatest opportunities for economic development both in Rhode Island and nationwide are found in business that protects the environment and creates new ways to improve it. He is a strong fiscal conservative, being an advocate of a greater reduction of taxes and the development of small business. He believes that more must be done to ensure that small business owners attain a better understanding of the services and opportunities available to help them grow. He feels the needs of seniors and veterans should be addressed more carefully and with consideration of the increasing demand for senior rights and privileges, as the Baby Boom generation grows to senior qualifying age. Ed Lopez has been a strong advocate of the concept of Visual literacy, the idea of broadening K- 12 education to include an understanding of the media and its impact from its inception to its evolution into the computer rich super-information highway. Lopez believes this knowledge is critical for our children as we work toward the goal of restoring a sense of citizenship and community involvement in a society that has become more consumer oriented and politically inactive. He believes this is a crucial element in the preservation of our country's Constitutional foundation as we begin a new century.

Ed Lopez is as a Political Consultant. He maintains an interest in Real Estate brokerage and has worked as an independent contractor for research on private investigations. His experiences in this field have included work in Brazil, Argentina and several U.S. cities. He continues to pursue his educational goals and balances his private and public commitments with ecclesiastical responsibilities and family duties. Lopez is a Witscheman trained member of the Boy Scout committee for Troop 4 in Warwick. He enjoys golf and basketball in rare moments of leisure time.

A Coming Of Age: Latinos Form PAC And Pols Zoom In

By M.Charles Bakst
The Providence Journal
Tuesday August 25, 1998

When they write the history of the Hispanic community's emergence as a full, powerful partner in Rhode Island elections, folks will note an event last Thursday at the Roger William Park Casino.

The Latino Political Action Committee made its debut with a fundraiser that brought in some $10,000, not a bad start on building a war chest and establishing clout. The bipartisan PAC is to support candidates - Hispanic and otherwise -it considers friends.

"We want to Play the game the way everybody else plays it," Dr. Pablo Rodriguez, PAC president, told me. "We think we are coming of age and are ready."

Bill Guglietta, a Democratic candidate for attorney general, had the. best read on Latinos' setting up a PAC: "It will send a message to all politicians: You've got to pay attention to them and their interests. PACs have a way of doing that."

in other words, money talks? "As I've found out," conceded the underfunded Guglietta.
Many pols who flocked to the event *contributed* money. Tickets were $50 apiece, $200 for sponsors.

Guglietta's primary rivals, Sheldon Whitehouse and Eva Mancuso, were there. Whitehouse said, "The Latino community is a fast growing community that is coming into its own politically in Rhode Island and is an important community for an attorney general to work with."

Top Democratic figures on hand included Sen. Jack Reed and candidates for governor (Myrrh York), lieutenant governor (Charles Fogarty) and general treasurer Paul Tavares). York said that "as someone who knows that political organization makes a difference in having your opinions and views and needs addressed," she can see why a PAC is important for Latinos.
Republicans on hand included candidates for treasurer (Jim Bennett) and secretary of state Ed Lopez). Lopez is a Latino. Still, Democratic Secretary of State Jim Langevin attended, and this was something of a pattern. One of

the community's brightest electoral hopes, Victor Capellan, a candidate for Rhode Island House, was there, but so was Joe Almeida, a black, and his opponent in the Democratic primary. And while Miguel Luna, a primary candidate for Providence City Council, was there, so too was Patricia Nolan, the incumbent he is trying to oust. She is white.

Mayor Buddy Cianci, an independent, made a brief appearance.

It also was an eclectic evening in this sense. Organizers were proud that they had broad representation from various Hispanic groups -including Puerto Ricans, Dominicans, Argentinians and Peruvians -who often have been rivals. Alina Ocasio, a state economic development aide who is PAC executive vice president, said outside challenges, such as immigration issues, "are forcing us to become more united."

Caterer Grizzel Rodriguez of Woonsocket served fried chicken fried sweet plantains, meat pies and meatballs.

PAC activities will include turning out the vote and lobbying. Pablo Rodriguez says key issues include education, economic development and health. In a speech, he emphasized that Hispanics are not looking for handouts but for investments in their community. "We are not here to ask for a bigger slice of the pie," he declared. "We are here to help bake a bigger one, so all of us can have a bigger slice."

And he warned pols not to think that dealing with the PAC relieves them of their duty to campaign in the community - they still must get out and shake hands and advertise in the Hispanic media.

Some pols are hiring Hispanic staffers - for example, Whitehouse has Carlos Lopez-Estrada as his scheduler, and Reed has Norelys Consuegra as a constituent aide. Reed, who studied Spanish at West Point - he also works on Portuguese with a tutor - wowed the crowd with a few words in Spanish. He went on in English and concluded, "I congratulate you. I look for-ward to working with you. And I'll still keep working on my Spanish. "*Buenas noches.*"

Haciendo Historia

August 20, 1998

Dear Friends:

The future of Rhode Island is inextricably linked to the health of its youngest and fastest growing community. It is impossible for anyone to walk through the streets of Providence, Pawtucket or Central Falls and not be aware of the Latino presence in our state. One of the few places where that influence is not as palpable, is in our political process. This is principally due to voter apathy towards a system that we do not perceive as our own, and which many times has harmed us instead of helped us. This lack of ownership in the political system threatens to unravel the fabric that has made this country great and this state a bastion of tolerance and multi culturalism.

We, the members of this PAC have committed our efforts to insure that all Latinos in the state become stakeholders in the future of Rhode Island It is our hope that through our efforts and that of our supporters, Rhode Islanders of all ethnic and racial groups will see the wisdom of advocating for the future of the Latino community as a way of improving their own lives. We will bring to the political discourse of the state the hopes and aspirations of this state's newest family members.

Our mission is not to address past discrimination but to build a better future, not to demand justice, but to illustrate the benefits of faimess for all, and not to demand a bigger share of the pie, but to help bake a bigger one together. Join us in the continuation of the dream of countless generations of travelers whose journey ended where our future **together** begins. Let us continue 'Haciendo Histona".

Sincerely,

Pablo Rodriguez. MD

RILPAC Founding Board of Directors

President: Pablo Rodriguez, MD
Executive Vice President: Alina Ocasio
Vice President: Juan Pichardo
Secretary: Michelle Torres
Assistant Secretary: Margarita Guedes
Treasurer: Tomás Alberto Ávila
Assistant Treasurer: Betty Bernal

Board

Alido Baldera

Victor F. Capellán

Francisco J. Cruz

Gladys Corvera-Baker, ACSW, RISCW

José González, Ed.D.

Nellie Gorbea

Ricardo Patiño

Vidal Perez

Tomás Ramirez

Jenny Rosario

Delia Rodriguez-Masjoan

Manuel Suarez, Esq.

Angel Taveras, Esq

OUR M ISSION

The Rhode Island Latino Political Action Committee is a nonpartisan organization formed to advance the following mission:

- To support candidates from Rhode Island for state and local office who are committed to improving the quality of life for members of the Latino and other urban communities.

- To endorse candidates who support issues benefiting Latinos and other individuals from urban communities while raising awareness on issues and/or candidates that could adversely impact the Latino community.

- To insure that elected officials, political leaders and candidates have a broad understanding of the concerns and priorities among Rhode Island Latinos.

Our Goals

The Rhode Island Latino Political Action Committee will focus on the following areas:
- Voter Education/Assistance and improved voter turnout
- Lobbying elected officials and securing public support for selected candidates
- Advocacy and get out the vote efforts
- Research and fundraising
- Coalition building and networking

Critiria F0r Membership

Membership is be open to Latinos and other persons who are at least eighteen (18) years of age and are approved by the Board of Directors.

Levels of Membership

Active Membership:
Active Members must attend all meetings and will have voting privileges.

Associate:

Associate members will receive a quarterly newsletter but will have non-voting status.

<u>Donor</u>:

Donors are supporters who contribute to RILPAC but are not active or associate members.

Commitees

- Political Education/Voter Registration
- Finance
- Membership
- Planning and Research
- Political Candidate Selection
- Legal

RILPAC Inaugural Invitation Letter

June 1998

Dear Friends:

Just about 1 ½ years ago most of us met at my house in what became a series of gatherings that helped solidify our bond as Latinos in this country. As Latino professionals, we found comfort in gathering and celebrating our common heritage. We enjoyed home-made foods and drink, made new acquaintances, and had a wonderful time.

As the parties continued and grew in size, several of us commented on the opportunity to build on the growing network of friends and colleagues. Some built business relationships. Some of our nonprofit leaders were able to connect with Latino professionals that were able to expand on the resources available to help our community. Still others became interested in the political arena, and it is because of this last group that I write to you today.

This is an important time in the history of Latinos and the U.S. Our community whether first or third generation is making itself increasingly known through our numbers and influence on American culture. Despite our many positive contributions Latinos are constantly being defined as lazy, freeloaders, criminals with no right to the American Dream. Many in the U.S. perceive us as members of an economic and a political under class. Our limited participation in the political process in Rhode Island has made it easy for those in positions of power to ignore the issues of concern to our community. It is time to change this situation.

Over the past several months, some of us have come together to develop ways to inject into the political debate, the wishes and aspirations of this state's fastest growing group. As Seinfeld said goodbye to viewers, we were welcoming into the political process of the state, Rhode Island Latino Political Action Committee (RILPAC). The mission of RILPAC is to ensure that candidates to political office in Rhode Island become increasingly aware of our people, as we become more informed about the candidates themselves and their views toward Latinos. Through political action, advocacy and education, we hope to include in the political agenda of the state, issues and ideas of importance to our communities. As expected, this does not happen without money and people. This is where you come in.

On Thursday, August 20th, we will celebrate the inauguration of our PAC. We are hoping to bring to Rhode Island, national Latino political leaders that will help us launch a serious and credible organization that will change the course of history in this state. I am not only asking you to save the date. If we are ever going to be respected as a political force, we must demonstrate not only our ability to gather people, but our ability to raise money as well. It is for this reason that I ask you to become a sponsor for this event.

Your $200 contribution will go towards the funding of this initial effort which hopefully should bring home the message that we are here to stay and to be heard. Your name on the invitation should serve to inspire others to come and contribute, especially if you have never participated in a political fund raiser before. So please, search for those wonderful moments of song and dance that we have experienced together, and turn them into political action that will benefit not only the Latino community, but the whole State. If we have been able to accomplish so much as a community under adverse circumstances, just imagine what we could accomplish if we had friendly lawmakers on our side. Please join us as we begin "Haciendo Historia". Gracias.

Saludos,

Pablo Rodriguez, MD

PS- Please make your check payable to RILPAC and fill out the enclosed contribution card. You may also become a sponsor by selling 5 tickets to the event at $50 each. Your response by August 3rd will ensure the inclusion of your name on the invitation. RSVP to me at 732-2443.

RILPAC Research/Policy Committee

April 1998

Short Range Plan

- thoroughly develop a working strategy for RILPAC's first election cycle
- become registered/incorporated with the appropriate state agencies
- adopt by-laws and endorsement criteria, and recruit members/donors
- conduct elections of a new board and constitute a membership
- continue to seek opportunities for further developments: training, experts, benchmarking, fundraising, etc.

Mid Range Plan

- research candidates by probing, interviews, survey and other methods
- continue to build the fund for RILPAC by having event(s) and individual solicitations
- endorse at least 5 candidates according to our criteria and mission
- work towards the primaries
- conduct GOTV efforts to win primaries and general elections

Long Range Plan

- work with the (5) elected officials to further enhance the work of RILPAC (lobbying)
- continue researching and providing accurate information to the community and to elected officials on issues that affect our target population
- work with the Census 2000 to ensure accurate representation
- position ourselves to be key players in the redistricting efforts of 2002
- continue the development of RILPAC for future years and elections

Training Opportunities/Necessities

- access the current expertise within the membership and ascertain the needs for development
- develop a strategy/systematic training program for RILPAC members
- develop a strategy/systematic training program for the community

Developmental Needs

- PAC's functions/limitations

- Campaigning
- Fundraising
- Mail in ballots
- GOTV efforts
- polling
- voter targeting
- lobbying

PAC Agenda

Develop an agenda: possible examples
- English only legislation
- immigration
- economic development issues

Develop a progressive message
Build coalitions: possible examples
- Blacks
- Southeast Asians
- labor movement
- churches and religious groups
- business

Winning Candidate Luis Aponte

Changing politics in Providence

By Gregory Smith
Journal Staff Writer
9.17.98

PROVIDENCE -- Luis A. Aponte, poised to become the first Hispanic member of the City Council, began his 1998 campaign the day he lost a race for the same seat four years ago.

Aponte, 35, whose occupation is training labor and community organizers, assembled a multicultural team to win his impoverished ward in the South Providence and Washington Park neighborhoods.

He appeared to have a formidable foe in Tuesday's Democratic primary election: Rep. George A. Castro, D-Providence, who was trying to ride an 18-year career at the State House to a berth on what Castro called his first love, the council.

Aponte won the Democratic nomination 526 to 200, and is unopposed in the general election.

``We worked harder'' than Castro, Aponte says. ``We covered the entire ward. And people remembered the campaign from 1994 and decided that I was the better candidate.''

A native of Puerto Rico who grew up in the Bronx and attended high school in Central Falls, Aponte is emblematic of a burgeoning Hispanic vote in Rhode Island.

That political participation, however, has trailed the growth in the Hispanic population.

In 1970, there were slightly fewer than 8,000 Hispanics in Rhode Island. By a few years ago the population had grown to 59,000 and is projected by the Census Bureau to reach 70,000 by 2000. Social-service agencies that work with Hispanics assert that the current population is at least 25 percent higher than officially calculated.

Hispanic leaders say obvious obstacles such as the language barrier and citizenship have delayed Hispanic political progress. Many of the Hispanics are poor, too, and the poor don't tend to vote.

Groups such as the Latino Political Action Committee and Quisqueya en Accion are doing everything they can to promote Hispanic politicians and causes. At the same time, however, those politicians are quick to say their appeal crosses ethnic and racial lines.

``There isn't this big Hispanic agenda out there to take over the city,'' Aponte said in an interview before the election.

There were three Hispanic candidates in the city Democratic primary, but Aponte was the only winner:

Miguel C. Luna, 40, a native of the Dominican Republic who emigrated to Rhode Island as a young man and whose political ideals were inspired by the resistance to the late Dominican dictator Rafael Trujillo, ran a credible campaign for a council seat, losing 536 to 413. He is director of transitional housing and special projects for AIDS Care/Ocean State.

Victor F. Capellan, 27, a Dominican native who 15 years ago was studying English as a newcomer at Roger Williams Middle School, suffered his second straight numbingly narrow loss for state representative in District 20. Capellan, student development coordinator at the University of Rhode Island, lost by 20 votes to Castro in 1996 and by 19 votes this time to Joseph S. Almeida. He has asked for a recount.

The Hispanic vote was evident in the primary, according to Pablo Rodriguez, president of the Latino Political Action Committee, and Santa ``Chary'' Espinosa, Republican candidate for City Council in Ward 9. ``I was very, very surprised by the Spanish turnout,'' said Espinosa. ``The turnout was unbelievable. . . . More and more Hispanics are becoming proud as American citizens.''

Remarked Rodriguez, ``I think it was a very encouraging race'' in the maturation of the Hispanic electorate. ``You only have to see the organizations that were created around all three candidates to see an increased professionalism in campaigning in our community.''

The Hispanic political phenomenon did not become obvious locally until 1990, when three Hispanics sought elective office in Providence. They all lost. But the first Hispanic was elected two years later Rep. Anastasia Williams, D-Providence, who is a native of Panama.

In 1994, Aponte got started late and lost the Democratic nomination in Ward 10 by six votes to longtime Councilman John H. Rollins. Rather than face Aponte a second time, Rollins got a job promotion from Mayor Vincent A. Cianci Jr. and quit the council this year.

``We came close. It was a learning experience in '94 and it prepared us for this election," Aponte said.

THE LATINO Political Action Committee donated money to all three Hispanic candidates in Tuesday's primary, Rodriguez said.

However, he and other leaders say, it would be a mistake to assume that Hispanic politicians or voters are marching in lockstep. For example, in Ward 9, Espinosa said Hispanics apparently split their votes between Luna and Councilwoman Patricia K. Nolan, who won.

``Candidates are not going to win on the Hispanic vote only," Aponte said before the election. They must be coalition-builders, as all successful candidates must be, he said. His program in Ward 10 knows no ethnicity, he said: To build a great neighborhood, with fewer vacant lots, faster and more sensitive police response to crimes and incidents, and economic development.

Aponte closely coordinated his campaign with that of Almeida, a disabled former city policeman who defeated Capellan. A key figure in the joint effort was Sen. Charles Walton, D-Providence, one of the city's black leaders. The Hispanic vote was no more a factor in his win than the vote of any other ethnic group, Aponte said yesterday.

However, as he said before the election, at the rate the Hispanic population is growing, the time may come when Hispanics can put candidates over on the strength of their vote alone. ``Maybe someday the Latino vote will be such that you can elect a mayor," he said.

Ethnic Issue Weighs In For Ward 10 Bout

Rep. George Castro, who is black, and Luis Aponte, who is Hispanic, square off.

By Gregory Smith
Journal Staff Writer
9.11.98

PROVIDENCE -- Will ``Georgie Walker" be in shape for this match?

A long time ago, Rep. George A. Castro, D-Providence, was a professional lightweight boxer, fighting under the name of Georgie Walker. But the old pugilist wasn't in fighting trim in 1994, when he was almost knocked out of his State House perch by a young Hispanic activist, Victor Capellan.

``I read my own press . . . and got lazy. I didn't walk the area" door to door, the 61-year-old Castro recalled. He had not been seriously tested since his first primary election, 14 years earlier.

But he said he is doing the necessary campaigning this time.

Leaving an 18-year career in the General Assembly, Castro now wants the Democratic nomination for City Council in Ward 10. His opponent in next Tuesday's primary election is Luis A. Aponte, 35, director of training and internships for Northeast Action, a progressive sociopolitical and labor group.

Just like the old days in the ring, when a boxer's following often expressed his race or ethnic origin, ethnicity could be an issue in this scrap.

Castro is black with Cape Verdean ancestry. In the other corner is the great Hispanic hope, Aponte. Aponte has said his campaign appeal is ethnically and racially diverse, but he is perceived as a symbol of growing Hispanic political power in Providence.

``There's always that (ethnic) attraction. We're not impervious to that," Aponte said. But Hispanic candidates must be coalition-builders to succeed, he said.
If he wins, Aponte would be only the second Hispanic elected to office in Providence.

Victory in the primary contest is tantamount to election, because there is no non-Democrat on the general election ballot. Ward 10 takes in parts of South Providence and Washington Park, generally south of Public Street and east of Broad Street.

In 1994, Aponte lost the primary election to Councilman John H. Rollins by a scant six votes. Rollins quit the council just before finalizing his candidacy for reelection this year and took a patronage job from Mayor Vincent A. Cianci Jr.

Racial and ethnic loyalties were in play in 1994. For instance, Joseph Buchanan, a prominent South Providence civic leader and Rollins supporter, commented then, ``When their time comes, it comes. But right now, the black community needs elected officials." Both Buchanan and Rollins are black.

This year Castro has distributed fliers bearing an illustration of the American flag and a request that the recipients vote for him. Aponte charged that the flier is a subliminal message that Castro is more of an American than Aponte.

As a native of Puerto Rico, Aponte was a U.S. citizen at birth.

Castro, who stresses his lifelong residency in the ward in another flier, could not be reached for comment on the flag flier. But he said previously that he often chides blacks for talking too much about their color rather than their nationality. Everyone is a minority of some kind, he said.

``I'm an American-African," he remarked.

Aponte is a former member of the Governor's Commission on Hispanic Affairs, a co-founder of the Latino Political Action Committee and a founding member of the Center for Hispanic Policy and Advocacy, among other civic affiliations. As the endorsed Democrat, he has the support of Cianci, an independent. Cianci and the local Democratic party are allied for now, and Cianci has donated $170 to the Aponte campaign in the last year. But Aponte does not appear ready to sign up for Cianci's ruling faction on the council.

Aponte and his wife, Gwendolyn, have not forgotten that the Cianci administration denied Gwendolyn Aponte an unpaid leave of absence from her job as equal employment opportunity officer for the city in 1994. Mrs. Aponte wanted a leave, as others had received, in order to work for Myrth York's campaign for governor.

Aponte friends alleged that the denial was retaliation for Luis Aponte challenging Rollins, a down-the-line Cianci man. ``The mayor is not sure of what he is getting'' if he is elected, Aponte remarked. ``He knows he is not getting another John Rollins in his pocket.'' Aponte's campaign chairwoman in 1994 and again this year is Councilwoman Balbina A. Young, D-Ward 11, who has little use for
Cianci.

``We'll go issue by issue with the mayor,'' Aponte added.

Both Castro and Aponte are vague about what they would do in office. Aponte talks about the need to improve city services in the ward and to stimulate economic development, and he promises to hold quarterly neighborhood meetings if he is elected.

Castro emphasizes community-building and the development of programs for youths.

Castro is employed as executive director of Blacks Interested in Communications, a nonprofit organization that trains people for careers in broadcast communications. He has a long history of crusading for minority groups. He co-founded, for example, Puerto Ricans in Action, a political and cultural group, in the 1970s. And he was instrumental in establishing the birthday of Martin Luther King Jr. as a state holiday. He also co-founded the Rhode Island Black Caucus of State Legislators in 1980, a group that he quit several years ago, apparently in a policy dispute.

But in the eyes of some people, he stumbled at least once, when he introduced legislation in 1987 to establish English as the official state language. Stung by complaints that the official-language movement is ``racist,'' he dropped the bill. Castro said that he thought an official-language law would help to attract government money for education and English instruction.

``All of my people learned to speak English. They knew they couldn't function'' without it, he said.

Ethnicity Is Big Issue In Ward 9's Primary

Hispanic activist Miguel Luna challenges Councilwoman Patricia K. Nolan.

By Gregory Smith
Journal Staff Writer
9.8.98 08

PROVIDENCE -- Miguel Luna is hoping that Pat Nolan's mouth has gotten her into trouble with voters.

Some political observers predicted that Councilwoman Patricia K. Nolan might have difficulty winning renomination in the Democratic primary election in Ward 9 because of her abrupt manner.

And Luna, a black Hispanic, has been busy portraying the white incumbent as less sensitive than he to the different social and economic classes in the ward, where about 80 percent of the population are members of ethnic and racial minority groups.

``With me running, a lot of good things are happening,'' Luna remarked. ``You can't ignore us any more.''

For one thing, Luna said, both sides are running slates of candidates for election to the Democratic ward committee that include Hispanics, ensuring that for the first time a Hispanic will be elected.

``I know I carry a big stick sometimes . . . and maybe I'm even a little abrasive,'' Noland conceded. ``But if people get to know me . . . they know what's in my heart.
``And I do get things done.''

The verdict on the Nolan approach is only a week away now. The nominee selected in the election next Tuesday will then go on to confront two Hispanics -- one Republican, one independent -- in the general election for a four-year term.

Ward 9 takes in most of Elmwood, north to Laura Street, and that part of Washington Park closest to Roger Williams Park.

The councilwoman is running a classic bring-home-the-bacon campaign, boasting that she has been personally responsible for bringing almost $15 million in projects and services into the ward and landing numerous city jobs for constituents and their children.

Keep Nolan -- according to the campaign pitch -- and because she is chairwoman of the council Finance Committee you will get even more of the same.

Nolan also prides herself on her work for minorities, including help in winning passage of the state gay rights bill and guiding to adoption a similar local ban against discrimination on the basis of sexual orientation or physical or mental handicap.

Luna contends that the resources coming into the ward still fall well short of the need. He promises to fight for more state aid to education and to redirect city finances to the neighborhoods and away from tax breaks for downtown businesses.

Without naming Nolan, he insisted that office holders must stop presenting public services as ``favors.'' He said he has been having some success in changing people's way of thinking that a sidewalk fixed or a
tree pruned is a personal favor from an office holder, even though taxpayers foot the bill.

Nolan, 56, grew up near Columbus, Ohio, and worked for many years in sales and training for Eastman Kodak and Danka, an office equipment sales and leasing company. Business brought her to Rhode Island in the 1980s, where she settled in at 230 Atlantic Ave., in a struggling part of Elmwood.

She wound up flanked by two crack houses, Nolan recalled, so she became involved in Elmwood Neighbors for Action. She eventually migrated to membership on the ward committee of then-Council President Nicholas W. Easton and was endorsed to succeed him in 1990.

Nolan emerged the winner of a four-way contest in her first primary, with 38 percent of the vote, but she has not been seriously tested at the polls since then.

Last January, Nolan took a buyout from her job as a training specialist at Danka, giving her the advantage of being able to work full-time on her campaign and paid council job. Luna, 40, of 146 Warrington St., in Elmwood, is a community organizer who, as a Dominican-American, is a member of the city's largest minority group.

He has highlighted his ethnicity, asserting, for instance, that Nolan was too hard on Dominican-Americans regarding misbehavior surrounding the Dominican festival last month. ``I have to ask myself if her criticisms are politically motivated because she fears me, a Dominican, as her opponent,'' Luna said in a news release. His campaign literature promises that he will be ``a voice for the whole community.'' Nolan replied that many residents, including Hispanics, joined her in complaining about the misbehavior.

Luna is a native of the Dominican Republic. His late father, a civil servant, refused to hang the obligatory picture of dictator Rafael Trujillo in his home. Luna emigrated to the U.S. in 1984, joining his mother in Providence. Over 80 years old now, she still works in a factory. Luna held a variety of blue-collar jobs.

He has been a fighter for political refugees, underpaid artists, farm workers and tenants, he said. He is married to Shannah Kurland, executive director of the local group DARE, or Direct Action for Rights and Equality, which he helped to launch.

Typical of Nolan's mixed-up priorities, Luna said, was her decision to spend money from a $50 million bond issue to replace a fence and fix the sidewalks around Locust Grove Cemetery. That money would have been better spent on eradicating lead paint from the homes of young children, he contended.

She has spent money on lead abatement, Nolan replied. As for the cemetery, she said, a community committee concerned about the condition of that prominent site determined the expenditure.

Luna currently works as director of transitional housing and special projects for AIDS Care/Ocean State. Luna said he is well-equipped to serve in public life.

``We need someone (on the council) who has a good understanding of oppression.''

URI Senior Takes Aim At An Incumbent Whose Star Is Rising

By Jonathan Saltzman
Journal State House Bureau

10.5.98

PROVIDENCE -- Of the five races for statewide office next month, none appears more lopsided than the contest for Rhode Island secretary of state.

James R. Langevin, the incumbent, is a well-financed Democrat in a traditionally Democratic state. A rising political star at the age of 34, he has carved out an image as a government reformer. For some, he is also a genuine inspiration, having overcome a 1980 shooting accident that left him a paraplegic.

His challenger is Eduardo Lopez, a 24-year-old senior at the University of Rhode Island, who hopes to become the first Hispanic elected statewide. Lopez is that rarest of New England commodities, a minority running as a Republican. A Mormon in the most Catholic state, he is making his first bid for elective office with little money but considerable pluck.

Lopez, whose finances are so limited that he strives not to waste campaign fliers, concedes it would be remarkable if he upset Langevin. But, he says, it's not impossible.

``I think it's been grossly exaggerated that he's that strong, that he can't really be defeated,'' Lopez says. ``He's beatable.''

Langevin, who led Lopez by a tally of 59 to 13 percent (with 28 percent undecided) in a recent Brown University poll, says he takes Lopez ``very seriously.'' Nonetheless, Langevin's ``campaign manager'' is a Brown senior who returns reporters' calls to his pager between classes.

The office for which the candidates are fighting is among the more obscure in state government. One of five general officeholders, the secretary of state is the custodian of state records and historic documents. He serves as independent recordkeeper of the General Assembly's activities and maintains filings for corporations and partnerships. He also helps set up federal, state and local elections.

From a political standpoint, the job is appealing because it seldom requires decisions that stir controversy or produce a voter backlash. Governors are ousted for mishandling hurricanes or fiscal problems; secretaries of state rarely get bounced for storing records poorly. There's another bonus: because the secretary of state's duties include informing the public about elections, he has many opportunities to shake hands with constituents during the election season. On the negative side, however, the office has little of the power or prestige of, say, governor or attorney general. Many Rhode Islanders would be hard-pressed to name the secretary of state, or say what he does.

Langevin, a former state representative from Warwick, won the office four years ago and, in the view of many, has energized it. Recognizing the public's revulsion with scandals that germinated in dark corners of the State House, Langevin pledged to make it easier for the public to scrutinize the activities of lawmakers.

``We've tried to be the office in state government that arms the people with the power that knowledge gives," said Langevin, invoking a quote by James Madison.

To that end, he transformed the office's ``record center," a dusty, paper-strewn warren where it was hard to find legislative bills, into a well-organized Public Information Center. Bills are stored by number in neat trays. Bulletin boards display committee agendas. Decorated with dark wood and antique lamps, the office even won a prize from the Providence Preservation Society.

Langevin, who has a master's degree from the Kennedy School of Government at Harvard University, also took the center into cyberspace. He created a secretary of state Web site, the first of its kind in Rhode Island state government. When the General Assembly is in session, more than 1,000 Rhode Islanders visit the site daily to track legislation, he said. Only last month, Langevin helped usher in another change by making the primary the first computerized state election in Rhode Island history.

Instead of pulling levers in election booths that dated back to the Eisenhower era, voters filled out special paper ballots and inserted them into optical scanners. There were some software glitches on election night. But Langevin loves technology -- reading Tom Clancy's techno-thrillers is one of his passions -- and has promised to iron them out.

In perhaps his defining moment in office, however, Langevin caught considerable flak from his former colleagues in the Assembly. In January he released a report titled ``Access Denied: Chaos, Confusion and Closed

Doors," which said that the General Assembly is so negligent about announcing meetings that the public was often excluded. The report, which was prepared with help from two Brown professors and three students, found that more than half the meetings in the 1997 session violated the letter or the spirit of the Open Meetings Law.

Legislators angrily complained that the report was unfair and gave them insufficient credit for improvements in recent years. Senate leaders, in particular, objected to being tarred with the same brush as the House, which had more violations.

Senate Corporations Chairman William V. Irons, D-East Providence, is still seething about the study, although he praises Langevin's tenure overall. He says the report illustrates Langevin's singular weakness, a ``penchant for making the legislative group the bogeyman because it plays well with the public."

Much to Langevin's chagrin, Brown's new president, E. Gordon Gee, quickly fell in step with General Assembly leaders after Gee got angry calls about Brown's role in the study. Gee said Langevin had given the report an inappropriately political title and tenor.

Sitting in a wheelchair -- which he has used since he was accidentally shot as a 16-year-old cadet in the Warwick Police Department -- Langevin says that had Gee's predecessor, ``President (Vartan) Gregorian been there, he wouldn't have had the same reaction that President Gee did. I think he would have been more quick to support the study."

Nonetheless, Langevin says he holds no grudge. And he says legislative leaders who immediately promised to provide a list of errors in the report never did. ``The findings are sound," he says. Since the report was issued, he added, the legislature has made vast improvements in complying with the Open Meetings Law. He plans to monitor the situation and issue a similar report every year.

Langevin, who is single, has spent $172,236 on his campaign so far this year. Because of term limits, he would not be able to serve a third term if he wins. Langevin, who has won plaudits from public interest lobbyists such as Common Cause of Rhode Island, says he would consider running for Congress or governor.

``I wouldn't rule out anything at all," he says.

His challenger, Lopez, wants Langevin to start looking for another job after Nov. 3. Lopez is an earnest and ambitious political science major at URI whose candidacy reflects the rising power of Latinos in Rhode Island.

Born in Puerto Rico, Lopez is the son of two college professors. He spent his early years in Syracuse, N.Y., returned with his family to Puerto Rico, then went to high school in Boulder, Colo., and began college at the University of Utah. Lopez, who was raised a Catholic, joined the Mormon church while attending the University of Utah. He left school for two years to serve as a full-time missionary in the Dominican Republic.

He got involved in politics while in his teens, working on Robert Bennett's winning Senate campaign in Utah in 1992 and volunteering on Ross Perot's unsuccessful presidential bid that year. After moving to Rhode Island, he volunteered on Rick Wild's ill-fated 1996 congressional campaign. Last year, he had a paid internship with Sen. John H. Chafee, working in his Providence office.

Lopez, who lives in Cranston with his younger brother, father, and mother, a professor of education at Rhode Island College, founded the Republican Hispanic Assembly of Rhode Island. Although Latinos in New England have traditionally favored the Democratic Party, Lopez had several Republicans in his family and says that Democrats are losing their hold on minority voters.

``The Democratic Party had their cycle with the ethnic community, and they were helpful in a lot of ways, but in a lot ways they also did a disservice," he said. He contends that the Democratic Party has fostered an overreliance on welfare. And he feels that affirmative action programs, while helpful to minorities, should be reformed so that the chief qualification is economic status, not ethnicity. Until this spring, Lopez had been considering running for a state Senate seat in Cranston. But he decided to challenge Langevin after speaking with Republican leaders, including state chairwoman Joan B. Quick, who were hunting for a secretary of state candidate.

Lopez recognized that the odds were daunting, he says, but went after Langevin anyway. He gives the incumbent high marks for character ``I wish we had more politicians that had that sense of sincerity and honesty" -- but middling ones for job performance.

Sitting in his campaign office on Park Avenue in Cranston, a former bicycle shop now decorated with bumper stickers and framed photographs of Republican stalwarts such as Jack Kemp, Lopez says Langevin's reputation is inflated.

If Langevin's Web site and the new voting machines are notable achievements, he says, it's only because Rhode Island lagged so far behind other states. ``This is technology,'' he says. ``It's bound to happen.''

And while Lopez gives Langevin credit for the ``Access Denied'' report, he says the secretary of state should have uncovered the problem sooner. He also feels Langevin dropped the matter after he issued the report, something Langevin denies. Lopez says he would establish a commission with the attorney general's office and citizens to monitor compliance with the Open Meetings Law.

Lopez's primary goal is to improve voter education and get more people involved in government, particularly young citizens, minorities and those who have been turned off by politics. He says he would enlist volunteers to get the Web site written in a variety of languages, from Spanish to Cambodian. Like Langevin, he vows to cut red tape to make it easier for citizens to open small businesses. Entrepreneurs typically have to file many forms with the secretary of state.

It hasn't been easy for Lopez to get his message across. He has raised about $9,000 and received about $11,000 in matching funds through the public campaign financing program. He only recently got a fax machine at his headquarters from the Republican Party, and good-naturedly admits that he doesn't know exactly how to operate it.

Marc Genest, one of Lopez's political science professors at URI and academic adviser, praises his academic performance and political savvy. ``He's running for office for the right reasons,'' Genest says. ``He's got a nice combination of ambition, intelligence and heart.'' Although Lopez's candidacy is a longshot, Genest adds, Lopez has already inspired other students to enter politics.

``He has a great future,'' Genest said. ``I fully expect him to be governor someday or congressman.''

RILPAC 2000 Political Strategy

Guy Dufault& Mark Ford
April 21, 1999

Per your discussion last week, the following outlines some of the steady, yet effective, steps your organization can make in the next twelve months to increase the electability of Latino candidates in Rhode Island.

Goals:

Specifically, we recommend focusing your efforts on General Assembly races. Not only do these positions offer broader involvement in the shaping of policy, but also gives higher exposure and unity to your caucus. Four or five Latino legislators is more effective than having a dozen or so spread out through city or town councils all over Rhode Island.

Similarly, instead of seeking out ten or more seats in a given election, run four or five well-financed and motivated campaigns. Picking up two seats per year, especially in 2000 before the 2002 redistricting will steadily increase the potency of the Latino voice in Rhode Island policy-making.

As a general organizational strategy for the RILPAC, focus on those things that help your candidates get elected. This pragmatic approach may at first run contrary to some more idealistic goals like voter participation, but in the long run having elected leaders who use their positions to make a real difference will go a long way toward accomplishing some of those goals.

Preparing for 2000:

RILPAC should make initial preparations for its 2000 General Assembly slate of candidates. Look to those legislative districts that both have large or growing Latino populations and have opponents who can be beaten. Once you select four or five key districts, then move toward voter research and identification.

Specifically, go to the local boards of canvassers and get the voter file for that district and the voter history file (this file, usually on disk in some of the larger cities, shows all those voters who participated in recent elections primaries or general). This is critical, Rhode Island General Assembly Democratic primaries are only among a couple thousand voters, at most. Being able to target your mailing and walking to those households who participate is a good way of making valuable resources like time and money work best for you. Sending three mailers to the two thousand likely voters will have a greater impact on the actual outcome of the election than sending one mailer to the six thousand registered voters.

Allow yourself a month or so to compile this data. Town Halls in Rhode Island are not known for accessibility of information. Plus, towns like Johnston and Cumberland, for example, may not even have the voter file on disk - you may have to recruit some volunteers to input the data manually. We understand you may have done this in some of your previous elections - so you may have a computer guru - if not, we can get you started.

Without question, your grassroots organization may be your strongest mechanism to victory. While Latinos may not yet have high rates of participation, your organization illustrates that those involved have a great deal of dedication and motivation. Begin to identify your volunteer base and find their areas of specialty.

While much of today elections are determined more by "wholesale" campaigning (mailers, radio, media, etc), local races can still be swayed if the "retail" (grassroots) is particularly strong. Volunteers can do the following: make phone calls, walk with candidates in their neighborhoods, prepare mailers, put up lawn signs, etc.

In particular, since most of your campaigns will be low-budget, a good group of phone callers may help with polling calls to find Out what issues are really effecting the voters in that district.

Creating Communications Tools:

Building strong lines of communications with your target audience is something that you should pay attention to. Delia's talk show, a weekly write-in column, and a quarterly newsletter. E-mail is a good way of communicating, but is limited to those who are active users; it is not good for mass communication. Particularly, a newsletter will allow you to start identifying your constituent base and get your messages out to them. You will be able to keep them informed about the issues and let them know how they can participate. Depending on the size of the mailing list - a two-color, four page newsletter can be very inexpensive and very effective.

When campaign season comes, if you have a strong line of communication with your voter base - you will be able to profile candidates and recruit volunteers in a way that reaches many of your favorable voters.

First Annual Bill Richardson Awards Winners Announced

September 1st, 1999

Providence, RI – The Rhode Island Political Action Committee (RILPAC) a nonpartisan political organization announced today the winners of the organization's first annual Bill Richardson Latino Advocacy Awards, to be presented at it's 2nd annual fundraiser to be held at the Rhode Island Foundation, one Union Station Building, Providence RI Saturday October 9th, 1999 6:00-8:00 PM.

According to Dr. Pablo Rodriguez, President of the Rhode Island Latino Political Action Committee, "These awardees best represent the mission of the PAC, based on their track record in support of the Latino community". Based on the awardees involvement in the Latino community, they know first-hand the issues affecting every one of us in the Latino community.

Their life experience, track record and advocacy on behalf of the Latino community of Rhode Island provide us with a clear choice in this selection. The award winners were chosen from individuals who were nominated by community residents and committee members attesting to their leadership in advocating on behalf of the Latino community of Rhode Island. The awardees are:

Senator Jack Reed, whose work in Congress on behalf of Latino immigrants has been invaluable to those most vulnerable to the 1996 Immigration Law. To him goes the First Bill Richardson Award for Latino Advocacy of an elected official.

Maria Luisa Vallejo, whose constant presence in the Legislature has made it possible for bills such as English Plus and Court Interpreters to become law, to the benefit of non English speakers in the State, goes the Latino Advocacy Award for Public Policy.

Leo DiMaio goes the Advocacy Award for Education, for having inspired a whole generation of Latino and minority students attending the University of Rhode Island to become the best that they could be.

Charles M. Bakst, whose column in the Providence Journal has made the case for Latinos as a political force worth reckoning with, and for constantly pointing out the lack of minority representation in the upper echelons of government, goes the Latino Advocacy Award in Public Education and Media.

The Rhode Island Latino Political Action Committee is a nonpartisan organization formed to influence the political process in the state of Rhode Island in order to improve the quality of life of Latino and urban communities.

###

RILPAC's Second Annual Fundraiser

September 1st, 1999

Contact: Dr. Pablo Rodriguez
              (401) 272-4050
              E-Mail: Pablo_Rodriguez@brown.edu

FOR IMMEDIATE RELEASE:

Providence, RI – The Rhode Island Political Action Committee a nonpartisan political organization will celebrate it's 2nd fundraising event, Saturday October 9th, 1999, 6:00 – 8:00 PM at Rhode Island Foundation, Union Station Building, Providence.

This event marks RILPAC's second annual fundraiser event and will have the participation of Secretary of Energy Bill Richardson as well as the presentation of our first Latino Advocacy Award.

RILPAC goal is to insured that elected officials, political leaders and candidates have a broad understanding of the concerns and priorities among Rhode Island Latinos. The event will get underway at 6:00 PM and close at 8:00 PM.

The Rhode Island community at large and local elected officials have been invited to attend the event. Admission to the event is $50.00 per person. The Rhode Island Latino Political Action Committee is a nonpartisan organization formed to influence the political process in the state of Rhode Island in order to improve the quality of life of Latino and urban communities.

###

Matthews' Tight Win Sets Up Showdown

By Douglas Hadden
The Pawtucket Times
Wed, Oct 06, 1999

CENTRAL FALLS -- It's going to be a horse race. That's what Mayor Lee Matthews' narrow 100-vote margin over Councilman Robert Weber in Tuesday's mayoral primary seemed to promise, with each candidate claiming later that the larger turnout expected for the Nov. 2 final will help him.

The two-term mayor bested the second-term councilman in four of the city's five wards, but often narrowly, in posting an 850 to 750 votes win, including mail balloting. Perennial candidate Wilfred "Pete" DeMeule ran a distant third with 67 votes, in official Board of Canvassers totals.

Matthews notched 50.99 percent of the vote, Weber had 44.99 percent and DeMeule 4.02 percent, with 13 ballots cast in other races left blank for mayor.
A total of 1,680 ballots were cast, or just under 28 percent of the city's 6,008 registered voters, in a light turnout.

Matthews won his home Ward 1 (voting at Calcutt School) by 128 votes to 79 for Weber; Weber took Ward 2 (Robertson School) by 180-174: Matthews won Ward 3 (Forand Manor) by 213-190, took Weber's home Ward 4 (Wilfrid Manor) by 197-194 and Ward 5 (Capt. Hunt School) by 138-107.

"This is exactly pretty much what we expected," Matthews said later at a small post-primary gathering at the Madeira Club. Matthews said November's larger turnout would help him, "no question about it," and said his campaign will have to "work hard to expand the margin of victory."

Matthews said as voters learn more about issues, he expected his support to increase. "It's pretty clear the unions own him (Weber)," Matthews said, "and if he wins, they will get what they want because there is no way he can win the election and say no," particularly to the firefighters union. Matthews noted several firefighters turned out to stump for Weber Tuesday.

Several firefighters, whose union has been in an arbitration battle with the city, were visible greeting voters outside polling sites Tuesday.

Other than Police Capt. Joseph Moran, who since Matthews first ran has worked on his campaigns, members of the police union appeared to stay out of active involvement in Tuesday's race.

Weber, at a large and enthusiastic gathering at the West Side Tavern, laughed out loud when told of Matthews' comments about city unions "owning" Weber.
"I've gotta laugh at that because the bottom line is I just came that close to beating a four-year incumbent," Weber said.

"I've promised (the unions) nothing and they know that. All I've said is that I'll be fair, I'll treat any and all fairly. (Matthews) doesn't care about them; he doesn't support city workers at all." Weber said the lower turnout out should have helped the incumbent. "It should have hurt me and it didn't."

Weber said he would have been "happy" to come within 200 votes in the primary and that the 100-vote difference could be turned around by November.

"I'm pleased. I'm real happy to be where we are," he said.

Three City Council races had primaries, and in Ward 2 a newcomer, 26-year-old Jason Leger, by a vote count of 198 to 152, topped Councilman Robert Ferri, a close supporter of Matthews who is seeking a third term. Joseph Cross came in a distant third with 15 votes.

In the Ward 3 primary, first-time candidate Rose Marie Canavan, a retired teacher and the wife of outgoing Council President Robert Canavan, topped vote-getters with 213 votes or 52 percent. Ricardo Patino, who operates a lead abatement company and is the only Latino in this year's political field, was a solid second with 142 votes, or almost 35 percent, in his first bid for office. Third-time candidate Douglas Pendergrass was a distant third with 42 votes and George DeLomba, who had already effectively quit the race, received 11 votes.

In Ward 5, Thomas Lazieh, the former three-term mayor, easily topped the field with 137 votes to 51 for Leonard Ryszkiewicz, an electrician who served on the former School Building Committee, and 46 for Alberto Moniz, a weaver who serves on the city Personnel Board.

The top two vote-getters in each race will face off in the November final.
One new trend Tuesday was active involvement by Providence-based Latino political groups, who worked on behalf of Patino. The groups included the Rhode Island Latino Political Action Committee, headed by Pablo Rodriguez

of Providence, and Puerto Rican American Political Action Committee, led by Osvaldo Castillo, who said he moved to Central Falls six months ago.

Those groups appeared to bring in new voters throughout the day. One was Alicia Sanchez, 29, of 99 Darling St., who came with her 8-year-old son to Forand Manor to vote. Sanchez, with Rodriguez translating her words from Spanish, said she came out to vote because "she wants change. She wants something better in her city."

Voters' biggest confusion was at Calcutt School, where Ward 1 voters had to go around the back of the newly expanded building to enter the building and vote but had no signs on Washington Street to advise them of the change.

Challenging Weygand, Licht Vies For Latino Support

M. Charles Bakst
The Providence Journal
10.17.99

Vying with Rep. Bob Weygand in the 2000 Democratic Senate primary, former Lt. Gov. Richard Licht asserts he has a real shot to win the support of the Latino community, which was a key to Weygand's success in getting to Congress.

Several Latinos tell me Licht -- because of his pluses or because of some disenchantment with Weygand -- indeed has a chance.

Licht already has the backing of Dr. Pablo Rodriguez, who is president of the Rhode Island Latino Political Action Committee and who supported Weygand against Joe Paolino in their hotly contested 1996 House primary.

Rodriguez says Licht ``absolutely'' could win the majority of Hispanic votes. ``He could take it simply because this community is one that is sophisticated, that is looking for leadership that responds to issues of Latinos."

Weygand concedes nothing, contends he enjoys robust rank-and-file Latino backing here and notes continued strong support from Rep. Loretta Sanchez, the high-profile Hispanic congresswoman from California.

With Weygand, a fellow House rookie, escorting her to several stops, Sanchez visited Rhode Island in 1997. She tells me she'll be here again for his Senate bid.

According to a Weygand Senate campaign-finance report filed this summer, he has received $1,000 from her reelection committee and $2,000 from Hispanic PAC, a political action committee operated by Democratic Hispanic members of Congress.

The 1990 census put the Rhode Island Latino population at 45,000, but it's been growing substantially, with estimates that it may now be close to 75,000. Two cities in which Hispanics especially are a presence -- Pawtucket and Central Falls -- are in the congressional district represented by Patrick Kennedy.

It may be that some in the Hispanic community aren't rushing to embrace Weygand at this point because they don't want Latinos to be taken for granted.

Sanchez says Hispanics must continually ask candidates what they'll do for them and look at the candidates' history. ``Hopefully, the Hispanic community is doing that up there,'' she says in a telephone interview from Washington. ``They'll see Bob has been good on issues that affect our community.''

She praises Weygand's constituent work visas, work permits and so on and his voting record in such areas as support for bilingual education.

She says she's never met Licht. But she can't say enough about Weygand. ``When I need a vote and I need him to round up votes, I explain the issue to him and he goes out and rounds up votes,'' she says.

Weygand, who was then lieutenant governor, became a darling of Latinos in 1996 after calls by former Providence Mayor Paolino to make English the official language of the United States, to crack down on illegal immigration and to take another look at bilingual education.

At the Biltmore Hotel, Hispanics thrilled to Weygand's victory on primary night. Victor Capellan told him, ``Our whole community is all excited.'' Carolina Bernal said, ``It's good for the whole state to have a person like you that we can trust.''

But today, Capellan, an aide at the Center for Hispanic Policy and Advocacy, says it's ``very possible'' Licht could seize Weygand's Latino support. And Bernal, a staffer at the Institute for Labor Studies, says, ``It's going to be a tough race.'' She calls both candidates ``excellent'' and refuses to give me a prediction on how things will go. That would be ``free publicity'' for one of them, she chuckles. ``They've got to do their homework.''

You could have seen both Licht and Weygand working the crowd at a recent Latino PAC reception.

Licht told me he has good prospects among Latinos because of a ``strong record'' in working with them. ``When I was lieutenant governor, I had an Hispanic advisory council. We met on a frequent basis.''
He also employed a Hispanic woman, Margarita Baez, as a policy aide. Licht largely disappeared from public view after he lost a 1988 Senate bid. He says he's making a concerted effort to reintroduce himself to Latinos. Licht says

147

it's too early to say whether there will be any Latinos on his campaign staff, but he definitely will have a Latino committee.

Licht contends his stands on issues -- including education and immigration appeal to Hispanics.

Rodriguez considers him a stronger voice than Weygand for an amnesty for undocumented immigrants, which is viewed as a way of keeping families united. Many undocumented immigrants, from such countries as Colombia, Mexico and Guatemala, work here and pay taxes. But because they came illegally, they cannot claim health benefits and they live in fear of being deported -- often to countries devastated by war or hurricane -- and separated from relatives, including American-born children, here.

Weygand is leery of an amnesty that would be so broad as to include criminals. On the other hand, there is debate over how to define criminals. And for the moment the amnesty topic may be more emotional or symbolic than real: Sanchez says that unless House Democrats find some magic bargaining chip in dealing with Republicans, the only way the legislation will pass is if Democrats seize House control in 2000.

Another problem Rodriguez has with Weygand is that the congressman does not have high-ranking Hispanic staffers.

Weygand boasts of having an Hispanic constituent caseworker, Yvette Jaquez, in his Rhode Island office. Overall, he says, his staff is ``very diverse,'' with more women than men and more minority representation than in the population at large.

Capellan, who has run unsuccessfully for the Rhode Island House and is eyeing another race, says he'd have liked to have seen Weygand immerse himself more in the Latino community, but he goes out of his way to praise Jaquez for being ``very active with us.''

In some Hispanic quarters, as with any other group, Weygand may be taking a hit for his opposition to abortion rights.

This is one area in which he and Rodriguez, medical director of Planned Parenthood, part company. Obviously, the two men also disagreed on abortion in 1996, but Rodriguez, who found the ``pro-choice'' Paolino unpalatable on other fronts, was willing to swallow the differences. Licht is ``pro-choice.''

Congresswoman Sanchez tells me, ``I am probably one of the strongest `pro-choice' votes here in Congress, as well as an advocate. When I look at candidates to support, that's one of the criteria I look very hard at. It's hard for me to work for `anti-choice' people. Bob is an exception. Overall, the rest of his agenda is very straightforward for working people: education, for children and vocational and lifelong learning. That's important, especially to the Hispanic agenda.''

Weygand says his relationship with the Latino community is ``extremely strong.''

He says it doesn't panic him if some leaders, such as Rodriguez, are not in his corner. In 1996, he says, some top Democrats weren't for him either, ``but the rank-and-file Democrats certainly were.''

Jenny Rosario, a high school teacher who was a close Weygand adviser in 1996, says she remains an enthusiastic backer, even though she also considers Licht a ``wonderful person.'' She says Weygand has done an ``excellent'' job representing average Rhode Islanders, including Hispanics.

Yet I also spoke with Francisco Cruz, who works for the Providence Plan, a nonprofit urban revitalization agency. Once a City Hall aide to Paolino, Cruz in 1996 sided with Weygand.

Today he says he leans to Licht, whom he knew through Margarita Baez and with whom he has cooperated over the years on several projects. Cruz says he's in the dark about the extent to which Weygand has maintained some of his connections in the Hispanic community. For example, in the Senate primary, ``I wasn't approached by his campaign.'' Cruz says Licht did seek his support.

It's not like Weygand to be lazy. This guy is driven. But I've never met any politician more driven than Licht. So if Licht says he's going to best Weygand in the Hispanic community, I'll keep my eye on the situation.

Suggest you do same.

Angel Taveras Announcement Speech

November 15, 1999

Thank you Senator Igliozzi. Thank you for your kind introduction and thank you for all your service as a Providence City Councilman and your tireless efforts on behalf of Rhode Islanders as a State Senator. I am very proud to have you as my Senator.

I cannot think of more fitting places for me to embark upon the journey I begin today than at a Providence public school and Rhode Island's state university.

I am here today in large part because I have had wonderful teachers who allowed me to dream, and a family that has always been there for me, in good times and in bad. I am here today because, through the grace of God, I was born in America and *because the promise of America was kept to me.*
I am here today because of a teacher that I had in Mary E. Fogarty Elementary School who believed in me and made me believe in myself. That teacher, Mrs. Donaldson, encouraged to dream -- *to believe that I could become something I had never seen.*

In the third grade, Mrs. Donaldson, asked me what I wanted to be when I grew up. I told her "I want to be a lawyer!" And when she asked why, I said, "Because I want to help people."

It never crossed my mind until years later that, even as a young child, *I wanted to be something I had never seen.* I wonder if Mrs. Donaldson knew at that moment -- I think she must have known-- that I had never seen a *Latino* lawyer in Providence, Rhode Island. That my dream was not reinforced with any living role model. I wonder if she quickly assessed the odds against me -- I think she must have figured those odds to be very great.

But Mrs. Donaldson not only didn't try to discourage me; she was *proud* of me. She used to take me to see the other teachers, and have me tell them about my dream -- about my vision of becoming something I'd never seen. And for reasons I couldn't even imagine then, but that now I recognize very clearly, my vision had an impact on those adults. It reminded them of a time when they weren't too jaded to dream. In a small way, maybe I helped make them young again.

I did it

Mrs. Donaldson. Thank you! I hope you are proud.

I'm here today to tell you that you can do the same as I did-- that you are limited not by society's vision, but only by your own imagination, by what *you* are bold enough to see. I'm here today to say that no one has the right or the ability to tell you how far you can go -- only *you* can choose your destination, and reaching it will be a function of *your* willpower. I'm here to assure you that the future -- your own and that of our society -- is not pre-determined by anyone or any force, but is waiting for you to shape it with compassion and intelligence and vision.

I'm here today so that you can see me, the son of Dominican immigrants, a product of the Providence public schools, a Harvard graduate, an attorney, and something more, and to offer living proof that the vision can be made real, that the destination can be reached, that the future can be shaped into a fair and hopeful future.

For all these reasons, I am here today to announce my candidacy for the United States Congress from Rhode Island's Second Congressional District. Political campaigns adopt mottoes. Mine is no different. On bumper stickers and billboards, as tags on television and radio ads, you will read and hear words that I will say often today: "keeping America's promise."

What is America's promise? That our children will do better than we have done. A promise of opportunity. A promise of equality. A promise that you and I know by heart because we recite it at the very end of the Pledge of Allegiance; it is a promise of "liberty and justice for all."

For those of you who don't know me -- yet -- and by the time voting day comes around, I will have shaken the hands and looked into the eyes of thousands upon thousands of Rhode Islanders an introduction is definitely in order.

I was born in New York in 1970, the son of Dominican immigrants whose education did not extend beyond the eighth grade. I came to Rhode Island as an infant. My parents divorced when I was seven years old, and I was raised by my working mother.
My education began exactly when it should I am a proud Head Start graduate, and as this campaign progresses, you will hear me talk at length, and from the heart, about the importance of early childhood education.

From there I began my journey through the Providence public schools, from Lexington Avenue School, to Mary E. Fogarty, to Roger Williams Middle School, to Nathanael Greene Middle School, to Classical High School.

Maybe I was lucky. Maybe it was as simple as being in the right place at the right time, but my teachers showed that they understood that education is about more than the "Three 'R's'". They cared about me. They nurtured my dreams. And I could not be standing before you today if they hadn't found the time to interact with me on a one-to-one basis. They never treated me as just another in a long list of names on attendance cards, but rather as a human being. One with dreams.

After graduation from Classical, I went to Harvard, where I graduated in 1992. During those years, I realized the importance of working with children and encouraging them to dream, as Mrs. Donaldson had encouraged me to dream. I worked on after-school and summer programs in Boston neighborhoods. I had many memorable experiences, but none more so than the first time I went with a group of Harvard students to Roxbury to tutor children in the Mission Hill After-School Program. It was my first day there, and I heard some of the children speaking Spanish. I joined the conversation, and the children stared at me and asked, "You aren't with the Harvard people, are you?" I told them that I was, and they looked at me with shock in their eyes. Over the next three years I became a very popular after-school and summer counselor. As I look back on that time now, I realize that I was probably something many of those kids had not seen before.

What I came away with that day was the powerful sense of responsibility that is felt by a role model. I accept that responsibility. It will inform every second of my life in public service.

Today I stand before you as a lawyer and a candidate for Congress, but none of this -- none of the degrees, none of the public service, none of the professional success ...none of it would have been possible without education.

An education that was life-sustaining and life-altering.
An education that encouraged me to dream.
An education that could not have come about without loans and grants from the federal government, without access to the public programs and facilities in which education is delivered, without teachers who gave of themselves in direct, personal ways that were truly above and beyond the call of duty.

And so you will understand why, as I begin to talk to the citizens of Rhode Island about my positions on the issues of our time, I begin with education.

I am committed to providing full and equal access to quality public education to every child in our state -- *because if even one child is being denied such access and quality, then we are betraying the trust of all of our children.*

I am committed to rebuilding our schools -- *because within the borders of Rhode Island, Providence, Johnston, Coventry and many other cities and towns are in dire need of new schools and reinvigorated educational resources.*

I am committed to establishing and maintaining a classroom student-to-teacher ratio that permits maximum opportunity for the teacher to teach and the student to learn -- *because every child is a unique miracle, and deserves as much individual attention as a teacher can possibly deliver.*

I am committed to providing and maintaining computer and other high-tech equipment in all of our schools -- *because our students will compete for jobs -- in a world that will offer little compassion to those ill-prepared to meet its challenges.*

Today's Republican-controlled Congress has turned a blind eye -- that is to say *an eye without vision* -- to the education and safety of our children.

We *can* do better!
As a member of the Democratic majority in the 107th Congress, I will commit myself to improving our education system to move us into the 21st Century and beyond. I will help create, develop and support legislation that rebuilds and rethinks where and how our children learn.

We *can* do better!
At the core of this campaign to keep the American promise of opportunity, equality and security is the issue of education. How important to this republic is free and equal access to quality public education? Eleanor Roosevelt, I think, said it best:
"*A democratic form of government, a democratic way of life, presupposes free public education over a long period; it presupposes also an education for personal responsibility that too often is neglected.*"

I am living proof that education makes all the difference between poverty and opportunity, between a government for the privileged, and a government of the people -- *ALL* the people.

So my vision encompasses a view of a new Rhode Island in which, strengthened by education, our children once again can dare to see, dare to dream, dare to become what they've never seen before. Just as I dare today to announce my candidacy for the United States Congress.

Throughout my campaign you're certain to hear about the issue of experience. The questions will come from the press and, I assure you, from my opponents. What kind of experience would Angel Taveras bring to the United States Congress? Does Angel Taveras have the experience he needs to survive in the political maelstrom of Washington?

These questions are valid. And I'm ready, willing and able to respond. But my answers won't be glib or superficial. I don't think in soundbytes. I'm *not* about politics as usual.

Allow me to address the issue of experience head-on.

Understand that the word has a broad definition. A definition that I want to expand for you now.

I know what it's like to punch a time clock. I know what it's like to live in public housing. I know what it's like to depend on public transportation. I know what it's like to live from paycheck to paycheck. I know what it's like to live with the threat of the loss of health insurance just a paycheck away.

This kind of experience counts in today's world. It is as relevant to my ability to serve as a member of the United States House of Representatives as is my education, my public service, my integrity, my ability to deal with complex social and political issues.

It is as relevant as my vision, my hope, my commitment to keep the promise of America.

It is the kind of experience that breeds compassion, that nurtures the instinct for public service, that strengthens the courage of convictions.

It is the kind of experience that cannot be measured in terms of time. Accept the fact that a *year* of experience like mine can be worth a *decade* of experience behind a desk or in an ivory tower.

As I've told you, I don't have to imagine the critically important role quality public education plays in the lives of all our children, especially those without great financial resources.

I also want working men and women, union members across the state, to know that I know what it is like to be a member of a unionized workforce -- and also know, all too well, the alternative.

I don't have to imagine working for a living. During high school I worked at the Star Market in Olneyville. I was a member of Local 328 of the United Food and Commercial Workers International Union. Conditions were pretty good, and I thought that better-than-minimum wages, regular pay increases and respectful treatment from management were the norm, available to all Americans.

Then, the summer before college, while I was living in Florida, I applied for a job at a supermarket in North Miami Beach. Before I was hired, the manager said to me in a very matter-of-fact way, words I'll never forget. "We don't talk to unions down here," he said. "And if you talk to unions, we don't want you around."

It was a tough summer. I don't have to imagine what it's like to have to go home at lunch after unloading tractor trailers all morning in tropical heat, because sweat had drenched my pants and shirt. I worked that summer because like many working men and women I needed the money to survive, but what an experience.

As your congressman, I will commit the full power of my intellect and the full breadth of my passions to organized labor, *because I've been there*!

I know, from *experience*, that a unionized America means a more prosperous America -- for everyone.

I know, from *experience*, that a unionized America ensures fairness, dignity and respect in the workplace.

Listen very carefully whenever a politician talks about experience. Experience is not meaningfully measured in terms of political offices held, but in terms of life experience.

Our vision must be as deeply perceptive of the past as it is keenly focused on the future.

I can't stand before you today and talk about who I am without thinking of my grandparents. My grandmother, who walked me to Lexington Avenue school and carried me anytime I saw a dog. She had no choice because I would cling to her leg and would not let go. Or my other grandmother who spoiled me and still does with her unconditional love, and who cried with me at my law school graduation.

And my grandfather who used to give me haircuts even though I didn't sit still. You don't want to see some of those pictures. I also think of my oldest grandfather, who, throughout my school years, never left my side without first making sure that I had cash in my pocket to go with the hope in my heart. I think of his serenity when he would say, "Angel, I know what you are trying to do and may not get there with you, but I want to help you get there."

He got here with me and you will always be with me, *abuelo*. All my grandparents did. I am profoundly grateful. Their strength is my strength. Their legacy is my future. So to them, and to all of our parents and grandparents who are with us in the flesh today, and to those who are here in spirit, I say that I will dedicate my political life to fulfilling our obligations to you all.

I am committed to strengthening and defending Social Security and Medicare with the same fervor, with the same sense of duty, that you brought to the building of America and the defense of America.

I am committed to making sure that never again will a single elderly American have to choose between being healthy and putting food on the table.

We *can* do better!

Let's pause to consider our country's history. Let's look beyond our borders and back on a time, not so long ago, when the greatest task facing Americans was the life-and-death struggle to defend our country. Focus, with me, on those who labored not only in factories and farms, but also on fields of battle --fields of honor.

I speak of our veterans, the over 106,000 veterans of the armed forces who live with us in Rhode Island, their millions of brothers and sisters across the country and around the world, the men and women referred to by Tom Brokaw as "the greatest generation," who won World War II and fought the Korean War, whose sons and daughters fought in Vietnam and Desert Storm.

Through the grace of God, and because of all they accomplished, we may never have to face what they faced. So I urge you to ask them to speak of things they probably would rather leave buried in the past. Together, with love and in peace, do what Robert Kennedy did so often:

" ... *think of the young men we have sent [to war]: not just the killed, but those who have to kill; not just the maimed, but also those who must look upon the results of what they do.*"

Ask an older relative or friend who was sent to war to speak of what it was like to don a uniform, bear arms, and awake every day with the certain knowledge that, before the day was through, he or she may be called upon to take a life, or even to make the ultimate sacrifice.

What you hear will leave you with one certainty. We live in a safer world in great measure because of the Americans who fought for and died for our country, against foes implacable and merciless.

And when those who survived the carnage returned victorious, it was with the realization that their work was incomplete.

And so they built for us our interstate highways and our cities, our schools and our factories. They plowed our fields and fished our waters, but in its fullness, what they built for us is beyond anyone's ability to measure.

Yet it can be *felt*, deep within us, as memories of warm family dinners on cold winter nights, of proud answers to the questions, "What did you do in the war?" and "What do you do at work?".

It can be as immense as a skyscraper, as limitless as millions of miles of highways, as compact as a folded triangle of white stars on blue cloth taken from the hands of a guard of honor.
It is a vision of America that we share.

And something more.

It is a promise of America that has been kept *to* us, and in turn must be kept *by* us.

May our vision never be so clouded by self-satisfaction that we lose sight of our veterans and how they kept the promise of America.

As your congressman, I will support and defend the rights of our veterans to health care that is delivered not with reluctance but with excellence, to social services that are provided not with resentment but with care and respect, to housing that is made available not with resignation but with eagerness and dignity and pride.

On the next Veterans Day, I want you all to remember that at your age, not too long ago, men and women were preparing to go to war for this country, to go to foreign lands and give their lives for this country. When you study the Vietnam War, remember that the average age of an American soldier in Vietnam was 19. Remember that number when you visit the thousands of names inscribed on the Vietnam Memorial.
We must not forget! We *can* do better!

Over the last several months, I've heard a persistent question:
"Why, Angel? Why are you doing this?"

Because there is no greater goal for any human being than to leave this world a better place than it was when he or she entered it.
How do we accomplish this task?

Each in our own way. But all of us begin with the word that is the motto of the state of Rhode Island. We begin with *hope*. Hope for a better day, for a better future, for the promise of America to be kept.
As I travel throughout the district, I am experiencing first-hand what I have felt in my soul for so long. When I sit down with a single mother in Warwick, or a schoolteacher in Coventry, when I am invited into their homes and their hearts, I am brought face-to-face not with the things that separate us, but with those factors that unite us.

Regardless of our neighborhoods, or the foods we place on our tables, or the music we play or the prayers we recite, we share values and dreams, burdens and fears.

We stand -- united -- on the shoulders of those who built and saved America, ordinary people with extraordinary dreams, common people with uncommon dignity, simple people with limitless hope.
People who have left this world a better place than when they entered it.

So we try to meet their standard. We listen. We see. We hear. We learn as much as we can about every aspect of life.

We seek the counsel of others, to be sure. But in the final analysis, we must never -- *NEVER* -- permit anyone else to set our personal goals for us. Because inevitably they will set them too low.

Again, I speak from experience. For there are those who have said to me, "Angel, you're aiming too high. Why start with Congress? Why not begin in a more traditional, safer way?

My answer? It's simple, really. From that day in the third grade, when I told Mrs. Donaldson that I wanted to be a lawyer, I trusted and followed my instincts. I set my own goals. I achieved those goals!

I am well and fully prepared -- intellectually, emotionally, and in the sum of my life experience to date -- to do the business of the people as your congressman.

I know that many of you might feel that there is nothing that you can do to change things. "Oh, I am only one person, I can't make a difference." Once again, I look back at Bobby Kennedy and the words he spoke in South Africa in 1966.

"Let no one be discouraged by the belief there is nothing one man or one woman can do against the enormous array of the world's ills—against misery and ignorance, injustice and violence. . . . Few will have the greatness to bend history itself; but each of us can work to change a small portion of events, and in the total of all those acts will be written the history of this generation.

It is from numberless diverse acts of courage and belief that human history is shaped. Each time a man stands up for an ideal, or acts to improve the lots of others, or strikes out against injustice, he sends a tiny ripple of hope, and crossing each other from a million different centers of energy and daring those ripples build a current which can sweep down the mightiest walls of oppression and resistance."

The time has come to act.
I challenge each and every one of us to help build a current that sweeps away our old outdated schools and replaces them with new modern facilities that take us into the 21st century and beyond.

I challenge each and every one of us to help build a current that sweeps away the opponents of affordable, universal health care …

… that sweeps away those forces that would not preserve and strengthen Social Security and Medicare …

… that sweeps away the demagoguery that would deny to women the right to choose …

… that sweeps away the heartless and the selfish who would deny to American workers the right to organize.
The time has come to turn dreams into realities. The time has come to define ourselves as either *givers or takers*, as *dreamers or sleepers.*

The time has come. Our time has come to acknowledge our roles in the promise of America … to care and to serve … *to dare to dream and become something we have never seen.*

On behalf of my generation, I accept the obligation to keep America's promise.

We *can* do better! We *can* do better! We *can* do better!

Prodigal Son

Angel Taveras, an appealing candidate in his own right, reflects growing political activity by Hispanics in Rhode Island

By Ian Donnis
The Providence Phoenix

Providence City Councilman Luis Aponte was recently having coffee in a Broad Street restaurant when he overheard diners debating Angel Taveras' uphill campaign for Congress. One side argued that Taveras, a 29-year-old lawyer making his first bid for public office, should have started instead by running for the General Assembly. Others insisted that the Harvard-educated candidate, who became an associate at a downtown firm after growing up poor in South Providence, is the right person to go to Washington. But regardless of which view is correct, says Aponte, "Just the fact that those discussions are happening in a restaurant on Broad Street is pretty telling."

Aponte should know. After getting elected during his second campaign, becoming the first Hispanic city councilor in Providence, he's well aware of the difficulty of getting people enthused about politics. And even though the consequences of a lack of clout are most evident around Broad Street, South Providence and other impoverished neighborhoods, it's that much harder to makes voters out of people, like recent immigrants and poor residents, whose lives are consumed by working and paying the bills.

Coming from this background, Taveras convincingly offers himself as a personification of the American dream. It's a personal story with widespread appeal and one with particular resonance for the state's burgeoning Hispanic community. Although some 65,000 Rhode Islanders, or almost 7 percent of the state's population (and many observers believe the actual number is higher) trace their heritage to Latin America, up from 45,000 in 1990, Hispanics remain seriously underrepresented in state and local politics. Of 150 state legislators, only one, state Representative Anastasia Williams (D-Providence), is a Latino. And, as noted by Aponte -- who with the Panamanian-born Williams is the most visible Hispanic elected official in the state -- there's a direct link between political representation and the way in which public resources are distributed.

Like Kate Coyne-McCoy and Kevin McAllister, Taveras faces a tough fight in challenging Secretary of State James Langevin for the Democratic nomination to succeed US Representative Robert Weygand in the 2nd Congressional District. As an affluent two-term incumbent from Warwick, Langevin enjoys a strong advantage in name recognition and he's happy to pour his own wealth into his campaign. Langevin, a pro-life social conservative, will also benefit from Taveras and Coyne-McCoy's overlapping appeal to liberals.

Still, the candidacy of someone as credible as Taveras represents an important step not just for his own prospective political career, but the civic development of Rhode Island's Hispanic community.

"I think it shows that we are coming of age politically," says Victor Capellan, executive director of the Center for Hispanic Policy and Advocacy (CHISPA) in Providence, who has twice run unsuccessfully for state representative. Besides reflecting the presence of other Hispanics who can capably represent a variety of constituents, "it empowers the community to come out and vote for one of their own," Capellan says. "You will see the number of Latino voters go up because of this race. People are enthused to see a young man with the education that Angel has, the good intentions that Angel has, and a plan. People are excited and they're hopeful."

NOT FAR from Superior Court and the attorney general's office, the Providence Washington Building on South Main Street is part of the landscape of downtown power. After graduating from Georgetown Law School in 1996, Taveras joined this rarefied world when he became a litigator at Brown, Rudnick, Freed and Gesmer. "Sometimes, I still can't believe I'm here," says Taveras, whose respected alma mater, Classical High School, and the hardscrabble streets that surround it, are visible from law firm's eleventh-floor office. "It's a short distance in terms of miles, but it's a long ways away. It's not something I envisioned when I was growing up."

As a third-grader at the Mary E. Fogarty School in South Providence, Taveras was precocious enough, however, to declare that he wanted to be a lawyer when he grew up. The statement from the boy, one of three children of Dominican immigrants who came to Rhode Island to New York, made such an impression on Taveras' teacher that she brought him to share it with other teachers. It didn't cross his mind until years later, he says, that he had never seen a Latino lawyer as a child.

Nor has Taveras seen a congressman of Dominican heritage -- because there hasn't been one. When he sounded out his colleague George Caruolo, a partner at Brown, Rudnick, Freed and Gesmer, the former House majority leader "really expressed how difficult it is to do what I'm trying to do," Taveras says. But despite the long odds of getting elected, the first-time candidate wasn't dissuaded from running for Congress.

Unveiling his campaign before an auditorium of Classical students in November, Taveras mined his own experience in saying, "I'm here to say that no one has the right or the ability to tell you how far you can go -- only you can choose your destination, and reaching it will be a function of your willpower. I'm here to assure you that the future -- your own and that of our society -- is not pre-determined by anyone or any force, but is waiting for you to shape it with compassion and intelligence and vision."

An early standout in school, Taveras was raised by his working mother after his parents divorced when he was 7, and he credits much of his success to the interest of relatives and teachers. After his freshman year at Classical, for example, he was encouraged by his guidance counselor, Mrs. Smith, to apply for a summer math and science enrichment program for minority students at Philips Andover Academy. "I didn't want to go to school during the summer," Taveras recalls. "I finally applied because I wanted to get her off my back." Looking back, he cites his three successive years of participation in the program as a big factor in his subsequent education at Harvard and Georgetown Law.

Clean-cut, amiable and articulate, Taveras lives in the Silver Lake section of Providence with his girlfriend, Agripina Garcia, and her two children. He says he's running to expand for others the kind of opportunities that he's had. Although the motifs of his campaign -- the motto of "Keeping America's promise," the virtual stars and stripes that flutters on his Web site -- would be trite for most candidates, they're more sincere coming from Taveras, who has been active in public service and could continue drawing a six-figure salary without taking on a long-shot campaign.

As a first-time candidate, Taveras contends he's qualified to serve in Congress because of his real-life experience in punching a time clock, living from paycheck to paycheck and experiencing anti-union sentiment during a summer job at a Florida supermarket. "You're going to hear a lot of candidates say, `I can imagine what it's like to be poor.' I can tell you what it's like," he says.

Although a little vague on some issues, Taveras cuts a progressive profile. He's pro-choice and describes himself as a strong supporter of gay rights, a greater commitment to early childhood education and steps to help the poor and working class, such as expanding the earned-income tax credit. Describing campaign finance reform as necessary, he doesn't have a specific plan in mind. Taveras, who has not signed on as a supporter of the Gore campaign, says he would not have supported the welfare reform deal that was embraced by President Clinton. He favors a robust foreign policy in which

US influence is brought to bear in foreign crises, even if US interests aren't threatened.

State Senator David Igliozzi (D-Providence), who introduced Taveras during his campaign announcement at Classical High and has contributed to his campaign, says, "there's no doubt that he has the intellect for any job. He also has the desire and the character." The legislator calls Taveras a perfect role model, and adds, "He's going to succeed ultimately in whatever he does." But the difficulty faced by Taveras can be seen in how Igliozzi, like the vast bulk of Rhode Island's Democratic establishment, is supporting Jim Langevin, who won the state party's endorsement in an overwhelming vote in April.

LUIS APONTE was motivated to run for the city council because of his frustration with the prevalence of subpar conditions, like crumbling roads and sidewalks, in the poorer parts of Providence near his home in Washington Park. "I didn't think there was an equitable distribution of resources city-wide, and I thought I could do something about that," he says. And after losing the Ward 10 Democratic primary by six votes in 1994, Aponte got busy. "I think I would have been less angry if I lost by 100 votes," he says. After walking the ward to meet residents once during the 1994 campaign, Aponte repeated the ward-wide door-knocking almost three times when the council seat came up for grabs in 1998.

In doing so, he followed in the time-honored tradition of grassroots democracy. As put by Aponte, who was born in Puerto Rico and grew up in Brooklyn, New York, and Central Falls, "The theory of representative democracy is that everyone has to participate in order for it to work."

Although the council job requires more time and encompasses more responsibility than he imagined, Aponte welcomes his multi-faceted role as a neighborhood leader, city official and spokesman for Hispanics in Rhode Island. While the pace of making change can be frustrating, "you can see the fruits of your labor," says the 36-year-old councilman, who works as an investigator for the Rhode Island Commission on Human Rights. And although something like replacing a missing stop sign may not seem like a big thing, he says, it offers an enhanced sense of security -- and a sign of responsive government -- for the parents of a small child who live on a heavily trafficked city street.

Aponte's persistence in pursuing election reflects how, at a time when the percentage of Americans who vote has plummeted, more Hispanic candidates are running in Rhode Island, organizing politically and wearing out shoe leather while courting votes. The trend emerged in the early '90s and continued as the Latino community -- most of whose members trace their heritage to Puerto Rico, the Dominican Republic, Colombia and Guatemala --- has grown and established stronger roots in the Ocean State.

A significant step came with the formation in 1998 of the Rhode Island Latino Political Action Committee -- a counterpoint to the historic division by nationality in the Hispanic community, which is often seen by outsiders as a monolith -- and the PAC's coming-out party at Roger Williams Park was attended by a spectrum of candidates and elected officials.

"People are recognizing we can be a key player," says CHISPA's Capellan, a 29-year-old native of the Dominican Republic, who plans to run for public office again in the future. "I'm very hopeful that we can build some strong alliances."

Maureen F. Moakley, a political science professor at the University of Rhode Island, cites Taveras' campaign for Congress as "a natural expression of the mobilization of the Hispanic community. They're well-represented and they're on the move. The next big step in the process is elective office. Over the next few elections, one would expect to see a couple of Hispanic representatives, at least, in the legislature." At the same time, Moakley says, Taveras is "a long-shot, and I think he knows that. I think he's out for next time."

Meanwhile, troubling social conditions, as evidenced by the recent Rhode Island Kids Count finding that 43 percent of Latino children in the state are living below the poverty line, remain an obstacle to increased political activity. And the hurdles facing Hispanic candidates can be seen in how voters in Central Falls, where close to 50 percent of the city's residents are thought to be Latino, have never elected a Hispanic city councilor. "We don't have the idea that your vote counts," says Ricardo Patino, a Colombian native who was defeated, 344-225, in running for a Ward 3 council seat last year.

Patino, a construction specialist for Rhode Island Housing, links the absence of Hispanic elected officials with the lack of any Hispanic police officers or firefighters in Central Falls (a cadet who is a native of Colombia has started police academy training). But Mayor Lee Matthews says Hispanics residents are reluctant to apply for police and fire department jobs, despite outreach and advertising in Spanish-language media. "I just think it takes a little bit of time for each ethnic group" to get assimilated, says Matthews, a view echoed by some Hispanic political observers.

Along Elmwood Avenue in Providence, notes Taveras, it's more common to see bumper stickers for candidates in the Dominican Republic than in Rhode

Island. "We've got to change the mindset," he says. "I think what we've got to do is convince people that what you do here makes a very big difference."

TAVERAS DISMISSES questions about future campaigns, saying he's focused on this one. The candidate relates well to people and he doesn't lack for confidence. "I believe if I met every person in this district, I would win this election in a landslide," Taveras says. "Rhode Island is a small enough state, so you can get around the district." True enough, but Taveras faces a tight window of opportunity in which to introduce himself, raise money and share his message with voters.

Langevin, probably best known for championing the cause of open government in Rhode Island, remains the front-runner to succeed Weygand, who, with Richard Licht and Lincoln Chafee, is running for US Senate. Among other factors, Langevin benefits from his status as a resident of Warwick, the second-largest city in the district, which stretches from Providence, south of Route 44, to Westerly? And although legislative leaders were angered when Langevin issued a report that showed how the General Assembly was violating the Open Meeting Law, the state Democratic Party, which is largely controlled by the legislative leadership, has since embraced him.

Kate Coyne-McCoy, executive director of the state chapter of the National Association of Social Workers, has proven herself an adept fund-raiser in challenging Langevin. She raised $394,000, about $30,000 more than Langevin through the March 31 federal reporting period, although Langevin swelled his war chest by adding $200,000 of his own money, according to the Center for Responsive Politics in Washington, D.C. Langevin was paralyzed below the waist when he was accidentally shot by a Warwick police officer in 1980, and the resulting lawsuit is thought to be the source of the fortune that has fueled his success as a candidate.

In contrast, Taveras, who recently hired Jane Asselta, a former fund-raiser for Myrth York, raised $65,000 through the March 31 period, although he hopes to bring in a total closer to $500,000 to run his campaign. Lawyer Kevin McAllister, president of the Cranston City Council, is running a deliberate low-cost campaign and came up with almost $27,000 during the same period.

Labor support was vital for Weygand in 1996 when a number of the state's most powerful Democrats supported his unsuccessful rival, former Providence Mayor Joseph Paolino. The Rhode Island AFL-CIO, the state's largest labor group, didn't endorse a candidate this time around since none of the four Democrats were able to muster support from two-thirds of 94 board members. A cluster of smaller unions have rallied behind Coyne-McCoy, whose father worked as a union plumber.

Within the next decade, Hispanics are due to supplant blacks as the nation's largest minority group. And regardless of what happens in the 2nd Congressional District race, the influence of Hispanics in Rhode Island politics will continue to grow in the years to come. With that in mind, Angel Taveras' Congressional campaign may well be remembered as a turning point.

Ian Donnis can be reached at idonnis@phx.com.

2002 Redistricting and Downsizing

Tomás Alberto Ávila
Policy Analyst
Center for Hispanic Policy & Advocacy (CHisPA)
November, 1999

Introduction

The Latino community is presently caught in the middle of deciding whether to invest it's efforts and resources in the vigilance of a fair and accurate reapportionment and the battle of repealing the downsizing legislature approved by the voters and ratify by the House in 1994.

As part of my research, I've read through many different documents provided by the different organizations and other publications to get a sense of what benefits each proposed agenda will bring to the Latino community. What continues is my report, based on my research and analysis of available information

As the 20th century draws to and end, and we prepare to welcome a new millennium and look forward to the 2000 census, battle lines are already forming on how the RI political map will be redrawn in 2002. This battle is brewing in the General Assembly over how to conduct legislative reapportionment the politically explosive issue of drawing a new political map to reflect Rhode Island's population changes over the decade of the 90's as well as in community organizations.

Adding ammunition to this battle is the upcoming down sizing of the Legislature from 150-member body to 113 approved by the voter in 1994 by a margin of 51.8%. This schedule downsizing is fuelling a lot of concern, from a variety quarters, over the impending size reduction for the Rhode Island General Assembly. This concept was flawed from the start, and now people are starting to realize that it would make the legislature less responsive to the people of Rhode Island.

Redistricting

Every ten years, following the census, the nation's political map undergoes an upheaval as political jurisdictions at the local; state and federal levels change district lines to comply with the constitutional requirement for equal representation.

At the federal level, the process of reapportionment is intended to ensure that each state has the number of U.S. Representatives proportionate to its population. The subsequent process of redistricting is intended to ensure that each congressional district in a state has exactly the same population as all other districts in that state. Similarly, state legislative districts are redrawn every ten years to reflect population changes, as are local district lines.

Next year, after the 2000 census, the reapportionment of the House of Representatives will be determined by a complicated mathematical formula (called the "method of equal proportions"), set by a 1941 federal law, that allocates the proper number of congressional seats to each state. Then state legislators who will be redistricting their own seats at the state level will undertake the process of redistricting the actual drawing of congressional district boundaries .

Because the redistricting process affects the political life and death of politicians, it has always been, and remains, an intensely political and partisan struggle. Incumbents of both political parties strive to have district lines drawn so that their reelection prospects are enhanced as much as possible. Where one party in a state is dominant and controls the drawing the lines, it inevitably strives to draw lines that favor its candidates.

The process of redistricting is extremely powerful. By packing or splitting concentrations of voters, those who draw district lines can often effectively eliminate competitive elections in a given district for a decade, by ensuring for all practical purposes that the candidates of one party or the other will prevail in that district, essentially without regard to who those candidates are.

The extremely partisan nature of the redistricting process, and the deeply-rooted reluctance of legislators to open up the process to reform, present formidable challenges to those interested in establishing a more fair and open process for redistricting, as well as more competitive elections.

According to information analyzed, the city of Providence has lost 2 House seats in the General Assembly during the 1980 and 1990 decennial census due to population lost to migration to suburbia. Census officials have announced that RI's population continues to decline since the 1990 census, reaching dip of 1.6 from the 1,003,464 in the previous census. At stake will be an uncertain but reapportionment of the General Assembly in 20002, causing more lost seats for the city of Providence. If the census officials predictions hold true in the decennial census result, it can cause a domino shift of House districts in the city of Providence similar to the one of 1992, when 2 seats were lost causing the following results.

Democratic Representative T. Elaine Bucci of Providence was placed in the same district with Representative Thomas Rossi, D-Providence

Edward W. Dodd of Warwick was placed in the same district with Representative George Zainyeh

Providence Representative Peter N. Waslyk and Alfred W. Cardente were placed in the same district.

East Providence Representative William H. Greene was placed in the same district with Representative Thomas E. Hodge of Pawtucket which was a newly created district.

Cumberland Representative Donald Large and Francis A. Gaschen were paired in a new district.

East providence Senators James P. McStay and James F. Correia were placed in a new district and faced each other in the primaries.

Senators John A, Sabatini of Pawtucket and William V. Irons of East Providence were place in a new district that had 70% of its population in Pawtucket wards 2 & 3 and the other 30% in Rumford East providence.

The commission plan also created 3 new House Districts in western and southern parts of Rhode Island. Meanwhile Providence Pawtucket and Warwick each lost a seat to accommodate the population changes.

Shifting a district from East Providence to western Rhode Island created one new Senate district.

During the 92 reapportionment, the commission proposed a shift of two South Providence districts into parts of Cranston that were challenged by the minority community. The proposal was opposed by the incumbent legislators Senator Robert Kells, D, District 10 and Rep. Jeremiah P' Murphy, D, District 17 who argue that the proposed shift would hurt minority voting interests and didn't think there was a need to dilute the voting strength of the minority groups they represent.

According to official electorate reports, district 10 contain the highest minority concentration in the state as follow: 35% Hispanic, 25% African American and 11% Asian. The legislatures were backed by the Rhode Island Minority Redistricting Committee strongly opposing the diluting of the minority voting strength in existing minority districts.

The downsizing of the Legislature

A Blue Ribbon Commission on the General Assembly appointed in September 1992 by then Speaker of the House, Representative Joseph DeAngelis, and then Senate Majority Leader, Senator John J. Bevilacqua, recommended the downsizing of the Legislature. The commission was charged with developing a broad blue print for the General Assembly in the 21st Century. The commission's efforts are part of a process, which has resulted in four-year terms for the State's general officers, and the adoption of comprehensive campaign finance reform and ethic reforms legislation.

The Commission began its work by laying out its vision of the General Assembly in the 21st Century.

> In the 21st Century, the General Assembly plays an active, creative and independent leadership role in state government it is accessible to qualified candidates and provides appropriate compensation and staff support for its members. Its structure and procedures help legislators speak and act for their constituents and it successfully reflects and embodies the kind of government the people of Rhode Island want for their State.

Based on this Vision Statement, the Commission adopted a Work Plan, which focused on the following questions:

➤ Does Rhode Island need a more effective legislature? Can the General Assembly be more effective 'and remain a citizens"' legislature?

➤ What changes, if any, should be made in the size of the General Assembly? Should the terms for legislators be longer? Should there be term limits?

➤ What resources does an individual legislator need to be effective?

➤ How should legislators be compensated?

➤ How can the lawmaking 'and oversight process be strengthened?
➤ Is information about the activities of the General Assembly readily available to the public?

As part of its Work Plan, the Commission held five televised public hearings and distributed a questionnaire to members and former members of the General Assembly. Briefing papers were developed by Commission staff on certain key issues. After extensive meetings, all of which were posted and open to the public, the initial findings and recommendations of the Commission were incorporated in a draft report. This draft report was released for public comment on August 1, 1993. A public hearing on the draft was held in October. Subsequent to that hearing the Commission met to formulate its final recommendations. This report reflects those recommendations. Taken together they constitute the Commission's blueprint for the General Assembly in the 21st Century[2].

A can be seen from the redistricting experience, the Latino and minority communities have a lot at stake when it comes times for redistricting. In my opinion this experience show us that if the legislature is down size as planned in 2002, the minority communities voting power risk being diluted and setting back their ability to elect their own legislators.

Providence minority population has exploded since 1980, up from 18% of the city to nearly 40%, but even with this overwhelming growth its Senate delegation remains disproportionately white. The current redistricting maps of Providence has three minority districts, with majorities of Latino, Black, and Asians. Except for Senator Charles Walton the incumbents in the other two districts are white.

Conclusion

All the talk that fewer districts will bring increased competition to legislative seats fails to take into account that a challenger will have an extremely more difficult time prevailing against an incumbent who represents a larger constituency. These new larger districts will make it much harder for a challenger to meet enough voters in a short period of time, while an incumbent has been interacting with these very voters throughout his/her term or terms of office. As most people in Rhode Island know, a challenger in our state who cannot meet enough voters in person before the election cannot expect to present much of a challenge.

A larger district means more voters to reach than before, and this translates into more money that a candidate will have to spend. This will result in a number of undesirables: the candidate pool may consist of wealthy individuals who can fund their own campaigns; candidates may have to seek more and more money from special interests; people in the middle and working classes will simply be unable to compete realistically. The days of running a grassroots campaign will be gone, and we will have an Assembly

---

[2] The General Assembly In RI, A Blue Print for the 21st Century

that will be less representative of and less responsive to the residents of our state.

That the Assembly size issue was presented to the voters in 1994 does not preclude the voters from having a chance to revisit this matter. The voters of the state of Rhode Island need to revisit the issue of Assembly downsizing.

Finally an emotionally charged debate in south Florida is offering a preview of what could become a flood of litigation over efforts to redraw congressional and other voting districts across the United States.

At issue is the extent to which officials may rely on racial criteria to draw new districts after the all-important 2000 Census. The issue has been the subject of several US Supreme Court decisions in the 1990s, but the legal standards remain murky. Thus the outcome here could have a direct impact on minority participation and representation in government - and eventually help shape the direction of democracy in America.

Depending on who wins the legal challenges, African-Americans and Hispanics across the country could find themselves losing voices in Congress and state legislatures. On the other side in this case are some white voters who feel disenfranchised because they live in neighborhoods included in strangely shaped districts designed to elect minority candidates. At the heart of the debate: Whether it is appropriate to use racial gerrymandering to compensate for generations of racial discrimination and segregation.

Based on all the information researched for this report, it's my conclusion that CHisPA should not involved itself in divisive decision making regarding a particular organization, but instead it should become the voice of the Latino community in the redistricting process and try to influence the voters of the state of Rhode Island need to revisit the issue of Assembly downsizing.

In 1994, the voters in the City of Cranston decided to reduce the membership of the school board, increasing the size of districts. Just four years later, the very same voters reversed their decision and restored the districts to their original size. No one in Cranston complained about revisiting this issue. Perhaps the voters in Cranston felt they were correcting a mistake.

As can be seen through this report, even without the inclusion of downsizing of the legislature, the minority communities face a monumentous challenge after the 2000 census and therefore The Latino community should start developing it's on agenda for the upcoming redistricting of 2002 that is base on the benefits for the Latino community, rather than preconceived agendas by other organizations based on their own interest.

This conclusion is based on the benefits and dangers presented in future negotiations in the reapportionment proceedings that will start in 20001 that will require the coalesce of minority communities with other organizations across the state and therefore the organization should not engaged itself in partisan redistricting and downsizing politics.

No ethnic group has a larger stake in the path our state legislature chooses between now and the year 2000 than Latinos. Latinos comprise more than 6 percent of this state, including almost 46 percent of the school age population. It is the youngest and fastest growing minority. Since 1990, Latinos represent the largest minority group in Rhode Island, and within 50 years 20 percent of the entire population will be Latino. As citizens with a substantial role and stake in the future of this state, we, Latinos of the state of Rhode Island should take the responsibility of our future in our own hands.

Energy Secretary to Visit Rhode Island

Press Release
December 13, 1999

Providence, RI – The public is invited to attend a breakfast gathering with U.S. Secretary of Energy Bill Richardson to discuss issues concerning the Latino community, Friday December 17th, 1999, 8:00 AM at Rhode Island Foundation, One Union Station Building, Providence.

This event marks RILPAC's continue efforts to empower the Latino community to become participants in the political process. RILPAC goal is to insured that elected officials, political leaders and candidates have a broad understanding of the concerns and priorities among Rhode Island Latinos. The event will get underway at 8:00 AM. Admission to the event is FREE. The Rhode Island Latino Political Action Committee is a nonpartisan organization formed to influence the political process in the state of Rhode Island in order to improve the quality of life of Latino and urban communities. For information call 274-5204

###

Campaign Taking Shape

Political Scene
The Providence Journal
2.28.2000

Providence lawyer Angel Taveras , one of four Democrats running for the congressional seat being vacated by Rep. Robert Weygand , has hired one of Atty. Gen. Sheldon Whitehouse 's former employees to manage his campaign in the 2nd District.

Andy Galli left a job as the program coordinator in Whitehouse's Consumer Protection Unit to run the Taveras effort. He is no newcomer to political campaigns; he volunteered on Whitehouse's successful 1998 bid for attorney general.

Galli, 37, a native of Cranston, graduated with a degree in modern history from St. Andrew's University in Scotland. He has worked as a teacher in Washington, D.C., Maryland and Puerto Rico. He also has been active in grassroots organizations and served as executive director of the Coalition for Consumer Justice. He is a member of the steering committee of Bill Bradley 's Rhode Island campaign organization.

Taveras has also hired the Chicago-based firm of Adelstein & Associates to handle political and media consulting. The firm has advised federal, state and local candidates across the country, he said. Taveras, incidentally, recently took a leave of absence from the law firm of Brown, Rudnick, Freed & Gesmer, where he was an associate. He said it was impossible to be a litigator and a congressional candidate at the same time.

``Now I'm devoting all my time " to the campaign, he said.

The other three Democrats in the race are Secretary of State James Langevin ; Kate Coyne-McCoy , the executive director of the state chapter of the National Association of Social Workers; and Cranston City Council President Kevin J. McAllister. The only Republican to announce his candidacy is John O. Matson , a South County carpenter who ran unsuccessfully for the seat in the last two elections.

6 Assembly Primary Races Heat Up

By Karen A. Davis
Journal Staff Writer
9.1.2000

PROVIDENCE -- A half-dozen candidates seeking to unseat incumbents in General Assembly primary races throughout the city say their main objective is clear: to give the voters in their districts a choice.

But incumbents are betting that voters will send them back to the State House to finish the job they started. Challengers have spent recent weeks campaigning door-to-door and holding coffee hours, determined to convince residents that a vote for them is a departure from the political establishment, with more focus on communities.

And incumbents have been just as busy canvassing neighborhoods and posting placards in yards and businesses, sending the message that a vote for them is a vote for continued improvements.

That's the way local races are shaping up, with less than two weeks until the Sept. 12 primary election. One of the fiercest battles is taking place in Senate District 9, where incumbent Robert T. Kells is seeking his sixth term, despite a tough challenge by community activist Juan M. Pichardo.

Here is a look at the primary races in Providence:

Senate District 9

Kells, 54, of 4 Falconer St., startled his colleagues in June by announcing on the Senate floor that he would not seek reelection. Kells later said that he was deeply hurt by a Senate colleague, who had endorsed Pichardo, who has been active in both the Rhode Island Young Democrats and the Hispanic community.

Numerous calls from constituents, however, persuaded Kells to change his mind in late June. After working 10 years on issues such as health care, economic development and the restoration of food stamps benefits to legal immigrants, Kells said his main focus continues to be "improving the quality of life of my constituents" in the Reservoir Triangle, Elmwood and West End neighborhoods.

"Basic human issues are of equal or greater concern to my constituents than some legislative matters that may generate lots of headlines," said Kells, a Providence police captain, who retired as a major from the Rhode Island

176

Army National Guard. "Taking care of those matters is my primary duty as the senator from this district."

Kells, Senate deputy majority leader, chairs the Finance Subcommitte on Public Safety and is a member of the Joint Committee on Veteran Affairs and the Health, Education and Welfare Committee. He said the issues he views as most important to his district are health care, medical coverage for seniors, improving the quality of schools and lowering the crime rate.

His challenger, Pichardo, 33, of 229 Atlantic Ave., said he is running to give voters a choice, given that Kells has run unopposed since 1994.

"Growing up in the neighborhood and being involved in different organizations and seeing that I could do greater good . . . has inspired me to run," said Pichardo, who works as a patient advocate at Rhode Island Hospital. "If I'm elected I would be an aggressive and accessible leader."

As he has campaigned in the neighborhoods over the last three months, Pichardo said, residents have told him the issues that most concern them are drug dealing, gun violence, the abundance of vacant lots, public safety and the relationship between community and law enforcement.

In addition, Pichardo said, the issues he views as most important are health care, education, economic development and the environment.

Pichardo said he has won endorsement from the Young Democrats and from such groups as the Rhode Island Latino Political Action Committee.

The winner of the primary will face Republican Sonya Zecchin O'Hara, 29 Laura St., in November's general election. Zecchin O'Hara's husband, Ian, is running as a Republican candidate for the House seat in District 18.

House District 19

The race between Democratic incumbent Aisha W. Abdullah-Odiase, 8 Quince St., and her challenger, Allene R. Maynard, 41 Moore St., is evident in the numerous placards placed throughout the district and along Broad Street.
Abdullah-Odiase, 45, who works in the city archives division, served a three-year term on the School Board before running unopposed for the House seat in 1998.

Abdullah-Odiase said she has been active in the community -- holding public meetings, bringing an early childhood reading program to local schools, supporting an increase in minimum wage that takes effect today, helping residents restore RIPTA bus service to Prairie Avenue, and encouraging the state to enforce federal law prohibiting schools from requiring children to take drugs to modify behavior. Yesterday, Abdullah-Odiase served as a panelist on children and drugs at a taping of the Montel Williams Show.

The most important issues facing District 19, Abdullah-Odiase said, are curbing a recent increase in gun violence by adopting new gun laws, improving education, bringing more jobs to the district and changing laws to allow prison parolees to vote after their debt to society has been paid.

Abdullah-Odiase, a member of the House Health, Education and Welfare Committee, said she believes her district needs more unity and should devote more resources to taking care of children and making sure that opportunities exist for all its residents.

Maynard, a long-time member of the state Democratic Committee, takes issue with the way Abdullah-Odiase came into office and says she is running to give the district a representative who has a long record of activism there.

The seat was for years held by Harold Metts, who pulled his name out of contention in 1998 and threw his support behind Abdullah-Odiase just before the primary election.

Maynard, who ran against Metts in 1986 and lost by 12 votes, said she believes residents of the South Side district deserve a representative with a long history of commitment and residency in the district.
Maynard was one of the plaintiffs who filed a lawsuit in 1986 against the City Council who tried to gerrymander the lines of the district, to allow would-be candidates who lived outside the district to run to represent it. A judge ruled in the plaintiffs' favor, causing the redrawn lines to be reversed and forcing a special election to be held two years later.

Maynard has a history of public service and governmental affiliation, including working in the Senate Majority Leader's office, the office of the General Treasurer and the Department of Employment Security.

From 1985 to 1986, she was a Rhode Island Constitutional Convention delegate and she was appointed to the Rhode Island Criminal Justice Commission. She is currently the only minority executive officer in the state Democratic Party.

The issues that Maynard believes are most important are economic development, affordable housing, health coverage for all and making the district "a better community."

The winner of the primary will face Independent Paul J. Degaitas, 32 Wesleyan Ave., in the general election.

House District 9

While primary races are merely the first in a two-part battle for some seats, other victors will be determined at the primary level.

Such is the case in House District 9, encompassing parts of the West End, Olneyville and West Broadway.

Democrat incumbent Anastasia P. Williams, 32 Hammond St., will take on challenger Barbara Thurman, 71 Bridgham St.

Williams, 43, who is seeking a fifth term, said she is running to "continue to represent the poor, underprivileged and underserved."

Williams, a native of Panama, said she believes jobs, education and safe, suitable and affordable housing are the most pressing issues facing her district. She also lists health care as an issue that must be addressed in the upcoming legislative session.

Williams said she has found that "individual constituents want your continued participation, one-to-one or in a group session" and "it's hard to be in more than one place at the same time."

However, Williams notes, just because a person is not always around does not mean they have stopped working in behalf of their community.

Williams, who sits on the subcommittee on Special Legislation, works as a monitoring specialist at the Providence Neighborhood Housing Corp. Thurman, who describes herself as "a healthy and energetic 69," said she is running because "I see and I feel more can be done in my community."

Thurman said she already serves as an ambassador of sorts for her community, helping residents in her Wiggins Village neighborhood with such problems as housing and immigration issues.

The issues that Thurman believes are most important to the district are education and whether young people are being prepared to obtain jobs that will allow them to raise families, affordable housing, the environment and pollution, health careand making medical expenses more manageable for residents on fixed incomes.

Thurman, who hails from Florida and spent years traveling in Latin America, is a mother of eight and a foster parent of 13 years.

Thurman, who several years ago joined with neighbors to run drug dealers off the corner of Bridgham and Cranston streets, said that, if she is elected, she would "be visible and available."

House District 20

Another seat that will be determined at the primary level is House District 20 . In that race, incumbent Democrat Joseph S. Almeida, 299 California Ave., will face Gonzalo Cuervo, 203 Calla St.

Almeida makes no bones about why he is running: "Because there's still a whole lot more work to be done."

Almeida, 42, a small-business owner and a retired Providence police officer, said he is focused on such issues as restoring the right-to-vote for ex-felons, working with the Narragansett Bay Commission to allow residents to pay off liens without losing their property and economic development in his South Side district. Lowering the crime rate is another issue that he believes crucial to his district's future.

A member of the House labor subcommittee, Almeida was active this past year in pushing for so-called "driving while black" legislation, which requires officers to document the race of the motorist and other specifics when making traffic stops.

Almeida said he believes he is a good representative for his district because he is "public service-oriented," he works hard and is a good negotiator in pushing for legislation that improves the lives of residents in his district.

Cuervo, 26, said he has canvassed the streets of his district, spreading the message that "real issues require real solutions" and has suggested that he could find those solutions.

"The problems that affect our urban neighborhoods have long been identified," Cuervo said. "To this date our leaders have talked the talk, nonetheless we have yet to reduce the incidence of gun violence on our streets . . . (or) improve an educational culture where minority youth find their aspirations quashed . . ."

Cuervo, who has operated several small businesses on the South Side, currently works as a marketing director for GFM Foodservice, operators of Mediterraneo Restaurant, and also works for AG Services, a Broad Street accounting firm.

He lists economic development and support for small businesses as other issues of importance in the district.

In order to better engage residents and make elected officials more accountable and accessible, Cuervo said he wants to establish a district committee of residents of all ages, with businessmen serving as advisors.

House District 18

The Democratic primary race for District 18 pits incumbent Marsha E. Carpenter, 98 Warrington St., against challenger Leon F. Tejada, 20 Miller Ave.

Carpenter, 53, was elected to the seat in 1994, after former Rep. Joseph Newsome decided not to seek reelection.
As a legislator, Carpenter has worked on school drop-out prevention, supported increased state aid to education and mandatory school breakfasts for all public school children and endorsed the phase out of the motor vehicle excise tax.

Carpenter, whose son was fatally shot several years ago, has also introduced proposals designed to stop gun violence and prevent youths from obtaining illegal weapons.

The district's other important issues are victim assistance, providing help to the families of murder victims, health care, childhood lead positioning, lowering taxes and increasing the minimum wage, Carpenter said.

Carpenter chairs the House and Senate Joint Accounts and Claims Committee and is a member of the House Judiciary Committee.

Her opponent, Tejada, 35, said he was inspired to run because he does not think the many problems of his district are being solved.

"We need something totally different," he said, saying he thinks more emphasis should be placed on prevention of a problem, as opposed to fighting a problem after it reaches a crisis point.

Tejada, a computer systems analyst who has run his own business for about a year, said he believes economic development and education are two of the most important issues facing the district.

Tejada said that, in working with several small businesses on the south side of Providence and filing tax documents for businesses and individuals, he sees the lack of resources and opportunities faced by community residents.

He supports appropriating more money for the local school system, improving poor housing conditions and providing job and educational opportunities to residents.

The winner of the primary will face Republican Ian O'Hara, 29 Laura St., in the November election.

House District 5

The Democratic primary contest on the city's East Side pits incumbent Gordon D. Fox, 146 Woodbine St., against Shannon M. Donahue, 230 Summit Ave.

Fox, a lawyer who has been a representative since 1992, said he considers it a privilege to represent the district in which he has lived all his life. He is running for reelection, he says, because "I believe I can make a difference" in the quality of life of his constituents.

Because he believes education is the key to opportunity, he has worked to make sure "all young people are afforded an education which will prepare them to succeed" by supporting the Mount Hope Learning Center and the Rhode Island Children's Crusade for Education.

Fox, 38, said his priorities include improving housing, education, health care and respect through civil rights and equality, as he believes they are the foundations upon which individuals are able to flourish.

"If I play a small role in improving such basic needs, I believe many of society's problems -- crime, breakup of families, business climate, etc. -- will ultimately take care of themselves," said Fox, a senior member of the House Finance Committee.

Donahue, 47, is a registered nurse who says her opponent's "politics are very different than mine."

Donahue said she would be a good representative of District 5 because "my issues and my beliefs revolve more around people than they do around finances."

Donahue, who is running as an openly lesbian candidate, has canvassed the neighborhoods with literature and coffee hours. During those sessions, Donahue said, residents expressed disapproval of standard political leadership that pays little attention to the needs and opinions of residents.

She said she believes the most important issues facing the district are health care, education and increased educational opportunities and safe streets. She suggests the creation of innovative programs to address recent violence, including opening safe havens for latchkey children.

On the issue of health care, Donahue said her profession and volunteer experience make her more knowledgeable about health care rights and the challenges facing many families. She said her knowledge could be valuable in drafting legislation designed to improve the health status of her constituents.

The winner will face Republican Charles L. Smith Jr., 33 Twelfth St., in the November election.

Board Rebuffs Election Challenges

Several campaign hopefuls in South Providence react with dismay.

By Marion Davis
Journal Staff Writer
9.19.2000

PROVIDENCE -- Candidates in three of five Democratic primaries held in South Providence last week told the state Board of Elections yesterday that the vote was marred by widespread fraud, poll workers' incompetence, and mayhem.

But one after another, the board rejected challenges to the primary results, saying that the alleged irregularities weren't significant enough to change the outcome.

The board's actions infuriated members of the South Providence political establishment, but even more, the Latinos whose aggressive efforts drew hundreds of new voters to the polls, making every primary a hot contest.

"It just seems to the casual observer that upholding the election law is not one of their priorities," said Gonzalo Cuervo, who lost to state Rep. Joseph S. Almeida by 26 votes in House District 20.

Cuervo's lawyer, Kevin McKenna, offered to prove to the board that 38 votes cast in that primary should be invalidated -- nearly three times as many as would be needed to change the outcome.

But after McKenna's opening statement, board Chairman Roger E. Begin said he believed Cuervo's petition should be denied without a full hearing, and his colleagues unanimously agreed.

Begin cited the state Supreme Court's ruling in Buonanno vs. DiStefano, a 1981 case, which said that to invalidate an election, the irregularities should be "sufficiently large . . . that the result would be changed by a shift of or invalidation of the questioned votes. . . ."

"This means that an election will not be overturned upon a mere mathematical possibility that the results could have been changed, when the probabilities all combine to repel any such conclusion." Begin said the 38-vote challenge didn't meet "that higher bar" of probability, not just mathematical possibility.

Cuervo said he would consider an appeal to the state Supreme Court, but he might not be able to afford the legal fees.

Cuervo's hearing capped an afternoon packed with complaints of alleged crimes, unethical behavior and carelessness by participants in nearly all the South Providence races, by poll workers, and by the city Board of Canvassers.

Before the Board of Elections started its hearings, it presided over recounts in a Warwick City Council race, in the Johnston mayoral and Town Council District 1 races, and in five House Democratic primaries Districts 18, 19, 20 and 83. None of the results changed.

Then the board heard and rejected challenges in the Johnston Town Council race and in House District 83, where incumbent state Rep. Maria J. Lopes lost to newcomer Brian Coogan.

Next came Juan M. Pichardo, who defeated Sen. Robert T. Kells at the polls in District 10, in South Providence, but lost by 94 votes after the mail ballots were counted.

Pichardo's lawyer, unsuccessful congressional candidate Angel Taveras, cited alleged irregularities that he said would invalidate at least 23 votes.

At Kilmartin Plaza, the master list used until 2:15 p.m. did not include voters whose names started with S or V, and at least two people were turned away, Taveras said. (Later, Laurence K. Flynn, executive secretary of the Board of Canvassers, said the master list was missing pages, but the other lists at the polls were correct, so no one should have been turned away.)

Taveras also alleged that poll workers had refused to allow anyone but a Kells volunteer to help Spanish-speaking voters with the ballots and instructions.

Fifteen voters registered as Republicans voted in the Democratic primary without having disaffiliated more than 30 days in advance, Taveras added. And at least four voters gave the addresses of vacant houses, he said.

Most important, Taveras said, the state police are investigating allegations of mail-ballot tampering by Kells campaign volunteers. That alone warrants a delay in certifying the results, he argued. The board unanimously rejected Pichardo's petition.

State Rep. Marsha E. Carpenter, who lost her District 18 seat by 89 votes to newcomer Leon F. Tejada, complained that the Sackett Street School polls were so badly understaffed that there was chaos (Pichardo agreed), and "horrendous" misconduct went unchecked. But Carpenter acknowledged that she couldn't meet the board's requirements, and her case was also dismissed unanimously.

Allene R. Maynard, a veteran Democratic leader in South Providence who lost to incumbent state Rep. Aisha W. Abdullah-Odiase by 17 votes, 320 to 303, forfeited her own hearing after watching others.

"I sat and listened and saw how futile it was," said Maynard, who had alleged that Abdullah-Odiase doesn't live in the district and that non-U.S. citizens had been registered to vote.

Latino Voters Win Praise of Candidates

At least one primary race was decided by Latino voters, with voter turnout in some Hispanic neighborhoods doubling the state turnout.

By Timothy C. Barmann
Journal Staff Writer

To see Angel Taveras shaking hands, hugging and kissing people who streamed into the Casino at Roger Williams Park yesterday afternoon, you might think that he was still running for office.

Taveras lost his bid for the U.S. House when he was defeated in the second district race by Secretary of State James Langevin in the Democratic primary last month.

But Taveras wasn't seeking voter support yesterday; he and two other Hispanic candidates held a party to celebrate the wide turnout among Latino voters in that primary.

"This is a thank-you from all the candidates for coming out in record numbers," Taveras said.

The other two candidates who sponsored the event were Gonzalo Cuervo, who narrowly lost in the primary to state Rep. Joseph S. Almeida in the House District 20 race; and Leon F. Tejada, who won the Democratic nomination in House District 18 against incumbent Marsha E. Carpenter.

Some 300 people gathered at the park to hear political speeches from Latino candidates, to eat, and to relish their newly realized political power.

During the primary, turnout in Providence's Hispanic neighborhoods reached as high as 38 percent in districts with tightly contested races, more than doubling the statewide turnout of 15 percent.

At least one of the races -- Tejada's -- was decided by Latino voters. Tejada beat Carpenter by 89 votes, a 7.4-percent margin, according to figures from the city Board of Canvassers. He will face Republican Ian O'Hara in the November election.

Gonzalo Cuervo lost in his to bid to unseat state Rep. Joseph S. Almeida by only 26 votes.

Taveras attributed the widespread interest in the election to the fact that there were several Latino candidates, as well as a campaign by Spanish newspapers and radio stations to get people to vote.

"We need to become more part of the political process, more involved overall," said Taveras. "That's the only way democracy can flourish."

The party yesterday seemed to be a continuation of that campaign.

In Spanish, a speaker at the podium got the crowd shouting a phrase that translates to "Latino united, we will never be overcome."

"I think this is the awakening process," said Tejada, in an interview. He said that while the turnout at the primary was impressive, he hopes that events like these will help raise it to 50 percent.

Over the past 10 years, the state's Latino population grew by 50 percent, to nearly 69,000 people, while the state's total population declined slightly, according to the U.S. Census Bureau. Latinos made up 4.5 percent of the state's population in 1990, but nearly 7 percent in 1999.

Latino Power Shows at Polls

"It's electoral participation catching up to the shift in the demographics," says Providence Councilman Luis A. Aponte.

By Ariel Sabar
Journal Staff Writer
9.14.2000

PROVIDENCE -- Tuesday's primary elections drew an extraordinary number of Latinos to the polls, a result not only of their surging numbers and clout here but of an unprecedented get-out-the-vote effort, Latino activists and political experts said yesterday.

Spanish-language radio stations trumpeted the elections for months, social-service agencies signed up hundreds of new voters in just the past few weeks, and Latino-owned cab companies shuttled dozens of people to the polls Tuesday, free of charge. The state's first-ever Latino congressional candidate, Angel Taveras, a 30-year-old lawyer with no political experience and a shoestring campaign budget, drew an astonishing one in three votes in Providence.

Leon F. Tejada, 35, a computer systems analyst, defeated three-term state Rep. Marsha E. Carpenter in the city's Elmwood section. Gonzalo Cuervo, a political newcomer, came within 26 votes of displacing state Rep. Joseph S. Almeida, a first-term incumbent from the Washington Park neighborhood.

And Juan M. Pichardo, 33, a patient advocate at Rhode Island Hospital who ran a savvy and aggressive campaign, came tantalizingly close to upsetting state Sen. Robert T. Kells, a retired Providence police officer and five-term senator. Asked late Tuesday about the closeness of the race, Kells, who is white, was blunt: "The diversity in the community had an effect."

A Journal analysis found that turnout in the city's Hispanic neighborhoods reached as high as 38 percent in districts with hotly contested local primaries, dwarfing the statewide turnout of about 15 percent. Those numbers follow a decade in which the state's Latino population grew 50 percent, to nearly 69,000 people, even as the state's total population declined slightly, according to the U.S. Census Bureau estimates. To put it another way: Latinos made up 4.5 percent of the state's population in 1990, but nearly 7 percent in 1999. Despite Taveras's third-place finish and Pichardo and Cuervo's narrow defeats, Latino activists said that the primary's turnout attested to the success of a dogged voter-education campaign. It was also a harbinger, they said, of wider electoral success within a few years.

"The giant is awakening," said Dr. Pablo Rodriguez, the chairman of the Rhode Island Latino Political Action Committee. "I think the Latino community has finally found its poltiical legs and people went out and voted. There are more candidates, better campaigns, and just a general coming of age."

He said that his mother was beside herself as she voted yesterday at the Sackett Street School, in South Providence, where the race between Pichardo and Kells made it far and away the city's busiest polling place.

Cars spray-painted with campaign slogans idled down the gritty street, and knots of campaign operatives shook hands and passed out colorful political fliers. "She told it me it was like being back in Puerto Rico during the elections," Rodriguez said.

"It's electoral participation catching up to the shift in the demographics," agreed Luis A. Aponte, who was elected in 1998 as the first Latino councilman in Providence. "I think that Angel's election and his campaign in particular motivated many people to come out and participate."

As she left the Sackett Street voting booths, Carmen Rosario, 30, a mortgage processor, said that Taveras had something none of the other congressional candidates had: he grew up in the neighborhood. "Angel's the man," she said Tuesday evening, after casting her ballot. "He was born and raised here. He knows what we need."

The scene would have been out of place even a decade ago, when Latinos held no seats on either the Providence City Council or in the General Assembly.

Anastasia Williams, who is Panamanian, became the first Latino state lawmaker in 1992. And Aponte became the City Council's first Latino member six years later.

But Latino activists said yesterday that it wasn't until recently that community leaders grasped the role even relatively small numbers of Latino voters could play in politics. A watershed was a set of state and local elections in 1998 in which the Latino candidates lost by painfully narrow margins.

"We learned from the last elections that a couple of voters can actually make a significant difference," said Luisa Murillo, the executive director of the Center for Hispanic Policy & Advocacy, a social-service agency in Providence that made interpreters available at the polls. "That was the message this time: Your vote most definitely can count."

For the last five months, Poder 1110-AM, the dominant Spanish-language radio station, has given large slices of airtime on its morning drive show to the nuts and bolts of elections. The show's hosts took calls on the air from listeners with questions as mundane as, "Where is my polling place?" The station also arranged for Latino-owned cab companies such as Gonzales Taxi to ferry people to the polls as a public service.

"We're a music station, but we took a lot of calls from people," said the station's CEO, Tony Mendez. "We explained the process."

In the congressional primary Tuesday, Taveras's odds-defying third-place finish was further proof of Latinos' swelling power at the ballot box. Though just 3 percent of voters in a poll late last month said they would support him, Taveras won four times that percentage. He captured nearly 12 percent of the vote, edging out the better-known Kevin J. McAllister, the president of the Cranston City Council.

More than half of Taveras's nearly 6,000 votes across the sprawling 2nd Congressional District came from Providence, where he was within 175 votes of beating Secretary of State James R. Langevin, the victor districtwide. A remarkable 635 of his 3,000 Providence votes were cast at Sackett Street School, the site of the hard-fought Pichardo-Kells race.

Though prickly about the label "Latino candidate" because of his desire to appeal to the entire district, Taveras acknowledged yesterday that he spent significant time and money courting the Latino vote. The son of Dominican immigrants, he did two dozen interviews with Spanish-language radio stations and newspapers, bought ads on Spanish radio and TV, and greeted voters at the city's Bolivian, Dominican and Puerto Rican festivals.

Taveras also tapped a network of Latino activists across the country for campaign money. "It was very hard to raise money in-state, essentially because people felt I was a long shot," he said yesterday.

Taveras said the phones were ringing yesterday with supporters urging him to run again. Exhausted by the campaign, he said he wanted to rest for at least a week before even thinking about his next move. Still, he sounded almost giddy as he described the outpouring of kudos after the election. "I'll tell you one thing," he quipped. "I've never been congratulated so much for losing."

He was not shy about casting his election bid, and Tuesday's turnout in Hispanic neighborhoods, in historic terms. "It's a huge step in the right direction of becoming more and more a part of American society," said Taveras, who has described his rise from the Head Start program to Harvard University as an archetypal immigrant success story. Despite what Latino leaders described yesterday as a banner day at the polls, some worried that it might a fluke.

Census figures show that voter turnout among Latino Rhode Islanders has swung wildly in recent years. In the 1996 elections, the year Latinos united to defeat U.S. House candidate Joseph Paolino, a supporter of English as the country's official language of government, nearly one in four Latinos 18 and older cast a ballot. Two years later, with no such races to energize Latino voters, just one in 17 voted compared to roughly one in two voters statewide.

For now, language barriers, an alienation from American politics, and the rigmarole of registering to vote are still stumbling blocks for many Latinos, advocates say. And some Latino leaders fret about the plan to downsize the General Assembly, a move that would enlarge districts and thus make it tougher for minority aspirants to win seats.

Aponte, the Providence councilman, is buoyed by the primary elections but wonders whether Latinos here have reached the political maturity to take part in elections that don't as clearly touch on their interests. "Will folks still come out and vote when there may not be Latino candidates running?" said Aponte, an investigator for the Rhode Island Commission for Human Rights. "That is the longer, more telling dynamic." -- *With reports from staff writer David Herzog.*

Latino Vote Influences Primary Races

Leon F. Tejada, who snatched the Democratic nomination in District 18 from incumbent Marsha E. Carpenter, attributes his win to a heavy Latino voter turnout.

By Marion Davis
Journal Staff Writer
9.14.2000

PROVIDENCE -- Three of the five Democratic primaries in South Providence were so close that many people yesterday weren't sure who had won: Did state Sen. Robert T. Kells keep his District 10 seat? How about state Rep. Aisha W. Abdullah-Odiase in District 19, or Rep. Joseph S. Almeida in District 20?

But when all the votes were counted -- including the mail ballots -- the three incumbents were in, though their opponents all challenged the results yesterday before the state Board of Elections.

Only state Rep. Marsha E. Carpenter, who has gained prominence for her fight against gun violence, lost her seat in the primaries. Newcomer Leon F. Tejada snatched up the District 18 Democratic nomination by 89 votes, or a 7.4 percent margin, according to figures from the city Board of Canvassers.

Tejada will face Republican Ian O'Hara in the November election.

Carpenter has also challenged the primary results, according to Robert J. Fontaine, executive director of the Board of Elections. She did not return a call from The Journal yesterday.

Tejada made no bones about why he won -- the Latino vote.

At all but one of the District 18 polling places, Latino voters had not one, but three Latino candidates on the ballot. Along with Tejada, there was Juan M. Pichardo, who was challenging Kells in Senate District 10, and then the even higher-profile Angel Taveras, a candidate in the 2nd Congressional District race.

Where one won, all three did well, a Journal analysis showed. On the left side of the Sackett Street School, for example, Tejada got 61.1 percent of the vote; Pichardo received 66.7 percent; and Taveras, 73.4 percent.

On the right side of the Casino in Roger Williams Park, by contrast, Tejada got 35.3 percent of the vote; Pichardo received 28.8 percent, and Taveras, 28.9 percent.

The results also roughly match the distribution of Latinos in the district -- the higher the concentration, the better the Hispanic candidates did. The ethnic pitch was pretty straightforward, too: Outside the polls, people were handing out fliers that urged, "Vote Latino."

Tejada, who was born in the Dominican Republic and became a U.S. citizen in 1992, said he knew from the beginning that "whoever wanted to win that district had to get the Latino vote." He had a clear advantage, he said, because "we need somebody who can speak in the same language."

A key part of his campaign effort was to register Latinos who had moved to Rhode Island from other states and weren't yet on the voting rolls, or who had lived here for awhile but hadn't registered.

Pichardo and Taveras were doing the same, he said, and between the three of them, "we registered over 900 people."

Tejada had a strong foothold among the South Providence Latino community because his Broad Street business provides a variety of services to them, such as translations and help with immigration papers and taxes.

The local Spanish-language media -- radio stations such as Poder 1110 and 1220 "La Inconfundible," and the newspaper Providence En Español -- gave all three Latino candidates ample opportunities to reach their constituents, and they helped to educate voters.

In Latin American countries, elections are traditionally festive and boisterous, "like a party," Tejada noted, and on Tuesday, the Latino candidates also built on that, getting people excited about going to vote.

Carpenter couldn't match that enthusiasm in her camp, Tejada said, because many people in the district didn't know her.

"She's not in contact -- she's not down here," he said. Many voters with whom he spoke thought he was running against Councilwoman Patricia K. Nolan, he added, because she is the one they see in the neighborhood. Nolan, who said Carpenter's defeat "breaks my heart," because they are friends and she admires Carpenter's work, acknowledged that Carpenter wasn't as visible in her district as she could be.

If Tejada could win District 18, why did Pichardo lose to Kells?

The race was painfully close. Pichardo actually won at the polls, with 1,179 votes to Kells's 1,161. But Kells snatched up 119 of the 126 mail ballots cast, besting Pichardo by 94 votes in the end.

Kells will face Republican Sonya Zecchin O'Hara -- Ian O'Hara's wife -- in the general election. Kells attributed his victory to his "grassroots community organization," his three decades in the neighborhood and his work as a Providence police officer (he holds the rank of captain), and lots of hard work.

"We left no stone unturned," he said. "We did our homework, and I think we got an A."

Nolan, who backed Kells, said many people in the district were turned off by the large amount of money Pichardo seemed to spend on the race, sending out numerous mass mailings.

Pichardo also had the backing of Senate Majority Leader Paul Kelly, Nolan said, whereas Kells supports Sen. William Irons, who is challenging Kelly for the leadership post. State Senators Rhoda Perry and Maryellen Goodwin both worked at the polls on Pichardo's behalf, Nolan said.

Both Nolan and Kells were critical of Pichardo's targeted appeal to Latinos. Kells said he was "overwhelmed" by the Latino voter turnout, especially at the Sackett Street School, where they showed up in droves. "I said, 'Oh boy.' "

But both Pichardo and Tejada said many Latino voters whom they had registered -- and others who had been registered for years -- were turned away at the polls because somehow they hadn't been put on the voting rolls. Pichardo, who has requested a hearing before the Board of Elections with regard to the District 10 race, said that was a key issue he planned to raise, because many Latino voters were disenfranchised.

The third Latino challenger in the Assembly races Gonzalo Cuervo, a son of Colombian immigrants who ran against state Rep. Joseph S. Almeida in House District 20 -- lost by an even narrower margin than Pichardo.

Almeida, who had the support of the city's only Latino councilman, Luis A. Aponte, Ward 10, defeated Cuervo by 26 votes, or 430 to 404 -- a 3.1-percent margin. Neither candidate could be reached for comment yesterday.

State Rep. Anastasia P. Williams, the only Latina candidate in the primaries who was also an incumbent, won handily in the District 9 race, garnering 459 votes to challenger Barbara Thurman's 219.

The only South Providence primary that didn't pit a Latino candidate against a non-Latino was in House District 19, where two African-American women went head to head: state Rep. Aisha W. Abdullah-Odiase and challenger Allene R. Maynard, who is active in the Democratic Party and supported Kells.

Abdullah-Odiase defeated Maynard by 17 votes, 320 to 303. Maynard, who has accused Abdullah-Odiase of living outside her district, said she was requesting a recount because "I owe it to myself and my supporters," but she acknowledged that, despite a tough fight, she had almost certainly lost.

"For all her million signs, though, I gave her a good run for her money, didn't I?" Maynard said with a laugh.

Abdullah-Odiase will face Green Party candidate Paul J. Degaitas in the November election.

Maynard attributed her loss to voter apathy, and she said Latinos may have also played a role in her race, because Abdullah-Odiase set up a table in front of a Latino-owned market on Broad Street over the weekend.

Reached at home, Abdullah-Odiase declined to discuss the primary results. Sounding exhausted, she just told a reporter, "I have no comment right now. I just want some rest."

Abortion Remains A Simmering Topic

M. Charles Bakst
The Providence Journal
10.12.2000

It may be low key, but abortion is a substantial issue in the Senate general election, and if you need proof, go to the Biltmore next Wednesday for a fundraiser for Republican incumbent Linc Chafee.

He favors abortion rights. Democrat Bob Weygand opposes them.

Chair of the $250-a-person 6 p.m. event is Dr. Pablo Rodriguez, medical director of Planned Parenthood, managing partner of a medical practice, and associate chief of obstetrics and gynecology at Women & Infants Hospital. During the Democratic primary, Democrat Rodriguez unsuccessfully backed the "pro-choice" Richard Licht. Rodriguez says organizers of next week's event largely represent abortion-rights sentiment.

Some comments Weygand made about Rodriguez the other day offended the doctor, and I don't blame him. They came about because the host committee features some very interesting names, especially if you recall that one of Weygand's big fans is former Providence Mayor Joe Paolino, who lost to him in a 1996 House primary and chairs Al Gore's campaign here.

I showed Weygand the roster. It includes Paolino's mother and stepfather, Bea and Martin Temkin; his sister Donna and her husband Bob Urciuoli; and Paolino's stepmother, Heather Paolino. ("All I can do is tell people how *I'm* voting," says the former mayor.)

As it happens, Bea Temkin is close to Chafee campaign aide Steve Hourahan and views him as a second son. She said she is "pro-life" but is not a one-issue voter. Martin reports he is pro-choice.

When Congressman Weygand saw the name of Bob Urciuoli, Roger Williams Medical Center president, he at first seemed surprised; he said he has worked hard to help the hospital. "But I also know that we opposed it when he tried to make it a for-profit hospital, and maybe he's still very upset."

Urciuoli told me the for-profit issue had nothing to do with it. He said he is a pal of Licht -- a hospital trustee -- and also has a longstanding relationship with the Chafees, especially the senator's wife, Stephanie, who worked at Roger Williams as a nurse. Urciuoli also is pro-choice.

Donna Urciuoli said, "I'm sorry that Richard Licht didn't win. . . . He would have made a great senator." She said of Chafee, "The fact that he's pro-choice really was the deciding factor for me. Maybe he can do something in the Senate and persuade some of the other Republicans."

When Weygand saw Rodriguez' name, he said, "He's a one-issue person" and abortion "is his livelihood."

Later, Weygand phoned to say that "the real leaders" of the Hispanic community are in his camp. For example, he cited former Democratic House candidate Angel Taveras, who confirmed he is indeed with Weygand.

But who asked Weygand anything about Hispanics anyway? Not I. It was obvious that Rodriguez was acting in his capacity in the choice community, not the Hispanic community. Weygand said, "Pablo immediately strikes me as being a representative of the Hispanic community."

I thought Weygand was typecasting him, and Rodriguez said by phone that I was right, that he and other Hispanics often are stereotyped, that people see them as Latinos instead of as individuals. Then he sent me an e-mail expressing dismay with Weygand's comments about abortion as a livelihood. Rodriguez wrote:

"One does not have to have a financial motivation to support a woman's right to choose and it is terribly insulting to the hundreds of physicians that put their life on the line for their patients when a sitting congressman needs to question the deep personal commitment we have. For the record, I can make three times as much doing pap smears in my office than performing abortions and with much less risk. My disagreement with Weygand is over policy."

On this issue, I stand with Rodriguez and women.

Democrats Raise Money For Chafee

The Republican senator is getting support across political lines, including from some who favor his pro-choice stance on abortion.

By Michael Corkery
and SCOTT MacKay
Journal Staff Writers
10.19.2000

PROVIDENCE -- A large "Lincoln Chafee for U.S. Senate" sign hung in the background as Dr. Pablo Rodriguez strode to the podium and posed the question on everyone's mind.

"What's a good Democrat like me doing in a place like this," asked Rodriguez, the medical director of Planned Parenthood, head of the Rhode Island Latino Political Action Committee and one of the few physicians in the state who performs abortions.

Rodriguez, a Democratic activist, was the host of a fundraiser for Republican Chafee last night at the Providence Biltmore hotel.

The $250-per-person event drew about 60 people, including a small, but prominent, group of Democrats who, like Rodriguez, said the abortion issue had driven them across party lines to publicly support Chafee, instead of Democrat Robert A. Weygand. Weygand opposes abortion except in cases of rape, incest or where the life of the mother is in danger.

The event reaped about $25,000 for Chafee's campaign, said Steve Hourahan, Chafee's campaign manager.

"I am a Democrat," said Rodriguez. "But first, I am an American who is tired of partisan politics and tired of politicians who say one thing and do another; that's why I am an American voting for the best man for the job, Lincoln Chafee."

Rodriguez praised Chafee for honesty and his ability to work with Democrats in Washington, but he and many of the guests -- though not all -- made it clear that Chafee's position favoring abortion rights led them to the event.

Antiabortion protesters picketed on the sidewalk outside the hotel as guests arrived for the fundraiser. They carried signs with Chafee's name crossed out in red, and with the slogan "Blood Money Kills Babies."

Protest organizer George Bedford, of Cristo Rey, said the group is a recently formed political action committee devoted to pushing antiabortion positions and candidates.

Chafee was busy in Washington and did not attend the event, but his wife, Stephanie Chafee, touted her husband's support for a "woman's reproductive rights," and lauded Democrats in the room for having the courage to support a Republican.

Stephanie Chafee made special mention of some of the Democrats, including former Lt. Gov. Thomas R. DiLuglio, former state Sen. Gloria Kennedy Fleck, of Warwick, and Carlo Pistaturo, a long-time Democratic Warwick city councilman, now an independent.

Several other prominent Democrats, who did not attend last night's event, but were part of the committee that sold tickets, included Donna Paolino Urciuoli, the sister of former Providence Mayor Joseph R. Paolino Jr., and Bea Temkin, Paolino's mother. In addition, Heather Paolino, wife of Paolino's father, Joseph R. Paolino Sr., was also on the ticket committee.

Joseph Paolino Jr. ran unsuccessfully against Weygand in 1996 for the Democratic nomination to the House in the 2nd District. Paolino Jr. is also chairman of Al Gore's Rhode Island presidential campaign.

Last night, Paolino said he is solidly behind Weygand, despite the support for Chafee among members of his family.

One of the elements Weygand must work on, Paolino said, is garnering votes among traditional Democrats in Providence and Pawtucket, where Weygand did not run well against Licht in the primary.

"He needs to work in Providence, where he lost to me [in 1996] and lost to Licht," Paolino said. "Warwick was always his base and now he's running against a former Warwick mayor [Chafee], so he's got to do well in Providence."

Latinos Celebrate Successes At Polls

The Rhode Island Latino Political Action Committee throws a party to honor candidates who won, or nearly won, primary races this past September.

By Michael Corkery
Journal Staff Writer
10.25.2000 00:36

The pollsters and pundits like to describe Latinos as the sleeping giant of American politics. They are one of the fastest growing ethnic groups in the nation, and as their population grows, so will their political clout.

But if this year's primary election was any indication, Latinos in Rhode Island are asleep no longer. On primary day, Latinos turned out to vote in extraordinary numbers after an aggressive get-out-the vote effort. Leon F. Tejada, 35, a computer systems analyst, defeated three-term state Rep. Marsha E. Carpenter in the city's Elmwood section. And other Latino candidates came within a few votes of ousting popular incumbents in the state Senate and House of Representatives.

Last night, the Rhode Island Latino Political Action Committee, a fundraiser for many Hispanic candidates, threw a party to celebrate their successes. And although not every race ended in victory, most candidates and their supporters gathered last night at the Rhode Island Foundation felt as though they had won.

"It's like a dream," said Tejada. "We showed the rest of the community that we count, and finally our message was heard."

The Latino Political Action Committee honored each of the candidates with a plaque, encouraging them to continue their political involvement. Among those honored were:

■Angel Taveras, the state's first-ever Latino Congressional candidate, who drew one in three votes in Providence in the race for the 2nd Congressional District.

■Gonzalo Cuervo, a political newcomer, who came within 26 votes of displacing state Rep. Joseph S. Almeida, a first-term incumbent from the Washington Park neighborhood.
■Juan M. Pichardo, 33, a patient advocate at Rhode Island Hospital who came close to upsetting state Sen. Robert T. Kells, a five-term senator.

■Anastasia Williams, who became the first Latino state lawmaker in 1992.

"It is a historic moment to know that I won't be alone up there," said Williams. She also encouraged more Latino women to run for office. "There is room in the House for you," she said. A sizable cadre of state and city officials joined in last night's celebration, acknowledging the growing importance of Latinos in Rhode Island's political landscape as they ate spicy meat pies and rice.

U.S. Sen. Lincoln Chafee and his opponent, Robert Weygand, Secretary of State James Langevin and Lt. Governor Charles Fogarty were among the guests. U.S. Sen. Jack Reed delivered a lengthy speech in Spanish.

"We are here to recognize the people who are trying to make things better not just for their people, but for all people," Reed remarked later. "This is just the beginning."

In the past decade, the state's Latino population grew 50 percent, to nearly 69,000 people, even as that the state's total population declined slightly, according to the U.S. Census Bureau.

Latinos made up 4.5 percent of the state's population in 1990, but nearly 7 percent in 1999. During the primary, turnout in Providence's Hispanic neighborhoods reached as high as 38 percent in districts with tightly contested races, exceeding the statewide turnout of 15 percent.

There are still many obstacles preventing the Latinos' political power from being fully realized, some speakers said last night. Language barriers and lack of citizenship are stumbling blocks in some cases, they said.

In his former home in the Dominican Republic, election day was like "a carnival," said Tejada. People waited for hours to reach the ballot box. Tejada hopes he and other candidates can instill the same excitement in Latino voters living in the United States.

"People didn't vote before because the candidates spoke a different language," he said. "Now we share the same culture."

On The Front Lines, Clashes, Nostalgia

M. Charles Bakst
The Providence Journal
10.24.2000

Early this evening, I plan to stop at a Rhode Island Latino Political Action Committee reception, hope to find Carolina Bernal, a RILPAC member, and try to usher her over to Pablo Rodriguez, its president.

Not that they don't know each other. This is so Rhode Island: He is her gynecologist. He is also Planned Parenthood Medical director, a top champion of abortion rights, and a Democrat who's been in the news for weeks because he backs the "pro-choice" Republican Sen. Linc Chafee over "pro-life" Democratic Rep. Bob Weygand.

Bernal, coordinator of education and research at the Institute for Labor Studies, is a Democrat who opposes abortion rights and backs Weygand. She and Rodriguez could have quite a chat. She approached me last week at a Weygand fundraiser -- actually, she was coming out of the Biltmore Hotel event; the press wasn't allowed in -- to say she thinks Rodriguez's embrace of Chafee is a disservice.

She said Weygand shows near perfect support of Latino issues. She said the community includes both proponents and opponents of abortion rights but that this "is not the main issue." She said Rodriguez, who'd be chairing a Biltmore fundraiser for Chafee the next night, was sending the "wrong message" by jumping across party lines. "He's a Democrat -- you can't have two ways about it."

Bernal said Hispanics are interested in a variety of issues, including minimum wage, immigrant matters and the like, and that Democrats are better on this agenda than Republicans.

The next night, I returned to the Biltmore, past the antiabortion pickets -- one sign called Rodriguez "the angel of death" -- and found the doctor at the Chafee party. He said such epithets don't bother him: "If that's the way they want to characterize me, so be it." (The pickets *are* entitled to their views, but they and their signs reminded me of harassment American women must often endure en route to having an abortion.)

Rodriguez did dispute Bernal's comments to me about Senate contest topics, such as immigration items, of special concern to Hispanics. "Who says

Lincoln Chafee is no good on those issues as well?" he said, adding that Sen. John Chafee, Linc's late father, was "very good on immigrant issues."

The party was organized largely to highlight Chafee's support of abortion rights. Meet Connie Worthington, a political independent and a professional fundraiser in the nonprofit world, who told me, "I'm here for choice. . . . Women will always be second class if we don't have a choice."

Chafee was in Washington. His wife, Stephanie, thanked Rodriguez and several others who crossed party lines; indeed, she thanked everyone. Pickets make many people uncomfortable, she said, and it's "human nature" not to want to confront controversy. "But that's what we do when we know in our hearts it's the right thing to do."

Of course, not everything in politics has to be this serious. Some stuff is just nostalgic. There were reminders at this event of the old John Chafee days. I ran into Jim Marshall, who, starting in 1963, was Governor Chafee's young press secretary and is now 70.

An eagle-motif ice sculpture called to mind the times the late insurance magnate Morton Smith hosted lavish Chafee fundraisers at the Biltmore. Several featured *six* ice sculptures -- C-H-A-F-E-E -- lifted with a hoist, propped on bases of plastic milk cartons covered by linen, and displayed on a long buffet table. Jim McDonnell, the Biltmore's director of catering services, last week sported a photo of one such tableau.

But there was one he didn't have a picture of. One year, he says, the hotel mistakenly ordered up an extra letter and installed *seven* sculptures: C-H-A-F-F-E-E. The event was under way before anyone noticed the extra F. By then, McDonnell says, it would have been too disruptive to remove it, so it remained on display all evening.

$8 Million Slated For R.I. Projects

The spending, approved Friday night as Congress belatedly finished its budget for 2001, will help build a museum, promote literacy in schools and pay for health research.

By David Herzog
Journal Staff Writer
12.17.2000

Before Congress wrapped up its work for the year, it left Rhode Island a Christmas gift: an additional $8.15 million for disaster planning, the proposed Heritage Harbor Museum and other projects.

The spending, approved Friday night as Congress belatedly finished it budget for 2001, also will help promote literacy in Providence schools and finance cancer research at the University of Rhode Island, according to lists of the projects provided by Senators Jack Reed and Lincoln D. Chafee.

The Rhode Island projects make up just a fraction of the $450-billion federal spending package that Congress approved Friday, two and one-half months after the 2001 fiscal year began. The measure includes hundreds of projects -- sometimes derided as "pork barrel" spending -- worth about $1.1 billion that lawmakers wanted for their own districts and states.

Representatives Patrick J. Kennedy and Robert A. Weygand voted to approve the measure -- part of the overall $1.8-trillion federal budget -- during the roll call vote in the House. The Senate approved the measure by voice vote. President Clinton has promised to sign the package.

The new money comes on top of the tens of millions of dollars set aside for Rhode Island in defense, transportation and environmental bills passed earlier this year. Some of that money will go toward improving rail lines for freight trains, building soccer fields in East Providence and creating the John H. Chafee Blackstone River Valley National Heritage Corridor.

With the final budget package, the Heritage Harbor Museum proposed for the Providence waterfront will get a $900,000 boost to its sagging fortunes. Last month, Rhode Island voters rejected a bond issue that would have raised $25 million for the proposed museum in the former South Street generating station of the Narragansett Electric Co.

The University of Rhode Island will be getting $2.8 million for health research and sports programs. Researchers at URI's Cancer Prevention Research Center will get $2 million for two studies: one to test smoking-cessation programs and another to target the most widespread and preventable causes of cancer mortality.

URI's Institute for International Sport is budgeted to get $800,000 so it can provide scholarships to 20 percent of the participants in its World Scholar-Athlete Games.

Congress approved roughly $1 million for the Rhode Island Disaster Initiative to fix shortcomings in the state's disaster medical preparedness. Some of the money will be used to help Rhode Island hospitals plan for taking care of victims of chemical and biological attacks.

Roger Williams Medical Center in Providence is set to get $700,000 for its Healthlink program. The medical center and other groups are developing a health-promotion initiative for elderly retirees.

Also, Our Lady of Fatima Hospital in North Providence will get $500,000 to help develop a comprehensive breast-cancer center, and the East Providence Senior Wellness Center will get $100,000 to help the elderly delay the degenerative effects of aging.

The other medical and social-service recipients are: Blackstone Valley Community Health Centers, $300,000 to run clinics in Pawtucket and Central Falls; Providence Smiles, $100,000 for its school-based dental program, and Progreso Latino in Central Falls, $100,000 to make a building accessible to the elderly.

Congress voted to give Rhode Island $1.65 million for education projects. Most of the money -- $1 million -- will go to Project Family Net, a partnership that links Providence students with their parents as partners in learning. Providence will get another $300,000 for literacy training.

Cranston Public Schools will receive $350,000 for its 21st Century Community Learning Center to provide after-school programs, particularly for middle school students.

Changing Political Landscape
An Opportunity for Latinos

By- Victor Capellán
April 2000

The announcement by Senator John Chafee, not to seek a fifth term in the United States Senate, provides the Latino community an opportunity to change the Political Landscape in the State of Rhode Island.

Such a move by a person at the "top" of the state political arena will cause a "moving up" fever among many in the state political arena. Once the announcements for bids to the coveted United States Senate Seat are said and done, we could be looking at many empty posts throughout the state and this could provide an opportunity for BIG gains in the Latino political scene.

The Latino community is the largest minority group in the state and one with a growing voting power in the state and certainly throughout the nation. However, we must ask ourselves a few questions, before we begin throwing our hats in for any specifics races or begin speculating which posts will become available.

However, it only takes one such move, as the one by Senator Chafee to change the face of politics and those that prepare and plan ahead might be well served in such a move.

From mayors of the cities, to state-wide office holders, Junior Congress members, to ex-candidates, state legislators, political aficionados, third party candidates, and wannabe's everyone wishes a shot at the big seat. Therefore, what will be created is a myriad of possible empty seats at entry level posts that an emerging political-immigrant force such as Latinos are well suited, qualified, and in demand fill.
This is an opportunity that must be garnished because we are facing one the most crucial times in terms of the need for Latino elected officials as well as opportunities to elect them.

The next election cycle will prove to be a key for Latinos. We have the opportunity the Census 2000 presents for us to be accurately accounted and we must fight to ensure that such accuracy happens. The dangers presented by Re-districting with the possibilities of Jerry Maundering, in 2001, worsened by the shrinkage of the state legislature in 2002 clearly point to the need for underrepresented communities to make their move in the year 2000.

Therefore, if we combine the announcement by Senator Chafee not to seek reelection, the myriad of Politicos scrambling to grab that seat, leaving a number of entry level post opened and the latter in terms of what the post 2000 events could bring, the Latino community needs to "Mobilize" the "Awakened" Sleeping Giant, make its numbers count and flex its political muscle in order to WIN BIG in 2000.

When you think about this also ponder the thought that, the last United States Senator Claiborne Pell served for 36 years before John Chafee who will have served for 24 years in the Senate. Add to this a Census that only takes place every decade and as Latinos we are in a sort of way "The Flavor of the Millennium." We must keep in mind that this scenario only happens once or maybe twice a life-time, then our moment to act is now!

Latinos, we must strategize, mobilized and realize the dreams that this change in Political Landscape offer us.

Juan M. Pichardo Announcement Speech

May 2000

Family, Friends, Neighbors; Welcome and thank you for coming. THANK YOU FOR BEING HERE…THANK YOU, GRACIAS!!! GRACIAS A TODOS POR SU APOYO EN ESTA TARDE.

I am here today because of you!

Your encouragement and support has brought me before you TODAY. This day is an important day for these neighborhoods, and for my family and i.

For several months, I have been meeting with many friends and neighbors, Activist, advocates and leaders. People like My good friend…_____…..

These conversation led me to reflect on my life and my future. This has been my home for 20 years. I enjoy living here, it is really a great place to raise a family. I am proud of my community. Yet, it can be so much better.

You know, as I look back at my life, it has not been easy. It has been a struggle from the day that my mother decided to leave Santiago, and come to the United States to be a Nanny. She worked hard and sacrificed to provide for me for nine years until she finally realized her goal of bringing me to the United States for a better future. Her sacrifices have been my driving force to make her proud and provide the same example to my family!

Today, I along with my wife Janet strive to raise our son, Cristian, with the same values and principles of hard work, dedication and respect that my mother taught me. These are lessons that have brought me here today. I am willing to work hard for my family and I now want to sacrifice and work hard for the improvement of our district.

That is why today, i am here to announce that i will be running to become a member of the Rode island state senate -- as your senator from the 10th district.

I am seeking the State Senate because:

I believe that I can make a difference for this district. The people of Elmwood, the West End and the Reservoir Triangle can truly elect a person who they can truly depend on, and someone that can represent US ALL. A person who will fight and advocate for the right issues that will benefit the entire district and the State of Rhode Island.

I am running for the State Senate because I want to work towards making a better future for my family, my son Cristian, for my neighbors and their children.

Like all of you, I want the best for my family and our district. I want District 10 and the state of Rhode Island to move forward together for a better future.

Our current Senator is not doing the job! He has not done the work necessary to improve our quality of life. Our Senator has not been able to respond to the changing needs of our neighborhoods, and this is apparent in the lack of trust and loss of faith from our youth and families.

I believe our system can work. I am a firm believer in our government and our country! For the last 11 years, I have been a member of the military because I am willing to fight and defend our country. This is the type of leadership our district deserves. Someone who realizes that the trust placed on it's elected official should not be taken lightly. They expect their civil servants to protect their freedom and rights. Our Senator has not. The reality in our district is that we need a Senator who will fight to bring resources to our neighborhoods and our current Senator has not been successful in doing that along with us. We can no longer live isolated in a system where only a few reap the benefits of one of the longest lasting economic booms in our state and country has seen. This must stop and our current Senator is tired and cannot deliver any longer for our youth, for our families, for our elderly and for us.

Together with you, I want to do something about making the future a healthier, Safer and better environment to live in.

As Martin Luther king said " we must continue to strive to achieve the beloved community"

As we stand on the gateway of a new century, we are also standing on the threshold of a point of reflection. John F. Kennedy once said, " Change is the law of life, and those who look only to the past or present are certain to miss the future."

We must reflect on our past while at the same time contemplating our future. If we as citizens do not take appropriate political action, we will have ignored the lessons that the past has taught us, and we will be blind as we move forward in this new century.

I am running because growing up in the Southside and the West End provided me with valuable insights of this diverse community. My involvement in little league, Quisqueya in Action, Elmwood Foundation, Providence Civic entrepreneur and Leadership R.I has shaped my personal and professional development.

As an advocate for the people in our neighborhoods, I have become a more proactive person. I am not afraid to express concerns that affect the quality of life for the people in our neighborhoods. Just as I fought the building of new school on a toxic dump site last year. My experience-as a family man, as a father, as a Soldier, as a patient advocate and as a community activist---have given me the leadership skills to lead this district. As a former President of the Elmwood Foundation, I was able to help increase home ownership and affordable housing in the Elmwood neighborhood. I fought for expansion of programs that benefited our neighborhoods. Today, we see other sections of Elmwood being developed. It is no longer just the historic district. I always stood up for equal economic opportunity so that we all can enjoy a better quality of life.

At the same time, as a Patient Advocate at Rhode Island hospital for the past 10 years. I see everyday the difficulties people face in getting access to health care they can afford. I see first hand the need that the elderly, the young and the newly arrived have. Everyday, I assist and I guide the most needy and helpless through a system in need of change. Change that I will FIGHT to bring about. So that every person can enjoy quality health care. That is why I will support and present legislation that will protect the uninsured. Everyone deserves and has the right to obtain quality health care. That is why I support the efforts of the Rite Care Program. I also support the expansion to allow small business to buy in to the Rite Care program.

I am running because I will fight for:

Higher quality standards and more resources for all of our children in the public school system. I will strongly encourage our community centers to become more active, and create new programs and community activities for our children. I will make sure that they have the proper resources to do so. Implementing these types of ideas will prevent our youth from trouble finding them. The issue of education is not one of the suburbs vs. the city schools…it is an issue of CHILDREN, THE FUTURE OF OUR CITY, OUR STATE AND COUNTRY! We need to support educational reform and fund it at a level where all children can succeed. I will be the Senator that will say YES to Diana Lam when she comes to the State House to ask for more funds to improve our school system. Because this is not an expense, this is an investment in our future. In addition, I can guarantee you that if we invest in education we will see tremendous returns when our youth succeed.

I will also fight for economic development opportunities for small businesses and micro-enterprises by supporting programs that will benefit the business community in this district and the state of Rhode Island. This district is in an Empowerment Zone. When businesses are established or relocated here, they qualify for tax breaks. Why haven't our businesses in the district actively participated? If residents in the Zone are employed then the

Tax breaks are increased. This promotes job opportunities for our neighbors. We have companies moving in and out of our district and the current Senator is not aggressively reaching out to the community that has brought these tax incentives. We are being shortchanged and we can not continue to allow this to happen. We too contribute a lot to the economy of this District and Rhode Island. The West End deserves better. Elmwood deserve better. And the Reservoir Triangle deserves better. Our district needs leadership and it needs a strong voice. And our Senator is not providing that!

<u>I am willing to be that voice.</u>

I am running because I want this District to change.

I believe change is possible in district 10--but it will not come from the current representation. It will come because we will work hard together to elect a senator, a leader who will respect and represent all three communities as one.

A leader who wants to move forward together for a better future. We are tired of our communities getting all the bad news. It is time that we take our destiny in our hands, this district has Roger Williams Park, which has the great zoo and is one of the most popular tourist attraction in our state. Broad Street Marketplace, the Elmwood Little League, the Industrial Park and a great diversity and ethnic representation from all corners of the world.

We are ready for a new leadership in District 10.

I intend to be a leader that will work hard with you to lift this community to new heights.

I want to be a member of the Rhode Island State Senate because I bring with me Integrity, Sensitivity, Respect, Trust, and most importantly Leadership.

I firmly believe in service before self.

I seek to represent AND SERVE the residents of the Elmwood, the Reservoir Triangle and West End. As a state senator, I believe that the experience I have gained in the community and the knowledge I have attained as an active member will make me a stronger & positive voice for District 10.

I cannot do this alone. My family, my friends and neighbors are currently helping in my campaign. However, believe me this is a lot of work. The more volunteers a campaign has the stronger it is. That is why I want your help, I want your financial support and most of ALL I WANT YOUR

VOTE; AND THE VOTE OF YOUR FAMILY AND THE VOTE OF YOUR FRIENDS AS WELL!

Before I end, I would like to take this opportunity to present my team so far. Campaign manager, Melba De Pena, Treasurer, Vernon Brown, and janet, finance director. Yamil Gomes, Rafael Martinez, Jenny Mercado, Marilyn Cepeda, Tomas Avila.

I need your help in this campaign for change.

We can do it. Cesar Chavez, an activist, a leader for better working rights said that the way can we make change is by contacting each person " one by one." "uno por Uno"

"MOVING FORWARD TOGETHER FOR A BETTER FUTURE" is a promise I plan to keep. I will be that person who will make sure that the three neighborhoods within District 10 are treated and represented EQUALLY. Remember on September 12 and November 7 of this year. I need your vote.

Vote Juan Pichardo for state senate.

Muchas Gracias a todos and come September and November we will win this election as we move forward together!

Juan Pichardo's Biography

Juan Pichardo is a 33-year-old Latino from the Dominican Republic, and he has resided in South Providence for 19 years. He is married to Janet and they have a son, Cristian. He is a graduate of the Community College of Rhode Island (A.S.), and he is pursuing a B.A. in Political Science at Rhode Island College.

Juan is employed at Rhode Island Hospital as a Patient Financial Advocate, and as Video Documentation Specialist at the Rhode Island Air National Guard for the past 11 years. He helped to found Quisqueya in Action, an organization for Dominican-Americans in Rhode Island that sponsors the Dominican Festival each year.

He also is affiliated with the Elmwood Foundation, Leadership Rhode Island, and the Rhode Island Latino Political Action Committee (RILPAC). He recently served as campaign manager for Victor Capellan, a candidate for the Rhode Island House of Representatives.

Public Service

Leadership Rhode Island, Upsilon Class
Young Democrats of RI, Member
Quisqueya In Action, co-founder/former president
The Elmwood Foundation, former president
Oasis Federal Credit Union, board member
State Committee Man, Member
Public Education Fund, board member
PROBE Advisory Council, member
La Unidad Latina Fraternity Inc., hermano
Providence Civic Entrepreneur Initiative,
RISD Museum Community Advisory Committee, advisor
9th Ward Project Area Committee, member
Saint Michael's Church, member

Biographical

229 Atlantic Avenue
Providence, RI 02907

Married t: Janet Pichardo
Children: Cristian M. Pichardo
Date f Birth: 10-21-66

Employment

Rhode Island Hospital
Patient Advocate
Rhode Island Air National Guard
Combat Videographer

Education

Gilbert Stuart Middle School
Mount Pleasant High School,
Community College f Rhode Island
Rhode Island College, Political Science.
U.S. Air Force, Security Place
Combat Videographer

Honor/Awards

Individual Community Award, 2000
Selected t Leadership Rhode Island, 2000
Selected as a Providence Civic Entrepreneur, 1998
Health Advocate Award, Progress Latin, 1998
Honor Guard, RI Air National Guard, 1992

Campaign Platform

1. Committed to policies that provide the highest degree of justice and social welfare for the people of the Senate district 10 of providence and the state of Rhode Island.
2. Committed to policies that preserves the fundamental rights of all
3. Access to affordable health care
4. The opportunity to earn a living wage
5. Access to a quality education
6. Freedom from discrimination
7. I believe in promoting social awareness and political activism.

Economic Development

I support programs for economic opportunity that encourage the development of good paying jobs. Thus, allowing people to work in the community and raise a family.

Tax Policy

1. I support a fair and equitable system of taxation.

2. I support the elimination of the "marriage penalty". A tax system with tax deductions for higher education tuition and student loans will promote education.
3. I support taxation that will support a balanced budget, reduces budget deficits, and discourages borrowing money to cover deficits.
4. I believe that tax incentives should be eliminated for businesses that violate environmental protection, and discrimination statutes.

Labor Relations

1. I support increasing the minimum wage, as a way to ease the growing income disparities between the wealthy and those stranded in poverty.
2. I support workers' rights to conduct organizing campaigns in order to gain union representation.
3. I support initiatives that will afford workers more protection from corporations that use fear, coercion, or termination to discourage unionization.

Health Care

I support the right of all Rhode Islander to have access to quality and affordable health care. The health and safety of our state's population is dependent upon all its residents being able to access comprehensive preventive and primary care.

1. Committed to ensuring universal coverage.
2. I support the right of every woman to make her own reproductive decisions.
3. I support a woman rights to choose because is a fundamental liberty.

Civil Rights And Social Justice

I believe in removing discrimination on all levels. The government should protect individuals and groups that are targeted because of race, color, gender, sexual orientation, religion, or disability.
1. I support bills that will be tough on those who discriminate people for housing, employment, health care, or safety.
2. I support domestic partnership.
3. I support hate crime bills.
4. I support welfare reform that not only encourages recipients to work, but also provides the tools necessary to make the transition from welfare to work, including job training, access to health care and childcare, and ensuring that jobs that pay decent wages are available.

Education

I believe that access to education will assure equal opportunities for success and that no one should be denied opportunities based on physical, emotional, or mental disability.
1. I believe that public education should be fairly and equitably funded to assure that our schools offer a variety of programs, and to assure that no groups are left behind.

2. I believe that schools and families should teach sensitivity to children, to promote understanding between diverse peoples.
3. I support initiatives to reduce violence in schools, and ensure that all children are able to learn in a safe and accepting environment.

Criminal Justice

I support programs that prevent recidivism through education and rehabilitation, including education and addiction programs for the incarcerated, and education and job training programs in the community.

1. Early intervention is an effective means of responding to juvenile crime and programs such as juvenile hearing boards; community and school based interventions. Day programming and foster treatment will help prevent such crimes.
2. I support community policing and crime watch programs, and expanding police presence in high crime areas.
3. I support a diverse police force that reflects the population of my district through out the city and the state of Rhode Island.
4. I support strong laws against domestic violence that include counseling, protection, and education to all. All crime victims should have access to assistance, including counseling programs.
5. I support strong child protection laws.
6. I support the development of community based treatment programs, including residential treatment, for non-violent juvenile offenders.
7. I support efforts to make my community a safe place to live, and drug free.

Environment

I support increased recycling through reduction of non-recyclable packaging, increased used of recycled materials, incentives for the private sector to invest in recycling technologies, and implementation of local curbside recycling programs.

1. I recognize the importance of protecting our natural resources and preserving open space.
2. I strongly support efforts to curtail urban sprawl and to develop responsible land use plans for our rural areas.
3. I support efforts to revitalize our community responsible without driving out anyone.

Medicare

1. I believe that we must make sure that Medicare remains an affordable health program for seniors.
2. I believe that the Medicare program must be fairly and adequately funded so that the program will remain comprehensive and affordable for future generations. This is important for all Rhode Islander, so that seniors can count on the program now, an others can count on the program in the future.

Campaign Staff and Key Personnel

Campaign Manager	**Melba Depeña**
Campaign Director	**Carlos Matos**
Finance Director	**Janet Pichardo**
Treasurer	**Vernon Brown**
Political Director	**Victor Capellan**
Campaign Strategist	**Tomás Alberto Ávila**

May 30, 2000

Contact: Melba Depeña
Phone: 401-941-2926

FOR IMMEDIATE RELEASE

Pichardo Announces Bid For State Senate

Providence — District 10 Committee is proud to report that Juan M. Pichardo will announce his candidacy for State Senate District 10, (communities of Elmwood, Reservoir Triangle and the West End). This event will take place on Thursday June 1, 2000 at 6:30pm in the parking lot of Superior Buffet Restaurant, located at 560 Elmwood Avenues (at the intersection of Reservoir Avenue and Elmwood Avenue),

"District 10 needs leadership in the State Senate and a strong voice that will bring the benefits of this booming economy and safeguard our communities against any future down turns", said Juan M. Pichardo. I am running for the office of State Senate so that all of District 10 will be represented. I am committed to moving forward together for a better future".

Juan M. Pichardo, has lived in Providence for 20 years. Juan has been in front of the issues, wether it is advocating for patient's rights, fighting to protect our children from the hazards of a toxic landfill, or assisting local business people to expand and grow their business, Juan has demonstrated the leadership that we need for District 10.

Juan's contributions are not limited to his community. He is a Traditional Guardsman with the 143rd Air Wing of the RI Air National Guard where he has served for 12 years and was recently honored with a community service award. Juan is a recognized leader. He is a member of Leadership Rhode Island, former president of the Elmwood Foundation, co-founder of the Washington Park Foundation and sits on numerous boards.

"There is a leadership vacuum in District 10, we need people in leadership positions that are not afraid to get in front of the issues".

A new Latino leadership paradigm

Tomás Alberto Ávila
The Providence Journal; Editorial
6.8.2000

THE LEADERSHIP STYLE shared by early Latino leaders in Rhode Island was one based on our traditional views of leaders as special people who set the direction, made the key decisions and energized the troops. These ideals were deeply rooted in an individualistic and non-systemic world view. These early leaders' prevailing leadership myths were still captured by the image of the captain of the cavalry leading the charge to rescue the settlers from the attacking Indians.

As long as such myths prevail, they reinforce a focus on short-term events and charismatic heroes rather than on systemic forces and collective learning. At the heart of the traditional view of leadership has been the assumption that the people are powerless and that only a few great leaders can remedy their lack of personal vision and inability to master the forces of change.

Because of this myth, the Latino community in Rhode Island has suffered from a lack of collaborating leadership that could work together toward a common agenda that benefits all Latinos regardless of place of origin.

As Providence Councilman Luis Aponte, D-Ward 10, so aptly put it during the 1996 elections: "Among the frequent mistakes Latino candidates have made over the years is concentrating on immigrants from their own country, instead of attempting to bridge differences." It's true, as he stated, that "candidates and campaigns tend to focus on that one community, and ignore the importance of all the other votes. You can't count on just one community to get elected."

Perhaps Hispanics are sometimes their own worst enemies when it comes to developing a unified movement.

Immigrants closely identify with their homelands -- the Dominican Republic, Puerto Rico, Guatemala, Mexico, Colombia and at least 15 other Latin-American countries -- making it difficult to agree on a single agenda. These myths were prevalent in the Latino leadership in the 1980s and '90s, during this community's emerging growth.

But since 1996, we have seen an evolution in the Latino leadership in Rhode Island that refuses to accept the old paradigm, and has instead accepted a new leadership of collaboration and co-existence. This new paradigm of inclusive leadership is producing changes in our community's sharing of power and agendas.

The heart of the new Latino leadership is based on the concept of belonging to a community and its common interests. No longer should techniques and positions be enough -- rather, it should be a broader reach for leadership possibilities and a true sense of belonging that win in the new paradigm.

Part of the challenge we need to overcome has been the recruitment of a broad base of people into places where they can exercise their leadership potential. The new leadership paradigm in our community shall reach out to everybody and call forth the leadership possibilities that exist in people from all circumstances and experiences, reminding them, and ourselves, that we all belong to one community and, therefore, we must share in its leadership.

We have to recognize and promote the idea that leadership is multidimensional in both application and participation. No longer is it desirable or even practical in our new paradigm to build leadership pyramids based on the hierarchical structures of traditional organizational charts. Rather, our practice should be to build flat leadership plazas or open, inviting and inclusive leadership that draws together a diverse citizenry.

This new concept of leadership has been promoted by some people in our community and can also be seen in some of our local organizations, such as the Rhode Island Latino Political Action Committee. These people and organizations have accepted the idea that leadership in its truest form is about collaborating, connecting and ultimately catalyzing actions focused on common interests.

We shall accept the reality of developing and building skills for inclusive leadership such as consensus building, collaboration, deliberation and strategy. We will know how to talk together, work together and act together.

Finally, this new paradigm of leadership is based on the principle that Latino communities and organizations must create working principles of process and action that not only allow but encourage opportunities for new leaders to participate in building and executing common priorities and common agendas.

We can become a united and thus a greater community, a community that values all of its citizens and leaders, one where communities and families are strong and prosperous, and where we can encourage and build on our rich diversity. We can be a more prosperous community, in which we bring together the enormous productive potential of all of our people. Our community can be a place where we all have an equal opportunity to contribute to our leadership and to our future -- to have a decent job, a good education, to be healthy, and to thrive through our enterprise and hard work.

We can become a community where every citizen can play a full and productive leadership role, and be positive and contributing voices in our community. It is our choice.

Tomas Alberto Avila, an immigrant from Honduras, is a policy analyst with the Center for Hispanic Policy and Advocacy in Providence.

Tomás Ávila, Advocate For Latinos

By Marion Davis
Journal Staff Writer
8.1.2000

PROVIDENCE -- Latinos have been an important part of Rhode Island society for more than a generation, but though they are becoming increasingly visible in business and in the schools, they have been slow to gain political power. Tomas A. Avila, 46, a policy analyst at CHisPA (the Center for Hispanic Policy and Advocacy), on Elmwood Avenue, is one of a core of Latino activists who are trying to change that. He was a co-founder of the Rhode Island Latino Political Action Committee and, in May, he worked to set up a monthly Latino Leadership Roundtable to promote networking and collaboration between Latinos in the state.

Born in the village of Trujillo, on the northern coast of Honduras, Avila moved to Boston with his mother and siblings in 1969, joining his father, a mechanic for the Coca Cola Co. who took a cleaning job here. After spending a year in an English immersion program, Avila completed his education in the Boston school system and earned a bachelor's degree in mechanical engineering from the Wentworth Institute of Technology, in Boston. He worked for General Electric for 15 years but lost his job to downsizing in 1992, then worked in the computer industry for two years. In 1994, he moved to Providence and took a job with Fleet Bank.

A year ago, when Victor Capellan became executive director of CHisPA, he asked Avila to join the staff.

Q: What do you do as policy analyst?

A: I look at government policies and bills that are submitted at the State House level and at the city level, analyze them, see what effect they're going to have on the Latino community, and then present them to the executive director and the board [of CHisPA] and they decide whether we're going to support them or oppose them. Then we build coalitions with other organizations to work on those policies.

Q: What kind of legislation do you look at?

A: It's very much the whole spectrum -- health care, economic development, everything that affects the Latino community and the community in general. A lot of the issues that we deal with, although we call them Latino issues, affect the general community. Health issues and health access, for example, is something everybody needs. The way we describe it, the only difference between the general community and the Latino community is the language barrier.

Q: How did you get involved in Latino community activism?

A: My heart has always been in the community. . . . I was very involved in the community in Boston, and when I moved here to Rhode Island, at first I wasn't very involved because, with the job I had at the time, I had to travel very much, so I didn't have a lot of contact with the community. In 1996, I made a conscious decision to get involved. Actually, it was through the Providence Journal that I found out about this leadership program for community leadership at CHisPA [and signed up].

Q: What did you get out of the leadership program?

A: What I was looking for, more than anything, was to get to know the community, to get involved, and . . . basically, it provided what I was looking for. I got to know the community, I got to know other leaders, and I got a firsthand look at the needs of the community.

One of the biggest things that it did was that, at that point, I realized that I had a lot of experience in the corporate world that the community was lacking. For example, my stronghold is organizational skills and planning. Through this program, I found that I could help the community by matching my experience to the community's needs, and that's how I started to get involved.

Q: How did you apply your corporate experience to your volunteer work?

A: One of the things I did was to document the things that were going on in the community. There was a lot of [talk] about issues in the community, but there were no concrete plans and no documentation as to those issues.

I started to document the community's needs and put together plans to address those needs.

Q: Can you give me an example?

A: The political empowerment of [Latinos] had been talked about for quite a while, and there had been many attempts to put something together to address that particular issue.

I got involved in a group that was putting together what today is the Rhode Island Latino Political Action Committee. There had been a lot of discussions in that regard, and there were a lot of ideas and very good planning, but there was a lack of execution. What I did was put those ideas together and prepare a plan to get the committee started.

Q: What has the committee done for Latinos?

A: I think the biggest impact the committee has made is getting the respect of the politicians toward the Latino community. One of the compelling issues that [Latinos] used to complain about was a lot of false promises from the politicians, and very much not taking them into account. They used to come to the Latino community only as an afterthought. Now, a lot of the elected officials look at the Latino community and consult with us prior to the issues becoming an explosive problem.

Q: Does the Latino community have strong leadership at this point?

A: The Latino community is twofold. Some of the Latinos who have been here for the longest -- such as Chicanos -- have matured as far as organization and political empowerment. On the other hand, we have a lot of new immigrants who started coming in the 1980s, and that's where we have the imbalance.

A lot of the people who came in the '80s have language barriers, a lot of them have immigration problems as far as being undocumented, and a lot of them came here running from persecution. Their involvement in the community and in leadership roles didn't really start taking off until, I'd say, the mid-'90s. What we're trying to do right now is trying to bring those people to participate in events and work and advocate for the Latino community.

Q: How far has Rhode Island's Latino community come?

A: I think we're in an evolution. Needless to say, we have had a lot of Latinos running for office, and a lot of people who have become citizens. One of the things I feel we've been lacking is, registering people hasn't been a problem, but getting them out to vote -- that has been an issue. With more Latinos running for office and the education of the community through leadership training and outreach, I'm starting to see people becoming more conscious that, after they register, they need to get out and vote. I'd say in the next four years, it's going to have an effect in Latinos getting elected to political offices and increasing Latino voter participation.

Q: Why have Latinos been so slow to become politically active?

A: Part of the problem that we realized was that most Latinos came here supposedly for two or three years, or to get enough money to build a house, and then they were going home.

Well, those two or three years turned into 20, 30, and in some cases even 40, and what happened was that they never became citizens, they never became homeowners, and they never really set roots in this country. These same people are now realizing that their children who were born here identify more with the United States than with their home countries, so something they had seen as temporary has become permanent. . . . As a result, they're becoming citizens, they're buying property.

Q: Does this also affect their community involvement?
A: Yes. Before, they always thought their responsibility was to their homelands. One of the things that amazes me is when you look at Latin American countries and see the biggest source of revenue besides the government is the money that is sent from here. A lot of people used to build their beautiful homes in their homelands, and here they lived in an apartment, and they never felt part of the neighborhood, they never felt part of the community. They felt, basically, 'I'm here until I get back home.' Now, they realize, 'This is my neighborhood. This is my community, so I have to become part of it.'

Q: Tell me about CHisPA's leadership program.

A: It started in January and went on for three months. Every Saturday from 9 a.m. to 2 p.m., we brought leaders from the community and elected officials to make presentations, and we taught them about the political process, community involvement, and how to access information and services that the community needs.

We had 24 people, from a high school student who wanted to get more involved to recent immigrants who want to know the system and also want to learn English, and people who just moved to Rhode Island and wanted to get connected with other people in the community, and we had some grandparents who now have time to dedicate to themselves and wanted to give something back.

Q: How do they apply what they learn with you?

A: Since January, I've seen three of the participants who have moved on to better jobs, and others have started to get involved in the community. This morning, we had a Latino Roundtable breakfast, and three people from this group attended. These are people who, prior to this, were not actively involved in the community and the leadership network. There are also people who have decided to go back to school to pursue a career, or get their credits from their country certified here. They're becoming empowered to make changes in their lives, and they also feel they need to give something back to the community.

We see it everyday -- people who are working outside their fields. In one group I participate in, we have architects, engineers, doctors working in factories because of the language barrier and, in some cases, because they need to get their certification. The highest poverty in this country is among Latinos, and a lot of them are professionals and could pull themselves out of it. By getting them back to their professions, we improve their economic standards, we empower the Latino community by raising the living standard. At the same time, they will be able to give more to the community.

Q: Does it also help Latinos to deal with mainstream America?
A: Definitely. One of the things in this country is that you can have all the knowledge that you want, but if you're not in a professional career, socially you're seen differently.

And the reaction of the general community toward these people is negative. But it's quite interesting that switching to becoming professionals and holding down careers, the outlook of the general community changes.
All of a sudden, it's like, 'You're at my level,' and we can deal on a one-to-one basis.'

Numbers Alter Political Landscape

The Census will be used to draw new General Assembly districts to reflect population changes. The numbers are also used to determine state and federal aid under an array of economic and social programs.

By Scott MacKay
Journal Staff Writer
3.30.2001

PROVIDENCE -- Political power in Rhode Island is shifting back to its Democratic roots in the ethnic neighborhoods of Providence and to the Atlantic coastal communities more familiar to generations of Rhode Islanders as beach destinations than polling precincts.

The surnames today may be Pichardo or Aponte rather than Roberts or Pastore, but the Providence neighborhoods that made the Democratic Party dominant in state politics from the New Deal to the end of the 20th century are on the upswing in the first decade of the 21st.

For political figures of all stripes, the surprising news from yesterday's release of U.S. Census numbers was the 8-percent increase in Providence's population, meaning the city grew almost twice as fast as the state as a whole.

As he gestured from his City Hall window toward the State House, an exultant Mayor Vincent A. Cianci Jr. said, "This is going to mean something else to our friends in the legislature. We're not going to lose seats as some had predicted."

"Our population increase is larger than most cities and towns in Rhode Island," said Cianci, who often complains that his city is shortchanged when money gets passed around at the Assembly. "The legislature will take note of that now."

The figures are important because they are used to draw new General Assembly districts to reflect population changes. The numbers are also used to determine state and federal aid under an array of economic and social programs. For example, Cianci said Providence receives about $4,000 in federal aid for each person counted in the Census.

THIS YEAR, the Census results will be more closely watched than at any time in the past century in Rhode Island because they will be used as a guide in cutting the Assembly by 25 percent -- 25 House seats and 12 Senate seats must be chopped out before next year's elections.

The Census figures are also used to reapportion the state's two U.S. House Districts. The 2nd District, anchored by Warwick, Cranston and southern and western parts of the state, is held by Democrat James Langevin. It has grown faster in population than the 1st District, anchored by the Blackstone Valley and the east side of Narragansett Bay, which is held by fellow Democrat Patrick Kennedy. That means that Kennedy must take over about 14,000 of Langevin's constituents to make the districts equal, as required by the U.S. Constitution.

Kennedy said in an interview yesterday that he would like to take from the 2nd District Block Island and the Providence neighborhoods of Elmhurst and Mount Pleasant, near Providence College, his alma mater. Kennedy represented those neighborhoods as a state representative, from 1989 to 1995.

"I'd love to be able to represent my old state representative district," said Kennedy. "Those people gave me my start and I'd love to have the opportunity to deliver for them."

Langevin declined to state a preference for which constituents he would be willing to give up, but said he expects that he and Kennedy will be able to negotiate an amicable agreement that would be acceptable to the Assembly, which makes the final decision.

THE JUMP in Providence's population was fueled mostly by Hispanics, who are just beginning to make their presence felt in politics. If they vote in proportion to their growing numbers, they will be a powerful presence in the city's future.

In fact, without Hispanics there was scant growth in Rhode Island in the last 10 years, so both parties will be vying for their votes in the future.

In the short term, the flexing of Hispanic political muscle may push some black political figures to the sidelines. This is the case because their populations are concentrated in some of the same neighborhoods on Providence's South Side.

"I think it means some growing pains in the urban centers, where folks will be competing for political power," says Councilman Luis A. Aponte, who in 1998 became the first Latino elected to Providence's City Council. "And it sort of reinforces that legislative downsizing could not have come at a worse time."

And while Providence surged, Warwick and Pawtucket barely grew at all, and Woonsocket, East Providence and Newport lost population. Those figures will become important to individual representatives and senators, whose political futures will be at stake when new districts are drawn. The Assembly's most powerful leaders are all from communities that were either stagnant or lost population -- House Speaker John Harwood (Pawtucket); Senate Majority Leader William Irons (East Providence); and House Majority Leader Gerard Martineau (Woonsocket).

"There is going to be a lot of infighting at the State House, a lot of battles behind the scenes before this is all over," says political science Prof. Maureen Moakley, of the University of Rhode Island. "It is going to make for an interesting election."

REPUBLICANS see an opening in the growth in South County, especially in such fast-growing communities as South Kingstown, North Kingstown, Charlestown, Exeter, Hopkinton and Richmond. And the GOP believes it may also be helped by the greater representation that population figures show must be given to some communities in northern Rhode Island, such as Lincoln, home of Governor Almond, Smithfield and Cumberland.

"This is a big opportunity for us," said House Minority Leader Robert Watson, R-East Greenwich. Watson said he hopes to work with some minority community groups to ensure that redistricting -- always among the most blatantly political action any legislature takes -- is fair.

"The fact is the Democrats control the candy store and the Republicans and the minority community are looking in the store window," said Watson. "We can work together on this issue."

Democrats took issue with Watson, saying the growing communities of southern and western Rhode Island are no longer solidly Republican.

"The Census numbers don't dictate which party is going to pick up seats," says William Lynch, state Democratic chairman. "We have a lot of good Democrats who have moved from urban communities in the northern part of the state to communities in South County."
"When this is all over, Democrats will still hold significant majorities in the House and Senate," Lynch said.

Martineau said the Republicans "may well" pick up seats, but it won't be due to any party advantage. Rhode Island voters pay scant attention to party labels anymore, and the success of the two parties will rest on how successful they are in recruiting good candidates willing to mount vigorous campaigns.

Martineau noted that Republicans now control traditionally Democratic Woonsocket's City Council. "In local races these days, the parties mean much less than the personality of your candidate and that candidate's work ethic," he said.

Election Reform Commission Recommendations

Tomás Alberto Ávila
Rhode Island Latino Political Action Committee
June 18th, 2001

Introduction

It has been decades since control of both the White House and Capitol Hill was so furiously contested. The presidential polls were close right up to Election Day, producing the most competitive race in a generation. Yet once again more than 100 million American adults abstained from the November 2000 elections[3]. This majority was disproportionately young, poor, less educated, and of color. Their absence provides the clearest evidence that we are becoming a post-electoral democracy: one where many civil institutions are strong and most rights reasonably well-protected, but where the elections at democracy's core are unobserved and their potential to mobilize, inform, and transform are deeply unrealized.

It doesn't have to be this way. In fact, most established democracies already provide their voters with better and more viable choices. In presidential elections, they have runoff elections that allow a sincere first choice rather than one for the "lesser of two evils." To elect legislatures, they use proportional representation systems that make every voter important, not just those fortunate few living in the handful of districts that are competitive in our system. Voters can cast meaningful choices not only between the major parties, but also within those parties and among smaller parties to the left, right, and center.

Reforms of the fundamental electoral rules can sometimes seem of secondary importance in the face of pressing issues and a laundry list of worthwhile but still-distant goals. But it may turn out that meaningful electoral reform is easier to achieve than fundamental policy changes. In fact, a closer examination reveals that only fundamental reform of our voting practices will liberate supporters of these goals to express themselves at the ballot box. Real support for these policies exist, but in our current system their proponents are virtually and sometime actually excluded from political debate and representation. With growing support among constituency

---

[3]   Reclaiming Democracy in the 21st Century: Instant Runoffs, Proportional Representation, and Cumulative Voting

organizations, voting system reform should be the cornerstone of the necessary movement to restore electoral democracy. Its value becomes obvious through imagining its impact on upcoming elections.

Comprehensive ballot reform is as much about political accountability as it is about improving the mechanics of voting. For too long, local governments have been left to conduct elections with insufficient resources and guidance. Florida was not the only place where confusion reigned. In jurisdictions around the South of Providence, unreliable poll workers, errors by ill-informed voters, inaccurate voter registration rolls, staffing problems at polling places contributed to the tangled and chaotic voting process.

Reliable and relatively trouble-free optical-scanner machines have decided Rhode Island's elections. So there can be no Florida-style debate about chads be they hanging, pregnant or dimpled. But state Board of Elections Chairman Roger Begin called for a task force to study the state's election laws in light of the U.S. Supreme Court's ruling on Florida election standards.

What follows are some recommendation to the commission, based on our experience working in many elections in the Latino community during the last six years.

Recommendations

Determining Voter Intent

Rhode Island presently has no uniform standard for determining voter intent on its optical-scan ballots. In most jurisdictions around the country, such questions have been left up to the discretion of local boards of canvassers and the Board of Elections. To avoid any legal challenges and potential lawsuits based on a lack of uniformity in this standard; the commission should make recommendations to the Board of Election for a uniform process in future elections. This uniform standards, shall comply with Supreme Court precedents set during the 2000 Presidential Election decision. To ensure uniformity of the law across city lines, the Secretary of State shall provide election officials with memoranda outlining the statewide guidelines of the uniform standard for determining voter intent that arise during the conduct of an election.

Bilingual Voting Material Requirement

Begin the process of complying with the Federal Voting Rights Act 1973aa(b) Bilingual voting material requirement before August 6, 2007. According to such requirement, states are to provide voting materials in another language when the census demonstrate that more than 5% of the citizens of voting age of such sates are members of a single language minority and are limited English proficient. Based on this law, the commission shall recommend the state begin the process of providing Spanish material in the following cities: Central Falls 47%, Pawtucket 13.9% and Providence 30%.

Spanish-speaking voters received no bilingual assistance at many of the polling sites in the South Providence community. In most precincts, the entire election staff spoke English only, and could not assist language minority voters.

Maintaining up-to-date lists of registered voters

The Secretary's highest priority should be to exercise authorization granted the Secretary of State under election law chapter § 6 17-6-1encouraging and assisting cities that have not yet done so to develop statewide electronic voter registration databases, linked to local registration offices, polling locations, and public agencies involved in the implementation of the National Voter Registration Act (e.g. departments of motor vehicles, public assistance offices, and the U.S. postal service).

Registration rolls are a mess in many cities and towns, with error rates as high as 25 percent or more. Listings for registrants who move out of the jurisdiction, die, or become ineligible for some other reason are often not removed in a timely fashion. This increases the risk of fraud. On the other hand, as we saw in Florida in 2000, efforts to purge the rolls of ineligible voters can lead to the erroneous removal of qualified citizens. Long lines and confusion at polling places and disenfranchised voters are the result.

Information-age technology, especially when combined with a unique voter identification number, can make a huge difference in facilitating new voter registrations, keeping registration rolls accurate, reducing election fraud, assisting election officials at polling places, and helping eligible citizens avoid being turned away from the polls on election day. Computerized state voter registration systems also have the virtue of making it easier to move the registration deadline closer to Election Day.

Voter File Security and Maintenance

Require board of canvassers to complete mandatory voter file maintenance procedures such as: obtaining address updates through the US Post Office, comparing undeliverable mail to the voter rolls, mailing to voters who have not voted in two federal elections, and working with jury commissioners to remove the names from the voter rolls of individuals who declined to serve on jury duty. Advise the board of elections to require the correction of voting lists by all local board as mandated by the RI Election Laws paragraph § 17-7-5 Powers and duties – Quorum, section 3 by the 2002 election season. Experience in the city's minority community, has shown the list provided by the local boards to challenging candidates are riddle with errors and usually are not provided in a timely manner.

Establishment of Central Voter Register

Established a Central Voter Register of all 39 communities' Voter registration that allows election officials to check for and remove duplicate voter registrations across community lines. California's CALVOTER Network can serve as an example to follow. Rhode Island Election Laws section § 17-6-1.1 Central voters register already grants authority to the Secretary of State for this purpose. This will do away with the fraudulent voting participation of individuals that no longer live in Providence but exercise their voting during election season to help keep their friend and relatives elected.

Every time Latino candidates ask for a list of voters at the Board of Canvassers to send them their political information, our experience has shown that they always get about 25 percent back as undeliverable. Many candidates have experienced that such outdate list system is used for fraudulent voting when a person that don't live in there particular district keep coming back to vote against them during the elections.

Furthermore no person shall be permitted to vote in any election precinct or district other than the one in which the person has his or her legal residence and in which the person is registered. There are many districts in the City of Providence, that use to be populated by previous immigrants to this nation, who have chosen to moved to the suburbs but retain their voting privilege active by utilizing fraudulent voting activities, by using old addresses or family addresses that remain in the voters list, to vote in Providence. This fraudulent process of voting has kept many incumbents that no longer reflect the diversity of the neighborhoods in power while defeating challengers from the communities. The commission shall advise the Board of Elections and elected officials to accept the reality that this wonderful country of ours and the state of Rhode Island are being transformed to Latino enclaves as has been proven by the recently released Census 2000.

Electoral process

Enforcement and implementation of electoral process education throughout the state consisting of instruction on how a person may become a candidate for electoral office and how a person registers and votes for candidates for electoral office as mandated by RI Election Law § 17-6-13 Electoral process education

Ensuring the integrity of absentee ballots

Experience in different campaigns in the Latino community has shown us that there is a thin line between making it relatively easy for people to vote absentee so as not to disenfranchise them and guarding against fraud. We recommend on a restriction Campaigns' Role in the Collection of Completed Applications for Absentee Ballots: In recent years, campaigns have collected completed absentee ballot applications from voters and forwarded those applications to election officials. Because of the delays this causes in the delivery of ballots to voters, applications should be sent directly to the election official from the voter.

Motor Voter Reforms

Work with election officials and the Department of Motor Vehicles to improve the procedures used to process registration forms collected at the DMV. Reforms shall include a revision of the DMV registration form, use of digitized signatures to automate the registration process.

Legislative intent

Submitting recommendations to the Governor, to strive to select a board of elections whose membership shall be representative of all citizens of the state and of their diverse points of view._As intended by the general assembly through RI Election Laws § 17-7-1 Legislative intent

Many of the irregularities brought up at many of the commission hearing across the state, were experienced by many of the minority candidates in the Southside of Providence and although they were brought to the board's attention, the board rejected challenges to the primary results, saying that the alleged irregularities weren't significant enough to change the outcome. Needless to say the board's actions infuriated members of the South Providence political establishment, but even more, the Latino candidates whose aggressive efforts drew hundreds of new voters to the polls, making every primary a hot contest.

The attitude shown by the board of elections to the minority community and the Latino community in particular, has been one of disenfranchisement and inattention to the issues raised by such community, as has been witnessed in the election of the mid 90's. The board acts as an arm of the democratic party delivering decisions to protect the incumbent elected officials, rather than enforcing the elections laws, amounting to patronizing of their favorite candidates and the protection of their jobs. The political apparatus over the

236

years has managed to infiltrate the board with members of their political circle and close the doors to any group that looks different than their members.

Voter Education

No aspect of the electoral process in the state suffers from greater under-investment than preparing citizens to cast their ballot. Mistakes made by voters account for a substantial portion of spoiled ballots and other errors on Election Day.

Every level of government—national, state and local—has a clear interest in developing and financing programs that educate citizens about their rights and responsibilities as voters. Registration instructions and confirmations, polling place locations and hours of operation, sample ballots, voter guides, and voting equipment demonstrations should all be provided to citizens on a timely basis. Civic, educational, political and media organizations should do more to educate citizens on the nuts and bolts of voting. Poll workers should be trained to assist voters, provide provisional ballots when registration status cannot be confirmed, and permit voters who spoil their ballot to receive a replacement. By increasing knowledge about when, where, and how to vote, these educational efforts might have the fortunate side effect of engaging more citizens in the democratic process.

Poll Workers

Although several citizens have testified of election irregularities by the immigrant community, such individuals have made claims about the Latino community in particular and gone so far as to request the commission to require poll workers to require voters to show proof of citizenship. Shall we consider requiring a BCI check to make sure voters don't have a criminal record also?

Based on our experience what these individuals have failed to mention is that due to the enduring power and control of District Committees by incumbents, poll workers and supervisors are usually drawn from the ranks of the established party network. Since the incumbents control these individuals, they in turn are there to protect the incumbent's interest rather than serve and help new immigrant voters. Such individuals are so engrained in their loyalty to the party and the incumbents, that any inability to communicate with Latino voters due to language problems, are reported as suspicious or illegal rather than doing their civil duty of helping such voters.

Many of the accusations levied against the Latino community in particular in the Southside of Providence have been done by individuals who refuse to accept the reality that demographics in that area have changed. Refusing to accept such reality individuals have resorted to try and influence the electoral process to secure their incumbency by making it more difficult for Latino voters.

Voting Procedures

These recommendations for upgrading registration lists and voting personnel are based on the premise of Election Day voting in hundreds of polling places across the state. Yet increasingly, this model of a community-based election day experience is being replaced by remote voting over an extended period of time. Oregon now conducts its elections entirely by mail. The state of Washington, with its liberal policy on absentee voting, may not be far behind. Many states have seen a dramatic growth in the percentage of absentee ballots cast, as parties and candidates to turn out their supporters in advance of Election Day quickly exploit liberalized laws. Early voting at polling places is also now permitted in a number of states and localities.

Voter Registration Advisory Board

Reviewing present voter registration advisory board established by § 17-9.1-31 Voter registration advisory board, to assist in the drafting of regulations and the monitoring of implementation of the National Voter Registration Act of 1993, 42 U.S.C. § 1973gg et seq., and to help recruit and train the volunteer registrars. I am of the opinion that this board shall be reorganized to truly reflect the demographic composition of the state population, as well as to insure that it's carrying the duties it was created to address.

Technology Consideration

Emerging technologies are revolutionizing political communication. Cable television, direct broadcast satellites, electronic mail, and the Internet are creating powerful new links between citizens and politicians, offering voters access to vast amounts of information, a diversity of perspectives, and new forums for sharing ideas. Although these technologies are still in their formative stages, they are already redefining traditional forms of political activity and transforming the character of political dialogue. Indeed, digital technology may ultimately have a greater effect on the American political system than radio and television did earlier in this century. And what we are now witnessing is only the beginning.

Electronic Voting

As digital technology continues to develop, there is no reason why citizens will not be able to register to vote electronically or even be registered automatically based on driver's license information or other official government records. We are already moving in this direction, as evidenced by the adoption of the motor voter law and the movement towards same-day voter registration, or the recent experiments in Oregon and a number of local communities with mail balloting. But even these path breaking reforms, which are designed to remove registration as an obstacle to voting and encourage higher participation, seem cumbersome when compared to the changes on the horizon.

Preparing for an Electronic Democracy

Because there is no guarantee that new technologies will promote the type of widespread, more informed participation that advocates expect, policymakers should proceed with caution in their efforts to promote electronic democracy. While the technology offers exciting prospects for direct voter participation in on-line initiatives and referendums, conference participants were careful to note that there are a number of concerns that must be addressed before these processes are established as part of our system of governance.

First, existing procedures for popular initiatives and referendums include a wide range of traditional safeguards that are designed to ensure that these processes are not abused and that any Initiative or referendum placed on the ballot enjoys support from a substantial share of the electorate. For example, petitioning procedures specify the number of valid signatures from registered voters needed to qualify an initiative for ballot; establish criteria for the geographical or jurisdictional distribution of signatures to ensure broad support; outline specific procedures to ensure due process; and, in some cases, limit the types of issues that can be determined in this manner.

Consider Relationship with Democracy Compact

The Democracy Compact is a non-partisan education and outreach campaign. The Compact's mission is to strengthen our democracy by making Rhode Island the most voting state in the nation. The compact, a volunteer, nonpartisan group established last year to increase voting, is starting anew to recruit volunteers, push voter-education programs in schools and lobby state officials to make voting more accessible. During the 2000 elections the Providence Board of Canvassers did not have a sufficient number of poll workers to efficiently process the Election Day voters at the Civic Center, the Democracy Compact helped by sending about 100 volunteers.

The compact recruited about 2,000 volunteers and in last year's general election used those volunteers to generate about 20,000 new voters more than in 1996, which was also a presidential election year.

Voter turnout increased in Rhode Island by almost 6 percentage points. Increases among young voters -- a group that the compact took special pains to reach -- were striking with a 41-percent increase over 1996 in voters ages 18 to 29.

Rhode Island moved from 24th among U.S. states in turnout to 14th, with a voter participation rate of about 55 percent. Voter participation is sometimes fueled by down-to-the-wire elections, but the state did not have close statewide races last year -- the U.S. Senate election and both U.S. House contests were blowouts.

Instant Runoff Voting

IRV simulates a series of runoff elections, but in a single round of voting that corrects the flaws of plurality voting–the spoiler problem and lack of majority rule–and runoff elections–having to pay for two elections. At the polls, people vote for their favorite candidate, but they also indicate on the same ballot their second, "runoff" choice and subsequent choices. If a candidate receives a majority of first choices, the election is over. If not, the candidate with the fewest votes is eliminated, and a runoff round of counting occurs. In this round, your ballot counts for your top-ranked candidate still in the race. The eliminated candidate is no longer a "spoiler" because the votes of that candidate's supporters go to their runoff choices. Rounds of counting continue until there is a majority winner. It's like doing a runoff election, but you do it all with one vote.

Conclusion

Census 2000 results released by the Census Bureau showed that efforts in the minority community were successful, by showing a racially diverse America. The Census Bureau also reported that Hispanics, who may be of any race, totaled 92,820, or about 9 percent of the total population.

The state's white, non-Hispanic population remained the largest single group with 891,191 people, roughly 91.1 percent. But that population grew more slowly than other groups and claims a smaller share of the overall population than it did in 1990.

The new information might erode some of the power of the traditional minority/majority categories. It will bring reexamination of many public policy & private sector. Policy makers and private industry have to understand that American culture and the state of Rhode island culture has ceased to be static, while still, most ethnic officials in decision making positions assume a static mainstream culture.

The acculturation models of the nation are reversing. Evidence of this dramatic change we're going through it's the fact that it's no longer necessary for immigrants to learn English to function and thrive in this society. The assumptions applied to diversity in the past were that the values of mainstream culture were superior to those of ethnic people, or even that ethnic values were corrupters of mainstream values.

Policy makers need to look at diversity as more than just language differences. They will have to conduct policy making in terms of what really matters to individuals, rather that what they perceive what they feel individuals should receive. Organizations and Policy makers that find it difficult to sensitize to cultural values and nuances will change their attitudes about the realities reflected in the census results, when other ethnic groups are allowed the opportunity to contribute interpreting what multiculturalism means. This document represents a first step by the Latino community towards this change.

As has been proven by the census numbers, the state urban demographic mix is rapidly changing. Our country, once dominated by Europeans, is fast becoming one where Europeans are in the minority. The influx of Hispanics from Puerto Rico, Mexico, and South and Central America; blacks from the Caribbean and Africa; and Asians from Vietnam, Korea, and China is causing the U.S. to move in a new direction demographically.

The reality in our district is that we need elected officials who will fight to bring resources to our neighborhoods. We can no longer live isolated in a system where only a few reap the benefits of the economic booms in our state and country because individuals that no longer represent our community interest try to squash challengers by trying to limit voter participation. This must stop and our current

We like to conclude with one President John F. Kennedy's quote, "Change is the law of life, and those who look only to the past or present are certain to miss the future."

We look forward to this commission and Rhode Island elected officials seeing the Latino community as what It's "the future" of this state and the nation. Let's look at the electoral process with an open mind and futuristic vision, rather than try to stay in the past and protect the present.

References

Barmann Timothy C. (2000, October 25) Latino voters win praise of Hispanic candidates: At least one primary race was decided by Latino voters, with voter turnout in some Hispanic neighborhoods doubling the state turnout, The providence journal, Providence RI

Bakst Charles M., (2000, June 8) State Senate seat: In changing district a new uncertainty: The only constant in politics is surprise, The Providence Journal

Bakst Charles M., (1999, November 28) Coming a long way, Angel Taveras now aims for Congress The Providence Journal,

Capellán Victor Campaign Announcement Speech, Providence, RI April 17, 1998

Corkery Michael, (2000, October 25) Latinos celebrate successes at polls: The Rhode Island Latino Political Action Committee throws a party to honor candidates who won, or nearly won, primary races this past September, The providence journal, Providence RI

Corrado Anthony, Firestone Charles M. (1996) Elections In Cyberspace: Toward A New Era In American Politics, A Report of The Aspen Institute Communications and Society Program and The American Bar Association Standing Committee on Election Law, Washington, DC

Davis Marion, (2000, September 19) Board rebuffs election challenges: Several campaign hopefuls in South Providence react with dismay, The Providence Journal, Providence RI

Davis Marion, (2000, September 14) Latino vote influences primary races in Providence: Leon F. Tejada, who snatched the Democratic nomination in District 18 from incumbent Marsha E. Carpenter, attributes his win to a heavy Latino voter turnout, The providence journal, Providence RI

Democracy Compact, (2000, September) Putting Leadership To Work For Our Democracy

Gearan Anne, (2000, December 17) Election Precedents Set By Court Associated Press Writer, Washington, DC

MacKay Scott (2000, April 29) Ex-City Year chief launches campaign to boost voting, The Providence Journal, Providence, RI
MacKay Scott (2001, May 19) Democracy Compact rallies to raise voter turnout: The state sees its voter count rise by 6 percentage points in the last election cycle following the volunteer group's first campaign to increase voting. The Providence Journal, Providence, RI

Pichardo Juan M, (2000, May) Campaign Announcement Speech, Providence, RI

Pina Tatiana (1998, May 5) Paolino apologizes for offense to immigrants: Joseph Paolino Jr. says he never meant to insult or demean the immigrant community by his stands during a political campaign two years ago. The providence journal, Providence RI

Richie Rob, Hill Steven, and Kleppner, Caleb (2001, March) Reclaiming Democracy in the 21st Century: Instant Runoffs, Proportional Representation, and Cumulative Voting, Social Policy Magazine, Washington, DC

Rowland Christopher (2000, December 15) Elections chairman calls for study of R.I. voting laws: The mayoral race in Johnston could have ended up in court because Rhode Island lacks a uniform standard for determining voter intent on its ballots, one of the flaws cited in Florida, The Providence Journal Providence RI

Rhode Island State Constitution website [Online] http://www.rilin.state.ri.us/gen_assembly/RiConstitution/riconst.html

Rhode Island State General Assembly [Online] http://www.rilin.state.ri.us/gen_assembly

Sabar Ariel (2000, September 14) Latino power shows at polls: "It's electoral participation catching up to the shift in the demographics," says Providence Councilman Luis A. Aponte, The Providence Journal Providence RI

Sachs Susan (2001, April 8) Give Me Your Tired, Your Poor, Your Vote, The New York Times, NYC
Secretary of State Bill Jones' 10-Point California Election Reform Plan, [Online] The Calvoter Project, California Secretary of State Bill Jones, http://www.ss.ca.gov/elections/elections_q.htm

Seelye Katharine Q. (2001, February 5) Panel Suggests Election Changes That Let States Keep Control, The New York Times, NYC

State of Rhode Island General Laws [Online] http://www.rilin.state.ri.us/Statutes/Statutes.html

Tenner Edward (2001, February 5) The Perils of High-Tech Voting, The New York Times, NYC

Taveras, Angel (1999, November 15) Campaign Announcement Speech, Providence, RI

The Center for Voting and Democracy [Online] http://www.fairvote.org/

U.S. Department of Justice Civil Rights Division Voting Section Title 42 - The Public Health And Welfare Chapter 20 - Elective Franchise website http://www.usdoj.gov/crt/voting/42usc/subch_ib.htm

Group's Goal Is To Elect First Latino To City Council

In addition, a nonpartisan Latino political action committee plans voter registration drives and transportation to and from polls in November.

By Tatiana Pina
Journal Staff Writer
6.6.2001

CENTRAL FALLS -- With a city population that is nearly half Latino, a statewide political action committee is making it its business to try getting a Latino elected to the City Council for the first time in November.

The Rhode Island Latino Political Action Committee is putting its full support behind Ricardo Patino, 43, an activist who lost to Rose Marie Canavan in his bid for the City Council's 3rd Ward seat.

But the committee's members aren't stopping there. The group is trying to recruit other candidates to run for the City Council, according to Dr. Pablo Rodriguez, RILPAC president.

Central Falls will hold an election for mayor and City Council in November. Political hopefuls have from Aug. 8 until Sept. 7 to declare their candidacies.

The nonpartisan political action organization is also planning registration drives during summer festivals to increase the number of voters, Rodriguez said. And the committee also plans to provide voters with rides to and from the polls.

The Central Falls elections will be closely watched by politicians elsewhere in the state, where there are large concentrations of Hispanic voters, says Tomas Avila, RILPAC treasurer.

"We have become aware that everyone is going to be looking. They know that the biggest concentration of Latinos in one area [of the state] is in Central Falls," he said.
"It presents a great opportunity for the Latino community," Avila said.
Consider the numbers, Avila says. According to the U.S. Census, 9,041 of the 18,928 people who live in Central Falls are Latinos.

In the city, 6,545 residents are registered to vote, according to City Registrar Gertrude Chartier. Chartier estimates that of the registered voters, 20 percent to 25 percent are Latino. But Patino estimates that the number of Latino residents registered to vote is about 35 percent. Despite the population figures, no Latino has ever been elected to the City Council.

Patino says he is running because he wants to have a say in what happens in city government and because he wants to encourage other people from ethnic groups to get involved in the political process.

"People have to understand the power that their vote has. [Latinos] are half the population of Central Falls. Once people see that others run and make it, they will get interested in running," he says. "This is a right we all have." A lead-abatement educator for Rhode Island Housing and Mortage Finance Corporation, Patino said that he is in favor of promoting owner-occupied housing in the city as well as bringing more businesses to the city.

RILPAC's efforts must be coupled with the efforts of Hispanic radio stations, Patino says. The stations led a get-out-the-vote drive during the 2000 elections, when a handful of Latinos ran for positions in the state legislature and for the U.S. House of Representatives. For weeks, Spanish-language radio stations informed the public about who the candidates were and continuously reminded listeners to vote. During the 2000 Primary, the voter turnout in Providence's Hispanic neighborhoods was as high as 38 percent in districts with tightly contested races, more than doubling the statewide turnout of 15 percent.

At least in one of the races, that of Leon Tejada, the outcome was decided by Latino voters. Tejada defeated three-term state Rep. Marsha Carpenter by 89 votes in House District 18, and went on to defeat Ian O'Hara in the November election.

Gonzalo Cuervo, a political newcomer, lost his bid to unseat fellow Democrat Rep. Joseph Almeida in House District 20 by only 26 votes. And Angel Taveras drew one in three votes in Providence in the 2nd Congressional District race.

Latino Voting Session Focuses On Redistricting

Fred Kuhr
The Pawtucket Times
May 14, 2001

PROVIDENCE -- According to the 2000 U.S. Census, the Latino population in Rhode Island almost doubled over the last decade.

But who is going to make sure that Latinos will be represented accordingly in the state legislature and Congress after the upcoming redistricting and legislative downsizing?

With that question in mind, staff members from the New York City-based Puerto Rican Legal Defense and Education Fund (PRLDEF) came to Providence this past weekend to help form the Statewide Latino Voting Rights Committee of Rhode Island.

The establishment of this committee was just one part of the Latino Voting Rights Conference of Rhode Island, held on Saturday at the Center for Hispanic Policy & Advocacy (CHisPA) on Elmwood Avenue in Providence.

The PRLDEF has already facilitated such conferences and established similar committees in Massachusetts, Connecticut, New Jersey, Delaware, Pennsylvania and Florida.

Local activists praised the idea of crafting a committee that would help to ensure better political representation of the state's Latino community.

"Part of our mission here at CHisPA is to look at this issue strategically," CHisPA Executive Director Luisa Murillo said. "€If we can ensure that the [district] lines are drawn to better represent our community in the legislature, that benefits CHisPA and our entire community."

Noting that the conference brought out a very multicultural crowd, Tomas Avila, treasurer of the Rhode Island Latino Political Action Committee, said, "We may call it the Latino Voting Rights Project, but redistricting doesn't know race or ethnicity. It affects everyone."

Redistricting is the process by which lawmakers redraw district lines for seats in the state Senate, state House, and U.S. Congress. The process, which takes place every 10 years, is based upon new population data garnered from the U.S. Census.

This year, the General Assembly has also been given the charge to downsize itself, further complicating the redistricting process. Angelo Falcon, PRLDEF's senior policy executive, impressed upon those in attendance that redistricting is not merely a political issue, but also a civil rights issue.

While Falcon noted that redistricting is an exercise in "€community empowerment,"€ he cautioned that it is not a cure-all. "We must also vote, field candidates for office, and raise money," he said.
Part of the new emphasis on increasing the Latino presence in different levels of representative government comes from Census numbers showing tremendous growth in the Latino population.

From 1990-2000, the Latino population grew 57.9 percent nationally and 98.5 percent in Rhode Island. Latinos now account for 8.6 percent of the state's population.

Central Falls has the heaviest concentration of Latinos in the state, with 47.8 percent of the city's population identifying as Latino. Providence is second with 30 percent. Pawtucket is third at 13.9 percent.

"Part of our problem used to be that we were invisible," said Falcon. "Now with Ricky Martin and salsa, I guess we're visible," he joked.

State Sen. Robert Kells, a Providence Democrat, represents the most Latino Senate district, with 49.7 percent of the district's residents identifying as Latino. State Rep. Anastasia Williams, another Providence Democrat, represents the most Latino House district, with 55.7 percent of the district identifying as Latino.

The problem for some activists, however, is that a number of the most highly Latino districts are not represented by Latinos. In many cases, this is because the districts include many non-Latino neighborhoods in neighboring cities like Cranston and Johnston which have very little in common with the Latino precincts.

This is where redistricting has civil rights implications, explained Falcon.

Even on the congressional level, Latinos can play a pivotal role in redistricting, he said. In District 1, which includes Pawtucket, Central Falls and the rest of the Blackstone Valley and is represented by Patrick Kennedy, the Latino population amounts to 7 percent. In District 2, represented by James Langevin, Latinos account for 10.2 percent of the population.

Due to population shifts, District 1 must give up 2.6 percent of its population to District 2. Falcon explained that since the line separating the state's two congressional districts cuts right through heavily Latino neighborhoods in Providence and other communities, where the line gets moved could have a significant impact on how Latinos are represented in Congress.

For more information, call the Puerto Rican Legal Defense and Education Fund at 212-739-7501 or 800-328-2322, ext. 9+7501, or call the Center for Hispanic Policy and Advocacy at 467-0111.

©The Pawtucket Times 2001

The Challenge Of Being Angel Taveras

It's a good time to be Angel Taveras

M. Charles Bakst
5.13.2001

Credited with an impressive, though unsuccessful 2000 Democratic primary bid for Congress, this 30-year-old lawyer, a son of Dominican immigrants, has landed a seat on a commission that is to oversee the General Assembly's 2002 redistricting and downsizing. With Buddy Cianci under indictment, Taveras also is being eyed as a potential candidate for Providence mayor, either in next year's regular election or in a special election before then. Or maybe lieutenant governor if incumbent Charlie Fogarty tries for governor in 2002.

Taveras says, "I've always felt like it was a good time to be Angel Taveras." Especially now. "I'm young. I'm learning. I have an opportunity to help people. I'm developing as a lawyer. I'm developing in politics."

Honors fall his way.

Chief Justice Frank Williams has asked him to serve on the Supreme Court disciplinary board. "I've got other plans for him, too," enthuses Williams. He wants to involve Taveras in such court efforts as outreach in the minority community.

Taveras has become a trustee of a charitable foundation at the Brown, Rudnick, Freed & Gesmer law firm, where he is an associate.

Johnson & Wales University has named a scholarship after him.

And he's signed on to help U.S. Rep. Loretta Sanchez, D-California, raise money across the country for Hispanic candidates and other politicians supportive of Hispanic issues. The census has confirmed that Rhode Island's Latino population is booming. Latino voters and leaders are becoming hot items, especially in Providence, where minorities now have huge numbers and in which Taveras ran strong in the congressional contest.

But Taveras knows it still won't necessarily be easy for him or for Latinos in general.

For example, he's flattered when people urge him to run for mayor. But he's clear-headed enough to ask them, "Are you going to give me $1,000?" When he ran for Congress, it was on a shoestring $150,000 budget. "I'm not going to run for mayor with $150,000, I can tell you that much," says Taveras. He says he'd need at least $500,000 to $1 million. He's not a candidate "at this time" but wants to see how things shake out.

As for the notion of Latinos being on the verge of making dramatic political gains, Taveras cautions, "There's no guarantee that people will remain united. People are independent-minded and will make up their own minds on candidates and on issues." He thinks some activists will gravitate to non-Latino candidates. To win, Hispanic aspirants will have to have broad appeal, he says.

And there's still much work to be done in registering people and getting them to turn out.

Taveras also knows the effort to redraw state Senate and House lines and reduce the number of legislative seats from 150 to 113 can create ill will. He worries about a "huge tension" he sees existing between Hispanics and blacks, who tend to live in the same areas and compete for the same slots. Mull two adjoining Providence South Side House seats held by Democrats. In one district, Rep. Joe Almeida, a black man, narrowly defeated a Latino primary challenger in 2000. In the other, Rep. Leon Tejada, a Latino, narrowly ousted a black incumbent in the primary.

Taveras fears the redistricting/downsizing exercise will exacerbate tensions.

He says it is not his goal to make both the Almeida and Tejada seats Hispanic. But he does want to make sure the two men are not thrown together.

Almeida, who helped Taveras in his congressional bid, insists there is less black-Latino tension than you might think. "More and more, blacks and Latinos have been joining hands politically," he asserts.

Taveras thinks several newly drawn legislative districts may be especially hospitable to Hispanics. Possibilities include Providence's Silver Lake, Mount Pleasant, and Federal Hill, as well as areas in Central Falls and Pawtucket.

Taveras, who rules out a 2002 legislative run, lives in a Silver Lake apartment but hopes to buy a home in Elmhurst-Mount Pleasant.

Everyone speaks highly of Taveras. But some admirers worry he may burn himself out running for the wrong office or at the wrong time and acquiring the label of two-time loser.

Former Rhode Island House Majority Leader George Caruolo, a Brown, Rudnick partner, says, "You've got one, maybe two losses in you. Generally speaking, after the second loss, you're damaged goods."

Caruolo says mayor could be a real possibility for Taveras, depending on the field.

Dr. Pablo Rodriguez, who heads the Rhode Island Latino Political Action Committee, says Taveras has great potential but worries about a flameout: "A lot of planning should go into his next campaign to make sure that he becomes a winner."

If any Latino has dibs on running for mayor, it might be Councilman Luis Aponte, but he says he does not plan to try. So would he like Taveras to go for it? "I'm not sure." He says Taveras thinks on such a "global" level he might be better off going next year for lieutenant governor. "I think he has that kind of promise where he could one day be governor." If Fogarty were to make clear he is running for governor, Taveras might have to make a quick decision on whether to join what undoubtedly would be a large field for lieutenant governor. Meanwhile, talk will continue of a run for mayor.

He is honored that Latinos would be rooting for him. He says he's less worried about losing another bid for office than about having to meet people's expectations should he win. For instance, he says, as mayor he would face tough challenges in such areas as schools.

He says he is not a miracle worker. "I'm an Angel," he chuckles. Later, he says he didn't mean to sound flip. "The times that I've been most disappointed in my life have been when people I most respect or admire let me down." He doesn't want to let you down.

Every day there is a new indication of the growing impact Latinos are having in America. The Latino stars on the Red Sox; the music played at Fenway Park. President Bush giving speeches in Spanish. Etc. Taveras says not everyone sees integration as positive. "We've got to let people know it's a good thing," he says.
He mentions the influx of immigrants. "You've got to give people a little bit of time to master the English language. My mom came here, worked to raise us, did all sorts of things. She didn't learn [fluent] English. I get upset a little bit when I hear people say, 'Well, you've got to learn English or go back.' Okay, in other words, work seven days a week like she did, raise three kids like she did, make sure they have food on the table, do everything else like she did, and then people are angry at her because she has not [mastered] one of the most difficult languages."

Taveras has a sense of proportion and of humor.

He says strangers, remembering him from the congressional campaign, often stop him, and it's exciting. On the other hand, he smiles and cites a day when he was in nice but casual clothes in the garage at the Brown, Rudnick building, waiting for the attendant to pull up with his car. A motorist drove in and asked Taveras, "You work in this building?" When Taveras said yes, the guy assumed *he* was the parking attendant and waited for him to take his vehicle. Taveras said, "No, I work upstairs." Taveras surmises the misunderstanding was due to his being young and Latino. "It keeps you humble," he says.

Hispanic Leaders Call For Seat At Table

Milton Valencia
The Pawtucket Times
05/11/2001

CENTRAL FALLS -- With Census 2000 figures showing the city's Hispanic population doubling in the past decade, minority community leaders are campaigning for "a better reflection of the community" in city government.

"This is a great opportunity to justify the need for Latino representation," said Tomas Alberto Avila, treasurer of the Rhode Island Latino Political Action Committee. "What we're trying to educate is that no one is going to know the community's needs like someone from the community."

Besides RILPAC, several minority leaders and agencies are recruiting Hispanic residents to become more involved, whether it is in the school district, the Police Department or City Hall.

Even Providence Espanol, a Hispanic-based weekly newspaper, printed an editorial in a recent edition pushing an enhanced Latino presence in politics. There has never been a Latino City Council member or a Hispanic mayor in this city, according to Board of Canvassers records.

That long-standing absence from City Hall is more striking considering that 48 percent of the city's population is Hispanic, according to 2000 Census figures. Statewide, the Hispanic population nearly doubled to 90,820 people, or 9 percent of the total population.

"The reality is everyone accepts the density and concentration of the Hispanic community in Central Falls," Avila said.

Police Chief Alan DeNaro agrees. The chief recently hired several Hispanic dispatchers, who may soon be training to become police officers.

Several senior officers on the force are either fluent in Spanish or are taking Spanish-language classes, and there are several Latino officers on the job as well.

"You have to reflect the community you serve," DeNaro said. "We're trying to branch out and get the people involved."

Schools Superintendent Dr. Maureen Chevrette said that her department plans to hire two home-to-school liaisons for the next school year, both Latinos, who will join a staff of several liaisons and translators that deal specifically with the Hispanic community.

"Our biggest challenge as a district is hiring bilingual professionals," she said, noting that a college graduate capable of speaking two languages is an asset to any workplace. Many of those graduates are opting for higher-paying jobs, she said.

The department has unsuccessfully tried to hire a bilingual speech therapist since September, she said, as well as bilingual counselors and psychologists. "The majority of our parents speak Spanish," Chevrette said. "We should have someone that can speak with them."

Hispanic-based businesses are booming as well, according to census statistics. Those numbers show that 100 businesses in the city garnered more than $6 million in revenue that year. And as businesses are growing, many Latino merchants and workers are campaigning for representation in City Hall, hoping to elect peers to the City Council.

Ricardo Patino, a construction specialist at the Rhode Island Housing and Mortgage Finance Corporation, has already announced that he will run for the city's Ward 3 seat. And Carlos Lopes, a project outreach coordinator at Project Hope/Proyecto Esperanza (a social-service agency), says he's contemplating a run for the Ward 4 seat.

"If we are 50 percent of the people, we have to be involved in politics," Patino said. "We don't want to be part of the problem; we want to be part of the solution."
Patino ran in the 1999 election, but lost by 119 votes to Rose Marie Canavan, who presently holds that seat.

This year, he said, he's looking to start campaigning earlier in the year and meeting every voter in the ward, not just the Hispanic voters.

"I want everyone to know I would be their councilor, for the whole community," Patino said. "We are taxpayers too."

Brown Power vs. Black Power

By Shannah Kurland
Spring 2001

Shannah Kurland discusses how Latino politicians targeted progressive black incumbents in Providence last fall.

An explosion of Latino voting in Providence, Rhode Island this fall should have been a cause for celebration. Instead, it has revealed an electoral quicksand that pits Latinos against African Americans and separates identity from ideology--conditions ripe for manipulation by an entrenched white power structure whose corruption is legendary.

Some people think that Latinos (backed by the white power elite) made a deliberate and reactionary grab at what little black political power exists in Providence; others see the conflict as a predictable, if frustrating, outgrowth of the demographic shift that has concentrated the potential electoral power of all people of color in the same few districts. Either way, there was no net increase in elected officials of color in a campaign marked by a complete absence of substantive discussions of policy or politics that would promote social justice.

The institutions that guided the surge of Latino voting emphasized themes of Latino pride and power, while the multi-racial teams supporting progressive black incumbents spoke of the courage and integrity of their candidates without articulating any racial justice message. All of this energy was squeezed into the three neighborhoods with the largest concentration of people of color. People of color throughout the rest of the city were left hungry for action, with no place to go. The white power structure was never called on to defend itself.

Providence is not unique; the effective electoral displacement of African Americans by Latinos is playing out from Southern California to Miami, and countless places in between. Does the expansion of Latino political power have to come at the expense of black representation? And beyond the identity of the individuals representing districts of people of color, are our communities even talking about racial justice when we engage in electoral work?

A Changing Population

For most of the last 26 years, Providence has been ruled by Mayor Vincent (Buddy) Cianci, a brilliant old-school Italian machine politician with illusions of mafia grandeur, who was once convicted of felony assault on his estranged wife's lover. Cianci's agenda of corporate welfare through downtown development is driven not so much by ideological preference as by a burning desire to consolidate personal power and wealth. He is currently the subject of a Department of Justice investigation that has so far resulted in the conviction of three members of his administration for various graft-related crimes and the indictment of his former chief of staff. Many folks feel that the best preparation for finding your way around City Hall is to watch *The Sopranos* a few times.

Cianci's relationship to communities of color has grown cruder over the years: when co-optation and crumbs fail to buy peace, as in the period following the murder by Providence police of a black off-duty officer last winter, he simply severs contact and writes off the black vote. Cooperation between various factions of Irish, English, and Italian ethnic politicians has created a solidly white political establishment at the state level as well, with more interest in creating personal wealth and appeasing the suburbs than dealing with messy "urban" issues of social or economic justice.

Providence is about half people of color. More than 25 percent of the city's population is Latino, about half of whom are immigrants from the Dominican Republic. They're joined by Puerto Ricans, South Americans, and an emerging population of Mexicans. Like the Cape Verdeans who immigrated to Rhode Island in huge numbers throughout the first half of the century, and like most other Caribbeans, Dominicans are part of the African Diaspora. African slaves, a few indigenous survivors, and European colonizers created a population that has as many degrees of oppression as it does skin tones.

In Providence, African Americans make up another 15 percent of the population. With about six percent share of the city population (and growing), Asians have not yet emerged as a potent force in the political scene. Due in part to the search for decent housing, a sort of reverse colonization process has taken place, with the result that not one working-class neighborhood in Providence remains predominantly white. Councilman John Igliozzi, whose family thinks they own the working-class Silver Lake neighborhood, recently lamented that not enough white people are moving into his ward.

The Latino Challenge

Despite the spread of Latinos throughout the city, all but one of the Latino candidates decided to try to unseat progressive black elected officials. The three races involving Latinos were focused in South Providence, which is still over 50 percent black and has been represented exclusively by black politicians for more than 20 years, and in the adjoining Elmwood and Reservoir Triangle neighborhoods, where white politicians have generally ruled despite a clear majority of people of color. South Providence has experienced a steady growth in Latino population, and the Latino presence in Elmwood has tripled in the last 10 years, while the black population has remained at 25 percent. Reservoir Triangle was mostly white until the residency rule for city workers was temporarily lifted in 1992, sending hundreds of white firefighters, clerks, and police officers stampeding to the suburbs as if they were escaping the seven plagues. Now Latinos and blacks together outnumber whites in the Triangle.

The September 2000 primary and the November general election were historic in terms of the number of Latino voters, but this high turnout had precedents. In 1994, Luis Aponte became the first Latino to run for City Council, and four years later he won. Anastasia Williams of Panama became the first Latina state representative in 1992, and in 1998, three Latinos ran for city or state office.

By election 2000, the other shoe dropped. At Sackett Street School, the city's most heavily Latino polling place, lines reached down a flight of stairs and out to the street, while Dominican-owned taxi and shuttle services dropped off vanloads of voters in 15-minute intervals, and dozens of campaign volunteers swarmed the sidewalks. Poder 1110, the city's most popular Latino radio station, pounded the airwaves all day, broadcasting live from the polls and exhorting listeners to get out and vote Latino.

In Elmwood, León Tejada, owner of an income tax service, beat Marsha Carpenter, a six-year incumbent black woman, for state representative by a mere 100 votes. A member of the political party currently in power in the Dominican Republic, the social democratic Partido Revolucionario Dominicano (PRD), Tejada was more a symbol of that group's emergence as local political power than a known entity in his own right. The PRD was instrumental in Tejada's victory, helping him overcome the fact that he moved into the district only a month before the filing deadline and had the very public backing of Joseph Voccola, a lawyer and state representative out of a mob-infested suburb, who trashes South Providence.

In South Providence, a young Latino marketing consultant named Gonzalo Cuervo ran against the social justice flag-bearer, Joe Almeida, a freshman black representative and former police officer who bucked the House leadership and led a successful charge to pass a law for collection of racial profiling data in Rhode Island. Almeida beat Cuervo by just 26 votes. Cuervo, whose political leanings are as much a mystery as his decision to run, works for a restauranteur who has a strong relationship with the Mayor. The latter has urged Cuervo to make a run against South Providence's militant black councilwoman Balbina Young. Nationalism got ugly at times in the Cuervo campaign--Gladys Gould, a Dominican who organizes with DARE (Direct Action for Rights and Equality), a multi-racial social justice community organization, spent the day hustling votes and working polls to support Joe Almeida, "because of his courageous fight on Driving While Black legislation. I know he makes a difference for all people of color." In response, Cuervo supporters screamed "traitor" in her face.

What Black Means

Almeida acknowledges that racism is a problem in getting blacks and Latinos together, and compares it to the privilege that lighter skin color carries within black communities. "Every Latino who ran is light- or white-skinned. What we have in common is that we come in shades, and we need to accept that within ourselves, as who we are." He explains that as people of color, "we're more apt to run against ourselves than someone white," since there is a fear of taking on the power structure.

Gwen Andrade, an African American political and community activist, warns that racism has created a wedge between blacks and Latinos rather than forging a bond. After running for state senate in the Elmwood and Reservoir Triangle neighborhoods in 1992 and managing successful campaigns including her Puerto Rican husband's bid for city council, she sees this election as a sign that many Latinos will respond to racism by more readily aligning with whites. This is especially frustrating because the Caribbeans who make up the vast majority of Providence's Latino population share not only African roots but also a history of slavery and brutal oppression with North American blacks.

"In America the further away from `black' you get, the better," says Andrade. "That's the perception that's been set up--it's the historical perspective of any group of people that has African roots. If you've got that African heritage that comes out in the skin color, or in the hair, you're fighting even harder to distance yourself from it because of what black means in this country." Or in this hemisphere, one could add.

The only local Latino candidate to challenge a white incumbent was Juan Pichardo, who lost a bid for state senate in Elmwood and Reservoir Triangle by less than 100 votes. Pichardo comes out of a new generation of Latino political operatives, having served as campaign manager for a young Dominican man who ran against Joe Almeida for state representative in 1998. His opponent this time was Bob Kells, a five-term white incumbent and current police captain with inconsistent positions ranging from progressive to fascist.

Pichardo tried to play the middle ground but alienated the black political establishment by failing to support Marsha Carpenter, the progressive black incumbent state representative from Elmwood. The PRD, on the other hand, was disappointed that Pichardo failed to give unequivocal support to Carpenter's opponent, León Tejada. Of all the local Latino candidates, Pichardo came the closest to building a base of black supporters, and also drew heavily on his strong relationships with white progressives at Ocean State Action (an affiliate of US Action) and the Rhode Island Young Democrats.

Most of all, Pichardo's race proved to be a test for RILPAC, the Rhode Island Latino Political Action Committee. Founded in 1998 by Dr. Pablo Rodriguez, a respected activist and philanthropist, the organization reflects its founder's solidly progressive politics and has a sizeable base of young Latino professionals. But RILPAC also plays the curious role of providing a "safe" space for white politicians of both major parties to get exposed to Latinos. The organization has raised eyebrows by endorsing black candidates, most recently by supporting Marsha Carpenter over León Tejada for state representative. In a reflection of internal struggle, RILPAC endorsed both Joe Almeida and his opponent Gonzalo Cuervo.

The Dominican Connection

If RILPAC has been up front in the political establishment's eye, then surely the PRD has been the stronger player on the street. Having this year recaptured the presidency in the Dominican Republic for the first time in 14 years, the PRD is no stranger to building membership throughout the hemisphere. It was founded in 1939 by exiled leaders during the brutal, U.S.-backed dictatorship of Rafael Trujillo, and soon had a strong leadership base in New York. In 1961, party members returned to the Dominican Republic and overthrew Trujillo's regime.

One of the heroes in the resistance to the 1965 U.S. invasion that (not surprisingly) followed was the young Francisco Peña Gomez, who went on to become the party's presidential candidate in 1996. He came in first, but lost the run-off when his opponent made an unholy alliance with Trujillo's successor.

Tragically, Peña Gomez died of a brain tumor two years after the election, but his legacy remains crucial. He laid the groundwork for dual citizenship for Dominicans, ensuring that participation in the U.S. political process would not require someone to sacrifice her or his Dominican political identity. Understanding the potential force of colonized people within an imperial power, he argued on countless trips to New York that Dominican immigrants must become U.S. citizens, involve themselves in their local communities, and win elections.

Equally important to the emergence of racial justice perspectives in local politics is the fact that Peña Gomez was black. Not mestizo, ni mulatto, ni any shade of brown, but dark black. In a country ravaged by racist imperialism, his leadership and expected victory represented a major accomplishment.

Locally, the PRD has built effective electoral operations but comes up short on multi-racial coalition. However, if the PRD is to reach its goal of expanded citywide and eventually statewide influence, it will require a broader base. Providence PRD President Rhadames Duran declares, "We believe it's necessary to work for the community as a whole. By uniting as minorities, as soon as we get ourselves organized politically, we can reduce the impact of racism." While the PRD's only major support went to Tejada, Duran claims that the party will be prepared to support any candidate who conforms to its mission.

In Providence's fall elections, concrete discussion of the values and policies that might promote racial justice was absent, but there may be nowhere to go but forward. Joe Almeida, for one, sees some black/Latino unity in the future, and suggests that leadership in that movement may come from today's multi-racial babies who embody both cultures. RILPAC spokespeople have been explicitly describing the links between Latino interests and those of other "urban" communities in public forums. Rhadames Duran speaks of redoubling the PRD's work, so that within six years there will be a viable "minority" candidate for mayor representing a unified front of Latinos, African Americans, and Asians.

As for the possibilities for creating a unified racial justice agenda, Gladys Gould of DARE says, "We're all in the same boat in terms of the struggle. Right now, the Latino community has the idea that the vote is a weapon, but they don't know how to aim it. Carrying a gun doesn't make me powerful--it's how I use that gun that makes me powerful."

Latino Community Becoming A Force

According to Census Bureau Redistricting Data

Tomás Alberto Avila
April 16, 2001

Providence, RI – Information released last month by the U.S. Census Bureau, shows that Political power in Rhode Island is shifting back to its roots in the ethnic neighborhoods of Providence and the Latino community, is poised to play a big role in the political arena into the new millennium. The data shows that the state's Latino population makes up 40 percent of the total population in 5 of the 50 Senatorial districts (**see table** 1), and 6 of the 100 House (**see table 2**).

This political empowerment is in line with the doubling of the Latino community during the 10 years since the last national population count was taken, jumping from 45,752 in 1990 to 90,820. Latinos now represent 8.7 percent of Rhode Island's total population. According to the data released by the bureau, eighty percent of the increase in the Hispanic population occurred in three communities: Providence, Pawtucket and Central Falls. This year, the Census results is being watched more closely than at any time in the past century in Rhode Island because they will be used as a guide in cutting the Assembly by 25 percent 25 House seats and 12 Senate seats must be chopped out before next year's elections. The Census figures are also used to reapportion the state's two U.S. House Districts.

TABLE 1					
Rhode Island Senatorial Districts					
Rank	**District**	**Total Population**	**Total Latino**	**Percent of Population**	**Percent 18+ Years**
1	10	21,043	10,450	49.7%	46.6
2	8	23,381	10,696	45.7%	40.9
3	35	21,879	9,326	42.6%	39.1
4	9	19,976	8,206	41.1%	37.1
5	7	23,420	9,278	39.6%	34.1
6	1	21,588	5,896	27.3%	21.9
7	4	22,270	4,238	19.0%	14.1
8	38	20,790	3,544	17.0%	14.1
9	40	20,464	3,067	15.0%	12.8
10	37	20,131	2,964	14.7%	12.2

The census data allow state officials to realign congressional and state legislative districts in their states, taking into account population shifts since the last census (in 1990) and assuring equal representation for their constituents in compliance with the "one-person, one-vote" principle of the 1965 Voting Rights Act. These data also are the first population counts for small areas and the first race and Hispanic-origin data from Census 2000

Redistricting could also create opportunities for Latinos. The surprising surge of Latinos could turn Senate districts10, 8, 35, 9 and 7 into Latino political power districts. House districts 9 and 19 have joined district 18 as districts where the Latino community makes up 50 percent of the population, along with districts 72, 17 and 12 in which the community makes up more than 40 percent of the total population.

| TABLE 2 | | | | | |
| Rhode Island Representative Districts | | | | | |
Rank	District	Total Population	Total Latino	Percent of Population	Percent 18+ Years
1	9	11,868	6,609	55.7%	52.60
2	18	10,565	5,842	55.3%	52.20
3	19	10,085	5,239	51.9%	48.50
4	72	10,662	5,074	47.6%	44.30
5	17	11,055	4,837	43.8%	41.40
6	12	10,975	4,728	43.1%	37.30
7	73	11,217	4,252	37.9%	34.50
8	13	11,574	4,132	35.7%	35.70
9	14	11,457	4,033	35.2%	29.60
10	20	9,831	3,299	33.6%	30.00
11	1	11,872	3,782	31.9%	25.30
12	7	11,193	2,686	24.0%	19.30
13	10	10,962	2,023	18.5%	14.80
14	6	10,832	1,650	15.2%	11.40
15	8	10,736	1,455	13.6%	9.90

US Census Bureau Redistricting Data (PL 94-171) Summary File 2000

The Census data contain population, race and Hispanic origin information for small geographic areas, as small as a city block in some cases.

City Woman Sets Sight On Legislaure

Russ Olivo, Staff Writer
The Woonsocket Call
August 29, 2001

WOONSOCKET -- Another Democrat filed for the District 62 House of Representatives vacancy yesterday, forcing a primary on Oct. 4.

Stella G. Brien, 29, of 513 South Main St., took out papers to run in the special election forced by the death of State Rep. Barbara C. Burlingame on Aug. 14. "I want to emulate her," Brien said outside City Hall yesterday. The other candidate is Jeffrey A. Burlingame, 26, of 565 Fairmount St., the son of Ms. Burlingame and a city firefighter. Town officials in North Smithfield, where a portion of District 62 is located, said no one filed papers to run in that town yesterday. Provided both candidates follow through in filing nomination papers, the two-Democrat race would be decided, in effect, on primary day, though the winner's name will end up on the ballot during the General Election just the same.

The General Election will be on Nov. 6, the same as candidates for City Council, School Committee and mayor for the city. Mayor Susan D. Menard, so far, is unopposed. The declaration period for the special state election ended yesterday at 4 p.m. For the local contests, it ends today at 4 p.m. A lawyer, Brien is the daughter-in-law of Albert G. Brien, who held the District 62 seat for about 13 years, until 1987, when he resigned to become the city finance director under then-Mayor Charles C. Baldelli. Brien's husband, also a lawyer, is Jon Brien, son of Albert Brien, and is serving as campaign manager for his wife.

Ironically, the elder Brien's resignation in 1987 paved the way for the election of Barbara Burlingame, who held the post until she died of melanoma earlier this month. In a brief interview outside City Hall yesterday, Stella Brien said she was inspired by Burlingame's agenda of fighting for victims of domestic violence. She said, "I feel I could be a good representative as a woman to take her agenda and go forward with that." A native of New York, Brien met her husband in law school and moved to the city with him a year ago. Brien said both of her parents are naturalized American citizens who were born in Colombia, South America. Her maiden name is Guerra and she speaks fluent Spanish, she said. Significant portions of District 62, such as Fairmount, are heavily Hispanic. According to the latest census, Hispanics overtook blacks and Asians as the city's dominant minority groups since 1990.

Canavan Faces Two Challengers

Milton Valencia
Pawtucket Times
September 28, 2001

CENTRAL FALLS -- A mayoral race and two tight City Council races are expected to have candidates campaigning until polls close on the municipal primaries Thursday.

Central Falls elections are nonpartisan, meaning a primary is held when there are three or more candidates, regardless of what political party each is affiliated with.

The two candidates with the most votes will continue on to the Nov. 6 general election.

The only City Council primaries will be in wards 3 and 4.

In the mayoral race, incumbent Mayor Lee Matthews is seeking re-election against former mayor and City Councilman Thomas Lazieh, political newcomer Charles D. Moreau and former government watchdog Wilfred "Pete" DeMeule.

In the Ward 4 race, incumbent City Councilman Ronald Robichaud is seeking re-election against Maurice M. Casto and former City Councilman Robert Weber.

Today, The Times is featuring profiles of the three Ward 3 candidates.

Rose Marie Canavan

Ward 3 City Councilwoman Rose Marie Canavan says she will be accountable to the voters and will hold the administration accountable and responsible for its actions.

The 60 Illinois St. homeowner is a lifelong resident of Central Falls, a retired schoolteacher and a mother of four and grandmother of six.

She is an English as a Second Language instructor at the Community College of Rhode Island, previously working as a teacher in the Central Falls School District.
She graduated from Rhode Island College in 1958 and from Central Falls High School in 1954.

"During my first tenure as a City Councilwoman these past two years, I have had the pleasure of meeting many of the residents of Ward 3 as well as residents throughout the city," Canavan said in a statement. "I would like to assure all of you that if re-elected I will continue to work toward improving this city.

"In addition to keeping taxes down and improving the quality of life for all residents, I will continue to push for open government in the city," she said.

Canavan says she has strived to improve quality of life for residents of Central Falls, having sponsored an entertainment ordinance that would hold clubs and organizations holding events accountable. The ordinance requires stricter guidelines for people looking to play music, whether it be live or electronic.

Also, as a former schoolteacher, she says she will work to make sure city streets are safe for children.

But she also vowed to continue serving as a government watchdog, saying the City Council has the responsibility of maintaining the "checks and balances" in city government for the benefit of the city.

"Open government is an issue I feel very strongly about," she said in a statement. ""I feel that every resident, along with council members, has the right and privilege to ask questions of the administration and receive proper and honest answers."

Ricardo Patino

If elected, City Council hopeful Ricardo Patino is vowing to work with the administration to bring progress to Central Falls government.

Patino, a construction specialist for the Rhode Island Housing and Mortgage Corporation, has been visiting residents, attending local events and talking to neighbors during his second campaign for the Ward 3 seat, after losing to Canavan two years ago.

"The needs of our city should take precedence over any personal or political interests that may exist," Patino said in a statement. "Together, we can work toward improving the quality of life in our neighborhoods and in our city. I am ready and willing to work with whomever it takes to deliver results."

The 43-year-old received his bachelor's degree in architecture and his master's degree in urban planning from the Pratt Institute of Design in New

York. After working for the Inter-American Development Bank, he married and moved to Central Falls.

Previously, he has worked as a lead inspector for the state Department of Health and an environmental consulting group.

Patino serves on the boards of directors of the United Way, American Red Cross and Latino Dollars for Scholars.

If elected, he pledges to work for more affordable housing, support for small businesses and programs to keep youth off the streets.

He says residents of Central Falls have had enough of "politics as usual," and want to move past the personal and political battles that have slowed the city's progress.

He has lived here for 12 years and owns his own home. He lives at 7 Darling St.

"As your councilman, I will work together with the administration toward our common goal: a safe and prosperous city for our children and families," he said in a statement.

Russell Rocheleau

Russell Rocheleau, of 16 Clinton St., is a lifelong resident of Central Falls.

He was born on Ledge Street and is the son of Leo and Violet Rocheleau, brother of Donald Rocheleau and Marie Rocheleau Sasso and wife of former police Chief Robert E. Sasso.

Rocheleau graduated from Central Falls High School in 1967 and went on to serve in the Navy during the Vietnam War.
He managed the Holiday Cinema on Broad Street for his father.
He also owned and operated City Limits Restaurant and Pub, co-owned Joseph's Catering and was president and owner of R and R Realty, Inc, which had holdings of several rental properties in Central Falls, Pawtucket, Scituate, Coventry, Johnston and properties out of state.

He has been employed by Osram Sylvania for 30 years as a water treatment controller and laboratory technician. He is a member of Union Local 1007.

If elected, Mr. Rocheleau's goals are as follows:

-- To work with fellow council members and the mayor in a team effort for the future of Central Falls.

-- As a union member, to never let politics interfere with municipal, police and fire unions and to settle contracts in a fair amount of time.

-- To work with residents in Ward 3 to clean up noise, drugs, prostitution, speeding cars and have live-in and absentee landlords repair homes that blight the neighborhood.

Saying he has no political aspirations beyond being a council member, Rocheleau vowed to dedicate his time and effort to gaining the trust and cooperation of the voters in Ward 3.

"Peace and harmony should prevail, not constant bickering," he said in a statement.

©*The Pawtucket Times 2001*

Latinos Seek Redistricting Input

Jim Baron
Pawtucket Times
September 28, 2001

WOONSOCKET -- Latinos, the fastest-growing portion of the Rhode Island population, fear that new redistricting maps for a downsized General Assembly could draw them into the political margins if their community is not represented and protected during the process. To ensure that it is, representatives turned out in force for the last of a series of public hearings held by the legislative Redistricting Commission Thursday night at Harris Hall.

"We are getting involved (in the electoral process), but we want the lines to be fair with us," said Ricardo Patino, a candidate for City Council in Central Falls.

As an example of unfairness to Latinos in the redistricting of 1992, Patino pointed to Senate Dist. 35, which straddles the Central Falls-Cumberland border and is represented by Sen. Daniel Issa.

"When you drew the lines 10 years ago," Patino explained, part of the district goes into Cumberland. Central Falls has nothing in common with Cumberland, we are different communities." He argued that the district should have instead gone into the Galego Court neighborhood of Pawtucket, a low-income, heavily minority housing project. "That is a community that we have more ties with," Patino said.

"All that we ask for is to have the chance to have a fair election, to have a fair distribution of the votes," he said, "so different people have the chance to be winners."

Lucia Gomez of the Puerto Rican Legal Defense and Education Fund underlined what she called "two important redistricting principles: that race can be a factor (in drawing district lines) and that states can create a minority majority district." A minority majority district is one drawn deliberately to give one or more minority groups a majority of voters in the district, making it easier to elect one of their own to office. Gomez fears that "other people are going to decide for the Latino community. I hear people talking about African-Americans and Latinos, but I don't hear African-Americans and Latinos talking about African-Americans and Latinos.

267

"Our people need to participate" in the redistricting effort, Gomez told The Times, "so we know what is going on. We know where our neighborhoods are. We know where the new boundaries are. We know where people are moving in and we know why they are moving there and we can anticipate where they are going to go. No one else can do that for us."

Another concern, she said, is that if Latinos don't get involved with the process of drawing the district lines, "I don't see them getting involved in campaigns or elections."

Juan Picardo of South Providence, an unsuccessful candidate for a state Senate seat last year, urged the commissioners to "carefully look" at Latino communities. "These communities have historically been disenfranchised, have not been provided the tools for empowerment. So I urge you to carefully look at the boundaries and, yes, look at race because race is a legitimate factor to be considered along with other legitimate factors."

"People want the opportunity to vote for someone they feel can represent them and their community," Picardo said.

Often, said H. Philip West Jr., executive director of Common Cause of Rhode Island, members of Latino and minority communities are interested in discussing issues with state legislators that have to do with immigrant concerns "and certainly with education concerns." And they may be very different in Central Falls as opposed to Lincoln; different in Providence as opposed to Cranston. With such a large Latino population in Central Falls, West told the committee, "we hope it would be a reasonable thing to expect they would be in a position to elect a Latino representative or senator. Again, I am not talking about a racial thing as much as about communities of interest that have great concerns about education, the kind of education and the funding of education." Thursday's meeting was the last at which the commission will solicit public input before preliminary lines are drawn, a job that is expected to start in two weeks. Once the commission has drawn proposed district maps, it will embark on another round of public hearings to get people's reaction to the plan.

The committee hopes to have a proposal to present to the General Assembly when it convenes in January.

Brien Takes House Seat By 14 Votes

Russ Olivo
The Woonsocket Call
Staff Writer
October 05, 2001

WOONSOCKET In a battle of newcomers with old names, Stella Guerra Brien pulled out a squeaker last night against Jeffrey Burlingame in the winner-take-all Democratic primary for the House of Representatives District 62 seat, 317-303.

It was an edge-of-your-seat race that had armchair pundits guessing until the last minute whether Burlingame's name recognition would be enough to outdo Brien's appeal to new Latino voters who have settled in parts of Fairmount.

In the end, Burlingame, 26, a Woonsocket firefighter, defeated Brien decisively at only one polling place, the Fairmount Fire Station, a few blocks from the home he shared with his mother, the late state Rep. Barbara C. Burlingame, who died of cancer in August. The vote there was 82-41.

Brien carried the heavily Hispanic Jimmy Ray Center in the Veterans Memorial Family Housing Development 97-60, and tied Burlingame at the Providence Street Fire Station, 64-64. Nevertheless, Brien was still trailing Burlingame at the Woonsocket polls by four votes, and it was the lone out-of-town polling place, the North Smithfield Fire Station, that gave her the victory. She outpolled Brien there 115-97.

"Not the way we wanted it to turn out," Burlingame said at Chan's Restaurant, where he gathered with friends after the polls closed.

Though the final tally includes five absentee ballots -- not enough to swing the outcome -- Burlingame said he would ask for a recount before he throws in the towel.

A lawyer and the daughter of Colombian immigrants, Brien, 29, swigged champagne and shared hugs with her husband and campaign manager, Jon, at the Village Haven in North Smithfield when the last poll runner arrived with the results. Though the town was crucial to her victory, Brien said the turnout of Latino voters in the Veterans Memorial Housing Development was at least as important. Brien, who speaks fluent Spanish, said she and her campaign workers made a strong push to identify registered voters in the housing project, get to know them and make sure they had transportation to the polls.

"I really connected with these people," said Brien. "I not only went door to door, I sat in their living rooms. What you hear from a lot of them is nobody ever paid attention to them before. They thanked me for coming to knock on their doors." Jon Brien said there has been a shift in the character of the Fairmount District that people seeking public office can no longer ignore.

"There's a new power base in the Fairmount district that's going to have to be considered," said Brien. "They've got to be taken seriously. They're not just a fringe vote."

The precise impact of the Hispanic vote is impossible to gauge, but John R. Dionne, manager of the Board of Canvassers, said it was "absolutely" a factor. There were enough Hispanic voters at the Jimmy Ray Center to create language problems, he said. He sent Gil Perez, a member of the Board of Canvassers who comes from Cuba, to help the poll workers.

The latest U.S. Census says Hispanics are now the fastest-growing minority in the city, outnumbering African Americans and Southeast Asians for the first time. Since the last presidential election, canvassing authorities said, more than 500 new Hispanic voters have been registered. Brien said he and his wife worked to register Hispanic voters during the campaign, working with a city grassroots group called Citizens In Action.

Barely 12 percent of the district's 5,205 eligible voters turned out for the election, limited to Democrats and unaffiliated voters.

Stella Brien said she worked especially hard in North Smithfield, where she preached against a proposed asphalt plant and listened to voters' concerns about improving state aid to education, preserving open spaces, and other issues they care about. "They want a professional," she says.

A corporate lawyer for Voicestream Wireless in East Providence, Brien, too, had something of a familiar name. Her father-in-law, Albert G. Brien, was the district representative for a dozen years before stepping down in 1987 to take a city job.

Brien Wins District 62 Primary

The victory in the Democratic Primary virtually assures the winner will serve in the General Assembly because there are no other candidates in next month's election.

By Michael Smith
Journal Staff Writer
10.5.2001

By a margin of 14 votes, Stella G. Brien yesterday won the Democratic Primary to fill the state House of Representatives District 62 seat that became vacant on the death of Barbara C. Burlingame, who had held the position since 1987.

Barring a recount that changes the outcome, Brien's victory in the primary virtually guarantees she will replace Burlingame in the General Assembly because there are no other District 62 candidates for the November election ballot.

In winning the election, Brien, 29, a lawyer for VoiceStream Wireless, defeated Barbara Burlingame's son, Jeffrey A. Burlingame, a 26-year-old Woonsocket firefighter.

Burlingame said last night he plans to request a recount today.

District 62 represents sections of Woonsocket, where both candidates live, and North Smithfield.

The final tally, including absentee ballots, was 317-303, or 51 percent to 49 percent, according to the Woonsocket Board of Canvassers.

The voter turnout was low, with 12 percent of registered Democrats and unaffiliated voters making it to the polls. There were 5,205 eligible voters in the district.

Barbara Burlingame, known for her work on domestic violence issues, died of cancer in August at the age of 54. A special election was called to replace her.
Brien will serve out the remaining year of Barbara Burlingame's term.

"My campaign committee was myself, my husband and my father-in-law, and we worked so hard at this," Brien said. "I had no doubt that my hard work would be rewarded."

Brien said she ran a shoe-leather campaign, trying to knock on as many doors as possible. She was assisted by a friend, Kerrie Blais, a mother who toted her young children around with her as they campaigned. Brien said she names Blais "most valuable player" of the campaign.

"I got out there and I connected with people door-to-door," Brien said. "They got to know me as an individual." Brien also has family ties to the District 62 seat. Her father-in-law, Albert G. Brien, held the seat until he resigned in 1987.

Stella Brien, of 513 South Main St., Woonsocket, grew up in White Plains, N.Y., the daughter of Colombian immigrants. She attended New York Law School, where she met her husband, Jon Brien, a Woonsocket native.

After shuttling between the two cities for about six years, the couple moved to Woonsocket permanently more than a year ago.

Asked whether she would run for reelection next year, Brien, in celebratory mode, said, "You can't ask me that tonight." It was both Brien's and Burlingame's first bids for public office.

Burlingame, of 565 Fairmount St., Woonsocket, had said he and his mother often talked about him replacing her in the General Assembly when she decided to step down.

Last night, Burlingame said he was surprised at the outcomes in some areas of the district. He won Woonsocket by a slim 206-202 margin, but Brien took North Smithfield by a 115-97 vote.

Woonsocket opened three polls in the district yesterday and North Smithfield opened one. "There were a couple places where I thought I would've done a little bit better," he said. "I had very much hoped to literally take North Smithfield."

Burlingame, who was supported by the Democratic leadership in the House, said he isn't ruling out a future bid for office.

Second-Place Finishes For Imcumbents

Douglas Hadden and Milton Valencia
Pawtucket Times
October 05, 2001

CENTRAL FALLS -- Incumbents were on the short end of the electoral measuring stick in the two nonpartisan City Council primaries Thursday, with former councilman Robert Weber romping over the man who succeeded him in Ward 4 two years ago when Weber opted to run for mayor, while the second time around was the charm in Ward 3 for Ricardo Patino.

Challengers Maurice Casto in Ward 4 and Russell Rocheleau in Ward 3 were eliminated from the Nov. 6 final, when Weber will face off against Councilman Ronald Robichaud and Patino will attempt to unseat Councilwoman Rose Marie Canavan, Thursday's respective second-place finishers.

In Ward 3, Patino, beaten by Canavan by fewer than 90 votes two years ago, became the first Latino to top the ballot in any city election, notching 227 votes to 176 for one-term incumbent Canavan. The race attracted Spanish language radio station WPMZ Poder-1110 to broadcast live from the parking lot outside the Forand Manor polling site on Washington Street. Political newcomer Rocheleau ran a distant third with 91 votes, but his candidacy was seen by political observers as drawing votes more likely to go to Canavan than Patino.

Those official Board of Canvassers totals included mail ballots. Voter turnout in Ward 3 was 34.56 percent, highest of any ward. Patino logged 45.95 percent, Canavan had 35.63 percent and Rocheleau 18.42 percent of the total. Canavan, of 60 Illinois St., said Patino "had the political action groups all working with him. They knew where they made their mistakes last time in turning out the vote," and got those voters out Thursday, many of them Spanish-speaking, she said. "They're professionals and they did a good job." Canavan, 65, a retired city school teacher, said she didn't think the past two years where the council and Mayor Lee Matthews often sniped with each other was a factor in the primary result. "If we all agreed on everything, we wouldn't be running a proper city government," she said.
Patino, 43, a Colombia native who moved to the city about 12 years ago and works as a construction specialist for Rhode Island Housing, celebrated with supporters at his 7 Darling St. home. Patino said that venue reflected the fact he is not allied with any mayoral or other candidate.

"I went and walked the entire community and I talked to everyone. This time I (also) approached the Anglo community," which he had not worked hard enough to appeal to last time, he said.

Among those celebrating with Patino and his wife, Diosa, were Providence-based key operatives in his campaign, who also helped him two years ago. They included Dr. Pablo Rodriguez, president of the R.I. Latino Political Action Committee; Andrew Galli, who ran Angel Tavares' unsuccessful campaign for Congress last year and has worked in elections for Attorney General Sheldon Whitehouse; and Providence activist Melba DePena. Also visiting the house was a Latino candidate for Woonsocket City Council, Grizzell Rodriguez.

But Patino said if elected he would work "with all the (ethnic) communities" in the city, first by organizing a neighborhood crime watch. He said Thursday showed the ward's voters are "tired of the system. They decided they were looking for a change."

In Ward 4, Weber received 272 votes to 159 for Robichaud and 45 for Casto in voting at Wilfrid Manor, Hunt Street. Weber, of 517 Hunt St., claimed 57.14 percent of the total; Robichaud, of 259 Fuller Ave., had 33.4 percent; and Casto, of 712 Dexter St., had 9.55 percent and was ousted from the final.

"The voters have spoken, and they want change," said Weber. "It's a good feeling the voters in Ward 4 haven't forgot about me. But we haven't won yet by any means," he said. "There's still November. We'll work hard through then."

Robichaud said he was proud of the turnout Thursday, and vowed to continue campaigning until Nov. 6. "It's a primary, we still got another month," Robichaud said. "We're going to work hard and keep plugging. It's not over until the fat lady sings. We'll be there," he said. Casto, who also ran unsuccessfully in 1999, said he was proud he participated in the democratic process, and congratulated Robichaud and Weber.

"The seat goes to who people want. But hey, I did it," he said.

Minority Groups Want Redistricting Voice

Hispanic populations in Providence and Central Falls should not have their political power diluted, activists say.

By Edward Fitzpatrick
Journal State House Bureau
10.24.2001

PROVIDENCE -- Hispanic and black leaders came to the State House last night, pressing their case for maintaining and gaining political power as Rhode Island takes on the twin tasks of redistricting and downsizing the General Assembly.

Members of the newly formed Latino Voting Rights Coalition began the evening with a news conference on the State House stairs, emphasizing that Rhode Island's Hispanic population doubled in the 1990s.

"Latinos are here and are ready to monitor the process and suggest solutions to improve our ability to translate our numbers into political power," Dr. Pablo Rodriguez, president of the Rhode Island Latino Political Action Committee, said prior to last night's redistricting commission meeting.

He introduced Lucia Gomez, a redistricting specialist from the Puerto Rican Legal Defense and Education Fund, saying, "We have in our possession the software and the information necessary to follow the process as it unfolds and stand ready to challenge any attempt at undercutting the voting rights of our communities."

Rodriguez said the coalition is now focusing on how redistricting will affect Providence and Central Falls, the two municipalities with the highest proportions of Hispanics in the state.

Central Falls, at 47.8 percent Hispanic, should not be lumped into legislative districts that include largely white Cumberland and Lincoln, he said. Rather, Central Falls should be linked with Pawtucket, which he called "a closer community of interest."

In Providence, which is 30 percent Hispanic, the coalition would oppose any attempt to eliminate or reduce districts that are now heavily populated by Hispanics, Rodriguez said. The group is particularly concerned, he said, about the future of Senate District 10, a 49.7-percent Hispanic district that includes Providence's West End, Elmwood and Reservoir Triangle neighborhoods.

Rodriguez noted the District 10 incumbent, Democratic Sen. Robert T. Kells, was named Lincoln police chief earlier this month, and reiterated the argument, made by Lincoln's Republican leader that the town charter prohibits Kells from being both senator and chief. If the district lacks an incumbent, he said, it would become vulnerable in the redistricting process. So, Rodriguez said, "We urge Senator Kells to do what he knows is right and resign his post in the Senate in order for District 10 to be preserved."

Reached later, Kells said he doesn't plan to seek reelection next year, but he doesn't plan to step down, either. He reiterated the argument, made by Lincoln's Democratic town administrator, that the charter does not bar him from being senator and chief. "That's absurd," Kells said of the call for his resignation. "I'm the senator elected for this district. It sounds like sour grapes on their part."

Among those at yesterday's news conference was Juan M. Pichardo, who lost to Kells by 94 votes after mail ballots were counted in last year's District 10 election. Pichardo said he plans to run for the legislature again next year in part because he wants to bring a Hispanic voice to the Senate.

The Senate, which will shrink from 50 to 38 members as part of the voter-mandated downsizing, now contains no Hispanics and one black member, Democratic Sen. Charles D. Walton, of Providence.

Former state Rep. Harold M. Metts, chairman of the Minority Reapportionment Committee, urged the redistricting commission to redraw maps to allow minorities to serve in the state Senate and House. "Senator Walton is a little bit lonely," Metts said. "He needs someone to help him carry that burden. It's time we had another minority senator."

That possibility would likely increase under maps submitted to the commission by Angel Taveras, a former congressional candidate who is now chairman of the Fair Redistricting Coalition. He said he drew the proposed maps without regard to race, but three of the Senate districts would contain substantial minority populations.

Taveras drew seven Senate districts within Providence, with just one of the districts crossing the city line. If districts in the southern part of Providence include parts of Cranston, he said, minority representation would be diluted.

H. Philip West Jr., secretary of the Fair Redistricting Coalition and executive director of Common Cause of Rhode Island, called for the commission to respect municipal borders wherever possible. He presented a map that divides the state into five regional clusters and then slices each region into legislative districts while crossing as few town boundaries as possible. He cautioned against "cracking" a town into multiple Senate and House districts, saying that often hurts the poorest communities.

West said municipal borders should be a higher priority than where incumbents live. But commission members immediately pointed out that Taveras's Providence map would put two Senate committee leaders in the same district -- Finance Chairman Frank T. Caprio and Health, Education & Welfare Chairwoman Catherine E. Graziano, who is on the redistricting commission.

Taveras said he did the maps without taking the location of incumbents into account. "When I saw that, I said 'Wow,' " he said of the Caprio/Graziano district. "I said other things, too, but I won't repeat those. I haven't been able to address it in a way that politically makes sense."

Latino Population Given Voice

Marcos Antonio, a longtime Providence resident, is named the director of the newly-created Office of Hispanic Affairs, to help serve the city's 52,000 residents of Hispanic descent.

By Gregory Smith
Journal Staff Writer
10.25.2001

PROVIDENCE -- "If you have a problem in the Latino community, here's your man, right here. Give him a call."

With that, Mayor Vincent A. Cianci Jr. yesterday introduced his director of the city Office of Hispanic Affairs, oil painter and former businessman Marcos Antonio.

The office, whose creation was announced at a news conference along with Antonio's hiring, is intended to serve as the mayor's liaison to cater to the needs and concerns of the growing Hispanic community.

There are now 52,000 residents of Hispanic descent in Providence, which represents more than 30 percent of the local population. That is an increase of more than 120 percent from the figures reported in the 1990 U.S. Census, according to Cianci.

And half of the students in the public school system are of Hispanic descent.

"The Hispanic community is playing a more prominent role in every aspect of our lives," the mayor said.

As for Antonio, who is a native of the Dominican Republic and a naturalized U.S. citizen, Cianci said, "He is intensely committed to his community and to the promotion of the Hispanic culture and will serve the people of our city well."

Said Antonio, "My brotherhood of Latinos" has grown remarkably in Providence and that population growth has "created both great promise for our people and new challenges."
The new office will help to integrate Hispanics into the general life of the community, Antonio said, while preserving and sharing with others the cultural traditions that distinguish Hispanics.

278

Although Antonio will carry the opinions of Hispanics to the mayor, Cianci made it clear that he would not be doing any tough political jobs such as fortifying Schools Supt. Diana Lam, who is Hispanic, or lobbying to save Senate District 10 in Providence, which Hispanic political activists want kept intact in the downsizing of the General Assembly.

Lam is under attack by the Providence Teachers Union, which has accused her of being dictatorial. Lam is "her own person," Cianci said, and "she'll get through what she's going through."

Senate District 10, which is now represented by Democrat Robert T. Kells, takes in the Reservoir Triangle and parts of the West End and Elmwood.

With Kells not intending to run for reelection, it is the "natural, normal, knee-jerk" inclination during reapportionment for legislators to carve up the district of a retiring colleague, Cianci commented.

He said there should be a Hispanic legislative seat but he does not know if the District 10 seat can be saved. That will be difficult to accomplish, he said, with the Senate being reduced from 50 members to 38.

In his $35,000-a-year post, Antonio will be expected to represent the mayor at public functions, stay in touch with the local Hispanic news and cultural media, coordinate cultural celebrations in which the city participates, help to identify and recruit potential Hispanic appointees to city boards and commissions, work with Hispanic organizations such as the Hispanic Chamber of Commerce, and help Hispanic residents get assistance from the city.

In the last election, only 1.5 percent to 2 percent of the Hispanics in Rhode Island voted, Cianci noted. He hopes Antonio can be a leader in encouraging Hispanics to vote.

Although the number of Hispanics is growing, the mayor said the figures reported in the 2000 census tend to exaggerate the growth because Hispanics were undercounted in the 1990 census.

"They've been here for years," he said, and the city has been reaching out to them. For instance, Cianci disclosed, the city is subsidizing the construction of a headquarters on Niagara Street in Elmwood for the Juan Pablo Duarte Society.

In recognition of Hispanics' growing importance, however, the mayor said that ABC6 television -- over-the-air Channel 6 -- is scheduled to begin simulcasting its news in Spanish on Monday. Antonio said other broadcast TV stations are expected to follow suit.

Antonio, 47, of 138 Sumter St. in Elmwood, was born in Baitoa in the rustic mountains of the Dominican Republic, where he spent his youth. He emigrated to New York City with his mother and siblings in 1971 and later moved to Providence, where he has lived for more than 25 years.

While holding a green card as a resident alien, he served in the U.S. Army and attained the rank of sergeant.

Antonio, who has a college degree in business, ran a cosmetic sales business for 11 years and also had a real estate investment business, buying buildings and then repairing and reselling them.

In recent years, he has been a self-employed painter and has exhibited his work internationally. He is a board member of the Hispanic Council for the Arts and the Providence Renaissance City Film Festival.

For the past three years Antonio has been director of the Providence Festival of the New Latin American Cinema, which the city subsidizes, and Cianci said he would keep that role.

Cianci Is Wrong; Hispanics Do Vote

Gonzalo Cuervo
Pawtucket Times
October 31, 2001

During a recent press conference, Providence Mayor Vincent "Buddy" Cianci, who always has something to say about everything, repeated his claim that few Rhode Island Hispanics actually vote. This time, however, Cianci went even further, stating that no more than 1.5 percent to 2 percent of the state's Hispanic population actually voted last year. I don't know how familiar the mayor is with any community outside of Providence, but I can say without a doubt that his numbers are all wrong.

According to the U.S. Census figures, more than 90,000 Rhode Islanders identify themselves as Hispanics. If Cianci is right, less than 1,800 Hispanics voted last year in the entire state, including heavily Hispanic cities such as Central Falls and Pawtucket. This is highly unlikely, as nearly 2,000 Hispanics cast their votes in Providence's South Side and Elmwood neighborhoods alone, catapulting the area's voter turnout to nearly 38 percent, or double that of the rest of the state.

Meanwhile, Hispanics in the Blackstone Valley have been making themselves much more politically visible in the past several years.

This should come as no surprise, as census figures indicate that Pawtucket's population is 14 percent Hispanic while Central Falls comes in at a whopping 48 percent Hispanic population.

A growing number of these Hispanic Americans participate in the electoral process and get out to vote.

In 1999, for example, Central Falls saw Hispanics voting in large numbers as they were mobilized for the mayoral race as well as the City Council race between incumbent Rose Canavan and Ricardo Patino.

Observers of October's primary elections in Woonsocket and Central Falls noted the increased number of Hispanic-American voters at the polling places.

In Woonsocket, Estela Guerra Brien won her bid to fill the vacancy left by Rep. Barbara Burlingame.

In Central Falls, Patino finished first in a three-way race against incumbent Canavan, who bested him and another candidate in 1999. A third Hispanic candidate, Al Baldera, has watched his campaign for the Central Falls City Council pick up momentum in the city's First Ward.

While all three candidates had plenty of mainstream appeal, they also benefit from a solid Hispanic voter block in each of their communities.

This is nothing new, of course; each emerging immigrant group -- Italian, Irish, French-Canadian has followed a similar course throughout the history of local politics.

However, an easily-overlooked fact is that a Hispanic voter is interested in the same issues as any non-Hispanic voter.

He or she works, pays taxes, is concerned with the safety of their neighborhood, the opportunities afforded to their children and the future of their community.

As a result, Hispanics won't vote for a Hispanic candidate just because he or she speaks their language. The candidate has to be able to deliver as well.

Next Tuesday's general election will determine the future of politics in Central Falls and the role that Hispanics play in developing that future for the benefit of all the city's residents for generations to come.

Gonzalo Cuervo is a columnist for The Times. You can contact him at: editor@pawtuckettimes.com

Courting Latinos:

Candidates Go Where Votes Are

M. Charles Bakst
The Providence Journal
11.1.2001 00:17

Dr. Pablo Rodriguez, president of the Rhode Island Latino Political Action Committee, said it with words. The three Democratic gubernatorial aspirants said it with their presence.

At a fundraiser Tuesday night at restaurant: PROV, Rodriguez said RILPAC, formed in 1998, has had its ups and downs. But, "none of our successes are as important as the fact that every time a political candidate throws their hat in the ring, they think about the Latino community as an important element that must be cultivated."

So here, cultivating, were Atty. Gen. Sheldon Whitehouse, two-time gubernatorial nominee Myrth York, and Rep. Tony Pires, all of them planning 2002 runs for governor.

When I asked Whitehouse what his campaign will do to reach out to Hispanics, he replied, "Everything we can think of. This is a very strong, active, growing political community."

It will be stronger if more Latinos register and vote.

Whitehouse asserted he has worked "very well" with the Hispanic community. When I asked him to identify his Latino backers, he referred me to Rodriguez, Juan Pichardo, Victor Capellan, and Tomas Avila. Rodriguez and Pichardo confirmed their support. Capellan and Avila told me they are undecided.

I recall Whitehouse's being blasted by Hispanics outraged by the execution-style slaying of scheduled murder-trial witness Jennifer Rivera, 15. Rodriguez says tensions have eased because of steps Whitehouse has taken, including improvements to the witness protection program. Still, he says Whitehouse's relations with the community "need work."

York said she'd appeal to Latinos the way she'd appeal to any group: "Speak to the issues that concern the people of Rhode Island, which have to do with being part of the process, having a governor that represents them, will work for them, on issues of health care, education, economic development."

Pires, son of Portuguese immigrants, said he will seek out Hispanics and will argue that someone from a first-generation, working-class family "really understands their hopes and dreams and aspirations."

Providence mayoral candidate David Cicilline -- whose Latino outreach aide, Gonzalo Cuervo, also was there -- applauded Buddy Cianci's appointment of Marcos Antonio to the newly created post of director of Hispanic affairs. Cicilline told me, though, "I'm disappointed that it took the mayor so long. He's 20 years into his term."

Antonio said Cianci has long been a friend to Latinos. He said that decades ago he and some other Hispanics experienced trouble with sewage and lighting and had rocks thrown at them. They called City Hall. "Cianci saw us and fixed it."

At the reception was Woonsocket's Stella Guerra Brien, set to become the House's third Hispanic member. She won a Democratic primary and is unopposed in a special election next week. Keeping the seat may be another matter. Redistricting models created by consultant Kimball Brace for mulling by the state Reapportionment Commission lump Brien in a district with House Majority Leader Gerard Martineau.

Martineau and Brien say they first learned this yesterday and need to get a handle on it. Martineau says downsizing may make such a pairing inevitable. Brien says she doesn't want to be squeezed out.

In a move toward closer ties between minorities, the RILPAC event drew such high-profile blacks as lawyer Casby Harrison, Sen. Charles Walton, and the Rev. Marlowe Washington. Harrison had the night's best line. When I asked what he was doing there, he said, "Some of my best friends are brown."

Patino Wants To Move City Past Battles

Central Falls Candidates' Statements
Pawtucket Times
November 02, 2001

Political statement from Ward 3 City Council candidate Ricardo Patino.

Since winning Central Falls' Oct. 4 primary election, Ricardo Patino says he has continued to visit his neighbors and discuss his plans for the City Council and for Central Falls.

Patino, a Rhode Island Housing construction specialist and 12-year Central Falls resident and homeowner, believes that the people of Central Falls want to move past what he called personal and political battles that he believes have brought the city's progress to a standstill.

"Our primary election results are proof that the people of Ward 3 are ready for progress," Patino said. "On Oct. 4, the Third Ward cast the highest number of votes in the city of Central Falls.The hard-working men and women of this ward want to move the city forward and I am ready to make that a reality." According to Patino, true change can only be achieved by establishing an honest, open dialogue with the residents of Ward 3.

"We must establish a partnership for progress," he said. "Together, we can work toward improving the quality of life in our neighborhood and in our city. "Our city is a little more than one square mile in size, yet we face many of the challenges of any urban city," he said.

"We need to improve access to affordable housing, create incentives to boost our small businesses and provide safe, productive alternatives for our kids. We need to keep our streets quiet, clean, well lit and safe for everyone." The 43-year-old candidate studied architecture and holds a master's degree in urban planning from New York's Pratt Institute of Design. Patino serves on the board of directors of the United Way, the American Red Cross and Latino Dollars for Scholars.

Baldera Tries To Unseat Noury

By Tatiana Pina
Journal Staff Writer
11.2.2001

CENTRAL FALLS -- Political newcomer Alido Baldera will try to unseat Gene R. Noury for the Ward 1 council seat.

Baldera, who works at Project Hope, said he decided to challenge Noury, an insurance agent, because it's "time for a change".

Noury is the council president.

Baldera, 41, one of the owners of the La Cabana Night Club in Lincoln, said he joined the council race after he grew frustrated with the constant fighting between the City Council and the mayor because it prevents work from getting done in the city.

"One of the most important issues in Central Falls is the city budget, yet the council and the mayor have not been able to come to an agreement on the budget. The people who pay are the residents," Baldera said.

An example of the deep discord that exists between the mayor and the council is the council's failure to confirm longtime city employee, Elizabeth Crowley as the city clerk, Baldera said.

As a councilman, Baldera said, he would work with the administration even if he doesn't always agree with its members.

He listed noise as one of the most important issues that concerns residents of the city. He said that he would work closely with the police to enforce a noise ordinance and to educate people about their responsibility to their neighbors regarding noise. He said money must be sought to repair sidewalks so that the elderly feel safe walking on them and that the city must continue to support after-school programs for children.

Baldera, of 55 Pacific St., is divorced and has four children.
Noury, 46, said he is seeking reelection so that he can continue the work he has been doing as a councilman.

Regarding the fighting between the council and the mayor, Noury said residents judge a representative on two things: if taxes are going to increase and if problems in the district are being solved.

Noury said he was able to pass a lower tax rate than what was proposed by the administration of Mayor Lee M. Matthews. He said he has continuously fought the wasteful spending of outside legal fees by the administration of more than three-quarters of a million dollars.

He says he also successfully lobbied the Planning Department to institute a program that gives people 62 years and older a $1,500 owner-occupant grant to do minor repairs in their home.

Noury considers himself a strong defender of the security of the city. He said he worked with police to eliminate prostitution on Clay, Broad and High Streets. He said he has supported the Police Department, helping to upgrade equipment and vehicles.

He was first elected to public office at age 20 when he was elected to the School Committee, on which he served for 12 years.

He lives at 1 Pacific St. with his wife and children.

Canavan Defends Seat From Patino

11.2.2001

CENTRAL FALLS -- The Ward 3 race will be a repeat of 1999 when Ricardo Patino tried to unseat Rose Marie Canavan for the council position.

Patino was the highest vote-getter in a three-way primary in October; Canavan came in second.

Patino, 43, is a construction specialist for the Rhode Island Housing and Mortgage Finance Corp. He said that the fighting between the council and mayor has worn the patience of city residents and could affect the outcome of the elections.

He said his top priorities are to control crime and to help residents obtain affordable housing in the city.

"People don't talk too much to each other and that's necessary in a small city. The way to do it is to have a neighborhood block watch," he said. "One of the great things about the neighborhood block watch is that you put criminals and others on notice that you are watching your neighborhood and that you are not going to permit them to do what they want with your city."

One of the first things he would like to do is clean the city. This could be done by starting educational programs in the schools and community centers. "There is no excuse for having a dirty city," he said.

Patino is married and does not have children. He lives at 7 Darling St.

Incumbent Rose Marie Canavan, 65, said that keeping taxes from going up and controlling the costs of the city are among her top goals.

Canavan is a retired school teacher from Central Falls who teaches English as a second language at Community College of Rhode Island in Lincoln.

She said that direct communication between the council and the mayor is another priority.
Canavan acknowledged that residents are dismayed with the discord between the mayor and the council. "The council cannot do its work without information from the administration, such as financial data from last year so that we can do the budget for the coming fiscal year," Canavan said.

This has been one reason that it has taken so long to pass a finalized budget, she said.

The conflicts come because of the council's lack of information, she said.

Canavan said she would continue to try to improve the quality of life for residents of the city. She has worked with the police to cut down on noise from loud music. "That's one of the biggest complaints. We haven't solved the problem but it's gotten better."

Canavan lives at 60 Illinois St. and has four children and six grandchildren

Patino Becomes City's First Latino Councilman

By Tatiana Pina
Journal Staff Writer
11.7.2001

CENTRAL FALLS -- Ricard Patino made history in Central Falls last night by becoming the first Latino to be elected to serve on the City Council.

Patino, 43, a Colombian immigrant, beat incumbent Rose Marie Canavan by an unofficial vote of 331 to 262 for the Ward 3 council seat.

Ward 3 had a total of 12 mail ballots.

Patino said the win came from a grassroots effort that targeted all sectors of the ward, both Spanish and English speaking. "We all have the same issues that concern us, crime, noise, garbage in the city," he said. "I will be working for everyone."

Patino, a construction specialist for the Rhode Island Housing and Mortgage Finance Corporation, celebrated at the headquarters of his colleague Alido Baldera, a political newcomer who lost to incumbent Gene Noury.

That Patino was making history was evident from the people who showed up to wish him well, which included a majority of Latino city residents, as well as state Sen. Charles Walton of Providence, Rep. Leon Tejada of District 18 in Providence, and members of the Rhode Island Latino Political Action Committee, some of whom had helped him on his campaign.

Patino will serve on the council for a city with more than 17,000 residents, nearly half of them Latino.

Canavan, 65, an English as a second language teacher at Community College of Rhode Island in Lincoln, said the race would be very close as she stood outside Forand Manor greeting voters with her son and granddaughter. "My family has been my campaign committee," she said. "I don't have a political action committee to help me," she joked.

Patino said one thing that helped him was that Russell Rocheleau, who lost to him and Canavan in the primaries, threw his support behind Patino and actually visited people and asked them to support him.

In Ward 1, Gene Noury, an insurance agent, beat Alido Baldera, an outreach worker for Project Hope, 280 to 191, according to unofficial results. There were 13 mail ballots in Ward 1.

Noury, who stopped by Baldera's headquarters at 801 Broad St., said, "The elections are over and it's time to move forward."

Noury said that perhaps Patino could help improve communication, which has been lacking between the council and Mayor Lee Matthews, who was reelected.

"He broke down an incredible barrier to be the first Latino to be elected in Central Falls; maybe he can break down the barrier with the mayor," Noury said.

In Ward 2, incumbent Jason R. Leger, a manager for Labor Ready, held on to his seat, beating Robert Ferri, 327 to 273, according to unofficial results. Ward 2 had 40 mail ballots.

In Ward 4, Ronald A. Robichaud became the second incumbent to lose his seat to a challenger. Robichaud, 38, owner of Buster's Trucking Inc., lost to Robert F. Weber, a former city councilman, 403 to 194, according to unofficial results. Ward 4 had four mail ballots.

In Ward 5, Jonathan Issa, 21, son of Dist. 35 state Sen. Daniel J. Issa, defeated Leonard Ryszkiewicz, 44, by a vote of 248 to 175. Ward 5 had seven mail ballots.

Blazing Campaign Trails

Ricardo Patino, Central Falls's first Latino councilman, says rethinking his pro-Latino campaign approach was the key to his success.

By Tatiana Pina
Journal Staff Writer
11.11.2001 00:22

CENTRAL FALLS -- Ricardo Patino keeps a large photograph of his hometown of Pereira, Colombia, on the wall of his den so he is sure to see it every day and remember his humble beginnings.

It's something he hopes will keep his thoughts in perspective when he goes about his duties as a new councilman in Central Falls.

Last Tuesday, Patino made history by becoming the first Latino to be elected to the City Council in Central Falls, where nearly half of the city's 17,000-plus residents are Latino. He was elected to Ward 3 and will take office Jan. 7.

While some Latinos hail Patino's election as a major breakthrough in the city and hope it will encourage other Latinos to participate in city politics, others see it as a natural course that previous immigrant groups have taken in the city.

Patino, 43, a construction specialist for the Rhode Island Mortgage and Finance Company Inc., says he has come a long way from six years ago when he first considered running for council.

For one thing, he changed his political focus and formed alliances.

"I was too pro-Latino. I was only thinking on the Latino agenda. After I lost two years ago [to Rose Marie Canavan], I got more experience. I realized the Latino agenda is the same as everybody else's," he said.

"All people want good government, no crime, affordable housing," he said. "It's the same agenda. I started to talk to people about what we could do together."

Patino emphasizes that he will advocate for all his constituents. "I'm going to work for everybody, not just Latinos as some people may fear," he said.

292

Patino, who is a participant in Leadership Rhode Island, says he has learned from his involvement in the leadership development program. "I know that the way you lead is by building up other leaders. That is one department where we are lacking, raising up young people to take part in the political process. In the next two years, I would like to see two other Latinos running for City Council who are better than I am," he said.

During his campaign, Patino preached about getting to know your neighbor and starting up neighborhood block watches so people could take care of each other. Melba Depena, who organized Patino's campaign, says that Patino never made big promises -- only things he actually thought he could do if he got elected.

"He ran because the Latino community is a forgotten community but won through partnerships with diverse people. He concentrated on the needs of all people who live in a poor city. That's where the campaign took a different turn," said Depena, 29, who is working for Matt Brown, a candidate for secretary of state.

This time around, Patino concentrated more on the Anglo community in his ward, a good percentage being residents of a housing complex for the elderly called Forand Manor.

But his campaign also sought out newly registered immigrant voters. Depena, Olga Silva, a few organizers and 30 volunteers made sure registered voters got constant reminders of election day. They gave rides to people. Showed them how to vote. They even watched their children while they voted.

Mayor Lee Matthews, a friend of Patino who was reelected to his fourth term in office, said he did not consider Patino's election a breakthrough but rather a normal process new immigrant groups have taken for years in the Central Falls melting pot.

"Ricardo is looking at the issues that affect all of us. He made that crystal clear during the election and that is what helped him. The Latino community has grown and now it's finally getting involved in elective office," Matthews said.

"All people care about in this community is are you going to work on core issues to make a better life for me and my children. Once you convinced them you are, it can be a woman, minority or a white Caucasion that gets elected," Matthews said.

Incumbent Councilwoman Rose Marie Canavan, who lost to Patino by a vote of 262 to 331, said that Patino's alliance with Matthews helped both men.

Canavan, who defeated Patino two years ago, said that this time around she saw a more mature and organized campaign that brought out a good number of Latino voters.

Angel Taveras, a former congressional candidate who chairs the Fair Redistricting Coalition, said Patino is a pioneer.

"Ricardo has helped open a door that hopefully will never be closed. It's important to get people involved in the process. That's vital to maintain a democracy," he said.

Patino says his wife, Diosa, helps him keep a healthy perspective.

"She says, 'At home you are still Ricardo. You still have to fetch your own shoes and take out the garbage.' "

RILPAC Group Elects New Officers

Pawtucket Times
November 30, 2001

PAWTUCKET -- The Rhode Island Latino Political Action Committee will begin the new year with newly-elected officers, including new President Nellie M. Gorbea, as the minority advocacy group assumes a role in state-wide issues such as the redistricting of the General Assembly. The officers, who will serve a one-year term, were elected at the board's regular scheduled meeting Tuesday at its Roosevelt Avenue headquarters.

"The new RILPAC board looks forward to continuing to build on the organization's recent success," Gorbeau said in a statement. "It is an exciting time for the Latino community of Rhode Island."

Under Gorbeau,Melba Depena will serve as executive vice-president; Victor Capellan will serve as treasurer; Sylvia Bernal will serve as assistant treasurer; Ana Cecilia Rosado becomes secretary; Claudia Cardona will serve as assistant secretary; and Carolina Bernal will become legal advisor and liaison. There was no candidate for the vice president seat.

There are also 18 members at large on the non-profit committee, which has organized to help elect Latino officials in cities throughout Rhode Island.

The at-large members are Luis Aponte, Ingrid Ardaya, Tomas A. Avila, Alido Baldera, Betty Bernal, Carolina Bernal, Ana Cabrera, Alberto Aponte Cardona, Gonzalo Cuervo, Maria Fernanda Escudero, Jose Gonzalez, Margarita Guedes, Andy Lemus, Miguel Luna, Tomas Morin, Ricardo Patino, Juan M. Pichardo, Tomas Ramirez, and former RILPAC President Pablo Rodriguez.

Minorities Blast Plan For Districts

With the legislative-redistricting panel's final vote looming, community leaders threaten suit over the Senate map.

By Edward Fitzpatrick
Journal State House Bureau
12.8.2001

PROVIDENCE -- Amid the threat of lawsuits and protests from black and Latino leaders, the redistricting commission last night narrowed its choices to one House map and one Senate map, preparing for a final vote Tuesday.

During a news conference before last night's meeting, a coalition of groups took aim at the Senate plan, saying it only gives the appearance of treating minority groups fairly. Several speakers charged that the map would "pack" a high percentage of minorities into one South Side district, depriving nearby districts of the numbers needed to elect another minority senator.

"The veneer of inclusiveness is but a cruel hoax on the disenfranchised and the poor," said Dr. Pablo Rodriguez, president of the Rhode Island Latino Political Action Committee. After last night's meeting, Senate leaders vigorously defended the proposal, saying it would create four nonwhite-majority Senate districts in Providence and provide fertile ground for minority senatorial candidates in the future. "The redistricting commission has done its best to empower the minority community," Senate Majority Leader William V. Irons said in an interview.

The redistricting commission is redrawing legislative district lines to reflect both new census data and a voter-mandated downsizing of the House, from 100 to 75 members, and the Senate, from 50 to 38 members. Before last night, there were two House proposals and two Senate proposals. The Senate now contains one black member, Sen. Charles D. Walton, D-Providence, and no Hispanics. And several speakers at yesterday's news conference said the proposed Senate map would make it possible to elect just one minority senator in next year's elections. They noted the proposal would put Walton in an 81.6-percent nonwhite district that would also include Juan M. Pichardo, a Hispanic candidate who narrowly lost a senatorial race last year.

"We will not allow African-Americans to be pitted against Latinos in a struggle for political crumbs," Rodriguez said. "We are here today together, we will protest together, and we will go to court together if that is the path we are forced into." While there would be four majority-nonwhite districts in Providence based on total population, that ignores the voting-age

296

populations in those districts and the proportions of minority members who have voted in past elections, speakers said. Many of the districts contain a lot of underage minorities and immigrants who can't vote, and minority voting levels have often been low in some of those areas, they said.

"Racial packing is a concern, and one super majority-minority district of 81 percent pitting blacks against Hispanics is not the answer," said former state Rep. Harold M. Metts, chairman of the Minority Reapportionment Committee. "Two districts could easily be created to protect the interest of both communities." Sen. Joseph A. Montalbano, vice chairman of the redistricting commission, said the panel followed the request of groups such as Common Cause of Rhode Island to keep Providence districts within city lines to avoid diluting minority populations. "And that parameter empowers minorities to win in these districts," he said.

Montalbano and Irons said they couldn't predict whether there would be more minority senators in 2003 because they don't know who the candidates are, but Irons said the proposed map offers the chance to have five minority senators in the future. And even if one minority senator is elected next year, he said it's better to have one minority senator in a 38-member Senate than one in a 50-member Senate. Montalbano said the overall number of minority members and the voting-age population of minority members are bound to grow in those districts in the years ahead. And Irons said that will create "the mathematical certainty" of electing more minority senators. Some critics are simply trying to elect Walton and Pichardo, Irons said, calling that the kind of political mapmaking that has been criticized in the past. "That's not about empowering minorities for the future," he said. "That's about anointing a few minority candidates."

The proposed Senate map unveiled yesterday actually contains just three majority-minority districts in Providence. Redistricting consultant Kimball W. Brace said that in making last-minute changes, one Providence district was unintentionally lowered to a 48-percent nonwhite population. Montalbano told Brace, "I know you were up till 4 a.m. working on these maps, but I would insist that between now and Tuesday you retain the number of majority-minority districts as four." Brace said, "It was an unfortunate click of the mouse. Certainly, we can put that back."

'It's Not a Spanish and English thing'

by Milton Valencia
The Pawtucket Times
December 10, 2001

PAWTUCKET -- Nellie Gorbea foresees a community moving forward. Dominicans, Colombians, Mexicans, Guatemalans, Puerto Ricans and, for that matter, anyone else who wants a better life, and is better able to pursue one through an improved education system, access to health insurance and a sense of affirmative action within state government.

"There are ways in which we can help each other out," the 34-year-old East Greenwich resident said. "The important thing is to keep our doors open, and to stay humble and open to learning."

Gorbea is the new president of the Rhode Island Latino Political Action Committee, a group that since its formation has gained greater clout in the realm of Rhode Island politics. Gorbea's goal, along with the other 40 members of RILPAC, is to unite a community to advocate for change. As she sees it, everyone -- not only relatively recent Latino immigrants, but also those whose families have been here for generations -- wants the same things in life: a safe home and health for their family.

"This is not a new thing, it's not a Spanish and English thing," Gorbea said, "It's a quality of life thing."

She says all Rhode Islanders are represented in RILPAC.

"The PAC looks at the bigger picture," Gorbea said.

Moving here from Puerto Rico some 17 years ago, Gorbea said she's always wanted to play a role in improving quality of life. In her admissions essay to Princeton University, from which she graduated with an international/public affairs degree in 1988, Gorbea wrote of her desire to help improve the government of her homeland. "I never wanted to be part of that generation, to leave and never come back and make things better," she said, in a modest but confident manner. After graduating from Princeton, she worked in New Jersey state government -- as an education policy analyst for the governor's Committee on Children's Services and Planning then continued her schooling at Columbia University in New York, where she received her master's degree in public administration. She moved to Rhode Island, where her husband,

Steve D'Hondt, is a professor of oceanography at the University of Rhode Island. She worked as a program officer at the Rhode Island Foundation, where she says she met many of the Ocean State's leaders in politics and economic development. In 1998, she returned to Puerto Rico. "I grew up there, my family was there," she said. "I expected to go back."

She first worked at a Puerto Rico government development bank, and later was part of Governor Pedro Rossello's department of economic affairs. Gorbea and her husband would see each other every three or four weeks, but "the important thing is we stayed together through all of it."

During those three years, she also stayed in touch with the friends she had made Rhode Island, through the Internet and e-mail. And she stayed in contact with the Political Action Committee, hearing of the advances the Latino community was making and the influence it had on Rhode Island's economy and politics. "We built a basis for success in the future," she said, pointing out that RILPAC at that time was in its infancy. These days, "we're at the beginning of engaging in the great political process in this state," she said.

As health insurance and living expenses increase, there's always a community that falls behind and needs to be represented, she said. Gorbea predicts RILPAC will play an important role in helping that community be heard. She noted a major grant for social-service agency Progreso Latino that Sen. Lincoln Chafee announced recently. And she pointed out there are more Latinos holding public office around the state, including Central Falls, where Ricardo Patino will be inaugurated as a city councilman on Jan. 7. Patino's campaign theme, she noted, was to represent the community at large, not just Latinos. Patino is a member of RILPAC. "This is not about electing Latinos for Latinos," Gorbea said. She said it's about electing officials who know and can help address the community's needs.

RILPAC is charged with letting candidates know what those needs are, as it did with Chafee, who helped Progreso obtain the much-needed grant. "This is a committee where people can come together to be heard for a common agenda," Gorbea said. "We try to find a common goal and that is what makes the PAC so exciting.

"People with a variety of differing opinions on subjects can come together in a group called the Rhode Island Latino Political Action Committee."

Commission Serves Up Its Plans

After four months of work, the 16-member commission will turn the maps over to the legislature for approval.

By Edward Fitzpatrick
Journal State House Bureau
12.12.2001

PROVIDENCE -- The redistricting commission last night voted for proposed new Senate and House district maps that represent a massive shakeup of Rhode Island's political universe.

The maps, which now go before the General Assembly for approval, reflect new census figures and a voter-mandated downsizing of the House from 100 to 75 members and the Senate from 50 to 38 members.

"It's a brave new world," said Sen. Leo R. Blais, R-Coventry, a member of the commission. "Everyone will be getting new territory. It's not John Smith's or Sally Smith's district anymore. None of us can be 100-percent happy, but the commission has achieved its goals."

The 16-member commission voted unanimously for the House and Senate maps as well as new congressional districts, completing four months of work that encompassed 22 public meetings. The legislature will need to vote on the plans by mid- to late-February so that cities and towns can adjust their voting districts in time for next year's primary elections, redistricting consultant Kimball W. Brace said.

One of the most contentious issues has been the drawing of Senate districts for the South Side of Providence. On Friday, black and Latino leaders made a last-ditch effort to avoid a district that would include the lone black senator, Charles D. Walton, and Juan M. Pichardo, a Hispanic candidate who narrowly lost a Senate race last year. They predicted the proposed map would result in just one minority senator in next year's elections.

But commission members kept the Senate plan intact, noting it would create four majority-nonwhite districts in Providence that would provide future opportunities for minority candidates.

Alma Felix Green, a Hispanic Providence resident appointed to the commission by Senate Majority Leader William V. Irons, defended the Senate map, saying, "our plan was not perfect or popular, but it was prudent."

300

Felix Green said she would have liked to have created an "open" seat by putting Pichardo in a district with no incumbents. But that was not possible with downsizing, she said, and it would have diluted minority populations in other Senate districts in Providence.

Critics claimed Senate leaders configured South Side districts to benefit Senate Finance Chairman Frank T. Caprio and Sen. David V. Igliozzi. "I've heard a lot about protecting the mythical interests of the Caprios and the Igliozzis," Felix Green said. "That was not what it was about."

Addressing her Hispanic friends, she said, "I didn't want to pack the future into the present. Through birth and immigration, we will truly lay claim to this land."

William Tammelleo, a Jamestown resident appointed to the commission by Irons, said, "The one burning issue is not having an open seat on the South Side of Providence." But the result was inevitable, he said, because of downsizing and because of the decision to keep Providence districts wholly within the city to avoid diluting minority populations. "If there is an evil, it's in the downsizing," he said. "It was a terrible mistake."

Another Hispanic commission member, Yahaira Placencia, asked how many of the proposed Providence districts have a nonwhite-majority when it comes to voting-age population, as opposed to overall population. The answer was three districts -- the ones that include Walton, Caprio and Igliozzi.

Rep. Joseph S. Almeida, a black commission member who is chairman of the Rhode Island Minority Caucus, asked if the panel could vote on the House and Senate plans separately. The commission chairwoman, Rep. Denise C. Aiken, D-Warwick, said the maps would be voted on as a package because the redistricting consultant dovetailed many House and Senate lines to avoid small pockets of voters.

Almeida, D-Providence, emphasized that new census figures show more than half of Providence's population is now nonwhite. "I know there will be a great coalition of black and Latino political power," he said, "and we are not going to wait 10 years or 5 years or even 3 years."
After the meeting, Dr. Pablo Rodriguez, president of the Rhode Island Latino Political Action Committee, said, "It didn't have to be this way. We could have had two districts where minorities could have been elected."

During the meeting, Sen. Catherine E. Graziano, a commission member, sought to dispel the idea that the redistricting plans were designed to target female incumbents. The Senate plan would put 7 of the 10 female senators in districts with other incumbents.

Graziano, D-Providence, said the commission tried to avoid pitting women against women. And while the plan would put Graziano in the same district as another Senate committee chairwoman -- Sen. Maryellen Goodwin -- she said that resulted from the simple fact that they live in adjacent areas of the city. "As someone who has consistently espoused women's causes and encouraging women to enter politics, I'd be the last person to support a plan targeting women," she said.

The commission also voted for a U.S. congressional district map that would shift nearly 14,000 Providence residents from Rep. James R. Langevin's 2nd Congressional District to Rep. Patrick J.

Kennedy's 1st Congressional District. The two congressmen each now represent 19 cities and towns, with Providence split between them. The new map, called Plan S, would give Kennedy the Mount Pleasant and Elmhurst neighborhoods, plus part of Smith Hill.

The commission rejected another map, called Plan T, which came under fire because it would have split up minority communities in South Providence.

Langevin and Kennedy, both Democrats, issued a joint statement saying they preferred Plan S. "After hearing the testimony of both the public and the members of the Rhode Island Reapportionment Commission at the commission hearing on Dec. 4, both of us agree that Plan T is not a viable choice because it splits the minority community of South Providence and is far too dramatic of a change for the simple task of moving approximately 13,500 people," the congressmen stated.

The Face May Change But The Spirit Endures

The 2000 Census showed that the growth of the Hispanic population brought the biggest shift in Rhode Island's ethnic mix since 1900.

By Scott MacKAY
Journal Staff Writer
12.31.2001 00:10

PROVIDENCE -- They are the phrases applied forever to Rhode Island: parochial and provincial, resistant to change, wary of outsiders, sealed off by its culture as New England's little backwater.

Census 2000 gave Rhode Island a multicolored portrait of itself at the dawn of a century. Along the way, it punctured some of those Rhode Island stereotypes -- but also reinforced a centuries-old theme: that of a state constantly reinventing itself through immigration.

During the 1990s, the state's population grew by 41/2 percent, to 1,048,319 people -- the most ever.

This growth was attributable solely to the presence of minority-group members, because the rest of the population -- the non-Hispanic whites -- decreased by nearly 38,000. Almost 1 in 5 Rhode Islanders is now a member of one of the state's minority groups.

A decade ago, only one small place in Rhode Island had a predominance of minority-group members: the South Side of Providence. By 2000 -- for the first time in history -- minority-group members dominated the numbers in both Providence and Central Falls, and in parts of Pawtucket.

The scales were tipped in these places by the growth of Rhode Island's Hispanic population, which during the 1990s doubled to 90,000. This growth represents the biggest shift in Rhode Island's mix since 1900, when European immigrants started competing in numbers with the Yankees and the Irish-Americans.

And, fueling Providence's 8-percent growth (almost twice the state's growth rate), Hispanics brought the city's total population to 173,618 allowing

303

Providence to surpass Worcester and reclaim its historical position as New England's second-largest city.

The growth in the state's minority numbers is consistent with that of most of the rest of the country, including Rhode Island's neighbors, Massachusetts and Connecticut. Minorities now compose about 31 percent of the U.S. population.

THERE WERE other trends in Rhode Island that the 2000 Census confirmed.

Many Rhode Islanders now want to live in communities they once viewed as summer destinations. The coastal and South County communities saw soaring growth, and many black and some Asian residents of Providence moved to such once-white cities as Pawtucket and Cranston.
To literally see some of this shift, take a walk.

Stroll down Broad Street, South Providence's lifeline, and note the names: El Malecon Restaurant, Pella Del Caribe Market, Pito's Restaurant, Hernandez Liquors, Asian Bakery, Sanchez Market, Mekong Market, and El Nanito Record Shop.

Fifty years ago, these buildings bore different names: Cohen's Market, Kolodoff's Liquor, Colarusso Bakery, Prescott Drug Co., McNeil's Children's Shop, Moran's Bakery, Hanley's Tap, and Celona Pharmacy.

Eavesdrop inside these places, and Spanish is what you'll mostly hear.

It isn't just on Providence's Broad Street that you'll encounter such change. Smith Street, running from the State House to North Providence, showed these names on a map from 1950: Cook's Fish Market, the Scottish Fish and Chips Store, Rinaldi's Variety, McPhillips Ice Cream, MacLachlan's Service, Zeitel's Radio and Appliance, and Max Weinberg Tailors.

These businesses are no more. Today's traveler down Smith Street passes Yun Nan Restaurant, Lao Lanexang Market, Patrick's Pub, Mandarin Garden, Cristina Market: Spanish and American Foods, and Alvarez Furniture.

BUT RHODE ISLAND'S new ethnic communities involve much more than business. A good place to witness all-encompassing change is Providence's Silver Lake neighborhood -- transforming faster than any other neighborhood in the state.
Ten years ago, Silver Lake had one of Providence's smallest concentrations of minority-group members. An Italian-American redoubt, the neighborhood

was 86-percent non-Hispanic white. Today, non-Hispanic whites make up just 34 percent of the population.

Silver Lake had produced such politicians as U.S. Sen. John O. Pastore, Gov. Christopher Del Sesto, and Mayor Vincent A. Cianci Jr. At midcentury, the names you would see on Pocasset Avenue included Dr. Vincent A. Cianci (the mayor's father), Buonanno's Pharmacy, Gelfuso Bros. Gas Station, Casali Brothers Liquors, Franco's Clothing Store, Zompa's Cleansers, Pannone Meats, DePasquale Fruits, Spadaro Shoe Repair, and Calabrese Variety.

Today in this neighborhood, even a business with a generic name is likely to be run by someone of Hispanic origin. Wendy Garcia, for example, is the principal broker at Silver Lake Realty.

St. Bartholomew's Church was founded by Italian immigrants, but its Spanish-language Mass now draws six times as many worshipers as its Italian-language Mass. And at the Silver Lake Little League field, middle-aged white coaches hit fungoes to mostly Hispanic, Asian, and African-American children.

When the coaches call the players' homes to schedule a practice, the parents answering the phone may not speak English; the children must translate for the adults.

English as a Second Language classes are common now at Webster Avenue School -- which 10 years ago had such a high proportion of white native English speakers that officials talked of busing out some of the pupils, to comply with desegregation laws.

Meanwhile, in other parts of Providence, other kinds of movement took place during the '90s. Many of the black inner-city residents moved to less urban settings in Pawtucket, North Providence, and Cranston -- reducing Providence's racial segregation to its lowest level since the 1930s.

LESS HEMMED in than ever by geography, Rhode Islanders nowadays commute much farther than in the past. Their forebears may have walked from wood-frame triple-decker to red-brick cloth factory, but today's residents live on the ocean or out in the country, while working in downtown Providence or even Greater Boston.

Every weekday, about one of seven employed Rhode Islanders crosses the line into Massachusetts for the many high-tech jobs and better pay. You can see them at 6 a.m. at the Providence train station, or on Routes 95 and 295, slugging coffee from behind the wheel.

In their retreat to the rural, many of these commuters have spread out into such once-quiet communities as Richmond, West Greenwich, and South Kingstown. To receive them, developers have plowed under fields of potatoes and turf, and erected subdivisions of single-family houses with multicar garages.

In their wake have come environmental pressures, traffic, and, to educate all the new children, soaring tax bills.

Some would say that this is the downside of the flourishing southeastern - New England economy of the late 1990s.

CHANGE in Rhode Island during the 1990s also occurred within the community of the elderly.

Some of the harsh truths of getting old are unwavering; the elderly will always face the death of spouses and friends, failing health, loss of independence, and depression.

Yet much has evolved in the last decade in the lives of the older residents of Rhode Island -- the state with the sixth-highest percentage of elderly residents in the country, and the highest percentage in New England.

Gone is the old "senior center," with its coffee-drinking, chain-smoking elders playing endless rounds of bingo or sitting in a corner knitting. In its place are such multipurpose facilities as Cranston Senior Services and, in North Providence, the Salvatore Mancini Resource and Activity Center.

The people who come to these centers are more likely to attend an exercise class than play bingo. They get blood-pressure checks, eat nutritious lunches, and enroll in high-school and college courses that they may have missed when they were younger and busier.

These Rhode Islanders -- many of them widows and widowers -- are getting involved with each other in ways that would have made earlier generations blush. Take 92-year-old Bill Della Valle, of North Providence, and 78-year-old Irene Pickles, of Smithfield. They have been inseparable since their eyes locked during a line-dancing class; they speak openly of their love for each other, and are physically affectionate.

306

The dating scene among the elderly is easier for the men. Women tend to live longer -- Rhode Islanders 85 years and older are about 74-percent female -- so there is a clear imbalance.

IT ISN'T just among Rhode Island's elderly, though, that there is a shortage of men. The census confirmed what all Rhode Island women seem to know: this state has a higher ratio of females to males than any other. For every 100 women, there are just 92.5 men.

The gender gap may be widest among the elderly, but look at this age group: on the college campuses in Rhode Island, 42,000 female students take classes alongside 33,000 males.

Another kind of gender gap exists in the world of work -- the gap in pay. The numbers show that, on average, Rhode Island women earn about 64 cents for every dollar earned by Rhode Island men. The difference is slightly more pronounced in low-wage jobs, those in which women make less than $20,000 a year. Yet it exists at all levels of the working world.

When it comes to gender roles, Rhode Island's biggest change in the last decade has been in the number of households headed by same-sex partners particularly those of male couples in what were once "Ozzie and Harriet" suburbs.

Rhode Island now ranks 16th among states in percentage of households headed by same-sex couples. While gay-rights advocates say discrimination persists in some quarters, almost everyone in the state's gay community says that things have gotten better since 1995, when Governor Almond signed into law the Gay Civil Rights Act.

Typical of male partners openly living together are Tony Caparco and Frank Ferri, of Warwick's Riverview section. Since 1985, Caparco, a store manager, and Ferri, a bowling-alley owner, have shared their home in this traditional suburban neighborhood of minivans and married couples with children.

Just like their neighbors, Caparco and Ferri hold neighborhood barbecues. One neighbor, who at first wasn't sure what to expect, refers to the two as "regular guys."

It is no longer unusual to see gay couples holding hands at Providence's *WaterFire* . And a magazine for lesbian women, Girlfriends, has ranked Rhode Island's capital among the cities most friendly to lesbians.

Meanwhile, Rhode Island households headed by a single parent are mostly headed by women. Yet a small but growing number of single-parent households now feature men. The census showed 7,300 male-headed single-parent households in Rhode Island in 2000 -- a 76-percent increase since 1990. Still, about 80 percent of the state's single-parent households in 2000 were headed by women.

WHILE the census showed Rhode Island blending the new with the old, that doesn't mean, of course, that every community is in flux. In many places, the Rhode Island of 2000 looks pretty much like the Rhode Island of 1990 -- or 1950.

Take Burrillville, the woodsy former mill town in the state's northwest corner. Roughly 98 percent of the 15,976 residents are non-Hispanic white; with Little Compton, this represents the highest proportion of such residents in the state.

Life in Burrillville still moves to the rhythms of church (mostly Roman Catholic), high-school hockey, rural roads, and open spaces.

Time moves similarly slowly in other outer suburbs of Providence, such as nearby Glocester and North Smithfield. In these towns, too, the minority population barely exceeds 2 percent of the total.

Another old mill community whose appearance has changed little is Woonsocket. Its distinction is that it is the one Rhode Island community to have steadily *lost* population since 1950.

While the city has a much larger minority population than it did a decade ago, it keeps losing non-Hispanic whites, and the economic boom of the 1990s bypassed its downtown.

Once a world-famous textiles producer its worsted wool was particularly prized -- Woonsocket has yet to find a modern engine. Few businesses, old or new, have succeeded in the graceful old red-brick downtown, although city officials keep searching for magnets to attract them.

The city has made a real effort. The Stadium Theatre has been reopened in all its Jazz Age splendor, and in October the Museum of Work and Culture, a tribute to Rhode Island's industrial past, attracted the most visitors it had ever had. Programs abound to fix up old houses downtown, where there is now even a skating rink.

Still, a drive around downtown Woonsocket is a trip to the past. The brick mills shadow the Blackstone River, their smokestacks though long extinguished still competing on the skyline with the steeples of the churches.

The northern part of Woonsocket, where the mill owners' stately Victorian houses can be bought for a fraction of what they would cost in Providence, increasingly serves as a bedroom community for Greater Boston.

FIDDLE with the car-radio dial, in Woonsocket or Westerly, and you can find a talk show that is a gripe session about state and local government. This, too, is an unchanging aspect of Rhode Island.

Rhode Islanders love to grouse about how much money their governments spend, and how high their state and local taxes are. The 2000 Census figures show, however, that the state ranks 27th nationally in expenditures. And its tax burden, though higher than that of many other states, is lower than the burden in Connecticut, Maine, New York, and New Jersey.

CHANGE and continuity: Despite all the new trends documented during the past decade, there is still much about Rhode Island that endures.

As the state's non-Hispanic white population has declined, new immigrants many fleeing the poverty of Latin America -- have poured in. It's part of a time-tested Rhode Island pattern. The newcomers, whether Latin Americans or Asians or others, arrive and weave a community. These new communities come to dominate neighborhoods that earlier received people from other parts of the world -- Portugal, Eastern Europe, Italy, Canada, Ireland initially, England.

Once again, the new Rhode Islanders are proving that the experience of immigration remains much the same from generation to generation and from one group to another. It is the oldest of American stories -- people moving here in search of safety, self-direction, betterment of their children, a satisfying spiritual life, and freedom from want.

City Furnishes Bilingual Ballots

The ballots are required because census figures show at least 5 percent of Providence's population are members of a single-language minority with limited proficiency in English.

By Gregory Smith
Journal Staff Writer
07/30/2002

PROVIDENCE -- Because of the federal Voting Rights Act, there will be a bilingual election ballot -- in English and Spanish -- in Providence for the first time this year.

The requirement has been in force in Central Falls for 10 years.

The U.S. Justice Department and the U.S. Bureau of the Census announced that Providence will have to comply with the minority-language section of the Voting Rights Act and "provide access" to all stages of its election process to people with no command or a poor command of English.

To qualify under the law -- the requirement was enacted in 1992 -- voters must be members of a minority group that meets certain literacy standards. In Providence, those are Hispanics.

The federal law means the secretary of state's office, which prints ballots for all Rhode Island cities and towns, will have to furnish bilingual ballots for Providence. And the city must have bilingual poll workers.

"This is a big step toward insuring that our Spanish-speaking citizens have an equal opportunity to vote," Secretary of State Edward S. Inman III said in a statement yesterday.

For citizens who have trouble speaking English, an English-only ballot can be confusing, said Mark Corallo, a spokesman for the Justice Department, which enforces the law for the Census Bureau. "So Congress said, 'Let's make it accessible to every citizen,' " he said.

The ballots to be used at the polls as well as mail ballots and applications for mail ballots will be printed in English and Spanish and there will not be separate ballots, according to Laurence K. Flynn, chairman of the Providence Board of Canvassers.

Because Inman anticipated the federal requirement, the state held off printing ballots for the Sept. 10 primary election in Providence, so the cost of reprinting will be avoided, Inman said.

Under federal and state law, the secretary of state said, a city is required to provide bilingual ballots when census figures show that 5 percent of the city population are members of a single-language minority who have limited proficiency in English.

The single-language minority group must also have an illiteracy rate in their native language that is higher than the national average.

In other places around the nation, the law requires ballots in Chinese, Korean and American Indian languages, among others.

Recognizing the need for bilingual poll workers, Flynn said the city has been arranging in recent years to have such workers available at certain polling places. But now a more concerted effort will be made to recruit them, he said.

For instance, polls in Wards 9 and 15 have a high concentration of Hispanic voters, Flynn pointed out.

The Democratic and Republican parties appoint poll workers and, if they fail to do so, the Board of Canvassers can appoint poll workers. The board will work with the parties, Flynn said, to encourage the recruitment of more bilingual workers.

The ballot requirement will not cost the city any money, according to Flynn.

Lawsuit Challenges Redistricting

Hispanic leaders announce the suit, saying the plan will dilute Hispanic voting power.

By Edward Fitzpatrick
Journal State House Bureau
07/03/2002

PROVIDENCE -- Calling it a "case that will make history," a coalition of Hispanic groups and individuals yesterday filed a redistricting lawsuit in U.S. District Court, charging that new state Senate districts in Providence are unconstitutional.

Senate mapmakers could have drawn a district in which the majority of the voting-age population is Hispanic, but instead they "split the heart" of the Elmwood neighborhood and in the process illegally diluted Hispanic voting power, the plaintiffs claim.

The map puts Juan M. Pichardo, a Hispanic candidate who nearly won a Senate seat in 2000, in the same district as the Senate's only black member, Sen. Charles D. Walton, D-Providence. And Hispanic leaders say the map is likely to result in just one minority senator being elected this fall despite the explosive growth in the state's Hispanic population.

Dr. Pablo Rodriguez, chairman of the Latino Voting Rights Committee of Rhode Island, and other Hispanic leaders announced the legal action while standing across from the federal courthouse in downtown Providence.

"Today we say to all that would listen that Latinos are here to stay, as full participants in the social, civic and political life of the state," Rodriguez said. "We will fight until we exhaust every legal option available to us in order to ensure that the future of this state takes into account the future of Rhode Island's newest citizens."

The suit represents the second legal challenge to a redistricting plan that reflects both new census figures and a voter-mandated downsizing of the House from 100 to 75 members and the Senate from 50 to 38 members.

A coalition of civil-rights groups and black South Providence residents have filed a suit that also targets the Senate map, alleging that it illegally dilutes black voting power in that part of the city. Chief U.S. District Judge Ernest

C. Torres has scheduled a hearing for July 17 on a motion to dismiss the case.

That suit's plaintiffs, which include the NAACP's Providence branch and the Urban League of Rhode Island, have suggested postponing some of the Senate primaries scheduled for Sept. 10.

The latest suit also seeks injunctions to halt use of those Providence Senate districts. But Nellie M. Gorbea, president of the Rhode Island Latino Political Action Committee, said it will be up to the judge to decide how the legal action affects the political calendar. The coalition would like new districts drawn as soon as possible, "but we realize this political year is already in full swing," she said.

Rodriguez said the two lawsuits are not working at cross-purposes and can help achieve the same goal. Indeed, yesterday's news release included a quote from Anita S. Hodgkiss, of the Lawyers' Committee for Civil Rights Under Law, which is representing the black plaintiffs: "We welcome the opportunity this creates to make sure that Providence's Senate districts are fair to all minorities."

Rodriguez said the suit was not filed sooner because the coalition wanted to analyze previous elections and show that "Latinos deserve a district where they could elect a senator."

The plaintiffs say they have proven it's possible to draw an Elmwood-area Senate district where the voting-age population is 51-percent Hispanic. Instead, the new Senate map creates two districts that have Hispanic voting-age populations of 40 percent and 43 percent. As a result, the suit states, Hispanic voting power is diluted, denying them an opportunity to elect candidates of their choice, in violation of the 14th Amendment to the U.S. Constitution.

Senate Majority Leader William V. Irons, D-East Providence, said, "I have great respect for the Latino community, but I disagree with their position on this issue."
"The problem Latinos have is they are a young population," Irons said. But as more Hispanics reach voting age, he said, the new Senate map will provide "significant potential" to elect five Hispanic senators -- four in Providence and one in Central Falls.

Rodriguez said, "We are being told to yet again wait our turn when the law is clearly in our favor. If we need to wait for 10 years, then what is the point of redistricting?"

Senate leaders point out that despite downsizing, the map maintains five majority-nonwhite districts. But Rodriguez said putting minority groups together in one district -- and counting Hispanics, blacks and Asians as one large minority community -- is not a "safe harbor" against claims under the Voting Rights Act. He said that is especially true in South Providence, where Hispanics can be the majority group all by themselves.

"Political power for one minority group cannot come at the expense of another," Rodriguez said, "and in this case, given the current maps, it comes at the expense of both African-Americans and Latinos."

Rodriguez concluded his speech, saying, "Together we row or together we sink. The words of Martin Luther King Jr. will be very appropriate once we win because 'Justice will flow like a river and self-righteousness like a mighty stream.' "

The plaintiffs in the latest suit include the Latino Voting Rights Committee of Rhode Island, the Center for Hispanic Policy and Advocacy of Providence, the Mexican Association of Rhode Island, Progreso Latino of Central Falls, Quisqueya En Accion of Providence, the Rhode Island Latino Political Action Committee, plus individuals such as Providence Councilman Luis A. Aponte, City Council candidate Miguel C. Luna, Francisco J. Cruz, Hilma Franco and Jacinta Pena.

A Light Roasting For Rodriguez

By Edward Fitzpatrick
Journal State House Bureau
06/24/2002

About 300 people came to Warwick's Crowne Plaza Hotel for a June 14 roast of Dr. Pablo Rodriguez , raising $42,000 to help launch the Rhode Island Latino Civic Fund.

Rodriguez, one of Rhode Island's best-known Latino and abortion-rights leaders, received a light roasting from Republican U.S. Sen. Lincoln D. Chafee and Democratic U.S. Sen. Jack Reed.

During his turn at the podium, Chafee joked that Rodriguez, a Democrat, is actually a Republican, drawing comparisons between Rodriguez and President Bush .

Both Rodriguez and Mr. Bush speak Spanish, Chafee noted, although he said Rodriguez is more fluent in Spanish and he joked that there's debate about who is more fluent in English.

Both Rodriguez and Mr. Bush are good dancers, Chafee said. While the president knows the "Texas two-step," Rodriguez has a wider repertoire, he said.

Finally, Chafee said, both Rodriguez and the president have fathers who worked for the federal government, although Rodriguez's father cut hair while Mr. Bush's father "cut many social programs."

Reed stood at the podium next to a cardboard likeness of Rodriguez, who was depicted in an Uncle Sam outfit. "I'm jealous of Pablo for many things," Reed said. "Among them is that even his poster is taller than I am."

Reed also joked about his limited Spanish vocabulary, recalling a phrase from a high school Spanish course that translates into "Crap, I forgot my notebook."

A biographical slide show followed, showing a younger Rodriguez sporting an Afro and a handlebar moustache.

Then Rodriguez came to the podium, saying, "Many of you have asked if I will run for political office, so this is a perfect opportunity for me to announce my intentions."

The room grew silent as he said, "Rhode Island needs new leadership -- someone respected in all circles." So, Rodriguez said, he was announcing his candidacy . . . to be the husband of his wife, the father of his children, etc.
"I got you all," he said, laughing.

Rodriguez emphasized the importance of the Latino Civic Fund, a nonprofit sister organization of the Rhode Island Latino Political Action Fund. The new group, headed by Nellie M. Gorbea , won't endorse candidates but will provide information in Spanish about what various government officials do, who is running in the elections and what their platforms entail.

"Latinos are the fastest growing segment of the population in the state," Rodriguez said. "And it's important that they step up to the plate, and voting is a big part of that."

Latino Politicians Launch Campaigns

M. Charles Bakst
On the circuit
The Providence Journal
05/28/2002

In the lunchroom of the Lillian Feinstein at Sackett Street Elementary School in Providence's Elmwood area, tape on the wall formed the outlines of the FOOD PYRAMID, or PIRAMIDE DE COMIDA.

More than 100 people flocked here recently to watch Juan Pichardo, 35, kick off his 2002 candidacy for state Senate. The crowd included Atty. Gen. Sheldon Whitehouse, whose drive for governor Pichardo supports.

In a 2000 Democratic primary, Pichardo, a Latino, barely lost to veteran incumbent Bob Kells. As a result of this year's legislative downsizing, Pichardo is now running in a primary in a reconfigured district against Sen. Charles Walton, the chamber's only black member.

Welcome to the new District 2, which takes in Elmwood, Lower South Providence, and Washington Park. Hispanics outnumber blacks. Putting Pichardo and Walton in the same district created an uproar. There were charges that lines were drawn to protect white senators while lessening the chances of minorities to elect two of their own. Pichardo and Walton back efforts in court to undo the situation.

Meanwhile, Pichardo, a Rhode Island Hospital patient advocate, plows ahead with his campaign. He says that in some ways he feels bad running against Walton, 53: "He certainly represents a lot of history in Rhode Island. But at the same time, I think that as a community and a state that are moving forward and are looking toward the future, we have to provide options to the voters."

A complication: the presence of another candidate, real estate developer Pedro Espinal, 37. Like Pichardo, he was born in the Dominican Republic. Pichardo frets that Espinal may split the Latino vote. Espinal, who announced first, says he's not doing the splitting.

Most of the new seat's territory is from Walton's old district. Espinal, like Walton, lives in Washington Park; he says Pichardo, of Elmwood, is "coming into my district." Pichardo says that until a couple of years ago he used to live in the district too and is a familiar face.

Walton, a CCRI administrator, has been in the Senate since 1983. He says he likes Pichardo: "I've encouraged him and others from the Latino community to get involved." But he also hints that, before running in District 2, Pichardo should have waited. "At some point I do expect to move on to perhaps bigger and better things."

Pichardo made his announcement in Spanish and English.

I went that same evening to the Metacomet Country Club in East Providence where Larry Shetler launched his Republican candidacy for lieutenant governor, a steep uphill run against incumbent Democrat Charlie Fogarty.

Shetler, 50, is community liaison officer for the Providence Economic Development Corporation, a quasi-public city agency. In the crowd: his "significant other," Linda Verhulst, an aide to Mayor Buddy Cianci.

Shetler was born in Pennsylvania of Puerto Rican parents, but was adopted from an orphanage at age 3 by an Amish-Mennonite couple. As for thinking of himself as Hispanic, Shetler told me, "When I was growing up, the nursery rhyme, 'Eenie, meenie, minie, mo, catch a ------ by the toe,' was real for me. I lived in a town where nobody was like me. I was never invited to other people's birthday parties because I was not perceived to be the right color."

Though identifying with Latinos, he says there's something that drives them to distraction. Here at Metacomet, confirming it, is his pal, Marcos Antonio, Cianci's director of Hispanic affairs. "I know he's Puerto Rican," Antonio says of Shetler, "but he doesn't know how to say one word of Spanish!"

Redistricting Suits Coming

The providence Journal
Political Scene
04/29/2002

Two months have passed since the redistricting bill became law, establishing new legislative districts to reflect updated census figures and a voter-mandated downsizing of the House and Senate. But no lawsuits have been filed, although at least one and possibly more are expected.

Nellie M. Gorbea, president of the Rhode Island Latino Political Action Committee, on Friday said it's just a matter of time. Hispanic groups and individuals are working together under the umbrella of the Latino Voting Rights Committee, and they plan to file a lawsuit soon, she said. The Hispanic coalition is also collaborating with the African-American community, she said. Gorbea said the lawsuit will target the new Senate districts in South Providence, charging that the districts dilute the voting power of both Hispanic and black communities. "Given the growth of the Hispanic population in Providence, we could have a Latino majority district," she said. "But the result of redistricting was to keep us under a majority."

So why hasn't the suit been filed yet? "It involves more than I ever imagined," Gorbea said. "You have to make sure you have your analysis done right, and we are collaborating with other groups." There's no deadline looming, Gorbea said. "But clearly, we are concerned with filing in a timely manner so that if we succeed changes would take effect this year," she said.

Redistricting grants

The Rhode Island Foundation has awarded three grants related to the legislative redistricting process. The largest grant, for $5,800, went to the Puerto Rican Legal Defense and Education Fund to support the Latino Voting Rights Committee. The money is supporting public forums to educate communities about new electoral districts, as well as providing for "coalition building." A $5,100 grant went to the Cranston-based Rhode Island Community Action Association to support a series of public forums on redistricting.

Espinal To Run For State Senate

Pedro J. Espinal is challenging an incumbent and fellow Democrat, state Sen. Charles D. Walton, in the new District 9.

By Gregory Smith
The Providence Journal
2.25.2002

PROVIDENCE -- Real estate investor Pedro J. Espinal has announced his candidacy for the Democratic nomination for state Senate in the new District 9 in Washington Park, Elmwood and South Providence.

The borders of the existing District 9, represented by Sen. Charles D. Walton, have been changed in the downsizing of the General Assembly.

Espinal is an elected member of the Democratic District Committee in the district now represented by Walton, a Democrat. It is unusual for a member of a General Assembly district committee to run against the incumbent legislator.

Walton is expected to seek reelection, and Juan Pichardo, a two-time Senate candidate whose political prospects have figured into the debate over downsizing, lives in the district now that it has been revamped and is a possible candidate.

"It could get crowded" in the Democratic primary election, Espinal said.

A legal challenge aimed at voiding the revamped Senate district boundaries remains possible, however.

Espinal said he wanted the District 9 Democratic Committee to be a forum for committee members to work with Walton for the betterment of the neighborhoods, and he is disappointed that Walton never called a meeting.

He said he wants to be a senator to help in the economic and social empowerment of residents.

"Many people have lost faith and cannot see a future . . .," the candidate said. He has worked on the political campaigns of Rep. Joseph Almeida, D-Providence, and former Rep. Marsha Carpenter, D-Providence.
Espinal, 37, of 162 Verndale Ave., is chairman of Direct Action for Rights and Equality, or DARE; chairman of the South Side Broad Street Committee;

and a member of the advisory board of the R.I. Victims of Crime Advocacy and Support Center.

He is also a member of the boards of directors of the Washington Park Citizens Association and the Washington Park Foundation.

Espinal said he is not to be confused with another Pedro J. Espinal, who is also a real estate investor and lives in the West End.

New Senate Map Is Unfair To Latinos

Nellie M. Gorbea
The Providence Journal
Editorial
2.6.2002

MEMBERS of the Latino community of Rhode Island have repeatedly testified at the legislature's public hearings on redistricting that the current plans for the Senate seats in Providence are unacceptable.

It is important to realize that this statement is not new. Latinos have raised these concerns at every opportunity provided by the Redistricting Commission. These are not a capricious concerns, they are concerns based on the fundamental rules of our legal system regarding redistricting and on the results of straight numbers -- the 2000 Census.

The U.S. Constitution requires that legislative districts be approximately equal in population size to each other. Thus, every person's vote has equal strength, from district to district. The Supreme Court also has indicated that legislative boundaries must be drawn so as to create compact districts with contiguous borders that respect existing political subdivisions or communities of interest. The Voting Rights Act of 1965 and subsequent case law forbid the dilution of minorities in the redistricting process. Section 2 of the Voting Rights Act states: "No voting qualification or prerequisite to voting, or standard, practice, or procedure shall be imposed or applied by any State or political subdivision to deny or abridge the right of any citizen of the United States to vote on account of race or color."

U.S. Supreme Court cases have further clarified this act by providing three defining conditions that must be present for minorities to demand a district in which they hold a majority. Those conditions are: (1) a minority group must be large enough and live in high enough density that a compact district can be drawn in which the minority is a majority, (2) the minority group must have a history of political cohesiveness or have voted as a group, and (3) the white majority has historically voted as a group so that minority group candidates are usually defeated.

The 2000 Census reported that the Hispanic population in Rhode Island had doubled from approximately 45,000 in 1990 to 90,000 in 2000. During this same period, Rhode Island's population increased from 1,003,464 to

1,048,319 -- an increase of 44,855. Basically, Rhode Island's population growth is due to that of the Latino community.

Because our system of political distribution is based on one person, one vote, any increase in population adds political power to a state. Let's keep this in mind as we look at Providence.

Population in Providence grew a total of 12,890, from 160,728 in 1990 to 173,618 in 2000. During that same decade, Latinos doubled their population from 24,982 in 1990 to 52,146 in 2000. According to the 2000 Census, Latinos now make up 30 percent of the population of Providence. You can see it in the school classrooms, in the home-sale transactions reported in The Journal on Saturdays, and in the thriving entrepreneurial activity that is essential to the vitality of the city. But we have not seen similar growth in Latino representation in elected office.

The Redistricting Commission claims to have created four majority minority Senate districts in Providence. There are several problems with that claim. First of all, if one looks at the demographics of those districts, focusing on such factors as voting-age population and voter registrations, one quickly realizes that those are not majority minority districts. They may be sometime in the future, but they are not so today. Second, the commission is treating all minorities as if they were one community of interest.

This is, sadly, not the case yet. African-Americans, Southeast Asians and Latinos do not vote together as one block. Any look at electoral races in Providence over the past 10 years will clearly demonstrate this. In fact, politicians frequently have taken advantage of this lack of unity and further fueled the divide between various minority groups in Providence. The placing of Sen. Charles Walton, an African-American who is the state's only minority senator, in a district with at least one very strong Latino contender is a clear example of this strategy.

Because of their numbers, their density and geographic compactness, Latinos in Providence should be able to gain at least one senatorial district where a majority of the voting age population is Latino. We will not be appeased by clever words that hide reality. The current Senate plan dilutes the Latino vote in all districts so that we are never able to elect the candidate of our choice. It also encourages confrontation with the state's only African-American senator.

Under the rules of redistricting, it is clear that we are not asking for special treatment. We are demanding that our community derive some of the benefits that we have granted the state by believing in Rhode Island enough to make it our home.

Like French-Canadians, Irish, Portuguese, Italians, Cape Verdeans and other immigrant groups, Latinos are in Rhode Island to stay. We exhort the legislature to live up to Roger Williams's legacy and recognize and welcome our community to the political power structure of Rhode Island.

Nellie M. Gorbea is the president of the Rhode Island Latino Political Action Committee.

Political Groups Give Nod To Cicilline

The Providence Journal
08/15/2002

PROVIDENCE -- David N. Cicilline has won the endorsement of two more political action committees.

The Rhode Island Latino Political Action Committee and APAC, the political action committee of the Rhode Island chapter of the Association of Community Organizations for Reform Now, both say Cicilline is the best Democratic candidate for mayor of Providence and that they will work to support him on primary day. Issuing the endorsement at Cicilline's Elmwood Avenue headquarters, Nellie M. Gorbea, president of the 35-member group, said yesterday: "David has long been known in the Latino community for his dedication and commitment to improving the quality of life for all residents of Providence. Our endorsement is natural, given his long track record in our community."

Cicilline said he was honored to receive the endorsement, saying that in the few short years since it has been organized, the Latino group's members have "'devoted themselves fully to improving the political opportunities for Latinos and all citizens in this state." The Cicilline campaign considers the endorsement significant because members of RILPAC encourage members of the Latino community to vote. The candidate said he has long been active in areas that affect the Latino community, including civil rights, community safety and access to government.

Cucy Cornejo, of the ACORN Political Action Committee, said the group is supporting Cicilline because "he is the candidate that will bring the downtown renaissance to our neighborhoods" and because "he will support our fight for jobs, affordable housing, improved city services and rat control."

RI ACORN, which is less than two years old, says it has more than 800 members throughout the state.

For Minorities, A 'Zero-Sum' Choice

By Edward Fitzpatrick
Journal Staff Writer
08/14/2002

As the result of a 1994 constitutional amendment, the General Assembly is undergoing a historic downsizing that coincides with this year's redistricting process. The House is shrinking from 100 to 75 members, while the Senate is shrinking from 50 to 38 members. The new maps have spurred lawsuits, pitted incumbents against each other and convinced some lawmakers to move or seek other seats. In the weeks ahead, The Journal will profile some of the races that will shape the new Assembly.

PROVIDENCE -- All of the political energy and intrigue, all of the venom and sadness of General Assembly redistricting and downsizing are most concentrated and most evident on the South Side of Providence this year.
There, amid a melting pot of blacks and whites, Asians and Hispanics, a new state Senate map has spawned two federal lawsuits and an unprecedented primary that pits Rhode Island's first and only black senator against a man who, two years ago, came within 100 votes of becoming Rhode Island's first and only Hispanic senator.

Sen. Charles D. Walton will take on Juan M. Pichardo in the Sept. 10 Democratic primary. The winner will square off against independent candidates Pedro J. Espinal and Rochelle Bates Lee, as well as Republican Yvon Chancy, in the Nov. 5 general election. The victor will go on to represent new Senate District 2, which spans all of Washington Park and most of South Providence and Elmwood. Only one other Assembly race has attracted five candidates, and no other Assembly district has spurred litigation.

Critics decry the new district, accusing Senate leaders of pitting blacks against Hispanics to protect favored white incumbents in other parts of Providence. Senate leaders vehemently deny that accusation, saying downsizing forced them to make a lot of difficult decisions, but that they took pains to protect the interests of Providence's minority voters. The debate is most pointed and passionate between Walton and Senate Majority Leader William V. Irons, D-East Providence.

"Irons should know better," Walton said, noting he and Irons were first elected in a 1983 special election, which was required because a Senate redistricting plan was deemed a gerrymander and tossed out by the courts.

"It's racial gerrymandering," Walton said of the latest Senate map. "What the leadership did was go in there with a meat cleaver and chop up minority interests in the South Side, Elmwood and the West End sections of the city."

Walton accused Senate leaders of drawing the map to protect two white Providence incumbents -- Sen. Frank T. Caprio and Sen. David V. Igliozzi -- and to avoid changes in Irons's East Providence constituent base. Walton said the leadership's alleged strategy is particularly galling because Igliozzi has since decided to run for mayor, and Irons has since clashed with Caprio and removed him as Finance Committee chairman.

"The Senate leadership has pitted neighborhood versus neighborhood and -- potentially -- racial group against racial group," Walton said. "That's the sad part of this whole thing. It didn't have to happen this way."

Irons bristled at Walton's remarks, accusing him of using "inflammatory rhetoric" and saying, "It's disgusting for him to say it's racial gerrymandering."

Irons said he can understand being upset about new district borders, because he was given an unfavorable district in the last redistricting plan. "But I didn't go to the press and accuse people of trying to cut my legs off," he said. "I went out and got reelected."

Irons noted the plaintiffs in one redistricting lawsuit have said they are not alleging "discriminatory intent" in the Senate map. The fact is, he said, that Providence's Hispanic population has grown rapidly over the past decade while many black residents have moved out of urban neighborhoods. "And that had nothing to do with Bill Irons," he said.

With downsizing, Senate districts had to grow by 25 percent, Irons said, and that resulted in some agonizing decisions, such as putting two members of the Senate leadership team in the same district -- Sen. Maryellen Goodwin and Sen. Catherine E. Graziano.

To avoid diluting minority concentrations, the Senate kept most Providence districts wholly within city borders, helping to create four majority-minority districts, Irons said. Igliozzi wanted to extend his district into Cranston, he said, "but we wouldn't let him do it because you'd dilute minority populations."

Irons said that when he became majority leader two years ago, he asked Walton to be the deputy majority leader in charge of minority issues. "But he wouldn't take it," Irons said. "He said, 'What happens if I lose an issue?

They'll blame me.' " The redistricting situation might be different, Irons suggested, if Walton "took the responsibility that I tried to give him."

Walton said he had a "philosophical opposition" to the title offered by Irons. "That shows white leaders would prefer to have one minority person deal with all the minority issues they don't want to deal with," he said, noting he'd been Senate president pro tempore under the prior leadership.

Darrell M. West, Brown University political science professor, described the District 2 Senate race as "zero-sum politics" for minorities, saying, "It's pitting Latinos versus African-Americans, so it's a very sad situation." But he said he doubts the lawsuits will overturn the Senate map because "with redistricting and downsizing, there really were no optimal solutions satisfying all the objectives."

H. Philip West Jr., executive director of Common Cause of Rhode Island and no relation to the professor, argued that much better solutions were available, but ignored.

West gave Senate leaders credit for keeping Providence districts within city borders -- something his watchdog group espoused. But he criticized them for lumping minority groups together to create the four majority-minority districts. "Counting all minorities as one is an illusion," he said. "It not only misrepresents the facts on the street, it also creates a hurt in a community that is already deeply hurt."

West, who lives in Elmwood, said Senate leaders "beheaded" Walton's former district, putting part of South Providence in a district that includes Federal Hill and Caprio's residence. At the same time, Senate leaders stuck Walton in a district that includes much of Elmwood and heavy concentrations of Hispanic residents. As a result, black voters could be "stripped of the only representation they have ever had in the state Senate," he said.

"African-Americans deserve a chance to elect someone that looks like them and to maintain some sense of empowerment, and Latinos deserve to be empowered," West said. "But it's an either/or scenario."
That scenario is just becoming clear to some voters.

As he campaigned door-to-door the other day, Pichardo approached a home in Washington Park. A Walton campaign sign was planted in the front yard, but Jose Hernandez emerged from the front door and greeted Pichardo warmly. Hernandez said he had not realized Walton and Pichardo were running against each other. "We thought we would be able to vote for both of them," he said.

"We know Senator Walton, and he's done a very good job," Hernandez said. But he said he supports Pichardo, a fellow Dominican Republic native whom he has known since the eighth grade. "We are really proud of Juan," he said. "He's very sincere. He speaks the language. And he's a young person -- a new generation of political leaders."

Walton went door-to-door in the Elmwood neighborhood yesterday along with state Rep. Leon F. Tejada, D-Providence, who is Hispanic, and City Councilwoman Patricia K. Nolan, who is white. The three have formed a coalition. "We are not going to kowtow to the Senate leadership and others who would pit our neighborhoods against each other," Walton said. "We are going to work together and show people you can have unity."

Tejada, also a Dominican Republic native, said he is supporting Walton because of his community involvement and because Walton is a "champion of education." He credited Walton with being one of the leading advocates for bringing the Community College of Rhode Island campus back to Providence. Walton is now CCRI's special programs director.

Pichardo, who is going door-to-door with Nigerian native Julius Kolawole, a campaign volunteer, said he doubts the Walton-Tejada-Nolan coalition will last long.

Pichardo said many people in the district desire a change in leadership. "Going door-to-door, I hear people saying, 'I don't know who my state senator is' because they haven't seen him," he said, referring to Walton. "I will be more accessible and present in the neighborhoods."

Walton called Pichardo's criticism "frivolous." He noted he has never represented part of the new district, and said, "People have no clue the hours you put in as a part-time legislator."

Pichardo says his community involvement shows he can provide the needed leadership. He is, for example, former president of the Elmwood Foundation, former president of Quisqueya in Action and a board member of the former Oasis Community Development Federal Credit Union.

Walton says his legislative records shows that he is already providing the required leadership. For example, he sponsored the 1986 Abandoned Property Act, which allows nonprofit agencies to take over abandoned properties. He helped create an arson prevention program and has repeatedly fought for increases in the state's minimum wage. "[Pichardo] wants change, but change for what?" Walton said. "You are going to have someone up there struggling for the next five to six years to figure out the legislative process."

Walton is the endorsed Democrat, but he accused Senate leaders of trying to steer the endorsement to Pichardo. He said Irons recommended a five-member Democratic district committee that included three of Pichardo's nominees and two of his. Walton said he only ended up with the endorsement because one of the women Pichardo nominated was a friend "who understood my track record" and ended up voting for Walton.

"Pichardo tried to grab the endorsement and get in bed with the person who tried to do this to us," Walton said. "The same damn people who have racially split our community and diluted our ability to elect more than one minority candidate to the Senate." Pichardo said the fact that Senate leaders chose three of his nominees "shows the credibility of my campaign." He said, "[Walton] should have worked very hard and had more standing in the Senate so this redistricting didn't affect us as much. It shows how effective he was in that whole process."

Walton said he fought hard against the Senate map -- submitting proposed amendments and helping to coordinate one of the redistricting lawsuits.
Walton said he encouraged Pichardo to get involved in the community and backed his last bid for Senate. But he said Pichardo "has failed to understand you never run against your mentor."

Pichardo said Walton has never been his mentor. "He's a person I respected who encouraged people to get involved and make a difference," he said. "And that's what I'm doing."

The New Senate District 2

Five candidates are running in the new state Senate district in Providence that includes all of Washington Park and most of Elmwood and South Providence:

Sen. Charles D. Walton, 54, of 82 Homer St., has been Rhode Island's only black state senator for 18 years and is running in the Democratic primary Sept. 10. He has worked at Rhode Island College and the Community College of Rhode Island for 24 years and is now CCRI's director of special programs. He graduated from Shaw University in North Carolina and received a master's degree in international education from the University of Massachusetts-Amherst. He is married and has a son. He said he has not decided whom to support for mayor and is "leaning toward" Democrat Myrth York for governor.

Juan M. Pichardo, 35, of 229 Atlantic Ave., narrowly lost a state Senate race two years ago and is running in the Democratic primary Sept. 10. He has worked at Rhode Island Hospital for 15 years, including 10 years as a patient advocate and now as a patient registrar. He graduated from the Community College of Rhode Island and is pursuing a political-science degree at Rhode Island College. He is a member of the Rhode Island Air National Guard. He is married and has two children. He supports Democrat David N. Cicilline for mayor and Democrat Sheldon Whitehouse for governor.

Yvon Chancy, 59, of 100 Carr St., is a Republican running in the Nov. 5 general election. He works as a behavior therapist at St. Mary's Home for Children in North Providence and is a part-time insurance agent. He graduated from Northeastern University with a degree in business data processing. He is married and together he and his wife have nine children. He supports Republican David B. Talan for mayor and Republican Donald L. Carcieri for governor.

Pedro J. Espinal, 37, of 162 Verndale Ave., is running as an independent candidate in the Nov. 5 general election. He is chairman of Direct Action for Rights & Equality and the South Side Broad Street Committee. He is a real-estate investor with 11 apartment buildings in Providence. He completed a one-year program at the Modern School of Business and has a semester to go for a social-science degree from the University of Rhode Island. He is married and has three children. He supports Democrat David N. Cicilline for mayor and Democrat Myrth York for governor.

Rochelle Bates Lee, 51, of 172 Ontario St., is running as an independent candidate in the Nov. 5 general election. She graduated from the University of Massachusetts-Boston and has a master's degree in African-American studies from Boston University, as well as a master's degree in regional and city planning from the Massachusetts Institute of Technology. She has worked on affordable-housing development since 1984. She worked seven years for the Local Initiative Support Corporation and two years for the affiliated National Equity Fund before being laid off this year. She is single. She supports Democrat David N. Cicilline for mayor and Democrat Myrth York for governor.

Mayoral Hopefuls Court Latinos

M. Charles Bakst
The Providence Journal
08/11/2002

The other day, former congressional candidate Angel Taveras, a prominent Latino, strode to a podium to endorse Rep. David Cicilline's Democratic primary bid for mayor.

Taveras declared:

"David Cicilline has uncommon courage . . . David Cicilline tiene un valor que no es comun."

Taveras cited Cicilline's launching his campaign months ago at a time when popular incumbent Buddy Cianci was still saying he was running.

Cicilline is counting on heavy support in the Hispanic community to help overcome former Mayor Joe Paolino and two other candidates in the Sept. 10 balloting. Cicilline boasts of long ties to the Latino community and pledges, "The city government I create will look like the city it serves." He talks of capturing as much as 80 percent of the Hispanic vote. (A more restrained Taveras says "at least 65 percent" is realistic.)

No one knows, of course, what the Latino turnout will be. The community has grown dramatically, but much of it -- partly because so many Hispanics are not yet of voting age -- is still unregistered. Several people I spoke with for this column think Latinos might constitute about 10 percent of the primary vote. In a close race, that could make a major difference.

Through such miscues as advocating English as the official national language, Paolino alienated Hispanic voters and bungled a 1996 congressional race; he later apologized. In the mayoral primary, he is mounting a Latino drive, and Councilman Luis Aponte is his campaign's general chairman.

Other Hispanic supporters include Jenny Rosario, a teacher and political activist who was so angry at Paolino in 1996 that, while emceeing the Puerto Rican Festival at Roger Williams Park, she refused to let him address the crowd.

But, over the years, at Paolino's initiative, she and he patched things up, and now she can't say enough about the former mayor's maturity: "What makes a good leader is to have the ability to listen, to reflect, to analyze, and to be flexible to change your point of view when it's needed."

Councilman Aponte says Paolino offers the experienced blend of policy and politics the city needs after the roller coaster Cianci years. "It's important to have a mayor who can stabilize city government right now," Aponte asserts. "Joe Paolino represents that stability."

Like Cicilline, Paolino has Spanish literature and advertises on Spanish radio and TV. Paolino employs former Cianci aide Carlos Lopez Estrada as deputy campaign manager. School Board member Bienvenido Garcia also is in Paolino's corner.

Paolino says, "We have made significant inroads from the outreach we have done in the Latino community and I'm happy with the support that we have and I want more."

But Paolino shies from saying what percentage of the Latino vote he can reasonably aspire to. Aponte sees the Hispanic vote breaking 50-50 between Paolino and Cicilline, with the other candidates, Sen. David Igliozzi and former Rep. Keven McKenna, not making major inroads.

I asked Aponte if there are Latinos who give him a hard time for embracing Paolino in light of the candidate's blunders in the 1996 primary won by Bob Weygand. "It happens every day," Aponte said. "But I say to them: 'Are you the same person that you were in 1996?' And, inevitably, everybody says no."

Aponte, who favored Weygand, believes Paolino took bad political advice back then and deserves a chance to redeem himself. In 1998, Paolino publicly apologized for his '96 campaign.

Paolino also had done some one-on-one repair work. One day he went to see Rosario, who'd been a key Weygand ally, and spent almost three hours clearing the air. Paolino, who as mayor had named Rosario to the Providence Housing Authority, says the primary had left him uneasy. "It bothered me a lot." Rosario welcomed his overture. "He showed character and I respect that," she says, and he has continued to seek her counsel.

IGLIOZZI AND McKenna also hope to attract Latino votes. For example, Igliozzi says he has a network of 20 Latinos working to drum up support through such activities as coffee hours. Rafael Ramirez, a volunteer regular at his headquarters, says he admires the former state prosecutor's law-and-order background and his working to pass the state law to require hospitals to provide interpreters. And Igliozzi's Silver Lake neighborhood is home to increasing numbers of Latinos. Still, when asked what share of the citywide Hispanic vote he could realistically hope to get in the primary, Igliozzi said one third. He rated Ciclline the front-runner.

McKenna points to pockets of Latino support and conjured the idea of the vote splitting four ways evenly.

All I know is that Cicilline and Paolino seem to have much more aggressive efforts and are signing up the big names.

For example, Cicilline's supporters include Rep. Leon Tejada and Senate candidate Juan Pichardo.

Pichardo says, "David Cicilline has been an effective legislator, an advocate of the community's needs." Don't bother telling Pichardo that Paolino knows what it's like to have to assume the mayorship in a post-Cianci crisis. Pichardo says, "We need a new mayor, a new era."

Or, as Angel Taveras put it in endorsing Cicilline, "It is time for a new page . . . Es tiempo para una nueva pagina."

The news conference took place outside South Providence's Mary E. Fogarty School, which Taveras, a 31-year-old lawyer, attended as a youngster.
You can expect Taveras, who nearly edged Jim Langevin in Providence in the 2000 congressional primary, to appear in a Cicilline radio ad.

Speaking of radio: Taking in the news conference scene was Tony Mendez, who is a part owner of a Spanish station, WPMZ, which styles itself as Poder 1110. Mendez, a Cicilline supporter and donor who lives in West Warwick, told me he remembers seeing Cicilline at Latino events when he wasn't even in politics. He was "just mingling with the people, just having a good time."

Rhode Island being Rhode Island, you will not be surprised to hear that Mendez' brother, Jose, who lives in Providence and is an account executive at the station, is a Paolino supporter. In a phone interview, he told me Paolino is a longtime friend and, "He was a good mayor."

BACK AT THE Cicilline scene, that fellow with the video camera, lobbing softball questions at the candidate, is Carlos Diaz, producer/director for Ritmo Latino (Latin Rhythm), a cable show on Cox. Diaz, who is running for House, is a Cicilline backer.

In talking with Diaz, Cicilline throws in a couple of Spanish sentences. The candidate tells me, "I speak it okay, but not well enough." He says he uses it at events like cookouts and in going door to door.

Gonzalo Cuervo, Cicilline's volunteer outreach coordinator, says the candidate understands everything he hears in Spanish. As for his speaking ability, Cuervo rates it 4.5 on a scale of 1 to 10 but aspires to see him at 7 by primary day. (Paolino does not speak Spanish.)

One of Paolino's Latino supporters, the School Board's Bienvenido Garcia, says the city, emerging from the Cianci experience, right now is on the edge and can go "real, real, deep down" if the wrong person is elected. (It's hard to imagine the city plunging further than the disgrace of having a twice-felon mayor, but I guess we'll have to see.)

Carlos Lopez Estrada says of Latinos and Paolino, "Some of the people who aren't with him don't remember or weren't here when he was mayor and they're stuck in the past when he ran for Congress and took a controversial misstep. Everyone's entitled to make one mistake, at least one, and he's made a mistake, and he's acknowledged it."
Which brings us back to Aponte, the campaign's general chairman, who speaks of Paolino in admiring, but clear-eyed, terms.

Aponte is 39. His wife, Gwen, was an aide to Paolino in City Hall.
Paolino says of Aponte, "He's smart, he's honest, he understands government, and he can help me from Day One bring the reforms necessary into Providence."

Aponte says the Paolino congressional platform that alienated Hispanics was "misguided" and "sent the wrong message." (Paolino says he was trying to be helpful and did a poor job of communicating what was in his heart.) Aponte says Paolino now understands better the politics of inclusion.

Aponte says Paolino got "bad advice" in '96, but he warns against assuming the candidate fell prey to bigotry. "In politics, you enter into this gray area," Aponte says. "One sort of sees the goal as winning." He also says, "You couldn't want to be the mayor of Providence if you didn't like Hispanics."

Aponte says Paolino was a good mayor with an "uncanny" ability to make good appointments.

WHILE CICILLINE may benefit from some backlash from 1996, and while many people may be impressed by his record, Aponte says Cicilline also gains from running for mayor early on, when Cianci was still out there and

Paolino was holding back. Aponte says this gave Cicilline "a lot of credibility" among Hispanics and that people who were down on Cianci saw Cicilline's campaign as a "viable opportunity" to get involved in the election.

Aponte says Paolino's hesitation, his willingness to defer to Cianci, is "something he has to answer for." Paolino says it took courage to stick by Cianci, whom he was hoping would be acquitted.

Aponte says, "As a politician, when you see things are going wrong, you can't sit by and not say anything. That says something about who you are . . . That's definitely one of the things that people ask: 'What took him so long?' "

York, Cicilline Endorsed By Latino Group

The Rhode Island Latino Political Action Committee likes York's recommendation to increase access to small business loans.

By Edward Fitzpatrick
Journal Staff Writer
08/10/2002

PROVIDENCE -- The Rhode Island Latino Political Action Committee is endorsing Democrat Myrth York for governor and Democrat David N. Cicilline for mayor.

The endorsement is of increasing significance because Rhode Island's Hispanic population doubled in the 1990s, "and the Latino community is more and more engaged in elections," RILPAC President Nellie M. Gorbea said, while noting the group does not speak for all Hispanic voters.

The committee picked York, although some Latino leaders, such as Dr. Pablo Rodriguez, are backing Atty. Gen. Sheldon Whitehouse in the Sept. 10 Democratic primary, which also includes Rep. Antonio J. Pires.

York received a majority of the 21 votes cast during RILPAC's endorsement meeting Thursday night, Gorbea said yesterday. "The vote was not against Sheldon; it was for Myrth," she said. "She did a bang-up job on her questionnaire responses. It was 15 pages, with very detailed policy recommendations."

For example, York talked about increasing access to small-business loans. "In terms of savviness, it shows she knows the bulk of [Latino] businesses are small businesses -- go down Broad Street and you see a ton of them," Gorbea said. "She really came across as very thoughtful."

The committee chose not to endorse anyone in the Republican primary for governor. Republican candidate James S. Bennett provided a "solid" response to the group's questionnaire, while his opponent, Donald L. Carcieri, never responded, Gorbea said.

The PAC picked Cicilline over his three opponents in the Democratic mayoral primary: David V. Igliozzi, Keven A. McKenna and Joseph R. Paolino Jr.

"He's been out there a long time, and from the beginning he came across as wanting diverse involvement in his campaign," Gorbea said of Cicilline. "A lot of Latinos liked his proposals. They think he represents a new beginning for the city."

The committee endorsed Democrat Matt Brown in his primary race against Secretary of State Edward S. Inman III. "Mr. Inman has done good things in office, but we feel Matt Brown would bring a new kind of energy to the job that is very positive," Gorbea said.

The PAC weighed in on a pair of state Senate Democratic primaries, picking Juan M. Pichardo in his race against Sen. Charles D. Walton, D-Providence, and picking Rep. Stella Guerra Brien in her race against Sen. Marc A. Cote, D-Woonsocket. "We could have two Latino senators," Gorbea said. "We would go from zero to two."

The committee endorsed candidates in a pair of City Council Democratic primaries, picking Miguel C. Luna in a Ward 9 contest against Patricia K. Nolan and Liandra Martinez in a Ward 15 contest against Josephine DiRuzzo.

Taveras Endorses Cicilline

The Providence Journal
08/08/2002

PROVIDENCE Angel Taveras, whose U.S. House candidacy in 2000 drew attention to the growing political strength of Hispanics in the city, has announced his endorsement of Rep. David N. Cicilline, a Democratic candidate for mayor.

"We need a mayor who has the courage to make difficult decisions and who will also bring the city together. David will be that mayor," Taveras said in an announcement outside the Mary E. Fogarty Elementary School in South Providence.

He said Cicilline had the courage to begin a campaign for mayor even as it appeared that Mayor Vincent A. Cianci Jr., with a high public-approval rating, would be a formidable candidate for reelection.

"I will walk any neighborhood, shake any hand, do anything I can to help David Cicilline become our next mayor," Taveras said.

The primary election is Sept. 10.

As a first-time candidate in the 2000 primary, Taveras finished third in a four-person race. But half of his nearly 6,000 votes were collected in Providence, where he finished only 457 votes behind the winner, Secretary of State James R. Langevin. Langevin went on to win the election.

Taveras, a lawyer, is the son of Dominican immigrants. He attended Providence public schools and graduated from Harvard University and Georgetown Law School.

Minority Voters Helped York Win

Contrary to Sheldon Whitehouse's predictions before the Democratic gubernatorial primary, York trampled the attorney general nearly 2 to 1 in Providence's minority neighborhoods.

By Mark Arsenault
Journal State House Bureau
09/22/2002

PROVIDENCE -- Shortly before the Sept. 10 primary, Atty. Gen. Sheldon Whitehouse downplayed his clashes with the African-American and Hispanic communities, and offered a wager that he'd carry those communities on Election Day. He lost his bet, and the election.

Former state Sen. Myrth York edged Whitehouse in the Democratic gubernatorial primary by about 900 votes statewide, but trampled the attorney general nearly 2 to 1 in Providence's minority neighborhoods. "In the Latino districts of Providence, there was a high turnout and weak political support for Whitehouse," said Darrell West, Brown University political scientist. Whitehouse has not responded to several requests for an interview since the primary. The four Providence voting districts with the greatest percentages of minority voting-aged residents, covering the West End, Elmwood and the south side of the city, were devastating to Whitehouse: throw out the results from those four wards and Whitehouse wins easily.

York won those districts over Whitehouse by a combined 3,488 votes to 1,834, a margin of 1,654. More than 70 percent of voting-aged residents in each of those neighborhoods are minorities, according to 2000 census data. Ward 9, the Elmwood neighborhood, has the highest percentage of minority voters in the city. Census data shows that just 17 percent of that ward's residents are non-Hispanic whites. In that district, York beat Whitehouse 1,111 votes to 558.

West said the numbers suggest that minority voters are still smarting over Whitehouse's handling in 2000 of the high-profile Cornel Young Jr. and Jennifer Rivera cases. Whitehouse was criticized after two white Providence police officers mistakenly shot and killed Young, a black colleague; and when 15-year-old Rivera, a witness in a murder case, was executed outside her home by a relative of the man she was to testify against.
"In both of those cases, minority community leaders were sharply critical of Whitehouse," West said. Those incidents "created a perception that Whitehouse was not interested in the minority communities and that he didn't

understand them. I don't think there was much he could have done in the campaign to repair the damage. The wounds were pretty deep and not subject to political spin."

Dr. Pablo Rodriguez, a leader in the Latino community who supported Whitehouse in the primary, offers a different take -- minority neighborhoods turned out to support York, not to punish Whitehouse, he said.

"I think there was probably more on-the-ground work by the York camp," Rodriguez said. "They had more volunteers."

He noted that York also had the endorsement of the Rhode Island Latino Political Action Committee. "That had an effect," he said. RILPAC President Nellie M. Gorbea said York ran an effective advertising campaign in Spanish, and that a great many Latino voters supporting Providence mayoral candidate David Cicilline also backed York. Cicilline worked very hard to woo minority neighborhoods.

"I don't think you can eliminate [the Rivera case] as a factor, but I don't think it was the deciding one," Gorbea said.

Whitehouse, before the election, had overestimated his support in the minority neighborhoods. In an interview in late August, he said his scraps with members of minority communities were exaggerated by his opponents and the press, and he predicted victory.

"Because of three-and-a-half years of really solid work in our urban communities I have very strong support in both the African-American and the Hispanic communities," Whitehouse said in August. "I'd be willing to make you a bet that on Election Day, I win in both those communities. "The perception [of trouble with minorities] is exaggerated by two things: I'm in a political race and I have political opponents who are only too happy to exaggerate that perception." "And second," he said last month, "we have a very white, generally very middle-aged suburban press corps that isn't really aware of what's going on down on Broad Street."

Cicilline's Win Signals Rise Of New Providence

The city's changing demographics is reflected in a victory that combined the votes of South Side Latinos with wealthy East Side residents.

By Scott MacKay
Journal Staff Writer
09/12/2002

PROVIDENCE -- Racing between campaign stops on a steamy afternoon in mid-August, David Cicilline mused that if the New Providence -- a diverse city where a majority of the 174,000 residents are members of minority groups -- showed up at the polls, he would win.

What worried him, he said, riding to a meet-and-greet in Olneyville, was an election dominated by the Old Providence of mainly white ethnic voters, the people who elected such mayors as Joseph Doorley and Dennis Roberts and had cast their lot with Vincent A. Cianci Jr. for so many years.

"We are getting a good response, I know that, I can sense it," said Cicilline, as he jumped out of the back seat of his campaign Buick that day. "If we can only get them all into the voting booth."

In an election Tuesday that signaled the demise of the Old Providence, Cicilline's masterful campaign took advantage of a new voter base -- South Side Latinos -- and fused it with his strong foundation among the wealthy residents of the East Side.

Remarkably, Cicilline's win came on an election day when Providence had perhaps its lowest primary voter turnout ever for such a competitive Democratic mayoral contest.

Voter participation was off in Providence, where about 27,000 went to polls in the four-candidate race. That compares to the 32,000 who voted in the last competitive Democratic mayoral primary, in 1990.

"This was a very impressive win for David Cicilline," said Anthony Pesaturo, a longtime Providence political consultant and pollster who did polling for the campaign of Cicilline's chief rival, former mayor Joseph R. Paolno Jr.

"The city is an entirely different place demograpically than it was," Pesaturo said. "It's changing by the minute and his campaign took advantage of it."

Tuesday's vote was a defining Providence election, probably the most significant since the 1974 Democratic mayoral primary that split the old Irish-American machine and set the stage for the first of Cianci's six victories.

The changes in the city's population patterns documented by the 2000 Census, which showed Providence a city where a majority of residents are members of minority groups, came home to roost at the polls.

Cicilline's victory tossed out two generations or more of conventional Providence political wisdom. Among the myths shattered by Cicilline: that the poor, minority voters of the South Side stay home on election day.

As good an example as any was the vote in the 9th Ward in the city's Elmwood neighborhood, which has the highest concentration of minority voters in the city. Census data show just 17 percent of the ward's residents are non-Hispanic whites.

A dozen years ago, barely 1,000 voted in the Democratic mayoral primary. On Tuesday, about double that turned out -- many of them Latinos who came to vote for Latino candidates in city council and state legislative races and also supported Cicilline.

Conventional Providence wisdom held that the East Side contributes about one in five votes in a Providence Democratic primary. On Tuesday that number increased to one in four. They backed Cicilline, who represented the neighborhood in the General Assembly.

"I am very grateful for the support I received from my base on the East Side," said Cicilline in an interview yesterday. About 40 percent of Cicilline's vote came from the East Side.

Beyond the glitz of the new downtown mall, the uncovered rivers, Waterplace Park and the fancy restaurants lies a harsh reality: Providence is one of America's poorest cities.

If the number of children living in poverty is the measure, census figures show that Providence ranks third among U.S. cities with a population of 100,000 or more, behind Brownsville, Texas, and Hartford, Conn. Providence is tied for third with New Orleans in the percentage of children --

roughly 40 percent -- who live in families with incomes below the federal poverty income threshold of $17,690 for a family of four with two children.

Census data also show that Providence has a declining middle class and an increasing number of families who live in poverty. The number of families living in poverty jumped by almost 6 percent between 1990 and 2000 and the median income of city residents dropped by 7 percent, according to census figures.

In such a city, the votes of the more stable neighborhoods of the East Side become more important, says Darrell West, Brown University political scientist.

Despite the increase in voter participation in the poorer South Side wards, the biggest turnouts were in the neighborhoods near Brown University and Miriam Hospital.

And Cicilline's East Side margins were remarkable; he harvested more than 70 percent of the votes in the three East Side wards.

The decline in turnout came in what once were the old white neighborhoods that controlled the city's politics for several generations: Mount Pleasant, Silver Lake, Smith Hill and the North End.

"A new day is dawning in Providence," said Cicilline, who also becomes the city's first openly gay mayor.

Latino Voting Bloc Spells Incumbents End

Charles D. Walton, the Senate's only black member, and veteran City Councilwoman Patricia K. Nolan are turned out of office.

09/12/2002
BY KAREN A. DAVIS
Journal Staff Writer

PROVIDENCE -- Two veteran incumbents who were unseated in Tuesday's Democratic primary election had more in common than a loss after years in office.

Both state Sen. Charles D. Walton and City Councilwoman Patricia K. Nolan lost to Latino challengers in heated races, bolstered by significant voter turnout in the heavily Latino South Side wards.

Both lost to challengers who worked together to send out mailings that endorsed Democratic mayoral candidate David N. Cicilline, who handily won his race with 53 percent of the citywide vote.

Miguel C. Luna defeated Nolan and Juan M. Pichardo defeated Walton.

Nolan and Walton said they believe their opponents were able to capitalize on Cicilline's overwhelming popularity and ride his coattails to victory.

Pichardo, who lost a close race in another Senate district two years ago, bested Walton 2,165 votes to 1,530. Walton is the Senate's only black member.

Luna, who lost a close race against Nolan four years ago, garnered 1,066 votes to Nolan's 741 in Tuesday's rematch. The victory ensures that the 15-member council will have a new Latino member in January, because Luna's opponent in the November general election is Reinaldo Catone, another Latino.

"I think the message that I was sending was that we're going to do things totally different; no more old-style politics," Luna said. "I was proposing a new vision and a new way of doing business. People like that."
Luna, 44, who served six years on the Providence City Plan Commission, said he wasn't surprised that he defeated Nolan by such a wide margin, having lost to her by 123 votes in 1998.

He said he started his campaign early and ran a reformist, anti-corruption platform, specifically targeting Latino turnout at the polls.

Nolan, 60, a 12-year veteran of the council and former Finance Committee chairwoman, said she thought the race would be closer.

She does not have regrets and believes she has always been there for her constituents -- not just a certain group.

She said she supported and pushed to use bond money to pay for the city's first traffic calming project in Elmwood, lobbied for the Civilian Review Board to oversee police misconduct cases and was the only council member to create a committee to oversee spending of neighborhood bond money.

Nolan, who is white, campaigned with Walton and Rep. Leon Tejada, a Latino who beat his primary challenger.

Nolan said she, Tejada and Walton walked the neighborhoods every day, and received a positive response to their multicultural allegiance.

"I think we did the best we could," Nolan said. "I had a good 12 years on the council. Now, I'm looking forward to a new life" and spending more time with her three grandchildren.

Walton, who served in the Senate for 18 years, and Nolan believe that redistricting hurt their bids for reelection. Minority leaders have criticized the plan for carving up minority neighborhoods and diluting the minority vote, while leaving intact the districts that have white legislators.

"You can't cut the heart out of the African-American community, which is my base, and then reasonably expect me to have a chance," Walton said.

But Walton praised Pichardo for running a strong campaign and praised Cicilline for working with Pichardo and Luna to bolster the Latino vote.

Pichardo did not return a call seeking comment yesterday afternoon.

Walton and Nolan criticized the voter registration system, which they said caused much confusion at the polls during the primary.

Walton said the voting list should be reviewed and purged of dead and ineligible voters.

If he had it to do over, Walton said, he would have educated voters about his accomplishments over the years. Among them, he said, was his push for the creation of the minority health division of the state Department of Health, initially to address the high infant mortality rate among minorities; crucial lobbying for passage of racial profiling legislation; legislation addressing housing, education and crime; and a call for the Community College of Rhode Islandto open a campus in Providence, so urban residents would have better access to education.

Luna praised Walton for the "tremendous work that he has done for the last 18 years" and for bringing a level of understanding to the legislature.

Without his work, Luna said, neither blacks nor Latinos "would be where we are."

Cicilline Ushers In A New City

M. Charles Bakst
The Providence Journal
09/12/2002

Change danced into Providence Tuesday night to a Latin beat.

That's what I'll remember most about the celebration of Rep. David Cicilline's momentous win in the Democratic mayoral primary -- the sea of Hispanic faces, the pride in their words, and the exuberance of their merengue. Also, the language skills the candidate employed in his victory speech. Along with his own East Side, the Latinos formed the backbone of his success.

With only token opposition in November, Cicilline, 41, is already, in the public's mind, mayor-elect. In a sense, we've had three mayors in less than a week: Buddy Cianci, John Lombardi, and now an Italian-Jewish gay man who speaks Spanish. Is that the secret to becoming mayor of Providence? "Not a bad start!" Cicilline beams.

(And, what, you were worried that journalists would lack for copy after Cianci?)
I will remember threading my way on a warm September night through the jammed winding roads of Roger Williams Park. I will remember the carousel lights in the distance. I will remember Cicilline's voice booming from his victory tent next to the merry-go-round.

I will remember talking with U.S. Rep. Patrick Kennedy, who said that this was "a great moment of empowerment for the Latino community, as they become great shareholders in the promise of Providence."

I will remember talking about Cicilline with Nellie Gorbea and Betty Bernal from the Rhode Island Latino Political Action Committee. Bernal: "He loves our community and we love him back." Gorbea: "We really have gotten to know him over the years. He didn't just show up."

A buoyant Allene Maynard, a veteran Democratic activist, told me, "He had a lot of black support too."

There were a number of blacks in the crowd. And plenty of gays: They'd approach me and say things like -- well, here's graphics designer Paul Grace declaring, "For a gay man from Providence, this is really just wonderful."

When I mentioned to Jack Cicilline, the candidate's father, that I didn't see many Italian-Americans on hand, he cracked, "Some of them are still in hiding. Most of them will be out tomorrow looking for my son, to congratulate him."

As for the Jewish mother, Sabra Peskin Cicilline, she said she was sure that her parents and father-in-law were up in heaven kvelling, or bursting with pride. (Though Spanish stands to be much in vogue in City Hall now, a little Yiddish can't hurt.)

It's easy to dwell on the idea that Cicilline's win on Tuesday represents a new era for Providence. But there was also something old-fashioned about it. He got a huge bounce from showing courage by announcing early, when Cianci was still running and still seemed popular. Cicilline's major opponents, former Mayor Joe Paolino and Sen. David Igliozzi, held back until Cianci was convicted of racketeering conspiracy and quit the race.

After the disgrace of Cianci's corruption and amid speculation that a financial disaster looms, Providence faces big trouble.

Cicilline, the candidate of change, has raised public spirits and hopes. But he says he's not worried that people are waiting upon him for miracles.

For one thing, he asserts, they understand the gravity of the city's problems.

And, he says, however much residents ask of him, it is no more than he will ask of himself. He says, "They should expect a lot, because I expect a lot of myself." A good attitude for a prospective mayor to have, and, by the way, in Spanish that would be, "Deberian esperar mucho, porque yo espero mucho de mi mismo."

Losing Candidates Seeking Recount,

Wilbur W. Jennings Jr. and Sen. Charles D. Walton want the state Board of Elections to investigate what they describe as "irregularities" at polling places.

By Richard C. Dujardin
Journal Staff Writer
09/12/2002

PROVIDENCE -- Two of Providence's General Assembly candidates have petitioned for recounts and hearings before the state Board of Elections because of what they say were voting irregularities in several polling places.

Wilbur W. Jennings Jr., who was 41 votes behind incumbent Rep. Thomas C. Slater in the race for the House seat in District 10, and Sen. Charles D. Walton, who was 626 votes behind challenger Juan M. Pichardo in the Senate District 3 race, filed their petitions yesterday.

In another race, incumbent Democrat Rep. Brian Coogan of East Providence won the new House seat in District 64, defeating fellow incumbent Raymond Coelho. Yesterday's Providence Journal incorrectly reported that Coelho won. The vote was Coogan 954, and Coelho, 836.

In the House District 10 race, covering areas of the West End, Reservoir Triangle and South Elmwood, Jennings, who retired as a deputy superintendent in the Department of Public Works, had a 41-vote deficit.
The machine totals gave Slater 657 votes, Jennings, 616, and challenger Carlos M. Diaz, 340. The mail ballots did nothing to close the gap, with Slater and Jennings each getting 61 mail-ins and Diaz getting 14.

Jennings said he asked for the recount not only because the vote was so close, but because of possible irregularities at three of the seven polling sites. He said that at the West End Community Center, on Bucklin Street, and the Kilmartin Plaza, on Benedict Street, some voters had trouble with the scanning devices that read the ballots . In at least two instances, he said, the machines rejected the ballots.

He said that while polling officials at Kilmartin solved the problem by leaving one machine idle, a troublesome machine at the West End Community Center was hauled away by the Board of Elections. He said he wants to make sure that votes from those machines were counted.

Jennings said he is also concerned with what he describes as an undercount in the totals. He wants to have a hand-count to verify that all ballots were counted. The candidate said he would also like to find out why the mail-in vote total for the three candidates was only 136 if the Board of Elections said there were 188 requests for mail ballots.

"This is a sensitive issue with me. Where are the rest of those ballots?"
Jennings also wants the board to look into a complaint that two people trying to vote at the Roger Williams Casino were initially denied by the warden because their names were "not on the master list," he said. He said the warden continued to deny them access even after securing affidavits from the city Board of Canvassers certifying they were registered voters, and relented only when a representative of the Board of Canvassers sent the police to the scene.

Jennings remains hopeful that the numbers will be reversed. "For all the time and effort I put into this, I have to pursue this, knowing there is a possibility that I won this primary. If not, I'll be back again in two years."
Walton, the state's only black senator, emerged from Tuesday's balloting 626 votes behind Juan M. Pichardo. Including mail ballots, Walton had 1,593 and Pichardo, 2,219.

In asking for a recount, Walton asked that the voting machines be impounded and that a hearing be held on possible "irregularities," such as multiple voting lists at one of the polling places, which he said made it possible for people to vote more than once.

Pichardo said he was surprised by Walton's request for a recount. "I had expected to be hearing from him since Tuesday night. I haven't and this may explain why." The candidates said he thinks people were motivated to come out and vote for him because "they have known me as a civic activist and advocate for the South Side, Elmwood and West End." There is no doubt, he said, the Latino community helped a great deal. "

The Board of Elections said that it plans today to begin scheduling recounts and/or hearings. State law requires that it be done by Tuesday.

Cicilline: Win Is Mandate From Voters

By Amanda Milkovits
Journal Staff Writer
09/11/2002

PROVIDENCE -- The candidate who promised to usher in change and clean out the corruption in City Hall became the winner in yesterday's Democratic mayoral primary election.

And that message, David N. Cicilline says, was sent by the voters. Only four days after Vincent A. Cianci Jr. was sentenced to 64 months in prison for running a criminal enterprise from City Hall, Democratic voters gave the party nomination to the young criminal lawyer and legislator who hammered repeatedly in his campaign about making government honest and accountable.

"The difference was a strong belief in the City of Providence, and the people who really love Providence and really care about it, and really want change," the 41-year-old Cicillinesaid last night at his Elmwood Avenue headquarters.

Shortly after 9 p.m., the roll started: poll runners came dashing into the headquarters with the written results in their hands. "We've got it!" they shouted in English and Spanish. By 9:45 p.m., as Cicilline arrived after a quiet dinner with family, his ecstatic supporters greeted him in the street, cheering and clapping, over and over, as he greeted each one with a hug and thanks. The result: Cicilline 13,818; Joseph R. Paolino Jr., 8,574; David V. Igliozzi, 2,920 and Keven A. McKenna, 699.

"That's a mandate! That's an absolute mandate, no question!" shouted state Rep. Thomas Palangio, a Cicilline supporter.

More people crowded in, people of different ethnicities, the people Cicilline had sought in his campaign and talked about representing the city's diversity. They were in his headquarters on Elmwood Avenue, cheering and applauding and hugging the smiling, soft-spoken Cicilline. Motorists leaned on their horns as they slowed while passing his headquarters. And by late night, they were joyous, dancing with Cicilline signs, and cheering, "Da-vid! Da-vid!" at his celebration at Roger Williams Park.

From the beginning, his campaign had aggressively sought the Latino vote. Some of his staffers were devoted to organizing and wooing Hispanic voters.

"The Latino vote is enormously important to the city. It's impossible to talk about Providence and not talk about the Latinos," Cicilline said.

Last night as the vote total began to climb, ecstatic supporters rushing into the headquarters congratulated Cicilline in Spanish and English.

"This feels wonderful, just wonderful," Cicilline said, his voice hoarse.
"This is an incredibly, incredibly exciting victory," Cicilline said, "It's exciting to see. I'm humbled by it. I'm excited about the work we're going to do." His mother, Sabra, interrupted Cicilline's first interview after the votes were tallied.

"This is a button that a man gave [former Mayor Vincent A. Cianci Jr.] during his first administration, and I'm giving it to you," Mrs. Cicilline said. "It's the seal of the City of Providence." They hugged, tight.

"I'm so proud of the City of Providence," Mrs. Cicilline said as others reached to hug and congratulate her son. "I kept saying to people, 'If he wins, he's going to change the city. I know he will. . .

"People came out and they wanted change, and he can do it. He can do wonderful things," Mrs. Cicilline said. "Of course, I'm his mother." "He ran a good campaign. He's sincere, he's honest," said his older sister, Roberta. "Everything he said he was going to do, he's going to do."
"This is like history for us," she added.

Cicilline, who launched his campaign before Cianci decided not to run again, was the one who other political leaders came to congratulate at Roger Williams Park, including acting Mayor John J. Lombardi -- who endorsed Paolino on Monday; City Councilman Kevin Jackson; and U.S. Rep. Patrick J. Kennedy. In November, Cicilline faces Republican David Talan, Green Party candidate Greg Gerritt, and independent Christopher Young. In a pointed note during his celebration speech, Cicilline sent a "cautionary note" to those still serving in city government -- "The trust you hold, until the next mayor is sworn into office, is a sacred one."

Judge Rejects RI Senate Redistricting Suit

It is the first court decision among three lawsuits over the state's redistricting in the General Assembly.

By Edward Fitzpatrick
Journal Staff Writer
09/10/2002

PROVIDENCE -- Chief U.S. District Judge Ernest C. Torres yesterday dismissed a redistricting lawsuit that claimed the new state Senate map illegally dilutes black voting power on the South Side of Providence.

The decision came a day before today's primary elections for the newly downsized General Assembly. Legislative districts have been recast to reflect new census data and a constitutional amendment shrinking the House from 100 to 75 members and the Senate from 50 to 38 members. The new Senate map has spawned three lawsuits, and this represents the first ruling in those cases.

Torres agreed with Senate attorneys, who had argued that such voting-rights suits can only be brought by minority groups representing more than 50 percent of a district. In this district, the black population is falling from 26 percent, under the old Senate map, to 21 percent under the new Senate map.

Torres said the lawsuit also failed to demonstrate that "the white majority votes sufficiently as a bloc." In this district, there is no "white majority" since the population is no more than 32 percent white, the judge said.

"Certainly, we are disappointed," said Anita S. Hodgkiss, of the Lawyers' Committee for Civil Rights Under Law, which filed the suit on behalf of seven plaintiffs. "It had seemed to us that [Torres] was willing to give us our day in court. I do believe we are right under the law and that we do have a Voting Rights Act claim."

Before deciding whether to appeal, Hodgkiss said she will talk with the plaintiffs, which include former state Rep. Harold M. Metts, the Urban League of Rhode Island and the Providence branch of the NAACP.

Senate Majority Leader William V. Irons, D-East Providence, said he was "very pleased" by the decision. "The redistricting commission and the legislature did a fair and accurate job of drawing these districts," Irons said. "So I have a strong belief the courts will uphold the plan."

The lawsuit centers on new Senate District 2, where the state's first and only black senator is pitted against a man who, in the last election, came within

100 votes of being the state's first and only Hispanic senator. Sen. Charles D. Walton is facing Juan M. Pichardo in today's Democratic primary.

Walton called the judge's decision "very disheartening," saying, "My sense is what his decision has done is put further strain on black and Latino voters in this district." With minorities making up more than half of the city's population, voters shouldn't be forced to choose between a black or Latino senator -- they should have both options, he said.

Pichardo called the judge's decision "a total disappointment," saying, "We fought very hard to go back to the drawing board and redraw the districts to effectively help elect minority candidates of choice." He said he hopes a second lawsuit, filed by a Hispanic coalition, provides a remedy that benefits both blacks and Hispanics.

In his 20-page decision, Torres noted that in its 1986 Thornburg vs. Gingles decision, the U.S. Supreme Court set three "preconditions" for proceeding with voting-rights lawsuits. The first precondition is that "the minority group must be able to demonstrate that it is sufficiently large and geographically compact to constitute a majority."

The plaintiffs said that requirement should be applied flexibly and not as a "bright-line rule." Even with less than 50 percent of the district population, blacks would have the ability to elect a candidate with help from a limited but predictable number of non-black "crossover" votes, the plaintiffs said.

Torres said the plaintiffs were "mischaracterizing" that precondition and distorting the meaning of the word "elect." He said, "In a democracy, candidates for political office are elected by a majority of the voters. Therefore, it is difficult to see how a group constituting less than a majority can claim the ability to 'elect' a candidate."

Some courts have said that two or more racial groups can form a cohesive majority and together elect a candidate they both favor, the judge said. But in this area of Providence, the plaintiffs say, blacks and Hispanics usually prefer different candidates.

Torres said the plaintiffs were essentially arguing that they should have "the ability to influence" elections in that Senate district. But courts would have a very tough time measuring the "ability to influence," he said.

"A voter may be influenced by matters such as the issues, party affiliation, a candidate's qualifications, a candidate's personal appeal, and so on ad infinitum," Torres wrote. "Consequently, voting patterns are likely to vary considerably from election to election, making it virtually impossible to reliably calculate the number of minority voters that would be required in order to 'influence' election results."

"In addition," Torres wrote, "recognizing 'influence' claims by minority groups rests on the insultingly stereotypical assumption that all members of a
356

racial minority vote alike, and it would encourage the kind of racial bloc voting that the [Voting Rights Act] seeks to combat."

Even if influence could be measured, the judge said, this district illustrates a "Catch 22" situation where "reconfiguring the district in a way that permits African-American voters 'to elect representatives of their choice' would deny the same right to Hispanic voters, who are an even larger minority."

The judge said the plaintiffs failed to meet another precondition for a voting-rights suit -- that they "must be able to demonstrate that the white majority votes sufficiently as a bloc to enable it . . . usually to defeat the minority's preferred candidate."

"In this case, there is no 'white majority' in District 2 that could prevent the election of candidates of the plaintiffs' choice," Torres wrote, noting that the district is 21 percent black, 47 percent Hispanic and, therefore, no more than 32 percent white.

Latino Vote Matures, Matters

And Could Affect Mayor's Race

More Latinos are working on political campaigns than in any previous year.

By Tatiana Pina
Journal Staff Writer
09/07/2002

PROVIDENCE -- At the community room of the Laurelmead retirement home on Blackstone Boulevard, Melba DePena keeps one eye on her candidate for secretary of state, Matt Brown, and another eye on the door in case any more elderly residents walk in so she can give them brochures about his campaign.

Across town on Broad Street, Dominican men talk politics in front of the new headquarters they opened to support Democratic mayoral candidate David Cicilline. One street over in front of the Center for Hispanic Policy and Advocacy on Elmwood Avenue, Ingrid Ardaya, a volunteer for Democraic gubernatorial candidate Myrth York, is waging a numbers' battle with Latino supporters for Sheldon Whitehouse, who are getting ready to announce their support for him in the governor's race. Ardaya is burning up her cell phone, calling on York's Latino supporters to hurry to the agency to counteract the announcement.

There are more Latinos working on political campaigns this year than in any previous year.

Community leaders, political pundits, and the campaign workers themselves say the Latino community's political time has come. They say that the large number of Latinos recruited to campaigns is an indication of the growth in that population and the belief that those numbers could tilt the balance in some candidates' favor.

"This is the year the Latino vote has finally arrived," said Darrell West, a Brown University political scientist.

"There have been so many changes in the census that candidates are scrambling to attract voters in the Latino community, West said. "This is the first election where the Latino vote is being taken seriously."

According to West, the race for the Providence mayor's office is so tight that "if Latinos tilt towards one candidate or the other they will most likely elect the next mayor."

Candidates are predicting that Latino participation will be between 3,000 and 4,000 in Providence.

On Broad Street, in front of Cicilline's headquarters, a group of men talk about why they decided to participate in his campaign.

Arys Batista, owner of Beeper Center on Broad Street, said he got involved because he believes Dominican business owners have given the South Side of the city its own renaissance and they deserve their due.

Batista said a new mayor will pay more attention to business owners in the South Side.

Ramon Nunez said he got involved in the Cicilline campaign because he hopes a new mayor will change the way things are done in City Hall.

"I have faced racism firsthand, Nunez said. "You don't know the countless times I have gone for permits only to face a mountain of barriers.

"I have hope that with the new mayor this will change."

One of the pivotal Latinos in Cicilline's campaign is Gonzalo Cuervo, who helps plan the Latino strategy for his campaign. Cuervo narrowly lost his bid to unseat Providence Rep. Joe Almeida in House District 20 two years ago.

Cuervo said there is no Latino working on any campaign that can deliver the Latino vote. It has to be done on a grassroots level, meeting people one on one, he said.

The participation of so many Latinos in campaigns comes from a maturing community , he said. "They have a solid base. They have homes. They have businesses.

"They are discovering that they only way to get things done is to participate."

Yvette Jaquez and Carlos Lopez work as paid deputy campaign managers for mayoral candidate Joseph Paolino Jr. Lopez puts in long hours at the Weybosett Hill office, coordinating Paolino's activities, recruiting volunteers and talking with other workers about issues that affect Latinos. Lopez helped Paolino come up with the Latino agenda for his campaign.

Lopez, 31, who worked as an aid to Mayor Vincent Cianci Jr., says Latinos are doing what previous immigrant groups such as Italians and Irish did before them -- taking part in the political process.

"In the future you will see Latinos running for statewide offices," he said.

Jaquez, 33, worked for former congressman Robert Weygand, who defeated Paolino in 1996 for the Democratic nomination for the 2nd Congressional District seat. Jaquez said that the immigrant bashing and opposition to bilingual education that was part of Paolino's bid during that race is "something in the past that he apologized for."

Working for Paolino, she sees that all written and verbal material directed at Latinos is worded correctly. She accompanies Paolino on visits to Latino elderly and, although it's not part of her job, she danced with him at the Dominican festival in front of 9,000 people.

As a paid field director for Matt Brown, Melba DePena's day starts at 8 a.m., when she goes to his headquarters in Pawtucket to analyze lists of previous voters and figure out how to reach them this time around. The latter part of her day is spent visiting potential voters in high rises for the and community centers around the state with Brown.

DePena got the job after working with Brown in 2000 during his statewide voter outreach drive, Democracy Compact. Before that, she ran the campaign of Ricardo Patino, who became Central Falls' first Latino councilman. She also ran Juan M. Pichardo's unsuccessful campaign two years ago to unseat state Sen. Robert Kells in District 10 in Providence. Pichardo is running this year in the Democratic primary for the new Senate District 2.

Her love of politics comes from her father, Narciso DePena, a member of the Dominican Liberation Party. Will she run for office one day?

"I'd rather work on people's campaigns, behind the scenes," she said.

Voters Alerted About Incidents Fraud

Callers to a Spanish radio talk show give accounts of people trying to "help" them fill out their ballots -- or who have told them that their ballots are defective.

By Amanda Milkovits
Journal Staff Writer
09/05/2002

PROVIDENCE -- One elderly woman's story about people pressuring her to give up her mail-in ballot has lit up the phone lines on Spanish talk radio with more tales of coercion and deceit. Those stories of possible ballot fraud prompted Latino leaders to call a news conference yesterday with state police Col. Steven Pare and Secretary of State Edward S. Inman III to urge people to be wary.

"The people in our community are concerned about this," said Nellie Gorbea, president of the Rhode Island Latino Civic Fund. "This is to educate our community that this is a crime."

The issue "has been absolutely on fire," said Pablo Rodriguez, the host of the Spanish radio program Hablemos (Let's Talk) on 88.1 FM (WELH), late Saturday mornings. Callers have talked about people pretending to be representatives from the state Board of Elections who want to "help" them fill out their ballots, Rodriguez said. Others said some people have told them their ballots are defective, he said. Yet, despite the numerous calls, very few have reported their allegations to the police. "People are afraid of coming forward. They're afraid for their safety," Rodriguez said. Pare said his detectives are investigating a few complaints in Providence and other towns. Providence police Maj. Martin F. Hames said that his detectives are investigating just one complaint -- the one filed two weeks ago that launched the attention. Relatives of Maria Martinez, an 85-year-old resident of the Stratford House on Elmwood Avenue, said that three men coerced her into giving them her mail ballot, saying they were there to help her vote.

Hames said the matter is still under investigation, and he plans to forward the findings to the attorney general's office soon.

Providence Primary Will Reveal More Than The Winner

The demographic makeup of the city has changed since the last competitive primary, but whether that influences the outcome of the Democratic mayoral race remains to be seen.

BY Scott MacKay
Journal Staff Writer

09/01/2002

PROVIDENCE -- Is the Sept. 10 Democratic primary for mayor the last election of the Old Providence, a city where white ethnic voters hold political sway, or the first election of the New Providence, a diverse city where a majority of its 174,000 residents are members of minority groups?

That is one of the big questions the primary will answer as voters choose a sucessor to Mayor Vincent A. Cianci Jr., who is scheduled to be sentenced to federal prison Friday on the federal racketeering conspiracy charge which he was convicted of in June.

The departure of Cianci -- who quit the campaign after his conviction -- has drawn four Democratic candidates to the primary: state Rep. David Cicilline, former Mayor Joseph R. Paolino Jr., former state legislator Keven McKenna, and state Sen. David Igliozzi.

The candidates have sounded similar themes, calling for city government to shift from Cianci's emphasis on downtown renewal and focus instead on neighborhood concerns, fighting crime, improving schools and putting the city's financial house in order.

Cicilline, who started running well before Cianci's conviction, and Paolino, who announced his candidacy after, have raised and spent the most money, been most visible on television and are viewed by Democratic Party leaders as the top contenders.

Experts predict that victory will take 12,000 or fewer votes -- meaning that less than 10 percent of city residents may decide who controls City Hall.

The winner of the primary is the overwhelming favorite to win the general election because the three remaining candidates are not well-known or well-financed; none of them -- Republican David Talan, independent Christopher Young or Greg Gerritt of the Green Party -- has ever won an election.

Census 2000 revealed what many Providence residents have known for years -- this is not the city of their grandparents, a place where the political divide was Irish-American and Italian-American and politics was dominated by the second and third generations of the great European immigration of the late 19th and early 20th centuries.

"This is definitely not the same city it was 20 years ago or even 10 years ago," says Angel Taveras, a 32-year-old lawyer who is one of a new generation of Latino political activists predicting that the primary will be a crucial election for Latino political power in Providence.

Like many young Latino activists, Taveras is working for Cicilline's election, while some more established Latino political figures, such as City Councilman Luis Aponte, favor Paolino.

WHILE THE CENSUS showed the majority of the city is black and Latino, the older generation of political observers in Providence say the white neighborhoods -- where voting is a biennial habit -- will largely choose the next mayor.

"The census city is not the voting city," says Bruce Mellucci, a longtime city political operative who is supporting Paolino. "The two highest voting areas, the crucial areas, will be the Mount Pleasant and East Side neighborhoods. And 40 percent of the vote will still be Irish-American and Italian-American."

Because Cianci has held office for a dozen consecutive years, there are few historical clues to the Sept. 10 primary. The last competitive Democratic primary was held in 1990; turnout was roughly 32,000. That race was won by Andrew Annaldo, a former city councilman, who took 30 percent in a four-way field. He lost to Cianci, an independent.

In an era when most voters statewide are not affliated with either major party, the majority of Providence's 93,000 voters are Democrats. The city has about 51,000 Democrats, roughly 37,000 unaffiliated voters and 5,000 Republicans.

Latinos are discovering what every generation of immigrants has learned: the one place -- some would argue the only place -- in Rhode Island where everyone is equal is in the voting booth.

Latino voter turnout will increase in this election, predicts Taveras, because several Latino candidates are running for General Assembly and City Council seats in neighborhoods to which many Latinos have moved in the past 20 years.

Besides the increase in the city's Latino population -- which now makes up more than 30 percent of the city -- there have been changes in the older and wealthier neighborhoods of the East Side, near Brown University, where an influx of single young professionals has changed neighborhoods once dominated by elderly and two-parent family populations.

"We have been learning for some time, but we have to start winning," says Taveras. Next Tuesday's voter turnout in Latino neighborhoods and in yuppie East Side areas will determine whether the city's newest residents flex their political muscles or whether traditional groups continue to dominate politics.

BEHIND THE GLITTER of the new downtown mall, the uncovered rivers, Waterplace Park and the fancy restaurants lies a harsher reality: Providence is one of America's poorest cities.

If the number of children living in poverty is the measure, Census 2000 figures show that Providence ranks third among cities with 100,000 or more population, behind Brownsville, Texas, and Hartford. Providence is tied for third with New Orleans in the percentage of children -- roughly 40 percent -- who live in families with incomes below the federal poverty income threshold of $14,269 a year for a family of three with two children.

Census data also show that Providence has a declining middle class and an increasing number of families who live in poverty. The number of families living in poverty jumped by almost 6 percent between 1990 and 2000 and the median income of city residents dropped by 7 percent, according to census figures.

Rhode Island is known as one of the more generous states in its social programs for the poor. Because of the RiteCare program, the state has the nation's lowest percentages of children who lack health care.

"So many state programs, such as child care and RiteCare, help to alleviate some of the effects of child poverty," says Elizabeth Burke Bryant, executive director of Rhode Island Kids Count, a children's research and advocacy group. "But these programs don't change family income."

After decades of decline and stagnation, Providence is once again reinventing itself through immigration. Between 1990 and 2000, the city saw a 45 percent increase in its foreign-born population. As a result, one in four residents of Providence are foreign born.

The dry statistics of the census report show that 43 percent of city residents speak a language other than English at home. It is a figure that sounds staggering to Rhode Islanders who come to Providence only to work, shop or attend college but is easily confirmed by a stroll down any of the city's neighborhood business lifelines: Broad Street, Smith Street, Pocasset Avenue.

Broad Street, which at the middle of the 20th century displayed such store names as Cohen's Market, Hanley's Tap, and Kolodoff's Liquors, now boasts Sanchez Market, Hernandez Liquors and Pito's Restaurant.

Silver Lake is a legendary Italian-American neighborhood that spawned such politicians as U.S. Sen. John O. Pastore, Gov. Christopher Del Sesto and Cianci.

Ten years ago, Silver Lake had one of Providence's smallest concentrations of minority-group members. Today, non-Hispanic whites make up just 34 percent of the population. St. Bartholomew's Church in Silver Lake was founded by Italian immigrants but on Sunday mornings its Spanish-language Mass now draws many times more worshipers than its Italian-language Mass.

The extent to which these new residents show up at the polls a week from Tuesday will also help determine whether Providence's political culture returns to the robust voter participation of a generation ago or continues to decline.

One number gleaned last week from the city Board of Canvassers hints at a healthy voter turnout. That is the number of absentee ballot applications, which as of last week was at 1,430, compared with the 1,009 absentee votes cast in the last contested Democratic mayoral primary, in 1990.

Attendance at a series of debates held in four city neighborhoods has been high and candidates have raced around the city, meeting and greeting voters. Candidates have paid special attention to the elderly, who are expected to make up 25 percent or more of the vote.

As recently as 1974, a Democratic primary drew almost 45,000 voters. That was the year a split in Democratic ranks weakened incumbent Mayor Joseph Doorley and dealt the party a blow from which it never recovered.

Today, Cianci's name is anathema in some East Side circles. But it was the neighborhoods near Brown, Miriam Hospital and Blackstone Boulevard that in 1974 launched Cianci's career by giving him the first of his six mayoral victories.

Cianci, running as a Republican, defeated incumbent Doorley 3-to-1 on the East Side, and that became the foundation of his victory citywide.

EACH OF THE four candidates has run a vigorous campaign; none is new to Providence voters. Paolino, 47, is a former City Council president who became mayor after then-Mayor Cianci was chased from office in 1984 following his felony conviction for assaulting his ex-wife's lover.

Igliozzi, 42, is a state senator from the Silver Lake neighborhood and a former City Council member. His father, Vincent Igliozzi, is a longtime ward leader in Silver Lake.

Cicilline, 41, is a state representative from the East Side and a lawyer who is one of the state's few openly gay political figures.

McKenna, 57, was a state representative from Mount Pleasant and a former municipal judge. He lost a run for mayor in 1984.

"I think it will be a good turnout in Providence just because it is a competitive race and and because it is the last chapter of the Buddy Cianci story," says Darrell West, a political science professor at Brown University.

Latino Civic Participation Reshapes Political Climate In Rhode Island

Tomás Alberto Ávila
Providence American News
10/01/02

If the story of America is one in which rising minority groups eventually seize control of local political office, many urban communities may well be their latest chapter. Expanding Latino population and rising Latino voter registration are expected to give many Latino candidates in this year's election their best showing in years.

As the political climate reshapes, the Latino population is showing a renewed commitment to demonstrating its political strength. The remarkable growth of the population and the significance of the Latino electorate has undergone intense scrutiny and become the subject of fiery debate across the nation. Policymakers and the public alike have voiced their need for a better understanding of the Latino community and the significance and actuality of the Latino vote.

The nation's Latino population grew by nearly 60 percent in the last decade, to 35.3 million, roughly equaling blacks as the country's largest minority. As Latinos strive to translate these numbers into the kind of political influence that blacks have achieved, the battle is on among Democrats and Republicans to court this still largely untapped and disparate voting group.

This unprecedented growth will increase Hispanics' political clout in the next years and will make an impact on the Congressional Races. Latino groups will be able to state their needs and policy maker will eagerly listen.

It often used to be assumed that Latinos were an easy target for aspiring politicians hoping to score political points by attacking minorities, as was shown by Pete Wilson in California and Joseph Paolino here in Rhode Island back in 1996. While Latinos are fully 13% of the United States population, conventional wisdom holds that their voter participation is low because many are not citizens. However, such thinking is dead wrong Latinos will be the pivotal vote in the country's future elections and any politician betting against this will pay for it at the polls.

While one quarter of the Latino population is not yet naturalized, applications for citizenship among the Latino population are at record levels.

Nationally, there has been a 100% increase in applications for citizenship. As a result of the amnesty program begun in 1986, 3 million more Latinos living in the United States are now eligible for citizenship. The statistics are clear more Latinos will be eligible to vote in elections than ever before.

The Latino community, threatened by the slew of anti-Latino legislation proposed in Congress and in state capitols across the country in the mid 90's heightened awareness of the importance of voting on their futures. We know that the only way to stop the political attacks on our community is to make our presence felt at the ballot box.

Latino organizations across the country have mobilized to educate and register more than 1 million new Latino voters. Voter registration projects are being conducted in Latino communities all over the United States as we speak. In fact, here in Rhode Island, the RI Latino Civic Fund has unveiled its effort to encourage Latinos to register and vote.

It is clear; the Latino vote will play a crucial role in the country's future elections and will continue to be more important year after year.

As a growing young electorate registering to vote at record rates, Latinos have attracted political attention from Democrats and Republicans alike. The parties spotlight certain issues in hopes of attracting Latinos, who tend to be conservative on some issues (such as abortion) and liberal on others (such as government programs). But rather than simply voting for one party or another, Latino voters like to keep their options open.

Indeed, many Republicans are pinning hopes on Latino conservatism to help Mr. Bush overcome Democratic voter registration drives to win Latino support in 2002 and 2004. There's no question the Republicans need a greater share of Latino voters to stay in the majority. More importantly to the politicians, Latinos vote, and with their numbers climbing and their willingness to cross party lines, Latinos could tip the scales in critical races and be the margin of victory.

Last spring's Census report showing that Latinos have officially replaced blacks as America's largest minority group may hold implications for political change far beyond urban communities. In some cases, Latinos are expected to make gains in cities long dominated by white officeholders. In multi-ethnic cities such as Providence, they may fight for seats held by other minorities.

Politicians need to expand their notion of civil rights and make sure Latinos are included in any future race initiatives. They need to take these voters and potential voters more seriously.

While shortsighted political strategists still dismiss the population as mostly young and nonvoting, the truth is that, at a time when voter participation rates for most groups have flattened, the rate for Latinos has risen in states like California and Rhode Island. They need to stop resting on their laurels and aggressively compete for Latino support. This is a community where a little attention and respect goes a long way. Politicians have to do better than simply adopting a philosophy of recruiting Latinos as unpaid volunteers in their campaigns.

The country is undergoing a period of profound change. It is estimated that by the year 2010, Latinos will account for one in every three American. By 2050, Latinos will comprise well over a quarter of the United States population. The Latino population will continue to grow in both numbers and levels of civic participation.

Latinos are naturalizing at much higher rates than in the past and they are becoming active in local elections. Increasingly, Latinos are becoming the margin of victory factor in electing candidates and changing policy. Despite the new surge of Latino participation in elections there is still an incredible amount to learn about the Latino vote. Latino voters tend to be younger, poorer, and less educated than the general population. The implications of this for the country remains to be seen. This is a new kind of voter, one we are not used to analyzing.

As the 2002 elections come to a conclusion, Latinos are settling into a position where we have worked very, very hard to be. We want to be in a place where our vote is not taken for granted by Democrats or Republicans, where candidates consciously reach out to Latino voters and work hard to convince us that they offer the better alternative to advance our interests, and that political parties think twice about pursuing policies that will alienate Latinos.

This is essentially where we want to be, and I think we are well on our way.

New Latin-American Group Backs Carcieri For Governor

By Karen A. Davis
Journal Staff Writer
10/14/2002

PROVIDENCE -- A newly-formed Latino political coalition endorsed Republican candidate Donald Carcieri for governor Saturday at a news conference at the Greater Providence Chamber of Commerce. Members of the Latin-American Political Independent Coalition said they made the unanimous decision to support Carcieri after determining that he is best-suited to "defend the values of the Latino community," according to Jaime Aguayo, a group leader. Citing the Carcieri's business experience, "wisdom and compassion," Aguayo predicted that the Republican candidate would be successful in turning around the state's struggling economy. The coalition, led by Aguayo, Jenny Rosario, Rene Taveras, Ana Morgan and Lydia Perez, was formed because its members believed that neither the Democratic or Republican parties were doing enough to cultivate Latino leadership within their parties, Rosario said. The coalition includes members who are Democrats, Republicans, independents and representatives from the state's diverse Hispanic communities.

Coalition members decided that they would join forces and support candidates who best reflect their positions on issues, regardless of political-party affiliation, Aguayo said. "Our focus will be in supporting candidates that could bring about changes with honesty, dignity and integrity during this historical time when our state is in crisis -- a moral and economic crisis," Rosario said. With his background as a parent, teacher, church deacon, businessman and entrepreneur, Rosario said the group believes that Carcieri will support its educational values by making sure that all children are equally-served and by embracing family values. Among them, Rosario said, coalition members agree with Carcieri's pro-life position. In accepting the endorsement, Carcieri told the group that he came from a family of teachers and the son of an Italian immigrant father and a Swedish immigrant mother. "As a candidate and as governor I will maintain an open-door policy to your community as well as to others to hear you out on the issues that concern you and to help you make your dreams and ambitions become reality," Carcieri said

Latinos Rejoice In Newfound Clout

A forum sponsored by Providence College celebrates the influence Hispanics have garnered in politics as well as the greater role they are playing in their communities.

BY KAREN LEE ZINER
Journal Staff Writer
10/18/2002

PROVIDENCE -- The headline regarding the Providence mayoral election was so excellent, Angel Tavares could barely stand it. "Latinos Give Cicilline Victory," it said, in bold black and white, and last night Tavares held it up to demonstrate just how far Latinos have come in Rhode Island. "Right now, I think we're in the infancy stage. We've stood up, and we're beginning to walk," said Tavares about the Latino community here.

The topic last night was "Welcome to Our World: The Lives of Latinos in Rhode Island." Sponsored by the Balfour Center for Cultural Affairs at Providence College, the forum drew several dozen people to the Slavin Center.

Tavares, an attorney and 2000 Democratic candidate for Congress, was one of five well-known Latinos from Rhode Island who offered their viewpoints. The others were: Nellie Gorbea, former economic adviser for the governor of Puerto Rico and current president of the Rhode Island Latino Civic Fund; Felicia Diaz, a housing counselor at the Elmwood Foundation; Alfredo Lorenzo, a well-known artist who trained at the Rhode Island School of Design; and Marcos Antonio, former mayoral liaison to the Latino community, a well-known painter, and director of the Latino Film Festival.

The discussion focused on politics, but also celebrated the growth and diversity of the Latino community, and the flourishing of Latino businesses, social service agencies and organizations -- including arts organizations.

Antonio, former mayoral liaison for Vincent A. Cianci Jr., spoke candidly about the nearly impossible task he faced at times as he tried to access police on behalf of Hispanics who were frightened or had a language barrier.
Antonio tried to intervene on behalf of one man who said his daughter had been raped, "but I got nowhere, and I realized there was nothing I could do to help him," he said.

Tavaras zeroed in on how the September election "has been great for Latinos. We were very very influential in the mayor's race [in Providence]. We basically decided the governor's [Democratic primary] race."

Tavares also gave former mayor Joseph Paolino Jr.'s electoral failures as a case in point.
In 1996, when Paolino ran for a seat in Congress, "He said English should be the official language, and we need to put a triple fence around Mexico," and take a tough stance on illegal immigration, Tavares said, in paraphrase. Paolino later apologized for any offense to the Latino community.

"If nothing else," said Tavares, "it woke people up" and galvanized the Latino community to vote against Paolino. This time around, "I thought it was important to show [Paolino] that we will not forget."

Gorbea, president of the Rhode Island Latino Civic Fund, noted that Latinos started arriving in this state "as early as the 1950s." They are a diverse group that includes Dominicans, Puerto Ricans, Guatemalans, Peruvians, Argentinians, "and the last group to arrive, and it keeps growing, is Mexicans," she said.

Recalling her first trip to the Warwick Mall more than a decade ago, Gorbea said, "I felt like I was the only Latino for miles. But five years later, you started hearing Spanish all over the place."

Broad Street, she noted, "is a completely different place today than it was 10 years ago. Now you have the Hispanic Chamber of Commerce, a very vibrant and wonderful organization in our community."

The other part of the political story, said Gorbea, is the Latino Political Action Committee, which has been influential since the early 1990s. "It really includes a cross-section of Latinos . . . the PAC became a very active player in Rhode Island, and this election crystallized it."

Laffey Lone Republican Endorsed By Latino Group

By SCOTT MAYEROWITZ
Journal Staff Writer, West Bay
10/22/2002

CRANSTON -- Saying that Stephen P. Laffey shows sensitivity to many minorities, the Rhode Island Latino Political Action Committee has endorsed the mayoral candidate. Out of the nine candidates statewide endorsed by the group, Laffey is the only Republican.

Laffey has also been endorsed by the local police and teachers' unions. His Democratic opponent, Aram G. Garabedian, has yet to be endorsed by any group.
Nellie M. Gorbea, president of the PAC, said that during an interview and in a questionnaire Laffey showed support for issues related to Latinos and "lot of things that carry beyond the Latino community," such as support for small businesses. Gorbea said Laffey showed a commitment to bilingual education programs, saying that besides learning English, students need to have a means to gain other tools to succeed.

During the interview, Laffey said he noticed that when he goes to the city's pool there are not many minorities there and that he wants to make the government's services more accessible to minorities, Gorbea said. "The endorsement by the Latino Political Action Committee of my candidacy for mayor is deeply moving and personal. From elementary school through my career as President at Morgan-Keegan, I have been conscious of the need to bring people of different backgrounds together and to help in their efforts to achieve the American dream," Laffey said in a statement. "With the growth of the Latino population in Cranston and the enrichment it brings to the community, as mayor, I would have the opportunity to assist and assure all our citizens of their importance to Cranston. Reaching out to the Latino community will be a major effort of a Laffey administration that will fit into my objective of an all-inclusive administration." According to the 2000 Census, 3,613 or 4.6 percent of the city's 79,000 residents are Hispanic or Latino.

Gorbea says that the Latino community is rapidly growing in Cranston, especially near the Providence city line. She said that even since 2000, there has been a large increase. Gorbea said Garabedian told her that he was going to send in the questionnaire, but never did. She said they set up an interview, but he never showed up or called to cancel.

Candidates Joined Forces For Victory

On the South Side, a coalition helped to elect Miguel A. Luna to the City Council and Juan Pichardo to the Senate.

By Karen A. Davis
Journal Staff Writer
11/07/2002

PROVIDENCE -- Voters on the South Side turned out in force at the polls Tuesday, helping to elect three Democrats -- a new city council member, a new state senator and Mayor-elect David Cicilline. Spokesmen for the candidates said they attractedvoters to the polls through hard work, widespread neighborhood canvassing and old-fashioned grassroots organizing.

"It was just so amazing -- putting together a strong plan, getting residents involved and getting our message out there," said Matthew Jerzyk, campaign manager for Miguel C. Luna, who was successful in his bid for City Council in Ward 9.

The campaign staffs of Luna and Juan Pichardo, a candidate for Senate in District 2, joined forces before the Sept. 10 primary. They were brought together by the ACORN political action committee, which had endorsed both Luna and Pichardo, said Jerzyk, who is also director of Rhode Island Jobs With Justice, a workers' rights advocacy coalition.. The combined campaigns led to a massive get-out-the-vote effort that drew voters from the Latino, African-American, Southeast Asian and white communities. It also included other organizations, including the International Association of Fire Fighters, Local 799, of Providence, the Rhode Island Latino Political Action Committee and PrSYM, a Southeast Asian youth group.

Dubbed "Operation 2 Victory," in reference to the Senate District 2, the effort included recruiting hundreds of volunteers to make phone calls, drive voters to the polls and visit every house in the district. The comprehensive campaign helped Luna, Pichardo and Democratic Mayor-elect David Cicilline into office, their campaign staffs said.
They point to the numbers as evidence that the organizing worked.

Pichardo defeated two independents and a Republican, winning more than 75 percent of the vote. Pichardo had defeated 18-year incumbent Charles Walton in the Democratic primary.

Luna defeated an independentwith more than 85 percent of the vote. In the Democratic primary, he defeated 12-year incumbent Patricia Nolan, 1,066 to 741. In two four-way races, Cicilline received 53 percent of the primary vote and 83 percent of the general election vote; he was helped in large part by significant voter turnout on the South Side. While the citywide turnout hovered around 32 percent to 35 percent, Senate District 2 had a turnout of about 42 percent.

Compared to turnout for the general election in 1998, the South Side saw a 43-percent increase in turnout. "I think we succeeded in making South Providence the strongest voice [in the city]," Jerzyk said. Pichardo believes the impact of the organizing effort "was huge" in propelling him to victory. "I couldn't have done this all by myself. . . ."

Pichardo said he feels good about his campaign, which was launched eight months ago and flourished because he had a relationship with individuals and organizations.

Luna, a longtime grassroots organizer, said he takes pride in having a multiracial contingent of supporters working with him. He said Tuesday's turnout should end the South Side's reputation as a district of nonvoters.

As part of its strategy, Operation 2 Victory launched its get-out-the-vote strategy in parts of City Council Wards 8 and 11. Workers spent Tuesday promoting Ward 11 Democratic incumbent Councilwoman Balbina A. Young, who defeatead Leo Beliveau III with more than 75 percent of the vote.

In Ward 1, which covers Fox Point, College Hill and the Wayland Square area,, Green Party candidate David A. Segal credited hard work, committed volunteers and grassroots organizing for his victory over three challengers. Segal received more than 38.6 percent of the vote to beat a Democrat, a Republican and an independent. He became the state's first Green Party candidate elected to office. "This summer, I worked long hours at the hotel and came home to cook for my family and then I hit the campaign trail to make sure that Luna, Pichardo and Cicilline won," said Carmen Castillo, a member of the Hotel and Restaurant employees Union Local 217. "On both election days, I worked the polls and the streets from 6 a.m. to 9 p.m. for a reason: We need candidates who will support working families and the right to organize."

New Secretary Of State Picks Pair To Lead Transition

Political Scene:
BY MARK ARSENAULT and EDWARD FITZPATRICK
Journal Staff Writers
11/18/2002

Incoming Secretary of State Matt Brown has picked his campaign manager, Albert Dahlberg, and Nellie M. Gorbea , the president of the Rhode Island Latino Political Action Committee, to direct his transition team.

"I've selected two people with the energy and commitment to help me organize our administration and assemble a team of talented people . . . " Brown said in a statement.

Dahlberg managed Brown's expensive campaign for the office, launched last February. Brown beat incumbent Democrat Edward S. Inman III in a contentious primary, and easily won election on Nov. 5.

Prior to managing the campaign, Dahlberg worked at the U.S. Environmental Protection Agency in Washington, and had previously served as a counsel to U.S. Sen. John H. Chafee

on the Senate Environment and Public Works Committee. He is a 1996 graduate of Boston College Law School, and received a bachelor's degree from Georgetown University in 1992.

Gorbea is a founding board member of RILPAC. She previously served as an economic affairs adviser to the governor of Puerto Rico and as program officer with the Rhode Island Foundation. She earned a master's degree in public administration in 1992 from the Columbia School of International and Public Affairs.

Thirtysomethings Step Forward To Lead State Democrats

They promise to bring a new look and fresh energy to the offices of the attorney general and the secretary of state as wella s the state Senate.

11/25/2002
BY MICHAEL CORKERY
Journal Staff Writer

As role models, they cite Howard Dean, the Vermont governor, and Cesar Chavez, the social-reform leader.

They hail from a political family in Pawtucket, an activist family on Providence's East Side and a Spanish-speaking one in the Dominican Republic. They all believe that civic participation is woefully lacking in Rhode Island.

Meet three of the youngest faces of the state's Democratic party, elected to office for the first time earlier this month:

Patrick Lynch, 37, was elected attorney general. Matt Brown, 33, will be the new secretary of state. Juan M. Pichardo, 36, was elected the state Senate's first and only Hispanic member.

Party leaders say these men demonstrate the depth of the Democratic farm team, a crop of young people who will continue to rise in the party ranks.

Others say these young Democrats are simply fresh faces who capitalized on an anti-establishment sentiment among voters, angered by the scandals at the State House.

Lynch and Brown will occupy two of the state's most high profile positions, while Pichardo's victory represents a Democratic inroad into the Latino community.

"In the long term, it bodes very well for the party and frankly for the state," said William Lynch, 45, chairman of the state Democratic Party, whose brother, Patrick, will be the new attorney general. "Old guys like me will be getting out of the way."

Other young Democrats, most notably Providence mayor-elect David N. Cicilline, 41, also vaulted into the limelight this election.

The Republicans boast about their impressive bench, too. But the younger GOP candidates did not fare nearly as well as the Democrats in statewide races, though they narrowly lost in a few cases.

Nineteen-year-old Republican Anthony G. Spiratos, a political novice, came within 134 votes of knocking out Democrat Paul Crowley, of Newport, a 22-year veteran of the House.

And Scott Avedisian, 37, cruised to easy reelection as Warwick mayor, keeping this key position in Republican hands for another two years.
"I don't think there is that much of a difference between the Democrats and Republicans in terms of age," said GOP party chairman Bradford Gorham. "It just happens more Democrats won than Republicans."

THE YOUNG Democrats are optimistic as they prepare their transition teams and get ready to take office for the first time.

"It's really a healthy time," said Brown during an interview in his transition office in the Foundry Building.

"The public is focused on putting an end to backroom deals and political-insider games that go on. We are going to open it up and let the public hold their elected leaders accountable."

Brown talked about his coming term recently amid stacks of papers and office chairs piled in the middle of his office.

The head of City Year in Providence and other Rhode Island cities, and former head of the Democracy Compact, Brown says he was "born a Democrat" and was reared on the sayings of John F. Kennedy.
His late mother, a dean at Wheelock College in Boston, worked for the Children's Defense Fund and on literacy issues in Rhode Island.

One of Brown's predecessors, James Langevin, now a U.S. congressman, transformed the secretary of state's office into an aggressive watchdog and advocate for open government.

Brown describes his plans to create more open government in largely nonpartisan terms and is careful not to bash his fellow party members.

He wants to increase civic participation by opening the system to more young people and creating fellowships in government agencies for college and high school students. He proposes that all cities and towns post their meeting schedules on the secretary of state's Web site, making it easier for the public to participate. "One of the most important things I can do is to encourage everybody of all backgrounds to get involved in politics," Brown said.

LYNCH LOOKS a lot younger than his 37 years. A former Brown University basketball star, who played the game professionally in Europe, graduate of Suffolk University School of Law and former lobbyist, Lynch is about to become one of the most powerful government officials in Rhode Island. "The greatest challenge is that people look at the office and say it's doing justice for everybody," Lynch said.

Munching on an M & M cookie and drinking a bottle of Coke, Lynch last week discussed his political upbringing and plans for the office. Nearby, his campaign manager sat reading a book of e.e. cummings poetry.

Lynch said he became interested in politics when he was 6, watching his father, Dennis, campaign as mayor of Pawtucket, and, of course, his brother, Bill, a lawyer, is the party chairman. During the campaign, Lynch took hits for being the ultimate insider in the Democratic political machine. But he takes pride that he has worked for both Republican and Democrat attorneys general.
He quotes Ronald Reagan, and he cites Vermont governor and presidential hopeful Howard Dean as a model of fiscal conservatism and social liberalism. He emphasizes that his job as a prosecutor must be nonpartisan.

The attorney general's office has been the graveyard for many political careers. Lynch said it doesn't concern him that few have gone on to higher office from that position.

Lynch acknowledges that there are problems with the public's trust in government. He believes that the responsibility to restore that trust lies not only with the Democratic majority at the State House, but also with the public itself. "I have faith in the public," said Lynch. "They can step up and make changes. They can put their name on the ballot and they can vote. People don't do enough of either."

ON THE OTHER hand, Pichardo said the scandals at the State House were never a factor in his race. The voters in his district, which includes South Providence, were more concerned about issues such as affordable housing and crime, he said. "They wanted to talk about things that were affecting them directly," Pichardo said. "How we can better our neighborhoods."

Nonetheless, Pichardo has sensed a disconnect between politicians and the Latino community, which includes a large number of young voters. Pichardo beat out Sen. Charles Walton, the first and only black in the state Senate, in a hard-fought primary.

A former member of the Young Democrats, Pichardo said the party needs to work harder to cultivate Latino voters. He believes that the Democratic platform is naturally suited to Latinos, but Latinos are not going to vote for candidates unless the party works for their votes.

Pichardo said he looks up to John F. Kennedy, Martin Luther King Jr., and Cesar Chavez as role models. He views politics as a basic struggle to improve the world around him. "That's why a lot of the immigrants come here. That's why I came here -- to make sure we did better than our parents and grandparents."

Minorities Hopeful Despite Few Gains

Black and Hispanic groups says they were energized by the elections even though they made minimal political gains and feel some of the redistricting was unfair.

12/01/2002
By Edward Fitzpatrick
Journal Staff Writer

PROVIDENCE -- The proportion of minorities in the General Assembly remained the same after legislative downsizing, but the status-quo statistics belie a series of hard-fought races, devastating defeats and groundbreaking achievements for black and Hispanic candidates this year. One of the biggest disappointments was the loss of Sen. Charles D. Walton, D-Providence, Rhode Island's first and only black senator who had served for 18 years.

But Walton's defeat in a Democratic primary set the stage for Juan M. Pichardo to become Rhode Island's first and only Hispanic senator -- and the first Dominican-American to win a state senate seat in the United States.

In another historic first, Rep. Gordon D. Fox, D-Providence, was selected to become the state's first black House majority leader.

Fox, whose mother is Cape Verdean and whose father is Irish, said people may not think of him as black because of his light complexion. He said people guess that he's Italian, Greek or Spanish.

But Fox identifies himself as biracial, saying, "I believe I am the first black majority leader in Rhode Island. It's important for me to talk about my minority heritage because it helps young people identify and say, 'You know what? That's something I can be.' It's about being a role model and breaking down barriers."

Fox's election did not come as a result of General Assembly downsizing. But he became majority leader in a year in which downsizing was one of several major changes shaking the state's political landscape. The House has shrunk from 100 to 75 members and the Senate from 50 to 38 members as the result of a 1994 amendment to the state constitution. The downsizing coincided with the once-a-decade redistricting process, which reflects new census figures.

Before downsizing, the 150-member Assembly contained nine minority members. After downsizing, the 113-member Assembly contains seven minority members. So the proportion has remained essentially the same -- going from 6 percent to 6.19 percent.

Rep. Joseph S. Almeida, D-Providence, president of the Rhode Island Minority Caucus, said he is disappointed that minority representation did not expand this year, given the growth of minority populations statewide and in places such as Providence.

"The minority political machine has a great body -- we are all working together -- but with redistricting we are stuck in neutral," Almeida said. "We haven't gained anything."

Fox's election as majority leader was "very big," Almeida said. "Gordon Fox is a very powerful black man. He represents the black community, and we are very proud of him. We expect a lot from him, and he knows it."

But the loss of Walton hurt and could have been avoided, Almeida said.

He said the new Senate district map should have been drawn to allow both Walton and Pichardo to be elected from separate districts. He claimed the map was drawn to protect two white incumbents -- Sen. Frank T. Caprio and Sen. David V. Igliozzi. He noted Igliozzi ended up launching an unsuccessful campaign for mayor instead of seeking reelection to the Senate. "Politics was played in the Senate," Almeida said. "It's not right."

Senate leaders have denied such charges. They say downsizing created difficult situations throughout the state, and they say they did their best in Providence by creating four Senate districts where the majority of residents are nonwhite. They say they kept districts within city borders to avoid diluting minority populations but couldn't help the fact that Providence's Hispanic population has grown rapidly while many black residents have moved to other parts of the state.

Almeida was a member of the state's redistricting commission. He noted he asked for a separate vote on the House and Senate maps, saying he would have voted against the Senate map, but the commission decided to vote on the maps as a package and Almeida joined in the unanimous approval.
Fox said he feared downsizing would diminish minority representation in the House. Before downsizing, the 100-member House contained eight minority members. After downsizing, the 75-member House contains six minority members. So the proportion remained the same -- 8 percent.

"We did hold onto seats," Fox said. "But it thwarted efforts to increase minority representation."

Two minority House members won't be coming back in January. A black incumbent, Rep. Aisha W. Abdullah-Odiase, D-Providence, lost a House primary against Almeida. And a Hispanic incumbent, Rep. Stella G. Brien, D-Woonsocket, lost a Senate primary against Sen. Marc A. Cote, D-Woonsocket.

"Look at Stella Brien -- a bright, articulate lady who I think could have been a dynamo in the House," Fox said, noting Brien had convinced him to restore funding for immigrant health care. "It's too bad that we lost her."

Before downsizing, the 50-member Senate had one black member and no Hispanic members. After downsizing, the 38-member Senate has one Hispanic member and no black members. So the proportion of minorities in the Senate has gone from 2 percent to 2.6 percent.

Civil rights groups are trying to reinstate a lawsuit that claims the Senate map illegally dilutes black voting power on Providence's South Side. A recent court brief noted that even if the state maintained one black senator (2.6 percent of the Senate), that would still not reflect the proportion of black Rhode Islanders (4.5 percent of the state).

"We fought long and hard to get black people involved in the electoral process," said Clifford R. Montiero, president of the Providence branch of the National Association for the Advancement of Colored People, one of the plaintiffs. "They are not going to do it if they don't see someone who looks like them in office." Montiero called Fox's ascension to a powerful political post a "big plus" but he described Walton's defeat as a "major loss."

"[Walton's] 18 years of seniority is gone away," Montiero said. "I am very happy that the Hispanic community has an elected official they can identify with, but it wasn't right that it was set up so that minorities had to fight each other. It didn't have to be either/or." The number of black Rhode Islanders increased by 21 percent in the 1990s, reaching 46,908, while the number of Hispanics doubled, reaching 90,820. Melba D. Depena, the new president of the Rhode Island Latino Political Action Committee and the Rhode Island Latino Civic Fund, called Brien's defeat "disappointing" but Pichardo's election "extremely important."

Nationwide, eight Dominican-Americans won elections this year, and three of them are Rhode Islanders, according to the Dominican American National Roundtable, based in Washington, D.C.

While Pichardo became the first native of the Dominican Republic to be elected to a state senate seat, Dominican native Miguel C. Luna was elected to the Providence City Council and Dominican native Leon F. Tejada was reelected to the state House of Representatives, the group noted.

Roundtable President Margarita Cepeda-Leonardo, a former Rhode Island resident who now lives in Florida, hailed the Election Day gains, saying, "This is a historical advancement in the ongoing empowerment of Dominicans in the nation." She said news of Pichardo's victory was broadcast on television and radio in the Dominican Republic.

"We are very proud of him," said Cepeda-Leonardo, whose cousin is married to Pichardo. "Everybody in the Dominican community on the national level is celebrating his victory." She said Rhode Island has a young, politically active Dominican community that is getting the chance to participate in a small, increasingly diverse state.

"Rhode Island has come a long way in the last 20 years. It's accepting, and there's an opportunity to be part of a bigger picture in Rhode Island," Cepeda-Leonardo said. "I really think Providence is a model city of what America can become with different communities working together."

She too, would have preferred to see a black senator and a Hispanic senator serving side-by-side. But one positive development, she said, was that the Pichardo-Walton race energized South Side residents. "You walked around the South Side and everyone was talking about it -- in stores, old people and young people," she said.

Looking ahead, both Depena and the NAACP's Montiero said their groups will be focusing on registering and educating voters and encouraging candidates for future races.

Election Spawns Shuffle RILPAC Seats

By Liz Anderson A Edward Fitzpatrick
Political Scene
Journal Staff Writers
12/02/2002

Melba D. Depea is the new president of the Rhode Island Latino Political Action Committee, replacing Nellie M. Gorbea , who is expected to join the staff ofincoming Democratic Secretary of State Matthew A. Brown.

Depea, who was field director for Brown's campaign, will also replace Gorbea as president of the Rhode Island Latino Civic Fund, a nonprofit sister organization of the PAC.

Gorbea left the two positions to avoid a conflict of interest. She has already been appointed to head Brown's transition team along with Albert Dahlberg, Brown's campaign manager, and she's expected to continue in some capacity once Brown takes office next month.

Gorbea, 35, of East Greenwich, was elected president of RILPAC a year ago, replacing Dr. Pablo Rodriguez , who had headed the group since its founding in 1998.

Gorbea said she feels bad about leaving halfway through a two-year term as the group's president. "But it's easier when you know good people follow you," she said. "And we have a lot of talented people in the community. Melba and Betty (Bernal) are prime examples."

Depena was campaign manager of Ricardo Patino when he ran for Central Falls City Council in 2001. She was campaign manager for Juan M. Pichardo when he ran for state Senate in 2000. And she was finance chairwoman for Victor F. Capellan's campaign for the state House of Representatives in 1998.

The new executive vice president is Bernal, who had been chairwoman of the group's outreach committee. Her sister, Sylvia Bernal, remains the group's treasurer. The vice president is Tony Affigne. The secretary is Ana-Cecilia Rosado, and the assistant secretary is Claudia Cardona

Diversity Key As Cicilline Fills Top Posts

The Providence mayor-elect appoints Gonzalo Cuervo as the city's chief public information officer.

12/12/2002
By SCOTT MacKAY
Journal Staff Writer

PROVIDENCE -- During his campaign for mayor, David N. Cicilline told voters that he would usher in an administration as diverse as Providence, a city where a majority of residents are members of minority groups and more than 80 percent of public school children are minorities.

Now, as mayor-elect, Democrat Cicilline is reaching out to the city's various communities and agressively recruiting women and minorities as he fills top jobs in his administration.

"I've been working very hard to ensure that we have an administration that is representative of the city," Cicilline said yesterday. "I've done some very specific things to make that happen."

So far, Cicilline has appointed two women to the two top jobs he has filled. Carol J. Grant, a lawyer and former Textron and telecommunications executive, was named as chief of operations in Cicilline's administration. And Carolyn Benedict-Drew, who was director of Family Service Inc., for 14 years, a social service agency, has been appointed policy chief.

Both jobs pay about $110,000 anually, Cicilline said. Neither Benedict-Drew nor Grant held a top position in his campaign, which Cicilline said yesterday is evidence that he is looking for the best employees rather than just the most politically loyal.

"These [Grant and Benedict-Drew] were not people actively involved in my campaign," Cicilline said.

Yesterday, Cicilline named Gonzalo Cuervo as the city's chief public information officer, a post that pays about $75,000 annually.

Cuervo has been active in the Latino community and was a Cicilline campaign supporter.

Cicilline says he has not been content to wait for résumés and job applications to come in to his transition office on Dorrance Street near City Hall.

He has held meetings with leaders of the city's Southeast Asian, African-American and Latino communities to seek recommendations on qualified people for City Hall and departmental positions. A job fair was held recently at the Elmwood Community Center, in the heart of the city's Latino community, that yielded 98 resumes, Cicilline said. And members of his transition advisory team have been told to look for qualified women and minority candidates for jobs.

Five of the 10 paid staffers in his transition office are women, Cicilline said.

The key to getting more minority applicants is recruiting, Cicilline says.

"This is a really serious effort," said Cicilline, the city's first openly gay mayor. "Diversity . . . is a very important commitment to me and my administration."

RI Democrats Have Reason To Party

Melba Depeña is the first female, and the first Latina, to be hired as their executive director.

BY SCOTT Mackay and TATIANA PINA
Journal Staff Writers
Wednesday, December 17, 2003

PROVIDENCE -- Just about every white, dark-suited and familiar male figure in Rhode Island Democratic Party politics -- Congressmen Patrick Kennedy and James Langevin, House Speaker William Murphy, Mayor David Cicilline, Attorney General Patrick Lynch, Secretary of State Matthew Brown -- went to a Latino hangout on the city's South Side yesterday to celebrate the appointment of a woman born in the Dominican Republic as the party's first female and Latina executive director.

Melba Depeña, of Providence, a 31-year-old community organizer and activist, the Democratic Party's new executive director, was cheered yesterday for both her political savvy and the path-breaking nature of her appointment to the $40,000-a-year post.
William Lynch, state Democratic chairman, said the appointment shows the party takes seriously its mission to embrace the new minority voters who have flocked to Rhode Island over the last 20 years.

"She has the perfect résumé for this job," said Lynch, brother of Attorney General Patrick. "This is an important confirmation that the Democratic Party in Rhode Island understands the demographic changes that have occurred and wants to expand."

"Finding a Latino woman with the the kind of talent that Melba has is very good for us," said Lynch.

More than 100 Democratic Party and Latino political activists flocked to Ada's Creations restaurant on Broad Street yesterday for speeches and a luncheon to celebrate Depeña's hiring.

The symbolism was clear in an event held in the heart of a neighborhood that has been the home to successive generations of struggling immigrants and minority groups -- from Irish, Italian and Jewish immigrants to blacks from Cape Verde and the American South and now the Latinos who have flocked here in the past 20 years.

Hispanics are the state's largest ethnic minority, according to 2000 U.S. Census figures. It is a fast-growing group that was crucial to Cicilline's 2002 mayoral victory and has flexed its muscles in local elections in Providence, Central Falls and Pawtucket.

There was irony. Lynch got to know Depeña well after she criticized state Democratic leaders for not doing a good enough job reaching out to young and minority voters. He met with her and was impressed, as was Murphy, said Lynch.

Depeña came to Rhode Island at age 12 and graduated from the University of Rhode Island with a political science degree. She has worked in several Democratic campaigns and is an ally of state Sen. Juan Pichardo, D-Providence. Depeña also has good relations with organized labor, a strong party base. "We think she's great," said George Nee, secretary-treasurer of the state AFL-CIO.

After the pols and other officials had left the restaurant, a tired Depeña sat down with friends who were eating the meal of rice and pigeon peas, ribs and salad that the restaurant had prepared for the event.

Depeña was nursing a cold so she had not been able to eat but was glad to sit and enjoy a low-key chat with friends. She sat with Gladys Baker, Ingrid Ardaya, Betty Bernal and Gabby Molina. Some of them are members of the Rhode Island Latino Political Action Committee, for which Depeña had served as president. Depeña noted that while a lot of Latinos came out for yesterday's event, one could count the number of blacks on one hand.

"That is one of the things we have to do, figure out how to reach out to other communities," she said.

"I haven't thought of a name but I want to have a caucus that would be comprised of blacks and Latinos. . . I personally have learned a lot from African-American leaders, like Tommy O'Connor and others," said Depeña, referring to Thomas O'Connor, a former Providence councilman long active in city Democratic politics.

Rep. Joseph Almeida, D-Providence, one of the few blacks to attend, said he was pleased with the Democratic Party's choice. "It's about time," he said. "She is equal right across the board. She is good for the black and Latino community. The black community will be calling her."

Depeña grew up on politics. Her father was an active member of the Dominican Liberation Party in the Dominican Republic and she learned at his knee as he read her the latest news on the political front from La Vanguardia newspaper. But Melba didn't just listen as Narciso Depeña read, she asked her father questions.

In Rhode Island, she and fellow Dominican immigrants Victor Capellan and Juan Pichardo served as members of Quisqueya en Accion, a Dominican organization geared to maintaining Dominican culture among its youth, through leadership and culture.

But while Capellan and Pichardo had political aspirations, Depeña preferred the strategy and grass-roots organizing necessary to get a campaign off the ground.

"Melba isn't one for the limelight. She prefers to work her butt off quietly in the background," according to her friend, Ingrid Ardaya, secretary of the Rhode Island Latino Political Action Committee.

Dr. Pablo Rodriguez, one of the founders of the Rhode Island Latino Political Action Committee, said that Depeña's appointment is a recognition of the rising political power of the Latino community. "It means that our point of view is important, that our point of view is becoming part of the point of view of the majority," Rodriguez said.

Central Falls City Councilman Ricardo Patino, the first Latino elected to the City Council in Central Falls, said that Depeña turned his campaign around and helped him clinch his first victory. It was Depeña who told him and his workers that they had to win the Anglo vote first before they could even think about getting the Latino vote. She had him stump in high rises for the elderly and speak English.

"Melba was born in the Dominican Republic but she was raised here," Patino said. "She knows the two worlds. She is able to know how people from there think and how the people from here think. She will be the one who can build that connection between the party and the long-forgotten Latino community."

RI Democrats Choose First Female Director

Melba Depena, 31, has worked on several political campaigns and is currently executive assistant to URI's vice provost in Providence.

By Tatiana Pina
Journal Staff Writer
Tuesday, December 16, 2003

PROVIDENCE -- The Rhode Island Democratic Party has chosen Melba Depena as the party's first female and first Latina executive director.

Depena's appointment will be formally announced today at a luncheon at Ada's Creations on Broad Street in South Providence.

Democratic Party Chairman William Lynch said Depena's energy, grass-roots organizing ability and reputation made her the choice to lead the Democratic Party in Rhode Island.

"She has done stuff from the ground up. She has established an incredible reputation throughout Rhode Island. Her name kept coming up," Lynch said.

Depena emigrated to the United States from Santiago, Dominican Republic, at 12 but she grew a love for politics early at her father's knee in her native country. At home, he was an active member of the Dominican Liberation Party, and he weaned her on politics from the time she was 8 by reading her political stories from La Vanguardia newspaper, she said.

Depena, 31, who holds a bachelor's degree in political science and a master's degree in human development and family studies from the University of Rhode Island, served on the political campaigns of Sen. Juan Pichardo, Central Falls Councilman Ricardo Patino, Secretary of State Matt Brown and gubernatorial candidate Myrth York.

The Rhode Island Democratic Party has been without an executive director for about a year, according to Lynch. He said the job pays around $40,000.

Melba Depena
Lynch said he was impressed by Depena's statements in a newspaper article about how the Democratic Party could be doing more in the state. He called her to talk about her ideas.

Asked what Depena's appointment might mean in terms of bringing in new members from the fast-growing Latino community, Lynch was careful to say that it was not the sole reason for her appointment.

"I don't want to paint her with that brush. I think it's going to help in general across the board. It should be further confirmation that the Democratic Party is committed to reflecting the people who make up our population."

Depena is working as the executive assistant to the vice provost of the University of Rhode Island in Providence. She will begin her new job as the executive director of the Rhode Island Democratic Party on Jan. 5. She is the former president of the Rhode Island Latino Political Action Committee.

Tomas Avila, the president of the Rhode Island Latino Political Action Committee, said Depena would bring a good understanding of the changing demographics of voters.

"As was proven in the last elections, the demographics of the state have changed. She understands the regular voter and the new voter. She will provide services to all those communities," Avila said.

House Speaker William J. Murphy, Senate President William V. Irons, U.S. Rep. Patrick J. Kennedy, U.S. Rep. James R. Langevin, Lt. Gov. Charles J. Fogarty, Secretary of State Brown, Providence Mayor David N. Cicilline, Lynch and other officials are expected to attend today's announcement.

New Director A Landmark Move

Tuesday, December 16, 2003
The Associated Press

PROVIDENCE -- The state Democratic Party today officially announced its appointment of Melba Depena as its new executive director, making her the first female and the first Latina to hold the post.

Depena, 31, has most recently served as executive assistant to the vice provost of the University of Rhode Island in Providence. She begins her new job, which pays about $40,000 annually, on Jan. 5.

The state Democratic Party has been without an executive director for about a year. Depena will focus on party-building activities, such as recruiting candidates, maintaining a voter file, and administering an internship program.

"Melba has the background and experience to ensure that the party is prepared for the upcoming election year, and I have every confidence in her grassroots organizational capabilities," Party Chairman William Lynch said.

Depena is the former president of the Rhode Island Latino Political Action Committee. She also was field director for Secretary of State Matt Brown's primary campaign last year, and assisted Myrth York in her unsuccessful gubernatorial run last year.

Depena emigrated with her family to the United States from Santiago, Dominican Republic, when she was 13.

Ready To Rumba

As Latinos in Rhode Island gear up for further gains, the nation's largest minority group is steadily wielding more political power

By Ian Donnis
The Providence Phoenix
Issue Date: June 27 - July 3, 2003

© Frank Mullin

ORGANIZE, ORGANIZE, ORGANIZE: in the face of heightened anti-immigrant sentiment since 9/11, activists like Garcia and Jerzyk (second from left, and far right) are redoubling their efforts to push for immigration reform.

ON THE MOVE: although Latinos remain underrepresented at the State House, efforts backed by Depena and the Latino Civic Fund are likely to yield gains in the years to come.

IN SHARP CONTRAST to the recent launch of President George W. Bush's high-stakes campaign fundraising, a decidedly grassroots political operation will come to Providence in the next few weeks: 50 high-school-age Latinos, clad in brightly colored T-shirts, will fan out through parts of Silver Lake and the South Side, seeking to transform fresh citizens into registered voters.

The registration campaign, sponsored by the Rhode Island Latino Civic Fund, with a $15,000 state Senate grant that followed tensions over legislative redistricting, is just one reflection of how Latino activists are promoting the message of participatory democracy. The civic fund hopes to cultivate additional voters by approaching other new citizens after monthly naturalization ceremonies at Bishop McVinney Auditorium. It wants to remedy the bad experiences of some Latino seniors with mail ballots by holding a series of ice cream socials at Providence high rises. The first 35 graduates of the civic fund's Latina Leadership Institute, an effort to build organizational capacity for campaigns and other efforts, are due to graduate in August. And, as the game plan has it, Latino voting power will expand from the newfound bastions of last November.

Such efforts won't come as a surprise for anyone who's been keeping a close eye on Rhode Island politics. After years of steady growth and quiet organizing, 2002 marked a watershed in which Latino voters were heavily courted, Latino candidates made history, (like Juan Pichardo, who became the first Dominican-American state senator in the US, and Miguel Luna, whose election doubled the presence of Latinos on the Providence City Council), and the state's Latino community, after toiling in relative obscurity, suddenly emerged as a significant political force. The evidence could be seen in those victories, like Myth York's Democratic gubernatorial primary squeaker over Sheldon Whitehouse, and Providence Mayor David N. Cicilline's resounding primary win, in which Latino voters proved decisive.

For all the progress, political representation doesn't yet come close to approximating the presence of roughly 100,000 Latinos in Rhode Island — about 10 percent of the state's population — up from 45,000 in 1990 and 20,000 in 1980. There are only three Hispanic members of the General Assembly — Pichardo, and Representatives Leon Tejada and Anastasia Williams, both Providence Democrats. And for all the enhanced political stature, Latinos in Rhode Island — a young (median age, 24) and heterogeneous group composed mostly of Puerto Ricans, Dominicans, Guatemalans, Colombians, and Mexico, are vexed by disproportionately high rates of poverty. Language barriers, competition with black candidates, a potential backlash against Latin nationalism, and rivalries based along national origin, although perhaps not as strong in the past, pose additional challenges.

This said, the gains of 2002 have engendered a sense of optimism, forward movement, and a belief that the passage of time and continued growth of the state's Latino population — the fastest growing in New England — will yield further elective gains.

"We still have to deal with our share of skeptics and people who don't understand how the system works," says Melba Depena, president of the Rhode Island Latino Civic Fund, and voting participation by Latinos has yet to match the high level in such places as the Dominican Republic and Puerto Rico. But generally, Depena says, there's a positive sense of momentum. "The census numbers have conveyed a message," she says, and the national political parties are certainly paying attention.

DEPENA, 31, who works as executive assistant to the vice provost at the University of Rhode Island's Providence campus, is a good example of the political maturation of the state's Latino community. A Dominican native who came to Rhode Island at 13, she graduated from URI in 1992 and was part of a band of young activists who, unaware of efforts by their elders, "thought we could come to Providence and change the world." But after working in different capacities for an array of candidates — including York, Victor Capellan in 1998, Pichardo in 2000, Ricardo Patino (who became the first Latino city councilor in heavily Hispanic Central Falls), and Secretary of State Matt Brown — Depena has gained a fair share of political savvy. (She hastens to add that she isn't interested in running for office.)

Similarly, the growing appreciation for the Rhode Island Latino Political Action Fund (the fundraising arm of the civic fund) could be seen when almost every statewide candidate of note — and hundreds of other people from a variety of backgrounds — came out for RILPAC's festive spring 2002 tribute to Dr. Pablo Rodriguez at the Crowne Plaza Hotel in Warwick. Rodriguez, one of the state's most veteran Latino activists, deliciously delivered on the palpable sense of a political coming-out; bringing the ballroom to a hush by saying he was about to make a very important announcement — triggering visions of an incipient campaign — he then vowed to be the best husband and father he could be.

All this marks a dramatic change from the time 15 years ago, when the since-deceased Juanita Sanchez and just a few other individuals advocated politically on behalf of Latinos. "It was very difficult in those days," recalls Rodriguez. "Now, there are a number of people who are working on issues, some together, some completely separately. I think that's a sign of a healthy community. Some people feel there should be a single group or a single representative, and I think that's inaccurate."

Indeed, the growing vibrancy of Rhode Island's Latino community is evident in any number of ways. Flourishing small businesses — bakeries, groceries, travel agencies, hair stylists, and the like — fill formerly vacant storefronts on Broad Street and Elmwood Avenue in Providence. Activists like Nellie Gorbea, Gonzalo Cuervo, and Patricia Martinez have landed prominent posts, respectively, in the Brown, Cicilline, and Carcieri administrations. And the predominant Anglo culture is paying a growing amount of attention — as seen by the copious selection of Hispanic foods at the new Shaw's Supermarket in Eagle Square, for example, or the issuance last week by Attorney General Patrick Lynch's office of a Spanish-language version of Durable Power of Attorney for Health Care.

The seriousness with which some members of the extended community view their civic responsibility can be seen in how Victor Cuenca, a 37-year-old Bolivian native, has abstemiously avoiding making political endorsements since starting his Spanish-language newspaper, *Providence En Espanol*, about four years ago. Other Spanish papers have tended to be irregular or fiercely partisan, so Cuenca's faced a struggle for credibility when he launched it with his wife from their North Providence home. Now, though,

Providence En Espanol boasts a payroll of 12, free weekly circulation of 25,000 copies at hundreds of locations, an office at a Seekonk, Massachusetts, industrial park, and after attracting a raft of campaign ads last fall, it's flush with news content and ads from Nordstrom, Ocean State Job Lot, and Showcase Cinemas. Cuenca now feels his paper has gained enough authority that he plans to start making endorsements after its fifth anniversary. Similarly, the Spanish-language radio station, *Poder* 1110, was a vital channel of political debate last year, arguably offering the most robust flowering of community-based radio in the Providence market.

It's these kind of developments that make observers sanguine about the outlook. Rodriguez, for example, says, "I think it's tremendous — what's happening and what's going to happen. The success that we had in the last election is going to translate into more political participation and activism. You can already see a number of groups getting together and trying to get more involved in the political process, because they've seen that we can make a difference."

Such optimism seems more than justified. At a time when most Americans are disengaged from politics, the growing involvement of Latinos — the nation's largest minority group, numbering almost 40 million — represents a healthy development for our civic culture. Voter registration efforts, like those sponsored by the Rhode Island Latino Civic Fund and Puerto Rico's governor (see "A new effort to tap Latino voting power," News, This just in, May 9), are poised to spread the influence of Hispanic voting from such natural bases as Elmwood, Washington Park, and parts of the South Side.

As Pichardo says, "They can see now if they are persistent in their goal in terms of participating, whether they're working in campaigns or they're candidates themselves, they have some hope. And I think that the gains we have made over the past couple of years gives them that hope, and gives me the great hope that we are becoming part of the American system and the Rhode Island system — because we're engaging and really being at the table when these decisions are being made."

© Richard McCaffrey

Still, while greater political representation would seem to offer a lift to the entire community, it remains far more difficult to improve the lives of the many Latino have-nots — the poor, undocumented immigrants, and others subject to exploitation — than to win even a growing number of elections.

PROGRESSIVE: following the path set by Luis Aponte (below), the first Latino councilor in Providence, Luna's election last year doubled Hispanic representation on the council.

IN THE SPIRIT of the civil rights freedom rides of the '60s, buses loaded with undocumented immigrants and their advocates will depart from nine US cities in late September, traveling town to town as the passengers share their stories, before converging for an October 4 mega-rally (hoped for attendance: one million people) in the Queens section of New York. The broad mobilization, sponsored by a coalition of unions, immigrants, and student and religious groups, is designed to build backing for changes in US immigration policy.

The conservative critique, periodically aired by WHJJ-AM talk-show host John DePetro and others, is that illegal immigrants flock to Rhode Island for welfare and other benefits. But the November 2001 death of Rosa Ruiz Barrera, a 22-year-old Guatemalan immigrant who was fatally injured in a single-vehicle accident in South Kingstown, tells another story.

As previously reported in the *Phoenix* (See "Justice delayed," News, April 5, 2002), Ruiz Barrera was among dozens of immigrant workers supplying the muscle behind the fish-processing industry in Narragansett, unloading boats, cutting open raw fish, and freezing and packing the seafood that winds up on restaurant and dinner tables across the world. She was killed when the driver of a van shuttling workers back to Providence lost control of the vehicle, and the driver vanished after his blood allegedly tested at more than three times the state's drunk-driving limit. Ruiz Barrera's death led fellow immigrant workers to charge they were being exploited — being paid below minimum wage and no mandatory overtime, among other things — by some of Rhode Island's fish-processing plants. But when 35 workers at one of the plants, including Ruiz Barrera's widower, lost their jobs after speaking out, it appeared as if they were the only ones who paid a price.

It's this dichotomy the way in which immigrant workers remain marginalized and vulnerable, even while taking on menial and undesirable jobs eschewed by most Americans — that has propelled growing efforts to reform US immigration law in recent years. As it stands, even hardworking and law-abiding undocumented immigrants are essentially ineligible for citizenship unless they've been in the country since 1972. (In another sign of the difficulties faced by undocumented immigrants, Rhode Island, which had been one of six states where people could use an Individual Taxpayer Identification Number to get a driver's license — an obviously vital document — is doing away with this practice.)

Juan Garcia, a 52-year-old Guatemalan native who coordinates the Immigrants in Action organizing project at St. Teresa's Church in the Olneyville section of Providence, seems tireless in his efforts. After nine years as an organizer — five as a volunteer — the steady buzz of his cell phone testifies to the constant demands of his work. And despite the prevailing clampdown on immigration after 9/11, Garcia enthusiastically outlines in accented English the proposal, backed by a coalition of labor, church, activist and student groups, to make it easier for undocumented immigrants to become citizens.

The idea is to create a three-year track toward naturalization for immigrants who demonstrate responsibility, self-sufficiency, and the lack of a criminal record. And with an estimated 10 million undocumented immigrants in the US, proponents describe the entry of these workers into the mainstream economy as a windfall waiting to happen. "We have the power to fly the country," Garcia says. "A lot of people have been waiting for 18 years."

Supporters cite globalization, the consequences of US foreign policy, and the North American Free Trade Agreement (NAFTA) as additional rationales for liberalizing immigration policy. As Garcia explains it, the migration of factories to Mexico and Guatemala has displaced small farmers, leading migrants to the US in search of a better living. "These people have no rights, no documents," he says. "People need to work two jobs to survive — $6 an hour. Who can survive $6 an hour if you have a family and two kids?"

But the difficulty of making progress on immigration reform can be seen in the stance of even a solid progressive like US Senator Jack Reed. Reed has supported changing the registry date — the starting point for citizenship eligibility for undocumented immigrants — from 1972 to some time in the 1980s. "If you've been in this country [that long], obeying the law, you should have the opportunity to become a US citizen," says Greg McCarthy, Reed's spokesman. But a blanket amnesty, McCarthy says, "would cover people who just entered the country recently as well," and could cause a rush of additional illegal immigration.

Prospects for an immigration bill were brighter a few years ago, and President George W. Bush, certainly cognizant of the growing Latino population in the US, had signaled his support. "But after September 11, there really hasn't been any talk of immigration legislation moving through Congress," McCarthy says. "September 11 has had a chilling impact on the immigration debate."

This helps to explain why 150 undocumented immigrants and their advocates were somewhat underwhelmed by the response from Reed and other members of Rhode Island's congressional delegation when they traveled to

Washington, DC, to lobby on the issue in May. In the absence of political support, advocates plan to press their case through grassroots organizing, including the freedom rides later this year. "At the end of the day, I think we're going to have the support of our congressional delegation, it's just going to take a lot more work than we'd like to have to do," says Matthew Jerzyk, director of the activist coalition Rhode Island Jobs With Justice. "With the federal election set for 2004, we can make immigrants' rights a political issue."

AS THE REPUBLICAN Party energetically strives to extend its control of the White House and Congress, the big question is whether the fast-growing Latino population in the US offers a greater advantage to Democrats or Republicans. It might seem like a curious query in heavily Democratic Rhode Island, but the political inclinations of Latinos — from the ultra-conservative Cuban expatriates of south Florida to California's GOP-leaning Mexican-Americans — tend to be far more heterogeneous around the US.

In politically important states with the largest Hispanic communities — New York, Florida, Texas, California, and Illinois — "It's a young community without the institutional memory, so allegiances can quickly be shifted if someone comes up with a message that resonates with Latino residents," says Pablo Rodriguez. "Luckily, for the Democratic Party, the policies of the Republican Party speak for themselves and are soundly anti-immigrant." Similarly, state Senator Juan Pichardo, a self-described Democratic partisan, points to Bush's support of cuts in the AmeriCorps national service program as an example of how GOP policies are contrary to the interest of Latinos.

A popular East Providence politician once told Dan Garza that being a Republican in Rhode Island is like trying to pee up a rope. And as Garza knows, trying to cultivate Latino Republicans is even more difficult. Even with the chairman's steady work and articulate manner, the Rhode Island chapter of the Republican National Hispanic Assembly has only about five members. But Garza, a pithy Ohio native and former Democrat who traces his heritage to Texas and Mexico, believes the GOP message of family, church, and self-reliance still has a lot of resonance for Latinos in the US.

Darrell West, a political science professor at Brown University, offers some backing for Garza's outlook. As West notes, Latinos from places with a social Democratic government, like Dominicans and Puerto Ricans, tend to back Democrats, while those from more Catholic-oriented countries, like Mexico, lean more to Republican candidates. Nationally, says West, "The Latino vote is up for grabs between the two parties. Republicans have made a major pitch for Latinos, although historically that vote has leaned Democratic. Republicans think that Latinos are more conservative than

399

African-Americans, so that gives them some hope of making inroads among that group."

The local Democratic-Latino relationship isn't without some degree of strain. Adopting an otherwise even tone during a recent interview, Melba Depena, president of the Rhode Island Latino Civic Fund, says, "The Democratic Party has been taking us for granted, locally and nationally." She cites a lack of sufficient support for some Democratic Latino candidates, but declined to elaborate beyond saying, "It's a growing issue," and "a big problem." (Bill Lynch, chairman of the Rhode Island Democratic Party, says he's mystified by the criticism, adding, "In Rhode Island, the Democratic Party has done everything we can do — and continues to do — to bring more and more minorities, including Latinos, into our party and the party system . . . We have worked very hard and have been fortunate to have some great Latino candidates elected.")

Another local source of division has been the rivalry between Latino and black candidates, sparking comparisons to the past competition between Irish-Americans and Italian-Americans. As Shannah Kurland, then the outgoing director of the activist group Direct Action for Rights & Equality (DARE), wrote in the spring 2001 issue of *Colorlines*, "Does the expansion of Latino political power have to come at the expense of black representation? And beyond the identity of the individuals representing districts of people of color, are our communities even talking about racial justice when we engage in electoral work?"

The question remained relevant last fall when Pichardo's election as Rhode Island's first Latino state senator came at the expense of Charles Walton, the state's only black senator. Critics blamed legislative redistricting, while legislative leaders said they tried to do their best with a difficult situation after downsizing in the General Assembly. But even though Walton's loss represented a bitter pill for some, the wider progressive gains of the 2002 political season (including the election of Pichardo, Cicilline, and Miguel Luna, Kurland's husband, to the Ward Nine seat on the Providence City Council) seemed to somewhat mollify concerns.

As far as the black-brown rivalry, Depena says new strategies are needed to avoid the pitting of one minority candidate against another in the future. "It's not easy," she says. "There's opposition from both sides, but there are some great people on both sides that are interested in a coalition, and I think we're headed in that direction."

In the minds of some, the grassroots organizing on behalf of candidates like Cicilline and Luna — in which Latino single mothers and other

400

unconventional political activists helped to chart the future of Providence marked a democratic high point in a city with no small tradition of political skullduggery.

"We really tried to build a multi-racial community that built Latino political power and recognizes that racism doesn't care whether you're Latino or Liberian, or Dominican or Puerto Rican," says Jerzyk, who took leave from his Jobs With Justice post to manage Luna's campaign. "That's a big obstacle, to try to bridge those perceived differences and to try to create a common agenda for immigrant communities, communities of color, [and the greater good.]"

There's little doubt that Latinos in Rhode Island are on the political rise. The more tantalizing question is how they will exercise their growing power in the years to come.

Ian Donnis can be reached at idonnis@phx.com

A New Effort To Tap Latino Voting

Talking Politics

By Ian Donnis
The Providence Phoenix
Issue Date: May 9 -15, 2003

For all the attention that Latino voters attracted as an increasingly influential voting bloc during 2002 political season, the fast-growing ranks of Latinos remain sorely underrepresented in elective offices in Rhode Island. Although this situation seems likely to change over time, it could get an immediate boost thanks to a new effort by the Puerto Rican government to increase voter registration among Puerto Ricans living in Rhode Island.

The registration drive — scheduled to be unveiled Thursday, May 8, at the State House, and entitled "*Que nada nos detenga!* ("Let nothing stop us!") — is part of a three-year, nonpartisan voter education campaign initiated by Puerto Rico's governor Sila M. Calder—n. The campaign is meant to narrow the glaring disparity between voting participation by Puerto Ricans on the island (86 percent, according to the Puerto Rican Federal Affairs Administration) and the US mainland (40 percent).

Luis A. Aponte, a Puerto Rican native who became Providence's first Latino city councilor when he was elected to the Ward 10 seat in 1998, attributes the gap to the high degree of attention paid by Puerto Ricans to local politics on the island, especially the perennial question of whether Puerto Rico should retain its current status as a self-governing US territory, become the 51st state, or strive for independence. "That struggle is one that permeates parties, and over the last 100 and something years has been an ongoing cause for political debate," he says.

Sandra Reyes of Providence, who will coordinate the voter registration campaign in Rhode Island for the Puerto Rico Federal Affairs Administration, plans to use door-to-door outreach and coalition-building efforts among nonprofit, business, labor, and faith-based groups to increase political participation. The message is simple, she says: "If you vote, you get heard."

Latinos have made steady political inroads in Rhode Island politics in recent years, emerging as widely courted voters in last year's gubernatorial and Providence mayoral elections. Along with other successes, Miguel Luna, a native of the Dominican Republic, won a primary fight in Providence's Ward Nine, going on to join Aponte as the second Latino on the city council. Still, it's clear that electoral representation has yet to catch up with the state's fast-growing Latino community, most of whose members come from Puerto Rico, Colombia, the Dominican Republic, and Guatemala.

With Republicans like Karl Rove demonstrating a high degree of political mastery in confounding Democrats, some liberals hold out hope that the growing Latino population in the US could tip the balance in a different direction. As it happens, the rate of growth among Latinos in Rhode Island — who have more than quadrupled, to almost nine percent of the state's population in 2000, up from two percent in 1980 — exceeds that of any other New England state.

Mayor Cicilline Announces Equity Force

May 8, 2003

PROVIDENCE - "In this majority-minority city, where 68 different languages are spoken in our homes, it is critical - more than ever - that our city government reflect the great and rich diversity of our community," said Mayor David N. Cicilline. He made that statement this morning as he announced the formation of an 12-member City Government Equity Task Force made up of community members, to review the City's affirmative action policy, minority contracting procedures, equal opportunity compliance, and other related issues.

The Task Force, appointed by the Mayor, includes Tomas Avila, real estate agent; Onna Moniz-John, Affirmative Action officer for the City of East Providence; Cliff Monteiro, executive director of the NAACP; Stan Cameron, head of the Black Contractors Association; Gertrude Blakey, deputy director of the Urban League; Molly Soum, president of the Cambodian Society; Judy Willis, director of employment with the South Providence Development Corporation; Cheryl Burrell, director of Diversity for the State of Rhode Island; Manuel Peguero, a Providence resident and community activist, and Marilyn Acevedo, a Providence businesswoman and head of the RI Hispanic Contractors Association.

The Task Force will assist the Mayor in redesigning and improving Affirmative Action recruitment and hiring practices, contracting procedures and outreach strategies. It will be staffed by members of the Administration responsible for these issues, including ray Rickman, the City's affirmative action/ equal employment officer in the public and private sector; Sybil Bailey, the City's Director of Personnel, Christine Roundtree, of the City's Human Relations Commission, and Kehinde Adegoke, a minority business representative with the City of Providence.

Part of the mission of the Task Force will be to examine the way in which new employees are hired, promotions and appointments are made, and there is outreach to minority and other contractors. "We live in a city rich with many languages and many cultures," Mayor Cicilline said. "As government officers, it is our legal and moral obligation to ensure that qualified people - irrespective of their backgrounds - are hired, but that every effort is made to enable all people of all backgrounds to seek employment and the opportunity to bid and be awarded public- projects."

How Did Life Change as a Result of RILPAC

Tomás Alberto Ávila
Address to Delaware Latino Political Action Committee
Inaugural Event
Wilmington, Delaware
January 26, 2003

Thank you very much for inviting me to visit with you today to speak about our accomplishments in Rhode Island and how the Rhode Island Latino PAC altered forever the political landscape of a state very similar to YOURS.

First however, let me state that I am privileged to represent and work on behalf of a dedicated group of Hispanic volunteers that through their perseverance, foresight, labor, and commitment formed the Rhode Island Latino Political Action Committee. Not only did this group of people change the political power structure in Rhode Island for the better but also through its other activities, it continues to build social capital and strengthen the bonds that unite us all as Latinos and Rhode Islanders. In brief, my message to you today is that the group that created the Rhode Island PAC in 1998 is no different from YOU and that YOU have it within your grasp to change the political landscape of Delaware for Hispanic Delawareans forever in ways that we can only imagine but for certain in ways that will benefit Latinos and all Delawareans – *SI TIENEN GANAS Y CORAZON!*

But let me go back in time briefly to 1996. At that time, many of the state's Latino leaders started to meet informally at the home of Dr. Pablo Rodriguez in what was to become a bonding experience for Hispanic Rhode Islanders. As Latinos, we found comfort in gathering and celebrating our diverse cultures and heritage. As you do, we enjoyed homemade foods and drinks, made new acquaintances, and had a wonderful time. Over time, these gatherings became a venue for building a strong Latino network in the community. Some built business relationships. Some of our nonprofit leaders were able to connect with Latino professionals that were able to expand on the resources available to help our community. Still others became interested in the political arena, and it is because of this last group that the RI Latino Political Action Committee became a reality.

We came to two important conclusions at that time. First, that our community was growing and making its presence felt by virtue of its numbers and spending power. Second, that despite our many positive contributions to the social and economic fiber of Rhode Island, we remained outsiders with no political strength or influence - invisible. We were not present at important government decision-making tables. In fact, Latinos were often stereotyped as lazy, freeloaders, and criminals with no right to the American Dream.

We were, for all intents and purposes, Rhode Island's economic and a political under class. Moreover, our limited participation in the political processes of our state made it easy for these stereotypes to be perpetuated and for our community to maintain its invisibility. Clearly, it was time to wake up, get with the program and drive some change. That is where Hispanic Delawareans find themselves today – at an important crossroad.

To the PAC, getting with the program first meant that we had to ensure that Latinos saw themselves as stakeholders in the future of Rhode Island. And conversely, that Rhode Islanders of all stripe embraced the notion that their success was closely tied to the success of Latinos. This in turn meant that Latinos had to be brought into the mainstream of the state's political and economic processes. It required the simultaneous education and collaboration of many communities within our state.

The vehicle to accomplish this goal was the Rhode Island Political Action Committee. The RILPAC was born on August 20, 1998. The original mission of RILPAC was to ensure that candidates to political office in Rhode Island were aware of Latino issues and that as a community; we were informed about the candidates themselves and their views toward us. In addition, we sought to inject ourselves into the political agenda of the state through political action, advocacy and education.

There were many challenges on the road to success. These included raising money, motivating volunteers and engaging the community on a broad scale. It was important that we publicly demonstrate our ability to rally voters and raise money. We did this and more.

As a result of the efforts of the PAC, the political landscape of Rhode Island underwent a transformation. Most notably, Latino voter participation increased to 38% in the 2000 election and 48% in 2002. In 2002, Juan Pichardo was elected as the first Latino state senator. Latino political appointments subsequent to the 2002 election include among others Jose Gonzalez was appointes Vice Chair of the Providence Democratic Committee, Nellie Gorbea as Director of Administration for the Secretary of State, Aida Patricia Crosson as Director of the Victims Unit, Office of the Attorney General, Gonzalo Cuervo as Director of Communications for the Mayor of Providence, Ernesto Figueroa as Director of Vital Statistics for the City of Providence, Patricia Martinez as Director of Community Relations for Rhode Island Governor Donald Carcieri and Nancy Garcia Ponte as Assistant City Solicitor for the City of Cranston. For the 2002 election, candidates endorsed by RILPAC won 7 of 8 primaries and 8 of 9 general elections. We believe these are significant accomplishments over a very short period of time.

How else did life change after the PAC? Well, before the PAC, political candidates made little to no investment in the Latino community. Generally, they recruited Latinos as volunteers but not as paid campaign staff. Post PAC, Melba Depeña was hired as Field Director for the Secretary of State campaign, Gonzalo Cuervo was hired as Director of Minority relations for one of the City of Providence mayoral campaigns and we saw the creation of Latino Campaign Committees for all statewide campaigns. RILPAC was also involved in a campaign for Providence City Council in 1999, and the endorsement of two Latino candidates for Central Falls City Council that resulted in the election of the city's first Latino elected official. Finally, RILPAC has worked with the Latino community of Woonsocket RI to help them organize a campaign of the city's first Latino at-large candidate.

In closing, let me say that the Rhode Island Latino PAC has been a breath of fresh air to the state's political process. The seeds planted by its activity will bear economic fruit in the years to come in the form of greater access to capital, increased educational and employment opportunity for our children, access to better paying jobs, a greater say on how the state's resources are deployed and integration of Latinos into the economic and political fiber of the state.

Do not let this opportunity slip through your fingers. The time to act is now because if not now when and if not you whom?

Thank you once again. Best wishes for success and don't give up the fight!

Martinez To Keep Carcieri In Touch

M. Charles Bakst
The Providence Journal
01/26/2003

In naming Patricia Martinez to be his director of community relations, Governor Carcieri has tapped a leader in Rhode Island's burgeoning Hispanic community. He says, "She's terrific."

Providence Councilman Miguel Luna says, "Her heart's in the right place. Her mind is in the right place. He couldn't have chosen a better person."

A Colombian immigrant whose father was a textile worker and whose mother toiled on an assembly line making boxes for jewelry and pens, Martinez knew no English when she arrived in Central Falls at 15. She was at first so miserable she begged her parents to send her back. Now she can scarcely believe where she finds herself, about to assume next week an $81,000 job at the right hand of the governor.

She says, "It's like, my God, how did I get here?"

With a Rhode Island College bachelor's degree in social work, she for years was executive director of Progreso Latino, a nonprofit agency in Central Falls that helps immigrants adjust to life in America. More recently, she's been working for the Providence School Department, reaching out to involve parents in their children's education.

In 2001, when Republican Carcieri was an unknown retired business executive mulling a longshot 2002 State House run, Martinez was one of the people he consulted. He went to her school system office and spent more than an hour shooting the breeze and picking her brain.

Democrat Martinez, 43, says he talked about his family and about having worked a stint for Catholic Relief Services in Jamaica. "He wanted to know more about the community in general -- Providence, not necessarily Latinos only, but the community -- and the school district and education in urban areas."

She was impressed with his people skills. "I was like, 'What a nice guy, down to earth.' " But, even after he formally announced, "I never thought he was going to be our next governor, never mind thinking that I was one day going to be working for him." Martinez, who says she picked up her party affiliation from her father, voted for then-Rep. Tony Pires in the Democratic primary. But when Myrth York won the party nod for the third time, Martinez went with Carcieri in the general election. Most Latinos preferred

York, but Carcieri worked to cut into her support. The fact that he opposes abortion rights appealed to some Hispanics. Indeed, Martinez shares his abortion views. But she says her real problem with York was, "Where had she been for the last four years?" Or four years before that. She calls York a "very, very wonderful person" but someone who seemed to surface only quadrennially, to run.

CARCIERI WANTS Martinez to help him avoid getting bogged down in government minutiae and instead stay in contact with everyday Rhode Islanders by going to community meetings or having groups come to him.
Carcieri, of Italian and Swedish descent, says he hopes to reach every segment of the Hispanic world and, in fact, every constituency in Rhode Island:

"I want to be out there, I want to be visible, and I want people to feel that I'm someone that's approachable and I do care."

How refreshing that would be. Too often over the years have I heard people ask, "Where's the governor?" Or complain, "The governor won't meet with us."

Rhode Island's Latino population, notably including Dominicans, Puerto Ricans, Colombians, and Guatemalans, has been booming. Hispanics are beginning to win elective office on their own as well as helping to determine the outcome in some other contests.
Miguel Luna, who has joined Luis Aponte on the Providence City Council, says, "What you're seeing is the Latinos waking up, participating in the political system just the same as the Italians and the Irish and the Jews have done."

For years the Hispanic community was held back by tensions among the various national groups within it. Martinez says the rivalries have substantially eased.

SHE AND I recently stopped by Progreso Latino, which is housed in an old convent on Central Falls's Broad Street. A classroom now occupies what once was the chapel; note the arched windows. A wellness center occupies what was once the office of the mother superior; note the private bathroom. Everywhere in the building are messages in Spanish, such as:

NO HAY EXCUSA PARA

LA VIOLENCIA DOMESTICA.

("There is no excuse for domestic violence.")

Progreso Latino offers English, citizenship, and literacy classes as well as health, day care and social work aid.

Martinez says case workers help out on such problems as utility bills, accident reports, restraining orders, and immigration paperwork.
The place is bursting at the seams. The organization has broken ground on an addition.
Wherever we went in the building, Martinez, who was the director from 1988 to 2000, was greeted like a treasured relative. I saw some of the same thing at El Paisa (The Peasant), a Dexter Street Colombian restaurant where we went for lunch. One customer hugged Martinez and told her, in Spanish, "I am so proud, I feel like I'm your mom now."

Martinez ordered salad and empanadas. I had what the menu called a "TYPICAL COLOMBIAN PLATTER." It included steak, rice, beans, yucca, potato, fried bacon, round maize bread, fried banana, and salad. Price: $11. Martinez assured me this was indeed typical fare, except for the steak, which she said would be considered a luxury.

Martinez lives now in Pawtucket. But Central Falls was her first American home. She was Patricia Hincapie then, one of 10 children. Through a combination of scholarships, loans, and money from their late parents, Emilio and Teresa, all of them would go to college.

You may think of Central Falls today as heavily Hispanic, but when Martinez arrived in 1974, Latinos were only beginning to move in. She went to Central Falls High and was placed in an English as a second language program. It was a jolt, and only partly because she missed her friends:

"You're Colombian and you leave your country and all of a sudden you land in a place that you don't know and you're no longer Colombian and you become 'Latino' or, at that time, 'Hispanic.' And it's a whole mix of identity issues"

Plus, the immigrant students had all kinds of academic backgrounds -- in fact, some had never gone to school.
Martinez has a lively personality. But back then, she says, "I was very withdrawn. I had a very hard time trying to adjust, making new friends,

trying to learn the language. I remember at times asking my parents, 'Well, can you send me back and I'll go live in a boarding school if you want me to, but I don't want to stay here.' "

But soon she made friends and began to learn English and things started to change. She'd go on to the Community College of Rhode Island and then to RIC.

More recently, she went through the high-powered Leadership Rhode Island business-community training and networking program and picked up a master's degree from Springfield College.

She also crossed paths with advertising executive Dave Duffy, serving with him on the board of Citizens Bank and on the race and police-community relations commission Gov. Linc Almond formed after the death of Cornel Young Jr. Duffy is a Carcieri pal -- he suggested in 2001 that Carcieri go to talk with Martinez -- and chaired the transition after the 2002 election.
As governor-elect, Carcieri sought Martinez out to come work for him. She says she was impressed with his interest in homelessness, inclusiveness, and open government, particularly the opportunity for individuals to come in and talk with him one Thursday a month.

"I'm a passionate advocate of the voiceless," she says. "I'm an advocate and an activist."

TO ARRIVE as an immigrant, to move in circles like Leadership Rhode Island, to be consulted by an aspirant for governor and then recruited for his State House staff seems to her like a dream. In fact, Martinez reports that her son Daniel, 15, told her, "My God, who would have thought that this little thing -- meaning my size and everything -- with her accent and all these things, is so well respected! I'm so proud of you, Mom."

My Disappointment with David Cicilline

Marylyn Acevedo
January 3, 2003

Starting with the interfaith breakfast, which was intended for religious and community leaders, all communities were represented except the Hispanic Community. If somebody from this group, (RILPAC), where most (if not all) Hispanic leaders belong to, received an invitation to the breakfast and did not go, please let me know. Well, my husband and I went to the breakfast along with my daughter and a member of our Hispanic group (Tony Guerrero), Melba Depeña, who went with us because we invited her, and the Hispanic Church Pastor Emilio Vasquez. To give every body some back ground, my husband and I started working for the Cicilline for Mayor campaign since January, before he announced he was running for mayor in February, and dedicated over nine months of our lives to work for somebody who we thought could do something different and in who we had faith would change the way the city works.

We went to the breakfast uninvited because we wanted to know what was going on, and we felt we deserved it. The first thing they did was to tell us that we had to move from the table were we were seating, because in effect, we were not in the list and the table was reserved for "staff" of the Cicilline committee. Then I ask, what were we? Weren't we "staff" of the campaign when we were outside on the streets, with temperatures of over 90 degrees, leaf fleeting houses, doing cook outs in different back yards, or in the different festivals? What are we? I ask again. Well, after going somewhere, somebody decided to leave us there, may be they thought it was too late to kick us out, and also the administration that talked so much about "diversity" will look bad with only five Hispanic people in the room, (that is counting Mr. Roberto Salcedo, Mayor of the City of Santo Domingo and his daughter).

After that, when the prayers started, it was very interesting to see that all the communities were represented. There were prayers from the Jews, the Catholics, the Baptists and the Buddhist. Where was the Hispanic Pastor that was going to say the Prayer is Spanish? Well, he was sitting on our table, and was almost kick out when they told us the table belonged to the "Staff". Why was not a Hispanic Pastor in the program? It is maybe that there is not Hispanic representation in the Cicilline's transition team? I am talking about the "Team" and not the Transition Advisory Committee, which I consider was done for "decoration". Was there Hispanic people in the Inauguration Committee, (I am talking about the real Committee, not the joke that was put

412

together to prepare the neighborhood parties, the one that prepared the program for the breakfast and the inauguration).

After the breakfast, we went to City Hall, to wait for the time of the inauguration. When we were there, the Mr. Mayor Elect called us and asked for the same Hispanic Pastor, who did not have the chance to say a prayer at the "interfaith" breakfast. He wanted us to find him to see if "he could be fit" somewhere in the program, which was already printed. After talking with four different people, (Mr. Mike Mello, Mr. Chris Bizzacco, Mr. Joe Brooks and Mr. David Pontarelly), they told us they were going to try to fit our Pastor in the program.

The day before, we received little blue tickets, which read "reserved seating". On the week before, the Mayor Elected promised us that there was going to be a row of chairs in the front, for the Hispanic Committees that worked for him at the election; he said we did not have to worry because our seats were going to be there. We were there at Noon, went outside to sit, and to our surprise the row of chairs promised were not there. Well, we tried to seat in the front row but in effect the chairs had names on, but to our surprise our names where not there. In addition, one of the ladies in the Cicilline "staff" who we used to see at the headquarters, told us that the chairs "were reserved for the "staff" and we could not seat there. Therefore, we had to move somewhere else, and she was following orders". I do not know how to explain the way I felt in that moment. Every time they needed us, there we were; they knew our names, our phones and addresses. And I ask myself, did the person writing the names on the chairs knew all the work we did? Did that person went out looking for votes, convincing the Hispanic people that this person was going to be different and that we were going to be taken into consideration at the moment of making the decisions?

We were there for almost one and half hours. We could not stand anymore. I wanted you to see the people seating on the stage along and behind the new Mayor. Even his biggest opponent was seating behind him, and we, the people that worked to get him where he is today, where sitting under ice and snow, freezing our bones, just to see if the promises he did in his campaign were going to be true. Well, we did not hear the Cicilline Merengue that bothered so many people, and which in each of the meetings and cook outs we did in the City of Providence, he promised was going to be played in his inauguration. Where was, the Hispanic Church Pastor who was going to say a prayer in Spanish? Where was the Spanish interpreter who was with him in all the meetings, cook outs and fund raisers? Where, I ask myself was every body?

After, when we were inside City Hall, the same people who we saw at so many meetings and who worked in his campaign were telling us that they did not understand anything, and were asking where the Spanish interpreter was. Later I found out from Mrs. Juana Horton, that she donated the interpreting and gave the Mayor Staff fifty little radios so the Spanish people could hear the translation. She also told them to do an announcement to the people of the service, but they did not bother. And the Hispanic Pastor, you may ask, did the prayer? Well, he froze to death and after he got tired of being standing outside the freezing cold, went home; not before telling us that he felt really bad for the lack of importance they showed to him.

In conclusion, I hope this can explain the way I fell about what is happening. We though things were going to be different, but I do not think they will. Does it matter that a few of our Hispanic brothers and sisters could get good paying positions, when all the decisions are made behind closed doors?? What did we work for? For a job? For recognition? I hope things can be different, but I lost all hope. What it really hurts me is how are we going to see in the face all the people who we said " las cosas seran diferentes" and all of them were there, under the freezing rain, waiting for the Spanish music to sound.

What I am really worry about is that our people can feel betrayed and come back to be not interested in voting again. I hope again, something can be done, because as far as myself, I lost all hope and it will take a miracle for me to believe again.

The only good thing I see in all this is the amount of good and marvelous people that we met in the nine months of campaign that we participated. I do not ask anything for myself but for all the people that worked with the hope of getting something. Please take care of them, since in four more years; they will have to vote again.

Thanks to Lidia Rivera for comforting me, (she was with us all the time). Thanks to every body and good bye, and God bless our new Mayor and our new Governor.

Nothing New with PAC's Endorsement

Tomás Alberto Ávila

August 2004

There is a very popular saying that states: "the more things change, the more they remained the same" and how fitting such saying to RILPAC's bi-annual endorsement process.

During RILPAC's first endorsement during the 1998 primaries, the committee endorsed Victor Capellán, District 20 candidate for State Representative, Miguel Luna, City Council candidate in Ward 9's primary, Sheldon Whitehouse for Attorney General, and Senator Paul Tavares candidate for General Treasurer. During the General Election we endorsed Myrth York for Governor, Sheldon Whitehouse for Attorney General, Paul Tavares for General Treasurer, James Langevin for Secretary of State, David Igliozzi for State Senate and Pat Nolan for City Council in District 9.

I remember vividly the discussion about the tight finish in the City Council District 9 between incumbent Pat Nolan and challenger Miguel Luna. This race became the most controversial of all the endorsement decisions since it was a race pitting a first time Latino candidate against an incumbent who had strong support among her constituency and among the members of RILPAC's first official endorsement committee and the start of what has become a very controversial process that pits friends against each other in a democratic process of endorsing candidates for state and local office who are committed to improving the quality of life for members of the Latino community.

I also remembered the controversy created when State Representative James Langevin was endorsed over Ed Lopez, a Republican Latino running for Secretary of State, Santa Espinosa not being given an opportunity to participate in the endorsement process, because she was an unknown Republican. Just as it has been questioned during this year's endorsement, the community questioned RILPAC's commitment to support and elect Latinos, regardless of their party affiliation and gave way to accusations of being a Democratic PAC rather than a nonpartisan institution which needless to say such doubt continues despite the endorsement the first Republican during 2002 and the first Green Candidate in the same year.

As can be seen from this first endorsement, Sheldon Whitehouse was elected Attorney General, Paul Tavares became Rhode Island's General Treasurer, James Langevin was elected Secretary of State, David Igliozzi became State

Senator in the Silver Lake and Pat Nolan was reelected City Council in District 9, setting up a trajectory of supporting winning candidates despite all controversies faced by the organization.

No sooner had the 98 endorsement season ended, we were back at it again during the PAC's 2nd endorsement in which we endorsed Juan M. Pichardo Senate District 10, Gonzalo Cuervo, State Representative District 20, Joseph Almeida State Representative District 20 and Marsha Carpenter State Representative District 18's primary elections. Once again RILPAC endorsement was being questioned and criticized. In particular the endorsement of both State Representative District 20 candidates Gonzalo Cuervo and Joseph Almeida, rather than reaching a conclusive and determining decision for either candidate. RILPAC also faced heavy criticism for it's endorsement of Marsha Carpenter in Representative District 20 an African American female being challenged by first time Latino candidate Leon Tejada.

This endorsement season also became very controversial in regards to Angel Taveras candidacy as the first Latino seeking a Congregational seat running against Secretary of State James Langevin, Activist Kaye Coyne-McCoye and Attorney Kevin McAllister. The sentiment in the community and some members of the PAC was very strongly that RILPAC should endorsed Attorney Taveras even though the organization initial board had decided to be a state PAC for the first 5 years. Just like any other races, the membership was divided as to whether the PAC should endorsed Angel or not, and as usual the issue was put for a vote with the outcome not modify the organization's operations and the decision was made not to endorsed the first Latino congregational candidate.

In 2002 the committee endorsed Myrth York, for Governor, Paul Tavares for General Treasurer, Matt Brown for Secretary of State, Patrick Lynch for Attorney General, Juan Pichardo for State Senator, District 2, Jeff Toste for Senate District 5, David Cicilline for Mayor City of Providence, Miguel Luna City Council and Stephen Laffey for Mayor City of Cranston.

During this election season, the heated endorsement was the Democratic gubernatorial race between Myrth York and Attorney General Sheldon Whitehouse, which was narrowly decided in favor of Myrth York, creating voting controversy once again among the voting members and even caused the loosing side to form their own RILPAC supporters for Sheldon Whitehouse and going as far as organizing a press conference to announce their support for Sheldon, and their disappointment that the general membership did not endorsed Mr. Whitehouse.

Needless to say despite individual members claims that Myrth's endorsement was obtained by their individual efforts, RILPAC's endorsement of Myrth during the 1998 gubernatorial elections and Sheldon Whitehouse for Attorney General shows that both candidates had a track record of supporters in the organization prior to the 2002 endorsement process. This also shows the evolution of the endorsement process, since Sheldon Whitehouse was considered a favorite by the majority of the PAC.

As can be seen so far, the experience faced during our 2004-endorsement process is nothing new or nothing different than in the past, but what has been consistent in this process is the evolution of the participants in the election process quite interestingly producing the same results and the same controversies. Looking at the participating embers in this year endorsement committee, the only members that remain participating in the process from the inception of the PAC are yours truly and Betty Bernal other tan that the participant have changed throughout the years which is a positive, but at the same time it has not allowed the process to evolve and mature with the agenda needs of the community rather than personal agendas. It's my opinion that if many of the senior members of the organization will remain active in the process while new membership keeps the organization growing and evolving the results may be different.

First of all I like to thank Tony for taking the initiative and starting the conversation regarding this matter. Secondly I like to say that I agree totally with your assessment of the matter.

As I stated prior to the voting, "every single one of us" have a personal agenda as to why we are members of this organization and why we invest the time that we do as active members and participants of the endorsement process. As I also stated that night my agenda "is the political empowerment of the Latino community, and as I shared with members of the labor movement, "to protect what we have and elect as many Latino as we can", but needless to say living in a democratic system and dealing with a democratic process within RILPAC, I like every other member should respect the decision of the voting majority and the decision of the voting results. This is the right thing to do and the democratic principle to respect.
I have spoken to many of the members of the endorsement committee and I'm aware of their disappointment with individuals who as soon as the voting was over called their particular candidates and reported to them their PERCEPTION as to who voted against them and then proceeded to create suspicion of the democratic process that took place in the endorsement voting, obviously this behavior leaves a lot to be desire of the professional ethics of these individuals and their commitment to the organization, the community the integrity of the process.

Let me assure you that there's absolutely no doubt in my mind that the endorsement voting was open, fair and democratic as it has been since the inception of the PAC. Let me also assure you that just like it has taken place since the beginning, there were individuals who promised and guaranteed endorsements to particular candidates and just like before, these same individuals are the ones trying to discredit the process and the organization.

I call this individuals to stop thinking about themselves and their dissatisfaction of not delivering their unmet promises and join the rest of the members that accept the fact that none of us is BIGGER than the organization and as such respect the choices made by the majority which is the appropriate and ethical decision to make.

As you may be aware I have been fielding many different interviews with the local media and many residents from the community, and I am very happy to report that beside the doubts that the disenchanted members have brought forward, the question that I am getting asked the most are: why RILPAC did not endorsed any of the candidates in district 11? Why RILPAC did not endorsed Senator Juan Pichardo? and why RILPAC did not endorsed David Quiroa? Needless to say once I explain the process we arrived to such decisions, most people have been understanding and receptive of the process utilized to arrive to our decision. They have also been very grateful of my openness, accessibility and willingness to discuss and clarify the perception with the reality.

I have also spoken with David Quiroa whom although disappointed that the committee chose not to endorse him, he expressed his surprise about the support the endorsement controversy has developed for his campaign and the interesting synergies developed among individuals who have personal disagreements, coming together around his campaign and their commitment to support him. Obviously there is a silver lining of not being endorsed by the PAC.

To end let me say that in my opinion the best "democracy" offers is the freedom to agree to disagree while respecting the decision of the majority and if we truly believe in democracy lets accept the decision produced by a democratic process and let us now FOCUS our energies to helping elect the candidates our organization endorsed. Let's concentrate our minds in considering what we need to improve in order to change the outcome; shall we consider automatic endorsements of individuals with proven track records? Shall we interview every previously endorsed candidate every 2 years? Shall we keep track of Legislative voting record? Shall we develop a Latino agenda to compare Legislative agendas to? Let's move on, very soon 2006 will be here and we SHALL do it again.

Departure Of Elections Administrator

Lucia Gomez "wasn't the right fit," says Mayor David N. Cicilline, who hired her less than a year ago.

By Gregory Smith
Journal Staff Writer
Wednesday, October 6, 2004

PROVIDENCE -- Lucia Gomez, city elections administrator, has quit under fire only 4 1/2 weeks before the general election.

Her departure has city officials scrambling to fill the void even as they try to correct widespread miscues in last month's primary election.
Some polling places had too few workers, workers were poorly trained and notices mailed to voters misdirected about one-quarter of the electorate to the wrong polling places, voters and political activists complained.

Bob Legacy, a representative of City State Computer Services, which has a municipal contract, charged at a special City Council meeting last night that Gomez erred in her handling of voter data and was responsible for the defective mailing of notices.

Gomez did not attend the meeting, which was called to discuss election issues, and she could not be reached for comment.

Gomez, who was one of Democratic Mayor David N. Cicilline's showcase Hispanic appointees, apparently wore out her welcome because she annoyed influential Democrats with her manner. She held her job for less than a year.

"I think there were some serious deficiencies with the primary process," Cicilline said when asked about the administrator's abrupt resignation. But he said he was not laying all the blame on Gomez.

It is not enough for an elections administrator to have technical expertise; she must be skillful in her interactions with candidates and voters, Cicilline said. I think she wasn't the right fit. I think she recognized that," he said.
Gomez met with Cicilline on Friday and resigned from her $50,474-a-year position that day.

Laurence K. Flynn, chairman of the Board of Canvassers, for whom Gomez worked, declined comment on her resignation. He said Maria Mansolillo, the former elections administrator who is now deputy tax collector, would help out this week in her old job.

He said he would like to have a temporary fill-in hired by Monday and that he is considering Dawn McCormick, the retired Pawtucket city registrar. McCormick would have the experience and knowledge of election law and regulations to handle the post.

Some politicians have said Gomez was overbearing. City Councilman Peter S. Mancini recalled being struck by Gomez' forcefulness when ward committee chairs met with her shortly after her appointment. Gomez dominated what he expected to be a chatty session, he said.

Joan S. Badway, city Democratic chairwoman, recalled an unpleasant telephone conversation she had with Gomez regarding the reassignment of a primary election poll worker on the East Side. Badway wanted the worker assigned to the polling place the worker had manned in previous years, and Gomez balked.

"I don't have to listen to you," Badway said Gomez snapped at her. "She hung up on me," Badway said. As it turned out, according to the Democratic chairwoman, Gomez did switch the worker. "I think if you talk to people throughout the city," you will find that Gomez irritated everyone, Badway said.

Badway was one of Cicilline's early political supporters and served as one of his campaign coordinators. Although she did not complain to Cicilline about Gomez' demeanor, word of their sharp exchange got back to the mayor, according to Badway.

Cicilline won office partly because of his Hispanic support, and he has obliged people in the Hispanic community by appointing some Hispanics to posts that generally are viewed as patronage opportunities.

Gomez was not a local person, however. She was employed previously as a project coordinator for New York State Senate Majority Leader David A. Paterson. She also worked as civic participation program coordinator for the Puerto Rican Legal Defense Fund, a national organization that presses for civil rights for Hispanics.

Gomez took a pounding at last night's meeting, with Legacy, of City State Computer Services, saying that she mishandled voter roll data that his company furnished to the Board of Canvassers from the city's mainframe computer. The information was formatted incorrectly pertaining to apartment numbers in addresses -- then was sent to a printing company that made up the problematic notice cards, according to Legacy.

"Nobody was overseeing what she was doing?" Councilwoman Balbina A. Young demanded to know.

"I'm not a computer expert," replied Flynn, who said the Board of Canvassers supervise the elections administrator. The bad notices were corrected and the board apologized, he said.

Under questioning by Young, Legacy said Gomez took a greater hand in managing the computerized voter data than her predecessors as elections administrator and he was less involved than he had been in previous elections.

"Her forte was computers," Flynn said of Gomez.

"Alleged forte," Young declared.

Council President John J. Lombardi interjected. "This is not a witch hunt," he said. "No one's trying to hang anybody."

At the meeting, members sought to assure themselves that the problems with the Sept. 14 primary election would not recur at the Nov. 2 general election, when voter turnout is expected to be much higher.

Several members insisted that another mass mailing be done to ensure that voters know where they are assigned to vote. A corrective mailing was done, but Councilman Kevin Jackson said he was misdirected by mail and he never received a corrected notice.

Flynn agreed to send out another mailing to the 23,000 voters who were the subject of the original erroneous mailing. It is expected to cost about $4,000.

Tejada Files Reports Pays Fine

However, the state Board of Elections says there are still problems in the campaign finance report filed by the outgoing state representative.

By Karen A. Davis
Journal Staff Writer
Wednesday, September 22, 2004

PROVIDENCE -- Rep. Leon Tejada filed delinquent campaign finance reports and paid $1,671 in late fees on Friday, in accordance with a state Board of Elections agreement that required him to turn in the documents by that day.

However, there are some deficiencies in the 12 reports that he submitted, said Richard Thornton, the board's supervising accountant. In one case, for example, one of the reports contained a math error, Thornton said. Board officials plan to send Tejada a letter notifying him of deficiencies that need to be rectified after all of the reports have been reviewed, he added.

Tejada, who represents District 11 on the city's South Side, had accumulated $6,687 in penalties through Aug. 19, for failing to file mandatory campaign finance reports for two years. Officials have said the two-term representative who was defeated by challenger Grace Diaz in last week's primary had not filed quarterly reports in 2003 or for the first half of this year. He filed one incomplete report in August 2002, but failed to refile the completed document, after receiving notice that more information was needed, Thornton said.

On Sept. 1, the board agreed to waive three-quarters of the original fine and impose a lesser penalty. The board also voted to place Tejada on a one-year probation within the elections system, which would allow for the reinstatement of the original fine if more reports are late.

Under state law, political candidates and office holders are required to file reports quarterly and just before and after an election to disclose the source of their financial support. In early 2002, the law was amended to give the board the authority to levy fines against delinquent filers.

Tejada, who took office in 2000, has said that he did not think he had to file reports because no contributions had come in during much of the time in question.

RILPAC Endorsements Under Fire

By Ana Cabrera
Providence American
Friday September 17, 2004

The Rhode Island Latino Political Action Committee, (RILPAC) a group that established itself about more than a decade ago in hopes of influencing political outcomes, last week held its yearly reunion at the Hi Hat lounge in Providence. But while a fair contingent of politicians showed up, some present noted that there were fewer members of the community itself attending than in prior years.

So is the group losing steam, or has it crystallized itself into a smaller, albeit more influential body? It's anybody's guess, because this year there was some infighting within the ranks, most notably over the issue of the PAC's endorsements and the process used by the group to grant them. Some in the community believe that any Latino candidate should get the nod because they think the group should support their own. However, some within the PAC say that there should be more to these endorsements, that they should go to any candidate who espouses the causes of interest to Latinos.

This year, RILPAC endorsed the Green Party's Jeff Toste, Senatorial candidate in district 5; Democrat Andy Galli, Senatorial candidate in district 7, incumbent Rep. Thomas Slater (D-District 7) and Republican Cranston Mayor Steven Laffey. They also endorsed Pedro Espinal in his Senate District 6 bid against fellow Democrats Harold Metts and Chris Lopes.

The PAC, however, did not endorse the candidacy of incumbent Rep. Luis Tejada (D-Providence) or his Democratic challengers, Grace Diaz and Richardson Ogidan. They also did not give the nod to Republican David Quiroa, who was challenging incumbent Rep. Maxine Bradford-Shavers in District 73. Tejada, Diaz and Ogidan all went through the questioning process, as did Quiroa: Bradford-Shavers did not.

The official answer to why they did not endorse in either case is that the votes just were not there. But Quiroa says there were more reasons why he did not get the green light. He claims that he suffers from geographic discrimination, because the bulk of RILPAC members live closer to Providence and simply have no interest in other parts of the state. Further, Quiroa has been quoted as saying that the PAC told him they were unlikely to support his candidacy against the Democrat Shavers.

423

Quiroa says he does not believe one bit that the group is non-partisan. "I think they are heavily philosophically controlled by the labor party wing of the Democratic party and the unions, and the status quo of the Democratic leadership. That's my personal opinion and I stand by that."

"What's going on with the endorsement is that the process works," said Pablo Rodriguez, one of the founders of RILPAC, who said he did not participate in the process this time around and denied anything less than a bipartisan effort, pointing out the Laffey and Toste endorsements as proof that the PAC will support candidates from other parties.

But some have criticized that same process this year because only about a dozen or so RILPAC members actually participated in the endorsement interview and voting proceedings, representing a miniscule fraction of the more than 100,000 Latinos who live in the state.

Historically, many of this state's Latinos vote Democrat, and some have charged that RILPAC, which is supposed to be non-partisan, has always shown a bent towards the Democrats.

Party chair Bill Lynch said he knew nothing about partisanship within RILPAC, but added that "the philosophy of the Democratic party and the philosophy of RILPAC are one and the same: working families, education, diversity, assisting people who need help" so he thought it natural that many members would support his party.

But several Republicans who were present at the RILPAC funder noted that their party is looking to change the situation not just in RILPAC, but within the entire state.

Governor Donald L. Carcieri said, "We are trying to reach out, frankly, because we have such an imbalance, partisan wise. We need debate…that's not fair to the voters, that they have no choice."

Warwick Mayor Scott Avedisian agrees. "The goal is to find quality people." Avedisian, who is seeking re-election this November, said he hoped to enlist the support of Latinos in his community towards that end.

Ditto for Cranston Mayor Steven Laffey, a man who that evening seemed to be almost continually surrounded by a small flock of certain RILPAC members. There has been some criticism levied against RILPAC in the past for allegedly cutting back room endorsement deals with some political figures in exchange for employment of a member of their ranks. Both Laffey and Pablo Rodriguez denied that any such promises had been made this year in exchange for the PAC's endorsement or in the past, for that matter.

Rodriguez said that Laffey was endorsed because he gave the right answers to the questions posed to him by the PAC and his history of hiring Latinos.

Some of Laffey's critics within the community, however, point out that even though Laffey indeed took on Latinos for city jobs, none have been very high paying positions.

Republican Congressional candidate David Rogers said that it has been very tough for the party to figure out what is the central mission of the organization. This year, he says, they have decided to break the Democratic stranglehold by simply recruiting more candidates to run in all races. He pointed to the support that Republicans have found within Miami's Cuban community, adding he believes this phenomenon could happen here in Rhode Island. Rogers commented on RILPAC's traditionally Democratic leanings, saying that "as long as one organization allows itself to be one sided, the party that it caters to knows it does not have to work for those votes."

The night also gave an opportunity to speak with some politicians about their future plans. One such person was Secretary of State Matt Brown, about whom there has been speculation he might run against Senator Lincoln Chafee in two years. But when asked this question outright, Secretary Brown guffawed aloud, and hemmed a little before stating that he was "entirely focused" on this upcoming election and doing continuing work to make government more accountable. He did not, however, deny the rumor.

It was a night to ask Greg Gerritt of the Green Party whether or not Ralph Nader's continued candidacy upsets the apple cart for Democratic candidates. "I'm not supporting Nader this year," said Gerritt, who blamed what he called the outdated electoral college system, not third party candidates, for what happened during the last election.

But Providence City Councillor Luis Aponte disagrees with Gerritt, saying that he wholeheartedly believes in the two-party system.

At the end of the evening, The Providence American was finally able to corral RILPAC president Tomas Avila for a quiet one on one chat. Avila pointed out that RILPAC is not geographically situated, noting that the group endorsed Woonsocket candidates in the past.

"As far as I know, nobody from the PAC is going to work for Mayor Laffey," Avila said laughingly when questioned about whether or not a deal had been cut to that effect. When pressed further about the perceived public notion that two of RILPAC's past presidents (Nellie Gorbea and Melba DePena) have gone on to politically bigger and better things as a result of deals cut by the group, Avila denied that this had been the case and emphatically stated that he did not have any such plans in his future.

"What I am looking for is what I have done for the last six years," said Avila, "to empower the Latino community, to influence the political process as the mission of RILPAC calls for. That is what I will do for the two years of my presidency."

Rep. Tejada Unseated By Newcomer

Grace Diaz, a home daycare owner, had the backing of House Speaker William Murphy and Providence Sen. Juan Pichardo.

By Karen A. Davis
Journal Staff Writer
Wednesday, September 15, 2004

PROVIDENCE -- Grace Diaz, a home daycare owner and mother of five, defeated incumbent Rep. Leon F. Tejada for the Democratic nomination in yesterday's primary election in District 11, according to unofficial Journal results.

Diaz received 789 votes to Tejada's 498. A second challenger, Richardson Ogidan, came in third with 224 votes.

Tejada was the only member of the city's House delegation who lost a primary race yesterday.

In another hotly contested South Side race, District 10 Rep. Thomas C. Slater defeated Wilbur "Billy" Jennings Jr. for the nomination.

Diaz -- who ran on a platform of honesty and integrity and assailed Tejada's failure to submit campaign finance reports to the state for two years -- said yesterday that residents were looking for a legislator who would better represent their interests.

Diaz -- who has been active in a movement to unionize childcare providers -- received endorsements from the AFL-CIO, Speaker William Murphy and Democratic Sen. Juan Pichardo.

"This race (was) close because there were so many resources put into this race," Tejada said before the polls closed last night. Tejada said yesterday he believed the race was evidence of a political struggle between Speaker Murphy and his political rivals.

Tejada also said he was surprised that Murphy -- who Tejada had supported in the past -- had endorsed his opponent.

Diaz will face Republican challenger Ryan P. Curran in November's general election.

In House District 10, Slater had 741 votes to 399 for Jennings.

Two years ago, Jennings lost the nomination to Slater by 41 votes.

Slater will face Republican challenger Matthew Camp in November.

In District 12, representing the South Side and Washington Park, incumbent Joseph S. Almeida defeated Leo Medina by 562 votes to 464 for the nomination.

The victory will send Almeida back to the House for a fourth term; he faces no challengers in November.

In District 2, serving Providence and East Providence, incumbent Paul E. Moura handily defeated Christopher F. Young by 387 votes to 151.

Moura, a six-term Democrat, will face Republican challenger Jason Kircher in November.

In District 3, incumbent Edith Ajello bested Dr. Howard E. Schulman by 577 votes to 273.

Ajello, who was elected to the seat in 1992, will face Republican Thomas R. Pizzuti in the general election.

In District 6, representing Providence and North Providence, Rep. Peter N. Waslyk bested Domenic Antonelli by 800 to 286 votes. .

Wasylyk will take on Republican Louis A. DiManni in November.

In District 13, representing Silver Lake and part of Johnston, incumbent Steven F. Smith outran newcomer Carla A. Ricci, 694 votes to 401. .
With no Republican or independent opponent on the November ballot, Smith will return to the House for a ninth term.

Yesterday's primary election wrapped up contests that drew much attention to the city's diverse South Side, where black, white and Hispanic candidates vied for seven seats.

At the Elmwood Community Center on Niagara Street, Latino music blared from a minivan parked outside and campaign workers passed out bilingual brochures to voters.

Poll workers reminded candidates and campaign workers to stay a mandatory distance away from the front entrance of the building.

At the fire station on Reservoir Avenue, where 371 residents had cast their votes by 7 p.m., supporters of Slater and Jennings distributed literature, while the candidates shook hands and greeted friends.

Jennings, who grew up in the Reservoir Triangle neighborhood, said he had spent all day outside the fire station, a block from his campaign headquarters and a block from the headquarters that Slater shared with incumbent Pichardo.

Metts Captures Redrawn Providence District

The longtime state representative says the district's black and Hispanic populations must learn to work together.

By Gregory Smith
Journal Staff Writer
Wednesday, September 15, 2004

PROVIDENCE -- The new Senate District 6 on the South Side and in Mount Hope, which was redrawn to improve the voting clout of blacks, produced what some people considered the desired result in yesterday's Democratic primary election.

Former longtime state Rep. Harold M. Metts of South Providence, the most prominent black candidate, emerged the winner.

According to unofficial vote totals compiled by The Providence Journal, Metts got 876 votes, or 42.5 percent, and runner-up Pedro J. Espinal, 664, or 32.2 percent, who counted heavily on Hispanic support. Trailing were Chris D. Lopes with 488, or 23.7 percent, and Mickeda S. Barnes, who did not campaign, with 35.

A potential 48 mail ballots could not affect the outcome.

The Democratic nominee will be elected senator because there are no other candidates for the seat.

Metts' supporters were fuming before the polls closed, talking angrily about allegedly widespread election irregularities, but when the result became clear, their frowns turned to wide smiles.

At his headquarters in the carriage house behind a community building known as The Center, on Broad Street in South Providence, Metts hugged one supporter after another. A slow chant welled up from the crowd: "Metts, Metts, Metts, Metts."

In the other hotly contested Senate battle in Providence, one-term Sen. Frank A. Ciccone III broke away from two challengers in District 7 to claim victory by a comfortable margin. The district includes part of North Providence.
Metts acknowledged in an interview the existence of "an undercurrent of division" between the black and Hispanic communities over what some see as their competing aspirations. He said it "really needs to be healed."

Having worked across racial and ethnic lines in South Providence and in the State House, he has said that he has a reputation as a uniter.

As a representative, he recalled last night, he was a member of a redistricting commission that took care to create a Hispanic-dominated legislative district on the South Side.

"We helped them, to a fault," he said.
"I can't go out there with just a black power agenda. And they can't go out with a Latino agenda. We have to work together."

Metts was the lead plaintiff in a lawsuit, backed by a coalition of minority groups, that challenged the constitutionality of Senate redistricting in 2002. In that year's election, Rhode Island's only black senator, Charles D. Walton, was beaten by the man who became the state's only Hispanic senator, Juan M. Pichardo.

Contending that the 2002 redistricting unfairly diluted the voting power of blacks, Metts and the others sued. In a settlement with the state, District 6 was created to gather as many black citizens as possible in one district.

The new district combined Washington Park and South Providence, south of downtown, with Mount Hope, to the east. The two pieces are connected by a skinny corridor through downtown.

Even with state officials agreeing to help the black community by entering into a settlement that gathered as many blacks as possible within the new district, only 25 percent are black. Hispanics, some of whom are black, make up 32 percent.

The candidates were Metts, 56, assistant principal and former basketball coach at Central High School and a church deacon; Espinal, 39, a real estate investor and community activist; and Lopes, 39, an information-technology project manager for Citizens Bank. Also listed on the ballot was the 29-year-old Barnes, a bus driver, who did not campaign. "It's been a very good campaign, a very clean campaign," Metts said recently. And he took a joking poke at Lopes and Espinal a week before primary day, saying, "They have a bright future ahead of them. But that's after I retire" from the Senate.
Last night he said he owes his victory to help from a bevy of current and former elected officials and the gratitude of the many people he helped during his nearly 30 years as a teacher and a coach. "Who would have known it would come back to bear fruit now," he marveled.

In Senate District 7, which was redrawn in the ripple effect from the settlement of the District 6 case, the race was fierce because there is no entrenched incumbent. Less than half of the new District 7 has been represented by Ciccone.

It includes Silver Lake, Manton and Mount Pleasant in Providence and Fruit Hill, Woodhaven and Lymansville in North Providence.

Ciccone, a labor leader and former state court employee who pinch-hit a couple of times as superintendent of the Rhode Island Training School, garnered 1,425 votes, or 47.4 percent, according to an unofficial Journal count. He outdistanced Christopher Nocera, vice president of marketing for Glass America Commercial Services and a veteran political operative, who collected 940 votes, or 31.3 percent, and Andrew E. Galli, campaign coordinator for the Fund for Community Progress, who picked up 640 votes, or 21.3 percent. Ciccone will face Republican Philip P. Stone, a U.S. Chamber of Commerce membership director, in the Nov. 2 election.

In Senate District 2 in Elmwood and the West End, one-term Sen. Juan M. Pichardo easily fended off housing consultant Rochelle Lee, 74.1 percent to 25.9 percent, to recapture the Democratic nomination.
He will face Republican Brian P. Mayben in November.

In Senate District 3 on the East Side and House District 2 in the Jewelry District and Fox Point, Christopher F. Young, an unsuccessful mayoral hopeful as an independent in Providence two years ago, tried to do double duty as a candidate for the Democratic nomination for both seats.
He was doubly drubbed.

In Senate District 3, veteran Sen. Rhoda E. Perry won in a landslide, with 80.5 percent of the vote to Young's 19.5 percent. The pattern was repeated in House District 2. Rep. Paul E. Moura swamped him, 71.9 percent to 28.1 percent. Perry will lock horns with independent Barry Fain in the November election and Moura with Republican Jason F. Kircher.

RILPAC Leader Pleased With Moreau

David Casey
The Pawtucket Times
09/13/2004

CENTRAL FALLS -- Rhode Island Latino Political Action Committee President Tomas Avila met with Mayor Charles Moreau and the city's only Latino Councilman and fellow RILPAC endorsee, Ricardo Patino, Wednesday to evaluate Moreau's efforts on behalf of the city's Latino population.

Moreau had the endorsement of RILPAC when he beat incumbent Mayor Lee Matthews by 16 votes in November 2003.

"My initial reaction was very positive," Avila said Friday, "We had a very cordial discussion and he presented some of the projects he's done. My first impressions were positive and I'm optimistic about the report."

RILPAC routinely "follows-up" on the candidates it endorsed for the previous election cycle, to measure how effectively that candidate has served his/her Latino constituents.

Moreau and Patino are two of nine elected officials who carry RILPAC's stamp of approval, a group that includes Secretary of State Matt Brown, Attorney General Patrick Lynch and Providence Mayor David Cicilline.

An official report on Moreau's performance will be released sometime after the primaries.

Avila said he was particularly impressed with Moreau's decision to hire the city's first Latino Municipal Court judge, Dan Carillo, and the bilingual business research center (reference area) that was recently established at the Central Falls Free Public Library.

"One out of five candidate for the Police Department were Latino and four were from Central Falls," Moreau told The Times Friday. "Thirty-three out of 45 Summer Work Program employees were also Latino, and for the first time, the point of contact in each of the city's most heavily used departments speak Spanish."
Patino, who publicly criticized Moreau for not hiring one of his Ward 3 constituents at a recent City Council meeting, called the RILPAC soiree "positive and productive."

433

Patino extolled the city's re-opening of the Ralph J. Holden Community Center and its decision to give Channel One Director Angelo Garcia double-duty as community center director.

Patino admitted he still has problems with Moreau's overall performance, a sentiment which surfaced at the City Council's Aug. 31 meeting. At that meeting, Patino asked Moreau why he failed to review a two-year-old resume from one of Patino's constituents when the city was conducting interviews for the newly instated trash service. Moreau responded that if any such resume existed, it left city hall with the previous administration.

After the RILPAC meeting, Moreau was optimistic that he would retain the organization's endorsement.

"I am confident we'll do well, and not just with what we have done for the Latino community, but what we've done for the entire community. We've fixed side-walks and streets, increased the numbers of police officers and work with local agencies to contribute to the community center. We haven't had that in eight years."

Voters Have Choices In Seven Races

Some of the closest races are on the South and Southwest sides.

By Karen A. Davis
Journal Staff Writer
Friday, September 10, 2004

PROVIDENCE -- The challengers are running on a platform calling for change and improvement.

The incumbents say improvement is best achieved by allowing them to continue the work they have started by returning them to office.

When voters go to the polls for Tuesday's primary, they will decide which message prevails in seven races throughout the city.

Two of the most hotly contested races are being staged on the South and Southwest sides, where incumbent Thomas C. Slater takes on repeat challenger Wilbur W. Jennings Jr. in House District 10 and incumbent Leon F. Tejada faces off against Grace Diaz and Richardson Ogidan in House District 11.

In District 12, representing the South Side and Washington Park, incumbent Joseph S. Almeida faces Leo Medina in race that has had candidates debating issues on Spanish talk-radio stations.

The District 10 race pits Slater against Jennings in a rematch.

Jennings, 60, of 115 Sinclair Ave., is a retired city employee who lost to Slater in 2002 by fewer than 50 votes, 657 to 616. Jennings said he believes he would have won had it not included a third candidate, who received 341 votes.

Slater, 63, of 70 Sawyer St., a salesman, said he is seeking a sixth term because "the job hasn't been done" and so he can continue to be an advocate for human services, which have been cut under Governor Carcieri's administration.
Slater said he has been actively involved in battling against Carcieri's cuts to the childcare subsidy and has lobbied for the state to fund the earned income tax credit for low-income families.

The top issues in his district, Slater said, are making sure that every child has a good education and access to after-school programs, and capitalizing on enterprise zones in order to create jobs. Those jobs, Slater noted, should give residents "a decent, livable wage . . . that makes workers feel proud of themselves."

Slater, who has been canvassing neighborhoods and distributing campaign literature, said he has received endorsements from city council members, Mayor David N. Cicilline, the Rhode Island Latino Political Action Committee, several labor unions, childcare providers and ACORN, a an organization of community activists.
Slater, a married father of three, who said he is committed to helping people with "action, not words," said he believes his experience makes him better qualified than his opponent.

"I'm running because I want to bring change," Jennings said of the year's "tight, tight" race. "It's all about change. People are sick and tired of the nonsense . . . and the bickering."

Jennings -noted that Slater has endorsements from House Speaker William Murphy and Cicilline. That leaves Jennings feeling he has "the whole army out there against me." He criticizes the fact that "things haven't gotten any better" since Slater took office.

If elected, Jennings said he would push for better education, bilingual eduation, affordable health care and affordable housing.

His first task, he said, would be to "be a champion for the elderly" and get them the health care that they need.

Jennings, who is married with two children, said he believes he is qualified because he is "very positive" and "a go-getter" who is not afraid to speak out on behalf of his community.

Jennings, who serves as Democratic Committee chairman for City Council Ward 8, has been canvassing his district, distributing campaign brochures and posting about 250 yard signs.

In District 11, Tejada, 40, a self-employed businessman, will have to fend off two opponents in order to retain his House seat.

Diaz, a home daycare owner who has been active in seeking organization of childcare providers statewide, and Ogidan, a project manager for the South Providence Development Corporation, are the challengers.

Diaz, of 45 Adelaide Ave., who was born in the Dominican Republic and has lived in Providence 14 years, said improving education is the top issue in her district.

"I will fight to increase our investment in public schools and adult education and open more doors for our young people who want to go to college or pursue job-training," said Diaz, who would be the second Latina in the state legislature.

Diaz has plastered the district with more than 400 signs, touting her candidacy as "A change we can trust."

She lists among the most pressing issues the need for jobs that pay a living wage, more affordable health care, particularly for small businesses, and creation of a fairer tax system that would reduce the property tax burden.
Diaz, has campaigned door-to-door and on debates on Spanish radio, has received endorsements from Speaker William Murphy, Democratic Sen. Juan Pichardo, ACORN, the Progressive Leadership Fund and the state AFL-CIO.

A mother of five, Diaz is active in the Center for Women and Enterprise.
Ogidan, of 127 Warrington St., has run on a platform of "jobs, jobs, jobs" as the primary issue in his district. However, he is quick to note that the district's most crucial issues -- jobs, affordable housing and education -- are closely related and could be affected by a boost in economic development.

A former business owner, Ogidan advocates for state funding to support the enterprise zones that could attract new businesses to abandoned commercial buildings and create jobs.

Having worked in the local community for 27 years, including serving on the boards of Youth Build, Community Prep and Stop Wasting Abandoned Property, Ogidan said his candidacy offers experience, leadership and integrity.

Tejada, of 197 Calla St., who is Dominican, has spoken out at recent community forums for higher taxes for the rich in order to help pay for education and spur economic development.

Tejada is seeking his third term and could not be reached for comment.
In District 12, Almeida faces Medina.

Almeida, a retired police officer and business owner who is seeking his fourth term, has campaigned on a platform that identifies one primary issue as economic empowerment, along with education and housing. Almeida said he is concerned about the lack of minority contractors hired by the state, and increasing utility costs.

If re-elected, Almeida said he would continue to work with Slater to dismantle the Public Utilities Commission, the agency that has approved multiple gas and electric rate increases this year.

During his tenure in the House, Almeida has led or supported legislation to fight lead paint poisoning and racial profiling and supported affordable housing and protection of the South Side enterprise zone.

Medina, 40, who ran for office in 1990, said he is returning to the political arena as a candidate who will work for the community and not to fulfill a personal agenda.

"I feel that I can bring the community and political sides together," said Medina, a married father of four who works as a legal assistant at Rep. John DeSimone's law firm.

If elected, Medina said he would work more closely with city leaders.
Born in the Dominican Republic, Medina has been in Providence since age 2 and said his platform focuses on youths and education, housing and economic development.

In District 2, serving Providence and East Providence, incumbent Paul E. Moura faces Christopher F. Young, of 238 Gano St.
Moura, 48, a union field representative, serves as senior deputy majority leader and is seeking his sixth term.
Young, 35, has said he is running against Moura because he disagreed with Moura's vote in favor of casino legislation and because he believes "it's time for change."

Young, who volunteers with Meals on Wheels and the Trudeau Center, said he believes his district is suffering from a housing crisis, fueled by a large tax rate increase.

Young, who made unsuccessful bids for the U.S. Senate in 2000 and for mayor in 2002, said he believes property tax relief is among the primary issues facing the district. If elected, he said, he would work to tax private colleges for property that is not used for education.

Young's campaign has including door-to-door canvassing and encouraging residents to vote.

In District 3, incumbent Edith H. Ajello, of 29 Benefit St., takes on Dr. Howard E. Schulman, of 14 Benefit St.

Ajello, 60, who works as an appraiser of Oriental rugs, said her message to voters has touted her experience and integrity.

In talking with constituents, Ajello said many have spoken out overwhelming against a casino and raised concerns about the funding of education.

Elected in 1992, Ajello said she was an early supporter of the separation of powers legislation and helped to get that measure passed. She said she has also actively worked on health care issues.

Ajello said she was recently praised by the ACLU as having the best record on civil rights issues in the General Assembly.

She has received endorsements from Clearwater Action, the Progressive Leadership Fund and a gay and lesbian political organization.
Schulman grew up in Westchester County, New York, and came to Providence in 1990.

While campaigning throughout the East Side district, Schulman said the issues that elicited the most concern were the casino, the legislature's attempts to grant a state-funded hotel deal to a former state legislator, and ethics questions surrounding legislative leaders.

Those comments from voters let Schulman to conclude that "the environment may be right for someone new."

If elected, Schulman said he would work to establish a school in his district, which he said is lacking local schools, and he would work for the overall improvement of education.

He believes he is qualified for the job because he said he is openminded, intelligent and able to get along well with people, he said. He also believes that the city of Providence needs to "get along better with the rest of the state."

In District 6, which covers parts of Providence and North Providence, incumbent Peter N. Wasylyk faces Domenic J. Antonelli.
Wasylyk, 47, of 168 Hillcrest Ave., said he is seeking his sixth term in order to continue working as a consumer advocate for health care, including taking an active role in helping to "try to reign in the increasing cost of health care."

Wasylyk, a lawyer, said his platform addresses such issues as health care, affordable housing, quality education and safe neighborhoods.

He said he is best qualified for the seat because of his experience and his commitment to serve asa an independent voice to make decisions that are in the best interest of the community.

His challenger, Antonelli, 46, of 92 Erie St., said he was inspired to run because he wanted to see improvements to the athletic fields at Mount Pleasant High School and because he believes he could do a better job representing the district.

Antonelli, a teacher, said he grew up in his district and has been active as a coach with the Mount Pleasant Little League, Elmhurst Little League and youth basketball leagues.

His campaign has included placing more than 50 lawn signs and canvassing neighborhoods to tout his candidacy, he said.

The primary issues facing his district, Antonelli said, are affordable housing, school improvement and affordable health care.
He said he is an honest candidate who has accepted campaign contributions.

In District 13, representing Silver Lake and parts of Johnston, incumbent Steven F. Smith takes on Carla A. Ricci.

Smith, 48, of 20 Neutaconkanut Road, who works as a school truant officer, is seeking his ninth term.

His platform, Smith said, is education -- improving the quality and "finding a better way of paying for it without going to the taxpayer."
Smith, who is a lifelong resident of Silver Lake, said he is better qualified to hold the seat because of his "leadership and commitment to the community."

"I've lived in the community my whole life and, quite frankly, my opponent hasn't," said Smith, who is actively involved with the Silver Lake Community Center, Silver Lake Little League and the Rosario Society.

If re-elected, Smith said he would continue the work in the community and on state issues, including working with the Rhode Island Public Expenditure Council to come up with a fairer and more equitable formula for funding education. He said he will also work to make sure school districts follow a law he advocated, which requires districts to create alternative programs to successfully educate all students.

Smith, whose campaign has included direct mailings, canvassing and coffee hours, said affordable health care and housing are also priorities.

Ricci, of 58 Merino St., who works as a third grade teacher, said she is running because she would like to be the state representative in the district where both of them happen to live.

The winners of the House District 12 and District 13 races face no Republican challengers and will be unopposed on the November ballot.

Latino PAC Takes Heat For Backing Only 1 Latino Candidate In 5 Races

By Tatiana Pina
Journal Staff Writer
Tuesday, September 7, 2004

PROVIDENCE -- The question on listeners' minds is the recent candidate endorsements made by the Rhode Island Latino Political Action Committee, so Dr. Pablo Rodriguez goes right to the point in his talk show.

The endorsements, or lack thereof, have tongues wagging on the airwaves and over the Internet, he says on Hablemos (Let's Talk) on Exitos 88.1 FM (WELH).

The Spanish-language talk-show host has invited mostly Providence candidates for the General Assembly to a "political barbecue" out in the backyard of the radio station in Cranston.

The first four candidates to show -- Grace Diaz, running for House District 11; Wilbur Jennings, running in House District 10; Leo Medina, running in House District 12, and David Quiroa, running in House District 73, in Newport, all have one thing in common.

"None of them was endorsed by RILPAC. That's the show right there," jokes Rodriguez, who once served as president of the Latino PAC.

"Why weren't these people endorsed?" Rodriguez asks.

RILPAC endorsed five candidates: Jeff Toste from the Green Party, in House District 5; Democrat Andy Galli, in House District 7; Democrat Rep. Thomas Slater, House District 10; Republican Stephen Laffey, incumbent mayor of Cranston, and Democrat Pedro Espinal, House District 6. Espinal was the only Latino who was endorsed.

No one was endorsed in the House District 11 primary race in Providence, one of the hottest races. There, Diaz, a political newcomer and a Democrat, is challenging Democrat incumbent Rep. Luis Tejada. Both are Dominican. The race has heated up as Tejada has been challenged by Diaz supporters and fined by the state Board of Elections for not reporting campaign finances. Both are regular guests on Spanish-language radio programs.

Diaz said RILPAC did the right thing by not endorsing a candidate in District 11. "Their regulations require a consensus and they could not come to one," she says. "What's important for District 11 is that people have more options when they go to vote."

When Tomas Avila, the president of RILPAC, arrives, Rodriguez tells him he is in the hot seat. The backyard is getting filled with candidates and people who have come to watch.

Avila said that neither Tejada nor Diaz garnered a majority of votes from RILPAC members to receive the endorsement. But he has taken heat because it's an important race, he says.

He said that RILPAC members plan to meet after the elections to talk about the endorsement process and what to do when members reach a verdict similar to the one for District 11. Does it matter if you get endorsed by RILPAC? After all, Tejada won without RILPAC's endorsement. "The fact that people are upset by the endorsements means it's important to them," Avila says.

When David Quiroa, of Newport, a Republican who will challenge the winner of the Democratic primary for District 73, did not get endorsed, there was a groundswell of e-mails decrying the fact. How could they not endorse a man who has worked with the Latino community and is making history by running? asked Julio Aragon, of the Mexican-American Association.

"David, there was a lot of controversy about you," Rodriguez says. "All those e-mails."

"I'M IN THE EYE of the hurricane," Quiroa says. "It's good that there is this type of energy. I did absolutely everything I had to do for the endorsement. I spent three hours on the essay."

Quiroa says that his candidacy is historic in Newport, a middle-class, Anglo community where a Guatemalan from the Republican Party has dared to run for office. Quiroa said Governor Carcieri asked him to run.

So it was a surprise to him when he went before the 12 or so members of RILPAC's endorsement committee and they spent more time talking about his participation in the Republican Party than what he stood for.

Avila says he stopped the talk "when I saw the direction it was going in." In the end, the members did not want to endorse Quiroa.

Asked whether the majority of RILPAC members are Democrat, Avila said that they reflect the state. Back in February, Avila said that he approached the Republican Party seeking members to join RILPAC to make the process more balanced, but as yet no one has approached the group.

In other primary races, such as Senate District 2 between incumbent Juan Pichardo and Rochelle Lee, and House District 12 between incumbent Joseph Almeida and Medina, none of the candidates turned in papers seeking endorsement. Avila said that in all, 21 candidates turned in endorsement papers.

After the talk show, Avila said that among the questions he has heard most is whether RILPAC is going to endorse Latino candidates. As it stands now, the organization endorses candidates whom it judges would best represent the interests of Latinos -- and that's not necessarily Latino candidates.

"This controversy goes way back to when we started, and Republican Ed Lopez ran for secretary of state and we did not endorse him. It has always been a question, and we are going to have to talk about it and decide what we need to do to respond to the community's desire," he said.

Among the other candidates who attended were Ed Morabito, a candidate for the 2nd Congressional District; Harold Metts, candidate in Senate District 6; Rep. Joseph Almeida, D-District 12, in Providence; Rep. Anastasia Williams, D-District 9, in Providence; Slater; Tejada, and Pichardo.

New Senate District A Win For Minorities

Three blacks and a Hispanic are candidates for the district's Democratic nomination in Tuesday's primary.

By Gregory Smith
Journal Staff Writer
Wednesday, September 8, 2004

PROVIDENCE -- The new Senate District 6 was born of conflict.

The defeat two years ago of Rhode Island's only black senator by the man who is the state's only Hispanic senator prompted a legal challenge to Senate redistricting.

After the state spent more than $1 million to defend its apportionment of the population for electoral purposes, a compromise finally was struck this spring to create a Senate district in Providence that would give black voters a better chance of electing a black.

Three blacks and a Hispanic now are candidates for the district's Democratic nomination in Tuesday's primary election. While the dispute sprang from strong feelings about the treatment of minorities, the resulting contest has been gentlemanly.

Former state Rep. Harold M. Metts, who is black, and a coalition of minority groups went to court to challenge the constitutionality of the 2002 Senate redistricting. They said it unfairly diluted blacks' voting power.

In the compromise, the lawsuit was dropped and 12 of the state's 38 districts were realigned, including all seven in Providence. No longer a litigant, Metts is a candidate.

"After fighting 2 1/2 years to win this district, it would be a shame not to win this election," Metts said of District 6. ". . . We need to win this election to make sure our [black] community is included in the state Senate."

Besides the 56-year-old Metts, assistant principal and former basketball coach at Central High School, who lives in South Providence, the candidates are Pedro J. Espinal, 39, a real-estate investor who lives in the Washington Park neighborhood, and Chris D. Lopes, 39, a technology project manager for a bank, of Mount Hope.

Bus driver Mickeda S. Barnes, 29, of Washington Park, also is on the ballot. But the other candidates say she does not seem to be campaigning. Barnes, who did not return telephone calls seeking comment, has not participated in any of the campaign's meet-the-candidates forums.

The Democratic nominee would be elected senator, because there are no other candidates for the seat.

The realignment gives blacks in Providence a fresh opportunity to elect one of their own since Charles D. Walton lost reelection to Juan M. Pichardo in 2002 after 19 years in the upper chamber.

It was a stretch, literally and figuratively, to form the district. Rather than combine contiguous neighborhoods, as is usually done when districts are drawn, Senate leaders and the plaintiffs stapled a small piece of the East Side to a large piece of the South Side.

The goal was to craft a district that would house as many black residents as possible. That meant using a skinny corridor through downtown as a link to connect Washington Park and South Providence to Mount Hope. As it turns out, 25 percent of the district population is black and 32 percent Hispanic. The district in which Walton lost his seat to Pichardo in a Democratic primary two years ago was 21 percent black.
Citywide, blacks make up 14.5 percent of the population; Hispanics 30 percent.

Espinal, a Dominican-American who grew up poor in Washington Park, worked for 16 years in the Facilities Management Department of Johnson & Wales University. He put together some money and began acquiring houses, which he fixed up and rented out. Finding success, Espinal was able to leave Johnson & Wales and concentrate on his property management business. He now touts as his number-one qualification for public office his ability to get things done, as a businessman and as a community activist.

A former chairman of Direct Action for Rights and Equality, a social-action group, as well as a mayoral appointee to a civilian board created to review police conduct, Espinal has been active in the Washington Park Foundation and the Washington Park Citizen Association. The latter organization oversees the Washington Park Community Center. In his only previous election attempt, Espinal lost as an independent in a three-way general election contest in 2002 for the Senate seat now held by Pichardo.

Pichardo, the only Hispanic senator, now seeks to represent the redrawn District 2. He is being challenged in the Democratic primary by Rochelle

Lee. The district, which includes some Elmwood and West End neighborhoods, is 50 percent Hispanic.

Espinal expects to spend about $30,000 on his campaign this time -- apparently two to three times as much as Lopes or Metts.

That would pay for Spanish-language radio and newspaper advertising as well as printing and distributing brochures by hand or by mail, producing signs and sponsoring catered get-togethers at the district's six housing-for-the-elderly projects. If elected, Espinal said he would concentrate on bringing more money to the city, especially for public education and adult education.

There are parts of South Providence, he said, in which 50 percent of the residents lack a high school diploma or a general-equivalency degree. In Mount Hope, he said, 24 percent of the residents lack them. That education deficit limits their job prospects, Espinal pointed out.

Lopes, son of former one-term City Councilman Donald J. "Danny" Lopes, had most of his political experience as a student at the University of Rhode Island in the mid-1980s. He was president of a minority organization called Uhuru Sa Sa, which successfully campaigned for the University of Rhode Island's disinvestment in South Africa. Uhuru Sa Sa had to overcome a move by the URI administration to close its house for budgetary reasons.

Lopes has given his financial and moral support to a variety of organizations such as the Mount Hope Neighborhood Association and the Men of Pride program. Men of Pride assists inmates at the Adult Correctional Institutions who are being released and tries to strengthen the bonds between single fathers and their children by, for example, organizing trips for them.

As he travels the district, Lopes said he tries to register people to vote as well as coax them to vote for him.
"A lot of people are frustrated and they don't want to participate in the process any more," he observed.

When knocking on doors on the South Side, Lopes often is accompanied by former Councilman John H. Rollins, a Washington Park resident who flirted with a run for the seat himself. If elected, Lopes said he wants to promote the development of more affordable housing, preserve intracity and intrastate bus service, and alleviate pressure on property taxpayers.
He also wants to ensure that corporations that receive tax breaks hire and train local people or at least provide demonstrable service to the community in which they are located. "I'm bringing in a new breed of lobbyist, the community," he quipped.

Metts, who has not run since 1996, is relying heavily on his 14 years' service in the Rhode Island House as his ticket to the Senate.

"When I first went in, it took me two terms to learn" the job, Metts said. He contrasted his readiness with that of his two opponents.

"I can hit the ground running because I've got that 14 years of experience," he boasted. He also has a foot planted firmly in each end of the district. While he is known as a South Providence legislator, he also is a deacon at Congdon Street Baptist Church in Mount Hope. As such, he also serves as a director of East Side Apartments, a joint project of the church and the Jewish community.

Metts is vice chairman of the South Providence Development Corporation and is active in the Urban League of Rhode Island and the Providence branch of the NAACP. He helps out as a volunteer lay minister at Sunday morning religious services in the medium-security unit of the ACI.

As for his policy ambitions if he wins, Metts is adamant about repairing a state program that seeks to award purchases of products and services to minorities and women, which he was instrumental in having adopted. He said the program has fallen far short of its goals, due at least in part to a lack of enforcement. It's a point of pride to Metts that, as he says, he successfully worked across racial and ethnic lines in the House, where he was president of the Rhode Island Caucus of Black and Minority Legislators.

"Whether it is the Africans or whether it is the Latino community," he said, "the key out of all of this is [which candidate] is committed to being a bridge builder to the various constituent groups in District 6."

Political Scene: No Negativity

By Scott Mayerowitz and Liz Anderson
Journal State House Bureau
Monday, August 2, 2004

No negativity allowed

The Rhode Island Latino Political Action Committee has banned any negative comments made about its endorsed candidates on its list-serve.

The group plans to announce its endorsed slate of candidates on Aug. 19, but last month started restricting messages on the 300-person e-mail list, according to *Tomas Alberto Avila* The edict came down in mid-July, right after somebody posted a negative comment on the list-serve about *Pedro J. Espinal* , a Providence Senate candidate. Avila said the prohibition had nothing to do with the Espinal posting and that the time was just coincidental.

In his e-mail to the list-serve, Avila announced the ban saying it is necessary "in order to avoid conflicting message being sent against RILPAC endorsed candidates. Therefore effective immediately and right through the primary elections, we'll be restricting political messages and will be using the list to promote RILPAC's endorsed candidates. . ."

New Senate Map Settles Lawsuit

The departures of Senators John A. Celona and William V. Irons allow for a new district that reunites parts of South Providence.

By Edward Fitzpatrick
Journal Staff Writer
Saturday, May 22, 2004

PROVIDENCE -- Senate leaders announced the settlement of a two-year-old redistricting lawsuit yesterday, saying they could have won the legal battle but chose to redraw the Senate map to bolster minority voting power.

The lawsuit claims the current Senate map violates the Voting Rights Act by dividing the black community on Providence's South Side into two districts.

The new map, if approved by the General Assembly and governor, would end that divide while changing 12 of the 38 Senate districts. That would leave 10 incumbents facing new territory in an election year while creating two new districts with no incumbents.

Senate President Joseph A. Montalbano said he is confident the Senate would have prevailed in federal court. But, he said, "We were presented with a rare opportunity when two districts abutting the city of Providence became unexpectedly open. That opportunity allows us to redraw the district lines to strengthen both the African-American and the Hispanic voting power in Providence."

That opportunity arose when former Senate President William V. Irons, D-East Providence, and Sen. John A. Celona, D-North Providence, resigned amid investigations into their financial ties to CVS and Blue Cross & Blue Shield of Rhode Island Their departures resulted in two vacant Senate seats, giving mapmakers the wiggle room to create a new Providence district that reunites parts of South Providence while reaching north to the Mount Hope neighborhoods.

The Senate map that triggered the lawsuit had pitted the Senate's first and only black member, Charles D. Walton, against Juan M. Pichardo, who defeated Walton in 2002 to become the Senate's first and only Hispanic member. The new map puts Pichardo and Walton in different districts. Walton is in the district reaching from South Providence to Mount Hope, which is 25 percent black and contains no incumbent. Pichardo is in an

Elmwood district that is 50 percent Hispanic and contains no other incumbent. Senate leaders believe the new map will increase the chance of electing more than one minority senator this year.

Montalbano, who was vice chairman of the redistricting commission, said no redistricting could have been more difficult than the one that took effect in 2002, which reflected a voter-mandated downsizing of the Assembly. The Senate shrunk from 50 to 38 members.

Given that "daunting task," Montalbano said, the mapmaking was fair and open. And, he said, "I want to make it very clear the Senate is not admitting fault."

But, Montalbano said, "They do refer to me as someone who knows how to build a consensus." And, he said, "We were sensitive to the needs of the minority community."

A SECONDARY FACTOR in the settlement, Montalbano said later, was that ending the legal battle could save the state up to $1 million in legal bills. The state has already spent more than $1.1 million defending against three redistricting suits. Senate Majority Leader M. Teresa Paiva Weed, D-Newport, said, "I'm so proud today to be a part of this proposed settlement agreement and of the 10 senators who put the principle of inclusiveness ahead of themselves."She said the plan is perhaps most difficult for Pichardo "because he's brand new, and he fought so hard for four years to get here."

Indeed, the new map gives Pichardo just 42 percent of his old district. "It's an ultimate sacrifice from my end," Pichardo said. So why did he agree to the plan? "It's the principle of more minority representation in the Senate," he said. The new map also changes Montalbano's district. While he'd retain 80 percent of his old district, Montalbano lives in North Providence, and the new map would give him a larger portion of Lincoln. "I hear now there's going to be real Republicans in my district," Montalbano said, adding that former Republican Gov. Lincoln C. Almond would be in his district. "So we are all personally affected, but we are all personally very committed to having this become a reality because of the importance of the issue."
The state's redistricting consultant, Kimball W. Brace, said, "Usually in these situations, cases do tend to go to trial, so it is unusual to see this kind of settlement, particularly when one side felt pretty confident they were going to win at trial." The key, he said, was having two Senate seats open up. Brace said he began "playing around with different possibilities" to reconfigure the map over the past two or three months. The plaintiffs presented a map that created a Providence district with a stronger black population, but that plan included "much more major change" for other districts. So he said he came

up with a map that achieved the same goal "without disrupting people as much."

AMONG THE SENATORS whose districts were redrawn, Sen. Daniel J. Issa, D-Central Falls, would be disrupted the least, maintaining 93 percent of his old district, while Sen. Frank A. Ciccone III, D-Providence, would be disrupted the most, keeping just 34 percent of his current district.

All 10 incumbents affected by the new map are Democrats, and Montalbano said he thinks all 12 districts will be won by Democrats. "The governor is not getting one of these seats, if I do my job," Montalbano said, referring to Republican Governor Carcieri.

The suit was filed on May 2, 2002, in U.S. District Court on behalf of seven plaintiffs: former state Rep. Harold M. Metts, Bryan Evans, Stephanie Cruz, Jean Wiggins, the NAACP Providence branch, the Urban League of Rhode Island and the Black Political Action Committee.

Metts, the lead plaintiff, said, "We believe the plan the Senate is now proposing, by uniting upper and lower South Providence in one Senate district, is fair to black voters. The plan is also fair to Latino voters because it allows them to elect their candidate of their choice to the Senate in a separate district."

Tomas Alberto Avila, president of the Rhode Island Latino Political Action Committee, said, "To our African-American brothers and sisters, I want to tell you that we are here to help you and work with you." He noted minorities make up 55 percent of Providence's population, saying, "Together we can achieve greater political power and truly be a force."

Clifford R. Montiero, president of the NAACP Providence branch, said, "This is a historical day." He said the plaintiffs also believed they would prevail in court. "So there was no need for a settlement," he said. "But in the interest of inclusion and justice, this settlement came about. Now we need it to pass through the legislature and be signed by the governor."

Reprinted with permission of The Providence Journal ©2004 All Rights Reserved

Senate Leaders Agree To Redraw District Lines

The Associated Press
Friday, May 21, 2004

PROVIDENCE -- Senate leaders have agreed to redraw district lines to settle a lawsuit that claimed Rhode Island's 2002 legislative redistricting was unfair to black voters, a move prompted in part by the resignations of two state senators earlier this year.

Today, minority leaders hailed the settlement, which changes the configuration of 12 Senate districts in and around the state's capital city, as a step toward more inclusive government.

"Our goals have always been to ensure that black voters and Latino voters each have a voice in the state Senate," said Harold Metts, a plaintiff in the case. "The new redistricting plan will help make Rhode Island more democratic."

The plan still must be approved by the General Assembly and the governor.

Minority leaders say the most significant change is in the Providence district represented by Democrat Juan Pichardo, the state's first and only Hispanic senator. In the last election he beat incumbent Charles Walton, who was Rhode Island's first and only black senator.

The new map would put Walton, if he runs again, in a different district than Pichardo. Each district would have a high concentration of minority voters.

Walton, who has served 18 years in the Senate, said after a State House press conference that he plans to run again. The new district will include about 60 percent of the area he once represented.

Pichardo said he agreed to the changes because they will improve the chances of "another representative of color" getting elected this year. Pichardo is the only minority in the 38-person Senate.

Senate President Joseph Montalbano said the resignations of former Sens. William Irons, of East Providence, and John Celona, of North Providence, made the settlement possible by allowing district lines to be redrawn without pitting two incumbents against each other.

"Without that, you'd be asking me as the leader of the Senate to place two Democrats in with each other," said Montalbano, D-North Providence. "I did that once before, and I didn't want to do it again."

Irons, who was Senate president, and Celona, a committee chairman, resigned amid questions about their business dealings.

All 10 Democratic incumbents whose districts are being redrawn agreed to the changes, Montalbano said.

Senate leaders noted the settlement was not an admission of wrongdoing. The agreement was endorsed by the Providence chapter of the National Association for the Advancement of Colored People and groups representing Hispanics.

The lawsuit was filed in May 2002 on behalf of Metts, a former state lawmaker, the Providence branch of the NAACP and other plaintiffs. A federal judge dismissed the lawsuit later that year.

The plaintiffs appealed. In March, the 1st Circuit Court of Appeals threw out the U.S. District Court's decision, and sent the case back to it.

Rhode Island's legislative districts were redrawn using updated census figures. The process coincided with a voter-mandated downsizing of the General Assembly.

The Senate has spent about $1.1 million defending the 2002 map against the now-settled lawsuit and two others.

A Hispanic group dropped another complaint and a Superior Court judge rejected a suit filed by the towns of Bristol, Little Compton and Tiverton.

5 Finalists Picked For District Court

Governor Carcieri has 21 days to nominate someone to fill the position.

BY EDWARD FITZPATRICK
Journal Staff Writer
Friday, May 7, 2004

PROVIDENCE -- Governor Carcieri yesterday received a list of five finalists for the District Court vacancy created by Judge Robert K. Pirraglia's retirement.

The Judicial Nominating Commission on Wednesday night picked these finalists from a field of 15 applicants: Debra E. DiSegna, Joseph P. Ippolito, Mary E. McCaffrey, Rafael A. Ovalles and Kristin E. Rodgers.

"We all wish we had 15 votes," said Girard R. Visconti, chairman of the Judicial Nominating Commission. "But these are all very, very qualified people."

DiSegna is a Family Court magistrate and former special assistant attorney general. She received a bachelor's degree from Rhode Island College and a law degree from Suffolk University.

Ippolito is the District Court administrator and Traffic Tribunal administrative magistrate. He is also a finalist for a Supreme Court vacancy. He received a bachelor's degree from Tufts University and a law degree from Suffolk University.

McCaffrey is a Warwick Probate Court judge and former Warwick Municipal Court judge. Her father is a former Warwick mayor, and her brother is Senate Judiciary Chairman Michael J. McCaffrey. She received a bachelor's degree from Georgetown University and a law degree from Boston College.

Ovalles has a Providence law practice and is a bail commissioner. He is a member of the Supreme Court Committee on Character & Fitness. He received a bachelor's degree from the University of Rhode Island and a law degree from Boston University.

Rodgers is a partner in the law firm of Blish & Cavanagh and is a former assistant town solicitor for East Greenwich. She is the daughter of Superior Court Presiding Justice Joseph F. Rodgers Jr. She received a bachelor's degree from Boston College and a law degree from Catholic University of America.

The governor has 21 days to select a nominee, who will face Senate confirmation.

The applicants who did not make the cut included three former state legislators: former Representatives Denise C. Aiken, D-Warwick, and Richard E. Fleury, R-West Warwick; and former Sen. James M. Donelan, D-Warwick; plus William R. Guglietta, chief legal counsel to the House Democratic majority leader, and Harris K. Weiner, legal counsel to the Senate Republican minority leader.

The group also included Patricia A. Coyne-Fague, Alan R. Goulart, Robert E. Hardman, George M. Muksian and J. Patrick Youngs III.

15 To Be Interviewed For District Court

Applicants will be interviewed early next month.

By Edward Fitzpatrick
Journal Staff Writer
Friday, April 2, 2004

PROVIDENCE -- Three former state legislators and legal counsels for the House majority leader and Senate minority leader are among the 15 applicants who will be interviewed for a vacant District Court seat. In all, 37 people applied for the vacancy created by the retirement of Judge Robert K. Pirraglia, and the Judicial Nominating Commission has decided to interview 15 semifinalists from May 3-4. A public comment hearing is set for 5 p.m. May 5 in the Department of Administration building.

The commission will pick from three to five finalists for Governor Carcieri to choose from. The nominee requires Senate confirmation. The group includes former Rep. Denise C. Aiken, D-Warwick; former Rep. Richard E. Fleury, R-West Warwick; former Sen. James M. Donelan, D-Warwick; William R. Guglietta, chief legal counsel to the House Democratic majority leader; and Harris K. Weiner, legal counsel to the Senate Republican minority leader.

The group also includes Robert E. Hardman, the son-in-law of former Gov. J. Joseph Garrahy, and Mary E. McCaffrey, the sister of the chairman of the Senate Judiciary Committee, which votes on judicial nominees. "The legal world and the political world are intertwined, and people migrate between them," said David L. Yas, editor of Rhode Island Lawyers Weekly. "It's especially notable in Rhode Island because it's such a small state, and there are only so many lawyers who are power players."

Girard R. Visconti, chairman of the Judicial Nominating Commission, said, "I think it's a very exciting group. We have some exceptional people." The applicants are:

Denise C. Aiken, Warwick's advocate for juveniles and families and a consulting attorney for Rhode Island Legal Services. She headed the commission that handled the politically volatile task of redistricting and downsizing the legislature. She received a bachelor's degree from Providence College and a law degree from Suffolk University Law School.
Patricia A. Coyne-Fague, senior legal counsel for the state Department of Corrections. She was deputy director of the attorney general's Medicaid fraud-control unit and a special assistant attorney general. She received a

bachelor's degree from Rhode Island College and a law degree from New England School of Law.

Debra E. DiSegna, a Family Court magistrate. She was an adjudicatory hearing officer under contract with the Department of Environmental Management and a special assistant attorney general. She received a bachelor's degree from Rhode Island College and a law degree from Suffolk University Law School.

James M. Donelan, a lawyer who served in the state Senate from 1985-92 and 1996-2002. He served on the Senate Judiciary Committee. He received a bachelor's degree from the University of Rhode Island and a law degree from New England School of Law.

Richard E. Fleury, a lawyer who served in the House from 1992-2002. He served on the House Finance Committee and has been a self-employed lawyer since 1977. He received a bachelor's degree from Georgetown University and a law degree from the University of Detroit.

Alan R. Goulart, deputy chief of the attorney general's criminal division. He was a special assistant attorney general from 1991-1999 and a U.S. Navy judge advocate general from 1987-1990. He received a bachelor's degree from the University of Rhode Island and a law degree from Western New England College School of Law.

William R. Guglietta, chief legal counsel to House Majority Leader Gordon D. Fox, D-Providence. He was chief of the attorney general's policy and prevention unit from 1999-2003, and chief of the attorney general's narcotics unit from 1987-1993. He received a bachelor's degree from the University of Rhode Island and a law degree from Catholic University of America.

Robert E. Hardman, a lawyer in the Providence firm of Kelly, Kelleher, Reilly & Simpson, and a former general counsel for the Rhode Island secretary of state. He is Garrahy's son-in-law. He received a bachelor's degree from the University of Rhode Island and a law degree from Suffolk University Law School.
Joseph P. Ippolito Jr., the District Court administrator and a District Court magistrate. He was an assistant attorney general from 1980-1987. He received a bachelor's degree from Tufts University and a law degree from Suffolk University Law School.

Mary E. McCaffrey, a lawyer and Warwick probate court judge. She was a Warwick Municipal Court judge from 1992-1994. Her father, Eugene McCaffrey, is a former Warwick mayor, and her brother is Senate Judiciary

Chairman Michael J. McCaffrey. She received a bachelor's degree from Georgetown University and a law degree from Boston College Law School.

George M. Muksian, an assistant state public defender. He was chief of legal services for the state Department of Labor and Training from 1995-2003 and city solicitor for Central Falls from 1990-1995. He received a bachelor's degree from Providence College, a law degree from Suffolk University Law School and a master's degrees from Wesleyan University and Harvard University Graduate School of Education.

Rafael A. Ovalles, a Providence lawyer and a bail commissioner. He is a member of the Supreme Court Committee on Character & Fitness and the Implementation Committee for Court Interpreter Certification. He received a bachelor's degree from the University of Rhode Island and a law degree from Boston University School of Law.

Kristin E. Rodgers, a lawyer in the Providence firm of Blish & Cavanagh and a former assistant town solicitor for East Greenwich. She is the daughter of Superior Court Presiding Justice Joseph F. Rodgers Jr. She is chairwoman of the Supreme Court Committee on Character & Fitness. She received a bachelor's degree from Boston College and a law degree from Catholic University of America.

Harris K. Weiner, legal counsel to Senate Minority Leader Dennis L. Algiere, R-Westerly. He was executive counsel to the state Department of Transportation from 2000-2003 and deputy executive counsel to former Republican Gov. Lincoln C. Almond from 1995-2000. He received a bachelor's degree from Bowdoin College, a master's of business administration from Bryant College and a law degree from Washington University School of Law in St. Louis.

J. Patrick Youngs III, head of the attorney general's white-collar crime unit. He has worked for the attorney general's office since 1987 and prosecuted the Christopher Hightower and Craig Price cases. He received a bachelor's degree from Providence College and a law degree from the Catholic University of America.

City Swears In Latino Judge
First To Head Municipal Court

By TATIANA PINA
Journal Staff Writer
Wednesday, March 3, 2004

CENTRAL FALLS -- Daniel Carillo was sworn in as the city's first Latino Municipal Court judge yesterday during a noontime ceremony at City Hall. The City Council selected Carillo last week.

Carillo, 59, will replace Ray Cooney, who resigned from the position he had held for the last 10 years to serve as the city solicitor.

Robert Weber, the president of the City Council, said that Carillo was chosen from among nine candidates.

Weber said that Carillo and one other candidate are bilingual. That gave Carillo an edge, he said, because some of the population he will work with speaks Spanish.

"Being bilingual gave him something extra. If the court has a problem with a Hispanic person who cannot speak English, the judge can speak to him directly," Weber said.

Municipal Court meets every other Tuesday at City Hall to hear the cases of people who have been cited for such things as traffic violations and excessive noise. Weber said Carillo will also serve as Housing Court judge to deal with housing code violations.

Weber said that he was impressed with Carillo's experience, which includes four years in the Air Force and time as an attorney in Colorado and Rhode Island.

Alberto Cardona, a community activist who is studying law and has known Carillo for years, said, "Dan's appointment will promote dialogue that it's about time to have a judge on the state bench."

Moreau Stomps Solis

David Casey
Pawtucket Times staff reporter
11/09/2005

CENTRAL FALLS -- Charles Moreau will serve a second term as mayor of Central Falls.

When the polls closed Tuesday night, Moreau had received 1,551 votes, his challenger Hector Solis 148. There were 15 write-ins.

The councilor election was somewhat less eventful.

Political newcomer Luis Gil and incumbents Agostinho Silva, William Benson, Ricardo Patino and Jason Leger all ran unopposed.

Moreau called the election results a "statement" by the people of Central Falls.

"The voters of Central Falls have spoken - it's obvious that the city's on the right track," Moreau told The Times. "I mean, 92 percent to 8 percent, that's a statement. It's a statement to my opponent and a statement that the voters are happy with what's going on. I am happy and proud to serve the residents of Central Falls for another two years and I'd like to thank everybody for their support."

Solis could not be reached for comment at press time.

The mayoral race between Moreau and Solis was brief but ferocious.

From the outset, Solis was criticized for past run-ins with the city council over his High Street business, Mufflers Unlimited, his lack of administrative experience and a perceived reluctance to offer substantive alternatives to Moreau's policies.

In September, Solis refused to participate in a live public debate hosted by the Rhode Island Latino Civic Fund, complaining that that entity's sister agency, the Rhode Island Latino Political Action Committee, was in Moreau's pocket.

On Nov. 1 Solis failed to show up for a televised debate on The Glenn Medeiros Show, a weekly political talk show hosted by local television personality Glenn Medeiros and former Central Falls Mayor Thomas Lazieh

461

The two candidates finally went head-to-head in a bilingual radio debate broadcast by WELH 88.1 FM, but Solis' arguments didn't gain him any traction with the Democratic City Committee, which unanimously voted to endorse Moreau shortly thereafter. In an interview with The Times, Committee Chairman Jason Leger said his decision was based on Solis' performance in the radio debate.

For his part, Solis has tried to paint Moreau as a power-hungry incompetent who couldn't care less about the well-being of his constituents. Solis accused Moreau of mismanaging the city's resources, claiming that he agreed to sell the city's water system to the Pawtucket Water Supply Board for considerably less than it was worth and that street crime under Moreau's administration was on the rise. Moreau, for the most part, campaigned on his first-term track record.

Since he was elected in 2003, Moreau has resurrected the city's defunct community center, appointed a Central Falls resident as police chief, pushed for the completion of the Francis L. Corrigan Sports Complex, deprivatized city trash collection and fostered one of the most successful recycling programs in the state and held the line on taxes.

Hector Solis, 57, emigrated from Guatemala in the mid-1960s to work in a Chicago factory.From Chicago he moved to New York, where he studied graphic design at Brooklyn College. He subsequently moved to Rhode Island, where he earned a degree in refrigeration, air conditioning, cooling and heating from New England Tech. After undergoing quadruple bypass surgery, Solis retired from the heating and cooling business, purchased a garage on High Street and started his own muffler and auto repair shop in 1997. He has two daughters, Alessandra and Danielle, from his first marriage and two sons, Michael and Anthony, with his wife Thelma.Moreau, 42, was born in Central Falls and received a bachelor's degree in business administration from Bryant College. In his early 20s, he opened Magee's, a popular Dexter Street restaurant.

Most recently, Moreau worked for the New England Patriots and the Central Falls Housing Authority. He currently lives in Central Falls with his wife Kristin and newborn son Aidan. He ran for mayor twice before beating incumbent Mayor Lee Matthews in 2003.

Moreau Racks Up A Landslide Victory

The mayor vows to "continue to have great things happen in Central Falls."

By TATIANA PINA
Journal Staff Writer
Wednesday, November 9, 2005

CENTRAL FALLS -- Incumbent Mayor Charles D. Moreau trounced opponent Hector Solis in yesterday's election by an unofficial vote of 1,551 to 148.

The mayor's race was the only one Central Falls voters decided as all the candidates for five seats on the City Council were unopposed. They included four incumbents: Agostinho F. Silva, of 82 Ledge St., in Ward 1; Jason R. Leger, of 21 Temple Place, Ward 2; Ricardo Patino, of 7 Darling St., Ward 3; and William Benson Jr., of 1100 Lonsdale Ave., in Ward 5.

In Ward 4, Luis A. Gil, of 255 Cowden St., Apt. 1, a radio journalist for WALE 990 AM, ran unopposed for the seat being vacated by Council President Robert Weber, who cited a busy new job schedule and frustration with politics in the administration as reasons for his decision not to seek reelection.

A total of 30 percent of the city's eligible voters turned out to vote.

Enjoying a victory beer at the Madeira Club with his supporters, Moreau, dressed in a suit and tie, said, "The people have spoken."

"People are happy with what is happening in the city. I'm happy with the confidence the people of Central Falls have put in me. We're gonna continue the progress of the programs we have put in place. We will continue to have great things happen in Central Falls."

City Councilman Jason Leger said the City Council had shown a united front and all had supported Moreau.

"We worked hard to have a full campaign to continue to build a base. It's a reflection of Mayor Moreau. I've never seen somebody who can bring so many people to the table. He is a master of networking," Leger said. Among the well-wishers was Attorney General Patrick Lynch.

Luis Gil, a Colombian native, became the second Latino member of the City Council. He, his wife, and friends sat in front of Wilfrid Manor, which is in his district, all day greeting people and getting their first taste of city politics. "We are learning a lot from this and it's really exciting," he said. "It is going to be great representing the people of my ward."

Earlier in the night, Solis, the owner of Mufflers Unlimited, visited Wilfrid Manor for a short time on his way to another precinct. He could not stop to talk but said he was doing well. "We are doing better than anticipated," he said. "It's going pretty well."

Solis could not be reached for comment after the results of the race were announced.

Former Mayor Lee Matthews showed up to vote at Wilfrid Manor about 8 p.m. with his wife. He would not say who he was supporting.

In the last days of the election, Solis had managed to tweak the noses of some Latinos, especially those from the Caribbean whom he named specifically when he sent out a letter through the Internet. In that letter he talked about some members of the Latino community being like crabs in a basket not letting him get ahead. He had lamented that as the first Latino to run for mayor, some Latinos did not give him their support.

Solis, a native of Guatemala, made history in 2003 when he became the first Latino to run for mayor. Central Falls has the largest percentage of Latino residents of any city in the state. In the three-way mayoral primary in 2003, Moreau, a former projects manager for the Central Falls Housing Authority, took 720 votes, Solis garnered 60 votes, and incumbent Lee M. Matthews won 766 votes. Moreau went on to beat Matthews by 16 votes in the general election.

In this campaign, Moreau pointed to what he said were his accomplishments over the last two years: hiring a police chief who lives in the city, new police officers, new firefighters, less overtime, development in the city, replacing private trash haulers with city workers, expansion of the Wyatt Detention Facility, and taking over the community center from the Pawtucket YMCA.
Reprinted with permission of The Providence Journal ©2005 All Rights Reserved

C.F. Candidates Meet Latino Group

David Casey
09/23/2005

CENTRAL FALLS -- Central Falls is an extraordinary place with extraordinary problems: high-density, high-cost housing, the state's lowest median income, a large tax burden coupled with a small tax base and a large population of people who do not speak English.

While most politicians grapple with some of these issues at one time or another, the candidates for Central Falls' upcoming municipal elections faced all of them in the Central Falls High School auditorium Thursday night.

Incumbent Mayor Charles Moreau, incumbent Councilmen Ricardo Patino and Agostinho Silva and council newcomer Luis Alfredo Gil, took on these issues and more at a public forum co-sponsored by Progreso Latino and the Rhode Island Latino Civic Fund.

Although Moreau's is the only contested race, all candidates fielded tough questions from Central Falls residents and officials from both organizations.

Incumbent Councilmen William Benson and Jason Leger were not present, according to Patino, because of prior engagements. Mayoral candidate Hector Solis, who had previously denounced RILCF as a part of Moreau's "political machine," boycotted the event as promised.

Spanish-to-English translation devices were made available to members of the audience, which included several members of both sponsor organizations and a couple dozen residents. Providence College Political Science Professor Tony Affigne served as moderator.

All of the questions dealt with the familiar themes of economic development, public safety and affordable housing.

The discussion over public safety quickly split into two themes: crime reduction and police/resident relations. While the moderator focused mainly on crime reduction, residents like Diosa Martinez shifted the conversation to the law enforcement officers themselves.
"A lot of people hate the Central Falls police because they are rude," said Martinez. "What can you do so the people of this city don't feel intimidated by the police?"

465

Moreau said the police department's new bicycle squad was already on the streets, interacting with residents on a "hand-shake basis," but stressed the importance of recruiting from within the community.

In addition to giving Central Falls residents hiring preference, Moreau said these resident-officers will replace out-of-towners as they retire. Moreau also announced plans to require officers who live in the city to take their cruisers home with them in an effort to increase police presence.

Silva called for an increased sense of civic duty.

"We need to get the community more involved," said Silva. "We need to give them a voice and then we need to listen. The residents are our eyes and ears on the street. We can't do it without their cooperation."

Residents also wanted to know how the city government intended to create jobs and help small businesses thrive.

Moreau cited the Donald D. Wyatt Prison expansion, Fortune Metals' new Higginson Avenue facility, which is expected to employ 40 workers, and a possible $300 million commercial development near Interstate 95.

Patino, who identified economic development and small business assistance as two of his top priorities, said he would continue and expand existing initiatives.

"Two months ago we met with the SBA and Progreso to form a partnership in which the city would (extend) Community Development Block Grant money to Progreso programs that promote economic development." Patino told the audience. "We also need to conduct a study and ask business owners what the city could have done for them but did not..e need to have a clear idea of what is working and what is not."

Gil, who also claimed that economic development was one of his main concerns, said he wanted to see more job and entrepreneurial training.

"We need to work with the SBA to get more training," he said. "Many people don't know how to get a small business loan."

Of all the questions asked Thursday, affordable housing caused the most trouble for the candidates.

Patino, who owns several rental properties in the city, said some form of rent control legislation might be imminent. Moreau and Silva mentioned existing federal and state housing programs and Gil suggested the problem was national in scope, and largely out of city government's hands.

The candidates difficulty with the affordable housing question, and, perhaps, their numerous references to the city's limited financial resources, prompted RILCF Executive Director Domingo Morel to accuse them of having a "defeatist attitude."

The candidates took immediate offense to Morel's comment.

"Don't take this the wrong way but what you just said was ignorant," Moreau replied. "We've been moving the city forward at a rapid pace and we wouldn't be sitting up here if we had a defeatist attitude. We're all here to make a difference."

"Not one of us came out to run for election because he didn't want to do anything," Silva added. "There's a lot of things we're doing behind the scenes that you're not aware of. We're all working very, very hard."

A Void Is Filled On State Bench

By Edward Fitzpatrick
Journal Staff Writer
Saturday, July 2, 2005

Judiciary welcomes Rafael Ovalles as first Hispanic member

PROVIDENCE -- Rafael A. Ovalles looked up in the State House rotunda yesterday, scanning the balconies of people who'd gathered to see him become the first Hispanic judge in the state court system.

Ovalles, 40, a Providence lawyer born in the Dominican Republic, had just put on the black robe of a state District Court judge. "Ladies and gentlemen, thank you," he said, slowly looking around at the faces of friends and colleagues. Somebody yelled: "Feels good, huh?" Ovalles beamed, and the crowd broke into applause.

"As we begin to celebrate the Fourth of July," Ovalles said, "I think it is fitting to note that the state of Rhode Island and the United States are reborn today as an American dream comes true yet again for another immigrant. An American dream coming true provides a catalyst for others -- immigrant or native born -- to strive, to work hard, with the hope that some day his or her dream will come true, also."

Ovalles fills the vacancy left by the retirement of Judge Robert K. Pirraglia, who stepped down about 16 months ago.

"It's been long in coming -- both in the appointment and a person of your ethnic background," District Court Chief Judge Albert E. DeRobbio said. "And we welcome that diversification in our court."

DeRobbio told Ovalles, "You are joining the people's court. I know you are people oriented, and I know you will be successful."

Supreme Court Chief Justice Frank J. Williams said, "Rafael's deep and personal connection with his Hispanic heritage only enhances his legal credentials. In addition to offering a fresh perspective to his fellow members of the bench, as the first Hispanic judge in Rhode Island, Judge Ovalles will undoubtedly inspire confidence in our judiciary from members of the minority community."

Senate President Joseph A. Montalbano, D-North Providence, called Ovalles "the personification of the American dream."

Montalbano, a lawyer, recalled meeting Ovalles when the future judge was a young lawyer. "It was clear that his talent and work ethic were going to take him places," he said. "Since he came to the United States from the Dominican Republic at the age of 10, with a limited knowledge of the English language, Rafael set high goals and he achieved them. He earned his way into Classical High School, he graduated magna cum laude from URI in three years, and he earned his juris doctorate degree from Boston University law school."

As the first Hispanic state judge, Ovalles "carries the weight of his community on his shoulders," Montalbano said. "But his are broad shoulders." Rep. Peter F. Kilmartin, D-Pawtucket, who is a police captain and a lawyer, said he's seen Ovalles at work as a bail commissioner.

"Be it a hot, humid Sunday morning or a freezing cold winter morning with ice on the ground, he always would show up, dapperly dressed," Kilmartin said. "And I'd say to him, 'Rafael, why are you dressed so nicely? The weather is terrible out, and you're looking like a million dollars, like you're on the way to your own wedding.' And he'd say, 'Because I'm representing the people and the court.' "

Kilmartin agreed it was a great day for the Hispanic community. "But this is a wonderful day for Rhode Island because they have a man of quality," he said. Before swearing in Ovalles, Governor Carcieri talked about how "we are all either immigrants or descendants of immigrants."

"We are a nation and a state built on immigrants who work hard," Carcieri said. "This is a young man who came from humble beginnings, like many of us, but worked hard."

Ovalles received a lifetime appointment and a starting salary of $112,116.
He had been scheduled to be sworn in June 3, but his brother died shortly before the ceremony, which was postponed. Yesterday, Ovalles said, "I want to thank everyone for the outpouring of support for my family and me with the recent passing of my brother, Angel Ovalles, who I am certain joins us today."

Martinez And Alston Confirmed

One senator says the governor "made two great appointments," for DCYF director and child advocate, respectively.

By Mark Arsenault
Journal Staff Writer
Thursday, June 23, 2005

PROVIDENCE -- The Rhode Island Senate yesterday confirmed Governor Carcieri's appointment of his former community relations director to a Cabinet post heading the Department of Children, Youth and Families.

Though Patricia Martinez has been acting director of the department since March 6, she called the 35-0 confirmation vote "overwhelming."

"It was one of those 'Wow!' moments," Martinez said in an interview after the vote, during a reception in the State House. "Although I have been in the department for three months, the vote today was a validation of some of the work we have been doing with very dedicated and talented staff members."

Martinez takes over for Jay G. Lindgren Jr.

In another vote yesterday, the Senate confirmed Jametta Alston, Carcieri's nominee for child advocate, a position formerly held by Laureen D'Ambra, who left to become a Family Court judge. The vote was 36 to 0.

Sen. Harold M. Metts, D-Providence, noted that he doesn't always agree with Governor Carcieri, "but I have to give credit where credit is due -- he made two great appointments."

Martinez immigrated to Central Falls from Colombia as a teenager. She has worked the past two years as Carcieri's director of community relations, as a liaison between the administration, community groups and other constituents. She has also worked for the Providence School Department, building relationships between parents and the schools.

From 1988-2000, she had been executive director of Progreso Latino, a nonprofit organization based in Central Falls.
She has a bachelor's degree from Rhode Island College, in social work, and a master's degree in the generalized field of human services from Springfield College, in Massachusetts.

"At the end of the day, when a child is safe . . . that's the reason we become social workers," Martinez said yesterday. "To lead a department [in charge of] something I have been doing all my life is so gratifying."

Alston is a Philadelphia native and a former Cranston city solicitor. She has also worked at Rhode Island Legal Services, and had her own practice. She earned a bachelor's degree from Temple University, in Philadelphia, and a law degree from Howard University, in Washington, D.C.

With reports from staff writer Scott Mayerowitz.

Latina Institute Graduates 17 Leaders

The program is aimed at young women who have a background in public service, education and government.

By Linda Borg
Journal Staff Writer
Tuesday, May 31, 2005

PROVIDENCE -- Patricia Martinez, the interim director of the state Department of Children, Youth and Families, was honored last week at the graduation of 17 women from the Rhode Island Latina Leadership Institute.

The graduates chose Martinez because she has been a pioneer for Latino women in civic participation and leadership in the community, according to Ana-Cecelia Rosado, a member of the Rhode Island Latino Civic Fund, which sponsors the classes.

The speaker was Melba De Pena, the executive director of the state Democratic Party.

The Civic Fund, which graduated its second class, originally asked 22 women to participate in an eight-week training program where they learned about leadership skills, grass-roots advocacy, media relations and the workings of government and media relations.

The group's mission is to "ensure that Latino women develop their personal and professional potential to serve as leaders in their communities and advocate for positive changes in the Latino community," said Doris M. De Los Santos, vice president of the Civic Fund.

Carmen A. Mirabal, coordinator of the Leadership Institute, said that she was "very proud to say that these . . . successful Latinas have the communication and motivational skills, the personal courage, the integrity and the honesty necessary to guide the Latino community."

The program, which runs for eight weeks on Saturdays, is aimed at young women with a background in public service, education and government who are interested in assuming a more prominent role in their community. The institute was created to address the large gender gap between Latino men and women who hold positions of influence.

The classes are sponsored by Sodexho School Services, the Neighborhood Health Plan of Rhode Island, Mayor David N. Ciciline's office and the Rhode Island Foundation.

The following women graduated Thursday:

Yolanda Baez, Evelyn Castillo, Martha Cedeno, Rosa Q. Crowley, Cynthia DeJesus, Irisonixa Diaz, Diana Figueroa, Judelkys Garcia, Alma Guzman, Judith Koegler, Katia Lugo, Olinda Matos, Vivian Moreno, Sonja Ogando, Patricia Patterson, Rosemary Raygada and Silvia Reyes.

The Latino Connection

Even with meaningful strides, some say the RI Democratic party has not done enough to tap political momentum among Hispanics

By Ian Donnis
The Providence Phoenix

PERSUASIVE: along with a compelling personal narrative, Diaz has a knack for politics.

IN THE SIX months since she won election, state Representative Grace Diaz has become a familiar presence at the State House, favorably impressing the House leadership and other observers with her warm personality and growing understanding of the legislative process. It's quite a contrast from how Diaz came to Providence from the Dominican Republic in 1990 with $40, two dresses, and no understanding of English. As the freshman Democrat from Providence's South Side puts it, "Sometimes I have to pinch myself — am I still dreaming?"

Beyond epitomizing the opportunity that America still holds for immigrants, Diaz offers a striking example of how Latinas of modest means can engage and win local elections, even when faced with significant odds. The election of Diaz, who last year ousted incumbent representative Leon Tejada, a fellow Dominican, was noteworthy considering the male-dominated nature of Rhode Island's Latino political establishment. As a leader in the organizing drive by home-based day care workers, Diaz also showed an ability to work simultaneously at several levels of the political process. After the watershed of the 2002 election, in which Democratic and Republican candidates courted Latino voters like never before, Diaz's rise can rightfully be seen as another harbinger of the steadily ascending political profile of Hispanics in Rhode Island. Indeed, the state is already a trendsetter, serving as the home of the first Dominican woman elected to statewide office in the US (Diaz), and the first Dominican state senator in the country (Juan Pichardo of Providence) — a distinction attributed to the Ocean State's small size. Elsewhere, Rafael A. Ovalles, a Dominican, last month became the first Latino judge in the state court system, and Latino representation on the Providence City Council doubled when Miguel Luna was elected in 2002, joining Luis Aponte.

Still, with just six Latino elected officials in Rhode Island — the others are state Representative Anastasia Williams (D-Providence), a native of Panama, and Colombian native Ricardo Patino, a city councilor in Central Falls — Hispanics remain underrepresented in elective office. And although the state

Democratic Party is cranking up several efforts to increase political participation by Latinos in preparation for the 2006 election season, a view persists among some that the party has not done enough to help realize their political potential. The situation is somewhat ironic, considering how Democratic Party chairman Bill Lynch tabbed Melba Depeña, then the president of the Rhode Island Latino Political Action Committee, as the party's executive director after her similar criticism was reported in the *Phoenix* (see "Ready to rumba," News, June 27, 2003).

Luna says the question of whether the Democratic Party is doing enough to cultivate more political participation by Hispanics is a hot topic in the Latino community. Since Myrth York edged Sheldon Whitehouse in the 2002 Democratic gubernatorial primary, a narrow victory attributed to Latino voters, he says, "There have been a lot of discussions about it, in terms of what are we doing, what is the Democratic Party doing, is it really putting in resources, does it really care about our agenda?" Luna, an outspoken and unabashed liberal, extends the critique to both of Rhode Island's major political parties. Ultimately, he says, "We feel, so far, we are used by politicians," because they tend to hire a few Latinos after wining a campaign, rather than working more actively to implement policies that expand opportunities for working people.

Victor Capellan, a former director of the Center for Hispanic Policy and Advocacy (CHISPA), who now works as an educator in New York City, takes a more nuanced view. Capellan, who continues to closely follow Rhode Island politics, says the Democratic Party has come a long way. Trying to engage the party when he ran for the legislature in the mid-'90s, he says, "was like pulling teeth." Capellan credits Lynch with having taken some major steps, such as hiring Depeña, and he notes how various candidates have hired key Latinos for their campaigns. "Some of the stuff that needs to happen is more of the organized or structured sort of outreach," he says. "Having Melba in there is great, but I don't think the Latinos are in the structure of the party, the caucuses . . . . I think that's the next level — getting it more into the community at large, not just the few individuals."

A related element is how the Rhode Island Latino Political Action Committee (RILPAC), which helped to raise the profile of the state's Latinos prior to the 2002 election, stagnated somewhat after Depeña's departure. In particular, the group drew criticism when its 2004 endorsements included only one Latino. Now, though, 28-year-old Domingo Morel, who succeeded Tomas Avila as RILPAC's president two months ago, cites plans to revitalize it, in part with more extensive monitoring of how officeholders act on issues of interest to Latinos. In terms of the performance of the Democratic Party, Morel, an academic advisor in the talent development program at the

University of Rhode Island, says he doesn't yet have enough information to make an assessment. He adds, though, that the hiring of Depeña, "in itself, is a huge statement. They've made huge progress, but it remains to be seen if they keep up with their promises, and we certainly hope they will back them up." For critics, the disconnect can be seen in places like heavily Latino Central Falls — not far from the Democratic Party's Pawtucket headquarters — where municipal elections will held this fall.

One would think that the party might want to cultivate someone like Patino, who became Central Falls' first Latino councilor when he was elected in 2001, as a way of showing its commitment to a diverse constituency, if nothing else. (He might also be a good ambassador in Woonsocket, which, despite the presence of a significant Hispanic community, has yet to elect one as a councilor; local elections will also be held there this fall.) Asked about how well the Democratic Party does in encouraging greater Latino political participation, Patino says, "Honestly, I never heard of the party. It's more the candidates who have been doing it. I never saw them [party officials] do anything for us, honestly."

ALTHOUGH SHE SAYS the grousing is "valid to a point," noting that it takes time to change public perception, Depeña points to a variety of fresh efforts, contending the party is doing far more than it was two years ago to increase political participation by Latinos and other minorities. Among the efforts: a new Providence-based caucus, co-chaired by Jim Vincent and Abigail Mesa, which is tentatively slated to hold its first meeting in June. Originally intended as an effort to promote cooperation among blacks and Latinos — who have emerged as rivals in some legislative races in recent years — the caucus is now envisioned as a wider initiative to forge closer ties between Democrats and various minorities.

Meanwhile, a youth outreach program staffed with three volunteers, also targeted to start in June, will target two groups: college students and young people, ages 18 to 25, who are not in college. A tentatively planned "Democrats in Action" tour will also seek to strengthen city and town committees throughout the state. "We don't want to concentrate on just Providence, Warwick, and Cranston," Depeña says. Summing it up, she adds, "I feel good that we've made some progress. I do agree that we need to do more."

For Lynch, who singles out such issues as Social Security, wages, and health-care, it's hard to imagine minority voters not recognizing Democrats as traditional champions of the working class. He says the party has worked hard to stay in touch with the Latino community, for instance, by buying advertising in Spanish-language media and mounting aggressive voter-registration drives in Hispanic neighborhoods during campaigns. Lynch attributes some of the griping to the difference between the heightened activity level of a campaign and the more staid state of normal affairs. "It's impossible to continue that kind of direct retail politics on a year-round basis," he says. [But] we don't take any vote for granted."

Latinos, of course, are not a monolith — those in Rhode Island have mostly come from Puerto Rico, Guatemala, the Dominican Republic, Mexico, and Colombia — although they do tend to lean Democratic locally. For all the political, entrepreneurial, and other strides made by local Hispanics, who conservatively number more than 100,000, they continue to suffer from disproportionately high rates of poverty and other social problems. Political representation, not surprisingly, given the history of the Irish, Italians, and other immigrant groups, is seen as part of the solution.

The strength of Latino voters is not to be taken lightly, considering how they represent a significant number of tallies in statewide elections. For now, however, given the dominance of primarily white Democrats at the General Assembly, and how freshly registered Latinos might pose an unknown quantity in some legislative races, the status quo might work well enough for some. If the Democratic Party went out and registered 500 fresh Latinos voters in a district, such a step could make clear the benefits of heightened activism.

As it stands, though, "In terms of the parties, people are looking for alternatives," says Luna, the Providence councilor. "People are hungry and none of the traditional parties are really filling that hunger. There is no excitement [for] these parties."
If the sense of dissatisfaction felt by some Latinos offers an opening for the perennially struggling Rhode Island Republican Party, even Patricia Morgan, the GOP chairwoman acknowledges that it has not done much to exploit the situation. As Republicans pressed a legislative push in 2004, one of the GOP candidates was David Quiroa, a native of Guatemala, who ran for a legislative seat from Newport. Republicans were disappointed when Quiroa didn't get the Rhode Island Latino Political Action Committee's endorsement.

Morgan holds out hope that the premium placed by Latinos on family and work represent a potential match with the GOP, and she says the party will do better. "We are going to start reaching out to them," she says, "and we hope that they will meet us halfway and look at the Republican Party." For now, though, Morgan acknowledges, "There is an incredible amount of pressure in their community to be Democratic."

CRANSTON MAYOR Stephen P. Laffey enraged at least a portion of his base when he announced plans on April 26 for Cranston to recognize identity cards issued by the Mexican and Guatemalan embassies. The talk-radio chatter that afternoon was thick with cries of disappointment and betrayal from Laffey supporters alarmed about the prospect of increased illegal immigration.

The controversial Republican mayor has made a practice of reaching out to Latinos — just, he says, as reaches out to Armenians, Portuguese, and members of other ethnic and racial groups. "I try to represent all of the people of Cranston," Laffey says. "If I have a soft spot, it's for people who want to live the American dream." His interest in the Latino community, including past trips to Guatemala and the Mexican border, have "nothing to do with politics, nothing to do with cultivating."

Laffey's denials notwithstanding, his efforts to strengthen ties with Latino voters seem like a deliberate attempt to craft a reputation as an inclusive fellow and blunt the more conservative components of his ideology. (There's also a certain irony in how Ronald Reagan, one of Laffey's political heroes, backed policies that resulted in egregious human rights abuses in Guatemala and elsewhere in Central America in the '80s. Reagan was also the last US president to sponsor an amnesty for illegal immigrants, in part to aid those forced to relocate because of the violence in Central America. Asked about this, Laffey says the US was wrong to support a 1954 coup in Guatemala, but he contends that Reagan, on the whole, "did a wonderful job," and supported freedom around the world.)

It remains to be seen whether Laffey will enter the race to challenge US Senator Lincoln Chafee, but regardless of which office he might pursue in 2006, his outreach to minority communities could prove to be a considerable asset.

Similarly, Chafee's Democratic challengers, Secretary of State Matt Brown and former attorney general Sheldon Whitehouse each cite Latinos as a significant part of their campaign preparations. "I think the Latino population is a very important political group in Rhode Island, very empowered, and very energized," Whitehouse says. "It's important for any candidate to have a serious strategy to reach out into the Latino community, and obviously we will." One signal of Whitehouse's interest in this area is Juana Horton's selection as his campaign treasurer.

Brown, who avidly sought Latino support during his successful effort to oust incumbent Ed Inman in 2002, and subsequently hired Nellie Gorbea, a past president of the Rhode Island Latino Political Action Committee, as his director of administration, has already made some meaningful inroads. State

Senator Juan Pichardo (D-Providence), seen by some as having the most elective potential of any of the current crop of Latino officeholders, will co-chair Brown's campaign in Providence. Sylvia and Betty Bernal, who have been active with the RILPAC, are involved with his campaign committee. Says Brown, "We start out with a lot of support in the community."

Asked about his efforts to increase Latino political participation as secretary of state, Brown cites a program launched in 2004, called First Voters, which targeted making first-time voters out of high school and college students, as well as freshly inducted American citizens. He says his office also started Civics 101, a pilot effort in Woonsocket and Central Falls that has since gone statewide, which promoted civic education. "Anecdotally, we get a good sense that we reached a lot of people," Brown says, although there are not hard numbers to quantify newly registered voters.

FOR HER PART, state Representative Grace Diaz has helped to break down cultural barriers, taking some of her legislative colleagues to lunch on Broad Street, for example, so they can see the strengths and struggles of her community. Recalling her own experience after coming to Providence to join an established friend in 1990, she says, "Like every immigrant, you just start at zero."

Diaz had worked in her native Dominican Republic as a secretary for the Dominican Revolutionary Party (PRD) and a customs officer. She lost her job when the party fell out of power, and she subsequently began traveling back and forth to Rhode Island. Diaz pursued classes at the International Institute and then the Community College of Rhode Island, serving as a factory worker, cashier, and bartender before graduating as a certified nursing assistant. By 1995, she was earning enough to bring over her five children from the DR, and her mother joined them four years later.

In 2002, she opened her home-based day care — a step that would propel her into activism, grassroots organizing, and her eventual victory last year over Leon Tejada as a state representative. "It's a big, big step and a challenge every day," says Diaz, who comfortably navigates the corridors of the State House, sharing a basement office with Representatives Anastasia Williams and Joseph Almeida, also Providence Democrats. For her part, she says, "Right now, the Democratic Party is trying to reach more Latinos than ever." Asked about Diaz, House Majority Leader Gordon Fox says, "I find her a very progressive legislator, and she can only get stronger."

The freshman representative has also impressed H. Philip West Jr., executive director of Common Cause of Rhode Island, who resides in the district represented by Diaz. "I think she's a natural political leader," West says.

"Not everyone who gets elected is. She has a quick grasp of the issues. She's clearly an extrovert in that she loves to connect with people and thrives on the energy of conversation. And there's something about her that I think people are inclined to trust."

With her upbeat personality and compelling personal story, Diaz is the type of person who can facilitate ties between Rhode Island's Latino community and the prevailing Democratic Party. In fact, it seems as if making such connections is practically part of her DNA. When it comes to building a wider and more symbiotic relationship between Democrats and Latinos, the 2006 election season will likely shed some light on the future.

Ian Donnis can be reached at idonnis@phx.com.

Grace Diaz: A Newcomer In The House

M. Charles Baskt
The Providence Journal
Thursday, May 12, 2005

You may have read that Grace Diaz, who is a freshman state representative, came to Providence from the Dominican Republic in 1990 with $40, two dresses and no English.

She's now swept up in the political whirl and was at a March 2 White House program for Dominican-American leaders. It turned out to be the day President Bush honored the Red Sox, and she got to see that. Diaz didn't lack for things to talk about over the cell phone with her 12-year-old daughter, Maria, the youngest of her five children, back in Rhode Island. "She's so excited about anything I do, and she's constantly calling: 'What are you doing now? What's happening now?' "

Diaz, 48, represents Elmwood, Washington Park and the West End, a largely Latino district. She owns a home-based daycare business. Backed by other child care providers and by House leaders, she ousted Rep. Leon Tejada in a 2004 Democratic primary. Tejada had run afoul of state campaign finance reporting laws and, in the House's internal politics, was on the outs with chamber powers. At a recent Diaz fundraiser, Majority Leader Gordon Fox said he'd been "very impressed" with her. "It happened to be a wonderful fit."

The event (chicken, rice, vegetable lasagna) was at Ada's Creations, a sprawling Broad Street restaurant and success story. "This represents prosperity for this community and also specifically for Latinos," said Sen. Juan Pichardo. Owner Ada Terrero is a Diaz pal. They both work hard. "We compete with each other," Diaz chuckles.

She rises at 5:30 a.m., receives her first young clients at 6, does errands in the afternoon, goes to the State House and attends political or community events until 9 or 10 at night.

After arriving here from the Dominican Republic, where she worked in government offices, Diaz studied English at the International Institute. She's been a bartender, cashier and metal polisher. She took courses at CCRI, became a nursing assistant, then a group home community living aide.

Diaz has submitted an ambitious agenda of bills. But one measure she did not join in sponsoring, though she certainly wants it to pass, is a bill to allow home-based child-care providers, whose services are state subsidized, to unionize and negotiate with the state. Governor Carcieri has threatened a veto of the bill, sponsored by Fox and many others.

Diaz calls daycare providers key to the community: "We're supporting who's working." She says providers had urged her to run for the House -- "We need somebody like us there," they said -- and that her winning impressed lawmakers with the providers' clout and ability.

She declined to co-sponsor the unionization bill in order to avoid a conflict of interest. As for whether she will vote on the measure, she is seeking an Ethics Commission advisory opinion on that and other matters regarding her roles as a provider and legislator. Until the ruling comes, it's not clear how free she is under ethics laws to talk up the bill with other reps. She told me she'd been doing that, but after meeting with Jason Gramitt, commission staff lawyer, she said that she'd now do so only if she, like citizens generally, comes upon legislators outside the State House.

Of course, there's no question about promoting issues of general concern to her district. Diaz says, "We are people who are working hard. . . . We want to be part of the economic development in Rhode Island. We want to have a better opportunity for education for our kids."

She hopes you'll drop by the area, see the businesses, hear the merengue and eat the food. I find the neighborhood interesting and lively; Latinos are a burgeoning population, and I feel I'm visiting the future.

Senators Endorse Ovalles

The Senate Judiciary Committee votes to recommend Rafael A. Ovalles as a District Court judge.

By Edward Fitzpatrick
Journal Staff Writer
Friday, April 1, 2005

PROVIDENCE -- One speaker compared him to Jackie Robinson, the first black Major League Baseball player.

Another compared him to some of the state's first Irish and Italian judges.
In all, 21 people spoke in support of Rafael A. Ovalles yesterday, saying he is the right man to make Rhode Island history by becoming the state court system's first Hispanic judge. The Senate Judiciary Committee voted 13 to 0 to recommend Ovalles as a District Court judge, and the full Senate is scheduled to vote on his confirmation Tuesday.

"Our legal system, unfortunately, is only as fair and just as those who come through the doors perceive it to be," said Senate Majority Leader M. Teresa Paiva Weed, D-Newport. "And one of the critical factors, I believe, is that those individuals who come into courtrooms see people who look like them on the bench, whether they be Latino, black, women, male."

Ovalles, 40, of Providence, was born in the Dominican Republic and came to Rhode Island at age 10. He graduated from Classical High School in 1983 and was twice named city cross-country champion. He graduated from the University of Rhode Island in three years, graduating magna cum laude in 1986. And he received a law degree from Boston University law school in 1990.

Fluent in Spanish, Ovalles has been a litigator for 14 years, working with criminal, family, bankruptcy, immigration and workers' compensation law. And he has been a bail commissioner in Central Falls and Pawtucket.

Governor Carcieri nominated Ovalles in January for the District Court seat that Judge Robert K. Pirraglia left a year ago. The governor picked Ovalles from among five finalists, including Family Court Magistrate Debra E. DiSegna; District Court administrator Joseph P. Ippolito Jr.; newly named Family Court Magistrate Mary E. McCaffrey, sister of Senate Judiciary Chairman Michael J. McCaffrey; and Kristin E. Rodgers, partner in Blish & Cavanagh and daughter of Superior Court Presiding Justice Joseph F. Rodgers Jr.

State Rep. Joseph S. Almeida, D-Providence, told the Judiciary Committee that his South Side district includes many black, Hispanic and Southeast Asian residents, and he told Ovalles that "everybody in South Side is proud of you." "Raf, you are about to be the Jackie Robinson of that Sixth [Division] District Court," Almeida said.

George E. Healy Jr., chief judge of the state Workers' Compensation Court, told the committee, "I think that this is an historic day today."

"I remember when I was a kid my mom talked with awe of Justice Edmund Flynn," Healy said. "To her, he was not simply the name on a school building. He was one of the first Irish-Americans to achieve a judicial appointment and become a member of the Rhode Island Supreme Court."

Referring to some of the first Irish and Italian judges in Rhode Island, Healy said, "These were role models and heroes that meant so much to the community from which they came." And he called Ovalles "an ideal role model," saying, "He is the ideal person for young Hispanic men and women to say, 'I can succeed just like Rafael did.' "

Supreme Court Chief Justice Frank J. Williams spoke in support of Ovalles and in written comments said, "Rafael is an ideal pioneer in the judiciary's continuing journey toward a truly diversified bench."

Sen. Juan M. Pichardo, D-Providence, the state's first Hispanic senator, said Ovalles has always gone "the extra mile," whether in high school track, academics or his law practice. "We are here to take part in a process that will once again demonstrate that Rhode Island is a place where all who work hard can achieve the highest recognition and responsibility," he said.

Retired Supreme Court Chief Justice Joseph R. Weisberger said, "I certainly concur with the senator in suggesting that we have the honor today to participate in the climax of an American dream."

District Court is "truly the people's court," Weisberger said. "And I believe that Mr. Ovalles will soon become a people's judge."

Community Activist Tapped As Director Of DCYF

Patricia Martinez, 45, has been serving as the governor's director of community relations.

By Scott Mayerowitz
Journal State House Bureau
Thursday, January 13, 2005

PROVIDENCE -- Governor Carcieri continued to shake up his Cabinet yesterday, replacing Department of Children, Youth and Families Director Jay G. Lindgren Jr. with Patricia Martinez.

Martinez, Carcieri's director of community relations, previously had worked for the Providence schools and spent 12 years as the executive director of Progreso Latino.

"We cannot forget that the work performed at DCYF touches the lives of some of the most vulnerable families in some of our most underserved communities," Carcieri said. "Ultimately, DCYF's success depends on its ability to work with the community to achieve a common goal, and that is the safety and well-being of Rhode Island's children. Patricia Martinez understands that."

The governor praised Martinez's community-based work and said her experience will move the department forward.

"I think you have chosen wisely," Elizabeth Burke Bryant, executive director of Rhode Island Kids Count, told Carcieri. "You have chosen a member of this community that all of us have worked with for many, many years. All of us can attest to her true devotion to children and families."
Carcieri said he decided to remove Lindgren because "it was time for a different direction" and he wanted "a lot more outreach into the community."

"I want to thank Jay Lindgren for nearly ten years of dedicated service to the people of Rhode Island. DCYF made some important strides during Jay's tenure," Carcieri said.

The DCYF has been under fire recently for the death last year of 3-year-old Thomas J. Wright, a Woonsocket boy allegedly killed by his guardians while in state care. Carcieri said Wright's death had nothing to do with Lindgren's departure.

"This is something I've been working on for some time," the governor said. Lindgren could not be reached for comment yesterday.

Carcieri said he wants the DCYF to focus on improving the licensing of foster care, constructing a new Rhode Island Training School for youth, and increasing the services available to children with mental problems.

Martinez, 45, of Pawtucket, said the department can only thrive with the support of the Family Court, community-service providers, business leaders and faith-based institutions.

"I'm prepared to bring all the stakeholders to the table," she said, "so that together we can develop family-centered, community-based programs which will address the needs of the entire family."

The governor's office was unable to say yesterday whether Martinez was the state's first Hispanic Cabinet member, but could not recall another.

LINDGREN'S REMOVAL comes just a day after Carcieri announced he would replace Dr. Patricia A. Nolan, the state's health director, with Dr. David R. Gifford; and a week after he removed Department of Business Regulation director Marilyn Shannon McConaghy, nominating A. Michael Marques to take her place.

Carcieri refused to comment yesterday on other possible changes to his Cabinet. He said there will be more announcements "shortly."

State Fire Marshal Irving J. Owens, whose five-year contract expired July 1, has submitted his name for reappointment. Carcieri's spokesman Jeff Neal said yesterday that Owens was recently told that Carcieri will conduct a national search for the position. Owens is a candidate, Neal said, but there is no timeline for filling the post.

Carcieri also refused to say what he plans to do with the Department of Environmental Management, where Frederick J. Vincent has been serving as acting director since November 2003.

Two other departments are also being run by acting directors: Human Services, led by Ronald A. Lebel since August 2003; and Mental Health, Retardation and Hospitals, run by Kathy Spangler since March.

Carcieri said that, when he took office two years ago, he held over a number of department heads from the last administration. Now, with a better idea about how state government works, Carcieri said: "I have my own views on where we need to move some of the agencies, and in the process, sometimes think it is healthy to have a fresh viewpoint."

MARTINEZ IMMIGRATED to Central Falls from Colombia at 15. She spent the past two years as Carcieri's director of community relations, working with community groups and other constituents, facilitating messages to and from the governor's office. The job paid $85,067 a year. If confirmed by the Senate as DCYF director, Martinez would earn $127,501.

Prior to that, she had worked for the Providence School Department for three years facilitating relationships between parents and the schools. From 1988 to 2000, she was the executive director of Progreso Latino, a nonprofit organization based in Central Falls.

State law requires the DCYF director to hold a master's degree in social work or "a closely related field" and have "demonstrated experience" in child welfare, children's mental health or juvenile justice."

The director must also have at least five years of "increasing responsibility in administering programs for children."

Martinez has a Rhode Island College bachelor's degree in social work. She also received a master's degree, in the generalized field of human services, from Springfield College, in Springfield, Mass., in 1999. The college has a school of social work, but Martinez earned her degree from the college's separate school of human services, according to a school spokeswoman. Neal said her master's thesis was on temporary employment agencies.

While Martinez has not spent five years administering programs, she and Carcieri said that a large part of her work has involved children and families.

Sen. John C. Revens Jr., D-Warwick, who wrote the law in 1979 creating the child-welfare department, said yesterday he did not know whether Martinez meets the qualifications.

If she does not, Revens said, the Senate cannot confirm Martinez without changing the law.

"We can't violate law, as much as the governor might want to advocate that we can," he said. "I feel strongly, and have for years, that the director of that department needs special qualifications and that's why the statute details some of those."

Senate President Joseph A. Montalbano, D-North Providence, said the appointment would probably go to the Judiciary or Health and Human Services Committee. He said, "it will be important that the nominee does meet the criteria."

The degree requirement was a problem in 1984 when then Governor-elect Edward D. DiPrete nominated Adelaide Luber for the post. Luber did not have a master's degree. DiPrete withdrew her name and she went on to head the Department of Elderly Affairs.

THE DCYF employs more than 820 people and has an annual budget of $143.6 million that could swell to $152 million by year's end because of cost overruns.

The overruns stem, in part, from the department's failure to implement changes planned when the budget was drafted. In particular, the DCYF has not created step-down facilities to ease the transition of children out of costly psychiatric hospitals.

Former Gov. Lincoln C. Almond appointed Lindgren to head the DCYF in 1995. Lindgren had previously worked as a Texas juvenile corrections administrator and in juvenile corrections programs in Minnesota. His annual salary was $133,876.

Lindgren will not become eligible for a state pension until August, according to state retirement system records. If he works until then, Lindgren, 61, could collect a pension estimated at $22,700 a year.

Neal said that Lindgren would be part of a short transition at the DCYF, and would then probably continue serving the state for another six months to a year, in a position outside the DCYF that is still being discussed.

With reports from Katherine Gregg and Liz Anderson of the State House bureau.

Martinez To Head DCYF

Jim Baron
The Pawtucket Times
01/13/2005

PROVIDENCE -- Calling it "one of the toughest jobs in state government," Gov. Donald Carcieri has named Patricia Martinez as director of the Department of Children, Youth and Families (DCYF).

Undaunted by that job description, Martinez said she believes "Rhode Island could become a national model for the delivery of services to our youth and our families."

Martinez, a longtime community activist who was director of Progreso Latino in Central Falls for 12 years, succeeds Jay Lindgren, who served nearly 10 years in the director's chair.

"I have observed Patricia and her work for several years now," said Carcieri, who hired her to be his administration's director of community relations in 2003, "and am confident that she will do a terrific job breathing new life into this important department."

"The issues at DCYF are incredibly complex," the governor told an assemblage of Martinez's friends and colleagues at a Wednesday morning press conference. "And the threats to the well-being of our children are very real. We cannot forget that the work performed at DCYF touches the lives of some of our most vulnerable families in some of our most under-served communities.

"Patricia's background and experience make her uniquely qualified for this post. Not only does she possess the skills necessary to manage an agency of this size and complexity.She also has a unique ability to work with the community.From her time as a community activist, and as the former director of one of Rhode Island's most important community organizations, Patricia understands the importance of building partnerships to achieve goals and of building programs to meet the needs of children."

A Pawtucket resident, Martinez, 45, will earn $127,501 at her new post, according to Carcieri spokesman Jeff Neal, up from her $85,067 salary as director of community relations. When Martinez was asked what her salary would be, she answered, "I honestly have no clue." Her nomination must be confirmed by the Senate.

After the announcement of her appointment, Martinez said DCYF is now poised to "develop a very strong system of care. That needs to be part of the framework. And that system of care is to look at the community engagement, developing service and programs that are community based, that are family-centered, where the family has a voice in their plan."

Asked about taking on one of the toughest jobs in state government, Martinez, said, "looking at my passion for what we need to do for kids and families -- after reflecting a lot, praying a lot -- I finally think we could make a huge difference in Rhode Island.

"Whenever there is anything to do with children," she told The Times. "I always look at the investments that we need to make to make sure that we don't lose a generation. A generation that is not only affecting the children who are being impacted by the lack of services or what have you, but a generation that will affect all of us.

"If we don't have a productive workforce, if we don't develop successful youth, it is going to affect your pocket, my pocket and everyone else's pocket."

Carcieri had to be prodded by reporters to acknowledge that he made the decision to replace Lindgren, saying "it was time for a different direction" at DCYF.

The governor emphasized that Lindgren's departure was not caused by the beating death of 3-year-old T.J. Wright of Woonsocket while he was in DCYF foster care.

"It's not a question of being a scapegoat for what happened, not at all," Carcieri told reporters. "I hope the media does not play this as somehow Director Lindgren is leaving because of the death of a 3-year-old child in Woonsocket. That is not the case."

Carcieri said Lindgren would stay on the state payroll temporarily in another capacity, which he did not specify. Neal said the details of Lindgren's new role has not been finalized, and he did not know whether Lindgren would keep receiving the $133,876 salary he earned at DCYF.

John Barry, Pawtucket city councilor and head of the secretariat of social ministry for the Diocese of Providence, said, "I have known Patricia since the late 1970s. She was one of the first people I hired at Project Hope. She has a tremendous ability to bring people together.

"She is assuming a tough job," Barry added, "but she has a great faith, and her faith will see her through."

Before joining the governor's office as director of community relations in 2003, Martinez worked for the Providence School Department as the facilitator for families and community partnerships.

She is the recipient of numerous leadership and achievement awards, and has served on many community boards and commissions. Martinez earned a master's of management, health and human services from Springfield College, and a bachelor's of social work from Rhode Island College.

Martinez has extensive experience working provide services to families and children who were involved with the Department of Children, Youth and Families, including foster care, case management, childcare licensing and working with youth in the training school.

Governor Nominates Ovalles For District Court Judge

Jim Baron
The Pawtucket Times
01/11/2005

PROVIDENCE -- Rafael A. Ovalles, a native of the Dominican Republic who immigrated to Providence at age 10, was nominated to be a District Court judge by Gov. Donald L. Carcieri Monday.

Ovalles, 40, is a lawyer practicing in Providence who also serves as a bail commissioner in Pawtucket and Central Falls. He is fluent in Spanish.

"Rafael Ovalles is an accomplished lawyer who will bring his legal intellect and extensive experience in the community to the District Court," Gov. Carcieri said. "He is a compassionate and caring person who is committed to making sure that every person is treated fairly. These qualities are integral to our judicial system. I am proud to put forward Mr. Ovalles as our state's next District Court judge."

Ovalles currently serves on two state court committees -- the state Supreme Court's Committee on Character and Fitness and the Implementation Committee for Court Interpreter Certification.

He previously served on the Court's Committee on Women and Minorities. Ovalles earned his bachelor of arts in history from the University of Rhode Island, where he graduated magna cum laude, and a juris doctorate from Boston University School of Law. As a law student, he was the president of the Hispanic-American Law Student Association. He is a graduate of Classical High School.

He is a member of the Thurgood Marshall Law Society of Rhode Island and has served on the board of directors for the International Institute of Rhode Island and the Federal Hill House Association.

He beat out four other candidates whose names the Judicial Nominating Commission submitted to Carcieri. They were Family Court Magistrate Debra E. DiSegna of Narragansett, Joseph P. Ippolito Jr. of Warwick, Mary E. McCaffrey of Warwick, and Kristin E. Rodgers of Warwick.

The Senate must confirm his nomination under its advisc and consent authority.

"I am grateful for the trust that Gov. Carcieri has placed in me," Ovalles said, adding he was honored by the appointment to the District Court.

"Serving as a judge is a tremendous responsibility and I look forward to serving in this capacity if I am confirmed by the Senate."

Ovalles lives in Providence with his wife, Gladys, and daughter, Katherine, 9.

Latina Leadership Class Puts Emphasis On Social Advocacy, Political Involvement

David Casey
The Patucket Times
01/04/2005

PROVIDENCE -- The Latina Leadership Institute's fourth annual leadership class is coming to Central Falls, Pawtucket and Providence in 2005.

The Institute, a program of The Rhode Island Latino Civic Fund, is currently accepting applications from a new batch of ambitious, upward-mobile Latinas from every corner of the Ocean State.

The idea behind the Institute is simple, according to President Tomas Alberto Avila: prepare Latinas for political leadership and social advocacy roles and, in doing so, increase political representation and social opportunity for Latinas -- burning the candle of gender and ethnic disparity at both ends, as it were.

In a related statement issued on New Year's day, RILCF noted that the "Latina Leadership Institute's commitment ..extends beyond helping Latino women succeed. The fellows are viewed by The Latina Leadership Institute as agents of a much wider transformation."

The Institute will host eight four-hour classes in each of the aforementioned cities starting on March 12.

Latinas of all ages and socio-economic backgrounds are invited to enroll, free of charge, by Jan. 28.

The Institute's curriculum is geared toward leadership development, networking, mentoring and community involvement.

Students will have the opportunity to hobnob with established and up-and-coming Latina leaders (this year's faculty includes Central Falls resident Carmen Mirabel, Section 8 director with the Rhode Island Housing and Mortgage Finance Corporation) while learning about public policy, leadership theory, strategic management, team building, political campaigning, public speaking, media relations and -- of course -- the myriad racial, class and gender issues facing the state's mushrooming Latina population.

Progreso Latino Executive Director Edwin Cancel, whose Central Falls-based organization will host classes this year, hailed the Institute as a valuable resource for local Latinas.

"There are not a lot of Latinas in political leadership roles in Rhode Island, and I think that any program that helps with skill development and encourages networking is good for our community," he said.

In 2002 the Women's Fund of Rhode Island, a subset of the Rhode Island Foundation, published "The Status of Women in Rhode Island," a statistical study of women's relative health, economic success and political activity in the Ocean State.

Avila and his RILCF colleagues were surprised to learn that female Rhode Islanders exhibited some of the lowest levels of political participation and representation in the country.

Avila would soon discover that Rhode Island's Latinas were much worse-off than their white counterparts.

The problem and its ostensible solution, the prototypical Latina Leadership Institute, crystallized when RILCF considered another sign of Latina detachment: a steady stream of requests for Latina board members, commissioners and councilors from a wide array of public and private organizations.

Latinas interested in enrolling should send their name, organization (if applicable), address, phone and e-mail address to RILCF at latinocivicfund@yahoo.com or Doris De Los Santos at goroi@cox.net or by fax at 633-6535.

State Senate District 5 Candiate
Alexis Gorriarán

Alexis Gorriarán is a candidate for State Senate in District 5, in Providence. The district includes parts of Federal Hill, Olneyville, the West End, downtown Providence, Silver Lake and Mt. Pleasant.

Alexis' talents span the non-profit, private and public sectors. He is a native Rhode Islander, of Cuban descent. Alexis speaks fluent Spanish, representing a progressive multi-cultural perspective. He was raised in a Spanish-speaking household in Warwick, in an environment of inclusion, equality and acceptance.

As a homeowner in the Federal Hill neighborhood for four years, Alexis' decision to run for public office is rooted in a deep desire to be a positive agent for change for the entire neighborhood and all Rhode Islanders. His passion for our community and energetic leadership will prove to be a strong voice on Capitol Hill.

Rev. Jesse Jackson and Alexis Gorriarán   Alexis at Providence City Hall Rally

Alexis attended Bishop Hendricken High School, where he excelled in sports including wrestling, football, and track. It was at this same time that Alexis became interested in community service and contributing his energy to many worthy causes and programs with a social conscience.

After graduating from the University of Rhode Island with a Bachelor of Science in Business Administration and Marketing with a minor in Spanish, he began his successful professional career. From 1995 through 2004, Alexis worked as the Director of Marketing for Hook-Fast Specialties, a local jewelry manufacturing company. During that period he also managed his own business Pride Promotions. He is currently employed at Advertising Ventures as the agency's Manager of Marketing and Multicultural Affairs. Through his work he has had the opportunity to provide strategic business solutions for the many challenges that organizations and individuals face in their respective industries in Rhode Island and throughout the country.

In 2004, Alexis graduated with the Omega Class of Leadership Rhode Island where he broadened his understanding of the diverse issues and challenges facing Rhode Island communities. He developed life long personal relationships with fellow public and private sector leaders through his participation in Leadership Rhode Island.

In 2002, Alexis served for the Mayor's Office in Providence as the Liaison to the Gay, Lesbian, Bisexual and Transgender (GLBT) community. In that capacity, he coordinated diversity & sensitivity training programs for the Providence Police Department, Progreso Latino, local businesses and city agencies in both Spanish and English. He also worked to enhance communications between various organizations in the arts and business communities.

From 1996 to 2005, Alexis served as the Co-chair of Rhode Island Pride. He developed various programs and services for the GLBT and Arts community and its supporters. Under Alexis' leadership, Rhode Island Pride forged partnerships with City and State agencies, businesses, organizations and the hospitality industry to make Providence and Rhode Island a welcoming place for all.

The Gorriarán family has contributed to the state of Rhode Island and the nation in many areas including business development, medicine, education and athletics. This legacy of community involvement and servant leadership has inspired Alexis and has been part of his development as an individual and community leader. Alexis has continued to embrace this family legacy through his dedication and commitment to non-profit organizations, businesses and community building initiatives throughout Rhode Island. Alexis has worked to address the social, health and political barriers multicultural individuals face in the community, at work, homes and schools due to their ethnicity, culture, religion, sexual orientation or well being.

Alexis will work for a healthy and safe neighborhood, economic revitalization, high quality, good paying jobs, small business development, arts and cultural initiatives, affordable housing, education reform, affordable healthcare, women's rights, civil and GLBT rights, and equality on all levels of government.

The Latinos Take It To The Next Level

More candidates, more challenges, and the quest for clout

By: MATTHEW JERZYK
8/18/2006

The latest US Census data showing a growing number of immigrants living in the US, including many from Mexico won't come as a surprise to anyone familiar with Rhode Island politics.

Indeed, with 11 Latinos running for the Providence City Council, and 11 more running for the General Assembly in communities extending from Newport to Providence this heightened level of participation is not just the next stage in the statewide development of Latino political power, but also a harbinger of things to come.

Building on earlier successes, Latino candidates can be expected to run in greater numbers, and for more offices. Once again, candidates as ideologically opposed as Sheldon Whitehouse and Stephen P. Laffey are aggressively courting Latino voters. And although a big increase in Latino representation in the General Assembly seems off in the future, it's probably only a matter of time before a viable Latino candidate runs for mayor in Providence.

Over the last 10 years, as Latinos became challengers in the political arena, and then winners, these newcomers are being forced to defend their record and their ability to advance an agenda for the common good. While difficult challenges remain, real progress has been made, and pacesetters like state Senator Juan Pichardo (D-Providence) are proud, "because we planted seeds, and the seeds have grown, and are producing many new leaders and civic-minded community leaders."

What about the results?

On a recent Saturday afternoon in Providence's Washington Park neighborhood, Pichardo and a friend celebrated 10 years of friendship in an unusual style: a combined pig roast and political fundraiser.

Pichardo and former local activist Victor Capellan, now a principal in Brooklyn, New York, mingled and laughed with about 100 of the people who have accompanied them on their journey to empower and educate Rhode Island's Latino community. Some told stories of past races lost. Some reflected with satisfaction on Pichardo's 2002 victory, when he became the first Dominican-American state senator in the US. Still others wondered about the unprecedented number of Latino candidates this year. And all could take pride in helping to bring fresh energy to Rhode Island politics.

Questions persist, however, as to just what kind of political power is being developed, and whether this power can influence high-level policy-making and thus bring needed change on such issues as public education, quality health-care, and affordable housing.

The difficulty of being part of the establishment no easy task has supplanted the challenges of running against the establishment. Creating a common agenda among minority legislators, building coalitions, and winning legislation will be the true test of the success of rising Latino political power in Rhode Island. As Gonzalo Cuervo, the president of Progreso Latino and the director of community relations for Providence Mayor David N. Cicilline, says, "Latino political power is growing at a phenomenal pace in Rhode Island, yet the absence of a common agenda has limited the community's true potential."

One of the most glaring examples of this is the national debate on immigration. While tens of thousands of immigrants mostly Latino marched in numbers not seen in Rhode Island in decades, almost all of the elected officials who had previously curried favor with the Latino community were noticeably absent.

Political analyst Luis Peralta concludes, "Latinos don't use the power that we have. We have the organizational strength and force to change that. We are many people. In each election, we demonstrate that. But we are not using our power. It is a serious problem in the immigration debate and in other areas." Ultimately, he says, "Political awareness needs to happen every day, and not just during election time. There needs to be more engagement with people to involve them in the political world, so that the power to win elections becomes the power to influence the policy-making process in Rhode Island."

Storming the gates

Four years ago, the 2002 election marked a watershed in the political maturation of Latinos in Rhode Island. Latino voters were courted like never before, and for the first time in US history, three Dominican-Americans Pichardo, state Repre¬senta¬tive Leon Tejada, and Providence City Councilor Miguel Luna represented a single community as elected officials. (Further, Ricardo Patino won his City Council race in 2001, becoming the first Latino elected in Central Falls.) This over¬night success, though, was long in coming.

Back in 1996, when Victor Capellan mounted a run for state rep, many Latinos were not registered to vote or eligible to vote. "On top of that, the apathy we encountered was so difficult that we brought a TV into the campaign office so that people could watch their *novelas* [soap operas] while volunteering for the campaign," recalls Pichardo, who managed the effort. "It was hard . . . battling years and years of disengagement."

Pichardo and Capellan would stay up late into the night, planning and strategizing. They recruited scores of college students and blitzed South Providence neighborhoods with literature printed in English, Spanish, and Portuguese. It was the first time that a multi-lingual campaign captured the attention of voters. And while Capellan lost the race by a mere 11 votes Pichardo still believes the election was stolen it sparked a wave of political organizing that built on the efforts of previous Latino candidates.

Inspired to keep fighting, Capellan and Pichardo joined with Tomas Avila and Jhomphy Ventura to create the group Latinos for Community Advancement (LCA). In meetings with the two dominant Latino organizations, Progreso Latino and the Center for Hispanic Policy & Advocacy (ChisPA), they discovered that these groups were not promoting civic engagement and political participation. They planned for LCA to fill this gap, with a focus on voter registration and political empowerment.

Pichardo recalls getting further motivation from then-Mayor Vincent A. "Buddy" Cianci Jr. "In meetings at City Hall, Buddy would always have the maps and the charts of voters in each ward, and he would tell us that we would be ignored until we registered our people to vote," Pichardo says. "He called us politically irrelevant. We wanted to prove him wrong."

New kids on the bloc
The state's most powerful Latino political voice, the Rhode Island Latino Political Action Committee (RILPAC), emerged from LCA. RILPAC's first projects included Capellan's second campaign, in 1998, for state rep. The candidate grew his support in the Latino community and among the political establishment. One example is Sheldon Whitehouse, then a candidate for attorney general, who publicly supported Capellan and called for a more community-based legal system. While other candidates for statewide office offered crime-laden stereotypes of places like South Providence, Whitehouse joined with Pichardo and Capellan in walking and talking to voters on Broad Street.

Once again, Capellan barely lost the election, this time by 23 votes. However, in the same neighborhood, Puerto Rican native Luis Aponte was elected as the first Latino member of the Providence City Council. And even Cianci started to take notice of the fledgling Latino political movement.

In 1999, a dinosaur exhibit that was coming to Roger Williams Park threatened to displace the annual Dominican Festival.

"After protesting the possible cancellation of the festival on PODER [the Spanish-language radio station], we met with Cianci," Pichardo says. "Buddy immediately got on the phone with the superintendent of the parks department and asked, 'Do dinosaurs vote?'

" 'No.'
" 'Well, then the Dominicans are going to have their festival.'

"Buddy then brought in the photographer and took a picture with all of us."

The number of Latinos candidates, and the influence of Spanish-language media like PODER, only increased with subsequent elections. In 2002, "We created a steady debate among the candidates, and the Latino community became involved and empowered," asserts Victor Cuenca, publisher of the newspaper *Providence en Espanol*. "We worked closely with the Latino Civic Fund to ensure that Latino voters knew about the process of voting and also about how the candidates stood on the issues."

Record turnout that year in South Providence propelled not just several Latino candidates to victory, but also Latino-backed candidates like Matt Brown, David Cicilline, and Myrth York, who won respective races for secretary of state, mayor of Providence, and the Democratic gubernatorial nomination. South Providence voter turnout was an astounding 42 percent higher than four years earlier, and the Ward 9 precinct of Elmwood and Washington Park went from the second-lowest voter turnout ward in the city to the second-highest.

PODER owner Tony Mendez believes that advertising on Spanish radio was instrumental for many campaigns. "There was a dramatic increase in political advertising at our station four years ago," he says. Candidates even developed their own *merengues* and *bachatas* to accompany their commercials.

With power comes responsibility

The challenge of using power won at the ballot box is the heart of the third shift in Latino political power. This transfer happened in 2004 when Latina challenger Grace Diaz ran against incumbent Latino Representative Leon Tejada (disclosure: I managed Diaz's campaign and am managing her reelection campaign this year). Diaz, who was politically active in the Dominican Republic before becoming a leader among home-based childcare providers in 2004, shocked the political establishment by winning a three-way race with more than 52 percent of the vote. This election demonstrated that a Latino in office was not as important as a Latino in office who could govern well: move resources, pass legislation, and respond to constituents' needs.

Diaz credits another emerging part of Latino political power women with fueling her victory. "For a long time, men were dominating political conversations in the Latino community," she says. "In my campaign, dozens and dozens of Latina women volunteered, and together we delivered a message of hope for children and families. I couldn't have won without the strength of so many childcare providers and women who gained campaign skills and training through the [the RI Latino Civic Fund's] Latina Leadership Institute."

With the growing political maturation of Latinos in Rhode Island, elections involving more than one in the same race were becoming less about identity politics and more about bread and butter politics.

As Pichardo says, "It was then that we felt significant pressure because it wasn't just about the politics of South Providence anymore, but it was the burden of representing all of Dominicans in the United States and showing everyone that we can work together and deliver results for all of our constituents."

This new stage of Latino political empowerment will play a key role in the 2006 elections, with an explosion of 22 Latino candidates running for office including many against incumbent Latinos. Indeed, the multiple Latino City Council candidates in Providence's wards 8, 9, and 11 will have to run on more than just being the "Latino" candidate.

The fading of identity politics

While multiple candidacies will require Latino candidates to offer innovative policy ideas to differentiate themselves, the increased competition in the Latino political community will also result in increased voter registrations and voter turnout in the Latino community which will inevitably help the statewide candidacies of Democrats Charlie Fogarty and Sheldon Whitehouse.

Yet, political leadership not only requires better performance at the polls, but elected officials who will deliver results and offer concrete solutions to real problems facing the Latino community.

502

"Our support of political candidates needs to be based on specific policy initiatives that have an impact in our communities," says Dr. Pablo Rodriguez, a prominent community activist and RILPAC's first president, "and not on their attendance at our events and having Spanish materials or staff. These policies need to be clear and disseminated in English and Spanish so everyone, including non-Latinos knows where the candidate stands."

The number of Latino candidates does not concern RILPAC president Domingo Morel, who suggests that it is a natural outgrowth in a state with a growing Latino population: "It is a positive step for democracy and a sign of political maturity for our community."

However, with so many Latino candidates running for office, there is a real chance that the Latino representation could slip. There's a good chance, for example, that the Latino vote will be diluted in Provi¬dence's Ward 9, where there is one African-American candidate and three Latino candidates. As notes Evelyn Duran, a recent Brown University graduate who was hired by the Rhode Island Democratic Party, "*Más, más, más* dialogue should be encouraged among Latino aspirants for power so the power is not divided and completely lost."

Like many of Rhode Island's politically empowered ethnic communities the Irish, Italians, and the Portuguese Latinos and their relative clout will depend on strong social movements, mass political participation at the ballot box, and the complex interactions of individual leadership. It remains to be seen whether increased competition in 2006 will dilute or strengthen their political power. Younger leaders like Duran and Morel, schooled on the pitfalls and the successes of the last 10 years, might very well make the difference.

Capital Power

Providence remains the political base for RI's Latinos

By: MATTHEW JERZYK
8/17/2006

In 2002, it was no mere coincidence that David N. Cicilline's Providence mayoral campaign placed its campaign headquarters on Elmwood Avenue, in the heart of the capital city's Latino community. Latino voter registrations and voter turnout in Providence surged in 2000 and grew further in city elections in 2002. That year, with the victory of Councilman Miguel Luna (Ward 9) and the re-election win of Councilman Luis Aponte (Ward 10), two of the 15 council members were Latinos, a first for Providence. This year, voter registration has surged and the number of Latino elected officials could easily double with candidates running in Wards 7 (Doris de los Santos), 8 (Leon Tejada and Eulogio Acevedo), 11 (Jose Brito) and 15 (Sabina Matos). Dozens of Latinos, looking to give a makeover to Providence's very white city Democratic Committee, are also running for ward committee seats.

Besides Providence, Central Falls is the only other Rhode Island city — based on Census data — that is required to have the ballot printed in English and in Spanish. Although Latino representation long lagged behind the growth of that city's Colombian and Dominican communities, Ricardo Patino (elected in 2001) was joined by Luis Alfredo Gil in 2005. The presence of the social-services group Progreso Latino on Broad Street, in the heart of Central Falls, has assisted in registering and empowering the Latino community.

In Cranston, Emilio Navarro recently won the Democratic endorsement for the Ward 2 City Council seat and could become the city's first Latino councilman. Also, Ivan Marte is running for the state Senate seat being vacated by Elizabeth Roberts. In Woonsocket, Stella Guerra-Brien mobilized the large Latino community in 2000 when she won her race for state representative. And in Newport, David Quiroa is registering more Latinos to vote as he makes a second bid for state rep. Meanwhile, across Rhode Island, in Pawtucket, Warwick, West Warwick, Johnston, North Providence, and South Kingstown, Latino communities are growing, but have yet to have made their political presence felt. As in the other cities mentioned, it will take a candidate, and an organization or an inspired leader, to turn presence into power.

Chafee Faces Critics Of TV Ad About Hispanics

Members of the local community say the advertisement, aimed at Stephen Laffey and paid for by a national GOP campaign unit, makes Hispanics look like terrorists.

By Karen Lee Ziner
Journal Staff Writer
Saturday, September 2, 2006

PROVIDENCE -- Latino immigrant advocates confronted U.S. Sen. Lincoln D. Chafee yesterday for delaying denouncement of a "divisive," "anti-Hispanic" and "highly charged" television ad aimed at Cranston Mayor Stephen P. Laffey, Chafee's opponent in this month's Republican primary.

The ad came off the air this week. It was not pulled; it ran its course of 9 or 10 days, according to the sponsoring National Republican Senatorial Committee (NRSC), which supports Chafee.

The ad warned that Laffey's acceptance of Mexican consular ID cards in Cranston poses "a threat to national security." During a news conference outside Chafee's office, critics said it made Hispanics look like terrorists.

Governments issue consular, or "matricula," ID cards to show the bearer is a foreign national living outside his or her country. Laffey announced last year that Cranston recognizes Mexican and Guatemalan consular IDs.
The ad in question stated:

"The matricula ID card. Used by millions of illegal Mexican immigrants . . .The FBI has warned the Mexican ID cards accepted by Steve Laffey can be used to gain access to other documents, to get a driver's license, gain access to government buildings, board airplanes . . .Mayor Stephen Laffey accepts Mexican ID cards that can threaten our national security. Will he put our security at risk in the Senate?"

"I think this commercial is anti-Mexican," said Julio César Aragn said the ad conveyed a message that "all Mexicans are not good."
Chafee, who stepped outside the office to face his critics, said he complained to an NRSC representative this week about the ad, but whether or not it contributed to the ad coming off the air, he couldn't say.

"I'm not sure, to be honest," Chafee said. "I made my feelings known."

Chafee empathized with his critics, but attributed his delayed response to "the reality of independent ads," over which he said he had no control.

"I never saw it until it was on everybody's TV. I saw it when everybody else saw it. I had the exact same feeling, and once you get into stereotyping or any kind of zeroing in on any population, it's not fair," the senator said.

Chafee aide Stephen Hourahan clarified that the topic came up while Chafee was speaking with an NRSC member at his Warwick campaign headquarters. The senator "just expressed his opinion that the ad had missed the whole point and he was dissatisfied with it, and the person he was talking to had no control over the ad either," Hourahan said.

"If people thought this was an ad done by Senator Chafee or his campaign, that would be incorrect," said NRSC spokesman Dan Ronayne. He said an NRSC "independent expenditure unit" controls the content, timing and message, and Chafee "has no input. If he did, he would break the law."

But critics, who included representatives of the Rhode Island Latino Political Action Committee, the Immigrants in Action Committee of St. Teresa D'Avila Church and the Mexican-American Association, didn't buy that. They pinned the blame on Chafee by noting that the ad was run on his behalf.

Senator Juan Pichardo, D-Providence, wrote a letter to Chafee a week ago, urging the senator to denounce the ad and try to get it pulled. Yesterday, Pichardo said, "The main point is we should not be portraying the immigrant community as terrorists -- it doesn't belong in Rhode Island."
Immigrant community ire heightened after Chafee called the ad "accurate" during a Saturday night debate broadcast on Channel 10 (WJAR).

Commenting on Chafee's complaint to the NRSC member, Pichardo and others at the news conference called it "too little, too late."

"If he felt that way, he should have tried to have it pulled in the beginning," Pichardo said, adding that the real focus should be on working toward immigration reform.

State Rep. Grace Diaz, D-Providence, said it's like being sick and waiting too long before getting a prescription. She added, "We are working so hard to make sure that [Anglo] citizens understand we are not terrorists."

The Laffey campaign weighed in yesterday as well.

"During the debate, Senator Chafee called the attack ad accurate, and now that the ad has run its course, he is conveniently changing his mind," said Laffey spokeswoman Nachama Soloveichik. "Rhode Islanders deserve a senator who knows where he stands, not a senator who keeps changing his mind."

Chafee likewise accused Laffey of a flip-flop.

"Three months ago, [Laffey] was in favor of consular cards," Chafee said. But now, "he doesn't call them immigrants any more. They're aliens. That's a flip-flop. He calls them aliens. That's the main point I want to make."

Not every Latino in the crowd agreed with the news conference sponsors. Reynaldo Almonte, host of a Hispanic talk show on radio station 88.1 FM (WELH), called the matter "a political issue for Juan Pichardo." He accused Pichardo of trying to bolster support for Democratic U.S. Senate candidate Sheldon Whitehouse.

Almonte said he concurred with the government's assessment that the consular ID cards were subject to fraud.

"You can buy them on Broad Street and Cranston Street," said Almonte, who is from the Dominican Republic. "It's not an anti-Hispanic commercial."

Latino Lawmaker Asks Chafee
To Disavow Ad

The television ad shows images of Hispanic men being herded into van by a law enforcement agent.

The Providence Journal
Tuesday, August 29, 2006

PROVIDENCE (AP) -- One of Rhode Island's top Hispanic lawmakers has asked Sen. Lincoln Chafee to denounce a television ad run by a Republican group supporting his bid for reelection because he said it could engender fear and prejudice against Hispanics.

The ad running on local broadcast and cable television accuses Cranston Mayor Stephen P. Laffey of being weak on national security because he has allowed the city to accept foreign identification cards presented by Mexican and Guatemalan immigrants.

Laffey is running against Chafee in the Sept. 12 Republican primary. Polls have shown it to be a very close race.

The National Republican Senatorial Committee, which backs Chafee, began running an ad last week that criticizes Laffey for Cranston's acceptance of matricula identification cards from Mexico. Laffey announced last year that the city would accept the identification cards Mexico and Guatemala issue to their citizens living abroad.

The NRSC ad shows images of Hispanic men being herded into van by a law-enforcement agent and says immigrants can use fake cards to get driver's licenses, enter government buildings and board planes.

State Sen. Juan Pichardo, D-Providence, sent Chafee a letter dated Friday asking him to renounce the spot.

"The ad's script and imagery are clearly meant to engender fear that, as a group, Hispanic immigrants present a threat to the security of Rhode Island and the nation," wrote Pichardo, a naturalized citizen who emigrated from the Dominican Republic. "I am deeply concerned that as a result, the ad will unfairly create feelings of prejudice and suspicion toward the Hispanic community as a whole."

Chafee described the ad as accurate during a Saturday night debate with Laffey.

But his spokesman Ian Lang referred questions to the NRSC after Pichardo's letter appeared yesterday on a Democratic Web site.

"This is not our ad, we have nothing to do with it," Lang said.

NRSC spokesman Dan Ronayne denied that the ad was anti-Hispanic in tone. "This ad is about our national security, and it speaks to concerns raised by the FBI," he said.

Latinos In R.I.: An Expanding Presence

The 2005 American Community Survey confirms what is anecdotally evident: Rhode Island's Latino population is growing.

By Karen Lee Ziner
Journal Staff Writer
Friday, August 18, 2006

New Census data confirms what is anecdotally evident in the state's increasing Hispanic commercial and political clout: the number of Latinos living in Rhode Island households has spiked by more than 24 percent in five years. That growth spurt follows an upward trend that has more than quadrupled the state's total Latino population since 1980, and as of the 2000 census, brought it within 9 percent of the state's total population. It also mirrors national findings that immigrants from Latin America constitute a majority (53 percent) of the 7.9 million new immigrants who arrived in the country between 2000 and 2005.

Unlike the once-a-decade full census that measures all population, the 2005 American Community Survey released this week measures only household populations. It excludes so-called group quarters populations, such as people living in prisons, universities and nursing homes.

The survey lists the number of Latinos living in Rhode Island households at 112,722. The data preclude an apples-to-apples comparison, but this is clear: the 2005 household population exceeds by 24.1 percent the 90,820 total Latino population measured in 2000.

Meanwhile, the black or African-American household population in Rhode Island increased by 22.4 percent during the past five years -- from 42,358 to 51,843 -- while the comparative number of whites dropped less than 1 percent. The state's total household population inched up from 1,009,503, to 1,032,662.

"Immigration has begun to appear in what we call nontraditional states of immigration, Rhode Island being one of them" for nearly a century, says Rob Paral, research fellow with the American Immigration Law Foundation in Chicago who includes Rhode Island statistics in a report he wrote that's based on the new Census data.

"What's happening to attract these people is that there's really been an explosive growth of a lot of jobs that natives are not so interested in, more specifically in the service sector" and the construction industry, he said. "We see this in quite a few states around the country."

The immigrant influx is stabilizing Rhode Island's population, as well as that of Massachusetts, Pennsylvania and Connecticut, Paral said.

"As you know, the U.S. population for some decades has been moving south and west. If you were to erase the immigrant population, your state would have a very flat population growth. It's really immigration that's been buoying the Northeastern states," said Paral.

"Massachusetts, for example would have lost population in the past five years without immigration. Yours wouldn't have lost population, but it would have been flat."

Paral sees economic benefit to all this. "You have an aging state, and the ratio of retired workers to [non-retired] workers has been going up. So, a beneficial effect of immigration is to keep the labor force up."

The burgeoning Latino population does not surprise Leonard Lardaro, professor of economics at the University of Rhode Island.

"We're a microcosm of New England, and what we're seeing is, there is an increasing population of Hispanics," says Lardaro. "Also, you're getting people from Central and Latin America going to places they [previously] didn't go to," he says.

Ladardo referred to what researchers call nongateway states, as opposed to gateway states such as California, Florida, New York and Texas.

Tourism and hospitality make up a substantial part of Rhode Island's economy, "so certainly there's a fair number of Hispanics" in jobs such as chambermaids, cooks and janitors, Lardaro said. They are also filling lawn-service, landscape, factory and agricultural jobs.

"I think what happens is that you get enclaves and you get families . . . you get a critical mass and that brings more in," Lardaro said.

That is certainly the case with Omar Perez, who co-owns Chilangos Taquieria and Tequila Bar in Providence, a Mexican restaurant on Manton Avenue that features Casa Vieja tequila, a family brand.

"The first one to move here was my uncle," said Perez. "He got a job at the [former] Bradley soap factory in West Warwick and found it was easy here."

Perez joined his relatives 10 years ago "basically for education purposes. They [his family] decided to bring me here, because there would be a better chance than in Mexico" for educational and economic success, said Perez. After graduating from West Warwick High School, Perez moved to Providence. According to the ACS survey, Mexican migration is largely fueling the national immigration growth. Perez' story echoes that of Enrique Sanchez, who arrived in Rhode Island from New York during the summer of 1988. Sanchez opened a Mexican market in Providence at a time when few Mexicans lived in this state. He also helped start Rhode Island's first Mexican soccer teams.

Since then the Mexican population has grown to almost 8,000, according to the 2005 American Community Survey. The number of Dominicans, Guatemalans and Colombians in Latino households has also spiked.

"Most of the increase, if not all of the increase, we had from 1990 to 2000 was Latino," said Marc G. Brown, principal planner with the state Department of Administration. Brown said that without the Hispanic immigration here, "we would have lost population. Some people refer to it as white flight."

"Certainly, once a group establishes itself in a community it's a lot easier for others to come," said Brown. While jobs in the jewelry and jewelry-related industries have largely disappeared, "where the immigrant community now has a foothold throughout the country is in the tourist industry."

Julio Cesar Aragon, president of the Mexican-American Association of Rhode Island, said that Mexicans have settled in communities throughout Rhode Island where job availability spreads by word of mouth.

"Everybody is asking by telephone. They say, 'What do you do in Rhode Island?' They say, 'I work in a factory, in landscaping. My supervisor is a very nice person.' And they ask, 'Do you think your supervisor has a place for me?' "

No Race Uncontested For City Council

"This is the most candidates I've seen since I've been here and I've been here 24 years," said Laurence K. Flynn, executive secretary of the Board of Canvassers.

By Cathleen F. Crowley
Journal Staff Writer
Thursday, June 29, 2006

PROVIDENCE -- Almost 50 people declared their candidacy this week for the 15 City Council seats, leaving no race uncontested.

The most crowded races are for the open seats in Ward 1, where Councilman David A. Segal is running for state representative, and Ward 8, where Councilman Ronald W. Allen is not seeking reelection.

Four candidates have come forward in Ward 1, which includes Fox Point and parts of College Hill. Eight candidates declared in Ward 8, which encompasses the Reservoir and West Elmwood neighborhoods.

"This is the most candidates I've seen since I've been here and I've been here 24 years," said Laurence K. Flynn, executive secretary of the Board of Canvassers.

Joan Badway, chairwoman of the Democratic City Committee, said "people have seen a change in the city with the mayor and I think they want to see it in the City Council."

All but three incumbents -- Ward 3's Kevin Jackson, Ward 6's Joseph DeLuca, and Ward 12's Terence M. Hassett -- face challengers in the Democratic primary.

Political lines are already being drawn in the Democratic Party. Two incumbents did not receive the endorsement from their ward committees.

Majority Leader Luis A. Aponte, of Ward 10, said he wasn't surprised he was not endorsed. Six of the Ward 10 Democratic committee members were appointed by Badway, who was a member of the the city's Board of Licenses when it approved a liquor license for the Cadillac Lounge. Aponte fought to get the licensing decision overturned. The decision was upheld but Badway was not reappointed to the board.

All six of Badway's appointees voted to endorse Pedro J. Espinal, Aponte said.

"Coincidence?" Aponte asked.

In Ward 9, challenger Kas R. DeCarvalho was endorsed over Councilman Miguel C. Luna. DeCarvalho decided to run after the council blocked his appointment to the Zoning Board of Review.

"It's the same committee that didn't endorse me last time and I still won the election," Luna said.
A few endorsements are still up in the air, including Ward 5, where Patrick K. Butler is running for a third term. The committee was expected to make a decision last night.

Incumbent Rita M. Williams was endorsed by the Ward 2 Democratic Committee over challenger Clifford J. Wood, who left Mayor David N. Cicilline's administration to run for the council.

Republican forces in the city have put up candidates for 12 of the 15 council seats. Only Wards 13, 14, and 15 do not have Republican candidates "unless someone comes out of the woodwork," said David B. Talan, chairman of the Republican City Committee.

Talan is pleased with the Republican turnout, which includes three black candidates and six Hispanic candidates.

"Republicans are going to file candidates or support [independent] candidates in 30 out of the 36 Providence races," he said. "It's the highest number ever."

In 2004, Republicans had only 12 candidates.

"It's a sign of the growing resurgence of our party," said Talan, who is running for mayor.

The three-day period to declare their candidacy ended yesterday. The candidates now must collect 50 signatures of eligible voters and return the papers by July 14.

"A lot of people file declarations but it's when you bring the papers back that it counts," Flynn said. "That's the real question of whose running."
According to an unofficial tally at City Hall last night, these people declared candidacy for City Council:

Ward 1, College Hill and Fox Point: **Ethan W. Ris** , Democrat, 90 Sheldon St.; **Seth Yurdin** , Democrat, 148 Governor St.; **Mark G. Teoli** , Republican, 22 Governor St.; and **Pasquale R. Petrunt** , 126 Governor St., independent.

Ward 2, College Hill, Blackstone and Wayland Square: Incumbent **Rita M. Williams** , Democrat, 76 Savoy St.; **Clifford J. Wood** , Democrat, 299 Doyle Ave.; and **Robert Farago** , Republican, 162 Freeman Parkway.

Ward 3, Mount Hope: Incumbent **Kevin Jackson** , Democrat, 91 Jenkins St.; and **James W. Kelley III** , Republican, 120 8th St.

Ward 4, North End: Incumbent **Carol A. Romano** , Democrat, 33 Manhattan St.; **Nicholas J. Narducci Jr** ., Democrat, 36 Langdon St.; and **Eze As** , Republican, 14 Squanto St.

Ward 5, Mount Pleasant and Elmhurst: Incumbent **Patrick K. Butler,** , Democrat, 63 Hilltop Ave.; **Michael A. Solomon** , Democrat, 174 Enfield Ave.; and **Laura Archambault** , Independent, 40 Roslyn Ave.
Ward 6, Mount Pleasant, Manton and Fruit Hill: Incumbent **Joseph DeLuca,** Democrat, 191 Carleton St.; and **Larry R. Shetler** , Republican, 507 Manton Ave.

Ward 7, Silver Lake: Incumbent **John J. Igliozzi** , Democrat, 19 Legion Memorial Drive; **Doris M. De Los Santos,** , Democrat, 61 Dewey St.; and **Edward R. Froehlich Jr.** , Republican, 10 Boundary Ave.

Ward 8, Reservoir and West Elmwood: **Eulogio Acevedo** , Democrat, 677 Cranston St.; **Janelle L. Costa** , Democrat, 55 Woodmont St.; **Wilbur W. Jennings Jr** ., 115 Sinclair Ave.; **Alexander N. Moore** , Democrat, 22 Ansel Ave.; **Julio C. Ramos** , Democrat, 617 Cranston St.; **Leon F. Tejada** , Democrat, 66 Stadden St.; **John P. Tomasso,** Democrat, no address available; **Evaristo Rosario** , Republican, 22 Calder St.; **Lauren Contursi** Independent, no address available.

Ward 9, Elmwood and Washington Park: Incumbent **Miguel C. Luna** , Democrat, 146 Warrington St.; **Kas DeCarvalho** , Democrat, 154 Miller Ave.; **Wellington P. Garcia** , Democrat, 2 Sackett St.; **Hector R. Jose** , Democrat, 560 Public St.; and **Yvon Chancy** , Republican, 100 Carr St.

Ward 10, Lower South Providence and Washington Park: Incumbent **Luis A. Aponte** , Democrat, 208 Washington Ave.; **Pedro J. Espinal** , Democrat, 179 Massachusetts Ave.; **Michael McSoley** , Democrat, 161 New York Ave.; and **Raymond Fay** , Republican, 1047 Eddy St.

Ward 11, South Providence, part of West End, North Elmwood and Jewelry District: Incumbent *Balbina A. Young* , Democrat, 1 Chestnut St., Unit 111; *Jose R. Brito* , Democrat, 603 Broad St., Unit 2; *Raymond Don Burns* , Republican, 64 Whitmarsh St.; and *Chester C. "Buddy" George* , who filed as a Democrat and as an independent, 162 Prairie Ave.

Ward 12, Smith Hill, Mount Pleasant and Capital Center District: Incumbent *Terrence M. Hassett* , Democrat, 15 Higgins Ave.; and *Daniel P. Martel* , Republican, 408 North Main St.

Ward 13, Federal Hill, West Broadway, Armory and West End: Incumbent *John J. Lombardi* , Democrat, 48 Grove St.; and *Leslie R. Papp II* , Democrat, 88 Dexter St.

Ward 14, Mount Pleasant, Elmhurst and Wanskuck: Incumbent *Peter S. Mancini* , Democrat, 104 Meridian St.; and *Robert J. Lennon* , Democrat, 26 Rome Ave.

Ward 15, Olneyville, Silver Lake Annex and West Broadway: Incumbent *Josephine DiRuzzo* , Democrat, 141 Roosevelt St.; and *Sabina Matos* , Democrat, 35 Florence St.

'A Day Without An Immigrant'

By Tatiana Pina
Journal Staff Writer
Tuesday, May 2, 2006

High noon: Dexter Street, in Central Falls, is nearly deserted at lunchtime yesterday -- and at Taqueria Lupita, below, the chairs remain atop the tables -- as many businesses stay closed, and workers and students stay home, to honor the national strike for immigrants' rights.

At Central Falls High School yesterday, Jandira Alves, 16, and Erick Reyes, 17, sit at the computers in their English-as-a-Second Language classroom as their teacher, Alicia Migliori, talks to Persi Severino, 18. Only 4 students were present, from a class of 18.

The national day of protest hits hard in Central Falls.

Central Falls' Dexter Street looked like a ghost town yesterday, the day of the national boycott for immigrants' rights.

Latino businesses, which account for the majority of the shops on the street, were closed. Restaurants were dark, some with their chairs on the tables. The barber chairs in the hair salons sat empty. Aloe plants looked out of store windows from darkened rooms. The street, wsually bustling with people walking to the stores and an abundance of traffic, was silent until about lunch time when some people started walking through.

Stanleys, a popular burger joint, and China House, a Chinese restaurant, were among the few eating establishments that remained open.

Some businesses had posted hand-written signs or posters saying they would be closed to honor the national boycott, staged to draw attention to the contribution of immigrants and the need for immigration-law reform.

In Rhode Island, the daylong general strike had been widely promoted as "A Day without an Immigrant." People participating in the boycott were asked to stay home from work or school yesterday, and spend no money, to show the economic strength that immigrants have.

In Central Falls, where half the city's 18,000 residents are Latino, many of them recent immigrants, many of the businesses are Latino-owned.

Ricky Petro, of Florida, who was visiting his mother, was unaware of all this. He crisscrossed Dexter Street, pulling on the doors of one variety store after another. "I had no idea this was going on," Petro said. He eventually found an open convenience store and bought a soda.

Zobeida Rojas, who manages Village Pizza, on Dexter, had a day off from work. "The boss said that if other stores were closing he would close, too," she said. Rojas said the workers at the pizza place are Latino. Last week, two organizers had visited area businesses to talk about the boycott and hand out fliers, she said. Latino businesses on Broad Street were also closed. Progreso Latino, the community-services agency, closed at 12:30 p.m.

City schools also felt the boycott.

At Central Falls High School, 507 of the 993 students did not come to school. The corridors were silent, and at first lunch, there seemed to be more tables than students. On a typical day at the high school, 80 to 100 students are absent. At Calcutt Middle School, 300 of 800 students were absent. That is unusual, said Schools Supt. Patricia Watkins. Usually, she said, only about 40 are absent.

Watkins said the elementary school students -- 1,700 in all -- showed no unusual absenteeism. "I expected that some students would be out of school today," she added, "but I am surprised by the number of students who did not come."

High School principal John Kennedy said students had been talking about immigration and the boycott last week, and some of them had told their teachers that they would not be attending classes yesterday.

Watkins had made it clear there would be school yesterday. The School Department used its computerized phone system to let parents know classes would be held as usual.

Kennedy said it was not surprising that students would participate locally on a national issue. "It's going to be a very good lesson in American civics. They will have some disappointments that go with it," Kennedy said. "The results remain to be seen."

In Alicia Migliore's high school class, just 4 of her 18 English-as-a-Second Language students were present. Those students sat around a computer learning English words. Erick Reyes said the boycott focused attention on the need for hardworking illegal immigrants to be able to work in the United States, but that was no reason for students to miss school.

Of the 21 students in Richard Kinslow's ESL class, 8 showed up yesterday. "What was surprising is that ESL students are usually serious about attendance," he said. "These guys are consistently here."

Kinslow had told his students to listen to what their parents tell them about the boycott.

"When you think about the lives of immigrants, their sacrifices and their pain, it would be a sign of disrespect to be home watching the Cartoon Network," Kinslow said.

Luis Yoimi De La Cruz, 14, one of Kinslow's students, said it is important that illegal immigrants who have been working here are able to work here legally, so they can get health benefits and life insurance. "Many immigrants are not insured, and they pay a lot for medical costs."

ELSEWHERE, In Pawtucket, at least 10 businesses closed to honor the boycott. John Garan's law office, on Main Street, was one of the businesses that closed.

"Our immigration law is desperately in need of reform," said Garan, who specializes in immigration law, as he did some paperwork before heading to the 3:30 p.m. rally. "There aren't many paths to citizenship in this country -- or, at least, the ones that exist are very limited."

Linda Bannon, a staffing coordinator at Morgan Health Center, in Johnston, estimates that between 12 and 18 workers there carry immigration "green cards." Only one person on the staff at the Johnston nursing home was out of work yesterday, and that employee isn't an immigrant, Bannon said.

George Nasuti, the principal at Woonsocket High School, said absenteeism was slightly higher than usual for this time of year, but not enough so that he could attribute it to the boycott.

Economic Impact Of One-Day Protest Minimal, Officials Say

Despite participation by many workers, the day of economic protest doesn't alter business as usual for the most part.

By Paul Grimaldi
Journal Staff Writer
Tuesday, May 2, 2006

PROVIDENCE -- Several hundred marchers, many of them children, walked past Union Station yesterday morning, curling into a circle at the confluence of Sabin, Fountain and Francis streets. Chanting and clapping, the marchers sat down, stopping traffic for a few minutes.

A knot of construction workers in hard hats gathered on a street corner to watch the action. One snapped pictures with a digital camera.

On a scaffolding above them, a pair of workers wrestled with a wooden concrete form at the Westin hotel construction site. Others wove steel bars into columns for the tower going up adjacent to the Rhode Island Convention Center.

The marchers split up, the bulk moving toward the Providence Place mall as a national day of economic protest got off to a start in Rhode Island's capital city.

The knot of hard hats broke up, too, as they turned their attention back to work, a blip on the economy's radar having passed by.

"It's like a snow day," said Edward Mazze, dean of the College of Business Administration at the University of Rhode Island. "It's going to have a very short-term impact any place where there is a large immigrant population.

"In Rhode Island, the numbers are going to be insignificant."

Yesterday's events are expected to have little effect on economic activity in the state or much of the country, said economists.
Like snow drifting on a blustery day, some locales might be buried to a standstill while others would be clear down to the pavement, they said.
"When everything stops in a neighborhood, it hurts that neighborhood," Mazze said.

There are about 3,400 Latino-run businesses in the state, which produced $250 million in combined sales last year, according to Mazze, who compiles an economic forecast on Rhode Island for the nonprofit New England Economic Project.

Places such as Providence, where nearly 2,000 Latino businesses are located, might have felt the effects, Mazze said.

Residents of Pawtucket and Cranston, which have 235 and 217 Latino businesses, respectively, might have noticed something as well.

The hospitality industry is a significant part of the state's economy, having added 7,900 jobs in the last decade, more than twice the clip of the job growth rate for the overall job market, according to the state Department of Labor and Training.

But restaurants and hotels were unaffected by the protests, said Dale Venturini, president of the Rhode Island Hospitality and Tourism Association.

"I had a little trepidation thinking this was going to hurt a lot of people today," Venturini said. "But it was business as usual."

The industry is noted for its varying work hours, which may have helped people participate in the protest without throwing off their employers, she said.

"We communicated to give people options," she said of the association's membership.

Businesses in other industries could work around yesterday's events if they chose, said Peter Morici, a professor at the University of Maryland's Robert H. Smith School of Business.

Goya Foods, the country's largest Hispanic-owned food company, suspended deliveries in the United States yesterday in recognition of the protest.

Woonsocket-based CVS Corp., the nation's largest drugstore chain by number of stores, kept its drugstores open, including its Broad Street location in a primarily Hispanic neighborhood in Providence.

There were no disruptions at airlines working out of T.F. Green Airport, said an airport spokeswoman.

"This is very different than the transit workers striking in New York City," Morici said.

A transit strike last December brought the nation's largest city to a halt and forced businesspeople and others to alter plans for traveling to New York.
"People who are staying home today aren't in critical positions," Morici said, in a phone interview yesterday. "A lot of the work is going to be put off."

Estimates put the number of illegal immigrant workers in this country at about 10 million, Morici said, less than 10 percent of the nation's 144 million workers.

But those illegal immigrants account for less than 2 percent of the nation's gross domestic product, he said.
"Those folks are earning about a quarter of what everybody else does," he said.

For a low-wage worker, losing a day's pay is significant, he said.
"These people don't have a lot of staying power," he said.

March Draws Thousands

In numbers not seen since the Vietnam War, immigrants take to Providence streets in a nationwide demonstration for immigrants' rights.

By Karen Lee Ziner
Journal Staff Writer
Tuesday, May 2, 2006

PROVIDENCE -- They started with a blessing of the mops and brooms; tools of the worker trades.

Then, as people chanted, "Si se puede" (Yes, we can), trumpets blared and banners snapped in the breeze, a jubilant immigrants' rights march led off from Central High School and quickly swelled to proportions that many said they hadn't seen locally since the Vietnam War.

Rhode Island's "Day Without An Immigrant" joined a nationwide demonstration intended to underline the significant economic and social roles played by immigrants -- legal and illegal -- in the United States.

Against a backdrop of stymied congressional debate, it was also a plea for comprehensive immigration reform, including "legalization without criminalization," and a path to citizenship for the estimated 12 million people living illegally in this country.

Rhode Island's boycott was organized by a coalition of organizations and activists under the name Immigrants United. Across the state, the strike included an estimated hundreds of business shutdowns in central Latino commercial districts, consumer boycotts and worker and student absenteeism.

By any standards, yesterday's march -- the main event in Rhode Island -- was enormous, a sea of many thousands. Demonstrators left Central High School at 4:15 p.m., and reached the State House at 4:40 p.m. where a rally began. A half-hour later, marchers were still streaming up Francis Street from below the Providence Place mall.

"The American dream is not just an idea; it's a reality, and that reality has a name -- your name," said Juan Garcia, key organizer for the march and head of the Immigrants in Action Committee at St. Teresa's Church in Olneyville.

"The fact that you are here, you are making history," said Garcia at the State House rally.

A legal permanent resident who came illegally from Guatemala years ago, Garcia spoke for the undocumented millions who live in the shadows:
"We are here, asking to start the path to citizenship, not in the darkness, but to come out into the light -- as citizens," said Garcia.

As the boisterous rally went on around them, Manuel and Cynthia Osorio held aloft a box of Kellogg's Cornflakes that featured photos of Cesar Chavez, Mexican-American founder of the United Farm Workers Union, and legendary Cuban singer Celia Cruz.

"This is beautiful," said Manuel Osorio, an immigrant from Colombia who washes cars for a living. "This has to be done. We are not criminals. We pay taxes. We work hard." Osorio, who has applied for permanent residency, said he has been studying English and taking courses on starting a small business.

"It's excellent. It's a victory," said Jose Brito, president of the Greater Providence Merchants Association, who marched with a dozen Latino business owners who'd closed their restaurants, insurance agencies, beauty salons and other businesses along Broad and Cranston Streets.

In Central Falls, Dexter Street looked like a ghost town. Latino businesses, which account for the majority of shops on the street, were closed. Restaurants were dark, barber's chairs sat empty, and the street was still.

Some 40 percent of Providence's 24,800 students skipped school yesterday, despite two taped phone messages from Schools Supt. Donnie Evans, urging them to come to class. In Central Falls, 807 students, primarily from the high school and middle school, did not attend.

Magdalena Franco, a secretary at a Massachusetts company, said her boss allowed her to stay out of work yesterday.

Draped in a Mexican flag, Franco said she joined the march because "even though I have papers, it doesn't matter," she said. She wanted to support illegal immigrants "because they struggle every day to get money, to support their families and to send money to their country. It's not fair -- they're not criminals."

State Rep. Grace Diaz, who came to this country from the Dominican Republic, overstayed her visa but eventually became a citizen, joined the march because she hoped that the same country "that opened its arms for me," will open its arms "for those [who live here] in silence."

Outside of the central Latino business districts in Central Falls, Pawtucket and Providence, some businesses that rely upon unskilled immigrant labor reported that it was largely status quo.

At Blount Seafood in Warren, some employees made arrangements in advance not to come to work yesterday, but Blount's human resources director Ronnie King said there had "not been a major impact."

On a calmer day, the strike might have affected some of the fish wholesalers in Galilee, but the wind kept most of the fishing boats at the docks.
"It has not affected us at all," said John McLaughlin, general manager at Pt. Judith Fishermen's Co. on State Street. "This is a very slow time of year for us, and it's been very slow to begin with. It's windy."

The day's events began with a morning rally at Kennedy Plaza that drew several hundred people.

Melissa Lopez, of West Warwick, said she attended the rally in honor of her husband, Fernando, who, she said, had been deported to Guatemala for working illegally on a farm.

"I just came back from [Guatemala]," she said. "We can't raise our children down there. They'd have no education." Lopez said she hoped the demonstrations will pressure Congress "and they'll put a law on the books allowing him to come back."

The rally at Kennedy Plaza was followed by a 1:30 p.m. Mass at the Cathedral of Sts. Peter and Paul, at One Cathedral Square, celebrated by the Rev. Gilberto Suarez of the Roman Catholic Assumption Parish. The service included a blessing of workers carrying mops, brooms, and buckets.

Edwin Rodas, a banquet server at the Westin Providence hotel and member of Service Workers International Union Local 217, boycotted work. He wore his white apron and carried a whisk and ladle to the service to be blessed.

"I think it's great, it shows we are united. Legal or illegal, we all deserve the American dream," said Rodas, a Guatemalan immigrant and legal permanent resident.

The Rev. Daniel Trainor, pastor at the largely Hispanic Assumption Parish, served as concelebrant. Afterward, he told a personal story about his mother, who emigrated from Ireland and graduated from high school in Pawtucket.

"She wanted to become a nurse," said Father Trainor. "She applied at a local hospital. They told her, 'You will not hear from us because you are Irish and you are Roman Catholic.' "

Father Trainor said, "I feel sorry that the sons and daughters of immigrants have forgotten their past -- the pain and perserverence" that they go through. Those sons and daughters of immigrants "use these people," he said, but do not appreciate them.

With reports from Tatiana Pina, Paul Grimaldi, Linda Borg, Mark Arsenault, Richard Salit, Michael P. McKinney and Kia Hall Hayes.

Thousands Of R.I. Immigrants To Strike

Organizers across the nation are calling for a May 1 boycott to underline the significant role immigrants play in the state.

By Karen Lee Ziner
Journal Staff Writer
Sunday, April 30, 2006

If tomorrow's boycott goes as planned, hundreds of businesses will close, trash will sit at the curb, floors won't get mopped, food won't get served, manufacturing plants will slow or idle, and thousands will march in Rhode Island as part of a nationwide demonstration for immigration reform.

"We are going to be peaceful. We are going to be orderly," says Julio Cesar Aragon, head of the Mexican-American Association of Rhode Island, and one of the boycott organizers. "We are not going to give anyone a bad impression."

Many elected officials, community leaders and clergy support the strike and demonstration -- known locally as "A Day without Immigrants" -- to underline the significant role immigrants play in the state's economy, and in society.

The strike also calls for a boycott on shopping, schools, alcohol, and use of computers, the Internet, and telephones. (Providence Schools Supt. Donnie Evans sent a phone message to students' parents noting that the city's schools will be open tomorrow, and "students are expected to attend class.")

Although the event's magnitude is hard to gauge, Providence Police Maj. Paul Fitzgerald predicted it might draw as many as 10,000 participants -- far more than the 5,000-plus people who joined an April 10 immigrants' rights march in the city (one of dozens of such nationwide demonstrations).

Three events are scheduled, all in Providence: a 9 a.m. rally at Kennedy Plaza; a 1:30 p.m. "Service in Honor of Immigrant Justice" in Cathedral Square; and a march from Central High School to the State House that is scheduled to assemble at the school at 3:30 p.m.

The 9 a.m. rally will honor boycott participants and draw attention to two current efforts: contract negotiations for hotel workers at The Westin Providence, and wage negotiations for contracted janitors in downtown Providence.

Marchers will gather at Central High School at 3:30 p.m. and leave at 4:30, walking down Broad Street to Weybossett Street, stopping in front of City Hall, and ending with a rally at the mall side of the State House at 5:20 p.m.

"We're going to have a lot of police out there, closing off traffic, closing off streets," Fitzgerald said.

Juan Garcia, the key organizer and head of the Committee of Immigrants in Action (Comite de Inmigrantes en Accion) at St. Teresa Church, in Olneyville, said the march culminates a 10-year effort through that parish and beyond, to give voice to immigrants' struggles.

"Right now, the people -- we create a movement" that centers on national immigration reform, Garcia said.

That nationwide movement calls for adjusting current immigration rules to avoid future backlogs; providing legalization, rather than criminalization, and a path to citizenship, for the estimated 12 million illegal immigrants in the United States; and including "comprehensive labor rights for all immigrant workers."

Garcia stressed, "this action is pacifist."

"All media have their eyes on this march," he said. "If something negative happens, it will cause damage to this movement." Participants have been instructed to be peaceful, and "if somebody calls a [racist] name, don't listen, just keep going."

Garcia called untrue the published reports and statements on local talk-radio shows, that some store owners have been pressured into closing, or threatened with retribution if they do not join the boycott.

"Nobody from this coalition called any businesses. The people we had do this -- they talked directly to the owner," Garcia said. He suggested that by citing such threats, "maybe some people are trying to create trouble."

The Rhode Island "Day of Action for Immigrant Justice" is being coordinated by the United Immigrants Coalition of Rhode Island (Inmigrantes Unidos). Besides the Immigrants in Action Committee of St.

Teresa Church, the coalition includes the Guatemalan-American Alliance; the Mexican-American Association of Rhode Island; English in Action; Jobs with Justice; American Federation of State; County and Municipal Employees; Council 94; and Service Employees' International Union, Local 615; the Rhode Island Latino Political Action Committee; Ocean State Action; ACORN (Association of Community Organizations for Reform Now), and Direct Action for Rights and Equality, among others.

Bishop Thomas J. Tobin, head of the Roman Catholic Diocese of Providence, said he will offer "prayers and a blessing" at a 1:30 p.m. service in honor of immigrant justice, at the Cathedral of SS. Peter and Paul.

"I try not to get involved in the political aspects," Bishop Tobin said Friday. But, although neither he nor the Roman Catholic Church condones undocumented immigration, Bishop Tobin stressed the need to recognize the human rights of all people, no matter their legal status in this society.

"My participation is meant to be spiritual and pastoral, he said. "I hope I, and the Church in general, can be a moderating voice in this whole debate, and that all members of the community can work together to resolve this issue."

The Rev. Raymond Tetreault, pastor of St. Teresa Church, in Olneyville, said he has watched the momentum grow since the April 10 demonstration. A lifelong Providence resident, Father Tetreault said it was the largest march he has seen in the city.

"What this is building up to on May first is quite an extraordinary moment in our history," said Father Tetreault.

"It's like from the bottom of the heap of the working people, raising their voices and making something move," Father Tetreault said, "where the average citizen has become kind of complacent and accepting things as they are. It's going to be interesting to see where this kind of people's movement leads to."

A random sampling last week of Hispanic-owned stores and private companies whose work forces are predominantly Hispanic indicated that the economic impact may be widespread. Organizers said they believe at least 500 to 600 immigrant- and non-immigrant owned businesses have pledged to close for the day.

That includes a wide swath of Broad Street in Providence, a Latino economic power base, as well as many stores and restaurants along Atwells, Academy, Manton and Douglas avenues. Likewise, stores and restaurants will close in Central Falls, Cranston, Pawtucket and elsewhere.

The impact will probably be felt at landscaping companies and nurseries, hospitals, hotels, trucking companies, construction sites, and jewelry, textile and other manufacturing plants.

One such company is United Workshops, in East Providence. Owner Ted Nataly will be letting his workers leave early to join the march.

"We have made a very nice agreement. They are all coming in," said Nataly, and although their shift ends 4:15 p.m., "my respect for them will be that they can leave at 3 o'clock."

Roxanna Parra, assistant to the president at Motivated Temp Inc., in Cranston, said that company will be closed tomorrow. Normally, it places 450 people a day at 10 or 20 companies, Parra said.

Cesar Alvarez, a driver for Waste Management of Rhode Island, a private company that does municipal trash-hauling, said he and many fellow workers -- perhaps as many as 50 workers and drivers -- plan to join tomorrow's boycott.

"Nobody's going to work in Providence and Cranston," Alvarez said.
But Jerry Dugan, district manager for Waste Management, said: "We want people to understand that we are going to operate on a regular schedule, with some anticipated delays. But we are open for business."

"As a company, we respect the beliefs of our employees," Dugan said. "We'll make adjustments as necessary. We're asking all the residents to put out their trash on the regular day. We may experience some delays, but we will collect by the end of the week. We are sure we can accomplish that."

Of the company's more than 150 employees, possibly up to 40 percent are Hispanic or of another minority group, Dugan said.

Tom Boyd, president of Blow Molded Specialities, in Pawtucket, a maker of hollow plastic parts for medical-device components, said he rearranged the four-day work week to accommodate his employees.

Boyd said the schedule has been changed from Monday through Thursday, to Tuesday through Friday.

"It was easy," he said. "I knew about it, through some of the workers, and I said, 'Let's just swing the day.' " Nearly all his 30 employees are Hispanic.

Providence City Councilman Miguel Luna, one of a number of elected officials who are expected to join the May Day activities, said, "I think there have been a lot of misconceptions regarding the immigrants in this country, in terms of taking jobs and not paying taxes and coming here and just being on welfare."

Luna added, "Immigrants get trashed all the time. They just don't get valued. What we're trying to show with this boycott is that we do play a role in society and in the economy, at the local, state and federal level."

House Members Push
For Immigrants' Rights

The members of Congress were at Brown University last night as part of the school's commemoration of Latino History Month.

By Scott MacKay
Journal Staff Writer
Tuesday, April 25, 2006

PROVIDENCE -- Four Hispanic members of the U.S. House joined Rhode Island Representatives Patrick Kennedy and James Langevin at a Brown University forum in calling for legislation to allow immigrants in the United States illegally to earn an avenue to legal residence.

The four members of Congress -- Democrats Raul Grijalva of Arizona, Grace Napolitano and Loretta Sanchez, both of California, and Republican Ileana Ross-Lehtinen, of Florida -- all denounced what they called the "punitive" approach on immigration taken by House Republicans and said they hoped that a compromise measure sponsored by Senators John McCain, R-Arizona, and Edward M. Kennedy, D-Mass., would become law.

"In the Senate, there was some lucid thinking," said Napolitano. "You need to realize you have every kind of immigrant from all over the world in America, especially those who look like us, brown."

Most Hispanic immigrants work hard, pay their bills, stay out of trouble and support their families, the Hispanic House members said, and want what other generations of immigrants have achieved -- good jobs, stable families, economic, religious and political opportunity.

The recent marches in favor of immigrants rights that occurred across the nation in the past few weeks have been beneficial, said Grijalva. "All we've been hearing is Lou Dobbs ranting on TV and Bill O'Reilly ranting on TV and the radio talk shows saying, 'Build a wall, deport them all, take them out of school.' "

"I feel the marches were good and productive and came at a necessary time," said Grijalva.

The members of Congress came to Brown as part of the university's commemoration of Latino History Month. Langevin introduced the panel, which was moderated by Prof. Tony Affigne of Providence College, a 1976

Brown graduate who said he was one of the few Hispanic students on the campus at that time.

Under the McCain-Kennedy measure, immigrants in the United States illegally would be allowed to apply for legal residence after undergoing criminal background checks, paying back taxes, and learning English.
Patrick Kennedy is the son of Sen. Edward Kennedy and a scion of one of the nation's best known Irish-American families. Kennedy said some of the opposition to any amnesty program for Hispanic immigrants is "about discrimination."

No one seems to get all that upset, Kennedy noted, when Irish students overstay summer work permits and remain in the country illegally. "There are a lot of Sullivans, and O'Neills, and Kennedys . . . who overstay their visas."

But Americans do not get so uptight about Irish or Italian immigrants, said Kennedy, whose great-grandfather, John F. "Honey" Fitzgerald, was Boston's first immigrant mayor.

Kennedy scored President Bush's administration and House Republicans for backing guest-worker programs aimed at keeping wages down for American workers. "They like the wages lower than they would otherwise be," said Kennedy. "Every American wants those jobs, if they pay enough."

Representative Sanchez said Kennedy was correct only to a certain degree. She said it is true that some American citizens shun jobs immigrants will take solely because of low pay.

But other jobs have such low status or are so difficult that only immigrants seem to want them. For example, Sanchez said, in her California district, there are decent-paying jobs at nursing homes taking care of Alzeheimer's patients that only newly arrived immigrants from Vietnam and Mexico seem interested in. Sanchez said she hears constituents say, "The Mexicans should go home so my kid can get a job."

When she mentions that there are plentiful jobs taking care of nursing home patients at $9.40 per hour, these same people say, "Well, you don't really expect my kid to be wiping old people's butts."

Broad Street Reflects
The National Debate

By Karen Lee Ziner
Journal Staff Writer
Wednesday, April 26, 2006

Carlos Arias and Winston Pena say they take in an average of $65,000 daily at their two Compare supermarkets in Providence. On Monday, however, their stores and what organizers predict will be hundreds of other Rhode Island businesses will close in support of a national May 1 general strike for immigrants' rights.

"I'm doing this from my heart -- it's something I feel that is right," says Pena, whose family emigrated from the Dominican Republic. Pena is also pragmatic; he says 75 percent of his customers are Hispanic, "and if you do not support them, maybe in the future they don't support me."

But some merchants say they do not intend to cooperate, and resent the request made by local strike organizers last week.

"I can't afford to close," says Richard Harootunian, whose grandfather opened Tony's Delicatessen on Broad Street in Providence in 1929. "I don't think people should tell you what you should do with your own business."

May 1 is especially bad, says Harootunian, "because food stamps, SSI checks, pension checks -- everything's [issued] on the first," and typically the first day of the month is one of the store's busiest.

The call for a nationwide boycott on Monday follows demonstrations in dozens of U.S. cities on April 10. Participants demanded "legalization, not criminalization" and a pathway to citizenship for an estimated 12 million illegal immigrants in this country, part of the divisive debate on immigration reform that has paralyzed Congress and heated the airwaves.

Rachel Miller, director of Jobs with Justice, a member agency of the Immigrants United coalition, says the May 1 strike is being called "to highlight and emphasize the important role immigrants play and the impact they have on society and the economy."
Rhode Island organizers are dubbing it, "A Day Without an Immigrant."

534

Nationally and locally, strike participants are being asked to boycott work, school, stores and banks, and not to make phone calls (unless it's an emergency), buy alcohol or use their computers or the Internet.

Miller says people who marched in the April 10 demonstration have been asked to honor the boycott. Word has also gone out on Spanish-language radio stations, fliers, "and announcements from the pulpits" of local Catholic churches.

Along the primarily Hispanic commercial district on Broad Street in Providence, posters that stating the business will be closed on May 1 in support of immigrants, are hanging in windows of automotive shops, beauty salons, restaurants, markets and check-cashing centers.

Juan Garcia, head of the Immigrants in Action Committee (Comite de Inmigrantes en Accion de St. Teresa) at St. Teresa Church in Olneyville, is part of an organizing group that has been going door-to-door or working a phone tree, asking businesses and individuals to join the boycott.

An estimated 500 to 600 Rhode Island businesses have pledged to honor the boycott, according to Garcia.

"We have people closing in Central Falls, Pawtucket, Providence and Newport. And right here in Providence, [businesses] on Manton Ave., Elmwood, Chalkstone, Broad Street, Atwells," have agreed to close, he says.

But Garcia said he was disappointed that some businesses plan to remain open. While not Hispanic owned or operated, those businesses have a largely Hispanic customer base, he says.

"That's their decision," says Garcia. "But we say to the people who don't close, right now is a time for business to support the [Hispanic] community," that has supported them "for years and years."

Garcia stresses, "We are not forcing anyone to close."

Roger Pelletier, who owns Providence Automotive Engineering Co. on Broad Street, does not want to close, "but I'm afraid if I do stay open, are they gonna ruin the place -- vandalize it?"

Pelletier says he was approached last week by two people whom he says "were Dominicans with a poster and everything -- they just asked me if I was willing to close [the shop] to help them support that immigration thing, whatever that is that they're fighting."

He adds, "I do a lot of business with Hispanic people. They're fine to do business with. But I can't see losing a day of wages for this whole thing. What are they gonna gain from this? I can't understand."

Pelletier says, "I've been here 46 years. I pay taxes, I pay workers' comp, I have Blue Cross" for his employees. "Now who is gonna come in here and tell me what to do? I was here first."

Juana Horton, chairwoman of the Hispanic Chamber of Commerce, and president and CEO of Horton Interpreting Services, says the chamber will honor the strike by closing its office in Providence.

"We have a respect and a belief that this is a very, very important statement," Horton says of the strike. However, for each of the chamber's 75 members, "it's an individual decision," she adds.

Horton says her own interpreting service likely will not close, "because we provide emergency interpreting services for the hospitals. So our business is kind of a little bit different. It's not a restaurant or a hair salon or a law firm. The person we would be hurting would be Hispanic."

An informal survey on Broad Street yesterday and Monday found numerous participants, including Adriana Carolina Delgado, owner of Carolina's restaurant, which specializes in piquant chicken, fried plantanas and other Dominican fare.

"We know a lot of illegal immigrants, and we will support everyone," legal and illegals alike, says Delgado. "Those people who are anti-immigrant, they don't have god in their life. The immigrants come here to work, to send money to their families," she says. "American people don't want to do the dirty jobs."

The Immigrants United Coalition includes: Local Council 94; The Guatemalan Alliance of Rhode Island; ACORN (Association of Community Organizations for Reform Now); The Mexican-American Association of Rhode Island; Immigrant Students in Action; SCIU Local 615; DARE (Direct Action for Rights and Equality); the International Socialist Organization; Ocean State Action, among others.

Politicians, Bankers Note Hispanic Business Growth

By Paul Grimaldi
Journal Staff Writer
Thursday, March 30, 2006

PROVIDENCE -- Bankers understand the meaning of numbers.

So it's no surprise that a handful turned up yesterday morning at Ada's Creations, the South Side restaurant that's considered an example of the state's growing Hispanic business sector. Representatives from Bank Rhode Island, Domestic Bank, Bank of America and Sovereign Bank wanted to be on hand as Hispanics displayed some new statistics.

The number of Hispanic-owned businesses in Rhode Island grew more than five times the national average for all businesses between 1997 and 2002 -- among the fastest in the nation, according to data released last week by the U.S. Census Bureau.

The Greater Providence Merchants Association wanted to make sure the state's business and political leaders took note of the data.
"You don't need to be a rocket scientist to know this is where we need to be," said Joseph Rochio, of Sovereign Bank.

In remarks to a crowd of more than 50 people, Rochio and the other bankers noted the lengths to which they are going to meet the demands of Hispanics -- offering micro-loans, hosting financial education classes and hiring bilingual staff, among other initiatives.

The efforts meet some of the association's key demands.

Formed three years ago by a group of Hispanic merchants in the city, the association has evolved into a nonprofit organization that promotes education, economic development, leadership and social progress for Latinos and other immigrants.

Its members say they want business education programs, access to capital, help navigating government bureaucracies and affordable health care, issues the association's leaders emphasized yesterday.

While commending the bankers and the various politicians on hand for their efforts to help Hispanic-owned businesses, Jose Brito, the association's president, urged them all to do more.

"We pay gas, electric [bills], taxes, but we don't get anything back," Brito said.

State and city politicians got the message, pledging their support, if not the money the bankers are offering.

"I'm trying to push them to get the money out," Governor Carcieri said of the state's development agencies.

Lt. Gov. Charles J. Fogarty noted that of equal importance to the business census data was the growth in Rhode Island's Hispanic population.

"If it were not for the doubling of the Latino community in the last census, our state would not have grown" in population, he said.

The number of Hispanic businesses in the state rose 56 percent, to 3,415, generating $213.7 million in revenue by 2002, according to the Census Bureau.

Rhode Island's growth rate placed it second with Georgia. New York had the fastest growth rate, 57 percent, during the period.

Across the United States, the number of Hispanic-owned businesses rose 31 percent between 1997 and 2002, to almost 1.6 million, three times the 10-percent growth rate for all businesses. Providence, with 2,022, has the largest number of Latino businesses in Rhode Island.

The business people gathered at Ada's apparently know how that growth affects the city and the state. The Providence Journal, for one, has joined the newly formed advisory board for the Greater Providence Merchants Association.

"There's no question the driving force behind the economy is the Hispanic businesses," said Tomas A. Avila, the association's vice president. "We understand what these numbers mean."

Latino Group Backs Roberts In Lieutenant Governor Race

The Providence Journal
Monday, March 20, 2006

PROVIDENCE -- Community leaders from throughout the state, including Democratic Represenatives Grace Diaz and Anastasia Williams, both of Providence, launched "Latinas for Roberts" last week at Ada's Creations in Providence. The organization is an effort to engage Latino voters for Sen. Elizabeth Roberts, D-Cranston, a candidate for lieutenant governor.

"The issues we face in Rhode Island require the full participation of the Latino community and every community throughout our state," Roberts said. "I want to engage Latinos so we can build a consensus and work towards creating a more healthy and strong Rhode Island together."

The chairwoman for Latinas for Elizabeth Roberts is Marisol Garcia, communications director for General Treasurer Paul Tavares. Diaz and Williams are the honorary co-chairwomen of the committee. In addition to the chairwomen, the founding members of Latinas for Elizabeth Roberts are Betty Bernal, Sylvia Bernal, Doris M. De Los Santos, Melba DePena, Grace Gonzalez, Dolores LeFlame, Marta V. Martinez, Sabina Matos, Carmen Mirabal, Delia Rodriguez, Ada Terrero and Adriana Vargas.

About 60 people attended the event, which raised about $1,000, according to the Roberts campaign.

Carcieri sounds off on Kass' comments

Although critical of his communications director, the governor says the barbs lobbed at him by the Newport GOP chairman "were untrue and unfair."

By Scott Mayerowitz
Journal State House Bureau
Thursday, February 23, 2006

PROVIDENCE -- Governor Carcieri yesterday continued to stand by Steve Kass, his $111,487-a-year communications director, but distanced himself from the specific words Kass used to defend the governor on an Internet forum.

Kass was responding to comments by David Quiroa, Newport Republican chairman, that Carcieri's proposal to cut 3,000 undocumented children from state-subsidized health care was "truly sad" and that Carcieri "is insensitive to all minorities."

"While I stand by Steve Kass' efforts to defend my record . . . I disagree with some of the language he used," Carcieri said. "I have made it clear to Steve that, as government officials, we should always avoid using sarcastic language that may be subject to misinterpretation."

Carcieri also took aim at Quiroa for attacking "me personally by stating that I am insensitive to the concerns of Rhode Island's minority community, and also by comparing me to a plantation owner in the Old South. Those comments were untrue and unfair."

The exchange in question started when Quiroa wrote of the governor: "This shows how narrow-sighted a policymaker can become when he or she surrounds him or herself with a non-diverse group of advisors (the inner circle). Although the official name of the state is Rhode Island and Providence Plantations -- We are not a Plantation!"

Kass responded that: "Speaking for myself, I would suggest that all proud Latino-American Republicans like Mr. Quiroa, should step up to the plate, say thank you for all the support they have been given by Rhode Island taxpayers, and then start a fundraising effort to assist those that do live on a plantation until our finances improve. I would be glad to make a contribution. Please tell me where to send the check."

"My remarks were aimed at him, no one else," Kass said yesterday. "I'm sorry that people have taken my comments and twisted them around. I never intended to offend anyone."

State Democratic Party Chairman William J. Lynch placed the blame with Carcieri, saying: "People are judged by those they choose to surround themselves with and Don Carcieri needs to take immediate action to assure Rhode Island's Latino community that Mr. Kass' biased and hurtful words do not reflect the official position of his administration."

Carcieri responded saying: "It was never Steve's intention or mine to cause offense to anyone. And I apologize to any Rhode Islander who was offended by Steve's statement."

The Kass flap: Carcieri slow to get it

M. Charles Bakst
The Providence Journal
Thursday, February 23, 2006

I see that Steve Kass, Don Carcieri's communications director, says his old talk show "rage" got to him and made him "crazy" when a Latino Republican blasted the GOP governor in an Internet discussion forum.

Thus, Kass sought to rationalize his over-the-top comments to Newport Republican chairman David Quiroa, who assailed Carcieri's proposed $4-million budget cut that would ax some 3,000 undocumented children from the RIte Care health program. Quiroa said Carcieri's inner circle lacks diversity and he's insensitive to minorities.

Rhode Islanders are not paying Kass $111,487 a year to indulge his anger.
Yesterday morning, Democratic state chairman Bill Lynch demanded that Carcieri apologize to Latinos for Kass' "degrading" statements. Carcieri waved off Lynch's move. Yet, in late afternoon, he did issue an apology to any Rhode Islander offended by Kass' words.

Ironically enough, Carcieri was scheduled for a 10 a.m. WPRO ask-the-governor talk show appearance hosted by Matt Allen, a gig Kass used to host. As soon as Carcieri walked in the building, I could see he wasn't grasping the offensiveness of Kass' comments and his own role in touching off a flap like this through budget cuts he promotes that target the poor.

Carcieri denounced Quiroa's portrayal of him as insensitive and a plantation owner. He said he named Latinas to head two state departments, appointed a black woman as child advocate, put a Latino on District Court, and has several Hispanic and black staffers. True, and good for him, though he still has no black department director.

Carcieri should realize that when he proposes cuts in health care, child care and welfare, he will be viewed as heartless. He deems himself a reformer and the friend of taxpayers. "I see retirees in my neighborhood who are struggling to pay health care costs and they say to me, you know, why are they having to underwrite health care costs for illegals?"

Let him quote to them from a Providence Sunday Journal story by Karen Lee Ziner about RIte Care: "Detractors of the governor's proposal point out that federal law permits undocumented children to attend public schools, and predict that eliminating their preventive health care coverage would pose a public-health risk, and would lead to more-severe illnesses, increased pressure on emergency rooms and costlier care."

To me and on WPRO, Carcieri defended Kass' rebuttal to Quiroa, though he said he wouldn't have been so sarcastic. He embraced Kass' comments on state finances, Rhode Island's generosity to the poor, etc. But he said he'd have deleted Kass' line that Quiroa and other "proud Latino-American Republicans" should "say thank you" for support from Rhode Island taxpayers and start a drive "to assist those that do live on a plantation."

I found Kass' language insulting. Carcieri wasn't sure what it meant. It was prompted by Quiroa's saying Carcieri needs reminding that Rhode Island isn't a plantation even if its full name is State of Rhode Island and Providence Plantations.

Carcieri should endorse removing the odious plantations phrase, but he said yesterday he's not keen on a change.

Testifying at a 2000 House hearing on a proposal to alter the name, then-Rep. Aisha Abdullah-Odiase said it was painful to be black and be pigeonholed as a descendant of slaves. She declared, "I wish that you could sit in my place one day and see what it's like to be a person of dark skin."

Let Carcieri and Kass think about that.

Latino 2000 Census Demographics

Tomás Alberto Ávila
May 2002

Communities across Rhode Island are feeling the effects of what observers are calling America's "second great wave of immigration." The fast growing Latinos

The work force is changing very fast. Your customers are changing. Your school systems are changing. Globally and locally. If you are not prepared for the diversity being developed by new immigration of Latinos, your competition will get the best employees. And expand into the customer base that is rightfully yours. That's not a potential threat. It is a reality today in nearly every community and every business. But successful organizations are turning the challenge into a competitive edge.

Everyone is affected by the changes occurring as society evolves multi-culturally through the immigration of Latinos to the state of Rhode Island. The private sector, the public sector, Not-for-profit organizations, School children and communities. Race, gender, age, sexual orientation, and religion are but a few of the points of bias causing problems and potential litigation in the workplace, the marketplace and the classroom.

Latinos Quick Facts will help you explores some of the assets of Latino communities and allow you and your employees to gain an appreciation for the role of cultural activities in the process of multi cultural relationship building and the impact the Latino community is having in our city and state.

Whether you live in a large metropolitan area where scores of different languages can be heard daily, or in a smaller town that is wrestling with the implication of new immigrants, Latinos Quick Facts has been designed to help you adapt to the new changes that come with immigration of Latinos to our state.

The goal of Latinos Quick Facts is to introduce critical areas for the multicultural social, government and corporate environment, and to visit the urban setting that composed the Latino communities of Rhode Island. Managers and Department heads often ask, after they have been exposed to the growing immigration of Latinos to our state and nation, "Who are they? How are they changing our community?

How are they changing the job market and the economy changing?, What should we do about immigration and our community change?, How do elected officials and corporate executives dealing with the immigration of Latinos?, Are Latinos a liability to our society or a valuable asset to it's future?

544

This report updates Latinos demographics in Rhode Island based on the must recent published 2000 Census data. According to these results, the Latino population in the state of Rhode Island experienced vigorous expansion during the 1990s. These results portray a profile of this rapidly growing segment of the state's population. This information should assist the general public in understanding some of the demography of the Latino community. It should also be useful to the many individuals and organizations who are concerned about the future of this fast growing community. Especially for those responsible for informed decision making: elected officials, policy makers, researchers, the business sector, the media, community based organizations, advocacy groups, community and labor organizers.

The areas covered include statistics in terms of population size and growth potential, employment, income, business, education and demographics.

From 1990 to 2000 the Latino community across the nation increased from 248,709,873 to 281,421,906 a 13.2% increase. The Latino community increased from 22,354,059 to 35,305,818, a 57.8% rate of expansion. Rhode Island's Latino population doubled in the 1990s, from 45,752 to 90,820 a 50.3% rate of expansion, propelling Providence to its fastest overall population growth in nearly a century and making it a majority-minority city for the first time in history, according to detailed numbers released from the 2000 Census. This constitutes 9% of the total population in the state of Rhode Island.

Most of that growth was in Providence, Pawtucket and Central Falls, where Latinos are filling the schools[i], opening hundreds of new stores and businesses and launching newspapers and radio stations. But the Census numbers also show Latinos following earlier generations of immigrants into suburbs such as Cranston and Warwick. These two communities experienced growth of 125% and 38% respectively between 1990 and 2000.

Latinos are treated as a homogeneous group throughout this report. However, readers should understand that the Latino community is made up of a number of different national origin groups with roots in various parts of Latin America and the Caribbean. Bound together by a common language of origin, Spanish and by many cultural traditions. Latinos are forging a new identity within the context of the American experience. Another important dimension of Latino identity is its multi cultural aspect, reflecting, African, European, and Indigenous heritage.

The 2000 Census is the most recent source of reliable data regarding the breakdown of the country demographics, and the foundation for this report. The Latino community is growing, and fast. Today there are 35.3 million Latinos in the United States and projected to hit 96 million by 2050 an increase of more than 200 percent.

The effects of these numbers are being felt everywhere. In the political arena, Latinos are decisive voters in many of the urban legislative districts of the state, and at the national level, eleven key states with 217 of the 270 electoral votes needed to win the presidential election. The growing Latino representation in almost every aspect of the Rhode Island's political system political parties, municipal and legislative branches of government is inevitable. In the economic arena, revenues from Latino-owned businesses currently exceed $200 million annually, and the purchasing power of Latinos, now over $17 million.

Despite Latinos extraordinarily vibrant and active presence in the United States and the state of Rhode Island, Latinos are far from enjoying the equal access and opportunities we need and deserve to both advance and contribute to the state and the nation. We continue to face serious challenges:

> ➢ Nearly a quarter of the Latino community continues to live in poverty.
> ➢ Latinos are more likely to live in inadequate housing.
> ➢ Eleven million of the 43 million uninsured individuals in this country are of Latino descent, and Latinos are disproportionately affected by higher rates of certain diseases such as diabetes and HIV/AIDS.
> ➢ More than three times as many Latino children drop out of school compared to their non Latino white counterparts.
> ➢ Latinos still lack representation at many levels of our political and civic institutions and face discrimination in the workplace, in housing, and in our educational and health care systems.

Everyone is affected by the changes occurring as society evolves multi-culturally through the immigration of Latinos to the state of Rhode Island and the nation. The private sector, the public sector, not-for-profit organizations, school children and communities. Race, gender, age, sexual orientation, and religion are but a few of the points of bias causing problems and potential litigation in the workplace, the marketplace and the classroom.

Latinos Quick Facts will help you explore some of the assets of Latinos and allow you and your constituencies to gain an appreciation for the role of cultural activities in the process of multi cultural relationship building and the impact the Latino community is having in our state, cities and the nation.

The goals that guide Latino Quick Facts are:
1. Identify, analyze, and shape public policies on Latino issues, based upon recent data from the U.S. Census bureau;
2. Prepare and disseminate a data-based factual report that specifies the nature and scope of Latinos throughout the state of Rhode Island; and
3. Promote greater awareness of attention to Latino concerns among the state's policy makers and civil and community leaders, as well as among the general public.

Population & Demography
2000 Rhode Island Latino Population

From 1990 to 2000, the U.S. Census Bureau reports the Latino population in Rhode Island grew by 50.3%, from 45,752 to 90,820. This growth raised the Latino community to 9% of the state's total population. Estimates predict that by the year 2010, the state's Latino population will grow to 133,000 accounting for 10.5% of the states total population.

Latinos find themselves concentrated in 10 cities across Rhode Island, also referred to as urban. One of every four Latinos live in these 10 urban centers including Providence has the largest number of Latinos: 52,146 people in 2000. Central Falls is the city with the highest proportion: 47.80%. Cranston and Warwick are the fastest growing cities with a Latino population each increasing by more than 33% in 1990.

The Census Bureau reported that Rhode Island's population grew by 4.5 percent in the 1990s, to 1,048,319 people. The figures show that the state's growth was entirely attributable to minorities. The state gained about 82,500 racial and ethnic minorities, slightly more than half of them Latinos. The combined population of the state's racial/ethnic minorities grew from 10.7% to 16.8%. Focusing on urban centers, for the first time in state history, Rhode Island has two communities like Providence and Central Falls where minorities outnumber non-Latino whites.

Latinos are more likely than non-Latino Whites to live inside central cities of metropolitan areas. Nearly half of all Latinos lived in central city within a metropolitan area (46.4 percent) compared with slightly more than one-fifth of non-Latino Whites (21.2 percent). In 2000 45.1 percent of Latinos lived outside central cities but within a metropolitan area compared with 56.2 percent of non-Latino Whites.

Table 1

1990 & 2000 Proportion of Total Rhode Island Population

RACE/ETNICITY	1990 Total Population	Percent of Population	2000		Percent difference 1990
			Total Population	Percent of Population	
White	917,375.00	91.40	891 191	85.0	-2.9
Black or African American	38,861.00	3.90	46 908	4.5	20.7
American Indian and Alaska Native	4,071.00	0.40	5 121	0.5	25.8
Asian	18,019.00	1.80	23 665	2.3	31.3
Native Hawaiian and Other Pacific Islander	306.00	-	567	0.1	85.3

547

Some other race	24,832.00	2.50	52 616	5.0	111.9
Hispanic or Latino (of any race) [3]	45,752.00	4.60	90,820	8.7	98.5
Total	**1,003,464.00**	**100.00**	**1,048,319.00**	**100.00**	**4.5**

Source: Table 3 in U.S. Census Bureau, 1990 & 2000 census.

Rhode Island Counties Latino Population Growth: 1970 - 2000

Growth in the Hispanic population and minority race categories support the general observation that Rhode Island has become more racially and ethnically diverse. At the same time, population in the minority categories still represents a relatively small portion of the state's total population.

The Hispanic population in Rhode Island has doubled during the past ten years, from 45,752 recorded in the 1990 census to 90,820 in Census 2000. The Hispanic population has increased by an additional 45,068 persons, representing a 98.5 percent gain.

Persons of Hispanic origin now represent 8.7 percent of Rhode Island's total population, an increase from 4.6 percent recorded in 1990. Eighty percent of the increase in the Hispanic population has occurred in three communities: Providence, Pawtucket, and Central Falls.

BRISTOL COUNTY

Bristol County's 3.7 percent population gain was primarily the result of an increase in the Black/African American and Asian populations. The White population decreased its representation from 98.8 percent to 97.8 percent, and the Hispanic population decreased by 14.9 percent.

Hispanic origin	1960	1970	1980	1990	2000
Population	-	-	928	672	572
As a percentage of total population	-	-	2.00%	1.40%	1.10%

Kent County

The Hispanic population grew by 62.8 percent in Kent County. The largest numeric increase (527) occurring in Warwick, the largest percentage increase (169.2%) in West Greenwich.

The Black/African American and Asian populations added an additional 3,699 individuals to the minority population in Kent County. The White population in Kent County has been reduced from 98.1 percent recorded in the 1990 census to 96.8 percent in Census 2000.

Hispanic origin	1960	1970	1980	1990	2000
Population	-	-	981	1,737	2,827
As a percentage of total population	-	-	0.60%	1.10%	1.70%

Newport County

Newport County experienced a 40.7 percent increase in its Hispanic population; from 1,790 in 1990 to 2,409 in 2000. The City of Newport counted the largest numeric increase, while the Town of Little Compton showed the largest percentage gain (181.8%).

Hispanic origin	1960	1970	1980	1990	2000
Population	-	-	1356	1712	2409
As a percentage of total population	-	-	1.70%	2.00%	2.80%

Providence County

The largest percentage of racial minorities resides in Providence County. Conversely, Providence County is home to the smallest percentage of Whites. The largest percentage of persons claiming more than one race was recorded in Providence County. The Hispanic population more than doubled in Providence County, from 40,569 reported in 1990 to 83,232 enumerated in Census 2000. Hispanics represent 13.4 percent of the County's total population.

The Hispanic population in the City of Providence also more than doubled, increasing the Hispanic presence in that community to 30 percent of the City's total population. Hispanics make up 47.8 percent of the resident population of Central Falls, and 13.9 percent of the population of Pawtucket. Today, 91.6 percent of all persons of Hispanic origin reside in Providence County.

Hispanic origin	1960	1970	1980	1990	2000
Population	-	-	14,929	40,569	83,232
As a percentage of total population	-	-	2.60%	6.80%	13.40%

Washington County

Population diversity in Washington County has remained relatively stable over the past decade. The White population has decreased slightly, from 96.6 percent to 96.1 percent. The Black population has increased by .1 percent, and Hispanics have indicated a decline from 1.4 percent recorded in 1990 to 1.0 percent enumerated in 2000.

Hispanic origin	1960	1970	1980	1990	2000
Population	-	-	712	1,062	1,780
As a percentage of total population	-	-	0.80%	1.00%	1.40%

Table 2

Rhode Island Cities With Largest Latino Population

Cities & Towns	Latino Population 1990	Percentage of Population	Latino Population 2000	Percentage Population
1. Providence	24,982	15.50%	52,146	30.00%
2. Pawtucket	5,211	7.20%	10,141	13.90%
3. Central Falls	5,119	29.00%	9,041	47.80%
4. Woonsocket	1,156	2.60%	4,030	9.30%
5. Cranston	1,532	2.00%	3,613	4.60%
6. Newport	789	2.80%	1,467	5.50%
7. Warwick	845	1.00%	1,372	1.60%
8. North Providence	571	1.80%	1,247	3.80%
9. East Providence	845	1.70%	922	1.90%
10. West Warwick	542	1.90%	918	3.10%
Total	**41,592**	**1.10%**	**87,897**	**1.70%**

Source: U.S. Bureau of the Census   RI Statewide Planning

Table 4

2000 Counties and 15 Largest Cities and Towns in Rhode Island Percent of Total Population that is Latino

Rank	Geographic area	Total Population	Latino (any race)	As % of Population
	Statewide	1,048,319	90,820	9%
	COUNTY			
1	Providence County	621,602	83,232	13%
2	Kent County	167,090	2,827	2%
3	Washington County	123,546	1,780	1%
4	Newport County	85,433	2,409	3%
5	Bristol County	50,648	572	1%
	CITY OR TOWN			
1	Providence	173,618	52,146	30%
2	Warwick	85,808	1,372	2%
3	Cranston	79,269	3,613	5%
4	Pawtucket	72,958	10,141	14%
5	East Providence	48,688	922	2%
6	Woonsocket	43,224	4,030	9%
7	Coventry	33,668	385	1%
8	North Providence	32,411	1,247	4%
9	Cumberland	31,840	667	2%
10	West Warwick	29,581	918	3%
11	Johnston	28,195	533	2%
12	South Kingstown	27,921	493	2%
13	Newport city	26,475	1,467	6%
14	North Kingstown	26,326	465	2%
15	Westerly	22,966	270	1%

Source: U.S. Census Bureau, Census 2000 Redistricting Data (P.L. 94-171) Summary File, Table PL1.

551

Persons Of Latino Origin As A Percentage Of Population By State, County And City & Town 1990 & 2000

Cities & Towns by Counties	Latino Population 1990	Percentage of Population	Latino Population 2000	Percentage Population
Barrington	125	0.80%	177	1.10%
Bristol	410	1.90%	289	1.30%
Warren	137	1.20%	106	0.90%
Bristol County	672	1.40%	572	1.10%
Coventry	260	0.80%	385	1.10%
East Greenwich	77	0.60%	117	0.90%
Warwick	845	1.00%	1,372	1.60%
West Warwick	542	1.90%	918	3.10%
West Greenwich	13	0.40%	35	0.70%
Kent County	1,737	1.10%	2,827	1.70%
Jamestown	45	0.90%	50	0.90%
Little Compton	11	0.30%	31	0.90%
Middletown	531	2.70%	508	2.90%
Newport	789	2.80%	1,467	5.50%
Portsmouth	175	1.00%	249	1.50%
Tiverton	161	1.10%	104	0.70%
Newport County	1,712	2.00%	2,409	2.80%
Burrillville	71	0.40%	132	0.80%
Central Falls	5,119	29.00%	9,041	47.80%
Cranston	1,532	2.00%	3,613	4.60%
Cumberland	440	1.50%	667	2.10%
East Providence	845	1.70%	922	1.90%
Foster	16	0.40%	34	0.80%
Glocester	46	0.50%	65	0.70%
Johnston	175	0.70%	533	1.90%
Lincoln	183	1.00%	343	1.60%
North Providence	571	1.80%	1,247	3.80%
North Smithfield	56	0.50%	50	0.50%
Pawtucket	5,211	7.20%	10,141	13.90%
Providence	24,982	15.50%	52,146	30.00%
Scituate	53	0.50%	77	0.70%
Smithfield	113	0.60%	191	0.90%
Woonsocket	1,156	2.60%	4,030	9.30%
Providence County	**40,569**	**6.80%**	**83,232**	**13.40%**
Charlestown	37	0.60%	87	1.10%
Exeter	30	0.50%	77	1.30%
Hopkinton	45	0.70%	83	1.10%
Narragansett	155	1.00%	204	1.20%
New Shoreham	8	1.00%	12	1.20%
North Kingstown	253	1.10%	465	1.80%
Richmond	48	0.90%	89	1.20%
South Kingstown	306	1.20%	493	1.80%
Westerly	180	0.80%	270	1.20%
Washington County	**1,062**	**1.00%**	**1,780**	**1.40%**
State Total	**45,752**	**4.60%**	**90,820**	**8.70%**

Rhode Island Profile of Latino Demographic Characteristics: 2000

HISPANIC OR LATINO AND RACE	Number	Percent
Hispanic or Latino (of any race).	**90,820**	**8.7**
Mexican.	5,881	0.6
Puerto Rican.	25,422	2.4
Cuban.	1,128	0.1
Other Hispanic or Latino	58,389	5.6
Not Hispanic or Latino.	957,499	91.3
White alone	858,433	81.9
Total population	1,048,319	100.0

Source: U.S. Census Bureau, Census 2000, Table DP-1. Profile of General Demographic Characteristics for Rhode Island: 2000

Providence

HISPANIC OR LATINO AND RACE	Population	Percent
Total population	173,618	100
Hispanic or Latino (of any race)	52,146	30
Mexican	2,237	1.3
Puerto Rican	12,712	7.3
Cuban	468	0.3
Other Hispanic or Latino	36,729	21.2
Not Hispanic or Latino	121,472	70
White alone	79,451	45.8

Source: U.S. Census Bureau, Census 2000, Table DP-1. Profile of General Demographic Characteristics for Rhode Island: 2000

Pawtucket

HISPANIC OR LATINO AND RACE	Population	Percent
Total population	72,958	100
Hispanic or Latino (of any race)	10,141	13.9
Mexican	581	0.8
Puerto Rican	3,298	4.5
Cuban	75	0.1
Other Hispanic or Latino	6,187	8.5
Not Hispanic or Latino	62,817	86.1
White alone	50,436	69.1

Source: U.S. Census Bureau, Census 2000, Table DP-1. Profile of General Demographic Characteristics for Rhode Island: 2000

Central Falls

HISPANIC OR LATINO AND RACE	Population	Percent
Total population	18,928	100
Hispanic or Latino (of any race)	9,041	47.8
Mexican	677	3.6
Puerto Rican	2,249	11.9
Cuban	38	0.2
Other Hispanic or Latino	6,077	32.1
Not Hispanic or Latino	9,887	52.2
White alone	7,577	40

Source: U.S. Census Bureau, Census 2000, Table DP-1. Profile of General Demographic Characteristics for Rhode Island

Woonsocket

HISPANIC OR LATINO AND RACE	Population	Percent
Total population	43,224	100
Hispanic or Latino (of any race)	4,030	9.3
Mexican	168	0.4
Puerto Rican	2,798	6.5
Cuban	22	0.1
Other Hispanic or Latino	1,042	2.4
Not Hispanic or Latino	39,194	90.7
White alone	34,503	79.8

Source: U.S. Census Bureau, Census 2000, Table DP-1. Profile of General Demographic Characteristics for Rhode Island

Cranston

HISPANIC OR LATINO AND RACE	Population	Percent
Total population	79,269	100
Hispanic or Latino (of any race)	3,613	4.6
Mexican	185	0.2
Puerto Rican	946	1.2
Cuban	88	0.1
Other Hispanic or Latino	2,394	3
Not Hispanic or Latino	75,656	95.4
White alone	69,104	87.2

Source: U.S. Census Bureau, Census 2000, Table DP-1. Profile of General Demographic Characteristics for Rhode Island

Newport

HISPANIC OR LATINO AND RACE	Population	Percent
Total population	26,475	100
Hispanic or Latino (of any race)	1,467	5.5
Mexican	227	0.9
Puerto Rican	626	2.4
Cuban	49	0.2
Other Hispanic or Latino	565	2.1
Not Hispanic or Latino	25,008	94.5
White alone	21,623	81.7

Source: U.S. Census Bureau, Census 2000, Table DP-1. Profile of General Demographic Characteristics for Rhode Island

Warwick

HISPANIC OR LATINO AND RACE	Population	Percent
Total population.	85,808	100
Hispanic or Latino (of any race)	1,372	1.6
Mexican	215	0.3
Puerto Rican	374	0.4
Cuban	58	0.1
Other Hispanic or Latino	725	0.8
Not Hispanic or Latino	84,436	98.4
White alone	80,920	94.3

Source: U.S. Census Bureau, Census 2000, Table DP-1. Profile of General Demographic Characteristics for Rhode Island

North providence

HISPANIC OR LATINO AND RACE	Population	Percent
Total population	32,411	100
Hispanic or Latino (of any race)	1,247	3.8
Mexican	131	0.4
Puerto Rican	241	0.7
Cuban	25	0.1
Other Hispanic or Latino	850	2.6
Not Hispanic or Latino	31,164	96.2
White alone	29,103	89.8

Source: U.S. Census Bureau, Census 2000, Table DP-1. Profile of General Demographic Characteristics for Rhode Island

East Providence

HISPANIC OR LATINO AND RACE	Population	Percent
Total population.	48,688	100
Hispanic or Latino (of any race	922	1.9
Mexican	111	0.2
Puerto Rican	306	0.6
Cuban	25	0.1
Other Hispanic or Latino	480	1
Not Hispanic or Latino	47,766	98.1
White alone	41,630	85.5

Source: U.S. Census Bureau, Census 2000, Table DP-1. Profile of General Demographic Characteristics for Rhode Island

United States

HISPANIC OR LATINO AND RACE	Population	Percent
Total population.	281,421,906	100
Hispanic or Latino (of any race).	35,305,818	12.5
Mexican.	20,640,711	7.3
Puerto Rican.	3,406,178	1.2
Cuban.	1,241,685	0.4
Other Hispanic or Latino.	10,017,244	3.6
Non Hispanic or Latino	246,116,088	87.5
White alone	194,552,774	69.1

Source: U.S. Census Bureau, Census 2000, Table DP-1. Profile of General Demographic Characteristics for United States

Rhode Island Sub-Divisions

Rank	Name	Hispanic or Latino	Not Hispanic or Latino	Population
1	Central Falls	47.80%	52.20%	18,928
2	Providence	30.00%	70.00%	173,618
3	Pawtucket	13.90%	86.10%	72,958
4	Woonsocket	9.30%	90.70%	43,224
5	Newport	5.50%	94.50%	26,475
6	Cranston	4.60%	95.40%	79,269
7	North Providence	3.80%	96.20%	32,411
8	West Warwick	3.10%	96.90%	29,581
9	Middletown	2.90%	97.10%	17,334
10	Cumberland	2.10%	97.90%	31,840
11	East Providence	1.90%	98.10%	48,688
12	Johnston	1.90%	98.10%	28,195
13	North Kingstown	1.80%	98.20%	26,326
14	South Kingstown	1.80%	98.20%	27,921
15	Lincoln	1.60%	98.40%	20,898
16	Warwick	1.60%	98.40%	85,808
17	Portsmouth	1.50%	98.50%	17,149
18	Bristol	1.30%	98.70%	22,469
19	Exeter	1.30%	98.70%	6,045
20	Narragansett	1.20%	98.80%	16,361
21	Richmond	1.20%	98.80%	7,222
22	New Shoreham	1.20%	98.80%	1,010
23	Westerly	1.20%	98.80%	22,966
24	Coventry	1.10%	98.90%	33,668
25	Charlestown	1.10%	98.90%	7,859
26	Hopkinton	1.10%	98.90%	7,836
27	Barrington	1.10%	98.90%	16,819
28	Warren	0.90%	99.10%	11,360
29	Smithfield	0.90%	99.10%	20,613
30	East Greenwich	0.90%	99.10%	12,948
31	Jamestown	0.90%	99.10%	5,622
32	Little Compton	0.90%	99.10%	3,593
33	Burrillville	0.80%	99.20%	15,796
34	Foster	0.80%	99.20%	4,274
35	Scituate	0.70%	99.30%	10,324
36	West Greenwich	0.70%	99.30%	5,085
37	Tiverton	0.70%	99.30%	15,260
38	Glocester	0.70%	99.30%	9,948
39	North Smithfield	0.50%	99.50%	10,618
	Grand Total	**8.70%**	**91.30%**	**1,048,319**

Source: U.S. Census Bureau, Census 2000 Redistricting Data (P.L. 94-171) Summary File, Table PL1 & RI State Wide Planning

Latino Owned Businesses

According to a report released by the Commerce Department's Census Bureau, the Latino owned businesses in the United States totaled 1.2 million firms, employed over 1.3 million people and generated $186.3 billion in revenues in 1997. Latino-owned firms made up 6 percent of the 20.8 million nonfarm businesses in the nation and 1 percent of the $18.6 trillion in receipts for all businesses.

The data for the state of Rhode Island shows that the state has a total of 2,186 Latino owned businessess with total sales and receip of $207,036,000 annualy. It also shows, that the state has 447 firms with paid employees with annual sell receipts of $157,405,000. and employing a total 1,890 individuals and annual payroll of $31,264,000.

The Census Bureau, an arm of the U.S. Department of Commerce, collected the information from 1997 tax returns and from 2.5 million questionnaires completed by business owners. The bureau collects the data every five years and in the coming months will provide similar information about other ethnic groups and by gender.

The report's Statistics for Selected Counties With 100 or more Latino Owned Firms shows that Providence County has the largest amount of Latino owned businesses with a total of 1,780 businesses with total sell receipts of $166,964,000 and a total of 377 Latino businessess with paid employees totaling 1,538 with an annual payroll of $23,854,000, follow by Newport County with 139 firms and sales and receipts of $8,760,000 and Kent County with 103 Latino owned businesses.

The City of Providence has the largest number of Latino buisnesses according to the information released by the Census Bureau, with a total of 731 and $61,893,00 Annual sales and receipts and 124 businesses with paid employees with $39,796,000 annual sales and receipts employing 445 with annual payroll of $6,619,000. Follow by Cranston with 274 businesses and $18,606,00 annual sales and receipts, Pawtucket with 190 and $46,167,000 and Central Falls with 100 businesses with annual sales and receipts of $6,060,000.

The survey data shows that four in 10, or 475,300 Latino businesses, had receipts of $10,000 or less; slightly more than 2 in 10, or 273,300 had receipts between $10,000 and $25,000; while 26,700, or about 2 percent, had sales of $1 million or more. Receipts per firm averaged $155,200 for Latino-owned firms compared with $410,600 for all U.S. firms, excluding publicly held corporations and firms whose owners' race or ethnicity were indeterminate (e.g., mutual companies whose ownership is shared by its members).

The largest number of Latino-owned firms (1 million) were sole proprietorships, unincorporated businesses owned by individuals. C corporations, all legally incorporated businesses except for Subchapter S corporations (whose shareholders elect to be taxed as individuals rather than as corporations), numbered 78,500. But C corporations ranked first in receipts ($71.8 billion) among all Latino-owned firms, the report showed. C corporations were included in the Latino portion of the Survey of Minority-Owned Business Enterprises, source of the data, for the first time in 1997.

Receipts of Latino-owned firms rose 49 percent, from $77 billion in 1992 to $114 billion in 1997, compared with a 40 percent increase for all U.S. firms of the same type over the same period. The data in the report were collected as part of the 1997 Economic Census from a large sample of nonfarm businesses filing tax forms as sole proprietorships, partnerships or any type of corporation, which had receipts of $1,000 or more in 1997.

This increased in Latino businesses, is in line with the doubling of the Latino community during the 10 years since the last national population count was taken, jumping from 45,752 in 1990 to 90,820. Latinos now represent 8.7 percent of Rhode Island's total population. According to the data released by the bureau, eighty percent of the increase in the Latino population occurred in three communities: Providence, Pawtucket and Central Falls.

Statistics for Latino Owned Firms by State: 1997

Rhode Island	All Firms[1]		Firms with Paid Employees			
	Firms Number	Sales and Receipts ($1,000)	Firms Number	Sales and Receipts ($1,000)	Employees (Number)	Annual Payroll ($1,000)
	2,186	207,036	447	157,405	1,890	31,264
United States	1,199,896	186,274,582	211,884	158,674,537	1,388,746	29,830,028

1 All firms data include both firms with paid employees and firms with no paid employees.
Source: Minority Owned Business Enterprises Table 3. **Statistics for Latino Owned Firms by State: 1997,** U.S. Census Bureau, 1997 Economic Census Mar. 6, 2001, pg 33

Statistics for Selected Counties With 100 or More Latino Owned Firms: 1997

Rhode Island	All Firms[1]		Firms with Paid Employees			
	Firms Number	Sales and Receipts	Firms Number	Sales and Receipts ($1,000)	Employees (Number)	Annual Payroll ($1,000)

		($1,000)				
Total	2,186	207,036	447	157,405	1,890	31,264
Kent County	103	20,767	37	19,037	166	4,883
Newport County	139	8,760	12	6,413	49	1,285
Providence County	1,780	166,964	370	124,172	1,538	23,894

1 All firms data include both firms with paid employees and firms with no paid employees.
Source: Minority Owned Business Enterprises Table 3. **Statistics for Latino Owned Firms by State: 1997,** U.S. Census Bureau, 1997 Economic Census Mar. 6, 2001

Statistics for Selected Places With 100 or More Latino Owned Firms: 1997

Rhode Island	All Firms[1]		Firms with Paid Employees			
	Firms Number	Sales and Receipts ($1,000)	Firms Number	Sales and Receipts ($1,000)	Employees (Number)	Annual Payroll ($1,000)
Total	2,186	207,036	447	157,405	1,890	31,264
Central Falls	100	6,060	24	4,564	25	833
Cranston	274	18,606	18	8,867	69	1,784
Pawtucket	190	46,167	32	42,068	542	7,024
Providence	731	61,893	124	39,736	445	6,619

1 All firms data include both firms with paid employees and firms with no paid employees.
Source: Minority Owned Business Enterprises Table 3. **Statistics for Latino Owned Firms by State: 1997,** U.S. Census Bureau, 1997 Economic Census Mar. 6, 2001, pg 108

Statistics for Latino Owned Firms by Industry Division for States: 1997

Rhode Island	All Firms[1]		Firms with Paid Employees			
	Firms Number	Sales and Receipts ($1,000)	Firms Number	Sales and Receipts ($1,000)	Employees (Number)	Annual Payroll ($1,000)
Total	2,186	207,036	447	157,405	1,890	31,264
Agricultural	12					
Construction	153	16549	41	d	c	d
Manufacturing	68	23,200	27	22,545	274	5,075
Transportation	66	D	8	D	a	D
Wholesale Trade	22	D	5	D	a	D
Retail Trade	454	93,042	137	80,023	692	9,287
Financial	61	D	24	D	a	D
Services	805	46,175	114	30,451	705	10,843
Not Classified	544	14,486	88	D	B	D

1 All firms data include both firms with paid employees and firms with no paid employees.
Source: Minority Owned Business Enterprises Table 3. **Statistics for Latino Owned Firms by State: 1997,** U.S. Census Bureau, 1997 Economic Census Mar. 6, 2001
See footnotes at end of table.

Statistics for Latino Owned Firms by Ethnicity for States: 1997

Rhode Island	All Firms[1]		Firms with Paid Employees			
	Firms Number	Sales and Receipts ($1,000)	Firms Number	Sales and Receipts ($1,000)	Employees (Number)	Annual Payroll ($1,000)
Total	2,186	207,036	447	157,405	1,890	31,264
Cuban	45	4,058	10	D	b	d
Puerto Rica	169	5,519	23	D	a	D
Mexican	S	S	S	S	S	S
Spaniard	61	6994	16	D	b	D
Latin American	933	81,304	172	D	e	D
Other	765	91.865	124	7,4381	1,089	17,167

1 All firms data include both firms with paid employees and firms with no paid employees.
Source: Minority Owned Business Enterprises Table 3. **Statistics for Latino Owned Firms by State: 1997,** U.S. Census Bureau, 1997 Economic Census Mar. 6, 2001
See footnotes at end of table.

Political Empowerment

For Latinos, the nineties were hugely political. Issues, agendas, and initiatives focused on Latinos seem unending. At first it was unclear how Latinos would react. The good news is we surprised most political pundits and reacted more strongly than anticipated. The bad news is that the battle rages on. Latino voter turnout drew headlines in the 1996 presidential election. As the 21st Century begins, Latino voters have demonstrated to continue their dramatic show of strength in the 2000 elections, providing the necessary support to candidates at the national and local level. In the last presidential election, 18.5 million Latinos voted, accounting for 5 percent of the total turnout, according to Hispanas Organized for Political Equality (HOPE), a nonpartisan organization formed to promote Latino participation in government.

Here in Rhode Island, the 2000 primary elections drew an extraordinary number of Latinos to the polls electing a second Latino to the Legislature, a result not only of their surging numbers and clout here but of an unprecedented get-out-the-vote effort, Latino activists and political experts said. A Providence Journal analysis found that turnout in the city's Latino neighborhoods reached as high as 38 percent in districts with hotly contested local primaries, dwarfing the statewide turnout of about 15 percent.

Those numbers follow a decade in which the state's Latino population grew 50 percent, to nearly 90,826 people, even as the state's total population declined slightly, according to the U.S. Census Bureau estimates. To put it another way: Latinos made up 4.5 percent of the state's population in 1990, but nearly 9 percent in 2000.

During the 2000 elections, in legislative district 18 in the Southside of Providence, at all but one of the District 18 polling places, Latino voters had not one, but three Latino candidates on the ballot to choose from. Along with Tejada, there was Juan M. Pichardo, who was challenging Incumbent Senator Robert Kells in Senate District 10, and then the even higher-profile Angel Taveras, a candidate in the 2nd

Congressional District race. The results also roughly match the distribution of Latinos in the district the higher the concentration, the better the Latino candidates did. State Rep. Anastasia P. Williams, the only Latina candidate in the primaries who was also an incumbent, won handily in the District 9 race.

The state's first-ever Latino congressional candidate, Angel Taveras, a 30-year-old lawyer with no political experience and a shoestring campaign budget, drew an astonishing one in three votes in Providence.

Leon F. Tejada, 35, a computer systems analyst, defeated three-term state Rep. Marsha E. Carpenter in the city's Elmwood section. Gonzalo Cuervo, a political newcomer, came within 26 votes of displacing state Rep. Joseph S. Almeida, a first-term incumbent from the Washington Park neighborhood. And Juan M. Pichardo, 33, a patient advocate at Rhode Island Hospital who ran a savvy and aggressive campaign, came tantalizingly close to upsetting state Sen. Robert T. Kells, a retired Providence police officer and five-term senator. Despite Taveras's third-place finish and Pichardo and Cuervo's narrow defeats, Latino activists said that the primary's turnout attested to the success of a dogged voter-education campaign. It was also a harbinger, they said, of wider electoral success within a few years.

Information released by the 2000 U.S. Census Bureau, shows that Political power in Rhode Island is shifting back to its roots in the ethnic neighborhoods of Providence and the Latino community, is poised to play a big role in the political arena into the new millennium. The data shows that the state's Latino population makes up 40 percent of the total population in 5 of the 50 Senatorial districts (**see table** 1), and 6 of the 100 House (**see table 2**).

TABLE 1 Rhode Island Senatorial Districts

Rank	District	Total Population	Total Latino	Percent of Population	Percent 18+ Years
1	10	21,043	10,450	49.7%	46.6
2	8	23,381	10,696	45.7%	40.9
3	35	21,879	9,326	42.6%	39.1
4	9	19,976	8,206	41.1%	37.1
5	7	23,420	9,278	39.6%	34.1
6	1	21,588	5,896	27.3%	21.9
7	4	22,270	4,238	19.0%	14.1
8	38	20,790	3,544	17.0%	14.1
9	40	20,464	3,067	15.0%	12.8
10	37	20,131	2,964	14.7%	12.2

US Census Bureau Redistricting Data (PL 94-171) Summary File 2000

The census data allow state officials to realign congressional and state legislative districts in their states, taking into account population shifts since the last census (in 1990) and assuring equal representation for their constituents in compliance with the "one-person, one-vote" principle of the 1965 Voting Rights Act. These data also are the first population counts for small areas and the first race and Latino-origin data from Census 2000. Redistricting could also create opportunities for Latinos. The surprising surge of Latinos could turn Senate districts10, 8, 35, 9 and 7 into Latino political power districts. House districts 9 and 19 have joined district 18 as districts where the Latino community makes up 50 percent of the population, along with districts 72, 17 and 12 in which the community makes up more than 40 percent of the total population.

TABLE 2 Rhode Island Representative Districts

Rank	District	Total Population	Total Latino	Percent of Population	Percent 18+ Years
1	9	11,868	6,609	55.7%	52.60
2	18	10,565	5,842	55.3%	52.20
3	19	10,085	5,239	51.9%	48.50
4	72	10,662	5,074	47.6%	44.30
5	17	11,055	4,837	43.8%	41.40
6	12	10,975	4,728	43.1%	37.30
7	73	11,217	4,252	37.9%	34.50
8	13	11,574	4,132	35.7%	35.70
9	14	11,457	4,033	35.2%	29.60
10	20	9,831	3,299	33.6%	30.00
11	1	11,872	3,782	31.9%	25.30
12	7	11,193	2,686	24.0%	19.30
13	10	10,962	2,023	18.5%	14.80
14	6	10,832	1,650	15.2%	11.40
15	8	10,736	1,455	13.6%	9.90

US Census Bureau Redistricting Data (PL 94-171) Summary File 2000

The census data allow state officials to realign congressional and state legislative districts in their states, taking into account population shifts since the last census (in 1990) and assuring equal representation for their constituents in compliance with the "one-person, one-vote" principle of the 1965 Voting Rights Act. These data also are the first population counts for small areas and the first race and Latino-origin data from Census 2000

Latinos caught up with the African Americans during the 2000 Census as the nation's largest minority group, something that is already true in most of the 10 largest U.S. cities). Politicians need to expand their notion of civil rights and make sure Latinos are included in any future race initiatives. They need to take these voters and potential voters more seriously.

While shortsighted political strategists still dismiss the population as mostly young and nonvoting, the truth is that, at a time when voter participation rates for most groups have flattened, the rate for Latinos has risen in cities like Providence, as demonstrated during the 2000 elections. They need to stop resting on their laurels and aggressively compete for Latino support. This is a community where a little attention and respect goes a long way. Politicians have to do better than simply adopting a philosophy of recruiting Latinos as unpaid volunteers in their campaigns. The country is undergoing a period of profound change. It is estimated that by the year 2010, Latinos will account for one in every three American. By 2050, Latinos will comprise well over a quarter of the United States population (CCSCE, 1995). The Latino population will continue to grow in both numbers and levels of civic participation.

Congressional District 1 Hispanic Demographics

HISPANIC OR LATINO AND RACE	Population	Percent
Total population	510,287	100
Hispanic or Latino (of any race)	**35,759**	**7**
Mexican	2,782	0.5
Puerto Rican	12,348	2.4
Cuban	487	0.1
Other Hispanic or Latino	20,142	3.9
Not Hispanic or Latino	474,528	93
White alone	425,620	83.4

Congressional District 2 Hispanic Demographics

HISPANIC OR LATINO AND RACE	Population	Percent
Total population	538,032	100
Hispanic or Latino (of any race)	**55,061**	**10.2**
Mexican	3,099	0.6
Puerto Rican	13,074	2.4
Cuban	641	0.1
Other Hispanic or Latino	38,247	7.1
Not Hispanic or Latino	482,971	89.8
White alone	432,813	80.4

References

Arteaga, Luis M., Flagel Cione, Rodriguez Guillermo, (1998, May 18) The Latino Vote 1998: The New Margin of Victory, Latino Issues Forum, Washington, DC

Avila, Alberto, Tomás (2001, Mayo 11) Mas de 2 mil negocios de propiedad Latina establecidos en Rhode Island, Providence En Español

Avila, Alberto, Tomás (2000, October 15) Latinos' Buying Power Rises, Study Finds Providence, RI

Avila, Alberto, Tomás (2000, October 1) Positive Economic Indicators For Hispanics Reveal Opportunity To Focus On The Nation's Working Poor, Providence, RI

Avila, Alberto, Tomás, (1999,August) NCLR 1999 Annual Conference; Launching a New Millennium Summary, Providence, Providence, RI

Avila, Alberto, Tomás, (1999, April) The 2nd Annual Harvard University Latino Law and Public Policy Conference, "Access To Opportunity" Summary, Providence, RI

Avila, Alberto, Tomás, (1999, June) 2nd Annual Dominican American Roundtable Summary, Providence, RI

Avila, Alberto, Tomás (1998, January 1) Community Leadership Development Initiative Structure & Vision, Providence, Providence, RI

Avila, Alberto, Tomás (1997, November 8) Community Latino Economic Empowerment in the Next Millennium, Providence, Providence, RI

Avila, Alberto, Tomás, Martinez Marta (1999, November) 6th Annual Latinos in the New Millennium Conference Report, Providence, RI

Bakst, M., and Charles (2000, October 24) Battle for Senate: On the front lines, clashes, nostalgia, The providence Journal, Providence, RI

Bakst, M., Charles (2000, October 12) In race for Senate, abortion remains a simmering topic, The providence Journal,

Bakst Charles M., (2000, June 8) State Senate seat: In changing district a new uncertainty: The only constant in politics is surprise, The Providence Journal

Bakst, M., Charles (1999, October 17) Challenging Weygand, Licht vies for Latino support The providence Journal

Bakst, M., Charles (1998, August 25) A coming of age: Latinos form PAC and pols zoom in, The providence Journal, Providence, RI

Bakst, M., Charles (1999, November 28) Coming a long way, Angel Taveras now aims for Congress, The providence Journal

Barmann Timothy C. (2000, October 25) Latino voters win praise of Hispanic candidates: At least one primary race was decided by Latino voters, The providence journal, Providence RI

Bakst, M., Charles (1999, October 17) Challenging Weygand, Licht vies for Latino support The providence Journal,

Branigin, William (1998, November 9) Latino Voters Gaining Political Clout, Washington Post, Washington, DC

Cabrera, Ana (2000, May 12) The Future Of This Nation Is In The Hands Of The Latino Community, Providence En Español, Providence, RI

Capellán, Victor F (1999, April) Changing Political Landscape: An Opportunity for Latinos, Providence, RI

Census Bureau Data Reveals Fewer Hispanics Living in Poverty (2000, October 12), The Providence American, RI

Center for Hispanic Policy & Advocacy (1999, March 22), Latinos at A Cross Road: Millennial Economic Empowerment Forum, Providence, RI

Christopher, Rowland (1996, November 22) Latinos becoming political force, The providence Journal

Community Design Partnership & Melvin F. Levine & Associates, (1999, June 15) The Southside/Broad Street Market: Market Analysis and Economic Development Strategy, Draft Final Report, Providence, RI

Corkery Michael, (2000, October 25) Latinos celebrate successes at polls: The Rhode Island Latino Political Action Committee throws a party to honor candidates who won, or nearly won, primary races this past September, The providence journal, Providence RI

Covarrubias, Amanda (1998, November 9) Hispanics score historic gains in 1998 elections, The Associated Press

Cox News Service (1998, November) Poll Shows Latino Voters are Optimists, Washington, DC

Davis, Marion, (2000, September 14) Latino vote influences primary races in Providence: The providence journal, Providence RI

Davis, Marion (2000, May 1) A Conversation with Tomas Avila, The providence Journal, Providence, RI

Democrats raise money for Chaffee, The providence Journal, Providence, RI October 19, 2000

Deaver, Mike, Penn Mark, (1999, April 23) The Latino Voter Survey, Washington DC

Devorana Frank, Latino Literacy: The Complete Guide to Our Hispanic History and Culture, Round Stone Press, New York, 1996

District 20 candidates seek support beyond core ethnic groups, The providence Journal, September 3, 1998

Farnsworth Riche, Farnsworth Riche and Associates, (2001) The Implications Of Changing U.S. Demographics For Housing Choice And Location In Cities Martha The Brookings Institution Center on Urban and Metropolitan Policy, Washington, DC, March

From Minority to Mainstream, Latinos Find Their Voice Washington Post, Sunday, January 24, 1999

Fox, Geoffrey, Hispanic Nation: Culture, Politics and The Construction of Identity, The university of Arizona Press, Arizona, 1996

Glaeser, Edward L. (April 2001) Racial Segregation in the 2000 Census: Promising News, Harvard University and the Brookings Institution, and Jacob L. Vigdor, Terry Sanford Institute of Public Policy, Duke University, Center on Urban & Metropolitan Policy, The Brookings Institution, Washington, DC

Gonzalez, Juan (2000) A History of Latinos in America: Harvest of Empire, NYC

Gounaris, Marilyn, Martinez, Marta, Cruz Francisco (1993, May 22) Under One Roof: The Juanita Sanchez Multi-Services Center, Providence RI

Harvard Journal of Hispanic Policy, (1989-1990) Volume 4, The Myth of Hispanic Progress: Trends in The Education and Economic Attainment of Mexican Americans, Cambridge, MA

Harvard Journal of Hispanic Policy, (1991) Volume 5, Policy Perspective: Hispanic Consciousness, Political Participation and the 1984 Political Election, Cambridge, MA

Harvard Journal of Hispanic Policy, Volume 6, (1992) Latino Electoral Participation, Harvard university, Cambridge, MA,

Harvard Journal of Hispanic Policy, (1992-1993) Volume 10, Latino electoral Participation, Harvard university, Cambridge, MA

Harvard Journal of Hispanic Policy, (1998-1999) Volume 11, A Decade In Review, Harvard university, Cambridge, MA

Harvard Journal of Hispanic Policy, (1999-2000) Volume 12, Health and the Latino Community, Harvard University, Cambridge, MA

Hearst Newspapers (1998) Poll Shows Power of Latinos as Swing Vote in Midterm Elections

Hernadez Andy, Ramirez Alfred, (2001, January) Reflecting an American Vista: The Character and Impact of Latino Leadership, National Community for Latino Leadership, Inc. Volume one

Indicadores economicos de hispanos revelan datos positivos, (2000, Octubre 6) Providence En Español, Providence, RI

Kids Count, 2000 RI Kids Count Fact Book, RI Kids Count, Providence, RI 2000

Lardaro, Leonard (2001, April 21)Rhode Island's surprising census data, The Providence Journal

Larmer, Brook (1999, July 12) Latin U.S.A: How Young Hispanics Are Changing America, Newsweek Magazine, Society, 48-51

Latino Voter Is Vivid in Parties' Crystal Ball, The New York Times, April 9, 2001

Latino Magazine, Absentee Ballot September 1998

Latino Magazine, Free to Choose: Issues, not party politics, impress Latino voters September 1998

Latino Yearbook/Anuario Hispano, Fourteenth Edition, 2000

Lardaro, Leonard (2001, April 21) Rhode Island's surprising census data, The Providence Journal

Making Connections: (1998, October 8) Providence, RI Designing Our Future, Providence, RI

Michaelson, Rita C. Report on the Hispanic, Portuguese and Cape Verdean Populations in Rhode Island, Providence, RI, September, 1986

Minority Owned Business Enterprises, Company Statistic Series Table 3. Statistics for Latino Owned Firms by State: 1997 U.S. Census Bureau, 1997

National Council of La Raza (1999) Defining an American Agenda for the 21st Century, National Council of La Raza Annual Report 1999, Washington, DC

National Hispanic Leadership Agenda, (1996, October 15) 1996 Policy Summary, Washington, DC

National Hispanic Leadership Agenda, 2000 Policy Agenda: An Agenda for Hispanic Advancement of Hispanic Americans, Washington, DC October 18, 2000

Navarrette, Ruben Jr. (2001, March 9) Census recasts the politics of race Dallas, Dallas Morning News TX

Navarrette, Ruben Jr. (2001, March 15) How the Democrats Mishandle Latino Voters, Dallas, TX

Oboler, Suzanne, (1995) Ethnic Labels, Latino Lives: Identity and the Politics of (Re) Presentation in the United States, University of Minnesota press, MN,

Pina, Tatiana, (2000, October 23) Aumentan los ingresos de la comunidad hispana, The Providence Journal, Providence, RI

Pina, Tatiana, (2000, January) Hispanos Viajan A la Capital del Pais, The Providence Journal, Pagina Latina, RI

Pina, Tatiana (1996, November 17) Coming into their own: In politics, business, music and the arts, RI Latinos are making their presence felt Providence, RI

Plan Providence The (1998, February 1) Improving Access to Jobs and Economic Opportunity: The Development of a Jobs Policy for Providence A Policy Concept Paper

Petrovich, Ed.D. Janice, (1987) Aspira Institute for Policy Research Northeast Hispanic Needs: A Guide for Action, Volume II

Polo Lillian , Ortiz Heather Ventura Jhomphy, Peña Federico, (1997) Latinos in Rhode Island, RI July

Politicians Court Latino Vote, Washington Post, September 16, 1999

Political futures on the line in redistricting, The Providence Journal May 4, 2001

Prodigal son: Angel Taveras, an appealing candidate in his own right, reflects growing political activity by Latinos in Rhode Island, The Providence Phoenix September 2000

Rhode Island Statewide Planning (2001, March) Race And Ethnicity Rhode Island (State, County, City & Town) 2000, Providence, RI

Rodriguez, Ralph, (1997, November 13) Governor's Advisory Commission on Hispanic Affairs Action Forum Report, Providence RI

Rodriguez, Ralph, (2001, April 4, 1997) Governor's Advisory Commission on Hispanic Affairs Nuestro Futuro/Our Future: Meeting The Needs of Rhode Island Hispanics Community; A policy Summary, Providence RI

Sabar, Ariel and MacKay, Scott (2001, April 29) With A New Wave Of Immigrants, A Storied Neighborhood Evolves: El Nuevo Silver Lake, The Providence Journal

566

Sabar, Ariel (2001, January 28) Climbing the ladder: A new generation of Latinos finds opportunity, success in RI The providence Journal

Sabar Ariel, (2000, September 14) Latino power shows at polls: "It's electoral participation catching up to the shift in the demographics," says Providence Councilman Luis A. Aponte, The Providence Journal

Sabar, Ariel (1999, November 28)`They had Atwells Avenue; we have Broad Street' The providence Journal, Providence, RI

Sachs Susan, Give Me Your Tired, Your Poor, Your Vote, (2001, April 8) The New York Times, NYC

Schmitt, Eric (2001, May 7) Most Cities in U.S. Expanded Rapidly Over Last Decade, The New York Times

Schmidt, Eric (2001, May 6) Segregation Growing Among U.S. Children The New York Times

Schmidt, Eric (2001, April 30) Whites in Minority in Largest Cities, the Census Shows, The New York Times

Smith, Gregory, (1998, September 17) Winning candidate Luis Aponte, The providence Journal, Providence, RI

Smith, Gregory (1998, September 16) Aponte: Wins Nomination in Ward 10, The providence Journal

Sum, Andrew M., Fogg, W., Neal (1999) The Changing Workforce: Immigrants and the New Economy in Massachusetts, Center for Labor Market Studies Northeastern University Boston, Massachusetts, Boston, MA, November

Survey Finds Latinos Optimistic About Direction of the Country and their Futures Los Angeles Times, November 1998

The Associated Press, Census Finds Whites Leaving Cities (2001, May 6) The New York Times, New York

The Associated Press, (1998November 9) Latinos score historic gains in 1998 election

The Associated Press, (1999, September 22) Top Latino leader to head Democrats' 2000 convention

The New Face Of America: How Immigrants Are Shaping the World's First Multicultural Society, Special Issue: Time Magazine, New York,

Tobar, Hector (1998, November) In Contests Big and Small, Latinos Take Historic Leap, Los Angeles Times,

Torres Andres, Chavez Lisa, (1998) Latinos in Massachusetts: An Update, Boston MA

Turnbaugh Lockwood Anne And Secada Walter G. Transforming Education For Hispanic Youth: Exemplary Practices, Programs And Schools, January

Univision Communications Inc. (1999, April 23) The Power of the Latino Vote," a conference, Washington DC,

U.S. Census Bureau Public Information Office (2001, June, 6), National Demographic Profile Summary

U.S. Census Bureau, Census 2000 (2001, May, 23), Table DP-1. Profile of General Demographic Characteristics for Rhode Island: 2000

U.S. Census Bureau (2001, March) Population Profile of the United States: America at the Close of the 20th Century, **Current Population** Reports Special Studies U.S. Census Bureau, Washington, DC

U.S. Census Bureau Census Bureau, 2000 Statistical Abstract of the United States U.S. Washington, DC March 2001

U.S. Census Bureau, The Latino Population in the United States, Population Characteristics Washington, DC March 2001

U.S. Census Bureau State and Metropolitan Area Data book, 1997-1998, Washington, DC March 2001

U.S. Census Bureau: Selected Summary Measures of Age and Income by Latino Origin and Race Washington, DC March 2000

U.S. Census Bureau, Minority Owned Business Enterprises, Company Statistic Series Table 3. Statistics for Latino Owned Firms by State: 1997

U. S. Census Bureau, Current Population Survey, March 2000 Ethnic and Latino Statistics Branch, Population Division, Washington, DC Internet release date: January 3, 2001

U.S. Census Bureau, Population Profile of the United States: America at the Close of the 20th Century, **Current Population** Reports Special Studies, Washington, DC March 2001

U.S. Census Bureau, 2000 Statistical Abstract of the United States U.S. Census Bureau, Washington, DC March 2001

U.S. Census Bureau, State and Metropolitan Area Data book, U.S. Census Bureau 1997-1998, March 2001 Washington, DC

U.S. Census Bureau, The Foreign Born Population of The United States: Population Characteristics, Washington, DC August 2000

U.S. Census Bureau, Selected Summary Measures of Age and Income by Latino Origin and Race U.S. Census Bureau: Washington, DC March 2000

U.S. Census Bureau, The Latino Population in the United States, Population Characteristics, Washington, DC March 2001

U.S. Census Bureau, Overview of Race and Hispanic Origin. Washington, DC, March 2001

U.S. Census Bureau, Population Projections 2000 – 2010 Washington, DC

U.S. Census Bureau 2000 Population Projections 2000 – 2010, August

U.S. Census Bureau, Resident Population and Apportionment of the U.S. House of Representatives, Washington, DC, March 2001

U.S. Census Bureau, Voting and Registration in the Election of November 1998: Population Characteristics, Washington, DC August 2000

U.S. Department of Commerce Economics and Statistic Administration Bureau of the Census, We the American Hispanics Washington, DC, September, 1993

US Department of Commerce Minority Business Development, Minority Purchasing Power: 2000 to 2045 The Emerging Minority Marketplace, Washington, DC September 2000

US Department of Commerce Minority Business Development, Minority Population Growth: 19950-2010, Washington, DC September 2000

U.S. Department Of Education, Improving Opportunities: Strategies From The Secretary Of Education For Hispanic And Limited English Proficient Students A Response To The Hispanic Dropout Project, Washington, DC February 1998

U.S. Census Bureau, Voting and Registration in the Election of November 1998, Washington, DC, August 2000

Valencia, Milton (2001) Latinos living the American dream of home ownership, The Pawtucket Times, January 31

Valencia, Milton (2001, January 31) Latino population, income rises locally in the past decade, The Pawtucket Times

Valencia, Milton (2001, January 31) Latinos find success in U.S., The Pawtucket Times

Valencia, Milton (2001, January 29) Latino immigrants make their mark in R.I The Pawtucket Times

Valdes Isabel M, (2000) Marketing to American Latinos: A guide to the In Culture Approach, New York

Williams, Anastasia; (1993, March) Moving The Hispanic Community Forward: Report of Anastasia Williams Economic Development Task Force, Providence, RI

Rhode Island Latino Candidates
1986 – 2006

Source: Rhode Island Board of Elections   **Bold**= Elected

Year	Office	District	Candidate	Party
1986	Governor	Statewide	Anthony D.AFFIGNE	Citizens
1990	City Council	10	Leonidas Medina	Democrat
1990	State Representative.	18	Jenny Rosario	Democrat
1992	**State Representative.**	**9**	**Anastasia Williams**	**Democrat**
1992	State Representative.	20	Juan Francisco	Republican
1994	City Council	10	Luis Aponte	Democrat
1994	Representative Committee	7	Corana	Democrat
1994	**State Representative.**	**9**	**Anastasia Williams**	**Democrat**
1996	State Representative.	83	Garza	Republican
1996	State Representative.	73	Leonel Bonilla	Democrat
1996	State Representative.	72	Vicente Caban	Democrat
1996	State Representative.	72	Mildred Vega	Democrat
1996	State Representative.	20	Victor F. Capellan	Democrat
1996	**State Representative.**	**9**	**Anastasia Williams**	**Democrat**
1996	State Senate	20	Delia Smidt	Democrat
1998	Ward Committee	13	Andy Andujar	Democrat
1998	Ward Committee	12	Sanchez	Democrat
1998	Ward Committee	11	Laura Perez	Democrat
1998	Ward Committee	9	Bienvenido Garcia	Democrat
1998	Ward Committee	9	Marcos Antonio	Democrat
1998	City Council	9	Miguel Luna	Democrat
1998	**City Council**	**10**	**Luis Aponte**	**Democrat**
1998	**House Comm.**	**3**	**Jose Marcano**	**Democrat**
1998	City Council	9	Santa Espinosa	Republican
1998	City Council	9	Jose Mendez	Independent
1998	**City Council**	**10**	**Luis Aponte**	**Democrat**
1998	**House Comm.**	**3**	**Jose Marcano**	**Democrat**
1998	State Representative.	20	Victor Capellan	Democrat
1998	**State Representative.**	**9**	**Williams**	**Democrat**
1998	Secretary of State		Lopez	Republican
1999	City Council	3	Ricardo Patino	Democrat
2000	United States Congress	2	Angel Tavares	Democrat
2000	**State Representative.**	**9**	**Anastasia Williams**	**Democrat**
2000	**State Representative.**	**18**	**Luis Tejada**	**Democrat**
2000	State Representative	20	Gonzalo Cuervo	Democrat
2001	City Council, Woonsocket	At Large	Grizzel Rodriguez	Democrat

Year	Office	District	Candidate	Party
2001	City Council, Central Falls	1	Alido Baldera	Democrat
2001	City Council, Central Falls	**3**	**Ricardo Patino**	**Democrat**
2001	State Representative	**62**	**Stella Guerra-Brien**	**Democrat**
2001	City Council, Central Falls	**3**	**Ricardo Patino**	**Democrat**
2002	State Senate	**2**	**Juan Pichardo**	**Democrat**
2002	State Senate	**1**	**Trevino**	**Republican**
2002	State Senate	**2**	**Juan Pichardo**	**Democrat**
2002	State Senate	2	Pedro Espinal	Independent
2002	State Senate		Stella Guerra-Brien	Democrat
2002	State Representative.	10	Carlos Diaz	Democrat
2002	State Representative.	**11**	**Luis Tejada**	Democrat
2002	City Council	**9**	**Miguel Luna**	**Democrat**
2002	City Council	9	Reynaldo Catone	Independent
2002	City Council	**10**	**Luis Aponte**	**Democrat**
2001	City Council, Central Falls	**3**	**Ricardo Patino**	**Democrat**
2003	Mayor, Central Falls	CF	Hector Solis	Democrat
2004	State Representative	5	Ramiro FERNANDEZ	Republican
2004	State Representative	**10**	**Anastasia P. WILLIAMS**	**Democrat**
2004	State Representative	**11**	**Grace DIAZ**	**Democrat**
2004	State Representative	**10**	**Anastasia P. WILLIAMS**	**Democrat**
2004	State Representative	**11**	**Grace DIAZ**	**Democrat**
2004	State Representative	11	Leon F. TEJADA	Democrat
2004	State Representative	12	Leo MEDINA	Democrat
2004	Rep District Committee	10	Aridia JENNINGS	Democrat
2004	Rep District Committee	10	Antonia MENDOZA	Democrat
2004	Rep District Committee	10	Isidro de LEON	Democrat
2004	Rep District Committee	11	Gonzalo CUERVO	Democrat
2004	Rep District Committee	11	Maryelyn ACEVEDO	Democrat
2004	Rep District Committee	11	Eulogio ACEVEDO	Democrat
2004	**School Committee, Cumberland**	**At Large**	**Rosa Quiñones-CROWLEY**	**Non Partisan**
2004	**State Senate**	**2**	**Juan M. PICHARDO**	**Democrat**
2004	**State Senate**	**2**	**Juan M. PICHARDO**	**Democrat**
2004	State Senate	6	Pedro ESPINAL	Democrat
2004	Senate District Committee	2	Rafael BLANCO	Democrat
2004	Senate District Committee	2	Abigail MESA	Democrat
2004	Senate District Committee	2	Maryelyn ACEVEDO	Democrat

Year	Office	District	Candidate	Party
2004	Senate District Committee	2	Eulogio ACEVEDO	Democrat
2004	Senate District Committee	6	Stephanie M. CRUZ	Democrat
2004	Senate District Committee	6	Patricia M. DELGADO	Democrat
2004	Senate District Committee	6	Melvin Douglas RIVERA	Democrat
2004	Senate District Committee	7	Delia C. RODRIGUEZ-MASJOAN	Democrat
2005	Mayor, Central Falls	CF	Hector Solis	Democrat
2005	**City Council**	**3**	**Ricardo Patino**	**Democrat**
2005	**City Council**	**4**	**Luis Alfredo Gil**	**Democrat**
2006	**State Senate**	**2**	**Juan Pichardo**	**Democrat**
2006	State Senate	5	Alexis Gorriaran	Democrat
2006	State Senate	28	Ivan G. MARTE	Republican
2006	**State Senate**	**28**	**Ivan G. MARTE**	**Republican**
2006	Senate District Committee	1	Andy Andujar	Democrat
2006	Senate District Committee	2	Maryelyn Acevedo	Democrat
2006	Senate District Committee	2	Rafael Blanco	Democrat
2006	Senate District Committee	2	Abigail Meza	Democrat
2006	Senate District Committee	16	Iris N. Castaneda	Democrat
2006	State Representative	5	Ramiro Fernandez	Republican
2006	**State Representative**	**9**	**Anastasia Williams**	**Democrat**
2006	State Representative	9	Noel Sanchez	Republican
2006	State Representative	10	Carlos Diaz	Democrat
2006	**State Representative**	**11**	**Grace Diaz**	**Democrat**
2006	State Representative	11	Laura Perez	Democrat
2006	State Representative	11	Teofilo Vasquez	Independent
2006	State Committeeman	1	Tomas Alberto Avila	Democrat
2006	State Committeewoman	2	Carolina Bernal	Democrat
2006	State Committeewoman	7	Dorothy Colon	Democrat
2006	State Committeewoman	9	Vivian Z. Medina	Democrat
2006	State Committeewoman	10	Aridia Jennings	Democrat
2006	State Committeeman	10	Rafael Colon	Democrat
2006	State Committeeman	11	Benny Cornelio	Democrat
2006	State Committeewoman	58	Elaine P. Ventura	Democrat
2006	City Council	7	Doris de Los Santos	Democrat
2006	City Council	8	Eulogio Acevedo	Democrat
2006	**City Council**	**8**	**Luis "Leon" Tejada**	**Democrat**
2006	**City Council**	**9**	**Miguel Luna**	**Democrat**
2006	City Council	9	Hector Jose	Democrat
2006	City Council	9	Wellington Garcia	Democrat
2006	**City Council**	**10**	**Luis Aponte**	**Democrat**
2006	City Council	10	Pedro Espinal	Democrat

Year	Office	District	Candidate	Party
2006	City Council	11	Jose Brito	Democrat
2006	City Council	15	Sabina Matos	Democrat
2006	Ward Coomittee (Warwick)	1	Angel V. Garcia	Democrat
2006	Ward Coomittee (Newport)	2	David A. Quiroa	Republican
2006	Ward Coomittee (Central Falls)	3	Ricardo Patino	Democrat
2006	Ward Coomittee (Providence)	4	Santos Bonilla	Democrat
2006	Ward Coomittee (Pawtucket)	4	Stella Carrera	Democrat
2006	Ward Coomittee (Providence)	4	Eva C. Hulse-Avila	Democrat
2006	Ward Coomittee (Providence)	5	Delia C. Rodriguez-Masjoan	Democrat
2006	Ward Coomittee (Providence)	6	Dorothy Colon	Democrat
2006	Ward Coomittee (Providence)	6	Angel Ramon Madera	Democrat
2006	Ward Coomittee (Providence)	8	Antonio Alba	Democrat
2006	Ward Coomittee (Providence)	8	Pedro Aponte	Democrat
2006	Ward Coomittee (Providence)	8	Isidro DeLeon	Democrat
2006	Ward Coomittee (Providence)	8	Rafael Genao	Democrat
2006	Ward Coomittee (Providence)	8	Aridia Jennings	Democrat
2006	Ward Coomittee (Providence)	9	Julieta O. Castellano	Democrat
2006	Ward Coomittee (Providence)	9	Bienvenido Rafael Garcia	Democrat
2006	Ward Coomittee (Providence)	9	Fabio Jose	Democrat
2006	Ward Coomittee (Providence)	9	Yolanda Langley	Democrat
2006	Ward Coomittee (Providence)	9	Ana E. Martinez	Democrat
2006	Ward Coomittee (Providence)	9	Mireya A. Mendoza	Democrat
2006	Ward Coomittee (Providence)	9	Rebeca Mendoza	Democrat
2006	Ward Coomittee (Providence)	9	Deyanara M. Rodriguez	Democrat
2006	Ward Coomittee (Providence)	10	Francisco Batista	Democrat
2006	Ward Coomittee (Providence)	10	Emelda Benitez	Democrat
2006	Ward Coomittee (Providence)	10	Maximo Garcia	Democrat
2006	Ward Coomittee (Providence)	10	Jose R. Cruz	Democrat
2006	Ward Coomittee (Providence)	10	Johany Urbaez	Democrat
2006	Ward Coomittee	10	Zulma Valenzuela	Democrat

Year	Office	District	Candidate	Party
	(Providence)			
2006	Ward Coomittee (Providence)	11	Jose M. Perez	Democrat
2006	Ward Coomittee (Providence)	11	Juan C. Funes	Democrat
2006	Ward Coomittee (Providence)	13	Bryan Principe	Democrat
2006	Ward Coomittee (Providence)	14	Ramiro Fernandez	Republican
2006	Ward Coomittee (Providence)	15	Noel Sanchez	Democrat

End Notes

[i] Providence Journal, March 30, 2001

www.ingramcontent.com/pod-product-compliance
Lightning Source LLC
Chambersburg PA
CBHW062146270326
41930CB00009B/1464